1759

France and the Jacobite Rising of 1745
The Jacobite Army in England
The Jacobites
Invasion: From the Armada to Hitler
Charles Edward Stuart
Crime and Punishment in Eighteenth-Century England
Stanley: The Making of an African Explorer
Snow Upon the Desert: The Life of Sir Richard Burton
*From the Sierras to the Pampas: Richard Burton's Travels
   in the Americas, 1860–69*
Stanley: Sorcerer's Apprentice
Hearts of Darkness: The European Exploration of Africa
Fitzroy Maclean
Robert Louis Stevenson
C.G. Jung
Napoleon
1066: The Year of the Three Battles
Villa and Zapata
Wagons West: The Epic Story of America's Overland Trails

1759

THE YEAR BRITAIN BECAME MASTER OF THE WORLD

Frank McLynn

GROVE PRESS
New York

First published in Great Britain in 2004 by
Jonathan Cape, Random House, London

Printed by special arrangement with Jonathan Cape

Printed in the United States of America

FIRST GROVE PRESS EDITION

Library of Congress Cataloging-in-Publication Data
McLynn, Frank.
    1759 : the year Britain became master of the world /
Frank McLynn.
        p. cm.
    Originally published: London : Jonathan Cape, 2004.
    Includes bibliographical references and index.
    ISBN-10: 0-8021-4228-1 (pbk.)
    ISBN-13: 978-0-8021-4228-3 (pbk.)
    1. Great Britain—History—George II, 1727–1760. 2.
Great Britain—History, Military—18th century. 3. Great
Britain—Colonies—History—18th century. 4. Great
Britain—Foreign relations—1727–1760. 5. Great
Britain—Foreign relations—France. 6. France—Foreign
relations—Great Britain. I. Title.
DA500.M24 2005
941.07'2—dc22   2004057397

Grove Press
an imprint of Grove/Atlantic, Inc.
841 Broadway
New York, NY 10003

06 07 08 09 10   10 9 8 7 6 5 4 3 2 1

For Pauline
With love

ACKNOWLEDGEMENTS

I feel privileged to have worked with a number of talented people on this book. Tony Whittome was an editor nonpareil, meticulous but never pedantic. Will Sulkin remains an author's dream publisher, in so many ways the last of the literary Mohicans. Paul Taylor drew the maps with his customary skill and panache. Among the other individuals who sustained, encouraged or otherwise aided me while writing this volume I must single out Lucy McLynn, Colette Bowe and Mike Bowe for special mention. Yet the palm must go, as ever, to my wife Pauline, the finest 'executive producer' any writer of serious books could ever hope for. I hope I have produced a narrative that matches their dedication and commitment.

Frank McLynn

CONTENTS

	Timeline	viii
	Illustrations	ix
	Preface	I
	Introduction	6
I.	The Struggle for New France	22
2.	The Bonnie Prince and the Crafty Minister	54
3.	Pitt and the West Indies	90
4.	Canada	122
5.	India	158
6.	Wolfe at Quebec	192
7.	Lagos Bay, Portugal	223
8.	Minden	254
9.	The Plains of Abraham	284
10.	Rogers' Rangers	314
11.	Quiberon Bay	354
	Conclusion	388
	Sources	393
	Bibliography	397
	Index	413

TIMELINE

12 December 1758– 16 February 1759:	French besiege Madras
20 December 1758:	Bougainville arrives at Versailles on mission for Montcalm
13 January 1759:	British fleet arrives at Martinique for intended conquest of the island
5 February:	Choiseul interviews Bonnie Prince Charlie in Paris
13 April:	French defeat Prince Ferdinand of Brunswick at Bergen near Frankfurt
1 May:	British complete conquest of Gaudeloupe
13 May:	Bougainville arrives in Quebec
4 June:	Wolfe leaves Louisbourg for the St Lawrence river
27 June:	General Amherst takes Fort Ticonderoga
23 July:	Frederick the Great fights the battle of Kay in Brandenburg, Poland
25 July:	British capture Fort Niagara
31 July:	French repulse Wolfe and the British at Montmorenci Gorge, Quebec
1 August:	Ferdinand of Brunswick and the British under Lord Sackville defeat the French at Minden, West Germany
12 August:	Frederick the Great defeated at Kunersdorf, East Prussia by the Austrians and Russians
18–19 August:	Admiral Boscawen destroys French Mediterranean fleet at Lagos, Portugal
13 September:	Wolfe defeats Montcalm on the Plains of Abraham
5 October:	Robert Rogers and his Rangers destroy the Abenaki village of St Francis (Quebec Province)
20 November:	Admiral Hawke defeats the French Brest fleet at Quiberon, Britanny
20–21 November:	Frederick the Great fights battle of Maxden, near Dresden, Saxony

Outstanding literary productions of 1759:

Candide by Voltaire
Rasselas by Samuel Johnson
The Theory of Moral Sentiments by Adam Smith
Gl'Innamorati by Carlo Goldoni
The Sublime and the Beautiful (2nd ed) by Edmund Burke
The Life and Opinions of Tristram Shandy (Part One) by Laurence Sterne

ILLUSTRATIONS

1. English ships in a storm (*National Maritime Museum, London*)
2. George Washington (© *Hulton Archive*)
3. Wesley and the Indians (© *Hulton Archive*)
4. Braddock on the march (© *Hulton Archive*)
5. Defeat of Braddock (*Library of Congress Washington D.C., USA/ Bridgeman Art Library*)
6. Louis Joseph, Marquis de Montcalm (© *Hulton Archive*)
7. David Hume (*Scottish National Portrait Gallery/Bridgeman Art Library*)
8. Edmund Burke (*By Courtesy of the National Portrait Gallery, London*)
9. Samuel Johnson (© *Hulton Archive*)
10. British Museum, Montague House (*The Stapleton Collection/ Bridgeman Art Library*)
11. Madam de Pompadour (*National Gallery of Scotland, Edinburgh, Scotland/Bridgeman Art Library*)
12. Duc de Choiseul (*The Art Archive/Musée Baron Martin Gray France/Dagli Orti*)
13. Louis XV (*Bonham's, London, UK/Bridgeman Art Library*)
14. Bonnie Prince Charlie (*Smith Art Gallery and Museum, Stirling, Scotland/Bridgeman Art Library*)
15. Pitt the Elder (© *Hulton Archive*)
16. Slaves felling ripe sugar (*British Library, London, UK/Bridgeman Art Library*)
17. Montmorency Falls (*The Art Archive/Musée du Nouveau Monde La Rochelle/Dagli Orti*)
18. The French Port (*Archives Charmet/Bridgeman Art Library*)
19. Niagara Falls (*The Art Archive/Musée des Arts Africains et Océaniens/ Dagli Orti*)
10. Voltaire (*The Art Archive/Musée du Château de Versailles/Dagli Orti*)
21. Elephant fight (*The Art Archive/John Meek*)

22. Tiger-hunting (*Yale Center for British Art, Paul Mellon Collection, USA/Bridgeman Art Library*)
23. General Robert Clive (© *Hulton Archive*)
24. General James Wolfe (*Private Collection/Bridgeman Art Library*)
25. Frederick the Great (*The Art Archive/Musée des Beaux Arts Nantes/ Dagli Orti*)
26. The war in Germany (© *Photograph RMN – Gérar Blot*)
27. Battle of Minden (*Mary Evans Picture Library*)
28. Plains of Abraham (© *Hulton Archive*)
29. Capture of Quebec (© *Hulton Archive*)
30. Death of Montcalm (© *Hulton Archive*)
31. Death of Wolfe (© *Hulton Archive*)
32. Robert Rogers of the Rangers (© *Bettman/Corbis*)
33. Rogers' Rangers in action (© *Corbis*)
34. Admiral Hawke (*National Maritime Museum, London, Greenwich Hospital Collection*)
35. Battle of Quiberon Bay (*National Maritime Museum, London*)

MAPS

The Indian tribes of eastern North America, 1759	16–17
The campaign of Guadeloupe and Martinique, January–May 1759	94
The campaign for India, 1759	166
The St Lawrence campaign, June–September 1759	209
The Battle of Minden, 1 August 1759	271
Rogers' Rangers' raid on St Francis, October 1759	329
The Quiberon campaign, 14–20 November 1759	367
The Battle of Quiberon, 20 November 1759	367

PREFACE

The year 1759 should really be as well known in British history as 1066, for this was when the British finally achieved the global supremacy they would maintain for at least another hundred years. Most of the other, better-known school history dates pale into insignificance. The Magna Carta of 1215 changed nothing; Philip II of Spain launched other armadas after 1588; and 1688 ushered in what was a very precarious 'revolution' for the first fifty years. The famous victories of Trafalgar in 1805 and Waterloo in 1815 are justly celebrated as outstanding feats of arms, but they changed little. Napoleon had already abandoned his invasion attempts by the time Trafalgar was fought and, even if Napoleon had won at Waterloo, he could not have prevailed ultimately against a coalition of Britain, Russia, Austria and Prussia. If we can trace the beginning of the British Empire to a single year, it must surely be 1759. The defeat of the French that year paved the way for the Raj in India and made the emergence of the United States possible.

The entire history of the world would have been different but for the events of 1759. If the French had prevailed in North America, there would have been no United States (at least in the form we know it), for it is inconceivable that France would ever have ceded any of its North American possessions and, without the Louisiana Purchase of 1803, even if we assume the thirteen British colonies had revolted successfully against their French overlords – a questionable assumption – they would have been hemmed in on the Atlantic seaboard, unable to expand westwards to the Pacific. If France had won in India, the global hegemony of the English language could never have happened. Some say that the worldwide struggle for supremacy had to complete another chapter, in the Napoleonic era, before it could be assured. But Napoleon never looked remotely like solving the problems of seapower that prevented him from invading the British Isles. He had no Jacobite fifth column to help him and, even if we posit the near-impossible – a successful invasion of England – the already independent

I

United States would eventually have risen to world supremacy. To some extent this is a simple matter of chronology. Napoleon's best chance for planting the French tricolour on the Tower of London came in 1805, but he had already sold the Louisiana Purchase (the vast territories on either side of the Mississippi River in what is now the south-central United States) to Thomas Jefferson.

This book concentrates on the deadly duel between Britain and France in the climactic year of 1759. Contemporaries were aware of the massive import of the struggle and frequently used analogies from the classical world to explain it. On one model, the struggle was freedom and civilisation (Britain) versus despotism and barbarism (France), with the British as the Greeks and the French as the Persians. Others preferred the analogy of seaborne Athens (Britain) against land-based Sparta (France). All such comparisons are useful provided they are not pushed too far in a deterministic, cyclical or ahistorical way, and I must plead guilty to 'analogy fever' myself, for in many ways the Seven Years War was, like the Second World War, a two-front conflict. Just as the European and Pacific wars in 1941–45 occupied separate spheres in every sense and rarely inter-penetrated, so the two different conflicts of 1756–63 were almost distinct wars. Frederick Great's land-based, European campaigns against France, Russia and Austria were wholly different in aims and conception from the global conflict of France and Britain which formed the deep structure of the war. Accordingly, in this volume the 'other' war (Prussia against France, Russia and Austria) is mentioned only when it impinges on our primary concern or is directly relevant. This book does not purport to be a complete history of the complex and crowded year of 1759, and some of the neglected themes are sketched in the Introduction. But I have tried to avoid the one-dimensionality of a purely military history by indicating some of the main cultural currents swirling around in this year of victory, and by underlining literature's highest peaks in 'prologues' at the start of each chapter. Above all, I wish to concentrate the reader's mind on what might have been. Counterfactual history is never popular with straitlaced students of socio-economic structures or devotees of *la longue durée*, but to my mind it is the essence of history. 1940, which likewise could so easily have turned out differently, may have been Britain's finest hour when backs were to the wall, but 1759 was the finest hour of the infant imperial nation.

Yet I must confess that, after years of study, I now find the year 1759 fascinating in its own right, almost as a thing-in-itself. An interesting social history of the Anglo-American world could easily be compiled from some obvious leads. In 1759 England was still a rigidly stratified society, with the oligarchy enjoying the best of everything in terms of conspicuous consumption while the masses suffered wartime dearth, warding off the misery with a per capita consumption of spirits 25 per cent higher than at the beginning of the century. Rapid population growth and a succession of poor harvests had driven wages down and prices – especially of food – up. With real wages depressed and with the high price of staples such as bread, the decline of gin and other spirituous liquors was starting to occur spontaneously as disposable income expended on alcohol was cut. On the other hand, one could cite at least one pointer in the opposite direction. In December 1759 the thirty-four-year-old Arthur Guinness acquired a brewery in St James's Street, Dublin (one of seventy in the fair city), and began manufacturing porter, which in the nineteenth century would be known as 'stout'. Nonetheless, optimistic reformers like Jonas Hanway concluded that, thanks 'to the hand of Providence interposed by the instrumentality of His Majesty's Ministers . . . the people themselves seem at length to have discovered that health and pleasure, food and raiment, are better than sickness and pain, want and wretchedness'. Other Panglossians pointed to the plummeting crime rates, always a concomitant of warfare in eighteenth-century England. Yet this was only a relative development. Opposition to forced enlistment and press gangs was acute and violent, and juries tended to be sympathetic to 'lawbreakers' in this context where the law itself seemed despotic. Local communities often turned out in force to give severe beatings to press gangs and there was loss of life on both sides in such encounters. A typical case from the north of England in March 1759 saw a barber named William Moffat first involved in such an affray, then arrested, then escaped, finally to be captured at Whitehaven and lodged in Carlisle jail before at last being acquitted at Durham Assizes.

But perhaps the most significant long-term development in Britain in 1759 was the emergence of a 'middling sort' of industrial inventors and entrepreneurs – that cluster of talented individuals sometimes referred to as the Lunar Men. Josiah Wedgwood was moving to the Ivy House and the English engineer Matthew Boulton was buying his land in Soho; meanwhile in Scotland James Watt opened a shop in Glasgow's Saltmarket. A notable ally of the Lunar Men, Francis, Duke of Bridgewater, got the first Canal Act through Parliament, allowing inland waterways to be built and thus, in the long term, leading to a nationwide network of canals. 1759 was indeed a year of building mania. The Yorkshireman John Smeaton built the Eddystone Lighthouse on a treacherous group of rocks fourteen miles out to sea from Plymouth. This was the fourth of five Eddystone lighthouses, of which the first had been constructed in 1703 and the last would be erected in 1882. Smeaton's lighthouse, designed in the shape of an English oak tree but made of stone, was lit by twenty-four candles and opened to great acclaim on 16 October 1759. Another British architectural triumph this year was John Barnard's Kew Bridge, which opened on 4 June 1759 after twelve months in the making. The British example was followed by that of their cousins in North America. For most of the eighteenth century the only land passage from the mainland to Manhattan Island had been via the King's Bridge, but in January 1759 the Free Bridge across the Harlem river, built by Benjamin Palmer and Partners, was completed, and to celebrate, thousands of New Yorkers from both mainland and city attended a party on the green near the bridge on New Year's Day 1759 and dined on roast oxen.

1759 was also a good year for literature and the arts. Apart from the literary classics of the year, which we shall consider in some detail later, there was Sarah Fielding's proto-feminist *The Countess of Dellwynn*, Charles Macklin's *Love à la Mode*, Alexander Gerard's 'An Essay on Taste' and Richard Hurd's *Moral and Political Dialogues*. James Paine and Robert Adam designed Kedleston Hall. On 15 January the British Museum opened to the public, exhibiting a variety of bizarre artefacts and fossils, including a tree trunk gnawed by a beaver and a mummified thumb found beneath St James's coffee house. Most scholarly interest centred on the soon-to-be-famous Reading Room, which issued six-monthly renewable tickets to readers; the librarians kept a record of who used the room and which books were consulted. One of the hot debating issues of the day was freemasonry: what exactly was it, was it anti-religion and could it be considered a secret society or a Jacobite fifth column? Particularly popular in Scotland, the lodges drew the wrath of the papacy, with the new Pope Clement XIII condemning both freemasonry and its links with the anti-clerical *philosophes* or freethinkers of France, citing Helvétius particularly in this regard. Clement was a busy and energetic pontiff, who found the time to promulgate an encyclical letter on 20 December 1759, stressing the spiritual advantages of fasting. Clement's 'interventionism' had already drawn the fire of Frederick of Prussia, who forged a papal brief, dated 30 January 1759, in which he congratulated the Austrian Marshal Daun for the victory at Hochkirch.

The future great and good, and the notorious and controversial, enjoyed mixed fortunes in 1759. George Washington married Martha Dandridge Curtis, a wealthy, twenty-seven-year-old widow and mother of two, and proceeded to lose much of her fortune in unwise speculation in tobacco plantations. Tom Paine, later the famous radical critic, settled in Sandwich, Kent as a master stay-maker; in September he married Maria Lambert, but she died within a year. The composer Thomas Arne received an honorary doctorate in music from Oxford University. Benjamin Franklin received the honorary degree of LLD at St Andrew's University and visited Edinburgh, where he met the doyens of the Scottish Enlightenment including David Hume, Adam Smith, William Robertson and Adam Ferguson. Another Scottish encounter would lead to more explosive results. In October 1759 the poet James Macpherson met John Home (one of Edinburgh's best-known literary figures) on the bowling green at Moffat in Dumbartonshire, just before the publication of his sensational *Fragments of Ancient Poetry*, which appeared in early 1760. Originally touted as translations of authentic Gaelic poems, the *Ossian* cycle actually comprises Macpherson's own inventions, albeit brilliant ones. Dr Samuel Johnson, who was Macpherson's most persistent critic, saw the poems as the concoction of a charlatan (on being asked if any man in the modern age could have written such poems, he replied: 'Yes, sir, many men, many women and many children') but failed to see that this does not necessarily mean they were 'fake', 'fraudulent' or 'forgeries'; the modern consensus is that Johnson missed the point of Macpherson's achievement.

Then there was the usual plethora of significant deaths and births. Among the many departing (apart from those who fell in battle) were the composer Handel and the *philosophe* Maupertuis. Among the births were those of the poet Robert Burns, the writer Mary Wollstonecraft, William Pitt the Younger, the French revolutionary Georges Jacques Danton, Napoleon's future police chief Joseph Fouché, the poet Johann von Schiller and the philanthropist William Wilberforce. Sadly, we must leave all these and other delightful byways to concentrate on our main theme: how Britain came to dominate the world.

INTRODUCTION

The Treaty of Aix-la-Chapelle, which ended eight years of fighting in the War of Austrian Succession (1740–48), was deeply unpopular on all sides ('as stupid as the peace' became a French proverb) and everyone was aware that it provided a mere breathing space until the great powers clashed again. The conflict was renewed earlier than expected. There were two distinct triggers for the Seven Years War of 1756–63. One was in North America, where the very remoteness of the European conflict has led some historians to regard the American warfare as a thing apart, designated as 'The French and Indian War'. The other was in Eastern Europe, where Prussian and Austrian interests collided. French expansion into the Ohio country in the early 1750s led the British government to respond with a major expedition sent from London under General Edward Braddock. When the French saw the scale of the Braddock mission, they sent six of their best battalions to Canada. The British Cabinet met in emergency session on 22 January 1755 and took the momentous decision to intercept the French convoy. Admiral Edward Boscawen cruised off Newfoundland, engaged three French ships on 10 June and captured two of them, although he failed to intercept the main convoy and clearly revealed Britain as the aggressor nation. France at once broke off diplomatic relations with Britain though it did not proceed to an outright declaration of war, constrained in part by Spain's unwillingness to help; Spain was at the time under an Anglophile king and an Anglophile Prime Minister. Yet throughout 1755 a bitter undeclared war raged in North America.

Historians normally date the formal outbreak of the Seven Years War to the late summer of 1756. In Europe Britain's position was immensely complicated, not to say compromised, by the Hanoverian dynasty itself, which made the Electorate of Hanover the Achilles heel on the continent. When France threatened retaliation for the piracy on the high seas with an invasion of Hanover, Britain asked for help from Holland, under the terms of the Treaty of Aix-la-Chapelle. But Holland, playing Spain to

England's France, categorically refused. The British turned for help to one of the hostile powers in the War of Austrian Succession. By the Convention of 16 January 1756 Britain and Prussia both agreed to guarantee each other's dominions and to resist jointly the entry of foreign armies into Germany. Russia, disgusted by British duplicity (since it already had a similar anti-Prussian agreement with Britain), thereupon entered into an alliance with Austria. The Austrian queen Maria Theresa then played her masterstroke. Aware that there was an ancient hostility at Versailles to Austria (the great battles of the last war – Fontenoy, Roucoux, Lawfeldt – had all been fought on the soil of the Austrian Netherlands), the Queen ingeniously decided to make overtures to Madame de Pompadour, Louis XV's mistress and confidante. Flattered by this royal deference, La Pompadour was instrumental in persuading the French king to undertake the famous 'reversal of alliances'. The Treaty of Versailles on 1 May 1756, which stunned Europe, stipulated that Austria would be neutral in the French war with Britain and that France would not threaten the Austrian Netherlands or sign any treaty with Russia; if attacked, however, both nations were pledged to come to the aid of the other.

Louis XV was playing a dangerous game. By the joint strategy of an invasion threat against England and an attack on Minorca in 1756 he hoped to avoid the entanglements of continental warfare, concentrating instead on the global struggle against Britain. But Austria had its own agenda, on which the principal item was the reconquest of Silesia. Realising that the Austrian army would not be ready to carry out this project until spring 1757, Frederick II, King of Prussia, got his retaliation in first and on 28 August 1756 sent his troops across the border into Saxony; by 16 October he had forced the Saxons to surrender. Austria immediately asked France to honour its obligations by sending 24,000 troops. The war was now declared and general, and Louis XV had failed signally to avoid the morass of continental warfare.

Britain and France were almost constantly at war during the 'long eighteenth century' from 1688 to 1815 – a war waged to determine who would be master of the world. The so-called War of the League of Augsburg ran for eight years until 1697; after a short breather, the two nations clashed again in the War of Spanish Succession (1702–13). A longish but tense interlude ended with the outbreak of the War of Austrian Succession in 1740. Seven years after the Treaty of Aix-la-Chapelle, the Seven Years War broke out. France tried, and partly succeeded, in recouping some of the catastrophic losses sustained in the Treaty of Paris in 1763 by a five-year war from 1778 to 1783, which ensured that the United States emerged as an independent nation but thereby bankrupted France and precipitated the

French Revolution. Finally, there were twenty-one years of revolutionary and Napoleonic warfare directed against Britain (with a meaningless 'half-time' interval in 1802–03), ending only with Waterloo in 1815. In 127 years, France and Britain were at war for sixty of them. It is customary to refer to the period 1688–1815 as the 'Second Hundred Years War', but the analogy is inexact in a number of ways, for in 1337–1453 the two combatants were backward, feudal nations, not even at the military cutting edge; in that era the Mongol Empire, especially as revived by Tamerlane, was the dominant warrior state.

By 1755, however, Britain and France truly were in competition for worldwide hegemony. Both China and Japan had retreated into fearful, self-imposed isolation, sealed off from the outside world. The other main difference from the Hundred Years War of the Middle Ages was that the two combatants were no longer symmetrical powers. Britain was a remarkably focused and homogeneous society; France a disparate and heterogeneous one. When Charles II was restored to the English throne in 1660, England was still a predominantly agricultural country, where five-sixths of the population derived its living from the soil. One single statistic brings this home: after London, the capital, with half a million inhabitants, there was only one significant city: Bristol, with a population of about 30,000. But by the end of the century the new institutions of the 'Glorious Revolution' of 1688 – the Bank of England, the East India Company, the National Debt – were rapidly transforming the situation and Britain was becoming a commercial nation, relying on overseas trade. Money rather than land became the index of wealth and power, commercial capitalism rather than agriculture became the hallmark of society, the class of yeomanry or free peasants disappeared, swallowed up in the burgeoning towns, and the beginnings of industrialism were discernible. The logic of trade and commerce led the British to seek out new lands to conquer, new overseas outlets for surplus capital and exports. The commercial revolution increasingly turned the British into a nation of warriors. Since Britain was an island, never successfully invaded since 1066, it relied heavily on its navy both to defend the shores and to protect its commercial vessels across the seven seas. In short, Britain was an irreducibly maritime nation, relying on seapower.

France, by contrast, was constrained by geography. Although it had two distinct coastlines (one on the Atlantic, the other on the Mediterranean) and thus had some potential to develop as a seaborne nation, sheer physical facts forced it to be mainly a land-based power. For centuries overland arteries had led south-west to Spain, south-east to Italy and, above all, due east to Germany and Eastern Europe. This was an historical destiny that

France could not evade. France was therefore forced to divide its resources between the navy and the army, and its peculiar geographical layout prevented the increasingly monolithic economic specialisation of England. France had its great commercial ports in Marseilles, Nantes and Bordeaux, with Marseilles specialising in goods of the Near East and Nantes and Bordeaux concentrating on colonial produce. There was a silk industry in Lyons and other types of factory in Rouen, Amiens and Orléans. Yet in the main France remained a predominantly agricultural country. History, geography and culture all prevented France from the ruthless concentration on global commerce that characterised eighteenth-century Britain, and the need to defend her frontiers against a number of potential foes meant that there had to be overwhelming emphasis on the army and corresponding neglect of the navy.

It is difficult to underrate seapower and the advantage it gave Britain in the global struggle in the eighteenth century, but one clue is the way in which it enabled London to nullify the advantages France seemed to have on paper. There were at most seven million people in Britain in 1759, as against more than twenty-five million in France (140 million in Europe as a whole and 800 million in the entire world). In normal circumstances, this kind of disparity in numbers between combatants is crucial and is often cited as the core reason for the victory of the North over the South in the American Civil War. France, then, appeared to hold the best cards in the global struggle, but it was seapower that opened the door to a world of massively increasing wealth; it is well known that in political struggles money can outpoint sheer numbers. A single statistic cited by the great French naval historian, Pierre Chaunu, is eloquent. Between 1750 and 1780 the number of vessels on the world's oceans increased tenfold.

In 1759 the exploration of the Pacific lay just a decade away, and there, under the aegis of the great navigators – Cook, Vancouver, Bougainville, La Pérouse – the two great nations would continue their rivalry. The Seven Years War was both prelude and precondition of Pacific exploration and the year 1759 was again salient, for it was then that John Harrison, the man who solved the problem of longitude, produced the fourth version of his chronometer, known as H4. It was H4 that Captain Cook would take with him on his epic voyages of discovery. This was also the year when the Russians, building on the pioneering work of Bering and Chirikov, began exploring the Aleutian Islands and launching out onto the broad northern Pacific in pursuit of seals. The geopolitics of the Pacific, however, still lay some twenty years in the future and in 1759 the global conflict between Britain and France was fought in three main arenas: North America, Latin America and India. It is part of the fascination of the year 1759 that in

9

each case one can discern another crucial element in our story: the presence of a third military force, affecting both the strategies to be employed and the eventual outcome. In Latin America it was the declining imperial power of Spain that complicated the situation; in North America it was the Indian or Native American tribes,[*] and in India it was the disintegration of the Mughal Empire.

The power vacuum in Asia, with the disappearance into self-sealed autarky of both China and Japan, became more pronounced in the eighteenth century when the Mughal Empire collapsed. Aurangzeb, the last emperor, who died in 1707, was an ascetic, industrious and courageous Sunni Muslim who spent the last twenty-five years of his reign trying to deal with the troubled Deccan. He sacked Hyderabad in a campaign that carried Delhi's sway to its farthest point south, but his successors proved utterly unable to hold the unwieldy imperial structure together. At his death Aurangzeb left no fewer than seventeen legitimate claimants to his throne – sons, grandsons, great-grandsons – and the result was a predictable chaos. For a time the Sayyid brothers, Husain Ali, Governor of Patna, and Abdullah, Governor of Allahabad, were the kingmakers, but one of their protégés, Muhammad Shah (who ruled from 1719 to 1748) turned the tables on the brothers, encouraging a revolt in the Deccan and engineering their downfall. By this time Aurangzeb's mighty empire was disintegrating rapidly. Hyderabad broke away and became an independent kingdom in 1724, and Oudh and Bengal soon followed suit, with Oudh slipping into the Afghan sphere of influence.

The collapse of the Mughal Empire in many ways echoed the decline of Rome 1,300 years earlier. The army declined in quality, there was factionalism among degenerate nobles, the empire was too big to be governed by ancient methods and required modern technology, and all the time it was assailed by external enemies, with Persians, Afghans and Marathas playing the role of the 'barbarians'. It scarcely helped that the Mughals were a foreign, Muslim dynasty with no popular support in India. The 1750s witnessed a new kingmaker in the shape of Ghazi-ud-din, who deposed the ruler Ahmed Shah (ruled 1748–54) and then murdered his successor Alamgir II. The assassination of Alamgir in November 1759 really marks the end of the Mughal story. The dominant powers in the north thereafter were the Afghans and the Marathas. The Afghans took Delhi in December 1759, bringing them into direct conflict with the Marathas; two years later the Afghans defeated them in the great victory at Panipat. But the result

---

[*] This book generally uses the term 'Indian', following the nomenclature of the time.

of all this was to leave south India wide open to European penetration. The Nawabs of Arcot and Hyderabad were blatantly used as pawns by the British and French and, when Hyderabad decisively switched to the British side, France countered by putting its money on Haidar Ali of Mysore, who checked the invading Marathas in 1758. It was Haidar's son Tipu Sultan who was later to be the great power in the south and a perennial thorn in the British side. But in the late 1750s there was a clear power vacuum which the Europeans filled greedily, the French based at Pondicherry, the British at Madras.

For a while the European encroachment on Asia halted at India, for the advance guards elsewhere met with unexpected checks. The French, it is true, set up a puppet named Dhon Bandara as Sultan of the Maldives in December 1759, leaving the 'ruler' hamstrung with a treaty of alliance with France and a French bodyguard. But an attempt by the British to establish a sphere of influence in Burma ended badly. In 1753 the East India Company had built a fort on the island of Negrais off the coast of Burma, and there were hopes that this could develop into a second Madras. But in 1755 the founder of the last Burmese dynasty, Alompra Aloung P'Houra came to prominence, founding Rangoon and conquering Pegu. A year later the Peguans revolted, Alompra suspected the British of having fomented the revolt and decided that the foreigners were just too dangerous on his flank. On 6 October 1759 he launched a surprise attack on the settlement at Negrais, attacking just when the British officers at the Fort House were assembling for dinner in the upper storey of the building. The Burmese killed four men and took the others prisoner to Rangoon, forcing the East India Company to abandon its foothold in Burma. But both France and Britain continued to be jumpy about their rival's ambitions in Asia to the point where, when Captain Cook departed for Australasia and the Pacific in 1769, the French Foreign Ministry at first thought his fleet was part of a British project to conquer Japan.

It had long been an ambition of both the British and French to break the Spanish and Portuguese monopoly of trade in Latin America. Officially all commerce with Latin America was conducted either by the Manila galleon in the Pacific or by the Cadiz fleet in the Atlantic. The annual Manila galleon sailed south from Acapulco to Callao, the port of Lima, to pick up the prevailing winds, then crossed the Pacific to the Philippines before returning by a very northerly route across the north Pacific and then dropping down along the coast of California to the starting point at Acapulco. The Cadiz fleet sailed twice yearly (in January and October), went first to the French West Indies and then split into two: one convoy proceeded to Vera Cruz and the eastern ports of Mexico and the other to

Porto Bello. Discharging cargoes of arms and ammunition, manufactured items and food, they took on gold, silver, precious stones, spices and quinine; the two convoys then united at Havana for the homeward voyage. It was a permanent grievance with France that its great commercial rival had been granted the *asiento* provision by the 1713 Treaty of Utrecht that ended the War of Spanish Succession. According to that treaty, Britain alone could supply Latin America with the black slaves needed to work the colonial plantations and she could also send two ships annually with merchandise to Vera Cruz and Porto Bello, free of all taxes. France constantly complained that although the tonnage of these ships was supposed to be limited to 500 tons, the British habitually used 1,000-ton vessels and there were numerous frauds and scams practised in addition. The French were really protesting too much, for the reality was that four-fifths of the supposed Spanish monopoly consisted of French goods. Despite their official doctrines, the Spanish could not supply their colonies with what they needed and thus the Cadiz fleet was bulging with silks, hats, stockings, sheets and even ironmongery of French origin.

By 1759 there was a further muddling of Anglo-French rivalry by the Spanish 'third force'. The campaign against the Jesuits by the Paris *parlement*, the Jansenists and powerful influences like Madame de Pompadour and the Duc de Choiseul had spilled over into Spain and Portugal, where the Marquis de Pombal proved to be an even more fanatical harrier of the Society of Jesus than his French and Spanish equivalents (Choiseul and Aranda). The Jesuits had established in Paraguay a society which its supporters claimed was Plato's *Republic* come to life and its enemies considered a mere cloak for Jesuit political intrigue and economic exploitation. The essence of the Jesuit 'reductions' (colonies) in Paraguay was that production was for use rather than profit and there was no extraction of surplus value. The Jesuit overlordship of the Guaraní Indians was certainly paternalistic but it did prevent their exploitation by Spanish capitalists. The removal of the Indians from an exploitable labour force, plus the sheer horror of such an anti-capitalist example and wild rumours about gold and other treasures salted away in the jungle by the fathers, won the Jesuits a host of enemies. By far the worst of them was Sebastião José de Carvalho e Mello, Marquis of Pombal, who had been appointed Minister of Foreign Affairs in 1750 and by 1759 was Charles III of Spain's first minister.

Pombal hated the Jesuits, as they opposed his South American projects. Moreover, like Henry VIII vis-à-vis the monasteries, Pombal calculated that if he could suppress the Society of Jesus in Portuguese domains, a huge economic windfall would accrue. But until 1750 the reductions of

Paraguay, in Spanish territory, were beyond his reach. Then, in that year the secret Treaty of Limits between Spain and Portugal transferred to Portugal about two-thirds of the present-day Brazilian province of Rio Grande do Sul, including the seven Jesuit reductions on the left bank of the River Uruguay. To their horror and consternation the missionaries and their Guaraní charges were told they would have to leave their ancestral homes and settle on the opposite bank of the Uruguay. The Jesuits themselves, and even the Spanish Viceroy of La Plata, protested to Madrid and Lisbon about this new arrangement, but Pombal was adamant. The Indians were in despair and finally, in 1758, despite the pleas of their Jesuit mentors, they rose in rebellion and were heavily defeated. While the survivors dispersed to fight guerrilla warfare, Pombal saw his chance, for at this very moment fate dealt him the most favourable possible hand.

On 3 September 1758 there was an attempt on the life of the Portuguese king Joseph I, a weak and feckless character who had agreed to the Treaty of Limits without understanding any of its implications. Pombal used this as an excuse to execute leading members of the powerful Tavora family in an act of private revenge. It was an easy task for Pombal to link the assassination bid and the Tavoras with the Indian revolt in the so-called War of the Seven Reductions and convince the feeble-minded monarch that he was the victim of a Jesuit plot. Moreover, Pombal claimed (it is uncertain whether he really believed this himself) that the British planned to seize Rio de Janeiro and were in league with the Jesuits to this effect – which was why he (Pombal) had closed all Brazilian ports to foreign shipping in 1755. In this way Pombal achieved the suppression of the Jesuits throughout Portugal and Brazil; the decree to that effect was promulgated in September 1759. Spain took longer to persuade but finally, in 1767, the Jesuits were expelled from Spanish America too. The luckless pope Clement XIII spent most of his pontificate vainly pleading for leniency for the Society of Jesus against its enemies in France, Spain and Portugal before finally accepting the political reality of superior power ruthlessly deployed. It took Frederick of Prussia and Catherine the Great of Russia to save the Jesuits from extinction. From the Anglo-French point of view probably the British were the greater losers from these events. Despite the supposedly historic ties of friendship between Lisbon and London, Pombal identified the British as the major threat to his ambitions in Latin America.

Spanish indecision about the Jesuits reflected uncertainty, dithering and sometimes chaos at the court of Madrid. It would be 1762 before Spain finally entered the war against Britain, thus ensuring that the geographical scope of campaigning widened still further, with notable British sieges of Havana and Manila in the Philippines. Ricardo Wall, the Spanish Foreign

Minister, was pro-England yet widely considered to be a crypto-Jacobite. The Spanish king Ferdinand VI was an extreme neurotic and borderline psychotic, obsessed with the fear that at any moment he would die a sudden and violent death. His corpulent wife Barbara was equally neurotic, equally afraid of sudden death, and monarch and consort simply wound each other up. When Barbara died in 1758, Ferdinand's fragile mental equilibrium collapsed; he pined away and never recovered.

One of the new king's first actions was to sever the connection between the Spanish and Sicilian thrones, which had complicated Spanish affairs just as much as the Hanoverian connection complicated those of Britain. Formerly Carlos VII of the Two Sicilies, the new king Charles III of Spain abdicated the throne of Sicily in the Pragmatic Sanction of 6 October 1759. The Treaty of Naples embodying the Pragmatic Sanction forbade the union of the Spanish Crown with the Italian dominions, abdicated the Two Sicilies to Charles's third son and his descendants in perpetuity, and set out new procedures for the succession. If the King of Spain inherited the crown of the Two Sicilies, he must then abdicate it to the next male heir in succession provided he was not the Prince of the Asturias. This at least cleared the way for a coherent Spanish foreign policy. Hitherto decisions about Spanish interests in the Americas had to be weighed against Sicilian interests in the Mediterranean, and this was one of the reasons why Spain did not ally itself to France until the eleventh hour of the Seven Years War.

But it was in North America that Franco-British rivalry was at its most intense. The effective French presence in Canada dated from the early seventeenth century, and France prided itself on a colony that was a perfect microcosm of France, with a similar class structure, its peasantry recruited mainly from Normandy, Picardy, Poitou and all western provinces except Gascony and Brittany. The early Canadian aristocrats tended to be those looking for peace and tranquillity away from the religious turmoil of the Thirty Years War, and it was notable that Canada became a fervently Catholic enclave. Contrary to the ill-informed propaganda of Voltaire and his fellow *philosophes*, France never used North America as a dumping ground for the criminal classes, the unemployable and the wretched of the earth, as England did. Partly because Canada was barred both to freebooters and the *canaille*, the colony's population increased at a painfully slow rate. Lucky to survive the first Iroquois war of 1647–67, the colony of New France contained only 4,000 people in 1667. It was Louis XIV's financial genius, Colbert, who saved it by sending out fresh emigrants and a regiment of troops. Even so, the population of Canada was just 19,000 in 1714. The Treaty of Utrecht, which ceded Hudson's Bay, Newfoundland and Acadia to Britain, alerted the French to the danger that they might be swamped by the more numerous British colonists. Determined efforts to increase Canada's population during the premiership of Cardinal Fleury brought the population up to 34,000 in 1730 and 40,000 in 1740. By the outbreak of the Seven Years War in 1756 this had more than doubled to over 70,000.

By contrast, the much more heterogeneous population of the thirteen British colonies along the Atlantic seaboard (where oligarchs and adventurers mingled with deportees, vagabonds, beggars and indentured labourers who were slaves in all but name) amounted to one million inhabitants by 1740. On paper the British colonists should have overwhelmed their French counterparts, but France dealt with the threat from the 'Anglo-Saxons' by penning them behind the Allegheny Mountains and expanding southwards and westwards. La Salle's great exploring expeditions of the 1670s and 1680s brought the Mississippi, the Missouri, the Ohio and the Gulf of Mexico into the French orbit. Not content to bask in their fortresses on the St Lawrence river, the French expanded across the North American continent. Even as they became masters of the fur (and especially beaver) trade, the French trappers and *coureurs de bois* penetrated inland as far as the prairies and the Rocky Mountains. The so-called *pays d'en haut* – Ohio and all areas west of the St Lawrence river – became an essential element in French power, allowing them to dominate the commerce of the interior and make treaties with the powerful tribes who lived around the Great Lakes. In the long term Franco-British rivalry in North America hinged on who would control the interior and who would be first to reach the Pacific by the overland route. This geopolitical imperative was constantly in the minds of the British adventurers and entrepreneurs who tried to manipulate the Indian tribes of the interior into abandoning their traditional friendship with France.

Yet even as the military balance seemed to be tipping decisively in Britain's favour by 1759, the Anglophone colonies had to confront a serious tribal war that had nothing to do with the collision between Britain and France; had the war broken out a year earlier it might have had a decisive effect on the outcome of the entire conflict. Suddenly in 1759 the most peaceable sector of the frontier, in the far south (South Carolina) burst into flames. For at least thirty years the powerful and populous Cherokee tribe had traded amicably with the colonists of South Carolina. Ensconced in three villages near the modern Tennessee–South Carolina border, they had traded deer skins and slaves with the colonists and even operated as a police force on their behalf, handing back runaway slaves in return for cash rewards. In 1758 they had volunteered 700 of their warriors to fight for the British. This turned out to be the trigger that detonated the rebellion the

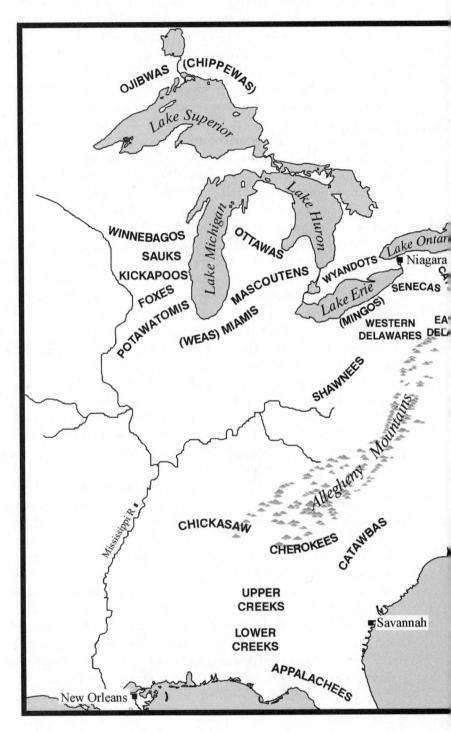

The Indian tribes of eastern North America, 1759

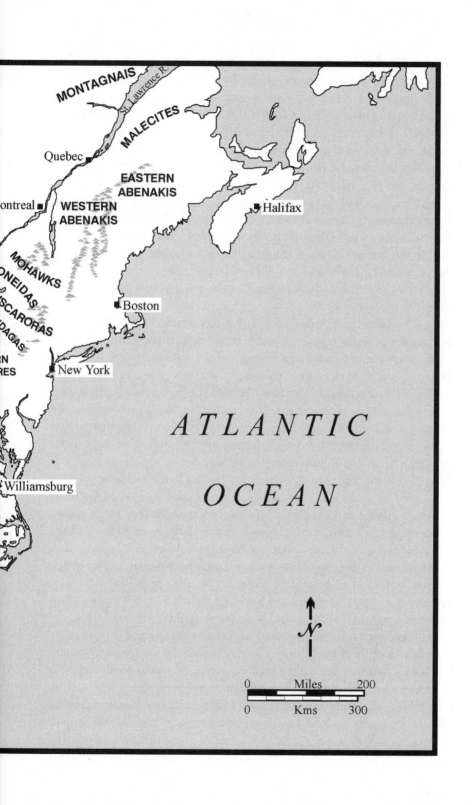

MONTAGNAIS

St. Lawrence R.

MALECITES

Quebec

EASTERN
ABENAKIS

ontreal

WESTERN
ABENAKIS

Halifax

MOHAWKS

NEIDAS

SCARORAS

DAGAS

N
RES

Boston

New York

ATLANTIC

OCEAN

Williamsburg

N

| 0 | Miles | 200 |
| 0 | Kms | 300 |

following year. Brigadier-General John Forbes treated his new allies with contempt, had no regard for their idiosyncratic folk ways and insisted they abide by the military discipline of the British regular army. Frustrated and disappointed not to receive the cornucopia of plunder and prisoners they had reckoned on, almost all the Cherokees left Forbes and headed south with the muskets and ammunition he had provided. On their way through the Virginia and North Carolina back country, they stole a few horses and butchered a handful of cattle. The reaction of the local militias was savagely punitive; there was cold-blooded murder and even massacre of the Cherokees. To add insult to injury, when the Cherokee warriors eventually staggered in to their homelands, they found that South Carolina colonists had taken advantage of their absence to poach game on the ancestral hunting lands of the tribe. Cherokee elders spent the spring of 1759 debating their options: either a sudden war of revenge or an embassy to Governor William Henry Lyttelton of South Carolina to seek substantial reparations.

The Cherokee chief Attakullakulla (Little Carpenter) was the leading advocate of a peaceful resolution of the tribe's grievances. In the spring of 1759 he spent many months negotiating with Lyttelton. But the Governor was duplicitous and stalled him, refusing to grant the gifts and peace offerings that Little Carpenter demanded. Scholarly opinion is still divided on whether Lyttelton was being stupid or wicked: either he underrated the seriousness of Little Carpenter's request and failed to realise that he was the one important 'dove' in a by now largely hawkish nation; or, more likely, he lusted after military glory and was looking for an excuse to wage war on the Cherokees. The tribal leaders played into his hands by losing patience with Little Carpenter's mission and launching a punitive raid on the frontier, which killed thirty settlers. Lyttleton escalated the conflict by telling the Cherokees that until the 'murderers' were surrendered to him, all the customary supplies of gunpowder and bullets would be embargoed. Since the Cherokees needed this ammunition for their autumn and winter hunts, they sent a second embassy to Charleston to treat with Lyttelton. The Governor then made war inevitable by taking them prisoner (October 1759) and announcing that no one would be released until the killers of the thirty settlers were surrendered. In a show of force he transferred his prisoners to the frontier fort of Fort Prince George, together with 1,300 troops and three tons of gunpowder which, he announced, he would hand over with the captive chiefs once the guilty warriors were given up.

Lyttelton's demands were unrealistic. Either he knew that and was being evilly disingenuous, or he did not, in which case he was criminally stupid. His actions played straight into the hands of the hardliners among the

Cherokees, but even if they had not, doves like Little Carpenter would not have been able to deliver on any promise made. Not only had the 'guilty men' dispersed into the forests where they could not be tracked down but, according to the Cherokee code, they had done no more than avenge their kinsmen massacred the autumn before and were thus acting honourably according to their own lights. Lyttelton then compounded his idiocy by leaving a small garrison behind with the Cherokee hostages and marching back to Charleston with the bulk of his forces – to avoid an outbreak of smallpox, he claimed. The inevitable upshot was that the Cherokees surrounded Fort Prince George and cut it off from the rest of South Carolina. The garrison troops responded by massacring their hostages. A general Cherokee uprising in early 1760 rolled back most of the frontier in South Carolina and by March the warriors were only seventy-five miles from Charleston. Lyttelton, promoted Governor of Jamaica for his 'sterling' service, dumped the entire problem into the lap of the British Commander-in-Chief, North America, Jeffrey Amherst. The bloody Cherokee rising lasted another two years; the British used scorched-earth tactics against them and finally, when the Cherokees ran out of ammunition, severely defeated them, in the process taking the previously thriving Cherokee economy back into the Stone Age. It was the luckless Little Carpenter who had to negotiate humiliating peace terms in 1761.

The southern frontier, detached as it was from the great Franco-British conflict in the north, proved particularly tempestuous in 1759. James Hamilton arrived in Philadelphia on 17 November 1759 as the new Lieutenant-Governor of Pennsylvania and Delaware. He had served in this capacity before and was reluctant to return but did so when it was agreed that he could have new taxation powers. On his arrival he ran straight into a frontier crisis. Shawnee Indians on the Pennsylvania/Virginia border attacked settlers in October 1759 and wiped out entire families. The militia overtook the marauders in Highland County and fought a few inconclusive skirmishes before the Shawnees broke off and withdrew. The dogged militia caught up with the raiders again near the present border with West Virginia and this time managed to kill some twenty warriors. But for a time the worry was that the Shawnees and Cherokees might make common cause and set the entire south alight, thus possibly enabling the French to avoid what otherwise looked like certain defeat in North America. That danger was averted, and ironically Hamilton went on to become a major factor in the downfall and death of the Delaware chief Teedyuscung, a major player in the 'French and Indian war' in the north. This was yet another of the salient intersections in the complex mosaic of Native American tribal politics.

Turbulent events in India, South America and North America – quite distinct from the bloody Anglo-French worldwide conflict itself – illustrate the general thesis that 1759 was an exceptionally violent year. Even the Spanish in North America were beset by problems with the contumacious tribes of modern Texas and New Mexico. Having narrowly averted an uprising of Orcoquiza Indians in March 1759 by the desperate expedient of executing the Spanish soldier who had killed a tribesman, the Spanish authorities of New Spain (Mexico) found themselves having to wage war on the tribes of the plains anyway. The trouble had really begun in 1748 when the Comanches attacked the Apache missions at San Saba (under Spanish protection), carrying off all surviving able-bodied men, women and children as slaves. The Spanish Governor of Mexico ordered Diego Ortiz Parilla, military commander of San Luis de Béjar (now San Antonio) to attack the raiders, who, he had discovered, were secretly backed by the French. Parilla marched out in September 1759 with 300 men (including 100 Spanish cavalry), two cannons, six wagons and a wealth of gunpowder and ammunition. His objective was the twin city-states of the Taovayan Confederation in present-day Oklahoma; this league comprised the Caddoes, Tawconies and Wichitas, who were close allies of the Comanches. Unfortunately Ortiz Parilla was heavily defeated after falling into an Indian trap; at the battle of San Teodor his men were massacred in droves and only sixty of the proud 300-strong force survived to limp back to Texas. Such was the ill-fated Red River campaign of 1759.

The cosmic violence seemed counterpointed in Nature itself this year, for there was a quite extraordinary number of seismic and volcanic outbreaks reported from all corners of the globe. A world still recovering from the earthquakes of 1755, which had killed 30,000 in Lisbon and 40,000 in Persia, was again convulsed by underground turbulence. An early warning was sounded by a quake in Tripoli in September, but this was only the beginning. Two massive earthquakes struck the Middle East in October and November 1759 (the latter 7.4 on the Richter scale), causing particular damage in Syria, Lebanon and Palestine and killing between 10,000 and 40,000 people along the Dead Sea Rift, causing structural damage and devastation in Beirut, Damascus and Aleppo. The 6.6 Richter-scale earthquake in October along the Jordan Gorge caused severe damage in the Holy Land, especially at Nazareth and Tiberias, and on the coast there were six-foot tsunamis and ships were tossed onshore. Tripoli was convulsed by a quite separate tremor in September. There was another severe earthquake in Scandinavia in December 1759, oddly coinciding with a spell of icy weather in the Baltic so severe that St Petersburg experienced its coldest-ever temperatures. In March 1759 Vesuvius, particularly active in the years 1744–60, spewed out a torrent of lava after a large portion of cinder cone collapsed, while in Mexico the Jorullo volcano in Michoacan province erupted with deadly effect on 29 September. In Africa Zambia experienced an annular eclipse in December following the earthquakes. Meanwhile on the night of 3–4 November a 'perfect storm', with waves at least fifty feet high and winds in excess of 100 mph, hit Nova Scotia, causing vast damage to wharves at Halifax. All the salt and sugar in the stores was destroyed, two schooners were driven inland, thousands of trees blown down, and the storm broke over the dykes in the Bay of Fundy, raising the water level eight feet above normal and overflowing the marsh lands, which remained unfit for farming for the next three years. But perhaps Nature's most dramatic manifestation of 1759 was the reappearance of Halley's Comet, clearly visible in European skies in March. Although the *philosophes* – and Maupertuis in particular – had gone out of their way to ridicule those who believed that astral phenomena presaged events on Earth, many still believed this was the case. As in 1066 (the first clearly recorded year of Halley's Comet) it was widely thought that catastrophe was just around the corner. Curiously, as in 1066, the superstitious were not wrong, for 1759 would shape British destinies more than any event since the Battle of Hastings.

ONE

THE STRUGGLE FOR NEW FRANCE

If we were to judge only by the long-term impact of human beings at the height of their powers in 1759, there is a strong argument for awarding pride of historical place to John Wesley, the founder of Methodism. Originally inspired by the notion of a return to primitive Christianity and the creation of a 'new man' who would be an exemplar of responsibility, sobriety, respectability, piety and probity, the vegetarian, teetotal, diminutive Wesley was, at fifty-six, still pursuing his punishing regime of itinerant preaching which would see him clock up 280,000 miles of horseback travel by the end of his long life. He had originally intended his 'Methodist Connexion' to be a splinter group within the Church of England, but the breach with the Anglican communion widened once Wesley began advocating ordination by priests rather than bishops, the institution of lay preachers rather than parsons with 'livings', outdoor worship, miracles and 'enthusiasm', and reaching out to the poor and dispossessed. As has been well said, the Church of England emphasised churches and pulpits, ordained clergy and local incumbent vicars, while Methodism emphasised open-air meetings, itinerant preachers and nationwide evangelism.

The year of 1759 was a busy one for the restless Wesley, whose flock had grown steadily to the point where his revivalist movement was already holding its fifteenth Annual Conference. Two very different snapshots from either end of the year evince the different faces of the would-be 'Pope' of Methodism. When French invasion threatened at the beginning of the year, Wesley appointed 16 February as a day of national prayer and fasting, in the hope that God would support England against France. That morning Wesley preached at Wandsworth at 5 a.m. and 9 a.m. and again at 3 p.m. at Spitalfields and at 8.30 p.m. at Methodist headquarters. The Countess of Huntingdon attended the evening service and afterwards invited Wesley to preside over a prayer meeting at her house. There he preached to a select company, including the Earl and Countess of Dartmouth, the Earl and Countess of Chesterfield, Sir Charles and Lady Hotham, plus assorted members of the Cavendish and Carteret families. But the autumn of 1759 found Wesley chiding his termagant wife Mary, with whom he lived in a marriage of quite exceptional unhappiness. His letter to her of 23 October listed ten things he disliked about her conduct, with ten items of advice whereby she could expunge her behaviour. 'I will tell you simply and plainly the things which I dislike . . . sharing any one of my letters and private papers without my leave . . . being myself a prisoner in my own house . . . talking about me behind my back . . . laying to my charge things which you know to be false.'

For all his religious fervour and undoubted achievements, John Wesley was not a very pleasant man. Disingenuous, duplicitous and mendacious, he liked to rewrite his own life story in his letters and journals, so that he appeared omniscient, omnipotent and infallible. But occasionally Wesley was faced by phenomena so overpowering that he confronted the truth with a steady eye. He liked to litter his autobiography with 'turning points' and lights on the road to Damascus, but one defining moment of truth certainly occurred. On his first visit to America in January 1736, Wesley endured a four-month voyage of tribulation before making landfall and was extremely lucky to survive a severe storm. His diary for 17 January explains the situation: 'The sea broke over us from bow to stern, burst through the cabins of the state room where three or four of us were and covered us all over.' On 23 January the storm renewed its full ferocity: 'The sea broke over, split the mainsail to pieces, covered the ship and poured in between the deck as if the great deep had already swallowed us up. A terrible screaming began among the English. The Germans (Moravians) calmly sang on.' According to Wesley, the steadfastness of the Moravians converted him to their view of religion though, naturally, it was not long before he had jettisoned them in turn.

What impresses the chronicler of the eighteenth century, rather than the student of religion, is the extreme hazard of a North Atlantic crossing. Historians talk blithely of entire armies crossing the ocean from Europe to America as if a mere train journey was at issue, but seldom is there any appreciation of what a truly terrifying and diabolical experience it was. In the age of sail the intrepid mariners had few defences against hurricanes, typhoons and high seas, and we now know that the usual track for America-bound vessels from northern Europe, passing the Newfoundland Banks is especially perilous. Tens of thousands of sailors and hundreds of ships vanished without trace in this area in the 300 years after Columbus's discovery of the New World, including some of the most gifted seamen of the times. In 1498 John Cabot left Bristol with five ships, hoping to consolidate the discoveries he had made the year before at Cape Breton and Cape Cod. Only one ship returned to Bristol, and Cabot was never seen again. In this era England's rivals for the fisheries of the Grand Banks off Newfoundland were the Portuguese, but even their most eminent mariners fared no better. Portugal's great maritime pioneers, the Corte-Real brothers, both perished in the North Atlantic. Gaspar Corte-Real left Lisbon in May 1501 with two ships, but disappeared for ever into the Atlantic maw. When his second ship limped back to Portugal in October with news that Gaspar was lost at sea, his brother Miguel organised another expedition to search for him. In May 1502 he departed Lisbon for Labrador but he too vanished without trace.

Modern science has conclusively established the main cause for the tragedy that befell so many brave men in the age of sail. Giant waves, almost vertical walls of green water seemingly appearing from nowhere, 100 feet or more from trough to crest, were long thought to be the tall tales of old salts who had spent too many years before the mast. Only recently has it been appreciated that such freak waves occur relatively frequently and are a deadly threat to shipping. No vessel ever constructed, even in the era of ocean liners, is equipped to deal with such monsters, and those ships that have had close encounters with these watery leviathans have survived more by good luck than anything else. To give just two examples of the perils posed by the rogue wave, we may cite the following chilling statistics. Even today most ships are designed to deal with maximum wave heights of forty-five feet, producing a maximum pressure of fifteen tons per square inch. Yet a 100-foot wave would produce a pressure of 100 tons per square inch. Similarly, even the largest ocean liner today is built on the principle that the maximum distance between two successive wave crests is 800 feet. Yet unimpeachable evidence has shown that ships in the North Atlantic caught between two different 100-foot waves fall into a trough fully 1,200 feet between the two crests.

Older maritime 'experts' hypothesised that freak waves of these dimensions could occur only in exceptional circumstances: off the coast of South Africa, where the wind pushes against a very strong current, thus piling up a pyramidal wave; or off the coast of Norway, where a shallow sea bottom focuses waves on one spot. But it is now known that previous models of wave behaviour at sea were seriously deficient, since they assumed that all waves obeyed a single 'linear' pattern. Unassailable research has now established as a certainty that there is a different kind of unstable, non-linear wave that can suck in energy from nearby waves, creating a monster that will quickly grow to massive proportions. Wave heights are normally determined by a threefold combination: speed of wind, duration of storm and extent of oceanic 'fetch' or open sea. But in a prolonged storm when the average wave height is already steep, several large waves can combine to produce the all-devouring Moloch of the oceans. The situation is made even worse when some 100-foot waves are preceded by a deep trough, producing the phenomenon known to sailors as the 'hole in the ocean' – another nightmare, like the rogue waves themselves, long thought to be the product of mariners' overwrought imaginations.

And so, as the French and British fought each other in the 1750s for control of the New World, they always faced a common enemy. The Atlantic in winter is a fearsome place, and for those limited by the technology of sailing ships, its terrors must have been so much greater. The unyielding, grey, white-capped, lumpy cross-seas and the pyramidal waves taxed the endurance of even the greatest masters of sail. For those coming from the St Lawrence and preparing to sail the mighty ocean to Europe, as a brilliant twenty-nine-year-old envoy did in the autumn of 1758, there were the additional perils of the Newfoundland Banks, notorious for its high seas, where waves 100 feet from crest to trough were encountered when the winds reached a three-figure velocity. Louis Antoine de Bougainville, mathematical genius but working within the limited scientific knowledge of his age, thought that the North Atlantic in this region was a statistical freak, for according to the laws of probability such heights should occur only three times in every million waves. But Bougainville was rarely surprised by anything, for he knew about life as well as mathematics. In many ways he was the perfect combination of French rationalism and Anglo-Saxon empiricism. And the sea was in his blood.

It is one of history's curiosities that all four of the eighteenth century's great circumnavigators served in the Seven Years War. The naval commander, George Anson, it is true, was past his glory days and largely sailed a desk at the Admiralty. But Bougainville, like his countryman the Comte de la Pérouse, and like the greatest navigator of all time, Captain James Cook, saw action in the Canadian theatre. Perhaps it is the prerogative only of the multi-talented near-genius to sample life in all its forms and to achieve a synoptic global vision. Bougainville certainly qualified on all counts. At the age of twenty-five, influenced by the French mathematician and *philosophe* d'Alembert, he published his *Treatise on Integral Calculus*, written two years earlier, a stunning achievement of great lucidity, which secured him election to the prestigious Royal Society in London in 1756. A great career in mathematics beckoned, but Bougainville's restless intellect had already sought out new domains. Joining the army in 1754, he was selected two years later to accompany the new commander in 'New France' (as the French termed Canada). Now it was as the Marquis de Montcalm's trusted envoy that Bougainville made the perilous crossing of the Atlantic to lobby Montcalm's political masters at Versailles. Ahead of Bougainville were all his greatest triumphs. In his circumnavigation of the globe in 1766–69 he claimed Tahiti and the Tuamotu archipelago for France.

His name would be given to an island in the Solomons group and to a brilliant tropical plant. An original member of the Institute of France, he lived to see Napoleon's greatest triumphs and died a Senator in his eighty-second year.

Bougainville left Montreal on 3 November 1758 and boarded the *Victoire* at the mouth of the St Lawrence eight days later. Landfall was at Morlaix after a month's tempest-tossed travail. When Bougainville arrived at Versailles on 20 December, he found his own fascination with the Indian tribes of North America matched by that of King Louis XV and the Marquise de Pompadour – formerly the King's mistress but now his confidante, procuress and, to all intents and purposes, Prime Minister in all but name. Much of the attention fastened on the Iroquois or Six Nations, in many ways the key to supremacy in North America. Who were they and why were they so consistently hostile to France? Bougainville, who would later popularise the notion of the Polynesians as 'noble savages', had no illusions, but his sociological flair was acute and he brought all his customary lucidity to bear. Properly known as the Hodenosaunee, the five original nations of the Iroquois (Mohawks, Oneidas, Senecas, Onondagas and Cayugas) lived in long strips of territory that ran in parallel north–south along the lakes of what would later be New York State. The people of the Hodenosaunee, or 'people of the longhouse', were so called from their characteristic dwellings – long bark-covered longhouses with barrel roofs, about 200 feet long and twenty-five feet wide. They were hunter-gatherers, who added corn, beans, squash, nuts and berries to the diet of deer, trout and salmon caught by the young warriors. Kinship was the key to Iroquois society. Since the longhouses could shelter up to a dozen families, from about AD 1000 clans tended to form from these extended families, and the clans in turn comprised the tribe; clan membership was by descent through the mother. But to prevent inbreeding and to foster solidarity in the tribe at large, each young person in a clan had to marry outside the clan – what anthropologists call exogamy.

Division of labour within the Iroquois was traditional. Men hunted and made war; women looked after children and oversaw domestic arrangements. But, as in many traditional societies, both males and females functioned as priests and seers. Like many North American Indian societies, the Iroquois prized power very highly. A complicated pantheistic cosmology was based on the overall notion of *orenda* – the totality of power, both material and spiritual. Since *orenda* was linked to population size, and the aggregate of tribal power was held to decrease with a single death, the Iroquois had a permanent motive for expansion and aggression, for they needed constant fresh blood, either from captives or newly adopted tribes.

At the end of Canada's bloodiest war, in 1689, after the rampaging Iroquois had slaughtered the French in their hundreds, Hodenosaunee warriors numbered 2,550, but after the warfare of the 1690s they were down to just 1,230. They recovered their fighting strength partly by adopting captives into the tribes, but most of all by absorbing an entirely new tribe, the Tuscaroras, into the Hodenosaunee League, which thereafter became the League of Six Nations. By 1720 the Iroquois could once again put 2,000 warriors in the field.

The great mythical founding father of the Iroquois was Hiawatha – mythical in the sense that the entire social structure of the Hodenosaunee confederation was attributed to him. Hiawatha was an Onondaga chief, who ended the self-destructive practice of vendetta and blood vengeance among the original five Iroquois nations and substituted a code of laws – according to Native American tradition a combination of the Ten Commandments, the laws of Solon and the US Constitution. This established a Grand Council of the Five Nations at the seat of the Onondagas. The oldest tribes, the Mohawks and the Senecas, traditionally sat on the eastern side of the council fire, the younger tribes of the Oneidas and Cayugas on the west, while the Onondagas sat in the northern position. A primitive form of grass-roots democracy was practised: first the individual tribes would hammer out and resolve their differences, then the inter-tribal disputes would be settled until finally (at least in theory) an overall consensus would emerge. Where there was a clear division of interests between the tribes – with, say, the Mohawks and Senecas ranged on one side and the Oneidas and Cayugas on the other – the Onondaga would exercise a casting vote (the paramount chief of the Onondagas, usually known as 'the Onondaga', was recognised as the supreme ruler). The overlordship of the Onondaga seems puzzling from our vantage point, since the Senecas were in many ways far the most important tribe: they could muster as many braves as the other four tribes put together. Each Iroquois tribal headman was known as a Half King and had considerable local power, subject only to the overlordship of the Onondaga. The Hodenosaunee League, in short, was a primitive form of federalism. This political structure was certainly a key factor in the rise and rise of the Iroquois as a military power. They reached their zenith in the seventeenth century when, armed with muskets obtained from Dutch fur traders, they conquered the Hurons, Eries, Monongahelas and Shawnees before stuttering to a halt around 1665–67. Exhausted by constant warfare, truncated by Jesuit conversions and deprived of the supply of weapons once the English conquered Dutch North America, the Iroquois throttled back on expansionism for the rest of the century.

The Iroquois always fascinated European observers: their admirers in the eighteenth century included Benjamin Franklin and Thomas Jefferson and, in the nineteenth century, Lewis Morgan, Friedrich Engels and Karl Marx. Three things particularly impressed the outsider: Iroquois democracy, the lack of a state apparatus and the role of women. To Europeans it was axiomatic that social consensus could not exist without the threat of force and the entire panoply of soldiers, gendarmes, police, kings, governors, nobles, prefects, judges, trials and prisons. But the Iroquois had society without the state – defined as a situation where no one has the full-time job of enforcing society's norms, values and laws. Moreover, the Iroquois achieved another 'impossible' target – a democratic system meshed with a communal economic system, or economic levelling without coercion. Their political sophistication was remarkable, and Franklin, an avowed white supremacist, paid them a grudging, backhanded compliment for their ability to form a harmonious federal league: 'It would be a very strange thing if Six Nations of Ignorant Savages should be capable of forming a scheme for such an Union and be able to execute it in such a manner, as that it has subsisted Ages, and appears indissoluble, and yet a union should be impracticable for ten or a dozen English colonies.'

The Six Nations operated on a kinship principle whereby the gens or clan was more important than the nuclear family. In its emphasis on clans and societies (phratries), as much as in its democratic decision-making, the Iroquois League recalled the city-states of Ancient Greece, although in some respects it was ahead of the Greeks. The female principle was highly valued among the Iroquois. Descent among them was matrilineal or through the mother, whereas the normal pattern among North American Indians was patrilineal. Moreover, women could take part in the Council of the Gens, the democratic assembly in which every adult male and female had a voice on questions before it. Women were particularly influential among the Senecas and did not hesitate to 'knock off the horns' from the head of a chief or to bust him down to the ranks, though capital punishment for members of the league was forbidden except in the case where a leader turned out to be unrepentant, incorrigible or abusive. But we should not exaggerate sexual equality or turn the league into a gender-free paradise. Males retained the ultimate power in an all-male executive council which determined 'emergency' issues (that is, all those relating to war), and naturally, as with all such 'senates' they themselves decided what constituted an emergency.

Yet it was not Iroquois mores, folk ways, politics or decision-making that most fascinated Bougainville's avid listeners at Versailles. They were more interested in the Indians' status as 'savages' and, lolling in comfort in the parkland of Versailles, indulged in the luxury of vicarious thrill as they listened to the young genius's description of Iroquois massacres and atrocities. Scalping, tomahawking, torture, war-whooping, arson, destruction and even cannibalism featured largely in Bougainville's recital for, as he wrote elsewhere: 'The very recital of the cruelties they committed on the battlefield is horrible. The ferocity and insolence of these black-souled barbarians makes one shudder. It is an abominable kind of war. The air one breathes is contagious of insensibility and hardness.' He told his entranced listeners that the mere sight of painted warriors in scalplocks yelling their war cries could freeze the blood of European soldiery. But this aspect of North American Indians was not restricted to the Iroquois. Bougainville also related that a party of 300 raw New Jersey provincials had once been ambushed by the Ottawas, who were allies of the French, and were speared like fish as they ran panic-stricken into a river: 'Terrified by the sight of these monsters, their agility, their firing, and their yells, they surrendered almost without resistance.'

It is worth stressing that, although his voyages in the South Pacific later popularised the notion of the 'noble savage', Bougainville himself was no Rousseau-like admirer of the primitive or of 'man in a state of nature'. He was habitually scathing about Native Americans and scoffed at the Ottawas, who were so dependent on their manitous or deified spirits; recently, he said with contemptuous condescension, they had added two Masters of Life to their cosmology: one brown and beardless, who had created the Indians, and the other white and bearded, who had created the French. He chafed at the necessity to form alliances with 'savages', to humour them and buy them off with presents, and complained particularly about the obligation 'of being a slave to these Indians, of hearing them night and day in council and in private, when caprice takes hold of them, when a dream, or an excess of vapours and the constant objective of begging wine or brandy leads them on . . . an eternal little detail, petty, and one of which Europe has no idea'.

Although Bougainville doubtless enjoyed curdling the blood of foppish courtiers and elegant ladies at Versailles, he was right to place so much emphasis on the Iroquois, for sober historical opinion inclines to the view that it was the Hodenosaunee League that triggered the global conflict known as the Seven Years War. The abiding ambition of the French in the first half of the eighteenth century was to secure the Ohio Valley as a kind of Suez Canal of the American interior, facilitating lines of communication between eastern Canada and New Orleans and the Mississippi. Yet it was on this precise Ohio Valley that a supreme Seneca chief of the Iroquois, Tanaghrisson (originally a Catawba captive), known as the Half King, who rose to power in the 1740s, had set his heart and he had already sent Indian settlers there. A meeting between Tanaghrisson and a French military delegation ended badly when the Seneca chief revealed his ambitions. The French commander raged at him: 'I am not afraid of flies or mosquitoes, for the Indians are such as those. I tell you, down that river [the Ohio] I will go. If the river is blocked up, I have the forces to burst it open and tread under my feet all that oppose me. I despise all the stupid things you have said.' He ended by throwing at Tanaghrisson the belt of wampum which the chief had brought as a sign of friendship, then stamping on it and kicking it around with heavy gestures of contempt.

The Iroquois and the French were on a collision course, but to muddy the waters, there were two major complications. Under the impact of British and French machinations in the early eighteenth century, the Iroquois Confederacy was no longer as solid as it had once been and was actually in danger of political fragmentation. Although the Hodenosaunee League was always inclined to be pro-British, some severe military setbacks early in the century made them more circumspect and inclined to hedge their bets: they therefore began to splinter into Anglophile, Francophile and neutral factions. By and large the policy of the Iroquois was to play off the British against the French and, under a guise of neutrality, advance a threefold strategy of war, peace and co-optation. They wanted peace with the French-allied Algonquin Indians of the upper Mississippi Valley and war against the southern tribes, especially the powerful Cherokees and Catawbas of South Carolina. Meanwhile the Iroquois sought accommodation with the colonial government of Pennsylvania with the ulterior aim of co-opting other important Indian peoples, such as the Shawnees and Delawares. The Treaty of Lancaster, Pennsylvania, in 1744 is sometimes set down in history as a defining moment, when Iroquois power was at its apogee, for here the confederacy received the green light for all three phases of its overall strategy. The colonial government acknowledged the Onondaga's suzerainty over the southern tribes; it paid the people of the longhouses £800 in cash and £300 in gold, with which they could buy off putative opponents or finance a new war; and Virginia granted Hodenosaunee warriors transit rights for the purpose of attacking the Cherokees and Catawbas.

But this was also the moment when the Iroquois League started to come apart at the seams. Basically, the Onondaga had duped the British into thinking that the Iroquois Confederacy was all-powerful and that it could control the Ohio Valley with a rod of iron. Official gullibility was increased by the confident pronouncements of Pennsylvania's Indian 'experts' to the effect that the Iroquois could put 9,300 warriors into the field; the true figure for 'effectives' (warriors that could actually be put in the field) was no more than 1,100. On paper this seemed plausible, for between 1713 and 1744 the Five Nations had staged a comeback by adding the Tuscaroras to their league as the sixth nation. But this seemingly powerful position masked all manner of cracks. The Senecas, the most westerly tribe, had settled the Ohio country from the 1720s, entering into informal alliances with the Delawares and Shawnees, who had also been forced west by European immigration. Now the entire political structure of the Iroquois depended on obedience to the Onondaga by the Half Kings. In the 1740s two things happened. First, Tanaghrisson increasingly asserted his independence from the Onondaga. Then the disgruntled Shawnees and Delawares in the Ohio Valley, making common cause with the Mingoes (the most westerly sept of the Senecas), grew increasingly restive and independent, asserting their autonomy not only from the Onondaga but even from Tanaghrisson. Some said that Iroquois hubris was finally beginning to produce its nemesis.

Yet even as the Iroquois geared up to confront French aspirations in the Ohio Valley, a third power staked its claim. By the Treaty of Lancaster, which they had considered such a triumph, the Iroquois, who did not understand the small print in European treaties and never had the subtle implications explained to them, gave up all claims to land in Maryland and Virginia, not realising that this would in fact negate their own claim to the Ohio Valley. Virginia's colonial charter granted its settlers rights to all land westwards to the Pacific – a point the Treaty Commissioners at Lancaster certainly did not spell out to the Iroquois. Nor was this some mere theoretical or paper right. In 1745 Virginia explicitly granted the land in the Ohio country to a consortium of twenty real-estate speculators. The Onondaga's neutralist strategy was further undermined in 1748 when the Mohawks, the most easterly and Anglophile of the Iroquois, abandoned neutrality in favour of cooperation with New York State. The Onondaga thus found himself outflanked and facing four lots of potential enemies: the British and their Mohawk allies in the east; the dissident Mingoes, Delawares and Shawnees in the west; the French in the north and west; and the ambitious Tanaghrisson on his own doorstep.

But British power did not manifest itself only in the form of the property speculators of Virginia. The government in London feared that unless decisive action was taken, its colonies would be confined for ever between the Appalachians and the Atlantic by a French cordon. The British government would then have to spend so many naval and military resources on defending the beleaguered thirteen colonies in North America that it would be reduced to impotence in Europe. So for its own reasons London wanted control over the crucial Ohio country. The fall of Louisbourg to the British in 1745, during the War of Austrian Succession, increased both motive and opportunity for British expansion into the Ohio Valley and seriously alarmed the French. The consequent closure of the St Lawrence river to French shipping opened up Ohio to British trade and entrepreneurship. Pennsylvanian merchants began to offer low prices as 'loss leaders' in order to gain a footing in the Ohio country; soon they were reaching and making over tribes like the Miamis and Wyandots, who had never previously traded with anyone but the French.

From 1749, when Virginia speculators started building a permanent settlement in Ohio, tensions quickly escalated to breaking point. Tanaghrisson rapidly found himself out of his depth. He agreed to the building of a 'strong house' at the confluence of the Allegheny and Monongahela rivers, but to get the Delawares to agree to this he had to accept their chief Shingas as another Half King; by this time the links between the ostensible Iroquois and their allies in Ohio and paramount chief Onondaga were the most tenuous imaginable.

Meanwhile, by the early 1750s the French were seriously alarmed. The advent of Anglo-American traders and land speculators into the Ohio Valley raised fears that the British would eventually drive a wedge westwards, cutting off New France (Canada) from the French hinterland in Illinois and from the Mississippi. Their fears were enhanced by growing uncertainty about the stance and likely behaviour of the Iroquois; their increasingly centrifugal factionalism introduced a dangerous element of unpredictability into the power equation. With whom should the French deal: the Onondaga, Tanaghrisson or Shingas? The problem was compounded by poor political leadership in North America. Had they been more subtle and nuanced in their approach, the French leaders might have spotted that the dreaded Anglo-Saxons no more constituted a monolithic entity than did the Iroquois. The government in London was at odds with the colonials, who were in turn divided among themselves. The Pennsylvania traders and Virginia speculators might have looked like a well-coordinated advanced column for British aggression, but they were in fact deadly rivals. But by opting to use force to solve the issue of the Ohio Valley, the French turned a some-what sordid jockeying for commercial advantage between Pennsylvania and Virginia into an issue of national credibility, setting Britain against France. This inevitably had the effect of uniting the Anglo-Saxon factions at a stroke.

First blood was drawn by the French. In 1752 thirty regulars, together with 180 Chippewas and thirty Ottawa warriors, attacked the Pickawillany settlement established by George Groghan in western Ohio, killed a trader and the post's head man, and burned the place to the ground. Since the provincial governments in the east declined to back up the ousted settlers, the French got clean away with their first act of aggression. Emboldened, they raised more troops and built four forts in Ohio, positioning one of them defiantly in the exact place that the newly formed British Ohio Company had chosen for its own post. This was something the government in London could not ignore, so it ordered Lieutenant-Governor Robert Dinwiddie of Virginia to make a vigorous response to the French. He in turn sent a twenty-two-year-old lieutenant named George Washington (America's future hero and monument) to the Ohio country. There he met Tanaghrisson, still smarting at his humiliation at the hands of the French and incandescent with rage as he contemplated the obvious fact that the Delawares and Shawnees would no longer obey him.

Tanaghrisson made common cause with Washington and in the bloody campaign that followed distinguished himself by slaughtering French prisoners after they had surrendered on the express understanding that their lives would be spared. The most notorious episode occurred when the French commander Contrecoeur, at the newly established Fort Duquesne, sent an ensign named Coulon de Jumonville on a reconnaissance mission. Tanaghrisson, accompanying Washington, murdered Jumonville and his men, scalped them, then sent word to the French that George Washington had killed their troops. The double game was an obvious ploy: the Half King knew that his only chance of hegemony in the Ohio country was by turning the French and British against each other. But the episode left a dark stain on Washington's reputation which has exercised his biographers ever since.

Contrecoeur's response was shrewd. He summoned the Delawares, Shawnees and Mingoes and, utilising the belt of wampum rather more skilfully than his fellow countryman had with Tanaghrisson, invited them to take up the war hatchet and drink wine as a pledge for the enemy blood they would soon spill. The Indians accepted, thus irretrievably splitting the Iroquois; they were now divided into the pro-English Mohawks, the pro-French Mingoes and the central rump of neutralists or undecideds. At all events, Tanaghrisson's dream of carving out his own fief in Ohio was over; perhaps fittingly, he died in October 1754 of disease (possibly smallpox) and did not live to see the conflagration that his scheming had produced. The French counterattacked vigorously. Contrecoeur's deputy, Coulon de Villiers, routed Washington, allowing him to depart in peace with a safe conduct on condition that he retreated from the Ohio country and promised never to return.

But Washington's well-publicised defeat simply screwed tensions up another notch and brought Britain and France closer to outright war. Dinwiddie's report to London panicked the never steely-nerved Duke of Newcastle, ace political fixer and machine politician who was the real decision-maker on colonial affairs. With his ally the Duke of Cumberland, with whom he had combined effectively during the Jacobite Rising of 1745, Newcastle concocted a threefold plan for a North American offensive. Two regiments would be sent to the New World under General Braddock, a tough, ruthless soldier wedded to Cumberland's own notions of butchery and repression. With this 'invincible' army, Braddock was to secure the Ohio country, destroy the French post of Fort St Frederic on Lake Champlain, and expel the French from the forts on the isthmus connecting Novia Scotia to the Canadian mainland. Behind Newcastle's back Cumberland expanded this plan and in effect hijacked it: he added to Braddock's instructions an order to occupy the whole of Novia Scotia and to destroy the French Fort Niagara on Lake Ontario. The departure of Braddock was essentially the start of a worldwide war between Britain and France, though the formal opening of hostilities had to await developments in Europe in 1756. Undaunted by London's aggressive designs, Louis XV dramatically raised the stakes in North America by sending eight new regiments to Canada. While he entered into protracted negotiations with London over the future of the American colonies, he also manoeuvred to overturn and reverse the system of alliances in Europe on which Britain relied for her security.

Braddock's arrival in North America in 1755 saw the first large-scale hostilities since the 1740s, but Cumberland's minion was the worst conceivable man to conduct a successful colonial campaign. A brutal sponger, fond of duelling, who lived off women and had a veritable harem of them in London (including the celebrated actress George Ann Bellamy), Braddock despised both colonials and Indians. His distaste for Native Americans was in one respect surprising for, according to his enemies, he himself was a kindred spirit under the skin; Horace Walpole declared that 'Braddock is a very Iroquois in his disposition'. He began by alienating the American colonists, rebuking them for their sordid economic self-interest and the jockeying for places and political advantage. Since the colonists at their conference in Albany in June–July 1754 had clearly shown themselves uninterested in concerting measures for common defence, Braddock should have tried to win them round by diplomacy instead of alienating them by giving a good impersonation of his dreadful master 'Butcher' Cumberland. But he went one better (or worse) by alienating his Iroquois allies, insulting them with his arrogance and high-handed, racist behaviour. The result was that when he marched out of Fort Cumberland at the beginning of July

1755 with a force 2,200 strong, almost all his putative Indian allies were absent and he had no more than a dozen Iroquois guides in his ranks.

Braddock's campaign was one of the great disasters in colonial history and convinced many that the French would win the war for North America. He divided his troops and sent a 'flying column' on ahead to advance on Fort Duquesne by forced marches. Contrecoeur, defending the fort with 1,600 men, sent his deputy with half of these troops and 637 Indian allies to intercept the British at the Monongahela river, ten miles away. Contrecoeur's Indians were a mixed batch of fighters from the most famous warrior tribes: Abenakis, Hurons, Potawatomis, Ojibwas, Ottawas and Mingoes. On 9 July Braddock's flying column fell into an ambush as classically sprung as Hannibal's encirclement of the Romans at Cannae. Brought to a halt in an Indian hunting ground which favoured the local snipers, the British sustained terrible casualties, with two-thirds of the column killed or wounded; the roster of fatalities fell just short of 1,000. Monongahela proved there could be no success in this frontier war without the cooperation or at least the acquiescence of the Indians.

Braddock's defeat left the frontier wide open, with more and more tribes sucked into the power vacuum. The Shawnees, Delawares and Mingoes formally declared themselves allies of the French, and were joined by Wyandots, Ottawas and others. Aware that Nova Scotia was in the British sights, the French counterattacked by stirring up the Micmacs and Abenakis of Maine and north-eastern Canada. But the British soon wrapped up their conquest of Nova Scotia and began a mass expulsion of French-speaking Acadians ('Cajuns') to the mainland: forced flight and deportation at gunpoint made Nova Scotia the scene of one of the first modern instances of 'ethnic cleansing'. Astonishingly, for nineteenth-century propagandists of Anglo-Saxon superiority such as Francis Parkman, this pogrom was somehow performed by the French, not the British. Parkman's study of the Jesuits had certainly taught him casuistry, for he commented in all seriousness: 'The government of Louis XV began with making the Acadians its tools and ended by making them its victims.'

Needless to say, Braddock's debacle was not allowed to redound to the discredit of his adipose, porcine master, Cumberland, George II's favourite and indulged son. But Cumberland drew the line at sending another of his cronies out to the New World; instead Governor William Shirley of Massachusetts became the new Commander-in-Chief. Yet it was the new dispositions of the French which were a more significant consequence of Monongahela. A new commander of the American theatre, Baron Dieskau, was appointed. Even more significantly there arrived in North America Pierre de Rigaud, Marquis de Vaudreuil, bearing the title of Governor and

Lieutenant-General for His Most Christian Majesty Louis XV throughout New France and the lands and countries of Louisiana. Vaudreuil made his headquarters in Quebec, where he had been born sixty years earlier and where his father had been Governor-General. The younger Vaudreuil had achieved his ambition of treading in his father's footsteps by his efficient administration of Louisiana from 1742 to 1753. But he was an unimpressive figure, described in a damning-by-faint-praise way by one of his contemporaries: 'Good sense, no insight, too much indulgence, an optimism about future events that often leads to precautions being taken too late, nobility and generosity of feeling, much affability – these are the principal traits which seem to me characteristic of M. le Marquis de Vaudreuil.'

The French, now perhaps over-confident, next tried to do to Shirley's advancing troops what they had already done to Braddock. Correctly intuiting that the Niagara campaign posed the greatest threat, Dieskau planned to use 200 French regulars, 600 Canadian militiamen, plus 700 Abenakis and contingents of Caughnawaga Mohawks, to ambush the redcoats as they advanced on Fort St Frederic. All seemed set fair for a repeat of Monongahela, as both sides had numbers almost identical to those at the first encounter. But when battle was joined at Lake George in September 1755, things began to go badly wrong for the French right from the start. Once again Iroquois factionalism was crucial: in this instance the Caughnawaga clan refused to attack their fellow tribesmen, the Mohawks, who were fighting for the British. Their refusal had a knock-on effect: the Abenakis would not move unless the Caughnawagas charged alongside them and the Canadian militiamen in turn would not attack without Indian support. The result was that the British won the day, but their victory was no Monongahela, for they seemed at once to lose heart, their morale doubtless affected by an epidemic of sickness that ran through the camp. Instead of advancing on Crown Point, they set to work constructing Fort William Henry, to consolidate their position on Lake George. The winter of 1755–56 saw both sides stalemated, with the French anchored at Fort Carillon at the north end of the lake and the British established at Fort William Henry in the south.

In 1756 new commanders arrived on either side. In a remarkably short space of time Governor Shirley fell from favour, was disgraced and eventually replaced by another appointment from England and another of Cumberland's henchmen, Lord Loudoun, a veteran of the 1745 Rising in Scotland memorably described by Parkman as 'a rough Scotch lord, hot and irascible'. More significant was the new French commander. The luckless Baron Dieskau got himself captured on his first military foray. Vaudreuil, who rated his own strategic abilities highly, loftily informed

Versailles that no replacement was necessary. Louis XV overruled him and sent out the forty-four-year-old Louis Joseph, Marquis de Montcalm Gezan, who had been a front-line veteran since the late 1720s, serving in Italy and Germany.

Born in the Château de Candiac near Nîmes, Montcalm had had an erratic childhood. The eighteenth century, the age of Rousseau and Pestalozzi, was a great era for educational innovation, but none of these ideas had percolated through to Montcalm's father, who entrusted his formation to a pedantic natural son of *his* father (i.e. Montcalm's grand-father) named Dumas. This unprepossessing pedagogue dinned a smat-tering of Latin, Greek and history into the young Montcalm, but left him with a taste for the classics and a vague ambition to become a member of the French Academy. The other peculiarity of Montcalm's boyhood was that he had a brother who was a genuine infant prodigy. The John Stuart Mill of his time, the brother mastered Latin, Greek and Hebrew by the age of six and had a good knowledge of arithmetic, history, geography and heraldry. His death at the age of seven deeply affected Montcalm and left him with a strong strain of melancholy.

At fifteen Montcalm joined the army, and was blooded at seventeen when he came under fire at the siege of Philipsburgh in 1734. The following year his father died, leaving him heir to a great titular fortune, but one, sadly, deeply encumbered by mortgages and liens. His friend and mentor the Marquis de la Fare rescued him from his financial embarrassment by arranging a marriage with a rich heriress – Angélique Louise Talon du Boulay. The marriage was happy and productive: the new Madame de Montcalm (for Louis Joseph's formidable mother was still living) bore him ten children, of whom four died, leaving two sons and four daughters. Montcalm had a deeply sentimental feeling for his children rare in the eighteenth century and was in many ways a simple soul, devoutly Catholic, conventional in his political opinions, staunchly royalist, with a profound love of the Château de Candiac, which he often remembered wistfully when in the Canadian wilderness. *'Quand reverrai-je mon cher Candiac!'* was a sentiment frequently repeated in his journal. Montcalm was an attractive human being whose uxoriousness and feeling for his children speak to us across the ages. 'May God preserve them all,' he wrote in his autobiog-raphy, 'and make them prosper for this world and the next! Perhaps it will be thought that the number is large for so moderate a fortune, especially as four of them are girls; but does God ever abandon his children in their need?'

Montcalm, with the rank of Major-General, was supposed to be the military commander, with the Chevalier de Lévis (a future Marshal of

France) as Brigadier and second in command, and the Chevalier de Bourlamaque as Colonel and third, but the confused chain of command in North America, which would eventually cost France her empire, bedevilled him from the very start. He made a leisurely journey from Candiac to Paris via Lyons to receive his orders, dutifully writing to his wife and mother at every stop. It was in Paris that he received the disconcerting news that he was to take just two battalions with him to Canada.

The contrast with British policy is striking. Even when Britain came under threat of invasion, the directing minds of the London elite would not withdraw a single soldier from the New World. But France, struggling for global supremacy in America, could spare just two battalions at the very time it was committing 100,000 troops to a campaign in Germany that had nothing to do with French national self-interest. After being presented at Versailles, Montcalm made his way to his embarkation port at Brest, travelling via Rennes on rough roads.

It was with Montcalm that Bougainville had his first taste of a deep ocean voyage when they left Brest in the *Licorne* on 3 April 1756. Stormy and terrifying as it was, it left Bougainville with a pronounced taste for adventure at sea. The French enjoyed good weather for a week, but then, on Monday 12 April, at the beginning of Holy Week, they ran into a heavy spring gale, which showed them the ferocity of the Atlantic at terrifyingly close quarters. For a whole week they endured high seas, with storm-force winds and waves lasting for ninety hours. Since the height of ocean waves is determined by wind speed, the duration of wind velocity and the 'fetch' of the ocean, it needs little imagination to picture the terrors the French endured. The forecastle was always under water and the waves broke twice over the quarterdeck. The ship and all aboard her were in severe danger, and the men accompanying Montcalm were shaken to the depths by the experience. All were violently seasick, and Montcalm's secretary found himself unable to eat for a week. One of his valets came close to death, as he could keep no food in his stomach and for seventeen days survived on water alone. Only Montcalm and Bougainville came through the ordeal relatively unscathed. From 27 April until 4 May there was an abrupt reversal in the weather pattern, with dense fog, great cold and myriad icebergs, which they luckily managed to avoid. On 30 April, when the fog briefly lifted, they counted sixteen bergs close by and nearly collided with one, being saved only by the cry of 'Luff!' from the deck officer. Montcalm wrote to his wife: 'I have taken very little liking for the sea . . . I shall not soon forget that Holy Week.'

Bougainville soon became close friends with Montcalm and shortly, on landing (11 May), had first-hand experience of the absurdly complicated chain of command in Canada. The *ancien régime* in France seemed to go out of its way to make all forms of administration arcane, Byzantine and impossibly difficult. Montcalm, despite being the designated military commander, did not command all forces in Canada but only the so-called land troops (*troupes de terre*) that he had brought from France. Outside his control were the colonial regulars, the citizen militia, the Indians and even the marines controlled by the navy (*troupes de la marine*). Louis XV's instructions to Montcalm stressed over and over again that he was under Vaudreuil's orders and should defer to him on ultimate decision-making. This was yet another of the multitudinous errors committed by the Bourbon king during the Seven Years War. Such a division of responsibility would have worked only if Vaudreuil had been an experienced soldier who could command Montcalm's respect. Instead, the Governor-General compounded military incompetence with vanity, pomposity, envy and jealousy. Vaudreuil hated Montcalm for his undoubted talent as a soldier and much preferred his Finance Minister, François Bigot.

The grandiloquently styled Intendant of New France, responsible for finance and trade and − in an evil hour − also given responsibility for supplying the armed forces, Bigot was an embezzler and larcenist on the grand scale, who had erected a pyramid of corruption and defalcation in which major scams ran in tandem with a casual network of backhanders, sweeteners, kickbacks and payola, extending all the way down to the simplest butcher and greengrocer. Vaudreuil knew all about Bigot's corruption and venality, but did nothing about it. Historians are undecided about the reason: perhaps Bigot had established a psychological ascendancy over Vaudreuil so that the Governor-General was afraid of him; maybe, having clashed bitterly with his Finance Minister when in Louisiana and having suffered for it in his career, Vaudreuil was determined not to make the same mistake again; or it could be that Vaudreuil was simply being paid to keep his mouth shut and covered his tracks well. Montcalm was to suffer hugely from the looming influence of the Intendant: this was a hidden and underrated factor in France's eventual loss of Canada. More seriously, Bigot's ascendancy disgusted many in Versailles who were vaguely aware of it but preoccupied by the war in Europe. Yet the 'trickle-down' effect was to make influential figures on Louis XV's Council conclude that maybe Canada was just not worth the candle and should be abandoned to its British predators.

Bigot's scams are worth dwelling on, since there is an entire school of thought that holds that France lost the Seven Years War because of the structural weaknesses and chaotic administration of its finances. Bigot had a large coterie of corrupt collaborators, ranging from entrepreneurs in

France to crooked officials in Canada, but his right-hand man was a speculator who had begun life as a butcher's son, Joseph Cadet. Because Bigot and Vaudreuil were not subject to an economic market in any significant sense but could issue edicts fixing commodity prices, they lived in a peculator's heaven. Since in theory all payments to army, navy and government were done in the name of His Most Christian Majesty, and the Intendant of New France enforced a monopoly by forbidding 'unauthorised' persons to sell to the King, Bigot and his cronies specialised in buying stores 'from the King' at an artificially depressed price, then selling them back at an absurdly high one. A favourite wheeze was importing provisions from Bordeaux (where Bigot's corrupt partners had a trading company) on the grounds that there were food shortages in Canada. Since prices were higher in Canada, there were already profits to be made, but Bigot increased his profit margins by escaping import duties: he simply had his officials at the customs house wave the goods through as the King's personal stores and therefore exempt from duty. The stores were then sold back to the government and the military at inflated prices fixed by edict, often with other rogues taking cuts along the way: the first buyer would make a profit, then the second, until finally 'the King' bought at a grotesquely distorted high price. One transaction netted Bigot and his associates twelve million francs: they bought for eleven million and managed to sell for twenty-three million.

But there was simply no end to the defalcation and embezzlement of which the 'Bigot ring' was capable. Bigot liked to force farmers to part with grain at a fixed, low price on pain of confiscation, on the grounds that they were 'hoarding', then sell to the highest bidder when dearth or famine threatened. He would bribe officers at the military forts to sign for, say, two million francs of goods, then deliver one million and pocket the difference. He bought up boats for military purposes, then leased them to the King at high prices. A favourite scam was cheating France's Indian allies. Let us suppose that Bigot had raised an invoice allowing him to give gifts to 2,000 Indians. First, 'payroll padding' would be employed, for there would be just 500 Indians, not 2,000. Then Bigot would charge the highest prices and *sell* one-third of the gifts to the tribes, keeping the other two-thirds as 'perks'. Another dodge was to employ free labour in the form of boatmen, drivers and porters in return for a year's exemption from military duty, then charge the government for their wages. All the time Bigot enjoyed the protection of Vaudreuil, who in turn was a beneficiary of the corruption.

Apart from jealousy and obstruction from Vaudreuil and Bigot, the newly arrived Montcalm soon realised that the underlying military preponderance overwhelmingly favoured the British. At full strength Montcalm could deploy just eight battalions of French regulars and about 2,500 Canadian regulars to face an enemy who could draw 7,000 seasoned fighting men from New York State and New England alone, in addition to the 6,000 British troops whom Loudoun brought with him. A coordinated effort from the Anglo-Americans, as they prepared to move out against Fort Carillon (at Ticonderoga) and Fort St Frederic (at Crown Point) could well have swept the French away in the first year of official, declared war, but Loudoun played into Montcalm's hands with his abuse of the vast viceregal power granted him. Governor Shirley had always paid for his troops' quartering costs, but Loudoun – a Cumberland man in this as in so many ways – insisted that he should billet his soldiers free; after all, was he not protecting the Americans' freedom and privileges? Bitter wrangling over this issue between Loudoun and colonial assemblies jealously guarding their traditional rights handed the initiative to the French. Although discord broke out almost immediately between Montcalm and Vaudreuil, with the latter keen on using France's Indian allies to the utmost and Montcalm believing that only European-style battles and sieges provided decisive outcomes, the new military commander scored a striking early success at Fort Oswego. After compelling British surrender, Montcalm found that he could not control his Indian allies. Even though he had given his word in the article of surrender that no prisoners would be harmed, he had to look on helplessly while the Abenakis and others went on the rampage, killing up to 100 Anglo-American soldiers and civilians and making captives of perhaps as many again.

The campaign of 1756 saw France apparently holding all the cards. Montcalm's army rolled back the frontier in Pennsylvania, advancing to within 100 miles of Philadelphia. The eastern Delaware Indians seemed on the brink of joining their western cousins on the warpath and held back only because of the wise counsel of their chief Teedyuscung. The chief warned the more intemperate young braves that economic chaos might follow a decision for war: in the first place the Delawares looked likely to lose their second harvest in a row and in the second the English traders on whom the tribe depended had left the area because of the war. Loudoun meanwhile was constrained both by orders from London to attack Louisbourg before advancing up the St Lawrence to Quebec and by his (admittedly self-inflicted) bad relations with the American colonists. Angered by the prevalence of smuggling in the New World, he was waging a war on contraband by ordering an embargo on all ships clearing from American ports, except military vessels.

In consequence it was not until the summer of 1757 that Loudoun felt ready to counterattack. Leaving the defence of the lakes frontier to General

Daniel Webb, he advanced on Louisbourg with 6,000 troops. Webb was supposed to dominate Lake George to prevent the French from bringing cannon from Fort Carillon to besiege the vulnerable Fort William Henry but he blundered badly by relying too heavily on the frontier irregulars known as 'Rogers' Rangers', who were severely defeated near Fort Carillon in January 1757. Thereafter the woods around Lake George teemed with France's Indian allies: Ottawas, Ojibwas, Nipissings, Menominees, Potawatomis, Caughnawagas and, especially, Abenakis, cutting off the British garrison in Fort William Henry from effective intelligence. 1757 was the last time the pro-French tribes would gather in significant numbers. Undoubtedly they were keen to campaign this year, as the story of easy pickings at Oswego the year before had lost nothing in the telling: there had been killing and scalping, rivers of brandy to consume, and Montcalm had paid out a small fortune to rescue white prisoners after the Indians had dishonoured the solemn assurances he had given in the articles of surrender.

Certainly vast numbers of warriors came to join Montcalm in the early summer of 1757. At least 2,000 braves joined 6,000 French regulars, some having travelled 1,500 miles to get there. There were Miamis and Delawares from Ohio; Ottawas from upper Lake Michigan; Ojibwas from Lake Superior; Menominees and Potawatomis from lower Michigan; Winnebagos from Wisconsin; Saux and Fox from even farther west. Thirty-three tribes were represented, and a careful analysis shows a clear breakdown between the heathen nations (Potawatomis, Ojibwas, Ottawas, Mingoes and Shawahoes) and the nominally Catholic ones (Caughnawagas, Hurons, Abenakis), with the Christians more than 800 strong and the pagans numbering 1,000 or so. This was the spearhead Montcalm used against the beleaguered Fort William Henry, defended by 1,500 troops and commanded by Lieutenant-Colonel Monro, in an episode immortalised by Fenimore Cooper in *The Last of the Mohicans*. Monro got a taste of things to come when he sent out a reconnaissance force that was ambushed by the Indians and badly mauled; dozens of men were massacred or taken prisoner. To make matters worse, Monro then received impossible orders from General Webb, who ordered him to hold fast while making it impossible for him to do so by decamping to Fort Edward. By the end of July 1757 Fort William Henry was down to 1,100 effectives plus some sailors, sixty carpenters and eighty women and children.

Monro realised that if the French got within range of Fort William Henry with their heavy artillery, they could blow it apart as if it were a hen-coop, and that there was nothing he could do to prevent the enemy from closing the range. Webb meanwhile, fearful of leaving Fort Edward inadequately defended, sent a mere 1,000 men as reinforcements to Monro, only 200 of them regulars. Montcalm continued to invest the fort ever more closely by land and water, and on 3 August began the siege in earnest. He started by cutting the road to Fort Edward then harried the defenders mercilessly with Indian snipers. In desperate plight, Monro sent a courier to Webb to warn that, though the fort was well defended, it could not resist a prolonged siege, and therefore begged the General to relieve him. The lacklustre Webb decided that he himself was under threat and could not even begin to consider relieving Fort William Henry until he in turn got reinforcements from New York and New England.

The inevitable end was not long delayed. The French opened up with cannon and howitzers and soon shattered the morale of the defenders with continuous bombardment. Monro surrendered on 9 August, having secured a promise of safe passage to Fort Edward and no reprisals. Fearing a repeat of the massacre at Oswego, Montcalm called his Indian allies together and warned them solemnly that they must not harm the departing Anglo-Americans. The Indians listened politely, but did not in any real sense hear, and how could they? By their own lights, they were campaigning for Montcalm in order to get the chance of loot, plunder and scalps; if they were denied these, what was the point of their being in the war at all? Consequently, as the surrendered garrison began to file out on the road to Fort Edward on 10 August, the Abenakis and others attacked them and a terrible massacre followed. By the time Montcalm managed to restore order, 185 lay dead and 500 had been taken as slaves or captives by the blood-thirsty Indians; another 500 took refuge with the French. By paying out large sums of money, Montcalm was able to ransom some 200 prisoners, but more than 200 were never seen again, having succumbed to illness, been tomahawked or simply been absorbed into the tribes.

Yet in a larger sense there were no winners from the 1757 campaign. The Indians realised too late that the British and Americans in Fort Henry had been suffering from smallpox and they themselves were decimated by the disease. Montcalm, virtually stopped in his tracks by the terrible harvest that year, did not press on to Fort Edward but withdrew to Fort Carillon. Loudoun failed to complete his assault on Louisbourg before the onset of winter, tried to save face with a daring winter assault on Fort Carillon (known as Ticonderoga to the British) that aborted in the snow and ice, and was then derailed by riots and passive resistance by Americans protesting at his recruitment drive. The new supremo and *de facto* Prime Minister in London, William Pitt, lost patience with Loudoun and sacked him. Before 1757 Loudoun, as a Cumberland protégé, would have been immovable, but Cumberland himself was disgraced that year after his military defeats in

Germany, so could do nothing for him. Pitt immediately reversed Loudoun's unpopular policies in North America. Instead of antagonising the American colonists, he planned to make them partners in the defeat of the French and to make patriotism and the desire for empire run in tandem with the colonial ethos and culture.

If 1757 was the year of the French in North America, by the end of 1758 they had suffered a dramatic reversal of fortune and were on the ropes. Pitt's strategy for that year was energetic, intelligent and remorseless, at last effectively harnessing the vast superiority which the Anglo-Americans enjoyed in numbers and resources. He began with an unimaginative appointment – simply bumping up Loudoun's deputy General James Abercromby, described by one historian as 'fat, fussy, indolent', to the role of Commander-in-Chief. But Pitt's general dispositions showed more flair. After a well-planned expedition that would finally take Louisbourg, he aimed to advance up the St Lawrence on Quebec and Montreal. The second prong of the campaign involved sweeping through the Lake Champlain corridor, taking Forts Duquesne, Carillon and St Frederic en route. Pitt asked the veteran Field Marshal Lord Ligonier to nominate four men to accomplish this twofold task. For Louisbourg and the St Lawrence he opted for two men recently promoted from colonelcies: General Jeffrey Amherst and an up-and-coming young officer, Major-General James Wolfe, as his second-in-command – both men with backgrounds in supply and logistics. For the offensive against the lake forts he chose John Forbes, with George, Viscount Howe, as his deputy.

The disparity in numbers between the rivals was striking. The entire population of Canada was 75,000, out of which, straining every sinew, Montcalm could put a maximum of 25,000 in the field. By contrast, even excluding sailors, marines, camp-followers and non-combatants, the Anglo-Americans had 50,000 under arms. Abercromby earmarked 25,000 men for the forts campaign alone, while Amherst had 14,000 men for the conquest of Louisbourg and the St Lawrence. And all this at the very time when the feud between Montcalm and Montreuil came to a head. Yet we should beware of a determinism by numbers in assessing the Franco-British struggle for North America. In the first place, logistical and commissariat problems, to say nothing of the weather, restricted the campaigning season to no more than four months in summer. And the French, as defenders, were operating on interior lines. The superior woodcraft of the French Canadian irregulars, fighting for their homes against often unwilling or press-ganged troops, weighed heavily in the scales; seldom has Machiavelli's point about the superiority of a civilian militia to a mercenary army been more clearly demonstrated.

Above all, there were the brute facts of geography, which General von Moltke famously declared was three-quarters of military science. Canada was fortified with natural ramparts and outworks in the form of dense forests, huge fast-flowing rivers often choked with fallen forest giants or broken up by precipitous waterfalls, man-eating quicksands and high mountains that handed the advantage decisively to the defender. The continuous waterway from Louisbourg to the Great Lakes via the St Lawrence allowed rapid movement of French forces, giving them local superiority. Often the problem for a slow-moving British army, encumbered by baggage and artillery, was how to find the French rather than how to fight them. Yet another factor hampering the British was that as they advanced they had constantly to leave behind garrisons for forts and block-houses and, beyond that, to police an entire frontier from Nova Scotia to South Carolina. Faced with a similar problem twenty years later, in the American War of Independence, the British would buckle under the effort.

So it was that the French could often bring to a pitched battle roughly equal forces to those of an enemy who was on paper vastly superior in resources. This explains why (if we exclude Monongahela, really a battle between the British and Indians), the French won five of the ten major engagements from 1755 to 1759. Perhaps insufficient praise has been given to Montcalm and his cohorts for the indomitable spirit with which they fought their corner, virtually abandoned as they were by the mother country. Throughout 1758 the French fought tigerishly. The British attempting to take Fort Carillon were heavily defeated on 8 July, taking severe losses, and Howe, the number two, was killed early in the campaign. But superior numbers and resources gradually told. Amherst and Wolfe took Louisbourg on 26 July – a triumph marred by atrocities when Amherst let the irregulars (both American colonial troops and the elite counter-insurgency group known as 'Rogers' Rangers'), off the leash, encouraging them to massacre all the Indians they could find. When the French surrendered at Louisbourg, Amherst refused to grant them the usual honours of war, arguing that Montcalm's parole at Fort William Henry the previous year had been vitiated by his inability to control his Indians. The atrocities at Louisbourg were thus partly tit-for-tat for the previous year and partly a system of terror designed to discourage any tribe from fighting for the French.

The policy of cowing the Indians was successful, but other factors played a larger part than mere terror. One of the notable things about 1758 was the way in which the legions of native warriors who had joined the French the previous year simply dissolved. The Indians blamed their French allies for the smallpox epidemic that had cut a swathe through their villages after the fall of Fort William Henry. They had also become disillusioned with the French, as there were no longer rich pickings to be had from fighting alongside them. The French armies were now seriously short of food and other supplies, partly because Canada's economy had been skewed by heavy wartime demand, partly because last year's harvest had been disastrous, and partly because of the British naval blockade; but probably, in the main, because of the corrupt regime presided over by Bigot. The result was that Teedyuscung and the Ohio Indians abandoned the French and made overtures to the British. Teedyuscung was a key figure at the conference at Easton in October 1758 where the authorities of Pennsylvania went out of their way to conciliate the Native Americans. All land from the Albany Purchase west of the Alleghenies was officially returned to the Iroquois; Teedyuscung acknowledged the Onondaga as overlord; and Iroquois control over the Ohio country was nominally recognised. The formal conclusion of the Treaty of Easton on 25–26 October saw chief Pisquetomen signing the peace on behalf of the western Delawares and other Ohio tribes. They knew they were conceding nothing, and that in reality they, not the Iroquois, were the true power in Ohio.

Even as the French found themselves deserted by their Indian allies, they deepened the feuds and rifts among themselves. 1758 saw Vaudreuil and Montcalm virtually at each other's throats. On 23 June, as Montcalm was leaving Montreal for the Lake Champlain theatre, he received 'impertinent' instructions from the Governor-General, in which he was advised, unless he had the support of a large number of Indians, 'not to expose himself to being compromised by a general and decisive affair'. Montcalm returned a dusty answer and an even more effective one two weeks later, when he trounced the British at Ticonderoga. But his withering contempt emerges in a journal entry for 23 June: 'This evening at ten o'clock the Marquis de Vaudreuil sent me his ridiculous, obscure and misleading orders.' Montcalm's anger and scorn escalated by the following year to the point where he could set down the following: 'M. le Marquis de Vaudreuil, Governor General and in this capacity general of the army, made his first tour; after all, youth must be instructed. As he had never seen either a camp or a work of defence, everything seemed to him as new as it was amusing. He asked singular questions. It was like a man born blind who has been given sight.'

The Vaudreuil–Montcalm rift became overt in a public row in Vaudreuil's own house. Supposedly hosting a soirée, Vaudreuil could not resist the temptation of jibing at his hated rival. He resurrected an old hobby-horse of his that Montcalm, after taking Fort Henry in 1757, should have gone on to take Fort Edward also. Since Montcalm had already dealt with this old chestnut a score of times in written memoranda as well as conversation, he replied with some asperity that if the Governor was not satisfied, he might consider taking the field in person himself. Almost beside himself, Vaudreuil ground his teeth and muttered that perhaps he would, and sooner than Montcalm would like. At this point the Governor's wife chose to put her oar in and began holding forth on military matters. Montcalm, who loved his wife and was chafing at the enforced separation, found this unbearable. Not only did the detested Governor have his wife by his side, but the woman was getting above herself. With icy condescension Montcalm cut her off: 'Madame, saving due respect, permit me to have the honour to say that ladies ought not to talk of war.' Winks and nods did not work with the loquacious Mme de Vaudreuil, who started up again. Even more frostily Montcalm drew himself up to his full height and said: 'Madame, saving due respect, permit me to have the honour to say that if Madame de Montcalm were here, and heard me talking about war with Monsieur the Marquis de Vaudreuil, she would remain silent.' This was the state of affairs as New France entered its supreme crisis, as the French fought for survival against the odds in Canada, just when Versailles seemed to have turned its back on America and given it up as lost.

The picture looked even blacker for the French that winter, at the end of the campaigning season. Colonel John Bradstreet led a daring surprise attack on Fort Frontenac on Lake Ontario; the French capitulated in less than twenty-four hours and ran up the white flag on 27 August. Bradstreet wanted to press on, attack Fort Niagara and achieve a complete conquest of the Ohio country, but was overruled by the circumspect Abercromby. Forbes, meanwhile, who had been advancing on Fort Duquesne (later Pittsburgh) at a snail's pace, making sure that he was vastly over-supplied before attempting a further day's march, left it until very late in the campaigning season before achieving his objective. Nonetheless, the fall of Fort Duquesne on 25 November was a further nail in the French coffin. Francis Parkman brilliantly summed up the results of the 1758 campaign: 'The centre of the French had held its own triumphantly at Ticonderoga; but their left had been forced back by the capture of Louisbourg, and their right by that of Fort Duquesne, while their entire right wing had been well nigh cut off by the destruction of Fort Frontenac. The outlook was dark. Their own Indians were turning against them.'

Such was the desperate context of Bougainville's mission to France. To make matters worse, Vaudreuil was already trying to sabotage it. Jealous of Montcalm's great victory at Fort Carillon, he wrote to Versailles in sibylline mode that this would have 'pernicious consequences for the colony' and recommended that Montcalm be recalled. When Bougainville and the other emissary, Doreil, set out for France, Vaudreuil wrote a formal letter recommending them to the court, but then sent a private missive warning that the envoys were 'creatures' of Montcalm. The position of Doreil, in charge of Canada's 'war commissary', was anyway clear: he had been deluging the Minister of War with doleful and pessimistic tracts for much of 1758. Since he had first come over with Dieskau and Vaudreuil, he wrote, things had gone from bad to worse, 'Rapacity, folly, intrigue, falsehood, will soon ruin this colony which has cost the King so dear. We must not flatter ourselves with vain hope; Canada is lost if we do not have peace this winter . . . it has been saved by miracles in these past three years; nothing but peace can save it now, in spite of the efforts and talents of M. de Montcalm.'

Bougainville and Doreil shipped out on separate vessels, so that if one was taken, the other would still have a chance of reaching Versailles. Bougainville made better time and got to Paris well ahead of Doreil, whose ship was driven by the winds into landfall in Spain, whence he had to travel overland to the French capital. The notes and aides-memoires Bougainville wrote during the voyage reveal the command of geography that he would later put to triumphant use in the Pacific. He put his finger on all the weak spots in Canada: the lack of fortifications at Quebec; the vulnerability of Saint-Frédéric; the precarious position of Fort Carillon covering the entrance of Lake Champlain, but open to outflanking movements; the state of the cannon in the towns of Saint-Jean and Chambly on the River Sorel; and, above all, the exposed position of Lake Ontario, which could be attacked by the English either from the River Chouagen or from Niagara. He also made a minute census of the available manpower, showing clearly that in the 1759 campaigning season the French would be outnumbered by five to one. He also prepared himself for the personal commission that Montcalm had given him, which, briefly, was to advance the family fortunes by marrying off his eldest son and daughter. No more signal instance of loyalty in the tawdry story of dysfunctional French personal relations in North America in 1758–59 can be found than the implicit trust Montcalm reposed in Bougainville, who repaid it handsomely. The commander wrote to his mother, Madame de Saint-Véran: 'He and I have two ideas touching these marriages – the first romantic and chimerical; the second, good, practicable.' Bougainville proved a brilliant diplomat and matchmaker. By early spring he had engineered a marriage contract for the Comte de Montcalm (to a sixteen-year-old heiress) and had already witnessed the marriage of Montcalm's daughter.

Needless to say, Bougainville was unable to perform similar miracles in the public sphere. Montcalm enclosed four separate memoranda with

Bougainville for the perusal of the King and Ministers of the Council of State (*Conseil d'en Haut*). He pointed out that although he had contemplated resignation on a high note after the victory of Ticonderoga, he was now determined to go down with the ship, as it were, if that was what was necessary. He pointed out – as indeed Vaudreuil himself had – that food, arms, ammunition and everything else were now in short supply in New France; that the St Lawrence was bottled up by British ships; that the harvest was poor and meagre, and a barrel of flour cost 200 francs; that most of the cattle and many of the horses had been killed for food. But, recognising the difficulty of sending substantial reinforcements to North America in view of the British blockade, Montcalm proposed a new strategy of making a strong diversion against Virginia or the Carolinas, forcing the British to lift the siege of Canada; the Royal Navy, moreover, could not guard all the approaches to America's eastern seaboard. The further advantage of the Carolinas was that the large slave population could perhaps be induced to revolt. Direct aid to Canada should be limited to replacements for battle casualties and those on the sick roster plus a new cohort of artillery specialists and, most importantly, small arms and ammunition in great quantities, food for the colony and trade goods for France's Indian allies.

Another paper outlined the strategic situation. Basically there were three different frontiers – Quebec, Lake Champlain and Lake Ontario – and the British could be expected to attack on each of them in 1759. To combat this three-pronged assault, New France could count on 3,500 regulars, 1,500 *troupes de la marine* and 6,000 Canadian irregulars. Short of ammunition, stores and food, the French also lacked specialised personnel, especially bombardiers and artillery officers; there were only two military engineers in the province and not a single sapper. Against this the British could throw 60,000 men into the field, including the colonial troops. It seemed, then, that even a reinforcement of 10,000 regulars, which presupposed at least temporary naval command of the Atlantic, would not alter the balance of power in North America. Faced with certain defeat, Montcalm was keen to employ palliatives such as the diversions in Virginia and the Carolinas, and to employ Fabian ingenuity to slow down the rate of inevitable British victory.

In a technical memoir Montcalm proposed making better use of the Canadian militiamen, grading them more efficiently and then dividing them into three corps, two of them to be incorporated with the regulars and the colonial troops and the third to function as a more streamlined militia proper. This was an honest attempt to make better use of manpower, but Vaudreuil's supporters claimed it was just a transparent attempt by

Montcalm to have direct control of the militia. In yet another memoir Montcalm faced the likelihood of military defeat in Canada and calmly discussed contingency plans for withdrawing all the best fighting men from Canada to Louisiana via the Mississippi, instead of meekly surrendering to the British. His intention was to show himself a 'lateral thinker', as against Vaudreuil, whose latest despatch, dated 3 November 1758, simply reiterated the old pleas for France to make an all-out effort to save Canada, even if this meant putting the war in Europe into cold storage for a while, leaving Frederick of Prussia to fight the Russians on the eastern front.

Bougainville duly presented the memoranda and added his own supporting comments. Given the normal tortoise-like process of decision-making under the *ancien régime*, the reply came back with amazing speed. The Council argued that France, with its back to the wall in Europe, simply did not have the resources to make an all-out effort in Canada: not only was the navy in no condition to take on the pride of the British fleet, but such a venture would leave the coasts of France unprotected at the very time the British were making frequent 'descents' in Brittany and the west to raid, burn and pillage. But Bougainville presumably already knew which way the wind was blowing, for the Navy Minister Nicholas Berryer was a friend and supporter of Vaudreuil and had received him (Bougainville) coldly on arrival at Versailles. When Bougainville stressed the grave state of affairs in New France, Berryer shrugged: 'Well, monsieur, when the house is on fire one cannot worry about the stable.' Whether Bougainville's alleged reply was what he actually said or simply *l'esprit de l'escalier*, it was certainly less than respectful: 'At least, monsieur, nobody will say you talk like a horse.'

Lamely the Council, influenced by Berryer, proposed sending four French warships with just enough food and ammunition to allow Vaudreuil to stand on the defensive and fight on until 1760 – by which time, it was hinted, dramatic new developments in Europe might well have solved the problems of North America. In a supplementary memoir, Berryer recommended the recall of Montcalm. He gave as his reason the fact that Montcalm was to be promoted to Lieutenant-General for his victory at Ticonderoga; the fact that Vaudreuil, as Governor of New France, was also a Lieutenant-General meant it was inconceivable that he could continue to give orders to Montcalm, for it was axiomatic that military rank always outclassed an equivalent rank in the civilian hierarchy. By recommending that the Chevalier de Lévis (who always got on with Vaudreuil) succeed Montcalm, Berryer alerted readers to what was really going on: he was attempting to use Montcalm's new rank as a means of removing his friend Vaudreuil's 'stone in the shoe'.

But Louis XV had a mind of his own and, in a rare display of decisiveness, quickly overruled Berryer on this point. He was not prepared to dismiss one of France's authentic military heroes – they were thin enough on the ground by now, especially after the horrific humiliation at Rossbach little more than a year earlier. Berryer had to swallow his pride and record the following: 'On mature consideration this arrangement is not to be made, M. de Montcalm being necessary in present circumstances.' The usual opinion is that Louis XV, faced with three choices, opted for the worst of the three: to prevent continuing discord and factionalism in Canada he should either have recalled Montcalm or preferably Vaudreuil. To allow the unsatisfactory 'cohabitation' in the New World to continue was to invite trouble. But perhaps he was mesmerised by Vaudreuil's reputation, assiduously peddled and boosted by his supporters at court, for influencing Canadians and being their natural favourite. Almost as if to make sure that matters would be worse than ever in Canada, Louis now ordered Vaudreuil to defer to Montcalm in all military matters – a dramatic reversal of fortunes, since the 1756 instructions had commanded exactly the opposite. Vaudreuil had asked for his rival's disgrace; he was now, in all but title and name, disgraced himself. The outcome was the worst of all possible worlds; Louis XV and his ministers had to dismiss either Vaudreuil or Montcalm to cut the Gordian knot. The law of excluded middle applied here as surely as in logic, but Versailles opted for poor logic and still worse politics.

There are even historians who think that Vaudreuil and his faction colluded to disobey the King's orders. Since the 'deference' order was sent to Vaudreuil, it is possible that he may never have revealed it to Montcalm, and the opaque nature of Berryer's communication to Montcalm increases the likelihood. Berryer simply told Montcalm that he had 'recommended' that Vaudreuil concert all military matters with him; no mention was made of seniority or chain of command. But Berryer was obliged by Louis to send Vaudreuil a pretty sharp letter, making it clear that he was not to interfere with Montcalm's military dispositions. Vaudreuil was ordered not to take to the field in person, to remain at the centre of government in a viceregal capacity and to venture forth only to bolster the morale of women, the old and agricultural labourers. Some have read the orders as a calculated insult; others as a ham-fisted directive from a 'friend'. Either way, they sent Vaudreuil into a massive combination of rage and sulk. Yet because of the Byzantine processes at Versailles, neither Montcalm nor Vaudreuil really emerged from Bougainville's embassy with what they wanted. Vaudreuil, it is true, had been awarded the Cross of St Louis, but then so had Bougainville, a 'mere' envoy. The man who really won his spurs was

Bougainville. Apart from Berryer, he made an impression on all the ministers and particularly caught the eye of Madame de Pompadour, whose influence over Louis XV could hardly be overstated. Pompadour was keen on the diversion in the Carolinas and would have pressed hard for it if the money had been in the exchequer.

Before returning to Canada, Bougainville sent Montcalm a note composed in a private cipher and written in a kind of telegraphese that Mr Jingle of the *Pickwick Papers* would have approved:

> For your eyes only. Incorporation of the militia approved and recommended. The retreat to Louisiana admired for its ingenuity but not accepted . . . The Carolinas project approved but not implemented through lack of money. Comprehensive coverage given by me to the lure and lore of the savage Indians, their character and that of the Canadians, their follies, fripperies, jealousies and interests. The Court furious about the expense of Canada and a stiff letter to go to Bigot . . . M. de Vaudreuil revealed as a man without talent but will be supported by the Navy, and he owes you the Cross of St Louis that I asked for in your name, which does you honour . . . You're the man of the moment. Keep going to the end but if you manage not to lose everything, claim whatever you wish, your star is in the ascendant.

Had the French had cryptologists capable of cracking Bougainville's code, they might have frowned at the over-close friendship between supposedly objective envoy and North American commander. But a *lettre de cachet*, or warrant of imprisonment, would surely have followed discovery of the following:

> The king is a nonentity and madame la marquise [Pompadour] is all-powerful and prime minister in all but name. They told her you were too quick-tempered and impulsive but I destroyed that impression . . . Choiseul impressive and is your friend, he is an audacious man who has dismantled Cardinal Bernis's system [in foreign affairs]. M. Berryer has a rough, bluff honesty, a good man but hard . . . M. le maréchal Belleisle is another good man who does not buckle under pressure . . . M. le prince de Soubise no longer has the support of the Army but is in the Council . . . Silhouette, the Finance Minister is a proud man, feared by the nation. M. le prince de Conti is discredited and angry, while the Comte d'Argenson and his nephew M. le marquis de Paulmy [both former Council ministers] are out of the reckoning. M. de Moras is now in the mud and M. de Chevert is ill, but at court. The Jesuits

are in the most critical position they have ever been in. In general there is no consistency either in decision-making in the Council or in who is in or out. The state of credit and the public finances is chaotic.

But Bougainville did not exaggerate. France faced the fateful struggles of 1759 with few financial or military shots left in her locker.

TWO

THE BONNIE PRINCE AND
THE CRAFTY MINISTER

In the eighteenth century the Venetian Republic enjoyed an Indian summer and by 1759 euphoria and confidence were at a high. A telltale detail was the decision that year by La Serenissima to build a small fleet, ostensibly for defence but really just for show, to let the world know that Venice was well and truly on its feet again. This was dramatic irony indeed, for the republic had less than forty years to live before its conquest and absorption by Napoleon Bonaparte, but some contemporaries genuinely felt they were living in a latter-day Athens of the Periclean age. Lady Mary Wortley Montagu, the English traveller who had been visiting the city for twenty years, was deeply impressed by its febrile energy and told her friend Lady Bute in December 1758 that there was no urban landscape so proper for the retreat of Old Age as Venice. What she meant becomes clearer from a letter to her daughter written a few months before, stating that there never seemed to be any old people in Venice since the pursuit of pleasure rejuvenated even those who were elderly in calendar terms. Venice's human energy always impressed foreign visitors to the network of canals. John Gay, the author of The Beggar's Opera, *expressed a thought that many still voice three centuries later:*

> *O happy streets! To rumbling wheels unknown,*
> *No carts, no coaches shake the floating town.*

The Venetian Carlo Rezzonico had just been elected Pope as Clement XIII, increasing the pride and self-confidence of the republic but, even as early as 1759, it was probably true that the most famous Venetian in the eyes of the outside world was the notorious rake, libertine and gambler Giacomo Girolamo Casanova. He had already worn as many masks as could be seen in the Venice carnival, having been secretary to a cardinal, an army ensign, a trainee priest, a violinist, an alchemist and a professional gambler. Making friends with the French ambassador, the Abbé (later Cardinal) de Bernis, he tried a ménage

54

à trois *with Bernis's mistress, only to be double-crossed by the jealous envoy. Arrested on the night of 25–26 July 1755, Casanova was imprisoned for five years without trial in the dreaded and unsavoury Piombi ('the Leads') prison across the Bridge of Sighs from the Ducal Palace. Bernis, it seems, had alerted the authorities that, in addition to being an adulterer, Casanova had clandestine contacts with foreign and even hostile envoys and practised the occult arts. After a year's patient tunnelling with an iron rod, Casanova and a monk named Balbi made their famous 'great escape' on the night of 31 October–1 November 1756. Restored to his life of gambling, spying and woman-ising, Casanova fled to Paris, where a guilty Bernis introduced him to the royal favourite Madame de Pompadour and got him a sinecure with the newly introduced State Lottery. Wealthy overnight, Casanova was employed as a secret agent by the French in Holland in 1758–59, but in 1759 he squandered his fortune by unwise investment in a silk-printing factory and, after another unsuccessful mission to Holland, was found guilty by a French court of forging bills of exchange. The irony of Casanova's career was that he was able to crawl back to his native city only by offering to be a police informer. Although indelibly associated with Venice, he was absent during the glory years of the city's 'silver age'.*

By 1759 Venice was enjoying an artistic boom not experienced for about 200 years. In music Antonio Vivaldi, the so-called 'Red Priest' who died in 1741, had put Venice on the map and produced compositions to rival his almost exact contemporary, Johann Sebastian Bach. Yet it was probably in painting that the Venetian renaissance was most marked. The city of Bellini, Carpaccio, Giorgione, Veronese, Titian and Tintoretto suddenly produced a 'silver age' of lesser but still substantial figures. Maybe Watteau kickstarted the process at the beginning of the century with his famous Fête Vénitienne. *Canaletto, who had returned to his native city in 1756 after doing important work in London, is sometimes dismissed as a mere 'topographical' painter, and it is true that he was in a sense a documentary artist, providing a faithful pictorial record of La Serenissima in the eighteenth century, but his best work has qualities that tran-scend these alleged limitations. For some tastes, his great rival and one-time pupil, Francesco Guardi, who extended the Canaletto* veduti *(views) by taking in the lagoons and islands as well as the city proper, was a more interesting artist, whose use of light and colour anticipated the nineteenth-century Impressionists. And to Pietro Longhi we owe an incomparable series of vignettes of everyday life in eighteenth-century Venice, dealing especially with women and featuring the odd, bizarre and quirky, such as the first rhinoceros ever exhibited on the Adriatic, in 1751.*

Yet without question the great painter working in and around Venice in 1759 was Giovanni Battista Tiepolo, the master of decorative painting and the major influence on Francisco Goya. Himself influenced by Veronese, Tiepolo was a phenomenon, a virtuoso of frescoes, chiaroscuro, movement and energy, amazingly fertile in ideas and probably the fastest worker with a paintbrush there has ever been: it was said that he could finish a picture before another artist got his palette ready. As inspired by conventional religion as by classical mythology, Tiepolo is instantly recognisable by his use of light, light-blue colours, fair-haired amorini, goddesses and naked women floating in the clouds. As a celebrator of sensual pleasure raised to the ultimate, Tiepolo was the perfect painter for eighteenth-century Venice. Although in 1759 he moved on to Udine to decorate the oratory of the Purità, he had just completed one of his masterworks in Venice. In 1757–58, working at his usual lightning speed, he painted two ceilings in the Palazzo Rezzonico. In one scene Apollo's four horses and chariot fly towards a fortunate young couple; in a second, Merit ascends to the temple of Immortal Glory, accompanied by Nobility and Virtue, and preceded by Fame sounding her trumpet. Tiepolo's work of genius in the Ca' Rezzonico, a dazzling mélange of perfect form, crystalline lucidity, colour and light, was his virtual swansong in Venice.

Even with this array of visual talents, probably for most Venetians the artistic highlight of 1759 was the première of Goldoni's new play, Gl'Innamorati (The Lovers). Carlo Goldoni was Venice's greatest writer, but his achievement is difficult to assess without an appreciation of the tradition of commedia del arte from which he came and which he tried, successfully, to transcend. The classic commedia worked along formulaic and ritualistic lines. Usually the first to appear when the curtain rose was the village bumpkin Pantaleone and the fake-erudite Dottore. After they had exchanged various bits of nonsense, the stock characters Brighella and Arlecchino (Harlequin) would appear as crafty servants, who would soon outwit and gull their masters. Soon an entire rogues' gallery would join in the buffoonery: low-life peasants, crooks, villains, heavies, simpletons, venal and artful ladies' maids. The commedia was the clear forerunner of British music-hall and American vaudeville, complete with slapstick, horseplay, parody, mimicry, repartee, catch-phrases, comic songs and Groucho Marx-like soliloquies 'confiding in' the audience. It was everyday Venetian life raised to the level of farce, the reductio ad absurdum of all that was most risible about La Serenissima. Into this brew Goldoni tried to inject realism, dealing with actual life, flesh-and-blood personalities and domestic conflict, concentrating particularly on manners and character.

Like Tiepolo, Goldoni was both phenomenon and workaholic. He began acting at four, wrote his first play at eight and had been diplomat, consul, bankrupt and – almost – a monk before he turned to writing full-time for the stage. Amazingly prolific – he rivalled Voltaire in his output – he wrote 149 comedies, eighty-three operas and ten tragedies. He worked at a furious pace, churned out no fewer than sixteen plays in the years 1750–51 alone, and in 1760 wrote La Casa Nova *in just seventy-two hours. He was a classic 'first draft' author, impatient and temperamentally incapable of slow, circumspect revision, and critics said his speed militated against a proper concern for structure. Naturally, with such an output, some of it lacked depth. His critics said Goldoni could never reach the heights of Molière, on whom he modelled himself, as he neglected social and philosophical issues and created no unforgettable characters. And prolific writers always have enemies: someone said of Goldoni that he could devise a play from the fluff out of his own navel. Kinder critics said he was like an early Mozart, who lacked the profundity to produce the dramatic equivalent of Mozart's late piano concerti or operas. Less attention was paid to Goldoni's formidable strengths. He was astonishingly fertile in the creation of plots and scenes, showed great comic invention, wrote sparkling dialogue and was a better craftsman than he was given credit for.*

The reason why Goldoni has survived while his rivals such as Chiari have not is that he held up a mirror to eighteenth-century Venetian society, making his theatrical work a prime historical and sociological source-book. Venice had a reputation as 'sin city', but Goldoni did not simply dwell on the (even then) rather clichéd picture of a town where hedonism, debauchery and bacchanalia were rampant. He also showed the Venetian class system in operation. One of his focuses was what we would now call 'distressed gentlefolk'. Out of a population that increased during the century from about 135,000 to 160,000, maybe 25 per cent fell into the category of aristocracy or nobility, but many of these (especially those who had possessions and wealth in the Levant) fell on hard times once Venice was overwhelmed at sea by the Barbary pirates. Goldoni shows the fallen aristocrats clustering in their favourite quarter of San Barnaba, trying to keep up appearances but eking out a precarious living on watermelon and polenta. He also has a broad cast list of working-class types: manservants, ladies' maids, gondoliers, caulkers at the Arsenal dockyards, Murano glass-blowers, fishermen, silkweavers, lacemakers, shellfish openers and simple layabouts. Then there are the cavalieri dei denti *– idlers, parasites, those addicted to* dolce far niente, *who lived off doles and battened off patrons who fed them in return for sycophancy. And there is* la bohème: *card-sharps, marginal types, petty thieves, sellers of fake relics, panders and shady middlemen.*

Yet even more of a Goldoni favourite was the middle class and its bourgeois banality, notably burlesqued in I Rusteghi (The Boors). *Middle-class males, as Goldoni shows, were unconcerned with politics, but fixated on notions of 'family honour'. They paid lip-service to Catholicism, but were religious only in the vague sense that they ritualistically went to church and detested free-thinkers, and the spiritual currents did not run deep. In* L'Uomo Prudente

(The Prudent Man) *Goldoni evinces the ludicrous bluster of the politically impotent and timid middle-class householder confronting a burglar. After warning him not to try to force himself on his wife and daughter, the bourgeois paterfamilias adds absurdly that there is a trapdoor somewhere on the stairs, which will drop any intruder into a pit full of spikes, nails and razor blades, but that only he, the home owner, knows where the lever is that works this contraption.*

As Goldoni shows, eighteenth-century Venice was both a liberal and a licentious city. It was keen on the French philosophes, *and the works of Diderot, Voltaire, Maupertuis, Montesquieu and Helvetius were widely available. The authorities in the guise of the State Inquisitors had banned only Rousseau, not for his freethinking or deism, but because of his unflattering remarks on Venice. Nonetheless, his books had a wide underground circulation; there were black markets for most things in Venice and poor Goldoni noted that by 1759 no fewer than fifteen pirated editions of his works had been published. For the working classes and foreign visitors not within the* cavaliere servente *system, the city could offer a vast army of prostitutes – morality in Venice was very loose, even by the generally permissive eighteenth-century standards throughout Europe. But most observers felt that Venice truly cut loose into the realms of the unbridled and lubricious at the time of Carnival, when most revellers went masked. The Venetian* bautta *was no mere highwayman's mask – a simple affair covering mouth and eyes – but an enfolding cape or mantle with black hood over the head and shoulders, a little tricorne hat and a mask (usually white) shaped like the beak of some large or possibly mythical bird. The huge domino-cloak or* tabarro *made it impossible to tell who was male and who female. Additionally, young men liked to dress in a variety of exotic garments so that they appeared as Moors, satyrs, Mongols, Iroquois, Royal Navy jack-tars, turbaned dervishes or well-known murderers.*

As the city of masks, waterways, sinister-looking alleys and mysterious deadends, Venice more than any other city was a place of fluid identity, and so no better place of safety could be imagined for political refugees, defeated rebels or those with a price on their head. This was why Venice after 1746 became a magnet for the defeated Jacobites, adherents of the House of Stuart. Here came so many of the great and good (and the mediocre, the bad and the ugly) who had fought in 1745–46 for Prince Charles Edward Stuart, grandson of King James II who had fled England in 1688. Lord George Murray, the military genius of 1745, Earl Marischal George Keith, the doyen of the exiled Jacobites and Lord Elcho, the Lowland warrior and hothead all congregated here in the late 1740s. And in 1749 there arrived the biggest fish of all, Prince Charles Edward himself. Successively expelled from France and the papal state of Avignon, Charles was minded to settle permanently in Venice, but the Doge and the Council of Ten who ruled the city knew this would mean running conflict with England; they could not defend themselves against the Barbary pirates, so how could they stand up against the mighty Royal Navy? And so, ignominiously given his marching orders, the wandering Prince set out on his travels once more.

Even before 1745, the Jacobites had been scattered across Europe in a diaspora that took them from Lisbon to Moscow. After the failed rebellion of that year, the process accelerated and acquired new momentum on the outbreak of the Seven Years War. By 1759 leading Jacobites could be found right at the heart of the various theatres of war. The Comte de Lally, who had tried to get French reinforcements to Charles Edward in 1746, now commanded French armies in India. The Chevalier de Johnstone, another veteran of the '45, was serving with Montcalm in Canada. The apostate Jacobite Earl Marischal was in Spain on a secret mission. The Chevalier Douglas had just returned to Charles Edward's side after a secret mission in Russia. And even John Grant, one of the fabled 'Seven Men of Glenmoriston' who had helped the Prince so valiantly during his 'flight in the heather' in Scotland in the summer of 1746, was in Canada although, bizarrely, as a pressed man, he was fighting against his erstwhile ally the Chevalier de Johnstone. 1759 saw the Jacobites with fingers in many pies around the world, and the whirligig of Fate was now once more to bring them to the centre of the political stage.

The evening of 5 February 1759 was cool and fine in Paris, and the French Foreign Minister waited in his garden for an important visitor. Etienne-François de Stainville, newly created Duc de Choiseul and newly promoted to his high office and the accompanying position on Louis XV's Council of State, had some reason for quiet satisfaction after little more than two months as Foreign Secretary. He had identified the major problems France faced in the third year of a gruelling world war and had solutions for at least some of them. His predecessor, the Abbé de Bernis, had let matters drift and, when he did decide to take action, he moved in the one direction that led to a cul-de-sac. In short he challenged the pro-Austrian policy that had been the King's brainchild and that of his adviser and ex-mistress Madame de Pompadour. This was dangerous folly. Louis had repeatedly warned Bernis not to query this cornerstone of French foreign policy, and yet Bernis had not simply had doubts, but had circulated them to friends in a memorandum. The 'reversal of alliances' whereby Austria, the enemy in the last war, became the staunch ally in this, was one of Louis's most prized achievements. In *l'état c'est moi* mood, he told his confidant the Comte de Broglie in a letter in January 1757: 'This alliance is my own work and I think it is a good thing.' When Louis thought Bernis was wavering, he sacked him in his usual brutal way, irrevocably and without any warning. But it was typical of Louis that he first threw a great party for Bernis to celebrate his recent elevation to the cardinalate. Having observed him in triumph in his red hat, Louis brought him down to earth a few days later with a letter that was at once a dismissal and a sentence of exile.

Choiseul was too intelligent to end up the same way. Bernis had a high opinion of his successor and was somewhat in awe of him. In a letter of congratulation Bernis told him he had boundless courage and an iron nerve; he (Bernis) admitted that he had felt the weight of adverse events crushing him, but Choiseul could bounce them off him. Bernis was right: Choiseul *was* France's last and best hope for success in the war. Aged thirty-nine, he had hitherto succeeded in everything he had set his mind to. He was a Lorrainer, born into a noble family; his father the Marquis de Stainville had been chief counsellor of the last two Dukes of Lorraine and had represented them in London and Versailles. Something of an international civil servant, Stainville became very close to the French Prime Minister Cardinal Fleury after 1726 and had also acted as ambassador for the Duke of Tuscany in Paris, in which sinecure position he became a notable epicure and gourmet. Stainville had five children (three boys and two girls) and all made their mark in the world. The second son distinguished himself in the service of Austria, the third became an archbishop, one daughter became a canoness and the other married the Duc de Gramont in 1759; the Stainvilles also had a numerous and closely knit extended kinship system. But it was the eldest son who achieved real historical fame. At twenty he joined the French army and took part in the Bohemia campaign and retreat from Prague in the early 1740s. Serving thereafter in Flanders under the great French marshals Saxe and Lowendahl, Choiseul rose rapidly in the military hierarchy: Second Lieutenant in 1739, he was a Colonel by 1743 and a Brigadier by 1748, ending the war as *maréchal de camp*.

In 1750 he married the granddaughter of the financier Crozat, Mlle de Châtel, then only fifteen. By common consent she was beautiful, charming, sweet-voiced and intelligent. Everyone thought her the perfect wife but within a year Choiseul had cheated on her. For Choiseul was a compulsive and frenzied womaniser, probably at root a misogynist; he liked to conquer women, humiliate them, lie to them, love them and leave them. One of the first of the many paradoxes about Choiseul was that, although probably the most successful philanderer of 1750s France – outdistancing even the legendary lecher (also his political rival) the Duc de Richelieu – he was an ugly man, short of stature with a large forehead, small eyes, thick lips and red hair. But, like John Wilkes in England, whose amatory career paralleled his, he had an almost magical appeal for the female sex. The most famous story about the young Choiseul – which more strait-laced historians have affected to disbelieve – explains how he established himself as the close friend and protégé of Madame de Pompadour. Louis XV took Madame de Choiseul-Romanet, a distant cousin of Choiseul, as a mistress in the early 1750s. Pompadour, worried about this challenge, needed proof that the King's relations with this woman were carnal. She enlisted the help of Choiseul, who seduced his cousin and stole from her boudoir a letter giving documentary evidence of the monarch's relations with la Choiseul-Romanet.

With Pompadour's support and patronage, he secured the French embassy to Rome in 1754. Ambassador during a particularly tricky time – when Louis XV wanted Pope Benedict XIV to help him resolve the religious disputes that were tearing France apart – Choiseul was a spectacular success. Although anti-clerical by conviction, he struck up a singular rapport with Benedict, the so-called philosopher-king and undoubtedly one of the great popes of the ages. Choiseul was transferred to Vienna as ambassador in 1756 and recalled only in November 1758 when Louis appointed him Secretary of State for Foreign Affairs. A workaholic, full of energy, imaginative, resourceful and brimming with ideas, Choiseul was brilliant at lobbying and networking to get what he wanted, as he proved in Rome. He had a limitless belief in his own abilities and his lucky star. Highly intelligent, quick-thinking and brilliant, he impressed the monarch by his dynamism and patriotism – in that he genuinely wanted France to be a great power and hated any sense of her humiliation – and by his courage, patience and charm. Two characteristics especially recommended him to the King. Since he had both a military and a diplomatic background, he melded easily into the team that Louis was building, and his *entente* with Marshal Belle-Isle, the War Minister (who regarded Choiseul as a genius), was particularly strong. And his analyses in the Council of State were so lucid and compelling that Louis, a neurotic ditherer and prevaricator, finally found decisions easy to make.

Choiseul was one of those people with amazing physical presence and charisma. His friends said he could spread joy and happiness through a gathering as if by magic, and that when he entered a room it was as if he took out of his pockets a boundless treasury of fun and jokes. His intimates praised his goodness, frankness and generosity and were amazed, rather in the manner of Goldsmith's villagers when contemplating the village schoolmaster, at a mind that could digest such a vast amount of factual information while being completely at home with general ideas and abstract speculation. Wit and humour were his forte, but sometimes toppled over into acidulous quips and cruel persiflage. He could always see the absurd in any situation, and some French critics have alleged that an inability to take things entirely seriously is a typical Lorrainer trait. A letter that Choiseul wrote to Voltaire in April 1760, when any other man would have felt overwhelmed by the Seven Years War, is sometimes cited by his critics as a sign that he was not really *sérieux*. Voltaire had written that Frederick the Great of Prussia admired him and, if Louis ever sacked him, would like to employ him in Berlin. Choiseul replied:

> I am mad about my pleasures. I have a beautiful and comfortable house in Paris; my wife is highly intelligent and – amazingly – has never cuckolded me. My family and circle of friends make me very happy. I like winding up d'Argental [his friend, the veteran councillor in the Paris *parlement*], or drinking and talking nonsense until 4 a.m. with M. Richelieu. People say I have passable mistresses but I find them exquisitely delicious. What could the king of Prussia, even if he commanded soldiers with twelve feet, have to offer me that could compare with that?

Despite his superlative talents and manifold qualities, Choiseul had a dark side, or rather several dark sides. The womanising misogyny has already been remarked upon, but there was also about Choiseul what one can only describe as a nihilistic cynicism. His enemies had a point when they said that he was frivolous, hedonistic and indiscreet. He wasted many hours on his pleasures, which he then made up for by getting through in an hour the work it would take a normal person a whole day to accomplish. He liked to write all important and secret despatches in his own hand, but his writing was so hard to read that ambassadors often sent back his instructions with a request that they be deciphered. He saw Louis XV virtually every day, and the King showered him with money and honours for twelve years, but Choiseul developed no real relationship with him and had no personal interest in Louis, seeing him merely as a source of the glittering prizes for which he was greedy. Louis for his part admired Choiseul for his intelligence, tireless energy and patriotism but was impatient with his overweening ambition and the coruscating success of the anti-clerical salon that he ran at the Hôtel Choiseul. Nobody pretends that Louis XV was a particularly attractive or admirable person, but one does not sense in the Louis–Choiseul relationship even any of the grudging tolerance that marked the Pitt–George II *entente*. When Louis finally dismissed him in 1770, Choiseul took his revenge by a merciless dissection of the monarch in his *Mémoires*. One often perceives in Choiseul the boredom of the cynic and the consequent need to act a role; his ability to switch from bonhomie to hauteur in a second suggests the born actor. Easily bored and impatient with detail, he was sometimes too readily satisfied with a superficial assessment of people and situations. All in all, he was a seductive but slightly disturbing person.

Apart from his desire to defeat England and show that he, not Pitt, was the true master of European politics, Choiseul had two abiding obsessions. One was nepotism. He worked tirelessly to catapult his siblings, cousins and remote kin to high office. He promoted his clerical brother successively to Bishop of Evreux, Archbishop of Albi and finally Archbishop of Cambrai. He intrigued to have his military brother made a Field Marshal by Maria Teresa of Austria, then enlisted him into the French army (1760) as Lieutenant-General. He set up his sister's marriage to the Duc de Gramont. And he later made sure that his cousin, the Comte de Choiseul, was in turn his replacement in Vienna, a Secretary of State and finally, as the Duc de Praslin, Minister of State on the Grand Council. His largesse was extended to members of the Lorraine aristocracy (such as Beauvan and du Châtelet), for he had a primitive, clannish feeling for his native county. Whatever he proposed for his cronies in the way of diplomatic, military, administrative or bureaucratic posts, he tended to get. He even secured the appointment as court banker for his friend Jean-Joseph de Laborde, in the process ousting the Paris-Monmartel brothers, who had not only controlled French finances since the Regency but enjoyed Pompadour's favour. Since the court banker's job was to transmit to French ambassadors the subsidies paid to foreign powers and secret agents, and he could draw on royal revenues – all tasks performed for premium fees – this was a prize worth having. The Paris-Monmartel brothers made the mistake of being anti-Austrian after 1756, thus enabling Choiseul to get Pompadour to cut them out of the loop.

Choiseul's other crusade was anti-clericalism. Although he remained formally a Catholic by performing his Easter duty, he was probably in his secret heart an atheist. He liked to evince his freethinking credentials by eating meat on Friday, corresponding with Voltaire, protecting the *philosophes* and making his house a haven for enemies of religion. In particular he had important friends and contacts in the Paris *parlement* and backed them in their pro-Jansenist stance against the devout party. Since he needed the *parlement* to vote him money for the war, he was prepared to offer them the Jesuits as a sacrifice. Choiseul promoted the line that the Jesuits meddled in politics, had huge temporal ambitions, aimed to control men's minds and wanted to establish a universal monarchy of the Pope. Choiseul's campaign against the Jesuits was systematic and ruthless, and in the year 1759 it was the Marquis de Pombal's expulsion of the Society of Jesus from Portugal that gave him his cue. His plans took time to germinate, but between 1764 and 1767 the Jesuits were expelled from all states controlled by the Bourbon kings: France, Spain, Naples, Sicily, Parma, and all their overseas territories – Peru, Paraguay, Argentina, Mexico and the Philippines; they had already been thrown out of Portugal and Brazil. Ironically, it was a Protestant king, Frederick of Prussia, who finally saved the Jesuits from extinction.

In early 1759 even the unflappable Choiseul had a mountain to climb, as France was simultaneously racked by religious, administrative and financial crises. In a sense there had been, since the early 1750s, what modern political science would term a crisis of legitimacy, and the crisis was now threatening to turn into a catastrophe. It was widely remarked that there had not been political instability on this scale since the days of Cardinals Richelieu and Mazarin, a hundred years earlier. At the simplest, financial level, France was nearly bankrupt, and the basic reason was that the wealthy aristocracy and the landed classes refused to pay taxes. No Finance Minister could alter the situation without vigorous and punitive commitment from the King, but Louis XV, absurdly, thought the level of tax in France was already too high. He compounded the problem by promoting the *grands seigneurs* of the high aristocracy to senior political positions in the 1750s, so making the job of Finance Minister even more difficult. Finance Ministers naturally enough came from Parisian financial circles and were thus considered not quite the social equals of the scions of the old families in political positions; when they attempted economic reforms or retrenchment they predictably ran into a brick wall. The King's policy was even more fatuous than he could have realised, since general political instability meant a rapid turnover of ministers, yet sacking one of the great aristocrats was a serious matter. Louis had got rid of the most talented members of the minor nobility – Maurepas in 1749, Machault and the Comte d'Argenson in 1757 – without making waves, but when he finally dismissed Choiseul and Praslin in 1770, he plunged France into a political crisis of a kind not seen since the Fronde of the late 1640s.

On an annual basis the Seven Years War cost France more than twice any previous war. Failure to balance the budget by taxation meant that the war had to be financed on credit, but by 1759 credit was becoming exhausted. Wearily the new Finance Minister appointed at the beginning of 1759, Etienne de Silhouette – a man whose phantom career made his name synonymous with a mere outline – projected the depressing budget for that year. With revenues of 286.6 million livres and expenditure of 503.8 million, he had to operate with a deficit of 217.2 million; his useless predecessor had underestimated the likely deficit by 84 million livres. For every year the war went on, the exchequer would have to be supplemented by about the same amount (217 million livres), so that, if peace ever came, all revenues would have been consumed in anticipation. Silhouette's projection was not far out since, whereas in 1755 France spent about 30 per cent of her revenues on debt servicing, by 1763 this figure had advanced to more than 60 per cent. Silhouette, a lawyer and an intellectual, began promisingly. He raised 72 million livres by clipping the profits of the tax-gatherers (farmers-general), a move that brought him great initial prosperity. Then he suspended all exemptions hitherto granted from direct taxation or *taille*. But still he could not raise enough money, and at times was led down the path of fantasy – as when he suggested an emergency capitation tax for every man, woman and child in the country designed to raise 325 million livres.

In September 1759 Silhouette finally carried his reforming zeal too far and issued an edict for a general subvention. He intended to mulct the rich via a property tax, to create new offices which the holders would have to pay to secure, and to farm a new tax on carriages, horses, velvet, silk, gold and silver, furs and foreign produce. Louis XV made a half-hearted attempt to support his minister by sending all his silverware to the Mint and exhorting his rich subjects to do likewise. But the wealthy had many ways of avoiding new taxation. One of these was the power which the Paris *parlement*, the financial supply granting body, had to order a *lit de justice* to look into the new taxes, and then to postpone the meeting of this body for an unconscionable time. In 1759 the meeting was postponed to November, by which time the vested interests had got rid of the pestilential Silhouette. In desperation, Choiseul was forced to go cap in hand to Spain and ask for a loan. In October he instructed Aubeterre, the French ambassador in Madrid, to petition for financial aid, but his hopes were always very slender since the year before Louis XV himself had been humiliated when making a similar request. Writing personally to King Ferdinand, Louis had asked for the relatively trifling sum of 36 million livres but Ferdinand, under the thumb of his termagant queen, had turned his fellow monarch down.

Although France suffered considerable price inflation in 1759, with the cost of sugar (the major import from the colonies) soaring and the costs of the war in North America crippling, the basic French economy was not in bad shape, with expanded trade with Spain and Germany compensating for her Caribbean losses (see the following chapter). Why, then, did France experience such difficulty in obtaining credit when Britain found it relatively easy? None of the usually proffered explanations convince. It was true that Britain could raise money at a lower rate of interest than the

French, but there was no shortage of usurious moneylenders in the international market. Some say that investors had been wary of France ever since the Regency period in the early 1720s, when France unilaterally reduced and rescheduled its debt as part of its reform of the collapsed John Law 'Mississippi bubble' system; but the British had done the same after the South Sea Bubble fiasco in the same era. A more plausible explanation was that in Britain the National Debt was a state debt, in which bondholders could have more confidence than was possible in France with its royal debt; but since all royal debts had anyway to be registered with the *parlement*, this argument finally lacks force. The most likely explanation is that the over-determined 'legitimacy crisis' in France simply made would-be investors nervous; a general issue of credibility in the system was involved.

Although the attempts to solve the French financial crisis would not founder definitively until the end of 1759, already at the beginning of the year Choiseul saw it as a Sisyphean task that he would somehow have to shoulder. More fully developed by 1759 was France's religious crisis. To follow this we must understand the role of the *parlement* in the *ancien régime*. Dating from the thirteenth century, the *parlement* was the most prestigious law court in France. Both a supreme court and an administrative tribunal, it oversaw public order in Paris and, by convention, the King had to send it all legislation, especially financial legislation, to check that it was in accordance with ancient practice; the *parlement* could protest or make remonstrances to the monarch, but only he could decide if these were to be heeded. If there was prolonged conflict, the King could compel obedience by a *lit de justice*, when he either visited the *parlement* or summoned it to Versailles where, in the presence of the princes of the blood and the great officers of the Crown, he would announce his will. The *parlement* was the power of the aristocracy in visible, institutional form. Roughly 450 grandees, recruited through wealth and social standing, comprised the body, and it was its adamant opposition to financial reform that made the life of Louis XV's Finance Ministers so difficult.

But for ten years after 1750 conflict between King and the *parlement* was not principally about taxation. Instead, it was recondite theology that caused the trouble. Jansenism had been a powerful force in France since the late seventeenth century, but a combination of contingent factors catapulted it to the headlines in the *ancien régime* of the 1750s. A form of predestination, taking as its starting point St Augustine's views on original sin as against the 'free will' views of Pelagius, and pushing them to an extreme point, Jansenism polarised religious opinion in eighteenth-century Catholic circles. In 1713 Pope Clement XI hoped to extirpate the heresy of Jansenism once and for all with the promulgation of the papal bull *Unigenitus*. In this exhaustive document, rehearsing the heresy through an examination of 101 unacceptable propositions, Clement expressly (in article 91) reserved the right to excommunicate the King of France. This was a direct challenge to Louis XIV who, in his 'gallican' law of 1682, declared that the French court was wholly independent of papal interference in all secular matters, including the exile and punishment of unruly clergy. In religious terms, the first half of the eighteenth century is often seen as the struggle between the 'ultramontane' clergy (owing primary allegiance to the Pope across the Alps in Rome) and the 'gallican' or Jansenist Church (supported by the overwhelmingly Jansenist *parlement*).

Cardinal Fleury, effectively Prime Minister of France during Louis XV's minority and until 1743, wisely dampened down the controversy by referring all difficult cases to the Council of State, thus cutting out both the Church and the *parlement*. But after Fleury's death Louis announced that he would never again tolerate a Prime Minister, and his own touch was much less sure. The appointment of the ultramontane Christophe de Beaumont as Archbishop of Paris stoked up the controversy again. A hardline, intolerant fanatic, Beaumont began refusing the sacraments to known Jansenists after 1750, and many bishops followed suit. The *parlement* sent in remonstrances to the King. After much vacillation, Louis sided with the bishops in May 1753. When the *parlement* hit back with a general strike of all judges, Louis lost patience and exiled the entire body for fifteen months. To get judicial business moving, he established a new court, the *Chambre Royale*. But lawyers and inferior courts proved reluctant to recognise it and Louis was soon forced to compromise. In 1754 he recalled the *parlement* from exile, amnestied those who had opposed him and ordained a law of silence on all religious matters; there were to be no public refusals of sacraments and everyone was to keep his religious beliefs to himself. Once again magistrates proved reluctant to cooperate and even when the judiciary accepted the law of silence, it added extra clauses to the legal code forbidding any innovation in the administering of the sacraments.

Louis bought himself a two-year breathing space, but in late summer of 1756, with the Seven Years War already raging, Archbishop Beaumont again broke ranks, started refusing the Eucharist to Jansenists and exhorted the faithful to disregard all laws and judgements passed by the *parlement*. A furious monarch exiled Beaumont and set about a definitive resolution of the issue by enlisting the help of Benedict XIV. The years 1756–57 were the time when Choiseul displayed his superb diplomatic skills by working closely with Benedict on a new encyclical that would give Louis the formula he wanted and bind up the nation's religious wounds. Benedict came up with a clever compromise: his encyclical *Ex Omnibus* confirmed that the faithful should accept *Unigenitus* as a general guideline but stressed that only notorious and egregious sinners, not Jansenists, should be denied the sacraments. This time it was the aristocrats of the *parlement* who turned out to be the fanatics. Because the encyclical was not 'registered' with the *parlement*, which reserved to itself the right to register all bulls, encyclicals and papal letters before they were promulgated, they took the line that *Ex Omnibus* was a 'rogue' pronouncement. This contumacity was too much for Louis, who adamantly refused to send the encyclical to be registered. When the *parlement* denounced the encyclical by a majority, Louis announced a *lit de justice* for December 1756. But at the meeting the majority of the aristocratic magistrates refused to accept the King's rulings and resigned; Louis responded by exiling sixteen of the 'ringleaders'. With France once again in internal crisis, Louis XV narrowly escaped death by an assassin's hand in January 1757. That event, and the dismissal of two of his long-serving Ministers of State (Machault and Comte d'Argenson) following conflict with Madame de Pompadour, left the King unable to deal firmly with the *parlement*. In September 1757 he climbed down and granted it the terms it wanted.

The conflict rumbled on. A small group of Jansenist magistrates wanted to continue the attack on the bishops and on *Ex Omnibus* and in the end Choiseul bought off the opposition by offering the hated Jesuits as sacrificial lambs. But until his accession to power, relations between King and *parlement* continued to be fragile. Because they needed the *parlement* to vote in taxes, Finance Ministers came and went in quick succession. When the Abbé de Bernis became Foreign Minister, he had the bright idea of printing all the King's proposals to the *parlement* and publishing them, so that the public could see how reasonable the monarch was being and how unreasonable the magistrates. This temporarily did the trick and the *parlement*, finding itself woefully out of step with public opinion, buckled, but not before successfully demanding that Louis rescind the sentence of exile on the sixteen so-called ringleaders. Secretly angry that he had to compromise in this way, Louis acquiesced. The entire affair had brought discredit both on the monarchy and the regime, and there are those who say, plausibly, that the religious quarrels of the 1750s did more to destroy the credibility of the *ancien régime* than all the more famous criticisms of the *philosophes*. 1757 was a particularly black year for France, with the attempted assassination of Louis by Robert Damiens and his subsequent hideously cruel public execution, the military disaster at Rossbach, and the dismissal of d'Argenson and Machault all contributing to the feeling that Louis XV's regime was not just, good, honourable or even competent.

Economic and religious woes were compounded at the political level by a paralysis of government and administration, as Ministers of State and Secretaries of State tumbled out of office in a process of accelerated chaos. In his memoirs Charles Hénault, President of the Paris *parlement*, remarked of the 1750s: 'Ministers were changing then like sets at the opera.' He was not exaggerating. In the first half of the eighteenth century a long tenure of office as Secretary of State or Minister Without Portfolio was considered essential for good government. Fleury lasted twenty-seven years at the top; the Comte de Maurepas, Navy Minister, served a similar stretch; Machault d'Arnouville was Minister of State for twelve years, and Philibert Orry, Finance Minister, was in post for fifteen years. Once Louis XV decided to be his own Prime Minister, and especially when Madame de Pompadour became his principal adviser, political anarchy began. Between 1747 and 1758 there were six Secretaries of State for Foreign Affairs: the Marquis d'Argenson, Puysieulx, Saint Contest, Rouillé, Bernis and Choiseul. Between Machault's move to the Navy Ministry in 1754 and the appointment of Henri Bertin in November 1759, there were no fewer than six Comptrollers-General of finance: Jean Moreau de Seychelles took over from Machault in July 1754 and lasted less than two years; François Marie Peyrence de Moras occupied the bed of nails from April 1756 to August 1757; Jean Nicholas de Boulogne then served eighteen months before handing over to Silhouette for his tempestuous eight-month stint. The Ministry of Marine was in no better case. Rouille handed over to Machault in July 1754, but on the dismissal of Machault in 1757 the Marquis de Moras took over for a disastrous sixteen months before resigning in May 1758. His successor, the Marquis de Massiac, lasted just five months before handing over to Nicholas Berryer in November 1758.

The rapid turnover of senior ministers was superficially due to the unpredictability of Louis's whims, the hostility of Madame de Pompadour to any who were not her protégés, and the protracted financial crisis which meant that ministers quickly became frustrated and found their tasks impossible. At a deeper level, it indicated a more profound malaise in the political system which would finally break out in spectacular fashion in 1789. Many historians are convinced that in the 1750s France entered a pre-revolutionary tailspin from which there could be no pulling out. One of the problems, as already noted, was that Louis stupidly allowed the return to power of the *grands seigneurs*. In this decade the high aristocracy began to reassert the powers they had lost during the reign of Louis XIV, the Sun King, and thus, unwittingly, Louis XV signed the death warrant of French absolutism. Yet another reason for political instability in the 1750s was that the nobility brought their ambitions into the realm of everyday administrative decision-making, thereby making functional tasks in the ministries subservient to their own personal schemes and ambitions. Patronage-hungry great families crowded to the trough, snouts a-quivering, their greed and lust for power encouraged by the King's indecisiveness. The resurgence of the aristocrats had another knock-on effect, since they thought it beneath their dignity to make economies in the ministries they controlled and, faced with this necessity, simply threw in the towel. The financial and political crises thus inter-penetrated and cross-pollinated. Louis XV either had to be a strong ruler himself (like Henry IV or Louis XIII) or he had to appoint a Prime Minister like Richelieu, Mazarin or Fleury. It was typical of the dog-in-the-manger monarch that he did neither.

The result was that by early 1759 Choiseul had a weak team to support him on the Council of State. Traditionally containing six members, the Council in 1759 comprised two failed Marshals (Soubise and d'Estrées); a Finance Minister (Silhouette) who was really a lawyer who did not understand finance, and who was anyway doomed to failure because of the opposition of the *parlement*; and a lacklustre Navy Minister Berryer. Choiseul's one ace in the hole was the able, energetic and sympathetic War Minister, Marshal Belle-Isle. A Marshal of France since 1741, the veteran Belle-Isle was old enough to be Choiseul's father, but worked with him in a spirit of fraternal solidarity. Rambunctious, brilliant, ambitious, seductive, energetic and popular, Belle-Isle was in personality not unlike Choiseul, with the same over-the-top extrovert disposition; it was his ability to get on well with a wide variety of people, even when they were deadly enemies of each other, like La Pompadour and the Comte d'Argenson, that doubtless accounted for President Hénault's judgement: 'he had enough admirers to found a religion'. The worst critics could say of him was that he liked to work in cliques and cabals. Belle-Isle became Secretary of State for War in April 1758 but he took some persuading. Some oligarchic prejudice made him feel that, whereas an aristocrat could be a Minister of State Without Portfolio, it was somehow undignified to occupy the office of Secretary of State. Bernis, then Foreign Secretary, worked hard to change his mind, though acidulous and snobbish critics said that Belle-Isle was not much of an aristocrat anyhow, being descended from Louis XIV's disgraced Finance Minister Fouquet.

Although the partnership of Belle-Isle and Choiseul was smooth, the new Secretary of State for War soon became disillusioned with his opposite number at the Navy, Nicholas Berryer. A former Lieutenant of the Paris police, and thus the kingdom's spymaster-general, Berryer was an undistinguished pen-pusher, nit-picker and number-cruncher who liked to pore over low-level accounts in his department in the hope of finding picayune errors. During his short reign he ordered that the cats kept by the navy at Toulon (to control the population of rats) should be put down, as they cost too much to feed. He also argued that navy veterans should not be paid pensions since, by feeding them over the years, the Ministry of Marine had saved that part of their wages that would have been spent on food if they were in civilian life. Since Berryer was a protégé of Madame de Pompadour, and Belle-Isle had also helped him on his way up the greasy pole, the War Minister imagined that he would have a compliant colleague at the Navy. Yet Berryer was one of those people who flatter and cajole to get to the top but, once in power, cast their former patrons adrift and are determined to do things their own way. Belle-Isle was confident that one of his favourite projects, the invasion of Jersey and the Channel Islands, would now come to fruition, having been rejected by the Council of State on two previous occasions. But to his fury, Berryer spoke out vociferously against the idea at a meeting of the Council of State and stuck to his guns, even when his patroness La Pompadour tried to intervene on Belle-Isle's side. An angry Belle-Isle confided to Choiseul the judgement that later historians have endorsed: Berryer was obsessed with bean counting and rooting out corruption and inefficiency in his ministery, but he forgot that his main aim was supposed to be fighting the British.

In addition to financial crisis, religious discontent, fragmented and fractured decision-making and incompetent colleagues, Choiseul had to contend with the vagaries of the King and the spirited political interventions of Madame de Pompadour. Louis XV shared Choiseul's taste for lechery and could compose a good minute for a Council meeting, but he had few of his Foreign Secretary's qualities. Neurotic, weak and indecisive – he favoured the devout party himself and disliked the *philosophes* and Jansenists but allowed Choiseul and Pompadour to side with them for political reasons and to expel the Jesuits whom he secretly admired – Louis had the weak man's dislike for strong and resolute characters. Excessively secretive, he reversed the pro-Prussian policy pursued until 1756 and worked in a cabal for a new pro-Austrian bearing, even as his Secretary of State for Foreign Affairs was still hard at work on the old policy. Even more incredibly, Louis had a secret foreign policy concerned with affairs in the Baltic, Poland and Russia, which he told no one about, not even La Pompadour, but directed with personal cronies. At first his henchman was the Duc de Conti, but Conti fell out with his master after the King, typically, double-crossed him over an army command. Louis then used the Comte de Broglie and a carefully placed senior official in the Foreign Ministry for the pursuance of the 'King's secret'.

Louis was also vindictive and vengeful, not a man it was wise to cross even inadvertently, since he would brood on slights and insults and bide his time until he could mete out sudden and irrevocable punishment. With the people at large he had lost all credibility. At the beginning of his reign and into the 1740s he was known as Louis the Well Beloved, but by 1759 he was universally perceived as Louis the well hated. Respect for the monarchy plummeted as the King, even after a series of disastrous military defeats, remained at Versailles instead of putting himself at the head of his army and trying to remedy the situation. To the working man of Paris Louis was a useless idler who preferred to make war on stags in his hunting lodges rather than lead his army at the front. And to the aristocrats in the *parlement* he was a weak bully who had to be stood up to, a cowardly autocrat who used *lettres de cachet* when he should have been using his mind.

Since Choiseul was himself a protégé of Madame de Pompadour, there was little he could do about her frequent political interventions. But, whatever he tried to do, whether it was concentrate on the war in North America or attempt the invasion of the British Isles, he had to take into account her likely reactions. Jeanne Poisson, later Marquise de Pompadour, was by any reckoning a phenomenon in the France of Louis XV. Born in 1721, the daughter of a wealthy farmer-general of taxes, she married Le Normant d'Etoiles in 1741 and caught the eye of the King four years later. As a young woman she was a notable beauty: slim, elegant, with a perfect oval face and luxurious fair hair (more light chestnut than blonde), big eyes, perfect nose, charming mouth, good teeth and marvellous skin, all topped off with a wonderful bewitching smile. Everyone remarked on the quality of her eyes, but few could agree on their colour, although it was agreed that they combined the vivid impact of dark eyes, the fineness of grey eyes and the tender languor of blue ones; this indeterminate hue seemed to make them suitable for all kinds of seduction and to express successively all the impressions of a very volatile spirit. The play of her physiognomy was infinitely varied; her face was regular-featured and suggested a soul at ease with itself; and her graceful movements conveyed a subtle nuance which was described as 'somewhere between the last degree of elegance and the first degree of nobility'. She had received a careful education in the liberal arts, spending four years with the Ursuline sisters of Poissy; a wag remarked that, apart from morality, she had been taught everything. All in all, then, she was a multi-talented woman with many different gifts and charms.

She was Louis's mistress in the carnal sense from 1745 to 1750. The King found in her company something he could not find elsewhere: he could be at ease, he could hear some common sense, he could be himself. This was why, even when he went elsewhere (after 1750) for his sexual satisfaction, he retained La Pompadour as a trusted adviser and confidante. She was certainly a good influence in some areas. Other Bourbon mistresses had antagonised the official royal consort by their haughtiness, their airs and graces. Pompadour went out of her way to be respectful to the Queen and, under her tutelage, Louis actually treated his wife better. For her part, she loved Louis with passion, sentimental feelings and sincere attachment. She was a member of the financial bourgeoisie and proud to be so; she had no aristocratic aspirations. Her enemies called her a whore and scoffed behind her back at her lack of savoir-faire; Voltaire, it was said, had taught her eloquence and conversation while Bernis had inculcated court manners and etiquette. She brought a bourgeois sensibility to bear on her life, excelling in running a house, improving the shining hour, presiding over a dinner. If she was a bourgeois, as her critics sneered, and cared excessively for money, then this was an attribute she shared with the King, so maybe he was a bourgeois at heart. Certainly Louis did not lavish money on her. There were occasional impulsive gifts but in general he watched the pennies. In 1745 he made her an allowance of 2,400 livres a month which he increased the following year to 7,200. In 1750, when she ceased to be his mistress, he cut the allowance to 4,000 livres and then to 3,000, and thereafter at no time did she receive more than 50,000 livres a year. Although Louis may be condemned for being tightfisted by the normal scale of benefices from monarch to mistress, Jeanne hardly needed his money, being immensely wealthy herself, from family bequests, real-estate investment and the ownership of houses in Paris and country factories, to say nothing of a huge collection of jewellery. Although she was a collector of art, porcelain and furniture, she never overdrew on her accounts, paid her bills scrupulously and would even sell her jewellery to settle her debts. During her lifetime she gave away the immense sum of 1,566,504 livres to charity and at her death left only thirty-seven louis.

In 1752 she was made a duchess and began to be devout, imitating Madame de Maintenon. Like the King she combined an official mask of Catholicism and probably genuine feelings for the faith with a hatred of ultramontane clericalism and of the Jesuits in particular. Her faith must often have been tested for from 1750 onwards she suffered from galloping consumption and was almost permanently ill. With myriad symptoms – fevers, coughs, chest infections, breathlessness – she used a variety of drugs to get relief. Soon she was having difficulty walking upstairs and had to have a primitive lift installed at Versailles. She hated the public life of a *maîtresse en titre* and the official duties and appearances, and often told her friends that the time she spent with Louis was the only good part about being the Marquise de Pompadour. Her enemies, drawing the ludicrous but intermittently fashionable analogy between physical illness and metaphysical evil, alleged that her physical suffering was 'God's punishment' for being the King's procuress. But La Pompadour had very little to do with Louis's infamous 'brothel', the Parc de Cerfs. In reality the much sensationalised and overhyped Parc de Cerfs was simply a quarter of Versailles where Louis entertained the women who really were what Jeanne was alleged to be: genuine *grisettes* and *filles de joie*. Here were the wholly carnal companions with whom the monarch disported himself and by whom he sired eight bastards: Louise O'Murphy, Jeanne-Louise Tiercelin, Ann Coupier and Lucie Citoyenne.

The other complaint her enemies made about La Pompadour was that she meddled in politics and was allowed virtually to run the country by a weak and complaisant Louis. Debate about Pompadour's exact role and influence has polarised historians. Some see her as the evil genius of the Seven Years War, the woman responsible for all France's worst defeats; others say that the legend of Madame de Pomapdour has been grotesquely overdone, that she had no real political clout and was merely the King's mouthpiece. It is natural for historians who emphasise structures and long-term forces to downplay the role of personality in history, but the extreme theory that Jeanne Poisson had no influence on political decisions cannot survive a close reading of the archives for the period. The obvious starting point is Maria Theresa of Austria's quest in 1755–56 for an intermediary who could introduce her to Louis confidentially and so promote her idea of getting France to abandon the Austrian alliance. Maria Theresa dithered about whether to approach the Prince de Conti or Madame de Pompadour for this delicate mission. She opted for Pompadour – shrewdly as it turned out, for Conti was out of favour with the monarch by the end of 1756. It was in August 1755 that Pompadour received a confidential letter from the Austrian queen, which she passed to Louis. The monarch, always intrigued by secret diplomacy, at once engaged Bernis as his agent in the clandestine negotiations with Austria. Pompadour was naturally delighted to be the go-between for a crowned head, as the confidence reposed in her by a 'real' monarch made nonsense of the lying and lubricious canards about her.

But the Austrian alliance was only the most dramatic manifestation of La Pompadour's behind-the-scenes influence. Louis used her as an arbiter in the disputes with the *parlement*, especially in 1756–57, and often delegated immense powers to her. There is even evidence of her persuading the King to make appointments against his better judgement, as in the elevation of Choiseul himself for, until she lobbied for him to become Ambassador to Rome, Louis still harboured a grudge against him for his role in the affair with Choiseul's cousin. She was always a highly intelligent and skilled politician. By 1756 she realised that she was acquiring an image of being always on the side of freethinkers and the *philosophes* and so, without abandoning her fondness for the Jansenists and her dislike of the Jesuits, she began to court the Queen herself, so successfully that she was appointed *dame du palais de la reine*. Her aim was to stay on at court by positioning herself as a peacemaker between the devout and the anti-ultramontanes, and the nuanced stance she adopted stood Pompadour in good stead when she survived the fall of the Comte d'Argenson in early 1757; it was thought that Louis, in shock after the Damiens assassination attempt, would cancel out the ousting of d'Argenson by getting rid of his enemy too. But Pompadour survived, and after 1757 was more powerful than ever. Soon all the great offices of state were filled by her protégés: Bernis, Berryer, Soubise, d'Estrées, Choiseul himself. It is impossible to underestimate her influence. It is true that she never secured anything against which Louis set his heart, and he often refused to dismiss ministers when she asked, simply because he enjoyed divide-and-rule, setting one ambitious would-be Prime Minister against another. But it is going too far to say, as some historians do, that she was always merely an echo or a reflection of the King. This assumes that Louis XV had fixed policies in all areas. In many spheres he did not, and his very indecision allowed La Pompadour to imprint her desires and make her wishes his.

Choiseul had time to revolve all these thoughts as he waited on that February evening of 1759, for his distinguished invitee was late for the appointment. Of all the difficult characters with whom Choiseul dealt in his political life none was more difficult than this visitor, for this was the prince Charles Edward Stuart, the Young Chevalier to his admirers, the Young Pretender to his enemies, but soon to be known to history and legend as Bonnie Prince Charlie. At thirty-eight, Charles Edward had experienced a plummeting fall as steep as Choiseul's rise had been meteoric. Ten years earlier he had been the most famous man in Europe. Only a year younger than Choiseul, he now looked older, for dissipation with the bottle had already taken its toll. Yet this was the prince who as a young man was regarded as the perfect young chevalier, tall, handsome, courageous, charming, magnetic. Born in Rome in 1720, he was the son of James Francis Stuart, who was in turn the son of James II of England and thus, to believers in the divine right of kings, the rightful King of England, Scotland and Ireland. James Stuart, known to his enemies as 'the Old Pretender', had tried to regain his father's throne in 1715 in the first of the Jacobite risings in Britain (so-called because supporters of the exiled James II were known as Jacobites, from the Latin *Jacobus* or James). Failing dismally in that rebellion, James married a Polish princess named Clementina Sobieska; from that union was born Charles Edward.

Sadly, the Prince's mother died when he was just fourteen. A devout woman who toppled over into religious fanaticism, Clementina Sobieska began a regime of fasts and strict diets, but this brought on the scurvy from which she died. Meanwhile James, a decent, fair-minded, but mediocre, timid, unimaginative and limited man, could never forge a relationship with his son, who always hated him, albeit unconsciously. From his earliest years Charles Edward had it dinned into him that it was his destiny to regain his grandfather's throne of the three kingdoms. The young Prince became a crack shot and a warrior, a master hunter who had steeled himself to physical hardship. The War of Austrian Succession gave him his chance. When France planned the first of its many would-be 'descents' on England, in the winter of 1743–44, the twenty-three-year-old Charles Edward left Rome, never to return while his father was alive. The 1744 invasion attempt fizzled out after a great storm wrecked a large number of French warships and transports. A frustrated Prince spent a year lobbying Louis XV and his ministers to stage another attempt, but in vain. Unwilling to admit defeat, he finally decided to go it alone. With just seven companions, Charles Edward bribed some Jacobite shipowners to land him on the west coast of Scotland, where he talked round some important clan leaders into raising the Stuart standard. By a combination of luck and the bungling of the Hanoverian government in London, the rebellion had already grown serious by the time the laggardly Scots authorities moved against it. In September 1745 the Prince and his tiny army won a great victory over government troops under Sir John Cope. The Jacobites held all of Scotland except for a few isolated government strongholds. In Versailles, Louis XV hailed the feat of arms by signing a formal treaty between France and the Stuarts.

France should now have revived the project of 1744 and sent a major expedition to England to support the Prince. But there were divided counsels about whether this was expedient at this stage in the war and Versailles spent October and November 1745 in dithering and procrastination; meanwhile the King and his ministers kept the rebellion alive by pump-priming, landing small detachments of troops in Scotland. When Louis XV finally committed to an all-out effort, it was too late. Realising that he was involved in a race against time, Charles Edward invaded England in November 1745 with an army of just 5,000 men. The little force performed miracles and arrived in Derby in early December, having outwitted their opponents at every turn. But at Derby the nerve of the Prince's Scots generals gave way. By this time they had expected reinforcements either from France or from the large number of alleged Jacobite sympathisers in England. When neither put in an appearance, the Prince's commanders insisted, over his frenzied protests, that the army return to Scotland. The decision at Derby was effectively the end of the rising of 1745. Charles Edward was right: had his army pressed on, it would almost certainly have prevailed against the demoralised and panic-stricken government forces. After an heroic retreat in the depths of winter, the Jacobites were back in Scotland by early January 1746. They defeated another government army at Falkirk, but failed to turn the victory into the rout it should have been. Having succeeded once more, the clan chieftains and other Jacobite leaders then made the extraordinary decision to retreat still further, into the depths of the Highlands. Penned in there during the winter by increasingly strong Hanoverian forces, and failing to get the supplies, money and men they expected from France, the Jacobites were ultimately forced to fight in highly unfavourable circumstances. At Culloden in mid-April 1746 the Prince and his army were heavily defeated. There was no attempt to regroup as a fighting force; a general *sauve qui peut* panic-stricken order was the upshot.

The five months that followed consolidated the Prince's legend for all time. With a price of £30,000 (£2 million in today's money) on his head, Charles Edward evaded his pursuers, dodging from outer islands to mainland, always one jump ahead of the enemy. When he was finally rescued by a French ship, he was regarded throughout Europe as the hero of the hour. On his return to France, the Prince was at first lionised. But relations between him and Louis XV turned sour in 1747 and even more so in 1748, when the French determined to make peace. One of the items the British insisted on as part of a general peace settlement was that France should expel the 'Young Pretender' from its territories. Louis XV asked the Prince to leave; he refused. There developed the most titanic clash of wills as Charles Edward, with many friends in Paris and wildly popular among the common people, defied Louis XV to expel him, going openly to the opera and other social events. There were even those who thought that the Prince was being put up to a trial of strength with Louis by his wife and her son the Dauphin, who wished to expel Madame de Pompadour and force the King to resign in favour of the Dauphin. Whatever the reason for Charles Edward's thinking that he was inviolable, he was soon disabused. In December 1748 Louis had him arrested, confined in the château of Vincennes and then taken to a remote frontier at Pont de Beauvoisin, near Chanbéry, Savoy, where he was dumped on the other side of the boundary like a parcel. The affair created a sensation. Sympathies were overwhelmingly with the Prince who, unfortunately unable to understand *raison d'état*, conceived the unshakeable idea that his expulsion by Louis was the result of personal dislike by the French King, who had violated all canons of solidarity with a fellow ruler by divine right in so humiliatingly truckling to the British.

The years that followed were dark ones for Charles Edward. After his expulsion he moved on to the papal territory of Avignon and later Venice, but found himself unwelcome in both. In the early 1750s he lived a twilight existence, commuting between secret lodgings in Paris and a more-or-less official address in Luneville, and later Liège, in Belgium. Forever on the move and changing his abode to throw British spies and would-be assassins off the track, the Prince even spent two unhappy years in Switzerland, before finally coming to rest in Bouillon. During these years he also made a daring visit in disguise to London and planned another rising, to be carried out simultaneously in London and the Highlands. After the grievous failure of that venture, known to history as the Elibank Plot, the Prince decided to invite his former mistress Clementina Walkinshaw to live with him. This decision caused consternation among his supporters, on two main grounds. Since Clementina had had another lover since she was the Prince's mistress, she was thought to be an unsatisfactory partner for him, and his comrades inveighed against her as a loose woman. Even more seriously, Clementina's sister was a lady-in-waiting at George II's court, and there were those who alleged that Miss Walkinshaw had been planted on the Prince by English spymasters, so that she could report back his every movement. The English Jacobite party insisted that he get rid of her before they could continue to regard him as their leader. But the Prince, obstinate, lacking all finesse as a politician, and by now drinking heavily reacted to this quite reasonable, if factually unwarranted, demand by digging in his heels and declaring that 'he would not put away a cat to please those people'. Charles Edward, sadly, always took the line that well-intended advice from any quarter, if if did not square with his own wishes and intentions, meant that other people were 'trying to give him laws'. The reference to 'those people' was particularly unfortunate, since those people (the English Jacobites) were his only source of money and sustenance during his existence as an incognito fugitive from English vengeance.

Ever since Monongahela and the likelihood that a general European war would soon erupt, the French and the Jacobites had been collaborating to see how their mutual interests could be dovetailed in the world conflict between Britain and France. There was one great, overarching problem. The failure of the '45 had left the Prince both with a massive grievance towards France and with a conviction that he should never again ignite a rebellion in Scotland. It was the Scots who had betrayed him at Derby, when complete victory was only just out of his grasp, and it was very clear that his so-called English supporters would declare themselves openly only when it was safe to do so, which meant after the landing of a French army and its triumph in arms. The Prince had, since 1747, always been adamant that he would only return to the British Isles if it was at the head of a huge expeditionary force. The French for their part wanted to use Charles Edward as a gadfly on the perimeter of events, to tie down British divisions and keep them guessing. They had offered to send a small force back with him to Scotland on many occasions, but the Prince refused, on the grounds that the French simply and cynically wanted to use him 'as a scarecrow'. In 1756 Marshal Belle-Isle visited the Prince at Bouillon and implored him to take command of the French expedition against Minorca, which was eventually led successfully by the Duc de Richelieu. Charles Edward had no interest in any of these schemes. The destination had to be England, the French had to be in earnest, and they had to provide him with incontestable proofs of their seriousness.

From 1756 onwards the Prince and his aides had assiduously lobbied the ministers at Versailles. Unfortunately they had done so in a highly unsystematic and unintelligent way; there was no mastermind in the Prince's service who had sufficiently sensitive political antennae to penetrate surefootedly through the labyrinth of intrigue, shifting alliances and changing ministerial personalities. The Prince used a number of agents, whose activities cut across each other and were self-contradictory, absurd and self-defeating. So little political talent did Charles Edward have that he often simultaneously targeted through these agents ministers and courtiers who were deadly enemies and who thus by no stretch of the imagination could ever support a common policy. At various times since 1755 he had employed the Comte de Lally (until he left to command the French armies in India); a dissolute ex-Church of England clergyman named George Kelly, who was hated and despised by everyone, French and Jacobite, apart from the Prince; George Jean Waters, son and heir of the Paris-based banking business; the discredited Alexander Murray of Elibank, who gave his name to the abortive Elibank Plot; and a seventy-plus-year-old Irish reprobate named Robert McCarthy, 5th Earl of Clancarty. Not content with this, Charles Edward also used on an ad hoc basis the Franco-Irish O'Heguerty brothers, the Prince's fellow freemasons: Pierre André O'Heguerty, the younger brother was deferential but his sibling Dominique, Comte de Magnières, was something of a hot-tempered loose cannon. There was also a French cavalry brigadier called the Marquis de Tournelle and Antoine Walsh, a Franco-Irish shipowner who had helped the Prince during the '45. Finally, there were the only two men who had any ability at all, William Stuart, Lord Blantyre, codename Leslie, was the leader of the Scots Jacobites in France and the main conduit to the Scottish Highlands; Sir Alexander Peter Mackenzie Douglas of Kildin, a Scots Catholic, was a veteran of French diplomacy. A protégé of the Prince de Conti, a fellow mason and friend of Charles Edward, Mackenzie Douglas had carried out two difficult missions in Russia for Conti and was instrumental in 1756 in getting Russian approval for the treaty between France and Austria. Not surprisingly, with such a plethora of agents targeting so many disparate personalities at Versailles, it was often very difficult to work out what Jacobite policy really was, or even if there was one to start with. The frequent changes of tactics by an impulsive, hot-headed and often paranoid Prince Charles did not help.

The only consistent supporter with real influence that the Prince had at Versailles was Marshal Belle-Isle but even his legendary patience was sometimes taxed to the limit by Charles Edward. The Prince fulminated continually about French perfidy, how he would never again be used as a 'scarecrow' by Louis XV, and how the French court would in future have to give unimpeachable proofs of the seriousness of its intention to invade England – and the Prince did mean England, rather than Scotland. Additionally, France would have to make reparation for the 'insult' of the arrest in 1748. Both the Prince's father and his sagest advisers had tried to counsel against such 'impossibilism'. What did 'making reparation' mean? All the ministers who sat in the Council of State in 1748 had since retired, so it was absurd and unphilosophical to visit their sins on their successors. That left Louis XV himself. The Prince surely did not expect the sovereign to abdicate or issue a public apology to an exile he was under no obligation to shelter in the first place. So why was he constantly harping about the need to make amends? The best amends the French could make would be to launch the invasion of England they had failed to complete in 1745–46. Everything else was moonshine. The French for their part wanted certain things from Charles Edward. Since he had refused over and over again to accept their offers of help on the Celtic fringes, the onus was on him to prove that he had a sizeable party in England. And there was something else. Surely if Charles Edward was serious about wanting to be restored to the throne of his ancestors, he should marry and beget an heir? Since his brother Henry was already a cardinal in the Catholic Church, the Prince needed to produce an heir to be credible. Otherwise, he might be killed during military action in England and the entire project of Stuart restoration would come to nothing.

The Prince stubbornly refused even to consider the idea of marriage. As for the English Jacobites, he was in an impossible position because the Jacobite party in England, such as it was, had virtually ceased to exist. When the Prince refused to put away Clementina Walkinshaw both the older Jacobite grandees like George Keith, last hereditary Marshal of Scotland (and always referred to as Marischal in Jacobite correspondence), and the younger devotees such as Jeremy Dawkins, who had won early fame by his exploration of Palmyra, washed their hands of the Prince and denounced him vociferously to their comrades in England. Again and again French ministers invited Charles Edward to come to Paris to discuss possible collaborative ventures between the French and the Jacobites. Always he refused to come, citing the alleged security angle: he explained that he thought Versailles was honeycombed with spies and special agents and could not enter into substantive discussions, involving the naming of names in England, as that might mean his friends in England suffering exposure and a cruel death, being hanged, drawn and quartered for treason as a number of his followers had been after the '45. The Prince realised that if he admitted candidly that he had alienated all his supporters in England, the French would have no further use for him. So he played a game of poker, bluffing as he sat at the table with no worthwhile cards in his hand.

As 1758 drew to a close, Choiseul reverted to the oldest wisdom of all: Rome can only be defeated in Rome. The contest in North America and Europe would be decided in the English Channel. If France could ever once get a substantial army across the Channel, than Canada, Guadeloupe and Madras might still be saved. Even after committing 100,000 troops to the venture, Choiseul reckoned that France still needed allies. He himself was sceptical about the utility of Charles Edward; he had heard the stories of the Prince's drunkenness, his instability and the circle of dubious friends with which he surrounded himself. There were also rumours that the Prince had changed his religion from Catholicism to Protestantism (the rumours were true), which would hardly predispose His Most Catholic Majesty in Charles Edward's favour. But Belle-Isle gradually won Choiseul round. Even though the British had tried to denude the Highlands of fighting men by drafting them and sending them to North America, thousands of potentially loyal clansmen were still available to the Bonnie Prince. In 1745 he had landed with just seven lacklustre comrades and had ended with an army 8,000 strong. If he landed with a large French force, he could raise at least as many again, even given the manpower shrinkage as a result of the British government's Machiavellian action. Choiseul took the force of the argument. Even though the Prince had already turned down three urgent invitations to come to Paris, one of them written in Louis XV's own hand, Choiseul summoned him once again. In the end, the Prince grudgingly agreed to make the journey, influenced most by a paternal letter from Belle-Isle, who said he would also be at the meeting at the Hôtel Choiseul. Choiseul added stick to carrot by sending a message through his own channels, stating that if the Prince refused to come to Paris, ministers might well decide to cancel the invasion project and sue for an immediate peace with Britain.

The Prince was so far from being a willing collaborator with Choiseul that he practically had to be dragged kicking and screaming to Paris. To reassure himself that he was doing the right thing and had not simply been persuaded against his better judgement by his followers, he went on a great drinking binge lasting all day on 5 February. The upshot was that he arrived at Choiseul's house very late in the evening, drunk and in the company of Alexander Murray of Elibank, one of the Jacobite agents most disliked by the French ministers and presumably chosen by the Prince for that very reason. No verbatim minutes of the conference survive but many letters referring to the points raised are extant, as well as Charles Edward's own jottings and Choiseul's reflections on the evening. Choiseul and Belle-Isle greeted the inebriated Prince cordially enough, though doubtless shocked by his condition. The Prince seems to have begun by repeating his old condition that he would not move a muscle until the French guaranteed him £20,000, twenty-five warships and 25,000 men destined for England. To his surprise, the ministers made no demur and assured him that an expedition was being actively prepared that very moment that would fulfil all the Prince's desires; the Prince de Soubise would be named as commander any day now. Choiseul then suggested that the maximum 'cost-benefit' could be obtained from the Jacobites if they were prepared to start a diversion somewhere on the periphery. What about Ireland? The Prince turned down the idea contemptuously. How often do I have to repeat, he blustered, that I am not interested in being King of Ireland only, or of Scotland only; it must be all or nothing, the three kingdoms or none.

Choiseul then suggested that the Prince might consider leading a relief expedition to North America; if the French beat the English in that hemisphere, the whole history of the world might be different, and the clear beneficiary would be Charles Edward himself. The atmosphere soured at this point. How could the French imagine that he would be interested in going to America, when he had not considered Minorca in 1756 or Scotland and Ireland any time since 1746? The Prince now took the line that if 'chimerical' ideas were being floated, he would put up a few of his own.

To Choiseul's consternation, Charles Edward announced that he wanted a formal treaty signed, with Spain as a co-signatory, committing the Bourbon monarchs to a Stuart restoration. Patiently Choiseul explained that he could not even persuade the Spanish to fight for their own objective interests in the Americas, so they would be hardly likely to go out on a limb for the House of Stuart. Very well then, said Charles Edward, I will accept a treaty with Louis XV like the one he signed at Fontainebleau with the Jacobites in October 1745. But, protested Choiseul, that was a treaty between crowned heads. Any such treaty could only be signed between Louis XV and James, the Prince's father, unless the Prince possessed a formal act of abdication from James, naming Charles Edward as *de jure* King of England, Scotland and Ireland. In 1745 James, having signed the Treaty of Fontainebleau, had waived his rights in favour of his son. But since that time father and son had fallen out badly, they were in total disagreement on relations with the French, and James had even written to the French court to complain about his son. 1759 was not 1745 and it seemed highly implausible that, in the circumstances, James would renew the act of abdication.

At this Charles Edward blustered and claimed that he could have an act of abdication back from Rome in the time it took a courier to make the return journey. But if he was bluffing on that point, he had to concoct some spectacular fantasies when Choiseul moved on to the subject of the English Jacobites. Who were they, where were they located and what were their names? Charles Edward replied that he had taken a solemn oath not to reveal their identities until the French invasion fleet was already at sea, such was the fear of security leaks and premature arrests in Britain. He tried to counterattack by asking what stage French invasion preparations had reached, since his friends in England were pressing him for news of French intentions. Choiseul replied coldly that, since the Jacobites in England were only to be contacted once the French fleet had cleared from the Channel ports, it followed logically that he could not give any precise information, for the selfsame security reasons. Charles Edward protested that he had to know beforehand in order to concert measures. But how can we concert measures when we do not even know with whom we are dealing, protested Choiseul. The conference was rapidly turning into a spectacular non-meeting of minds. It seems that Belle-Isle tried to intervene and bring the two principal negotiators together again, but Choiseul had lost confidence in Charles Edward's intelligence and the Prince, not liking the Foreign Secretary's rapier-like ripostes, was coming to the conclusion that the Lorrainer was trying 'to give him laws'.

The meeting finally petered out. Both sides agreed that they would send a written précis of their understanding of the conference, and that the ministers would be in touch again with the Prince as soon as the expedition to Britain neared completion. In his usual headstrong manner Charles Edward insisted on leaving Paris immediately and heading home, even though further meetings had been arranged with the Prince de Soubise and Madame de Pompadour. Choiseul concluded that the Prince was hopeless and that nothing should be looked for at his hands. However, there was an obvious value to keeping the Jacobite card in play until the expedition took shape, and it might still be useful to use the Prince's name as a rallying cry if a second army was sent to Scotland. Choiseul therefore devised the anodyne but meaningless formula that was to be used as a mantra throughout 1759. Pointedly cutting the detested Elibank out of the loop, he wrote to Mackenzie Douglas on 14 February, summarising his sense of the meeting and adding: 'Nothing will be done without the prince but only by him and for him.' Privately he told Belle-Isle that they should proceed with their plans, leaving the Prince completely out of the reckoning. When everything was ready – which he expected would be around midsummer – they would see whether there was any role Charles Edward could play and if there was still mileage to be had out of him.

As soon as the Jacobites in France realised that the French were in earnest about their invasion plans, they bombarded Choiseul with ideas about landings and 'descents' in England and Scotland. Choiseul found himself deluged with memoranda from Stuart supporters at court and from Jacobites in the Church, the army, the navy, the East India Company and the masonic lodges. His own brother Antoine, Cardinal Archbishop of Cambrai, interceded on the Prince's behalf, as did the Dauphin, always an admirer of Charles Edward Stuart and animated by the same sort of distaste for his father that Charles entertained for James. Back in Bouillon, the Prince fumed at the 'duplicity' of Choiseul who, he alleged, had called him to Paris on a fool's errand. The refusal to enter into a treaty particularly nettled him. He also claimed, disingenuously, that he had informed his followers in England and Scotland that a French invasion was imminent, and there was now the danger that they would show their hand and rise prematurely. Another of the Prince's fantastic drink-fuelled falsehoods was the transparent nonsense that he went to meet Choiseul on the assumption that the 25,000 troops and twenty-five ships of the line were ready and waiting, but he then found they would not be ready to sail until late summer. According to Charles Edward, he had gone to Paris to trigger a pre-existing expeditionary force not to discuss the preparation of one. He wrote to Mackenzie Douglas on 9 February that it was still his hope that

France would restore him as they had restored Charles II almost exactly 100 years before but in that case 'then what resentments the French may expect for all the injuries they have done to him'. Charles Edward was now adding ingratitude to his many other faults.

While the Stuart prince brooded, fumed and raged in his eyrie at Bouillon, Choiseul turned to the serious task of trying to construct an anti-British coalition that would assail Pitt on many different fronts and prevent him concentrating all his efforts on the French invasion force. Having concluded that the Jacobites were a busted flush, he looked for more solid support from supposedly friendly nation-states. His first inclination was to try to bring Sweden into the fight, preferably alongside Russia. On 21 January he told the French ambassador in Stockholm, the Marquis d'Havrincourt, that he should lobby the Swedish court for 12,000 men to be part of a Franco-Swedish invasion force; while France sent its troops across the Channel to England, the Swedes should land their men in Scotland, citing English piracy on the high seas as the reason for war. But d'Havrincourt made no progress in Stockholm. The Swedes proved singularly reluctant to collude with the French, citing a number of reasons. In the first place, any putative plans for an invasion of Scotland could not be kept secret, since such a scheme would have to go before the Diet and its secret committee, and not just the Senate; moreover, the ruling Hat party hated the Russians and would never collaborate with them. In any case, both Sweden's objective interests and public opinion made a Franco-Swedish descent on the British Isles chimerical: on the one hand Frederick of Prussia was regarded as the defender of Protestantism; and on the other Sweden was far too dependent on British markets for her iron and maritime products. Even those Swedish senators who were Anglophobe and supported Choiseul warned him that they could not collaborate in anything as audacious as an invasion of the British Isles – a point made to Choiseul in no uncertain terms by the Swedish ambassador in Paris, Ulric Scheffer. Choiseul's overtures to Sweden turned out disastrously and were even counterproductive, since the Swedish envoy in Denmark told the British envoy in Copenhagen all about Choiseul's designs. Even the arms and ammunition ordered in Sweden and paid for by France ended up in enemy hands, since the arms shipment was routed via Amsterdam where it was seized by the Dutch, acting on a tip-off from British secret agents.

Enraged by this grave setback to his plans – which he blamed on the 'utopianism' of the Swedish court – an embarrassed Choiseul hid his failure from his colleagues on the Council of State and cast about for alternative allies. He did not seek Austrian help, since he knew the Hapsburgs were the ancient enemy of the Stuarts. But the Austrian alliance did offer a slight consolation prize, since, as a guarantee of the neutrality of the Low Countries, Vienna had allowed the French to occupy Ostend as long as the war lasted. Ostend was a useful base for a descent on England, and there were many 'Wild Geese' (Irish soldiers in exile) in the Austrian army who flocked to volunteer with Choiseul once they heard the invasion rumours. More solid support might be expected from Russia following the signing of the 1756 Franco-Russian treaty, so Choiseul proposed to Chancellor Vorontzov that Russian forces proceed down the River Oder to capture Stentin from the Prussians; from there, 10,000–12,000 Russian troops could be embarked on Swedish ships, ready to carry out combined operations in the north of Scotland. Choiseul argued that the Hanoverian dynasty might be quite easily toppled, since George II was close to death while his favourite son the Duke of Cumberland was locked in a deadly struggle with the Prince of Wales and the rival court at Leicester House. But would Sweden provide the shipping? Anders Johann von Hopken, President of the Swedish Chancery, did not play straight with Choiseul but instead pretended to be interested provided there was a cast-iron guarantee of Russian participation, Sweden was granted the island of Tobago in the Caribbean and France hugely increased its subsidies to Stockholm. But Vorontzov was no keener on collaborating with Sweden than the Swedes with him. He too strung Choiseul along, always superficially polite but never a serious player in the invasion game.

Finally Choiseul did persuade one of the Baltic countries to his way of thinking but unfortunately for him, it was not one of the giant fish in the northern sea but a relative minnow, Denmark. At first Denmark shared the reservations, voiced privately by Sweden and publicly by Holland, that Choiseul's invasion scheme seemed too much like a Catholic crusade on behalf of the Stuarts. Choiseul replied that his personal aim was neither a revolution in the British Isles nor even Stuart restoration, but merely to hurt England as much as she had already hurt France and thus to get an equitable peace settlement. Choiseul's case was hardly helped by the blundering efforts of Jacobite agents who tried to quell Protestant fears by bruiting it around Europe that Charles Edward had abjured his Catholic faith and embraced the Church of England. It was true that the Stuart prince had gone through a form of Protestant conversion in 1750 purely out of political expediency (the Prince himself was a deist, if not an outright atheist), but far from reassuring Protestant Europe, this new canard lost the Prince many old friends without gaining him any new ones. Finally Choiseul was able to concentrate Danish minds on *realpolitik* and convinced the Chancellor in Copenhagen, Baron Johan Hartvig Ernst von Bernstorff, that Britain was already far too strong, both navally and commercially, and that the long-term interests of Denmark were threatened. Although the Danes took the force of this argument, they drew back from the provision of troops for the invasion. The farthest they were prepared to go was to form a defensive alliance in the Baltic – as happened in March 1760 when they combined with Russia and Sweden in a league of armed neutrality. But they wanted neither to help revive Sweden as a major military power nor to risk the wrath of Britain by taking part in a full-scale project for a descent on the British Isles.

Choiseul's best hope always lay with Spain, whom geopolitical considerations finally forced into the Seven Years War in 1761. The Spanish Prime Minister in 1759 was Ricardo Wall, a man of Irish Jacobite ancestry with an emotional attachment to the Stuarts but an even greater attachment to his career which meant paying attention to *realpolitik* rather than sentiment. His favourite device was to pretend sympathy for French pleas for assistance while claiming that his royal masters prevented him from acting. There was little Bourbon solidarity in evidence for, though Louis XV often solicited him in his own hand, Ferdinand VI never advanced beyond abstract sympathy. Choiseul and his agents used many persuasive lines of approach with Spain – and indeed Bernis had used most of them in 1758. Apart from offering the Spanish court Minorca – as an inducement to join France in the struggle against the natural and necessary enemy, England – Versailles employed at least three main arguments. The first was what would later be known as the 'domino' theory: if Canada fell, Louisiana would be next and after that the British would look for their next target in the New World, probably Mexico but certainly some other part of the Spanish 'Indies'. Wall always denied that there was any linkage between Canada and Mexico and professed himself unmoved by the domino theory. The second French line was to get Wall to agree to supply New France from Spanish Florida, hoping thereby to embroil Spain with Britain. But Wall was alert to that possibility, and always replied that it was impossible to supply Canada from Florida since British seapower would interdict any such commerce. The third argument was that the Spanish treasure fleets themselves were in danger and that, once France was defeated in the New World, the British would make themselves masters of the Caribbean and cut Spain off from its American empire. Wall always said that he would take this threat seriously only when he saw evidence of definite British aggression against Havana or Cartagena.

Wall was himself constrained by a number of considerations. While Ferdinand VI was alive, the King was obsessed by the idea that he could be a peacemaker, a mediator between France and Britain. Although Wall told his confidants that the idea was fanciful, since Britain would never accept a Bourbon king as 'honest broker' and anyway a general peace would have to include Frederick of Prussia, he was bound to humour his royal master. When Charles III succeeded and Wall admitted that he was worried by British advances in North America, he nonetheless used the 'newness' of the King as an excuse to do nothing and veto the sending of Spanish warships to help the French at Brest. Moreover, Charles III, though more sympathetic to the Stuarts than his predecessor, always claimed that he wanted to see the Jacobites rise in Britain *before* he sent an army of invasion, whereas it was clear from the events of 1745–46 that this was the one thing that would never happen again. Most of all, though, Wall listened to the advice of the erstwhile Jacobite Earl Marischal George Keith, a renegade in all but formal protestation who, while claiming continued attachment to James Stuart in Rome, was privately advising Wall in 1759 that the Stuarts were a hopeless cause and that the Hanoverian dynasty was too firmly planted in Britain. It did not help that the Jacobite lobbyists in Madrid were not of the highest calibre. The Comte Walsh de Serrant was a shipowner and slave-trader who never conferred with the French ambassador Aubeterre or the other French diplomats and tended to leave the detailed lobbying to his deputy Bernard Ward.

Throughout 1759 Choiseul continued to hope that something might yet come of his assiduous overtures to Russia, Sweden and Spain and he even thought it worth keeping the Jacobite card in play just in case Charles Edward turned out to be not quite the paper tiger (or at any rate the drunken sailor) he had appeared to be in Paris on the night of 5 February. The Stuart prince meanwhile remained in Bouillon, demanding and expecting that the French approach him as the next move, when the reality was that Choiseul had largely written him out of the script. Charles Edward's inactivity was the despair of his friends and supporters; one of them, Sholto Douglas, could finally bear it no longer and burst out with: 'Your enemies now wantonly exult and express themselves as Peter the Great did of Charles XII of Sweden, that he kept his Swede chained at Bendar. They say they have you in a bottle at Bouillon and have the cork in their pocket.' Whatever the Prince's erratic behaviour, even his enemies could scarcely deny that his name and presence were worth half a dozen regiments. Whereas in 1745–46 the French commander, the Duc de Richelieu, intended to land in England with no more than 15,000 men, counting on massive support from the supposedly pro-Jacobite English Tories and the fighting power of the Scottish clansmen, Choiseul laid his plans on the assumption that he might have to operate entirely without Jacobite support. This meant earmarking up to 100,000 men – a huge effort but one that Choiseul was determined to fulfil. As he remarked ominously, this was now a do-or-die effort: 'If 50,000 men perish in a first expedition, the King has determined to send out another force of equal strength, and we shall not give up as long as there are men in France.'

THREE

PITT AND THE WEST INDIES

By 1759 belief in the supernatural was encountered less and less among the intellectual classes of Europe, but it is difficult to be certain about the extent of the scepticism, since a curious two-way process was observable. On the one hand, there were Enlightenment abbés, *dedicated to the deistic or even atheistic principles of the* philosophes, *who hid their lack of Christian faith so as not to lose valuable benefices or livings. On the other hand, intellectual sophisticates probably affected a greater degree of disbelief in the supernatural than they really felt. Yet a curious case occurring in July 1759 made even some unbelievers sceptical about their own scepticism.*

The case involved the Swedish mystic Emanuel Swedenborg, a man whose impact was to be profound, since he influenced Kant, Blake, Goethe, Emerson, Dostoevsky and the French Symbolists. Already in his seventy-first year in 1759, Swedenborg was one of that curious class of people whose careers fall into two distinct halves, when the early achievement (however considerable) is repudiated in favour of an entirely new and mystical bearing (Annie Besant, Sir Francis Younghusband, A. N. Whitehead, Ludwig Wittgenstein, Carl Jung, etc, etc). As a man Swedenborg looked undistinguished: he had quiet clerical habits, sipped tea and coffee in a timid, spinsterish way and was known to be kind to children. Old-fashioned even in eighteenth-century terms, he wore a sword and full velvet dress in company and, when he went for his daily walk, carried a gold-headed cane. Although habitually described as having a wandering or vacant air, Swedenborg would end his life with a huge coterie of followers, including Sweden's royals.

Swedenborg had a distinguished early career as a scientist in many different fields – anatomy, physiology, metallurgy, engineering, astronomy, pure mathematics – but in 1744 (when he was fifty-six) he underwent a religious crisis in which he claimed to have been given a direct vision of the spiritual world. He then produced thirty volumes expounding his revelations in Latin. He claimed to have had supernatural visions, to have travelled 'astrally' to the planets and to have conversed with Jesus. According to Swedenborg, humans exist simultaneously in the physical and spiritual worlds, but only the memory of the spiritual world survives after death. The afterlife is a relatively mundane place, where even angels have sexual intercourse; there is a Hell but no Satan or devils and Heaven is much like Earth, except peopled by spirits. The core of Swedenborg's message is that God, Heaven and Hell are not transcendental or 'out there', but located within us. To the mortification of orthodox Christians, Christ, it seems, did not suffer crucifixion to atone for the sins of mankind since all genuinely numinous phenomena take place inside us, not in the external world. The props of Protestantism and Catholicism whether the Trinity or the doctrine of predestination have to be jettisoned, since redemption is solely concerned with personal striving in the spiritual life.

In June 1759 Swedenborg returned from England to his native Sweden and made Gothenburg his first port of call. On 19 July he was dining in that city at the home of a prominent burgher, William Castel. A distinguished company had assembled, and the other diners noticed that Swedenborg looked pale and seemed ill at ease. After a while Swedenborg excused himself, saying he needed a breath of air, and went out into the garden. When he returned, he told the diners that a terrible fire had just broken out in Stockholm (which was 300 miles away) and was spreading rapidly. Later, at about 8 p.m. he said: 'Thank God, the fire is extinguished three doors away from my house.' The provincial Governor heard about this extraordinary dinner party, summoned Swedenborg, questioned him and took down a detailed account of his vision. A few days later a courier arrived from Stockholm, confirming that there had indeed been a great conflagration on the evening of 19 July and giving an account of the fire that matched Swedenborg's in every detail. The reputation Swedenborg already had as a clairvoyant was enhanced and he was taken up by the Swedish royal family, to whom he gave other proofs of his spiritualistic and mediumistic powers. The philosopher Immanuel Kant was deeply impressed by Swedenborg, and some Kant scholars claim that his philosophy is a never-ending struggle between the mysticism of Swedenborg and the scepticism of David Hume. But probably Swedenborg's greatest advocate in later times was the psychologist Carl Jung, whose views about 'one world' (the unity of the physical and spiritual), God as a power within us, and 'synchronicity' (the simultaneity in space-time of significant events, which the unsophisticated read as coincidences) matched the Swedish mystic's perfectly. Thus does Jung explain the strange events of 19 July 1759: 'there was a . . . lowering of the threshold of consciousness which gave him access to absolute knowledge. The fire in Stockholm was, in a sense, burning in him too.'

The mixture of science and mysticism in Swedenborg is an apt symbolisation of the Janus face of the eighteenth century in general. While philosophers like Berkeley, Kant and Hume raised epistemological issues that still baffle the world's best minds today, ordinary people went to public executions, and the thief who stole an apple could be hanged at Tyburn Tree under England's 'Bloody Code'. Hume's devastating *Dialogues Concerning Natural Religion* were so subversive of normal Christian belief that the great Scottish philosopher did not dare publish them in his lifetime. But meanwhile, in benighted areas of the world coming within the European orbit, primitive people worshipped sharks, crocodiles and snakes. These primitive beliefs were borne in on Europeans very forcibly in 1759 when France and Britain contended for mastery of the West Indies. Of the fifteen million slaves taken from West Africa to the New World in the eighteenth century, at the height of the slave trade, about 42 per cent went to the West Indies, and many of these (10,000–12,000 a year) were uplifted from the kingdom of Dahomey, whose great period was in the eighteenth and nineteenth centuries. Along with the slaves Dahomey exported the dark pagan religion of voodoo or snake worship, which underwent various changes in the Caribbean and was in turn re-exported to French Louisiana. The island of Martinique, the cockpit for Anglo-French rivalry in the Caribbean, was second only to French-speaking Haiti as a centre for voodoo, to the point where in 1782 the Governor of New Orleans, alarmed at the arrival in North America of this new devil-cult, forbade the import of slaves from that island. His alarm was understandable. Voodoo involves snakes, animal sacrifice and the drinking of blood. In the classic voodoo ceremony, priests designated as a 'king' or 'queen' would open a box inside which was a snake. A boiling cauldron would then be prepared into which chickens, frogs, cats, snails and, always, the snake, would be thrown. A male dancer, representing 'the Great Zombi' ('*Le Grand Zombi*') would then officiate and all participants in the rite would drink from the cauldron, washing down the disgusting mixture with raw alcohol; the evening would then end in an orgy. The white rulers feared voodoo, not so much that black magic would actually be used against them but that voodoo could be used by troublemakers to 'legitimate' plots, slave revolts and revolution itself.

The West Indies were widely perceived as a prize supremely worth fighting for, since sugar was the biggest business of eighteenth-century colonial empires. In 1775 sugar made up one-fifth of all British imports and was worth five times Britain's tobacco imports. What this meant was that to British ministerial minds, the West Indies was a more important area than North America and Britain's great leader in 1759, William Pitt explicitly stated that he thought the French sugar island of Guadeloupe was worth more than the whole of Canada and that the West Indies were worth more than North America: 'The state of the existing trade in the conquests of North America is extremely low; the speculations of their future are precarious, and the prospect, at the very best, very remote.' He had a point, even though a limited and unimaginative one – since even at the time of the Boston Tea Party in 1773 the value of British imports from Jamaica was five times greater than from all the American colonies. The island of Nevis on its own produced three times more British imports than New York in the years 1714–73, and Antigua three times more than New England. But trade between North America and the West Indies was equally important to the white plantocracy in the islands; whether we are talking of the Dutch in the seventeenth century or the British and French in the eighteenth, North America and the Caribbean had complementary economies, with each depending on the other. The French supplied the Antilles from Louisbourg and vice versa, and for the British the trade fulcrum was New York, which supplied the British West Indies with food and allowed the islands to devote more land to their cash crops. New York's shipping took beef, lamb, pork, wheat, rye, corn, bread, butter, cheese, apples, peas, onions and pickled oysters to the islands and returned with sugar, molasses, hides, lumber and silver together with bills of exchange (credit notes) that enabled New York's merchants to buy manufactured goods from Britain. New York also participated in the triangular slave trade, joining ships from Bristol and Liverpool on the West African coast, where they traded rum and manufactures for slaves to be sold in the West Indies.

The French slave trade was carried on from its Atlantic ports but by 1759 the position of the islands in the French Antilles was not nearly so favourable as its British-controlled counterparts in the Caribbean. The French Antilles trade concentrated on white sugar, indigo, cotton and coffee, with brown sugar very much a poor relation; but Martinique, the jewel of the French West Indies, suffered badly during the early period of the Seven Years War, both because of the British blockade (particularly effective in 1758 under Admiral Sir John Moore) and because of lack of shipping in which to export its crops. There was scant sympathy in Versailles for the plight of the Antilles. Navy Minister Machault told the islands in 1756 that Louis XV would not protect their ships by the old convoy system as he had better uses for His Majesty's warships, but would simply station squadrons at landfalls, to protect the entry and departure of shipping. In 1759 Minister Berryer stopped payment on all colonial bills of exchange, thus drying up the credit of the Antilles. He recommended that the islands seek their salvation through neutral shipping; unlike his predecessors Maurepas, Machault and Moras, he thought that not enough neutrals were

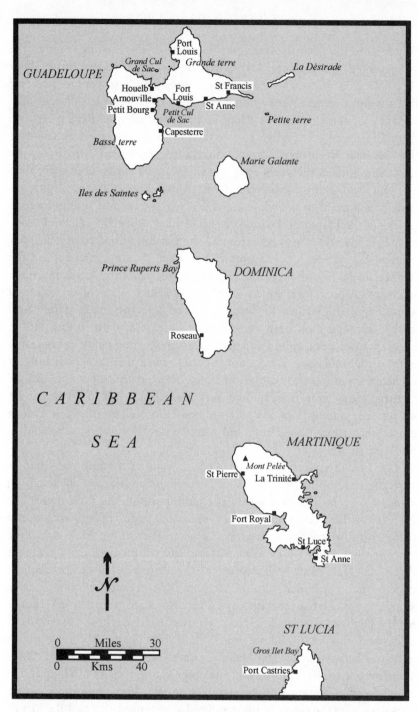

The campaign of Guadeloupe and Martinique,
January–May 1759

admitted to the islands; they had all thought too many were. There was considerable disillusionment in the French islands by early 1759 and William Pitt thought he saw an opportunity to capitalise on their lack of morale.

William Pitt, Prime Minister in all but name, was one of Britain's greatest assets in the Seven Years War. Although his arrogance and aloofness could alienate even close friends (or at any rate those who thought themselves friends), as a politician he possessed a formidable arsenal of weapons. He was cynical and ruthless: the original 'desiccated calculating machine', he only ever did anything out of political considerations. He was the perfect Machiavellian, in that he understood that in politics one must 'look like the innocent flower but be the serpent under't'. He would never lift a finger to help even those supposedly close to him if it did not serve his political ends, but he was a great hand at feigning concern and pretending to help. He had many of the attributes of a natural actor, with an imposing physical presence and a powerful voice: his bell-throated oratory was said to have been second only to Danton in the entire eighteenth century. Always the most histrionic of statesmen, he gave himself theatrical airs, could pose and preen like the most hammy thespian and was even said to flash stage lightning from his eyes. His command of actorly gestures was complete, from the raised and supercilious eyebrow to the dismissive wave of the hand. He had the vanity and narcissism of the great actor-managers. But, like the famous French Marshal Villars, who boasted that he could fight the Duke of Marlborough to a standstill, was universally disbelieved, and then proved his point at the Battle of Malplaquet, Pitt was a man equal to his vainglorious posturings. 'I am sure that I can save this country and that nobody else can,' he bragged. His ingenious mind was essentially pragmatic; he was flexible and open to new suggestions and could think divergently. He could temper contempt with political know-how, as he proved in his notoriously difficult relations with George II and in his (on paper) implausible alliance with the Duke of Newcastle.

Aged 50 in 1759, Pitt had served in a previous administration as Paymaster-General, but his big break came at the outbreak of war in 1756 when he was appointed Secretary of State in a coalition government. Violent antipathy from George II forced his resignation in April 1757 but popular clamour led to his recall just two months later. George II's dislike was a compound of three main factors. In the first place, Pitt favoured a war against France on the imperial periphery and was against continental entanglements, whereas for the monarch the defence of his beloved Hanover was always the priority. Second, Pitt felt dislike and contempt for George II's favourite son, the Duke of Cumberland, and added insult to injury by favouring Prince Frederick (George II's eldest son) and his coterie at Leicester House; the King, on the other hand, following the fashion of the Hanoverians, loathed Frederick, who returned the hatred with interest. Yet even George II had to endure the unendurable when reasons of state were involved, and it was clear to everyone that Pitt was indispensable to the war effort. To many contemporaries the political alliance with the Duke of Newcastle was the more amazing phenomenon. The sixty-six-year-old Thomas Pelham-Holles, 1st Duke of Newcastle, was a veteran of more than thirty years with his hands on the levers of power. As an ally of the avatar of 'Old Corruption', Sir Robert Walpole, he had often been the target for Pitt's acidulous tongue. But for all his manifold faults, his venality and mediocre intellect, Newcastle was, in his own way, a shrewd operator. He realised that Britain needed Pitt, so he swallowed the taunts, forgot the insults and allowed the go-between Lord Chesterfield to forge an alliance between himself and the 'Great Commoner'.

Pitt's common sense and flexibility emerge most clearly in this alliance with Newcastle, whom in his heart he must have despised. Newcastle was a pure machine politician, described by one historian as 'ignorant of most things except the art of managing the House of Commons and careless of all things that could not help his party and himself'. Congenitally timid, he lived in terror of personal unpleasantness and devoted much of his political skill to avoiding 'scenes', even if this meant ducking the issue. Essentially an amoral, cowardly, unprincipled, vacuous man, Newcastle was one of those people who was never nasty to anyone until he felt sure it was safe; sycophantic to the powerful and influential, he could be merciless to those who he was sure had no power, nor ever would have. His jerky physical movements, rapid and garbled speech, neurotic restlessness and air of always being in a hurry, his taste for hyperbole and impossible promises, were much commented on, parodied and burlesqued. Horace Walpole said of him: 'A borrowed importance and real insignificance gave him the perpetual air of a solicitor . . . He had no pride, though infinite self-love. He loved business immoderately; yet was only always doing it, never did it. When left to himself, he always plunged into difficulties, and then shuddered for the consequences.' An age that values political fixing over principle or ideology, such as our own, has seen unconvincing revisionist attempts to rehabilitate Newcastle, but it is difficult to argue with Parkman's verdict that 'a more preposterous figure than the Duke of Newcastle never stood at the head of a great nation'.

To Newcastle, America was a distant and unimportant blur on the map. The story is told that General Ligonier once suggested that Annapolis should be defended, to which Newcastle replied: 'Annapolis, Annapolis!

Oh, yes, Annapolis must be defended; to be sure. Annapolis should be defended, – where is Annapolis?' According to Tobias Smollett, Newcastle was entirely ignorant of all geography, and Smollett reports the following 'exchange' in his novel *Humphry Clinker*:

Captain C treated the Duke's character without any ceremony. 'This wiseacre,' said he 'is still abed; and I think the best thing he can do is to sleep on till Christmas; for when he gets up he does nothing but expose his own folly. In the beginning of the war he told me in a great fright that thirty thousand French had marched from Acadia to Cape Breton. "Where did they find transports?" said I. "Transports!" cried he. "I tell you they marched by land."

"By land to the island of Cape Breton!"

"What, is Cape Breton an island?" said the Duke.

"Certainly."

"Ha. Are you sure of that?"

When I pointed it out in the map, he examined it earnestly with his spectacles; then, taking me in his arm, "My dear C – !" (cried he), "you always bring us good news – egad! I'll go directly and tell the king that Cape Breton is an island!"'

But Newcastle admired Pitt's willingness to shoulder responsibility and perform well under stress, and was content with a division of labour whereby Pitt occupied the public stage while he was the behind-the-scenes fixer: intriguing, bribing, cooking up shady political deals, dispensing patronage, places and pensions. Pitt, for his part, took the line that as long as he could appoint generals, admirals and ambassadors, Newcastle could have the rest. 'I will borrow the Duke's majorities to carry on the government,' he declared. The two men drew closer together. While considering Pitt a child in financial matters, Newcastle gradually evolved into a stubborn defender of his old tormentor. He was happy with the title of First Lord of the Treasury while Pitt was Secretary of State. Pitt, on the other hand, came to appreciate Newcastle's expertise in finance and patronage. It was, as the historian Francis Parkman remarked, 'a partnership of magpie and eagle'.

Pitt's power base was unusually secure for someone operating in a parliamentary rather than absolutist system. The key to his power was three-fold. In the first place, the alliance with Newcastle made him impregnable in the House of Commons since Newcastle was the only man in Britain who could topple him and Newcastle refused to grant offices to Pitt's opponents and critics. It was difficult even for an informal opposition to arise, for Pitt, with his track record of previous opposition to Newcastle and Walpole, could claim to be above party, a patriot who believed in wartime coalition rather than strife and faction. Pitt also neutralised the potential opposition among 'country' MPs by refusing to increase taxes on land and relying on the militia rather than regulars to defend the island against invasion, thus heading off the pressure for further revenue through taxation. The 1757 Militia Act, controversial though it was, was a clever piece of politics. As the cynical Horace Walpole pointed out, the country squires 'by the silent douceurs of commissions in the Militia . . . were weaned from their opposition, without a sudden transition to ministerial employment'. Secondly, Pitt set himself to court and flatter George II and began laying it on with a trowel. He started by ruthlessly severing his contacts with Prince Frederick and Leicester House, to the fury of the Prince who regarded him as a backstabber. Pitt committed substantial subsidies and troops to the defence of the monarch's beloved Hanover, while simultaneously (and paradoxically) enthusing the King about his grand scheme for the conquest of Canada. He even manipulated George so that Newcastle's complaints about the multiplying costs of the war fell on deaf ears. Thirdly, because British institutions, and particularly the armed forces, had not yet become bureaucratised, a powerful individual could gather immense decision-making power to himself. Pitt took full advantage of the situation, working in small ad hoc committees with men he really trusted, like Admiral Lord Anson of the navy and Field Marshal Lord Ligonier in the army. Major military expeditions were despatched by Pitt after a lack of consultation that looks incredible to modern eyes; sometimes an entire army corps could be sent to a destination on what looked like no more than one man's whim. The inevitable quid pro quo was a workload that even a titan like Pitt could not sustain indefinitely. One-man rule, even in a not quite modern state like eighteenth-century Britain, is an impossibility in the micro-managing sense.

Pitt's versatility and adaptability meant that he often seemed to be able to square the circle. One of the oldest debates in English foreign policy in the eighteenth century was whether to make affairs in the wider world or overseas empire the priority or to concentrate on the balance of power in Europe. Pitt's preference was overwhelmingly for defeating France in North America, India or wherever the two powers came into conflict. But he was nudged back towards Europe not just by George II's obsession with Hanover but by the general military situation there. By late 1758 Frederick the Great had lost 100,000 fighting men to death, wounds, disease, desertion and capture and seemed close to collapse. Pitt showed solidarity in two ways. He sent more troops to Europe to ease the pressure on his ally, and he began a policy of 'descents' on the French coast, that is to say, landing armies in some strength on the western coast of France to harry, destroy and irritate coastal defences and generally to undermine the credibility of Louis XV's war effort. But he failed to ride the two incompatible horses of the monarch and Prince Frederick. Pitt needed George II's confidence, as even the favourite son Cumberland had learned to his cost when he was disgraced in 1757. Since Frederick and the Leicester House clique opposed making Hanover a cornerstone of foreign policy, Pitt was increasingly forced to choose between his old and new patrons. As a *realpolitiker* he chose the King, but his cold, callous and offhand reply to overtures from Leicester House angered Frederick and made him vow vengeance on the viperous ingrate he had previously nurtured.

By January 1759 William Pitt could derive some satisfaction from the shift in policy he had engineered the year before. The first plum to be plucked from the French orchard was in West Africa. A Quaker merchant from New York named Thomas Cumming suggested to Pitt that there were easy pickings to be had in Senegal and the Gambia, where the French guarded colossal wealth – in slaves, gold dust, ivory, silver and gum arabic – with minuscule military forces. The opportunistic Cumming offered to put his local expertise at the service of the British in return for a trade monopoly in Senegal. Pitt accepted and sent a nugatory force – two ships of the line and some 200 marines – to West Africa. The French commandant at Fort Louis on the Senegal river had evidently grown used to a sinecure, for when this tiny force appeared outside his walls he promptly surrendered. The resident traders swore allegiance to their new British masters and Cumming got his heart's desire. When his ships duly returned to England laden with the promised spoils, Pitt woke up to the scale of what could be achieved on the African coast. He was particularly impressed by the 400 tons of gum Cumming brought back. Gum arabic, the sap of the acacia tree, was crucial in silk manufacture but hitherto British textile makers had had to buy it from the Dutch at premium rates. Equally impressive was the haul of slaves bound for the West Indies: the sugar planters there had been complaining for years about the shortage of slave labour. Euphoric at this African serendipity, Pitt sent out two more expeditions. One seized the French post of Fort St Michael on the island of Goree, and the other took over the slave-trading factory on the River Gambia.

Maybe it was the association of ideas between West African slavery and the sugar plantations, but Pitt's next idea was to knock out French power in the West Indies as he had expunged it in West Africa. Once again the proximate 'push' for the exploit was a profit-hungry entrepreneur. William Beckford, MP, an absentee landlord of Jamaica and a crony of Pitt's, wrote to his friend to point out the vulnerable position of the French on the island of Martinique: it was entirely dependent on French control of the sea lanes, could not support itself and its slaves without food convoys from France, but at the same time contained a body of slaves and stores of wealth worth more than £4 million (at least £200 million in today's money). Arguing that Pitt would have a walkover victory every bit as easy as that in Senegal, Beckford concluded his exhortation with the words: 'For God's sake, attempt it without delay.' Yet Pitt was very aware that all analogies between West Africa and the West Indies were facile. The former could be acquired by opportunism, but the latter would need a formidable effort. His position was complicated by the need to further his true objectives – the expulsion of France from the Americas – while conciliating both Newcastle, who fretted about the costs of global warfare, and George II, who insisted on making Europe the primary theatre. To keep them happy Pitt had already given hostages to fortune by promising that the attacks on Goree and Senegal would be the only significant new overseas venture in late 1758.

Yet a host of other considerations tugged Pitt towards a campaign in the West Indies. At the most basic level, he was under pressure from a powerful coalition of economic and financial interests to take decisive action in the West Indies where competition with France for slaves, sugar and furs was intense. The 'golden age' for French sugar began at the end of the seventeenth century when French planters switched their endeavours to sugar cane and began to undersell the British West Indies in much the same way as the British had undersold the original sugar planters of Brazil. Slavery was another bone of contention. French competition in the 1750s had thrown the slave trade into crisis; until Pitt's expeditions against West Africa, British planters in the Indies had experienced severe labour short-ages, mainly occasioned by the odious fact that the life expectancy of black slaves in the plantations was no more than seven years. The French, by contrast, had made the West Indies a prime target for economic warfare. Not only did they subsidise their own slave trade but since the early 1700s they had controlled the beaver catch of the Hudson Bay, making them serious rivals in the hat trade. The French also had the edge in world fishery markets. The Treaty of Utrecht gave them the northern shores of Newfoundland as a base for curing and drying cod, while the British, confined to the more humid southern side, could not match the quality of cured cod and therefore suffered by comparison in the global fish trade.

Privateering and smuggling were also big issues in the West Indies. The principal reason that the French sugar islands showed more profit than the British ones was because of contraband between the French islands and British North America. The highly valued rum of Rhode Island was made from French molasses brought in clandestinely; in a word, the American colonists could smuggle in molasses more cheaply from the French West Indies than they could buy it from British sources on the open market. So, in addition to a cheaper labour supply and greater areas of fertile soil, the French had a ready market for their product in British North America, and this was vital to the economic life of the islands, since the French bought food and lumber with the contraband revenue. Molasses from the French West Indies was banned in France to protect native manufacturers of brandy, so without the North American market the island French would have been hard pressed, and could certainly not have basked in the reputation of being the richest and most prosperous colonies of any empire in the world. Faced with this situation, the British West Indies would have gone under but for the monopoly they enjoyed in Britain itself and the great expansion of the home market. But here was one of those 'contradictions' that would manifest itself immediately after the Seven Years War in the struggle between home country and North American colonists. In flat contradiction of mercantilism, the economic interests of Britain and her North American colonies were divergent. From the colonists' point of view, the French supremacy in the islands was desirable. From the metropolitan point of view it was vital that the British colonies in the West Indies survived, since Jamaica alone bought more British manufactures than Virginia and Maryland combined.

Quite apart from the direct economic interests at stake in the islands, Pitt had to weigh two other, even more important, factors. First was the general military, naval and strategic implication of the West Indies, for his new bearing in foreign policy meant moving away from simple commerce protection and the destruction and harrying of enemy commerce towards an outright war of conquest. The general strategic position held by the British in the West Indies was unpromising, for the imperatives of geography favoured the French. At the beginning of the Seven Years War four nations shared the Caribbean islands. Spain possessed Trinidad, Puerto Rico, Cuba, the Bahamas and the eastern half of Hispaniola which they named Santo Domingo (the modern Dominican Republic). The Dutch Republic had Curaçao and shared the Virgin Islands with the British, who additionally had Jamaica, Barbados, St Kitts, Nevis, Antigua and Montserrat. France occupied the western half of Hispaniola (modern Haiti) and most of the other islands as far south as Grenada, including their cynosures of Martinique and Guadeloupe. There were in addition a number of officially neutral islands – St Lucia, St Vincent and Dominica (not to be confused with the Dominican Republic) – which were in fact dominated by the French on Martinique.

The British islands were awkwardly distributed, with Jamaica far to the leeward of the rest and Barbados, the most windward island, with no harbour fit for a naval station. Since 1745 the Royal Navy had maintained two stations, one at Jamaica, the other in the Leeward Islands. The French, on the other hand, had their two bases in much more favourable strategic niches: one on the north coast of Santo Domingo dominating the windward passage into the Caribbean, and the other in Martinique. This strategic superiority was reinforced by trade routes. British merchant navy vessels, making for two widely separated landfalls, parted company before entering the Caribbean and were particularly vulnerable as they sailed into the waters to the windward of Barbados and Antigua respectively. French privateers preyed mercilessly on English shipping on both outward and homeward journeys and on vessels plying between the entrepots with a particular fondness for the Antigua passage. Martinique and Guadeloupe were notorious nests of privateers, the indented coastlines making them perfect for predatory raids. British small cruisers were not strong enough to attack these corsairs inland, as their headquarters were too far up the tropical 'fjords' for warships to reach them. The French meanwhile were relatively secure, since their islands all lay to the windward of the British base in each area. The Royal Navy's task was particularly onerous since it additionally had to protect trade between the British West Indies and North America. Naval commanders tried to use the convoy system to counter-attack the French threat, and employed a threefold seaborne strategy. Ships of the line watched the French bases at Santo Domingo and Martinique; the biggest warships patrolled the waters to the windward of Barbados and Antigua; and small cruisers and frigates concentrated on surveillance of the privateer nests, with particular emphasis on the Leeward Islands.

But over and above all these complex day-to-day dispositions, Pitt had to fit the West Indies into a mosaic of global strategy and geopolitics. In one sense the West Indies was a locus for convergent economic interests from outside, since the lumber trade of North America and the slave trade of West Africa both had their focus here. Overwhelmingly, fear was the spur for, although the British seemed on paper to be winning the struggle for the Orient – the British East India Company had factories from St Helena to Borneo – they were uneasy about increasing French encroachments and their burgeoning volume of trade. Fear sometimes became paranoia, with the British imagining that the French were trying to 'encircle' their North American colonies and the French apprehensive that the British would cut Canada off from the Louisiana territory and then conquer both separately. Each area of the world had its 'boosters', but Pitt considered the West Indies a more important theatre than India. The Royal Navy's commitment was significant: in India the British deployed four ships of the line and three cruisers, but in the West Indies the respective figures were twelve and twenty. Both the objective interests and the sheer volume of trade in the Caribbean were so much greater than on the subcontinent. It was not surprising, then, that when Pitt felt strong enough for warfare on a truly global scale, he opened the second front in the West Indies, not in India.

Pitt had yet another motive for his proposed West Indian campaign. Eighteenth-century warfare was not *guerre à outrance*, nor would anyone have dreamed of modern war-fighting objectives like 'unconditional surrender'. Newcastle constantly warned his colleague of the ruinous expense of his projects and advised that the time would come when the financiers of the City of London would no longer lend the government money. When that day arrived, the resulting crisis of credit would force any conceivable government to sue for peace terms. Pitt agreed that the enormous cost of the war alone meant that it would have to end at the earliest plausible moment, and his definition of a good peace was one where the French were driven from North America altogether and British supremacy in the Mediterranean maintained. So, although in 1759 Pitt aimed at a genuine war of conquest in the West Indies, which marked a new departure in the Caribbean, it was not intended as a war of permanent conquest, as the campaign in Canada was. At the peace table Pitt needed Martinique as a powerful bargaining counter, which he could exchange for Minorca. The obvious question then arises: if Minorca was so important, why did Pitt not send an expedition there instead? Here we see clearly the quality of his strategic thinking. In the first place, Minorca was a tougher nut to crack than Martinique and, in the second, he saw an ingenious way to kill two birds with one stone: to take out France's equivalent of Jamaica and to achieve a conquest which the French would be glad to have back by giving up Minorca. Martinique, after all, was an island that exported 20,000 tons of sugar a year. And France would be desperate to get it back in order to reinforce the tenuous links between the St Lawrence and New Orleans, always assuming that Canada, or New France, was still in existence as a French territory.

Painstakingly Pitt explained his thinking to his inner Cabinet. Newcastle reiterated his opposition to widening the war on the periphery when the military situation in Europe was so parlous and British credit stretched almost to snapping point. It was bad enough that Britain was fighting both on the continent *and* in North America, but now Pitt was proposing warfare in the West Indies as well. Where would it all end? If Pitt was really serious about Martinique, economies would have to be made in other theatres and the obvious candidate for cutback was the series of 'descents' on the French coast, intended to take the pressure off Frederick of Prussia. But Pitt insisted that these attacks would have to go on, to cover the Martinique expedition; otherwise the French could mobilise resources to strike back in the West Indies.

Anson took Newcastle's side and weighed in with the argument that the Martinique project was dangerously quixotic: too many ships would be absent in the West Indies if the French suddenly decided to launch an invasion of Britain. But Anson was never prepared to push really hard against Pitt once the Prime Minister had made up his mind, so the main opposition in September 1758 continued to come from Newcastle. Things reached the point where Pitt angrily threatened to recall all British troops from the continent if he could not have his way over Martinique. He was surely bluffing, for he could scarcely have made an enemy of George II *and* Newcastle at the same time. As a sop to Newcastle, he promised that, aside from the expedition to West Africa which had already been despatched, after Martinique there would be no more global adventures. Grudgingly Newcastle acquiesced, encouraged by the change of mind at the Admiralty. By early October Anson was telling Newcastle's confidant Lord Hardwicke that he foresaw few barriers to a successful outcome in the West Indies. Anson thought the amphibious operation ingenious, and commented that the entire venture was singularly well thought through: there was a good beach for landing marines and failsafe plans were in place in case they had to retreat. Yet whatever opposition there was at the highest level, there was little in Parliament. In November the House of Commons approved a war budget of £13 million for 1759 – the largest wartime appropriation ever granted. Horace Walpole remarked, half-admiringly, half-aciduously: 'You would as soon hear NO from an old maid as from the House of Commons.'

Pitt's great West Indian expedition finally cleared from Portsmouth on 12 November 1758: 9,000 men and a handful of women sailed to Barbados in seventy-three ships commanded by General Peregrine Thomas Hopson, a favourite of George II, who liked the fact that the commander was an old man. With a quasi-senile prejudice against young men, George II deliberately chose this method of putting Pitt in his place for, as the gossip-monger Horace Walpole, homosexual son of Sir Robert, put it, the choice of the elderly and reluctant Hopson was 'not consonant to Mr Pitt's practice, who, considering that our ancient officers had grown old on a very small portion of experience, which by no means compensated for the decay of fire and vigour, chose to trust his plans to the alertness and hopes of younger men'. Pitt had to be content to see his choice as commander, John

Barrington, occupying the second-in-command slot. It was difficult to find adequate officers for the lesser commands, as those who had purchased their commissions or obtained them through influence used their prerogatives to avoid service in dangerous, disease-ridden theatres like the West Indies. On the other hand, the high casualty rates in the Caribbean, especially from disease, meant that a career officer could take a calculated risk: entering as a Captain at the beginning of the year, he could be Colonel by the end of it.

Coffee-house opinion was divided on the wisdom of this venture, especially as it was widely known that half of the war budget was to be borrowed and that half the tax revenues would go in servicing the debt. Walpole, though, with his characteristic pessimism, vastly overrated the odds against success. 'Martinico is the general notion; a place the strongest in the world with a garrison of ten thousand men. Others now talk of Guadeloupe, almost as strong and of much less consequence. Of both, everybody that knows, despairs.' The truth was that the French had grown careless and the number of defenders was far, far less than Walpole's hyperbolic estimate. Guadeloupe, in particular, was almost absurdly ill guarded, to the point where a modern historian has commented that this island in 1759 was 'one of the few examples in history of a time when the best apple hung lowest on the bough'. Maybe the French had grown over-confident because of the sheer success of their privateering operations; of the 113 enemy ships seized by their corsairs in the West Indies in 1758, eighty-one were prizes taken either to Martinique or Guadeloupe.

The expedition made its way slowly across the Atlantic. The track of the fleet was south-west from Plymouth to latitude 13° north, then due west to Barbados, running before the trade winds. The ships were out of sight of land from the middle of November until they anchored in Carlisle Bay, near Bridgetown, Barbados on 3 January 1759. There were sixty-four transports, eight ships of the line, a frigate, four bomb-ketches and a hospital ship. The idea was that the four regiments and their naval back-up would sail first to Barbados, where Commodore John Moore would take over the naval forces. The combined forces would next attack and take Martinique, which would then be garrisoned. But plans began to go awry almost immediately. The fleet suffered badly on the way over, not so much from storms but from disease: scurvy, dysentery, smallpox and 'shipfever'. And because the fleet had to wait to allow stragglers to catch up – including the all-important hospital ship – it was impossible to take the French by surprise, even if they had not already been aware of what was about to descend on them. In fact Cardinal de Bernis, then acting as French Foreign Minister, knew the fleet's destination before it had even left Portsmouth, and immediately informed the Marquise de Pompadour (whose creature he was). Captain Gardiner, who left the classic account of the 1759 expedition to the West Indies, produced this purple passage to describe landfall: 'As the ships approached, the island rose gradually out of the sea with a delightful verdure, presenting a most inviting prospect of the country all around, which looked like a garden; the plantations were amazingly beautiful, interspersed at little distances from each other, and adorned with fruits of various colours.'

Moore assumed command of the naval squadron, and he and Hopson decreed ten days' rest, revictualling and rewatering, giving the stragglers time to arrive. But by the time the united battalions left the Barbados rendezvous on 13 January, tropical disease had cut a swathe through the armada and the attack force had already been reduced by one-third to little more than 5,000 effectives. Yellow fever, smallpox and scurvy were the principal scourges. 'Yellow jack' was *the* most dreaded disease in the Caribbean. Borne by the *Aedes* mosquito, yellow fever had as its most common symptoms headache and agonising pain followed by the vomiting of large amounts of blood, made greasy and black by the action of the gastric juices. About half the fever's victims vomited themselves to death within a few days; those who survived had immunity for life. Yellow fever had already made its presence felt among British invaders of the Caribbean, most notably during Admiral Vernon's siege of Cartagena in 1741, when two-thirds of the British force besieging the town died of it. Smallpox, a bacteriological rather than insect-borne disease, also caused havoc. Symptoms were high temperatures, followed three days later by purulent blisters; the patient then either died or recovered, bearing disfiguring scars for the rest of his life. Scurvy was the usual effect of the notorious vitamin C deficiency in the diet of the Royal Navy before the late eighteenth century.

While profoundly worried by the growing sickness roster and especially the yellow-fever cases, the British commander pressed on. The attack on Martinique began on 13 January, but it soon transpired that the British had seriously underestimated the problems of a successful assault. The island was fringed with dangerous, rocky and rugged shores, where 300-foot cliffs often beetled almost perpendicularly from the sea. In the interior mountains reaching almost 5,000 feet in altitude, their lower slopes and foothills covered in thick, mosquito-infested rain forest, posed another formidable obstacle. On the western coast, where the British tried to land, there were thorn and cactus forests, alternating with mangrove swamps and salt grass. Moore decided to make his first assault on Fort Royale on the west of the island rather than on St Pierre farther up the coast. To take Fort Royale, an invader first had to silence the battery at Negro Point, and here the redcoated marines acquitted themselves well, even though they were taken aback by the defenders' novel method of irregular warfare. The French and their mulatto soldiers hid in trees, bushes and cane plantations, often behind entrenchments not visible to the British, from which they directed heavy fire on an enemy that could not see them. When they retreated, and a party of British skirmishers advanced to 'mop up' in the bush, the defenders would then open a withering fire from the next of a series of defensive positions, compelling the skirmishers to retreat. Even Highlanders found the terrain – woods, mountains, ravines, sugar-cane plantations – difficult and particularly the steep approach to the mountain passes 'interrupted by broken rocks and furrowed by a variety of gullies, which were extremely difficult to pass, and which rendered it very hazardous to make any attempt to force it'. These conditions badly affected morale. A British deserter later told a court martial that the reason he and his comrades quit was because they 'saw no enemy to fight with, and yet bullets were flying about them from every leaf and bough they came near; that the country was afull of ambuscades and that, if they proceeded further, they must all be cut to pieces'.

Nevertheless, on 16 January, after a naval bombardment, the British swarmed ashore, took the fort, spiked the guns and destroyed all gunpowder. They then abandoned the fort and proceeded to land unopposed on the beach at Cas Navires. Pleased with results so far, Moore then changed his mind and decided to land a permanent garrison at Negro Point. On 17 January the French counterattacked. The garrison at Negro Point came under heavy fire, when British troops fanned out from the fort into the nearby woods, hoping to clear a distinctive track towards Fort Royale, French snipers and skirmishers started to take a heavy toll on them. In a foretaste of the conditions redcoats would face less than twenty years later in the American War of Independence, the British soon found themselves in a parlous state, unable to come to grips with an elusive enemy, dropping in their tracks from heat, fatigue and shortage of water.

Hopson began to surmise that Fort Royale might conceivably hold out for ten days or more, during which time his own troops well might melt away, even if they did manage to build a road to the French citadel. Only five miles separated the British beachhead from the fort, but the intervening country was a morass of woods, canes and ravines. The last straw was when Hopson's engineers reported that, to bring the citadel within cannon range, they would have to cross a ravine. But how was that possible, Hopson asked. Only by making a further five-mile diversion, the engineers replied. Hopson's calculations quickly showed him that the manpower needed to portage thirty cannon, plus cannon balls, mortar and stores, far exceeded his own labour force. The clincher was that there was no water on the route either. This meant that to build a credible road to the fort so that his heavy artillery could be deployed, Hopson would need 1,000 pioneers for road building and another 1,000 as water carriers. He was in a position remarkably similar to the one General John Burgoyne would confront at Saratoga in 1777: short of water while being unable to deploy his big guns. Not surprisingly, Hopson concluded that this was mission impossible. He ordered an evacuation, having taken losses of twenty-two dead and forty-eight wounded.

But Hopson was still unwilling to admit overall defeat on Martinique, so he decided to probe at St Pierre instead, even though this lacked the strategic significance of Fort Royale. On 19 January the British fleet appeared off the commercial capital, which was built in a crescent along the bay with the volcanic Mount Pelée (which would erupt so devastatingly on 8 May 1902) as the dramatic backdrop. HMS *Rippon* began shelling the town but St Pierre's batteries made a vigorous riposte. After exchanging fire for four and a half hours, the *Rippon* was the worse for wear and in imminent danger of being sunk. Moore withdrew her to safety and hastily conferred with Hopson. Both men were by now pessimistic about the military possibilities on Martinique. Moore repeated his earlier opinion that there was no strategic advantage in taking the town, while Hopson concluded that he could not maintain a garrison there, as it would have to be continually supplied by sea. They were not to know that French morale was low and their resolve signally lacking; and, in general, the British commanders overrated the problems of Martinique, which was captured easily three years later by a British combined operation. What they should have done was what was done in 1762: make a number of feints on the island before delivering the main attack, thus sapping the defenders' fighting spirit still further; the militia's initial enthusiasm would soon drain away and, even if he spotted the feint, the French commander would have to disperse his forces against his better judgement to still the laments and clamours of the planters.

Official opinion privately (there was no public censure) blamed Hopson for the debacle at Martinique and absolved Moore, though the Admiralty was simply rewarding him for his fawning attitude over the Byng affair two years earlier, when Admiral John Byng had been shot for neglect of duty after failing ignominiously to relieve Minorca. Perceptive critics outside the establishment saw that Moore was as much to blame as Hopson. Neither man acquitted himself well, but the bizarre events of the early years of the Seven Years War in a sense contrived to let them off the hook. Not to press an attack with full vigour was inevitably to invite comparison with Admiral Byng at Minorca, who had been shot, as Voltaire said, 'to encourage the others'. But, on the other hand, both Moore and Hopson alleged that to tangle with the guerrillas, snipers and sharpshooters in the ravines outside Fort Royale was to invite Braddock's fate at Monongahela. Fortunately for them, it was this version of events that was endorsed by the power elite in London.

Hopson and Moore also escaped censure by pressing on to Pitt's secondary target of Guadeloupe, separated from Martinique by the officially neutral (but really pro-French) island of Dominica. Guadeloupe had many advantages for the British marauders. It was the chief producer of sugar and molasses; it produced more cotton and coffee than any other island in the West Indies except Jamaica; its trade was more valuable than Canada's; it was a nest of privateers who preyed on British shipping; once taken it would be an invaluable base, enabling the Royal Navy to guard shipping and dominate the Leeward Islands; it was scantily defended, with a population of just 2,000 Europeans and 30,000 blacks; and in short its loss would be an utter disaster for France. But Guadeloupe also had many disadvantages. The heat and humidity were terrific, with temperatures never below 70°F and more usually above 90°; malaria and dysentery were frequent in the low-lying areas (below 1,500 feet in altitude); and it would have to be conquered before the hurricane season in July–October. Additionally, Guadeloupe was really two islands in one. There was the volcanic, so-called Basse Terre and, separated from it by a sea arm, the limestone Grande Terre, with an indented coastline full of small inlets and river mouths, the haunts of privateers. The British campaign was therefore planned as a threefold operation: first, destroying resistance on the leeward side of Basse Terre; secondly, crushing the enemy on Grande Terre; and finally the conquest of the windward side of Basse Terre.

The bombardment of the town and citadel of Basse Terre began on 22 January. The Royal Navy had perfected bomb-ketches – sturdy fore-and-aft vessels built with heavier frames and beams – for use against shore installations. Each one contained at least one mortar, which could throw a bomb on a high parabolic trajectory for a distance of two to three miles. Normal bombs were like shells, spherical in shape and packed with powder, with the wall of the shell given an extra thickness so that the bomb would not fall to earth with the fuse on the downward side. British gunners were supposed to cut the wax and gunpowder fuses in such a way that the bomb exploded on contact with the ground or some other object, but eighteenth-century bomb-making was an inexact science and many bombs exploded in the air. A refinement of the ordinary bomb was the carcass, like a shell but incendiary rather than explosive. Used both to gut buildings and as a flare to guide night artillery fire, it was often packed with charged pistol barrels of various lengths, which fired intermittently and irregularly, so that even experienced members of bomb squads approached them with caution. The best ordnance evidence from 1759 suggests that the carcasses in use during the West Indies campaign were loaded with a mixture of wax, sulphur, nitre and gunpowder, making them inextinguishable by water.

Even with the help of these formidable weapons, the British at first experienced tough going. The numbers of shore batteries initially made the spirits of the attackers quail, and the British chief of engineers gloomily declared the place impregnable. Moore persisted and ordered a day-long fusillade from his warships. Finally the French batteries were silenced but by this time darkness was falling and Moore postponed the amphibious landing to the next day. At 10 p.m. that night, the British bomb vessels began lobbing carcasses into the town – whether through simple boredom or to keep the enemy guessing appears uncertain. At any rate the wooden houses and laden warehouses were soon ablaze and both citadel and town gutted. Vast amounts of sugar, rum, tar and other produce were needlessly destroyed in a peculiarly mindless act of vandalism. Although Moore later assured Pitt that the inferno was an accident, the fact is that the bombing continued all night. The terrified enemy fled to the hills from the scenes of a Hieronymus Bosch horror, even abadoning the wounded in their panic, and a good general would have capitalised on their confusion and demoralisation. But Hopson had his men stood to all night, fearing a French counterattack or some underhand ruse. In the morning he counted the cost. He had lost seventeen killed and thirty wounded; the Royal Navy ships had been badly damaged in their rigging and because of the fire no loot or significant prizes had been taken. Worst of all, Hopson now decided to dig in and retrench, condemning his men to idleness, inactivity or deadening boredom while labouring on the citadel's fortifications.

The result was what all old West India hands would have expected. Disease cut a swathe through the army and by 30 January 1,500 men were on sick parade. Mosquitoes, untreated sewage, contaminated water, back-breaking toil in the heat, incompetent surgeons and poor diet all played their part. By early February Hopson was down to just 2,796 men fit for duty. By mid-February eight transports cleared for Antigua bearing 600 of the most seriously ill, the majority of whom died during the passage or soon after arrival. Hopson sent out companies of redcoats to scour the countryside, but the French, adopting guerrilla warfare, easily evaded them and began to harry them with hit-and-run attacks. Every day snipers and sharpshooters became more of a menace and on 30 January a French guerrilla group, hidden in lofty sugar cane, showed its mettle by ambushing and killing four sailors.

Emboldened by this success, the French became over-confident and sustained a bad check on 1 February, when thirty prisoners fell into British hands. Skirmish and counter-skirmish continued but there was no decisive breakthrough. Secretly champing at the bit over Hopson's incompetence, Moore tried to fight his own war by sending his cruisers out to blockade the entire island and prevent food reaching the guerrillas. His mood grew blacker by the day as the army continued to be decimated by disease.

During this period of 'phoney war' there was one notable success. To sever all communications between Basse Terre and Grande Terre and so prevent any aid from reaching the guerrillas, the English had to capture Fort Louis. By begging a few companies of Highlanders from Hopson to add to his own marines, Moore thought he had the strength to do it. On 6 February the commandos set sail and on the 13th the military action began. For six hours Moore's task force bombarded Fort Louis and took out both the shore batteries and the four-gun redoubts on each of the nearby hills. Initially all went to plan, and the Highlanders and the marines of the landing party were happy to watch while the two ships of the line blew the fort apart. But once the assault party clambered into the flat-bottomed landing craft – each carrying sixty-three men, rowed with twelve oars and drawing no more than two feet of water – the barrage was lifted for fear of hitting the invaders with 'friendly fire'. Whereupon hundreds of French troops reoccupied the battered positions and opened such a heavy fire that the Colonel of marines ordered the boats to retreat.

This led to one of those bad-tempered scenes that should act as a cautionary tale for triumphalist theorists of combined operations. As the flat-bottoms returned alongside HMS *Berwick*, the irascible commodore Captain William Harman shouted: 'Don't give the damned cowardly felloes a rope.'

Enraged, Captain William Murray of the Highlanders stood up and yelled back: 'Captain Harman, we are under command and were forced to obey, but rest assured that you shall answer to me for the expression you have used.' Not fancying a duel with a claymore-wielding Highlander, Harman blustered that he was not referring to the Highlanders but to the marines. Yet Murray was so indignant that he ordered his boats to put about for the shore; the marines were then shamed into following him. As Fort Louis suddenly seemed to burst into spontaneous combustion – actually the pent-up impact of yet more deadly carcasses – the Highlanders and the English marines waded ashore under cover of the thick pall of smoke. They too had been pent up – cramped in readiness for five hours in the longboats – but now they surged through the foam with gusto, making for the sandy strand.

There were some nasty moments when they hit the booby-trapped shoreline – for the French had driven pilings into the seabed and interlaced them with mangroves, which acted as a home for the dreaded *Anopheles* mosquito; there was therefore a chance of malaria at the very moment of securing a beachhead. But finally the beachhead was secured and the marines and the Highlanders, who could have been deadly enemies just thirteen years earlier in the last Jacobite rising, came boiling out of the foam like sea monsters. To their consternation, French veterans and black irregulars heard the dreaded cry 'Claymore', as the Highlanders were on them in a trice with broadsword and bayonet. Lieutenant Grant of the Black Watch, who ached to be a hero, came a spectacular cropper. 'Getting out of the boat, I stumbled over a stone and fell forward into the water. My servant, thinking me mortally wounded, seized me and was dragging me on shore, in doing so he scraped my shins against the grapwall. We all rushed on pell-mell, and the French ran like hares up the hill at the back of the battery.' Not without some deaths among the landing party by dusk the deed was done and Basse Terre could no longer be reinforced from the other side of the island. But it had been a grim affair, with terrible wounds inflicted. The British did not open fire with their muskets until the French were ten yards away, at which range the volley was devastating and murderous. All in all, it had been a close-run thing. As Grant rightly remarked of amphibious operations: 'Of all species of warfare that of landing is the most unpleasant [as] you present a mark for your enemy and you are not in your element.'

Yet as long as the ailing Hopson lived, and more and more men went down to tropical disease, stalemate was still the most likely long-term result. Again Moore chafed and fretted at the lack of action. But at last, on 27 February, his prayers were answered when the despised Hopson succumbed to fever. His replacement, General Barrington, whom Pitt had originally wanted to command the expedition, proved as energetic as Hopson had been listless, although from the first day of his command he had a mountain to climb. Moore and Barrington, who enjoyed an amazing unanimity on the way forward, agreed that the next step was to transfer the bulk of the force to Fort Louis, leaving just a garrison of 500 to oversee Basse Terre. Leaving behind one battalion and transferring the worst of the sick cases to Antigua, the commanders effected the move on 11 March, after having been at sea for a full four days, beating up against the trade winds. To mask their departure from Basse Terre they used a ruse worthy of Greek mythology, for Barrington ordered tents struck and huts built as though they were settling in for a long stay. They were now in a race against time in a double sense: they had to complete the conquest of Guadeloupe before the hurricane season and while they still had a credible army. Tropical disease seemed to become more virulent every day, so that by the time they landed at Fort Louis, their effectives numbered no more than 1,500.

Scarcely had the British landed at Fort Louis than they received a piece of dramatically bad news. Despite the urgings of many of the ministers on Louis XV's Council, who despaired of ever making inroads against British seapower and wanted to concentrate on the war in Europe, the King had sent Admiral Maximin de Bompart to the Leeward Islands with a powerful counterattacking task force, comprising eight ships of the line, three frigates and a battalion of Swiss and other troops. Even though the British enjoyed the incontestable advantages of naval dockyards in the West Indies and being provisioned from North America, Versailles was determined that Martinique would not be abandoned without a fight – the ministers were of course unaware that the British had now switched operations to Guadeloupe. Moore and Barrington were placed in a peculiarly difficult position by this new development. With the hurricane season approaching, Moore would soon have to detach some of his warships for convoy duties and the protection of the homeward merchant fleet. Even worse, when Barrington opened Pitt's sealed instructions to Hopson, he read that Pitt ordered the Highlanders to be sent to North America once the Martinique operation was complete. If he stuck to the letter of the orders, Barrington would leave himself far too weak to maintain himself against Bompart's incursions.

Yet another of the numerous councils of war that beset this West Indies expedition was convened. The idea of taking the offensive and blockading Bompart in Martinique was ruled out, on the grounds of supply and communication lines; for a start, there could be no search-and-destroy mission against the French armada without an adequate water supply, which not even the troops at Fort Louis had. Instead the commanders hit on the idea of concentrating the British fleet at Prince Rupert's Bay in the north of the neutral island of Dominica so that it could intercept any French move against Fort Louis. Meanwhile Barrington, aware that he was vulnerable at Fort Louis to possible French attacks from a number of directions, opted for the strategy of offence as the best means of defence. He reasoned that the enemy could never unite for a push against Fort Louis if he kept them disunited by striking at several points at the same time; accordingly in the third week of March he sent 600 men to attack the towns of Le Gosier, Ste Anne and St François simultaneously. The strategy was a brilliant success and the thrust against Le Gosier even produced an unexpected bonus when the jubilant attackers pressed on and took in the rear a French force moving against Fort Louis. Barrington followed this up with a brilliantly executed war of movement, continually harrying the French, forever appearing in their rear when they were expected in the van, continually switching the angle of attack and the military objective. The French became more and more demoralised, and desertions from the militia reached record levels.

By the beginning of April Barrington was satisfied that he had completed the first two phases of his campaign. He had wiped out resistance on the leeward side of Basse Terre and had crushed the defenders on Grande Terre even more effectively. There remained the windward side of Basse Terre, the most populous area and the region where all the richest plantations were located. Barrington had done the difficult parts first, for this final phase favoured conventional forces more than the other two phases. A gently rising coastal plain extended from one to three miles to the foothills of the mountains, and on this fertile paradise between the sea and the peaks lay a series of wealthy sugar plantations that probably generated more wealth per acre than any other terrain in the world in 1759. On 12 April the British disembarked some 1,450 men at Arnouville. A hard-fought action followed, with British artillerymen and the Highlanders particularly distinguishing themselves. They won the day but left fourteen of their men dead on the field and carried off fifty-four wounded. The French retreated only slightly before digging in again. They proved doughty defenders, pegging the British back to an advance of just two miles a day. Yet in the end the combat between regulars and militiamen in open terrain could have only one ending. On 21 April the brave but demoralised defenders finally surrendered. The formal capitulation was signed on 1 May, allowing for an immediate exchange of prisoners.

Incredibly, the very next day (within hours of the capitulation according to some melodramatic reports) Bompart suddenly landed at Ste Anne, now no more than a burnt-out shell after its recent destruction. He arrived from Martinique with his fleet, 600 Swiss regulars, spare arms and ammunition for another 2,000 fighters and a large force of irregulars, described in some reports as '2,000 buccaneers'. Whether these militiamen and volunteers quite numbered 2,000 or in any way merited the bloodthirsty (and at this date somewhat anachronistic) description of buccaneers is doubtful, but the fact remains that they made up a formidable fighting force. Learning of the capitulation and the prisoner cartel, Bompart apparently tried to persuade the French Governor of Guadeloupe, Nadau du Treil, to find some technicality for reneging on the deal, but du Treil refused. Bompart accepted the inevitable and sailed back to Martinique. Learning of his arrival to the east, Moore tried to get his ships under way to bring Bompart to a decisive action, but the winds were against him and he spent five frustrating days trying to reach the island of Marie Galante. But not even a Nelson could make easting against the trade winds, and in fifty-seven hours Moore's ships managed to beat eastward just six miles. What had happened? How was Bompart able to sail from Martinique to Guadeloupe and back again without being intercepted? Moore's main mistake was to base himself at Rupert's Bay in Dominica. His critics said he should have sailed for Martinique and attacked Bompart at Fort Royale, but Moore knew the strength of the defences there and did not want to tangle with an enemy fleet and shore batteries. That decision was sound enough, but basing himself at Rupert's Bay meant that Moore lost contact with the French. The usual view is that he should have positioned himself to windward of the enemy and within sight, ready to pursue wherever Bompart went. But Moore thought he had all the options covered. He expected Bompart either to attack Basse Terre and Fort Louis or to proceed to Jamaica. Nobody on the British side had considered the possibility that the French might land on the windward side of Grande Terre. So it was that Moore failed to intercept Bompart both on the outward and return journey between Martinique and Guadeloupe. Moore had got to the windward of the enemy's putative objective but not of the enemy himself. His later protestations were of the same kind as those of the punter who complains that the favourite in a horse race did not win: reason, logic and the form book did not prevail. Bompart defied all normal expectations by passing round the southern end of Martinique instead of coming inside the islands.

The British had won the battle for Guadeloupe, but it had been touch and go. If the French commanders had cooperated better and shown more energy, the British would have been defeated. If Bompart had arrived just a day earlier, the balance of forces would have shifted irremediably in the French favour. Barrington admitted that he was at the limit of his resources and could not have fought much longer. He told Pitt that disease was making such inroads on the expeditionary force that he would soon not have a credible fighting body and he therefore dreaded the consequences. Aware that he could be criticised for having agreed to very lenient terms of capitulation, he wrote to the Prime Minister on 9 May: 'I hope you will approve of the arrangements for I can assure you that by force alone I could not have made myself master of these islands nor even of maintaining a garrison at Fort Louis, which I would have had to blow up after withdrawing the garrison . . . [whatever troops I left behind] would have succumbed as soon as my army departed.' Whatever criticisms can be made of Moore, Barrington emerges with a clean sheet from the Guadeloupe campaign. He has been criticised, anachronistically, for not fighting a war of attrition instead of accepting a negotiated surrender. But it is simply a fact that eighteenth-century armies aimed at victory but not annihilation, and still less at unconditional surrender. Moreover, if Hopson had simply accepted a truce and allowed experienced negotiators time to arrive, Bompart's force would have reinforced the defenders and ultimately defeated him.

Meanwhile new orders arrived from London. Pitt, having learned about the switch from Martinique to Guadeloupe, ordered Barrington to take the island of St Lucia and to that end rescinded his previous orders about sending the Highlanders to Louisbourg. Barrington, though, did not have nearly enough manpower for the conquest of St Lucia. He sent the Highland regiments to Louisbourg, having first conducted a face-saving exercise by conquering the small islands in the Guadeloupe group – Marie Galante, Deseada, The Saints, Petit Terre. On 25 July he sailed for home with three battalions.

Moore moved on to Antigua to protect merchant navy commerce, which had been preyed on incessantly by the privateers once they saw the Royal Navy preoccupied with Bompart. Moore was not able to make any further contact with his French rival, but sailed for home with a huge convoy of 300 merchantmen in September. He took with him a blackened reputation. Not only was he in bad odour for failing to search and destroy Bompart but, as the Barbados authorities complained bitterly to London, he had failed to protect their commerce, as the facts proved: the privateers had taken ninety British ships between January and July. Moore's defence was twofold. Dealing with the privateers was a Herculean labour against the hydra's heads, as the terms negotiated required a simple exchange of prisoners; since the corsairs had to be released as soon as they were caught, they simply went back to their piratical activities. As for his unpopularity in Barbados, this was because Moore had tried to find out who was running the illegal but highly profitable slave trade between Barbados and St Vincent as well as the commerce in foodstuffs to the neutral islands which the French had occupied.

The armed forces of George II had learned a lot from their tropical campaign in the West Indies. Richard Gardiner of the marines testified that the Martinique and Guadeloupe campaigning was particularly arduous. The troops were 'exposed to dangers they had never known, to disorders they had never felt, to a climate more fatal than the enemy, and to a method of fighting they had never seen'. If by the end of the campaign they knew nothing about fighting irregulars in the bush, they also had no answer to the ravages of yellow fever and other diseases. From Barrington's departure after the conquest of Guadeloupe in June to October 1759 eight officers and 577 men had succumbed to disease while performing nothing more strenuous than garrison duty. In such a context admirers of the land-scape were rare, yet George Durant, one of the British officers, contributed to the growing cult of the picturesque, finding the island 'prospects both noble and romantic . . . hills whose tops reached the clouds, covered with stately woods of ten thousand different shades of green'.

Yet in the short term the many critics of Moore took a back seat, while euphoria in London at the conquest of Guadeloupe was given free rein. Newcastle was in full burbling mood, writing to the Admiralty of 'great good news . . . I want something to revive my spirits and this has done it . . . must be great in its consequences . . . hope will refresh our stocks . . . great affair.' Pitt remarked more sparingly: 'Louisbourgh and Guadeloupe are the best plenipos at a Congress.' The news was particularly welcome as Pitt's government had been under great strain through financial crisis. Ministers could not agree which taxes should be earmarked to finance the massive debt voted so facilely by Parliament the previous autumn; and the kingdom was seriously short of specie, since gold and silver coins had been exported in large numbers to maintain the war in Germany and North America. Financial confidence was shaken and government bonds began selling at the steepest discounts since the Glorious Revolution. The conquest of Guadeloupe proved a massive shot in the arm, even though London was at first slow to appreciate the wealth of the sugar islands. The 350 plantation owners of Guadeloupe and Marie Galante began shipping their sugar, coffee, cocoa, cotton and other products to Britain in return for much-needed slaves and manufactured goods. Within a year of the conquest, from 1759 to mid-1760, Guadeloupe sent 10,000 tons of sugar, valued at £425,000, to Britain and imported 5,000 slaves plus wrought iron and other manufactures. Guadeloupe also supplied Massachusetts rum distillers with half the molasses they needed – three times the volume exported from Jamaica.

If Britain achieved the serendipity of riches gained while pursuing what were primarily military ends, France by contrast was sunk in the deepest gloom by the news from the West Indies. Marshal Belle-Isle at the War Office confessed himself devastated by the loss of Guadeloupe. The French took the setback hard and went looking for scapegoats. They fastened on the Governor of Guadeloupe, Nadau du Treil, whom they blamed for signing the articles of capitulation to Barrington. Du Treil received a sentence of life imprisonment. But the real culprit, François, Marquis de Beauharnois, Governor of Martinique, who took three months to decide to help Guadeloupe, even though the island was just a few hours' sail away, escaped serious censure on the grounds that he had repelled an attempted British invasion of his island. The French position in the West Indies was bedevilled by a number of factors, principally the lack of inter-island co-operation and the militia system. Because of the class system on the islands (out of Guadeloupe's population of 50,000 more than 80 per cent were black slaves), most of the Frenchmen were grandees of one sort or another, who would not take orders willingly; it was a classic case of too many chiefs and not enough French West Indians. And the different islands failed to cooperate with each other largely because militiamen and their native levies would not serve 'abroad' – that is, away from their own islands.

Bompart, who eventually returned to France in November and slipped through a British naval blockade to reach Brest, is a good source for the endemic French weaknesses. Two weeks after anchoring in Fort Royale, on 20 March, he wrote to the Navy Minister Berryer as follows: 'I have found everything chaotic and disorganised, the people terrified, order and hierarchy virtually annihilated . . . I have not been consulted or warned about conditions here and the governor lets everything go to pot and does nothing.' Two months later, after the capitulation, Bompart was even more acidulous, wrote despairingly of the loss of French prestige and spoke of the way the neutral islands were going over wholesale to the British side. A letter to Berryer on 22 May contains the following: 'Dominica is now removed from the orbit of His Most Christian Majesty and has signed a pact of neutrality (i.e. friendship) with the British. The French on that island sell our enemies their best produce . . . Guadeloupe's favourable economic position now under the British is making people in Martinique think . . . Grenada now has a glut of sugar and the French West Indies are now in economic crisis, since exports to Canada and Louisbourg have ceased.' Now the only outlet for French sugar and coffee was France itself, with whom the islands had secure communications only in neutral Danish or Dutch shipping. And even the neutral flag did not protect such shipping against British privateers. Needless to say, British tribunals invariably declared such captures lawful prizes.

The letter to Berryer is worth following up, for it expresses the fundamental truth that Guadeloupe did very well out of the four-year British occupation from 1759 to 1763. The planters in the islands of the British West Indies wanted and expected draconian treatment of the conquered Antilles isles and required as an absolute minimum some of the following: expulsions, high taxation, oaths of allegiance, land expropriation, a ban on the production of sugar, cocoa and coffee. Yet almost the reverse happened. In the four years of their occupation, the British developed Pointe-à-Pitre as a major harbour, opened English and North American markets to Guadeloupean sugar and allowed the planters to import cheap American lumber and food. After being boosted by imports, Guadeloupe overtook

Martinique's slave population, and until 1763 half of all French slave carriers had Martinique and Guadeloupe as their destination (the other main ones being Guyana and Grenada). To general stupefaction in the islands, the French planters were not expelled. How was this possible? The main reason was that Moore and Barrington allowed exceptionally generous terms at the surrender, which in turn reflected uncertainty in London as to whether Guadeloupe was to be taken over as a permanent conquest or simply subject to temporary occupation.

In the articles of capitulation, Moore and Barrington allowed the Guadeloupeans to be neutral, to have complete religious freedom and security for both church and lay property, to enjoy their old laws, to pay no more duties than at present and, if Guadeloupe was retained after the peace, to pay no more than 4.5 per cent taxes on exports (the lowest rate in the Leeward Islands) – in effect granting the island most-favoured-nation status; moreover the people would not have to provide barracks for the British army or supply forced labour – all labour would be paid for and blacks employed only with the consent of their masters. This last was a remarkable concession, as it put Guadeloupe planters ahead of any other slave-owners in the West Indies, whether British or French. As an added bonus, it was agreed that anyone free of debt could leave at once for Martinique and/or send their children to be educated in France. The most remarkable concession of all was Article Eleven of the capitulation which promised that, until peace came, no British subject could acquire land in Guadeloupe.

Guadeloupe's position improved almost magically once removed from the domination of Martinique. American merchants supplied all the goods of which the island had hitherto been starved. The only problems remaining for the French planters were how to export coffee to England and how to import wine from France, and they solved these easily by smuggling. Slave merchants did particularly well, and there were 7,500 more black slaves on Guadeloupe in February 1762 than there had been in 1759. In the general atmosphere of bonanza the British authorities had one overriding problem: tightening up the nexus that bound debtors and creditors. Under the lax pre-1759 laws, creditors had rarely been paid, and the British feared that if they advanced credit to the planters and Guadeloupe was returned to France as part of a general peace, they would not get their money back. Indeed, certain shrewd operators in the French mercantile community had worked out that, having escaped their French creditors when the British took over, they might in turn escape their British ones once peace came, and thus complete a double-whammy of debt evasion.

Soon the prosperity and special concessions made to Guadeloupe led to jealousy and bitterness in the other islands of the West Indies, both British and French. Barbados began to complain that market prices had increased because of the huge demand in Guadeloupe, while in London absentee West Indies planters were angry at plummeting prices when Guadeloupe sugar starting flooding the market in 1760. Martinique was deeply resentful of the favourable deal obtained by its fellow countrymen in Guadeloupe, and this may have been a factor in the speedy surrender of Martinique to the British in 1762. Martinique, however, managed to live on the proceeds of privateering in the three years between the first and second British attack, partly because its own corsairs were more successful after 1759 than previously and partly because British privateers, discouraged by a recent decision in the Court of Prize Appeals in England, largely ceased their depredations; moreover, the Royal Navy blockaders spread themselves too thinly among the islands. Besides, Versailles belatedly decided to do something for the Antilles and, as a reward for repelling the British, Martinique was opened to neutral shipping after February 1759; no special trading licence was required and the normal fee of 3,000 livres was waived. For all these reasons Martinique was able, if not quite to hold its own against Guadeloupe, at least to enjoy, paradoxically, greater prosperity after 1759 than before.

The West Indian campaign was an unusual venture in eighteenth-century terms, when amphibious operations were rare. Anachronism is the enemy of history and 1759 can be understood only if we realise how far the mentality of warriors of that time was from the twentieth-century sensibility, inured to combined land and sea assaults like those in Operation TORCH in North Africa in 1942, the assault on Sicily in 1943, the D-Day landings in Normandy in 1944, to say nothing of an entire chapter of seaborne invasions in the Pacific War (in the Gilberts, Marshalls, New Guinea, the Philippines and Okinawa). Nonetheless, all the elements of modern combined operations were there in primitive form in 1759: naval bombardments, flat-bottomed naval craft, perilous landings in the teeth of underwater obstacles, beachheads secured only at great cost in human life.

Although Pitt's conception of Guadeloupe as a trading counter for Minorca inspired the enterprise, when peace negotiations to end the Seven Years War began in 1762, the British proved remarkably reluctant to give up their acquisitions in the French West Indies. There was a powerful lobby that wanted to hang on to Guadeloupe and was even prepared to return Canada to France if that could be accomplished. The Canada-versus-Guadeloupe debate became one of history's most famous controversies. There are even those who argue that if Britain had retained Guadeloupe and returned Canada to France, the impossibility of an independent United

States would have been doubly determined, both by the French presence in North America and by the absence of the French seapower in the Caribbean that ultimately made Yorktown in 1781 possible. 1759 changed world history in more ways than one.

FOUR

CANADA

Although Jacobitism as a doctrine was in full retreat by 1759, the diaspora of those who had fought and suffered for the House of Stuart had by then reached the point where the Jacobites had a finger in virtually every pie. It may seem a far cry from the Scottish philosopher David Hume to Bonnie Prince Charlie, but Hume was in fact intensely interested in the exiled dynasty and often quizzed his friend the ex-Jacobite Earl Marischal George Keith on the personalities of the Old and Young Pretenders. By 1759 Hume was internationally famous – Kant claimed he had awoken him from his dogmatic slumbers through his work – and the most celebrated figure of the Scottish Enlightenment. Hume has always divided the philosophical world. For the Anglo-American empiricist tradition he remains the one man in the history of philosophy who posed all the important questions, and his method of scepticism remains the nonpareil in methodology. In terms of the Franco-German continental tradition, Hume was more of a psychologist and intellectual gadfly than great philosopher, though this can largely be set down to the continental preference for 'gigantism', which for a long time elevated Beethoven and Wagner far above Mozart as composers. The truth is probably somewhere between the two viewpoints: Hume was neither the supreme figure in philosophy that empiricism requires him to be, nor was he the second-rater (trailing behind Leibniz, Kant and Hegel) of continental prejudice.

In April 1759 Hume, in correspondence with Adam Smith, drew his fellow Scot's attention to the second edition (just then appearing) of an original work by an up-and-coming thirty-year-old Irish Protestant politician. Edmund Burke, he pointed out, 'wrote lately a very pretty treatise on the Sublime'. In fact Burke's Philosophical Inquiry into the Origin of our Ideas of the Sublime and Beautiful *has usually been considered the first serious work in the study of aesthetics. Burke distinguished between the beautiful, on which many philosophers and poets had already offered theories and explanations, and the sublime, which combined the normal notions of beauty with ideas of pain, danger and even death. Whereas beauty could be approached through rationality, the sublime lay beyond reason and defied human understanding, control or activity. Beauty involves love, pleasure and smallness but the sublime entails admiration, pain and greatness. Some have likened the distinction Burke makes to that later made between Eros and Thanatos by Freud in* Beyond the Pleasure Principle, *and the inference of a sexual subtext certainly seems warranted by Burke's own remarks: he says that seduction relates to the domain of beauty but rape to that of the sublime; that pleasure (beauty) cannot be forced on us but pain (the sublime) can. Indeed, many later quasi-philosophical notions seem adumbrated by Burke in this seminal work. He tells us that certain kinds of absence, all presaging the unpredictable, are sublime: vacuity, darkness, solitude, silence; all of this seems a clear pre-echo of Jean-Paul Sartre's treatment of 'nothingness' in* L'Être et le néant.

Like Voltaire's Candide *and Sterne's* Tristram Shandy, *two other famous and influential literary productions of 1759, Burke's essay on the sublime does not proclaim its originality from the rooftops but proceeds slowly and soberly. All eighteenth-century writers liked to parade their knowledge of the ancient classics, and in his 1759 preface to the second edition Burke justifies his philosophical quest with a quote from Cicero: 'To consider and contemplate nature is the essential food for our spirits and intelligence.' Much of Burke's treatise is taken up with quotations from classical authors: Homer, Virgil, Horace, Lucretius, and so on, or from those heavily influenced by the classics such as Milton; the home-grown genius Shakespeare has to be content with a single citation. But Burke also tries to make his meaning clear by homely allusions. So: wild horses are sublime, but tame ones are not; bulls are sublime, but oxen are not; wolves are sublime but not dogs; kings and mythological gods are sublime, but ordinary people are not. A classic example of the sublime is the horse in the Book of Job that 'swalloweth the ground with fierceness and rage'. Yet Burke soon muddies this simple message by introducing nuances, showing that the beautiful can shade into the sublime and that the sublime itself can be subdivided into categories. Looking at the body of a beautiful woman, for example, is 'like a deceitful maze through which the unsteady eye glides giddily, without knowing where to fix or whither it is carried'. And the sublime in art is productive of delight but in nature simply of fear and paralysis; one need only compare our reactions when faced with murder in Greek tragedy, where catharsis comes into play, and murder in actuality where fear and horror are the dominant emotions.*

Burke's essay on the sublime looked forward to motifs that would be developed more fully in a number of manifestations: in the Gothic movement (Mary Shelley's Frankenstein *is an obvious spiritual descendant), in the mysticism of Blake and in the Romantic movement in general. Images of flight abound in Burke's treatise, linked to the innate human fear of heights for, as Burke says:*

'No passion so effectively robs the mind of all its powers of activity and reasoning as fear.' This emphasis on fear worried Samuel Johnson, who was as sceptical about Burke's essay as he was about Tristram Shandy, *and who always argued that the commitment to the notion of the imagination unbound, increasingly fashionable after 1759, was sure to end in madness. Johnson's argument with Burke was essentially a variant of a very old one: is one awed by contemplation of the stars and the concomitant realisation of human insignificance (Burke), or does one despise the vastness of the cosmos because the stars cannot write poetry, crack jokes or experience emotion (Johnson)? Yet the one aspect of the sublime that Johnson could not argue around relates to a general post-1750 Zeitgeist. In Nature the sublime was a feeling of terror and awe evoked by landscape and scenery, not a feeling of pastoral pleasure or bucolic relaxation. To feel the sublime in Nature was to be swept by incomprehensible powers. And increasingly men and women observed gigantic geographical features and intuited the truth of Burke's point. Whereas in the 1745 Jacobite Rising hardly any of the participants made mention of the grandeur of the Scottish Highlands, by the time of the Seven Years War one can discern a very different attitude to landscape.*

By the end of the 1750s, in an era when society was showing a growing awareness of the picturesque and formal gardens were being landscaped, the grandeur of Canada, with its extensive wilderness, forests, mountains, lakes and waterfalls, made a special impact. This was a particularly acute experience for troops who had never before left European shores and had campaigned in the flat terrain of western Germany or the Low Countries, but not even service in the Scottish Highlands fully prepared men for the awesome and sublime geography of North America. Most fearsome to the troops, especially after the debacle of Monongahela in 1755, were the dark forests where they feared they would be swallowed up by an unseen enemy, just as Varus's three Roman legions had been when ambushed by Arminius and his terrible German warriors in the Teutoburg Forest in AD 9. In Canada's gloomy forests the very vegetation seemed to be alive in an uncanny, loathsome, reptilian way. The black mould of the forest floor, frightening in its fecundity, spawned a million seedlings which engaged in a fearful struggle for existence where only the fittest survived by blighting their comrades. The interlocking of boughs, and the mutual suffocation of branches and foliage in the primeval evergreen darkness seemed to complement the murderous combats with Indians to which all who entered the Stygian depths of the forest were condemned. Some observers compared the crazed prodigality of Nature in the forests to the emission of spermatozoa, since only one in a thousand trees survived to maturity and those that did seemed to endure an arboreal form of the Black Hole of Calcutta, 'pressed together in struggling confusion, squeezed out of symmetry and robbed of development' as one observer of the woods put it. The forests seemed to reproduce in Nature Hobbes's nightmare of a war of all against all or suggested a society based on violent anarchy where the mob was permanently in control. The rotting vegetation at the level of the forest floor, a gallimaufry of sere and yellow ferns, feculent toadstools and mossy trunks, serpentine roots, clotted and matted bushes, rotting tree trunks and musty mulch, added a further connotation of evil.

Colonel (later General) John Forbes, who served in North America from 1756, spoke of those 'hellish woods' and 'an immense forest . . . impenetrable almost to any thing humane [*sic*] save the Indians'. When he advanced against Fort Duquesne, Forbes's troops had to cut a road through woods, mountains and swamps, trying to fashion a highway twelve feet wide, following a trail into leafy mulch, ascending precipitous heights, tentatively crossing narrow ridges and then descending again through the tree canopy into the damp shadows of the forest floor, where distant mountains could be vaguely descried through flickering leaves and jagged boughs. Only the sensuously minded noticed the myriad colours of red and brown in the foliage, soon prismatically enhanced by the green and blue of streams and waterfalls and only the botanically inclined noticed the profusion of trees: pine, dark birch, Douglas fir, alder, swamp-maple, pitch pine, silver birch. Where the trail ran down to rivers there was particular chaos and confusion, with dead trees littering the watercourse, blanched and bark-stripped in the shallows, rotting yet with limbs raised above the surface in deeper waters, while forever there was the barrier of the newly fallen giants, which storms or old age had flung down to produce a porcupine effect of bristling, matted boughs. The overall effect of this temperate jungle was profoundly depressing: one of Braddock's men wrote in 1755 that 'the very face of the country is enough to strike a damp in the most resolute mind . . . I cannot conceive how war can be made in such a country.'

Another aspect of the Canadian sublime that impressed observers were the multitudinous lakes, and especially the Great Lakes – that freshwater Mediterranean of the western hemisphere, and Midwestern America's equivalent of a coastline. Some thought there was something uncanny and vaguely sinister in the way the lakes were not walled in by mountains and other natural features, as in Europe, but seemed to merge flatly and seamlessly with the plains and prairie. Others recorded horrified reactions to these huge expanses of water: it seemed contrary to nature that, once out of sight of land, sailors on even sturdy vessels could endure all the terrors of open-ocean voyaging, with the pitching, rolling and yawing to be expected on the North Atlantic. Although the maximum wave height on the Great Lakes was about twenty-five feet because of the limited fetch, veteran mariners confided that they had endured worse storms on Lake Superior than on the China Sea. There appeared to be something hideous in the very idea that one should suffer such gales in the heart of a continent. The Great Lakes seemed an unnatural monstrosity: neither proper fresh water nor honest oceanic brine, but some terrible hybrid – ominous, hellish, cruel, treacherous and, in the true sense, God-forsaken. The Great Lakes were the sea and yet not the sea, producing a kind of ambiguity of vision with their vast expanses and landless lines of the horizon, yet with a shortness of wave pulse that did not quite convince as belonging to pelagic wastelands. The Great Lakes had all the blankness and vacancy ('vacuity' to use Burke's word) of the ocean but without the telltale swell.

Yet, as Burke himself had suggested, the sublime often merged with the beautiful, and the sunsets on the Great Lakes could inspire diarists and annalists to purple passages. Sunsets that could meld water, rainbows and sun in a fabulous kaleidoscope, so that the sun could successively appear as a golden urn, an ochreous acorn, a glowing aureate disc and a pillar of fire excited superlatives from the writers. Standing at Fort Holmes (near the modern-day Straits of Mackinac), so that she had clear views over both Lakes Huron and Michigan, the early nineteenth-century traveller Harriet Martineau described a scene that had not changed since 1759:

I can compare it to nothing but what Noah might have seen, the first bright morning after the deluge. Such a cluster of little paradises rising out of such a congregation of waters, I can hardly fancy to have seen elsewhere. The capacity of the human eye seems here suddenly enlarged, as if it could see to the verge of watery creation. Blue level waters appear to expand for thousands of miles in every direction; wholly unlike any aspect of the sea. Cloud shadows, and specks of white vessels, at rare intervals, alone diversify it. Bowery islands rise out of it; bowery promontories stretch down into it; while at one's feet lies the melting beauty which one almost fears will vanish in its softness before one's eyes; the beauty of the shadowy dells and sunny mounds, with browsing cattle and springing fruit and flowers. Thus, and not otherwise, would I fain think did the world emerge from the flood. I was never before so unwilling to have objects named. The essential unity of the scene seemed to be marred by any distinction of its parts.

The ultimate test for all partial to sensuous ravishment by water was Niagara Falls, already a source of wonderment to both sides. The falls, 165 feet high and a quarter of a mile wide, seemed almost to have been designed to clarify Burke's famous distinction between the beautiful and the sublime. The beauty lay in the proportion and symmetry, and the devout claimed this was surely God's masterwork, for even the rolling clouds of spray at the base of the cataract seemed fixed and ordered as if constructed by a master architect. The more reflective among the God-fearing were apt to reflect that the selfsame scene of seething waters and giant sprays had taken place here since the day of Creation. Some saw the falls in metaphorical terms as Nature's version of the Trinity with the boiling flood over the lip, the rising mist and the indeterminate middle zone, part cascading water, part rising spray, conveying a mystical meaning, denoting the passage of body to soul, matter to spirit, human to divine. But the idea of beauty was mainly available only to those who observed from a distance. Those who approached closer were overwhelmed by feelings of terror and dread and perceived themselves as insignificant alongside the gigantic, thundering body of water. Some felt that they had departed the sublunary world for the upper sky. Others felt an overpowering desire to throw themselves into the water and become as one with the seething cauldron and described the feeling of gazing into the waters as producing dizziness or a curious mixture of pain and pleasure. Niagara Falls were the classic instance of the sublime manifesting itself in Nature.

But the combatants of 1759 did not experience Canada only as landscape in three dimensions; climate and the weather added another layer. As Voltaire was fond of pointing out, in Canada winter tended to fuse with spring and autumn, so that only four clear campaigning months in the summer could be relied on. By December the snow and ice had the entire country in a deadly grip; a twenty-four-hour snowfall could easily produce three-foot snowdrifts. Everywhere the white silence appalled the luckless troops in winter quarters as they gazed on glaring snowfields and blinked half-blindedly into the fierce light and cold. Men on garrison duty were frostbitten as they dug away dry, powdery drifts piled up by the wind against the forts, and he was a rash man who touched the metal of gun or sword with his bare hand, for the flesh would immediately cleave to the metal like the sucker of a giant squid and have to be cut loose. Sentries were relieved every hour, yet feet, fingers and other extremities were still frozen stiff. In December 1759, when all the fighting was over, no fewer than 153 men suffered severe frostbite in the week before Christmas while out hunting for firewood. On a reconnaissance expedition to Ticonderoga in March 1759 the weather was so cold that the scouts had to cut up their blankets and wrap them round their frozen feet. During the march from Crown Point to Ticonderoga in the same campaign 166 men were frostbitten and army surgeons amputated more than 100 toes. The one advantage of winter to European minds was that the Indians did not like to fight in it. The cold aside, the barren trees and bushes could not hide them, while the snow betrayed the tracks of their shoes.

The troops' problems in winter were compounded by inadequate clothing and fuel. Although stoves were supplied in guard and barrack rooms, supplies of fuel were woefully short and soon ran out, necessitating woodcutting expeditions into the wilderness. Felling timber and chopping lumber in fact comprised the main tasks of garrisons in winter. Strongly guarded parties of axemen ventured into the forests, where the winter silence resounded to the hum and thwack of a thousand implements; the logs would then be dragged back to the fort on sledges, usually eight huge logs to each sledge. This was truly a Herculean task; after labouring all day with axes, the woodsmen often spent the twilight hours having to cut fresh trails through the snow after new drifts had piled up over the outward track. Since normal military clothing for the redcoat (uniform coat with long skirt and tricorne hat) offered little defence against the sub-zero temperatures, soldiers increasingly improvised their own winter uniform, which officers connived at. Lieutenant John Knox, whose journal is one of the prime sources for 1759 in Canada, encountered one woodcutting party and reported that the men looked more like Hungarian or Croatian guerrillas than British regulars, being unshaven with long beards, wearing a motley assortment of clothing and misshapen tricornes, with the uniform skirts cropped short, the brims of the hats lopped off and – a significant detail – swords replaced by tomahawks. Knox later made another entry in his journal:

Our guards on the grand parade made a most grotesque appearance in their different dresses; and our inventions to guard us against the extreme rigour of this climate are various beyond imagination. The uniformity as well as nicety of the clean, methodical soldier is buried in the rough, fur-wrought garb of the frozen Laplander; and we rather resemble a masquerade than a body of regular troops, insomuch as I have frequently been accosted by my acquaintances, whom, though their voices were familiar to me, I could not discover, or conceive who they were.

Troops brought up on European campaigning had to adjust to these very different conditions and in general they adapted well. Gradually they became alpinists and learned to march in Indian fashion along narrow defiles, where one false step meant plunging over a precipice or into a crevasse. Longingly they waited for the telltale crack in the frozen rivers and lakes that would signal that the ice was beginning to lose its grip and that winter was beginning its death-throes. But spring in Canada was a long time coming. In April the sap was still not rising or the buds sprouting, and many was the false dawn when the forest was merely dappled and patched with snow, and men thought they could finally discard their winter modes. Often soft rain would viciously turn into a heavy snowfall and the low-hanging clouds and morning mists that seemed to herald spring would suddenly be replaced by hoar-frost, powdery snow and rime-covered pine trees. The utmost vigilance was necessary now, for early spring was the time when campaigning by rangers and *coureurs de bois* was technically feasible, and they could use the frozen lakes as a fast travelling surface just before the ice became too thin to bear their weight. But for most of the warriors late spring was the favourite season, neither too cold nor too hot, with every-thing seemingly in Nature's perfect equilibrium as swallows and bluebirds whizzed in and out of the trees. Lieutenant Knox described the rapture that such a late spring day could engender: 'I think nothing could equal the beau-ties of our navigation this morning: the meandering course of the narrow channel; the awfulness and solemnity of the dark forests with which these islands are covered; the fragrancy of the spontaneous fruits, shrubs and flowers; the verdure of the water by the reflection of the neighbouring woods; the wild chirping notes of the feathered inhabitants.'

Summer brought mixed blessings. This was the high campaigning season when men were most likely to lose their lives. Moreover, the heat made the troops' coarse woollen uniforms and full pack exhausting; many, again with the connivance of their officers, slimmed down by jettisoning shoulder and waist belts, swords, sidearms, buff belts and spare kit. And the summer was the season of disease: dysentery, typhus and scurvy – the last a particular problem as the basic army diet was salt pork and hard bread. Heavily dependent on Indians for supplies of venison and corn, British troops tried to combat scurvy with 'spruce beer' – made from molasses and boiled spruce boughs. But summer contained other menaces. Although rattlesnakes were not present in such profusion as on the great plains, the farther west the fighting extended, the more the reptiles were encountered. Far the worst of all pests, though, were the mosquitoes and black flies which attacked humans in great clouds. The troops were forced to put on long linen trousers and make improvised mosquito nets to go over their hats. The best time in summer was during a soft rainfall by the lake shore, when Indian allies refused to exert themselves and took time off by bivouacking in the coves and inlets that indented the lacustrine littoral. To the fury of men like Amherst, who always hated Indians, the Iroquois would often upend their canoes on the shore during rainfall and smoke their pipes under a roof of bark or birch.

October brought the definitive advent of a Canadian autumn. The clouds returned to the sky, and mist and rain hid the mountains and trees. A chill was felt in the air and all around the landscape seemed to be breaking up with trickling and oozing noises under the impact of rain. Forage was getting scarcer and around the camps gaunt, spavined nags chafed at the gushing sound of water and the pattering of rain drops. Soon the drizzling rain turned to sleet, and then to snow, forming beautiful crystalline patterns in the forests but simply getting absorbed and churned up in the muds of the primitive roads, deepening the quagmires into which supply wagons sank. All regulars now huddled in their winter quarters, and only the bravest Indians prowled the woods. The sole winter fighters the British had at their disposal was the crack force of Rangers under Major Robert Rogers, whose all-weather capability was famously and memorably described by Parkman:

> The best of them were commonly employed on Lake George; and nothing can surpass the adventurous hardihood of their lives. Summer and winter, day and night, were alike to them. Embarked in whaleboats or birch-canoes, they glided under the silent moon or in the languid glare of a breathless August day, when islands floated in dreamy haze, and the hot air was thick with odors of the pine; or in the bright October, when the jay screamed from the woods, squirrels gathered their winter hoard, and congregated blackbirds chattered farewell to their summer haunts; when gay mountains basked in light, maples dropped leaves of rustling gold, sumachs glowed like rubies under the dark green of the unchanging spruce, and mossed rocks with all their painted plumage lay double in the watery mirror; that festal evening of the year, when jocund Nature disrobes herself, to wake again refreshed in the joy of her undying spring. Or, in the tomb-like silence of the winter forest, with breath frozen on his beard, the ranger strode on snow-shoes over the spotless drifts; and, like Dürer's knight, a ghastly death stalked ever at his side. There were those among them for whom this stern life had a fascination that made all other existence tame.

The Canadian landscape meant contact with an entire range of wildlife that Europeans had never seen before: elk, moose, brown bear, black bear, puma, lynx, wolverine, beaver, muskrat and many other species. Yet it was not the animals that scared European soldiers, but the flitting shadows in the forests and the bark canoes appearing suddenly and as if by magic on the limpid lakes, which always spelt just one thing: Indians. Combat between regulars and Indians was one of the novel features of the Seven

Years War; before 1750 Indian attacks affected colonists and settlers almost exclusively. Another factor in the late 1750s was that large numbers of captives fell into Indian hands: it has been estimated that some 2,700 whites were taken prisoner in Pennsylvania, Virginia and Maryland alone during the years 1755–65. After Monongahela British troops lived in mortal terror of the painted red men, to the point where Pitt actually appointed Wolfe to an independent command on the St Lawrence and concentrated a major expedition there so that the redcoats could avoid fighting Indians in the lakes and forests. Monongahela undoubtedly made a huge impression on British troops. One veteran said afterwards: 'The yell of the Indian is fresh on my ear, and the terrific sound will haunt me to the year of my disso- lution.' Armchair theorists in England affected to despise the British fighting man for such an attitude, and Dr Samuel Johnson suggested, only half in jest, that troops be inured to the noise through 'a proper mixture of asses, bulls, turkeys, geese and tragedians'. But it was not the good doctor who had to face the spectral apparition in the forest, smeared in bears' grease, daubed with paint and shaven-headed except for a central tuft.

Both the British and French perceived the Indian tribes to be preter- naturally cruel and the huge gap in culture, folk ways and mores between the white and red man naturally accentuated this perception. From the Native American standpoint, scalping was the means whereby a warrior supplied definite proof of his prowess in the field, the key to prestige in a martial society. Loot and captives also represented both proof of courage and a form of wealth, and the Indians beheld with incomprehension the European practice of allowing prisoners to go free under parole. The other relevant factor in the 'cruelty' debate was that by its very nature wilder- ness warfare was a savage and ruthless business, and males were most at risk when taken prisoner. White children were usually absorbed and women also, as breeders. On the other hand, there is little point in denying that many European captives did die horrible and painful deaths and were tortured first. Indian tortures included the laying of hot stones on the soles of the feet, running hot needles into the eyes, shooting arrows into victims, pulling them out, then shooting again. The speciality of the Abenakis, a pro-French tribe on the Vermont/Canada border, was to make their pris- oners 'run the gauntlet' or run between lines of warriors wielding sticks and clubs. The toughest victims survived badly beaten; the weakest simply died. Other tribes liked to divide captives into two groups: those to be burnt alive to assuage grief and vengeance for the fallen and those to be adopted or enslaved. Slavery could often mean a fate worse than death, or rather death by a thousand cuts, since slaves were set to back-breaking toil, regularly beaten or made to run the gauntlet. But, in any balanced assessment, we must not forget the many whites who were adopted by their captors, who became tribal mascots or favourites and subsequently 'went native', refusing to return to white 'civilisation' even when given a clear chance or pressurised by anxious relatives. And it must be remembered that in the Seven Years War Europeans encountered Indians who had degenerated from previously higher standards of behaviour. Partly this was because contact with whites, and particularly the white man's liquor, had eroded traditional values. Partly it was because the advent of firearms meant that the ritualised combat of the pre-seventeenth-century era gave way to deadly quarrels fuelled by European armaments technology. Heavy casualties from firepower required retaliation and revenge, and thus there was a vicious circle of escalating violence.

The differential experience of Native Americans by the French and British makes an interesting study. At the height of the conflict between Wolfe and Montcalm in 1759, Montcalm had 1,000 Indian allies, Wolfe almost none. The British in general tried to keep the Indian tribes at arm's length because of the possibility of linguistic misunderstanding. There is the additional consideration that the Commander-in-Chief, North America, General Amherst, hated and despised Indians and in later years would become infamous as the man who deliberately traded blankets with them that were infected with smallpox. In February 1759 he wrote to Pitt about the Stockbridge Mahican tribe: 'They are a lazy rum-drinking people and little good, but if ever they are of use to us it will be when we can act offensively; the French are more afraid of them than they need to be, numbers will encrease [sic] their terror and may have a good effect.' Yet another factor in the differential experience was that the British had far less knowledge of the Indian tribes than the French. This ignorance persisted into the American independence era. Fenimore Cooper, whose classic The Last of the Mohicans deals with events at Fort Henry in 1757, managed to conflate the entirely different septs of Algonquin Indians, the Mahicans of Massachusetts and the Mohegans of Connecticut and rename them 'Mohicans'.

The French, by contrast, enjoyed the advantage that their fur trappers had lived among the tribes and even intermarried with them. Against this was the disadvantage that France drew its allies from many different tribes, some with outstanding feuds and vendettas of their own, and so experienced the greatest difficulty in controlling them. Montcalm and his lieutenants, beset by a persistent numerical inferiority to the British, regarded their Indian allies as a necessary evil. As Bougainville remarked: 'In the woods of America one can no more do without them than without cavalry in open country.' But it was difficult to meld their fighting spirit with the discipline of the French infantryman. Indians liked to fight from long range, when sure of victory and thus likely to lose few men. They preferred to surround an enemy; to fight in scattered bands, not a compact body; to melt away before a frontal challenge and re-form later. If forced to fight large-scale battles, they would try to use techniques perfected when hunting animals: drive opponents within a 'half moon of musketry', then close the jaws of the trap and pin them down within a ring of fire. Crack shots, the Indian warriors had learned total mastery of the smooth-bore musket through repeated target practice, and could also used grooved rifles – slower to load than muskets but more accurate and with a longer range. Choosing their war chief on the basis of past martial performance – not according to seniority or the ability to buy a commission as in the European armies – they presented an awesome military spectacle, armed with musket or rifle, tomahawk, powder-horn, shot-pouch and scalping knife, seemingly the perfect killing machine. Yet they had to be used sparingly by their allies. Bougainville remarked that it was always 'better to have on hand only a specified number of these mosquitoes, who would be relieved by others'.

Someone once said that the only fun to be had in wartime is fighting your own side. While Bougainville was away in Paris, Montcalm and Vaudreuil proved the truth of the observation by continuing their cat-and-dog cohabitation in Canada. Each wrote to the relevant minister in Paris with slanders and calumnies about the other. Furiously angry about Montcalm's great victory at Ticonderoga, Vaudreuil set out to belittle it. Against all the evidence, he claimed that Montcalm would have been beaten but for 'divine intervention'. Incandescent with fury that Montcalm's regulars had secured the victory on their own, without the help from the Canadians and Indians that Vaudreuil had begrudged them, the Governor now sent these in large numbers, trying to rewrite history by insinuating that they had been present at Ticonderoga. On 8 April 1759 he wrote to Berryer a missive which can only be described as a masterpiece of mendacity. Even though he had ordered Montcalm to avoid battle – and Montcalm had won at Ticonderoga by ignoring those instructions – Vaudreuil had the gall to claim that the English escaped only because Montcalm ignored his (Vaudreuil's) precise battle plans. He then added (self-contradictorily) that the victory would certainly have bad results, though he refrained from specifying what they might be. He added that Montcalm had been indulging in 'infamous conduct and indecent talk', by which he clearly meant that Montcalm had criticised him and the venal Bigot. Once again he asked for the recall of Montcalm. Most despicable of all his effusions was this lying estimate of his own influence and charisma: 'The people are alarmed and would lose courage if my firmness did not rekindle their zeal to serve the king.'

Montcalm meanwhile was fulminating about Vaudreuil's regime in private correspondence with his friend the Chevalier de Bourlamaque. Repeatedly he complained that he was kept in the dark about everything, never consulted by the Governor, and that his troops were treated as an alien force or an army of occupation rather than as the thing that stood between Canada and perdition. Once again it was the corruption that most exercised Montcalm. Everyone in Canada, it seemed, was peculating, looting, pillaging and defalcating. Even the army officers were at it, though they could not match the Canadians in sheer rapacity: their commanders reckoned they had done badly if they did not return from a campaign with 300,000 or 400,000 francs in their pockets, and even a junior ensign stood to make 15,000. His letters to Bourlamaque typically expressed fervent sentiment for the fatherland, disillusionment and longing for the château and orchards of his beloved Candiac. At the end of every outburst he asked Bourlamaque to burn the epistle, afraid that his savage indignation might be construed by a third party as lack of patriotism. Here is an extract from the letter of 18 March 1759: 'Oh, when shall we get out of this country! I think I would give half that I have to go home. Pardon this digression to a melancholy man. It is not that I have not still some remnants of gaiety; but what would seem such in anybody else is melancholy for a Languedocian. Burn my letter and never doubt my attachment.'

The mutual antipathy between Montcalm and Vaudreuil appears in disguised form in their official letters during the winter of 1758–59, with Montcalm making detailed suggestions for the coming campaign and Vaudreuil brushing them aside with declarations of absurd optimism. Montcalm wanted to defend one of the three frontiers – Quebec, Lake Champlain and Lake Ontario – in depth, abandoning the other two to the British until events in Europe enabled Louis XV to mount a major rescue attempt in North America. Where Montcalm's preference was to concentrate at Niagara and to pull back from the other two theatres, Vaudreuil wanted to defend all three simultaneously and even to make a quixotic foray into the Ohio country, though with what resources he was unable to explain. The only point on which they agreed was the assumption that the main British offensive in the summer of 1759 would be against Lake Champlain; they discounted the possibility of an assault on Quebec. Vaudreuil, it is true, stated that he would not fight for Quebec even if attacked, as the fortifications were not strong enough and the town could not be properly provisioned. But, such was the duplicity of the man, that he used the hypothetical case of an attack on Quebec as the means whereby he would set at nought Berryer's strict orders that he should defer to Montcalm in all military matters. Vaudreuil dealt with this hated memorandum, whose existence he barely acknowledged even to himself, as follows: 'If the English attack Quebec, I shall regard myself free to go there in person with most of the troops and all the militia and Indians I can muster. On arriving I shall give battle to the enemy, and I shall do so repeatedly, until I have forced him to retire or he has crushed me by sheer superiority of numbers.'

Montcalm had staked a lot of his hopes on Bougainville's mission, but all the news he received from France in the early spring of 1759 made him realise how parlous his position was. The Minister of War, Marshal Belle-Isle, advised him in February that no large-scale reinforcements would be available in 1759 and that Montcalm should fight a holding action until 1760, by which time events in Europe might have changed dramatically. He gave two reasons for what looked like Louis XV's cold-blooded abandonment of North America. In the first place, if a huge armada with massive reinforcements were sent across the Atlantic, there was a real fear that the British, with their naval superiority, might intercept it in mid-ocean with disastrous results. Secondly, France doubted whether the conflict in the Americas could ever be resolved by warfare in the New World; even if a massive reinforcement was landed at Quebec, the British would simply redouble their efforts and land further armies, and so ad infinitum. Belle-Isle hinted that the solution would be sought in Europe that very summer:

> As we must expect the English to turn all their forces against Canada and attack you on several fronts at once, you must limit your plans of defence to the most essential points and those most closely linked so that, being concentrated within interior lines, each part may be supported and reinforced by the others. However small the redoubt or salient you defend, we must keep a footing in North America, for if we once lose the country entirely, it will be almost impossible to recover it.

Montcalm, though replying that he and his men would shed the last drop of blood to defend the colony, was not sanguine and replied to Belle-Isle: 'Unless we have unexpected luck, or stage a diversion elsewhere in North America, or the British commit egregious military errors, Canada will fall during the coming campaign season. The English have 60,000 men, we have 11,000. They are well organised and our government here is worthless. They have food and we have none.' The reference to food was not just rhetoric, for the harvest of 1758 had been one of the worst in living memory, and the winter the coldest. Worst of all problems was the issue of morale. The French colonists had hung on through a long period of adversity but they had no confidence in Vaudreuil and Bigot and their nerve was beginning to crack. Montcalm again directed Belle-Isle's attention to the massive corruption in Canada, which was why the French were losing their Indian allies. Bigot and his cronies were diverting into their own coffers the subsidies that were supposed to be paid to the Indians to keep them as allies. 'If the savages had actually received a quarter of what has been allocated to them, the King would have every last red man on his side, and the English would have none.' Moving on to the campaign proper, Montcalm said he would defend at Lake Champlain, since British naval supremacy made Lake Ontario a lost cause. While discounting the likelihood of an attack on Quebec, Montcalm added that if the British did approach the St Lawrence from the Atlantic, the French certainly did not have a fleet that could stop them.

Such was the situation when, on 12 May, Bougainville arrived in Quebec, with further letters and despatches from France. This time it was not the winds and waves that had delayed him, but ice; his ship had been held fast in Newfoundland ice-fields for twenty-two days. Adept at news management, Vaudreuil gave out that in the envoy's wake was a fleet of seventeen vessels from Bordeaux, full of supplies and ammunition. Although it was true that ships bearing vital war supplies did get through, the information Vaudreuil did not underline was that only 328 new troops were arriving. But in the context of bread and meat rationing, which had been Quebec's fate throughout the winter, the first consideration was for food supplies, so that for a short while there was general rejoicing and French morale noticeably picked up. Bougainville scarcely noticed. He arrived in Quebec at 8 p.m., but pressed on downriver to Montreal, where he found Montcalm. 'A little is precious to those who have nothing,' said Montcalm with a shrug. The two men conferred about the personal business which Bougainville had commissioned. Bougainville brought sad news. Just before sailing from France he had heard that one of Montcalm's daughters had died. Montcalm's stoical sadness on receiving the news is one of his appealing characteristics. 'I think,' he wrote to his wife, 'that it must be poor Mirete, who was like me and whom I loved very much.' But he tried to look on the bright side. 'Our daughter is well married. I think I would renounce every honour if I could be with you, yet the king must be obeyed. The moment when I see you once more will be the greatest of my life. Goodbye, my heart, I believe I love you more than ever.' This revelation of the tender Montcalm beneath the soldierly exterior explains in part why he has always been a favourite with historians.

However depressing the general picture that Bougainville painted, Montcalm could at least take comfort from the fact that Versailles at last seemed to have woken up to the extent of corruption in its North American colony, even though, as Bougainville added, it was a case of the doctor arriving after the patient was dead. Two things had finally contrived to put the noose around intendant Bigot's head. Versailles was outraged that the royal prerogative had been infringed by Bigot's promissory notes or *ordonnances*, which he issued on his own authority as legal tender. But meanwhile Bigot was caught in a trap of his own devising. The more henchmen and cronies he enrolled in his great schemes of graft and fraud, the more difficult he found it to control them and to keep the lid on the whole simmering cauldron. When his underlings came to him for signatures to frauds too outrageous even for Bigot and he demurred, they threatened exposure of the whole rotting edifice unless he signed. Seeing a crevasse opening up before him, Bigot tried to detach himself from the impending scandal and attempted to resign. But Vaudreuil would not let him go, so Bigot had to batten down and await the hurricane. The verbal typhoon was every bit as ferocious as he had feared, for as early as January 1759 Berryer had the bit between his teeth.

On 19 January he reprimanded Bigot as follows:

The ship *Britannia*, laden with goods such as are wanted in the colony, was captured by a privateer from St Malo, and brought into Quebec. You sold the whole cargo for eight thousand francs. The purchasers made a profit of two millions. You bought back a part for the King at one million, or two hundred thousand more than the price for which you sold the whole. With conduct like this it is no wonder that the expenses of the colony become insupportable. The amount of your drafts on the treasury is frightful. The fortunes of your subordinates throw suspicion on your administration.

Poring over the accounts, Berryer found even more to enrage him, and wrote a second letter the same day:

How could it happen that the smallpox among the Indians cost the king a million francs? What does this expense mean? Who is answerable for it? Is it the officers who command the posts, or is it the storekeepers? You give me no particulars. What has become of the immense quantity of provisions sent to Canada last year? I am forced to conclude that the king's stores are set down as consumed from the moment they arrive, and then sold to His Majesty at exorbitant prices. Thus the King buys stores in France, and buys them again in Canada. I no longer wonder at the immense fortunes made in the colony.

But the most gloomy news Bougainville brought was confirmation of the British strategy for 1759. Among the voluminous memoranda he laid before Montcalm and Vaudreuil was clear confirmation from French intelligence sources that the British intended to open yet another front and to this end were assembling a fresh army and flotilla for despatch to North America. This was part of Pitt's determination to make 1759 the decisive year in the struggle for mastery in the New World. His 1758 strategy had worked well in the Ohio Valley and on Lake Ontario but came to grief at Fort Carillon (Ticonderoga) when General Abercromby foolishly sent his much larger army on a frontal assault on Montcalm's entrenchments, where it was shot to pieces. For 1759 Pitt ordered the new commander General Amherst to invade Canada either via Lakes George and Champlain or by way of Lake Ontario and the upper St Lawrence; and to proceed against Fort Niagara and French strongholds farther west. Additionally, Pitt gave a wholly independent command to the thirty-two-year-old colonel James Wolfe. Promoted to Major-General, Wolfe was to leave Louisbourg in May and make a direct seaborne attack on Quebec by the St Lawrence. The theory was that he would coordinate his assault on Quebec with Amherst.

Wolfe was given lavish resources to accomplish the deed. Pitt envisaged an army of 12,000, though Wolfe was actually able to take only 8,500 with him up the St Lawrence, as the regiments he picked up in Nova Scotia were sadly under-strength. But the troops he had were the pick of the British army: ten regular British line battalions plus a battalion of Grenadiers from the below-strength garrison in Louisbourg – the so-called 'Louisbourg Grenadiers'. There were also three companies of the Royal Regiments of Artillery and six companies of Rangers. The Rangers were supposed to be North America's equivalent of the modern-day SAS and Amherst liked them, but Wolfe emphatically did not: he despised their reputation for rapine and atrocities and described them as 'the worst soldiers in the universe'. Apart from a handful of Indians serving with the Rangers, Wolfe's force was a white man's army. As a favourite of Pitt's, Wolfe was able to hand-pick his brigadiers, Robert Monkton and James Murray; he also raised no particular objection to the third brigadier, George Townshend. That France faced an uphill task is evident when we consider that the total military manpower in Canada was only just numerically superior to Wolfe's army alone. And instead of defending in depth at one selected location, the French had troops scattered around the continent: some on Lake Ontario, some at Niagara, others at Ticonderoga and Lake

Champlain and still others at Quebec. Even more absurdly, Vaudreuil still had soldiers probing towards the Ohio country, which at this late hour he should have regarded as definitively lost. Vaudreuil's thinking was that the future of New France depended on alliances with the tribes of the 'upper country' (*pays d'en haut*), for their ravages, if they were still employed as allies of France, could in the end force Britain to sue for peace. If then the west was the key to mastery in North America, any last stand by France should be made farther upriver, possibly at Montreal. Vaudreuil's long-term objective was not the defence of Quebec, but a final reckoning somewhere in the interior, and to this end he bent his energies to contingency plans for getting his manpower evacuated upriver in case Quebec fell.

Montcalm's view was almost exactly the opposite. For him Quebec was the only defensible site and the dispersal of forces in the face of a three-pronged British attack utter madness. He never placed any value on Indians and thought Vaudreuil's grand strategy chimerical. The chasm between his views and the Governor-General's was partly a matter of personalities, partly the natural dichotomy between professional soldier and civilian administrator, but it was also in a larger sense cultural: the sensibility of the Canadian versus the French, the provincial aristocrat against the Paris-formed military mind and ultimately an entire American ethos ranged against a European one. But Versailles had now given Montcalm the green light, so it was the military commander's view that prevailed.

Apart from being outnumbered five to one, Montcalm had to contend with three other major disadvantages in the 1759 campaign. In the first place, British seapower meant that the Royal Navy controlled the Atlantic and the supply lines. In many ways the fleet Pitt had put at Wolfe's disposal was even more impressive than the army he had given him. Forty-nine ships sailed with Wolfe, including twenty-two vessels of fifty guns or more, including Saunders's flagship, the ninety-gun *Neptune*. The fifty-gun *Centurion* had been Lord Anson's flagship when he circumnavigated the globe in 1740–44. Among Saunders's officers were Rear-Admiral Philip Durell and captains of the calibre of Edward Hughes and John Jervis (later Lord St Vincent). Among other future celebrities along with Saunders was the thirty-one-year-old James Cook, currently master of the *Pembroke*. When the fleet reached Louisbourg it became a veritable armada with the addition of 119 transports, ordnance and commissariat vessels. Wolfe's army, in short, was backed by nearly 200 ships and some 13,500 sailors and marines. A mere recital of army manpower gives no idea of the real odds the French faced.

The second disadvantage for Montcalm was that New France was a sparsely populated colony and there were no external sources of manpower on which to draw. Amherst and Pitt by contrast could tap the resources of the English-speaking colonies in North America. Pitt had very early seen the fallacy of Loudoun's draconian policies, whereby the American colonists were treated as an inferior species and made to pay the full cost of army quartering and requisitions. Not only did Pitt go out of his way to treat the American colonists as equal partners in a crusade to rid the continent of the detested French but he was prepared to absorb the costs himself. The case of Massachusetts is instructive. War expenditure by the colony was estimated at £500,000 for the years 1756–61, whereas the total annual revenues from taxes on polls, land and trade yielded no more than £100,000. To save Massachusetts from bankruptcy, Pitt had to bail it out with subsidies voted in Parliament. In this regard the arrival at the Bay Colony in January 1759 of seven huge chests of gold and silver made all the difference to how the war with France was perceived. Reassured that any expenditure on the war would be reimbursed, the Massachusetts assembly proposed to raise 1,500 new recruits, on top of the 5,000 already enlisted, paying a bounty of £14 to each man. The combination of guaranteed reimbursement of all expenses plus the payment of a bounty did the trick also in Connecticut, New Jersey, New York, New Hampshire and Rhode Island. In each colony recruitment targets were met without the need for a draft. The upshot was that in 1759 the northern colonies were able to raise 17,000 provincials to assist the invasion of Canada. Army cash-flow crises were also solved. Whereas earlier commanders, short of funds, had had to go cap in hand to American bankers to secure very high-interest loans, a delighted Amherst found that the New York assembly was prepared to advance him the necessary funds against a future refund from the Treasury in London. Pitt and Amherst praised the colonists' patriotism, though cynics said it was simply that money had talked on this occasion, as it always does. Self-interest can certainly be discerned, but perhaps self-interest of a more subtle form. The southern colonies did not manifest nearly the same level of commitment or recruiting but they were geographically remote from Canada and were not potentially menaced by French arms.

Yet the third strike against the French was possibly the most serious of all. Montcalm, who two years earlier had almost been overwhelmed by his out-of-control Indian allies, now found he had no friends left among the red men, while British subtlety had almost succeeded in winning over the Native American tribes in their entirety. The situation should not be overstated, for in the American colonies *in general* British success was not uniform and their policies would ultimately lead to serious warfare in the 1760s with both Cherokees and the Indian League under the Ottawa chief

Pontiac. In 1758 General John Forbes had tried to recruit the Cherokees to his banner and actually mustered more than 700 of them in May. But the high-handed Forbes had no experience of Indian customs and took it for granted that the warriors were inferiors who should defer to him. When the Cherokee chief Little Carpenter showed that he had a mind of his own and refused to be simply a pawn on Forbes's chessboard, the General arrested him as a deserter. By the time he realised his cross-cultural error, Little Carpenter was in high dudgeon. Not only did he refuse to serve further with the British but he and his braves decamped with the expensive weapons and trade goods with which Forbes had tried to bribe them.

Despite his ineptitude, Forbes was a man who grasped the importance of Indian alliances, so he tried to learn from his mistakes. He built superficially close relations with Teedyuscung, using him as a conduit to the western Delawares in the Ohio country. What he aimed for ultimately was a general treaty binding the various tribes, such that France would be left without native allies. Forbes's difficulty was that Teedyuscung's ambitions and interests collided both with those of the Iroquois and of the white property speculators who hoped to make a killing in the Ohio country. Teedyuscung particularly wanted a formal repudiation of the fraudulent treaty of 1737 whereby raw and gullible Delawares had been deprived by the Penn family of two-thirds of a million acres in eastern Pennsylvania. Forbes's envoy to the tribes of the Ohio country, Christian Post, forged a particular rapport with the important Delaware Indian sachem Pisquetomen. Together the white emissary and the sachem proselytised for a general peace treaty with the English, but everywhere they went they encountered the cogent argument that if the Ohio Indians abandoned the French, the English would simply move in and steal their lands. To this the tribes made the unanswerable riposte that if the war was not being fought over Indian lands, why did the French and British not settle their differences in a purely European war?

Nonetheless, between them Forbes, Post and Pisquetomen achieved the near-impossible and convened a congress at Easton in late October. In contrast to Teedyuscung's apparent triumph the year before, when he had negotiated with the British (with the Iroquois present merely as observers), this time he was just one of many important chiefs. Altogether 500 Indians from fourteen different nations were present at Easton: the western Delawares, the eastern Delawares, the Six Nations of the Iroquois Confederacy, the Nanticokes, Tuteloes, Chugnuts, Minisinks, Mahicans and Wappingers. Tired of Teedyuscung's contumacity, Onondaga had sent as his delegates three paramount chiefs from the Mohawks, Senecas and Oneidas, charged with reasserting Iroquois hegemony over its traditional fiefdom, including the Ohio lands. Too late Teedyuscung realised that his 1757 triumph was actually a political trap – that by concluding a separate agreement with the British then, he had thrown away all his best cards. Realising to his horror that he had no leverage, and was even from the British point of view a disposable asset, he spent most of the conference comatose with drink, emerging in lucid intervals to rant in bellicose fashion. This simply played into the hands of the Iroquois chiefs, who argued with circumstantial cogency that such a drunkard was unfit to represent anyone and could be disregarded. Eventually, after a poignant plea for a homeland for his people, Teedyuscung accepted the inevitable and bowed to a formal reassertion of Iroquois suzerainty.

Only Pisquetomen stood between the Six Nations and a clean sweep at Easton. Before accepting the general peace protocol, he insisted that the rights of his people to represent themselves in land negotiations with the Penn family and other white speculators were guaranteed, in return for acknowledgement of formal Iroquois overlordship. This was guaranteed by Pennsylvania Governor William Denny. Pisquetomen considered he had done well: he had secured an end to warfare which his people could not afford; Iroquois recognition of their virtual autonomy and a British promise that the white man would not found permanent settlements in Ohio when the war with France ended. The Iroquois came away from the conference having learned the lesson that if they wanted to keep control over their traditional western territories and nip breakaway movements in the bud, alliance with the British was the only way, for they alone had the power to make their writ run across the continent. The main Indian loser at Easton was the lachrymose Teedyuscung, but an even bigger loser was France. Once the Iroquois switched from neutrality to a pro-British stance, the balance of power tipped decisively, the French lost their Indian allies and never won another war. Even admirers of Montcalm must face his limitations. In his mind the French had won the great victories of Monongahela and Fort William Henry by their own skill in arms, not because of their Indian allies. Montcalm always looked on the Indians as auxiliaries, somewhat lower than the militia and never as genuine allies. Louis XV, the ministers at Versailles, Vaudreuil and Bigot were all major culprits in the fall of New France, yet Montcalm cannot be absolved of all blame.

But Pisquetomen and the Delawares soon had cause enough to regret their acquiescence in the treaty of Easton. When the French withdrew from Fort Duquesne, they took with them or destroyed all their provisions and trade goods. The incoming British troops had to endure a winter of half-rations and, latterly, near-starvation because of bottlenecks in the supply chain. Put briefly, there were no longer enough wagons and horses to ferry provisions and, until the winter snows ended and there was grass in the meadows to feed the huge herds the British intended driving westward to feed their garrisons, the only relief from dearth and hunger was the occasional pack train. By the time drovers brought the first cows to the newly named Fort Pitt, the troops were eating their own horses and cats and dogs. When the first cattle arrived, the famished soldiers slaughtered forty of them on the spot and ate the meat raw, making no distinction between offal and choice cuts. The knock-on effect of this winter of famine bore down most heavily on the Delawares, Shawnees and Mingoes. The immediate effect of their switch of allegiance from the French to the British was that they were now starving. British credibility depended on feeding the Indians at the very moment when they could barely feed their own, while French commando and guerrilla groups took a heavy toll of the winter pack trains with ambushes and surprise attacks. The overwhelming likelihood as the winter of 1758 merged with the early spring of 1759 was that the Ohio tribes would switch their support back to the French.

Even when the British managed to ease the supply situation – which was not until late April 1759 (though the first cattle did not get through until mid-June) – the Delawares had other worries. Echoing the later St Petersburg–Petrograd–Leningrad transformation, the former Fort Duquesne became Fort Pitt and then Pittsburgh, the change in nomenclature reflecting the tenfold increase in size of the settlement. Not only were there large numbers of white soldiers present by summer 1759 but white traders, speculators and get-rich-quick low-lives and *canaille* from Pennsylvania. Pisquetomen and his fellow chiefs had been led to understand that the British would withdraw their troops once the French threat in Ohio was extinguished, leaving behind merely a small trading post. But by July 1759 it was obvious both that the French were not coming back and that the British had no intention of leaving. Even worse, their army engineers were laying out a pentagonal fort extending over seventeen acres. By August soldiers and civilians were collaborating in all the features of a large, permanent settlement: a sawmill, a brick kiln, a smelting works, a forge, to say nothing of a moat and a glacis. Pisquetomen and his colleagues were far from stupid, but by the time they realised the true scale of British ambitions, it was too late to throw their alliance into reverse and rejoin the French. Active and imaginative diplomacy by the French in the winter of 1758–59 might have worked wonders with the Delawares, but Montcalm was not the man for that particular endeavour.

In any case, once Bougainville returned from France, Montcalm had no leisure to consider the Indians. The threat to Quebec was clear and, four days after his envoy's return (16 May 1759), Montcalm entered the town and was at once hailed as a deliverer. It was time to think how Quebec might be more effectively fortified and defended. Nature had already done its best for, situated on the left (northern) bank of the St Lawrence, the town sat on a peninsula that thrust in phallic fashion into the broad river. The ancient fortress sat on a rock 200 feet above the St Lawrence, where the river suddenly widened to give the stream an altogether different character. One statistic is eloquent: at Quebec the river was 1,000 yards wide, but thirty-two miles downstream the width was twelve miles; only the Île d'Orléans, cleaving the lower river in two, temporarily distracted attention from the dramatic change in river size at this point. Located 700 miles from the open Atlantic, wedged between the St Lawrence and its tributary the St Charles, were the seat of the French Governor and the two different settlements, the Upper Town and Lower Town. The lofty Upper Town looked out across the basin and down upon the docks and straggling houses of the Lower Town, where it petered away into the suburbs of St-Roch and Palais. The confluence of the St Lawrence and the St Charles brought the city to an abrupt end with a steep escarpment. Quebec was thus protected partly by water and partly by steep, beetling cliffs, ranging in height from 200 to 350 feet on the western side of the peninsula. There was just one vulnerable spot: the land facing open country to the south-west known as the Plains of Abraham. Named for Champlain's pilot Abraham Martin in the early 1600s, this narrow plateau was farmland, where the ground rose gently upward through small farms, first to a broken ridge and then on to the walls of Quebec. This was where the French had to build artificial defences and fortifications, but the sloping and uneven ground made it impossible to construct a continuous line of bastions covering each other.

In 1759 there was no proper citadel in Quebec (and there would not be one until 1831). For nearly a hundred years the French had tinkered with the defences on Quebec's western front without achieving anything significant. A report by a French engineer in 1744 said that Quebec was highly vulnerable to attack, but this was disregarded until the following year, when the British capture of the 'impregnable' fortress of Louisbourg finally sounded the alarm tocsin in Versailles. Serious work then began on Quebec's defences but was periodically halted while Paris went through another of its chronic financial crises. By 1759 the west of Quebec was supposed to boast a complete stone-wall defence, but Montcalm's inspection soon convinced him that the city's fortifications were 'so ridiculous and so bad that it would be taken as soon as besieged'. He saw clearly enough that the stone wall itself was useless unless there were external works that could protect it from artillery fire or being taken by escalade. Against all the canons of fortification lore, the French had neglected to dig a deep ditch in front of the wall *before* they built the wall itself; since the ground was rocky and a ditch could be made only by blasting, Montcalm now faced the absurdity that any such blast would bring the wall down. Nor could external fortifications to cover the wall be built at this time, since this would require 4,000 workers who would consume the food being held by Montcalm as a reserve in case future convoys from France were intercepted. The consequence was that the city walls on the west remained a sitting duck for enemy artillery. To compound this incompetence, the French had wrongly sited all their guns to deal with an escalade and had none that could fire towards the open country. As the *pièce de résistance* they had neglected to occupy and fortify Point Lévis, immediately across the St Lawrence from Quebec and less than a mile from the city. This immediately opened the possibility that the British might occupy these heights from which they could shell the city and blast a passage for their ships to land men on the Plains of Abraham. The French apparently thought they could use fireships against any enemy vessels coming within close range of Quebec.

Although Montcalm was in the proverbial situation of stable doors and bolting horses, he did what he could to shore up Quebec's rickety defences. He pressed all sailors from merchant and marine vessels into manual labour and had them begin work on a trench line along the right bank of the St Charles. Ships were sunk in the navigation channels of the St Lawrence, while buoys and markers were removed and false ones substituted. Eight large vessels were converted into fireships, hulks were sunk in the St Charles, waterside batteries erected in the Lower Town, three new bridges built over the St Charles and a floating battery started. The provision ships were stationed fifty miles upriver, with the supply line running from the west. Assuming that the British could not get through to the upper St Lawrence and attack from the west, Montcalm decided not to keep a food supply in the city itself, lest it be lost if the city fell; his men could then retreat west to the food dumps. But there was fatal confusion here. The British could take Quebec only if they had already blasted a passage to the west, in which case they would also have severed the French supply line. But to Montcalm's stupefaction, his engineers reported that the St Lawrence channel was too wide to be blocked. Despite their presence in Quebec for 150 years, the French knew next to nothing about the St Lawrence itself, and their laziness and ignorance now returned to haunt them. Montcalm wrote to Bourlamaque that 'our best seamen or pilots seem to me either liars or ignoramuses'.

If everything in both Nature and history seemed to have conspired against him, Montcalm did at least enjoy one slice of luck in the spring of 1759. On the one hand Wolfe did not move as quickly as expected; on the other, most of the French supply ships got through. Delayed by ice, which forced him to divert to Nova Scotia instead of making an immediate land-fall on Cape Breton Island, Wolfe did not reach Halifax until 30 April and Louisbourg not until 15 May. Meanwhile he had been poorly served by Admiral Durell, who had wintered at Halifax. Durell was under orders from Pitt to move into the St Lawrence at the earliest possible date in 1759 to intercept any French ships trying to reach Quebec from France. But both his reconnaisance vessels and British merchant navy captains reported more severe ice than usual for the season, so Durell played safe. When he was finally ready to get under way at the end of April, an accident to one of his ships delayed him. After an infuriating hold-up, Durell tried to clear from Halifax only to find that the winds had changed and he was further delayed until 5 May. More trouble with ice meant that his flotilla of ten warships and three transports did not reach Bic until 21 May, where he learned that seventeen French ships had passed that way en route to Quebec on the 9th. Some historians are convinced that if Durell had managed to intercept that convoy, the damage to French morale would have been incal-culable and Wolfe would have had a walkover victory at Quebec. Certainly Durell's protestations about the ice seem weak in the light of the progress of the French convoy.

But if Fortune had given Montcalm a sop, his larger problems remained. He might have had a chance if he could have retained all of New France's military manpower to deal with Wolfe, but 3,000 men were assigned to hold Amherst at Lake Champlain, another force took off to garrison Fort Niagara and yet a third to guard the approaches to Montreal from Lake Ontario. Myth-making has Wolfe as the hero of 1759, but Amherst played a vital if indirect role in the campaign for Quebec. Amherst had to over-come a number of obstacles. Bedevilled by shortage of money, he was able to continue campaigning only after an appeal for paper money to the Governor and Assembly of New York; bad weather and the late arrival of the colonial troops further hampered him. In May 1759 he sent Brigadier-General John Prideaux with 5,000 men (three battalions of regulars and two of colonials) to take Fort Niagara. Prideaux left Schenectady and proceeded up the Mohawk river on 20 May making for Oswego (Chouagen). On the way he left behind a strong garrison at Fort Stanwix and estab-lished posts at both ends of Lake Oneida. He then descended the Onondaga river to Oswego. When he arrived there on 27 June he found the so-called 'Mohawk Baronet', Sir William Johnson (a man who had 'gone native' and lived polygamously with at least two Iroquois wives), and 1,000 Iroquois warriors waiting for him. This was an unprecedented display of pro-British martial endeavour by the Six Nations. Hitherto only the Mohawks had evinced any sympathy for the British; most of the Iroquois, and especially the Senecas, had hired themselves out as mercenaries to the French while not committing themselves to formal alliance. Yet Prideaux's welcoming committee contained braves from all Six Nations, even the Senecas.

The Onondaga and the Iroquois leaders had brooded on the implications of the Easton treaty over the winter and had not entirely liked what they concluded in the cold light of the short December days. True, they had regained formal suzerainty over the Ohio territory, but the Delawares had blunted the impact of this by securing the right to negotiate directly with the authorities in Pennsylvania. The Iroquois League Council therefore decided that the only way to liquidate these strivings towards Delaware independence was to cooperate fully, formally and wholeheartedly with the British. Their chosen transmission belt was the powerful Indian trader and Superintendent of Northern Indian Affairs, Sir William Johnson. Beginning as a merchant in the Mohawk Valley, Johnson had parlayed his assets into land speculation and army contracting and was now diversifying into diplomacy as an informal power broker. The Onondaga's emissaries offered Johnson military aid in a campaign against Fort Niagara. Johnson at once informed Amherst and asked for a massive subvention of gifts, in return for which he pledged himself to bring over the Six Nations in their entirety to join 'His Majesty's Arms'. Even Johnson was surprised by the Iroquois volte-face but it was sheer pragmatism that actuated the Six Nations. They feared – and with reason – that the Shawnees and Delawares intended to create an independent Indian confederacy in the west that might embrace the Miamis and Munsees. Only an alliance with the British could nip this inchoate movement in the bud. If Fort Niagara fell, the French would be cut off from the Ohio country, but this alone was not enough. To stymie the plans of Pisquetomen and his henchmen the Iroquois had to get the British to establish a permanent presence in the west. Doubtless the Iroquois thought that once the French were driven from Ohio and Pittsburgh made a regular feature of the landscape, they could go back to their old game of playing off the European powers against each other. But if so, they were fatally shortsighted. They did not seem to envisage the possibility that the French might be driven from North America altogether and that, in that case, the British might then turn their devastating power against their erstwhile Indian allies.

At Oswego Prideaux left just under half his troops behind with Colonel Haldimand, with orders to rebuild the fort that Montcalm had devastated three years before and hold the Chouagen position in an iron grip; otherwise a French counterattack could leave the assaulting force at Niagara hopelessly cut off. It was as well that Prideaux made these dispositions, for a force of French irregulars came within an ace of achieving exactly what he feared. Not long after he embarked on Lake Ontario for Niagara, the French Colonel Saint-Luc de la Corne, one of their Indian liaison experts, led a mixed force of about 1,000 French and Canadians in a surprise attack on the English builders and woodcutters at the proposed fort. But the Canadians were undisciplined and failed to capitalise on the element of surprise. They decided to retreat to their boats and, by the time la Corne rallied them, the English had formed an effective defence. Secure behind a rampart of felled trees, the French directed an inconsequential long-range fire on the enemy for two hours and, next morning, when the English wheeled up their cannon, the French re-embarked, having sustained losses of nearly thirty dead and wounded (la Corne was one of the latter); the defenders meanwhile incurred a loss in single figures.

Prideaux's troops and the Iroquois warriors spent four strenuous days rowing westward along the inhospitable southern shore of Lake Ontario. They made landfall on 1 July about three miles from Fort Niagara, a formidable target that overlooked the lake from a bluff at the mouth of the Niagara river. A successful siege of the fort was far from being a foregone conclusion, for one of Montcalm's best officers, Captain Pierre Pouchot had spent two months strengthening the defences. Fort Niagara was now the best-defended fortress in North America, screened by extensive earthen outworks, a ditch, glacis and covered walkway sheltering the castle and citadel. Pouchot had 600 well-provisioned troops under his command as well as some Indians under the direction of the Franco–Indian Joncaire brothers. He could also count on the intermittent support of a mixed force of Indians, guerrillas, bushrangers and irregulars under Captain Lingeris, a veteran of the 1755 campaign against Braddock, though some 2,000 of these had unfortunately just been sent as reinforcements to the French outposts in the Ohio country. For these reasons, and because a British attack would have been expected that spring while the fort was still vulnerable, until Prideaux's force actually arrived to begin the siege, Pouchot had been sanguine – and indeed over-confident – that he could ride out the storm. Pouchot's first disappointment occurred when the flotilla he had constructed as his advance guard not only failed to attack, impede or impair Prideaux's canoes on their arduous haul along Lake Ontario's southern shore but did not even manage to warn Pouchot that the enemy was approaching. The first the French commander knew of the coming of the English was when he heard the crackle of gunfire. Panic-stricken scouts rushed in to tell him that an Iroquois war party had just attacked woodcutters outside the walls of the fort. From this event, too, Pouchot learned to his alarm that the local Senecas, hitherto dependable allies, could no longer be trusted and might even have gone over to the English already.

Pouchot could scarcely be faulted for being unable to second-guess a genuine reversal of traditional Iroquois policy, but does not the despatch of so many men to the Ohio country argue for a kind of hubris, crying out for the nemesis that actually descended? Here the strategic thinking of Vaudreuil must be arraigned as the culprit and, in particular, his refusal to concentrate on a single objective or even to obey the explicit orders of Belle-Isle that he was to fight behind interior lines. Vaudreuil's idea was that, if Ligneris and his troops could descend the Allegheny before the British were at full strength in the Ohio country, they might regain the overland passage to Louisiana. If that happened, Indian raids on the back country of Virginia and Pennsylvania would resume, and the British would have to pull back their offensive forces (or a large part of them) to defend the clamorous colonists. This would buy New France crucial breathing space until 1760, when Versailles had promised to retrieve the position in North America. Pittsburgh was the prime target, and three separate forces of French irregulars under Ligneris, Aubry and Marin were assembling at the jump-off points of Le Boeuf, Venango and Presque Isle.

The formal siege of Fort Niagara began on 9 July but the British engineers disappointed Prideaux by botching the first attempt at trenches, so that there was a delay while new trenches were built and the batteries could open fire. As if in biblical or mythical fashion, Prideaux paid for his impatience by being killed instantly when a shell from a cohorn fragmented immediately on discharge from the mouth and struck him on the head. Johnson, the 'Mohawk Baronet', took over and proved just as energetic as the late Captain. On the 14th, British cannons opened up from an advanced battery about 250 yards from the glacis. On the 17th, British howitzers started a crossfire from across the Niagara river, dominating all riverine, littoral and lake-front aproaches and effectively enfilading the French. By the afternoon of the 20th, the covered walkway came under fire from a battery just eighty yards away, which threatened to blow a hole in it. Within two weeks more than a hundred French defenders had been killed or wounded by an endless hailstorm of mortar bombs and sizzling shot, and the rest were jumpy and exhausted from lack of sleep. Morale had plummeted and many shellshocked men were now mutinying, refusing to mount the walls. Two weeks into the siege, the British had tightened the noose to the point where their trenches stretched right across the peninsula and the nearest was a mere musket shot away from the fort. No defence or counterattack was possible, since the big guns in the bastion had been silenced or blown off their carriages. There was a gaping hole in the parapet which could not be repaired as the defenders were under constant fire; the most they could do was stuff bales of fur or animal skins into the breach.

Even while Fort Niagara was being blown apart, another chapter in the complex story of the Iroquois was being written. The Niagara Senecas had been France's reliable allies, acting as scouts, boatmen, couriers and porters on the tricky Niagara portage but now they seemed to have deserted. In fact they were taken unawares by the arrival of warriors from all Six Nations of the Confederacy and needed time to ponder their next move. Before his death Pouchot was able to arrange a truce that enabled Kaende, chief of the Niagara Senecas, to parley with his Iroquois cousins. Tense and protracted negotiations stretched over three days while Kaende exhorted his kinsmen not to attack the fort and they in turn explained why it was now in the overriding interest of the Confederacy to do so. Kaende's eloquent argument that the Six Nations were being made the dupes of the English, especially by the egregiously duplicitous Johnson, almost won the day. To prevent his warriors withdrawing from the fray completely Johnson had to promise that on its fall Fort Niagara would be given over to whole-sale plunder. But when the conference ended on 14 July, 'his' Iroquois informed him they would not fight their brothers, the Niagara Senecas. Since none of the Six Nations braves wanted to fight each other, a reluctant Pouchot agreed with Kaende that it would be best if the Niagara Senecas withdrew to smoke the pipe of peace with their blood brothers. Johnson had had a narrower escape than he realised, for Kaende's rhetoric at one point came close to persuading the other Iroquois to switch sides or at least revert to their traditional neutrality. In terms of *realpolitik* the Iroquois decision was the shrewdest one, for they avoided fratricidal bloodletting while ensuring an English victory.

By 23 July Pouchot was beginning to despair but that day he received word from Ligneris that the French irregulars, recalled from Ohio, were nearing the fort. Ligneris's relief force, which departed 2,500 strong, had somehow been whittled down to about 1,600 (doubtless because large numbers were Indians who came and went at will) but even so, as they appeared on the Niagara river above the falls they made an imposing sight, like 'a floating island, so black was the river with bateaux and canoes'. Johnson, amply warned by his Indian scouts, took effective measures: he blocked the road from the portage to the fort, tried to suborn Ligneris's Indian allies by pointing out the strength of the Iroquois forces in the neighbourhood and constructed a log breastwork across the road near La Belle Famille up the Niagara river where the non-combatant Iroquois were camped: it is clear that he hoped to inveigle the Iroquois into the coming

1. The terrors of the North Atlantic

2. George Washington's inauspicious début

3. Wesley and the Indians

4. Braddock on the march to Fort Duquesne

5. Catastrophe for Braddock, 1755

Louis Joseph M⁹ de MONTCALM GOZON
29 fevrier 1712 + 14 Septembre 1759

6. Louis Joseph, Marquis de Montcalm

7. David Hume,
sceptic and rationalist

8. Edmund Burke,
prophet of the Sublime

9. Samuel Johnson.
His *Rasselas* was a hit in 1759.

10. The British Museum opens to the public in 1759

11. Madame de Pompadour,
the power behind the throne

12. The Duc de Choiseul:
cunning and hedonism personified

13. Louis XV, a neurotic ditherer

battle and, significantly, the Confederation's warriors deployed themselves in the surrounding woods, on the flanks of the defenders. But Johnson had no illusions about the coming test of strength. Ligneris and Aubry had left Presque Isle a few days before with the flower of the French irregulars. Traders, trappers and bushrangers, many of whom had 'gone native' and were 'white Indians', may have presented a gruesome spectacle with their deerskin shirts, painted faces, long hair and even headdresses, war bonnets and battle-paint, but they were crack shots, expert marksmen, deadly snipers and probably the best bushfighters in Canada.

Johnson's propaganda worked well. Ligneris's Indian allies did indeed decide to take no part in the battle, so that perhaps only 600 (some authorities say 800) French regulars and irregulars made the assault on the abatis defended by Colonel Eyre Massey and the 46th Regiment. But Johnson and the British could not rely on localised superiority in numbers, for he had to divide his forces into three: one to face Ligneris and Aubrey, one to guard the trenches and another to secure the English boats. Since the besieging cannon had now ceased firing, Pouchot at first thought all the enemy had withdrawn to face the new threat from the Canadians, so he contemplated a sortie to take them in the rear. But when the remoralised French sallied from the fort and began doubling along the covered walkway, suddenly there was life in the seemingly abandoned trenches, and the bayonets glistened in the sunlight like porcupine quills. Disconsolately Pouchot withdrew. He spent the rest of the afternoon of 24 July listening to the rattle and clatter of distant gunfire, fervently hoping that Ligneris and Aubrey had the skill and elan to turn the tide for him. Through his field glass he could see smoke around La Belle Famille, but for hours he was in suspense, buoyed up by hopes and lacerated by fears.

Unfortunately for the French, the 464 redcoats under Massey had been skilfully deployed. He sprinkled men of the 46th among three companies of light infantry to contest the road to Fort Niagara. The main strength of the regiment was stationed on the right of the light infantry, and the 46th's own flank was covered by a Grenadier company backed by a 'picket' of the 44th Foot. Aware that the French were largely regulars, Massey ordered his front rank to fix bayonets, to lie down and to refrain from firing until he gave the word. Firing as they came, the French sortied from the wood-fringed track into the La Belle Famille clearing and began to deploy from column into line. The discipline of the redcoats was superb, as they took punishment from the popping shots of the French as they emerged from cover. Timing his movement perfectly and waiting until another second's delay might have seen his men panic and scatter, Massey finally gave the order to fire. Their volley was devastating. More than 130 men under Massey's personal command delivered a withering fire in massed volleys; this was lethal musketry unleashed at very close range. Massey reported: 'The men received the enemy with great resolution and never fired one shot, until we could almost reach them with our bayonets . . . I never saw a Grand Division (for so I must call my number) give so plump a fire. After firing standing seven rounds I gave the word for the whole to advance by constant firing, which was done in great order and the most of the 46 fired sixteen rounds.' The Grenadiers won special praise, for they 'behaved most gloriously, and by their pouring in all their fire, in the enemy's flanks, killed great numbers, and in my opinion was the occasion of breaking them'.

So Pouchot's worst fears proved justified. The French and Canadians were brave and skilful but poorly led, and the tactics of their leaders beggared belief. Seeing the enemy dug in, the regulars, marines and bushrangers simply made a frontal charge into a hailstorm of musketry, finally running into a wall of fire as the 46th Regiment and their supporting Grenadiers gunned them down from a lethal range of thirty yards. Of the 600 only about 100 survived the cauldron of death, to be taken as prisoners and maybe another 100 fled in panic, to be picked off by the Iroquois who, predictably, lent a hand once they saw the turn of the battle. Massey was furious that later reports credited the Iroquois with fighting valiantly, since in his opinion their behaviour was 'most dastardly'. Almost all the French officers were killed or wounded, some by being pulled out from beneath logs and scalped by the Iroquois; among the maimed was Ligneris, veteran of Monongahela in 1755 and one-time commander of Fort Duquesne. Those of the survivors who reached their canoes above the cataract, paddled frantically back to Lake Erie, gutted Presque Isle, Le Boeuf and Venango and with their shattered brethren in these garrisons, retreated to Detroit. The whole of the upper Ohio was now in English hands, and the French would never again make inroads in the Ohio territory.

The first Pouchot knew of the debacle was when the British ceased shelling his position and sent an envoy with an offer of surrender on decent terms. At first Pouchot refused to believe the scale of the reported defeat and sent his own envoy to see for himself. When denial was no longer possible, Pouchot accepted Johnson's surrender terms. Particularly important was Johnson's personal guarantee that there would be no Fort William Henry in reverse, and that the Iroquois would not be allowed to massacre the garrison. Johnson ensured this by taking two days to load the French prisoners onto boats, whence they were taken to New York and imprisonment. He bought off the Iroquois by allowing them free range through the fort. Rapine, pillage and looting were rampant as the warriors cleaned out warehouses and stores of furs, skins and other trade goods, but there was no arson, no rape, no mayhem and no murder. Iroquois forbearance puzzled many then and since. The most likely explanation is that, having sustained very light losses, they saw no need to replenish their ranks with adopted captives.

Johnson tightened his hold on the western end of Lake Ontario, using his Indian warriors before they dispersed. He sent a flotilla of whaleboats to probe towards Fort Toronto but they returned with word that the French had abandoned the fort and gutted it. Johnson then made a treaty of alliance with the Chippewas, as part of his forward policy for making over all the tribes of the Ohio. Then, leaving Fort Niagara in the charge of one of his colonels, he returned to Oswego. Amherst sent out General Thomas Gage, who had a reputation as an administrator, to take command of the western posts. For the French, the gateway to the *pays d'en haut* was now closed. The British and their colonist allies had rolled back the frontier to Oswegatchie, little more than 100 miles upriver from Montreal. The knock-on effect was considerable: the French immediately pulled out of Forts Presque Isle, Le Boeuf and Machault and left their settlements in the Illinois country to fend for themselves. Although they retained a foothold on the Great Lakes, through a network of trading posts from Detroit to Michilimacknic, these posts were cut off from New France and were hard put to survive, since they now received no supplies. Montcalm was forced to despatch his deputy, the Chevalier de Lévis and some troops he could ill spare from the defence of Quebec to shore up the position at Montreal. He was not to know that Gage was far too circumspect a commander to contemplate striking at Montreal down the St Lawrence from Oswego. But perhaps worst of all, it was clear that Indian warriors from the west would never again come to the aid of the French.

Meanwhile Amherst began what was supposedly the main operation of the year: the attempt to prise open Canada by seizing Ticonderoga and Crown Point, which would also effect a diversion in favour of Wolfe. He began in typical fashion by running late, insisting that supplies be exact and roads built before he ventured even as far as Lake George. Commissariat problems (which not even the talents of John Bradstreet, the Quartermaster-General, could wholly solve), the late arrival of colonial pioneers and their slow progress with pick and shovel further delayed the commander's departure. At the end of June Amherst finally arrived at a valley at the head of Lake George, which since 1755 had been the traditional mustering point for armies engaged on summer campaigns. Here were assembled about 11,000 men, roughly half regulars and half colonials. Amherst did not immediately lead them into the wilderness, but instead displayed his characteristic penchant for delay and indecision, killing time by starting work on a fort that was never completed or used in any way. As Parkman waspishly remarked: 'Amherst was never long in one place without building a fort there.' So it was 21 July before his army finally embarked for Ticonderoga and then it proceeded with great caution and circumspection, forever clearing the next stretch of wooded littoral because of Amherst's fear of ambush. Slowly the unwieldy force threaded its way through the islands of Lake George, taking twenty-four hours to cover the short distance to Ticonderoga, lashed by high waves and winds in the latter stages.

On 22 July the landing began. Outwitted, the French retreated via a portage road to a sawmill by the waterfall, but were soon in turn winkled out from there. Amherst's troops occupied the heights commanding Fort Carillon and then advanced to the trenches where Lord Abercromby had taken such a beating from Montcalm the year before. The French had totally recast the defences, with logs and impacted earth but made no attempt to defend the entrenchments, even though the commander, General François-Charles Bourlamaque, had roughly the same numbers as those with which Montcalm so signally defeated the British in 1758. Sheltered by these defences, Amherst's men were largely secure from the booming cannon of the fort. No sooner had Amherst brought up his own artillery, on the 23rd, than he learned that Bourlamaque had retired down Lake Champlain, leaving 400 men under Captain Hébécourt to make a last stand. Bourlamaque's conduct at first sight seems bizarre, but he was actually obeying the strict letter of instructions he had received in June from Vaudreuil, ordering him to abandon both Ticonderoga and Crown Point on the approach of the British. The thinking was that a stubborn defence of Ticonderoga might result in the surrender of Bourlamaque's entire force, whereas if he retreated to Île-aux-Noix at the outlet of Lake Champlain, he could fight a protracted holding action, thus preventing Amherst from securing outright victory in this theatre. As Montcalm put it to Bourlamaque in a supplementary letter on 4 June: 'Your task is not to beat the enemy but to avoid being beaten.'

On 26 July the desultory cannon fire that had claimed five dead and thirty-one wounded among the Anglo-American attackers suddenly ceased. At 10 p.m. that evening French deserters brought word to the English camp that Hébécourt and his men were escaping in their boats and that the magazine in Ticonderoga had been primed to blow. After vainly offering 100 guineas to anyone who would attempt the suicide mission to cut the gunpowder trail, Amherst could do nothing but wait for the inevitable explosion. Around eleven o'clock there was a tremendous thunderclap and the night sky was lit up as by a thousand flares. From the falling wood and fragments of Fort Carillon, it seemed certain that the whole of Ticonderoga had been blown sky-high. Then it was realised that the French explosives experts had been incompetent. Only one bastion of the fort was destroyed, and the French flag could still be seen fluttering on the ramparts, though fire was raging through the rest of the fastness. The French failure to detonate the entire fort was scarcely surprising, for Hébécourt's sudden withdrawal was a shambles. Most of his men were drunk; he had given orders for the flag on the battlements to be taken with them, but the orders were ignored; and, worst of all, a party of forty scouts, who had been told nothing about the change of plans, returned next day to the fort, believing it to be still in French hands, and were taken prisoner. Amherst had succeeded where Abercromby had failed, and the reason was his fussy, infuriating Fabian progress. This he exhibited once more by tarrying to repair the damaged fort before advancing on Crown Point, to which Hébécourt and his troops had retreated, to join Bourlamaque's 3,000-strong force.

Amherst was just working round to preparations for the next advance when his scouts came in with word that the French had abandoned Crown Point also and had withdrawn northward down the lake. Amherst duly occupied Crown Point and pondered making good the rash promise he had made to Pitt 'to make an irruption into Canada with the utmost vigour and despatch'. But he thought better of it and instead set his men to building a new fort at Crown Point. He sent small diversionary parties to explore the local creeks and waterways and put his pioneers to work both on a road into what is now Vermont and on the old French road between Ticonderoga and Crown Point. Once again Amherst can be faulted for dithering, but the very lack of French resistance made him suspicious. Were they tempting him forward to fight on terrain where they would finally have the advantage? He knew the enemy had a small fleet of warships on Lake Champlain while he had none. Boasting thirty-two cannon, the French schooner and three three-masted xebecs could cut his bateaux to pieces on the open lake. Characteristically Amherst decided to wait until his shipbuilders at Ticonderoga could construct a brigantine and a large armed raft that would cover his army's advance down the lake. Three weeks later, alarmed by the information he had received about the four French warships, Amherst ordered a further armoured sloop built. These demands overtaxed the exiguous resources of the saw-mill. Needing to provide timber both for Amherst's three new ships and for the rebuilding of the fort at Crown Point, it cracked under the strain and the continual breakdowns meant that it was autumn before Captain Loring, Amherst's naval commander, could launch the vessels.

The other factor that constrained Amherst was that he had heard nothing from Wolfe and therefore did not know how to interpret the lack of French resistance to his forces. Clearly he could advance against Bourlamaque if the campaign on the St Lawrence was consuming all of Montcalm's defensive energies, but was this indeed the case? Amherst's innate pessimism and circumspection led him to conjecture that Wolfe's campaign would probably fail and he would be forced back to Louisbourg. In that case an enterprising commander like Montcalm would almost certainly shift his forces to the defenders at Île-aux-Noix and achieve local superiority against the British. Certainly it was untypical of Montcalm to hand his enemies such easy victories as they had won at Ticonderoga and Crown Point, so the suspicion increased that he was baiting a trap. Moreover, Île-aux-Noix was a good eighty miles down the lake and Amherst knew nothing of the terrain, the landscape or the defences there. Was it wise to risk a three-day boat journey so far from his base, supplies, reinforcements and the realm of certainty? This was a job for a gambler, and Amherst was never that. His decision was prudent. At Île-aux-Noix, Bourlamaque awaited his coming with aplomb. He had 3,500 men dug in with confidence, in a natural defensive position in the mid-channel of the River Richelieu soon after it issues from Lake Champlain, with an arm of the river on each side of the fortress. A frontal attack would be costly and possibly suicidal but otherwise a long siege loomed. As Bourlamaque wrote: 'I await his [Amherst's] coming with impatience though I doubt if he will venture to attack a post where we are entrenched to the teeth, and armed with a hundred pieces of cannon.' Amherst meanwhile took the sound but unadventurous line that until he heard from Wolfe he would be content to continue with his building programme, to watch and to wait. The entire fate of North America now indubitably hinged on Wolfe's campaign on the St Lawrence.

Amherst eventually settled in for the winter, aiming to make 1760 the year for settling accounts decisively. His 1759 campaign had secured control of the Great Lakes and the back country (*pays d'en haut*) and when he finally heard from Wolfe, he knew that French defeat was only a matter of time. Already by late 1759 Amherst began looking ahead to the Indian problem, for it had always been his intention, once the French were defeated, to extend British hegemony over the unruly tribes. Finally the Iroquois saw the danger and by the end of the year their suspicions about British intentions were at fever pitch. Slowly Amherst turned the screw on them. First he insisted that all white captives taken in Indian villages must be given up, even if the whites had by now integrated with their captors. Then he started cutting back on the traditional presents made to the Indians, and particularly on ammunition supplies, thus making it difficult for the tribes to wage war or have an effective military presence. Moreover, it alarmed the Iroquois that at Crown Point Amherst immediately started building a fort many times the size of the previous French one. Particularly suspicious and resentful were the Senecas, who felt that the British had broken all their promises and were now charging sky-high prices for trade goods. But the worst grievance of all was settler encroachments on their land. It was clear that, despite what had been said, the British had no intention of withdrawing from the ancestral territories but instead planned to plant colonies there.

Too late the Iroquois realised that by making themselves Amherst's poodles, they had diminished their influence with other tribes. Even the Mohawks observed with trepidation that their blood-brother Sir William Johnson was more interested in becoming a great land baron than in helping them. Johnson made his position clear, telling the Iroquois chiefs that they 'have it in their power now . . . to become once more a happy people but if . . . they should act a different part, they must expect no quarter from us'. The Delawares too realised that when the British promised they would leave the Ohio territories once the French were defeated, they were lying. So acute was Delaware discontent that in the summer of 1759, absurdly late, they planned an ambitious campaign to seize as many forts as they could, including possibly Pittsburgh and Fort Duquesne; their plan was to enter the forts as friends and then overcome the garrisons once inside. In an evil hour the Delawares finally decided to wait and see whether the French could defeat the British on their own; by the time it was clear the French could not, it was too late and the Delawares stood alone. In the last days of 1759 were laid the gunpowder trails that would explode a few years later in the great Pontiac uprising.

FIVE

INDIA

1759 was a good year for the fifty-year-old Samuel Johnson, though he would have to wait another three years before a state pension would give him financial security. The most-quoted man in the English language after Shakespeare, Dr Johnson certainly filled his annual quota of quips, sallies and apophthegms. Perhaps his most famous saying, dated to 16 March 1759, was that life on a ship was like being in jail with the added chance of being drowned; moreover, on a ship you cannot get away from other people or see those who are not on board. The good part of shipboard life is that it is like being on retreat in a monastery but the bad part is that it is not your choice when the retreat is brought to an end. But his essays in The Idler *series are full of gnomic utterances: 'Nothing is more hopeless than a scheme of merriment' (May 1759); 'As gold which he cannot spend will make no man rich, so knowledge which he cannot apply will make no man wise' (June); 'Criticism is a study by which men grow important and formidable at very small expense' (June). Admittedly, some of his 1759 utterances strike one, with the immeasurable advantage of hindsight, as merely naive. 'The trade of advertising is now so near to perfection that it is not easy to propose any improvement' raises a wry smile in the twenty-first century, as does his lament on the over-production of books: 'One of the peculiarities which distinguish the present age is the multiplication of books. Every day brings new advertisements of literary undertakings and we are flattered with repeated promises of growing wiser or living easier than our progenitors.' It was no wonder that Tobias Smollett, author, Scotsman and pro-Jacobite, in a letter in March (surprisingly written to the arch anti-Scot and anti-Jacobite John Wilkes) referred to 'that Great Cham of literature, Samuel Johnson'.*

Yet Johnson's greatest triumph in 1759 was Rasselas, *his most sustained and successful attempt at fiction. Clearly influenced by Ecclesiastes, the satires of Juvenal and Jonathan Swift,* Rasselas *tells of the eponymous Prince of Abyssinia who lives in a changeless society rather like that of Plato's* Republic, *yet yearns for answers to ultimate questions about the meaning of human life.*

Leaving his life of luxury in Abyssinia's Happy Valley he, together with his mentor Imlac, his sister Nekayah and her servant Pekuah, escapes to Egypt in a quest for the happiest way of life; need one add, this being Samuel Johnson, that they never find it. Supposedly written because at the time Johnson was too poor to pay for his mother's funeral (she died at eighty-nine in January 1759), the novel was cast in the form of an 'Eastern tale' and was so similar in structure, plot and general sensibility to Voltaire's Candide *that James Boswell, Johnson's biographer, declared that, but for the simultaneous publication of the two different philosophical fables, Johnson would certainly have been accused of plagiarising the great French master. There is the same delight in the exotic, the same satirical intent, and the same pessimistic view that life is something to be endured rather than enjoyed. The simultaneous appearance of* Candide *and* Rasselas *alerts us to the point that much so-called plagiarism is no such thing but merely a synchronistic response to the spirit of the age; Laurence Sterne made similar sceptical points about plagiarism in yet another 1759 production,* The Life and Opinions of Tristram Shandy. *The cases of Leibniz and Newton and Darwin and Wallace are well known but there are many more in the history of thought and literature. Like* Candide, Rasselas *is powered mainly by dialogue and, given the eighteenth-century popularity of philosophical fables involving exotic locations, it is not surprising that Johnson with this one work acquired a European reputation, and that he never repeated that success with any other prose work.*

Rasselas is addressed to those 'who listen with incredulity to the whispers of fancy and pursue with eagerness the phantoms of hope; who expect that age will perform the promise of youth and that the deficiencies of the present day will be supplied by the morrow'. Like Sterne with Parson Yorick in Tristram Shandy, *Johnson uses the character of Imlac, the sage, to express his views about science, philosophy and a range of social questions, especially marriage, on which his cynical conclusion is that 'marriage has many pains, but celibacy has no pleasures'. In Egypt, when visiting the Pyramids, Imlac says: 'I consider this mighty structure as a monument of the insufficiency of human enjoyments.' There are some interesting reflections on the strategy and tactics of dealing with kidnappers and a warning against fantasy which Marie-Antoinette, had she read the book, might have heeded: 'And I,' says the Princess, 'will not allow myself any more to play the shepherdess in my waking dreams.' Johnson/Imlac explores many philosophical and theological issues, discusses the virtues and drawbacks of the monastic life and is harsh on those, like Pliny the Elder (the famous workaholic of the Ancient World) or like Laurence Sterne in his own day, who live the scholarly or creative life at the expense of life itself. The remarks on the ambiguous face of good and evil would not be out of place in nineteenth-century writers like Herman Melville and Robert Louis Stevenson,* as when Imlac remarks: 'The causes of good and evil are so various and so uncertain, so often entangled with each other, so diversified by various relations, and so much subject to accidents which cannot be foreseen, that he who would fix his condition upon incontestable reasons of preference must live and die inquiring and deliberating.' Most interesting to a twenty-first-century reader are the fantasies of flight, which clearly admit of a psychoanalytical explanation, and Johnson's premonition of the possibility of war in the air with aeroplanes, of which he says: 'What would be the security of the good, if the bad could at pleasure invade them from the sky? Against an army sailing through the clouds, neither walls, nor mountains, nor seas could afford any security. A flight of northern savages might hover in the wind, and light at once with irresistible violence upon the capital of a fruitful region that was rolling under them.'

Like Candide, Rasselas finishes his wanderings convinced that he might as well have stayed quietly in his room. Happiness and the quest for meaning are alike illusions and the final chapter is explicitly entitled 'The Conclusion in which nothing is concluded'. 'Imlac and the astronomer were contented to be driven along the stream of life without directing their course to any particular point. Of those wishes they had formed they well knew that none could be obtained. They deliberated awhile what was to be done, and resolved, when the inundation should cease, to return to Abyssinia.' Yet for the historian what is more interesting than Johnson's pessimism is his fascination with the exotic and the 'Country' ideology (dislike of money over land, city over country, conspicuous consumption over spartan austerity) that finds eastern 'luxury' deplorable. Imlac has in his time travelled throughout Persia, Arabia, Syria, Palestine, India and Asia and was once adviser to the Moghul Emperor in Agra; his travels are to the eastern hemisphere what Candide's are to the western. In Rasselas we discern the mania for foreign travel and exploration recently popularised by Jeremy Dawkins, the 'discoverer' of Palmyra, and by Lady Mary Wortley Montagu; and the same sensibility that would, little more than ten years later, thrill to the tales of Polynesia which Bougainville and Cook would bring back from their Pacific rovings. Rasselas, indeed, is sometimes credited with having inspired the Scots explorer James Bruce to make his ground-breaking explorations of Abyssinia ten years later. As for eastern 'luxury' – one of the things Prince Rasselas so disliked about the Happy Valley – Johnson was tapping into the old 'Country' ideology that drew on classical models like the Roman poet Horace, one of whose most famous lines was: Persicos odi, puer, apparatus ('I hate Persian luxury, boy'). The idea that economic surpluses spent on luxury and high living inevitably spelt disaster, for in its train came weakness, lack of civilian virtu and dependence on mercenary armies was an idea that went back at least as far as Machiavelli and was to reach its culminating statement in Edward

Gibbon's famous work on the decline and fall of the Roman Empire, a classic example of 'Country' thinking. For the eighteenth-century Englishman the focus for these concerns was always mainly the British presence in India.

For most British travellers and observers in India before about 1780 the abiding impression of the subcontinent was a place where the squalor of the majority contrasted with the wealth and splendour of the few, making it a perfect specimen of Oriental despotism. A century earlier the traveller Peter Mundy had contrasted the magnificence of the Mughal Emperor in Agra with the plethora of brothels and 'common stews' to be found there. Robert Clive, the great English conqueror of Bengal, called Calcutta one of the most wicked places in the universe and the establishment of British rule there after 1757 did not improve the impression made on fastidious lady travellers like Jemima Kindersley and even on much tougher characters such as William MacIntosh, who reported about Calcutta (though how he can have known anything about Spanish California or hermetically sealed Japan is a moot question):

> It is a truth that, from the western extremity of California to the eastern coast of Japan, there is not a spot where judgement, taste, decency and convenience are so grossly insulted as in that scattered and confused chaos of houses, huts, sheds, streets, lanes, alleys, windings, gullies, sinks and tanks, which, jumbled into an undistinguished mass of filth and corruption, equally offensive to human sense and health, compose the capital of the English Company's Government in India. The very small portion of cleanliness which it enjoys is owing to the familiar intercourse of hungry jackals by night, and ravenous vultures, kites and crows by day. In like manner it is indebted to the smoke raised in public streets, in temporary huts and sheds, for any respite it enjoys from mosquitoes, the natural productions of stagnant and putrid waters.

Concern about luxury, degeneracy and Oriental despotism was one of three main eighteenth-century motifs that informed English metropolitan discourse about India. The second, a much more positive response to the subcontinent was enthralment with its exotic flora and fauna, itself part of the rage for faraway places and captivating tales of savage lands. It is probably true to say that a bedazzled response to Indian wildlife has, at least until the recent near-extinction of many species, been a staple of the European response to India. As early as 1616 Edward Terry in *Purchas his Pilgrimes* emphasised this aspect of the East:

Lest this remote country should seem like an earthly Paradise without any discommodities, I must needs take notice there of many Lions, Tigers, Wolves, Jackals (which seem to be wild dogs) and many other harmful beasts. In their rivers are many Crocodiles and on the Land overgrown Snakes with other venomous and pernicious creatures. In our houses there we often meet with Scorpions, whose stinging is most sensible and deadly, if the patient have not presently some Oil that is made of them, to anoint the part affected, which is a present cure. The abundance of Flies in those parts do likewise much annoy us, for in the heat of the day their numberless number is such that we can be quiet in no place for them, they are ready to cover our meat as soon as it is placed on the table, and therefore we have men that stand on purpose with napkins to fright them away when we are eating; in the night likewise we are much disquieted with Mosquitoes, like our gnats but somewhat less; and in their great cities, there are such abundance of big hungry rats, that they often bite a man as he lieth on his bed.

The only difference in sensibility between Terry and Mark Twain writing almost 400 years later is that Twain evinces the Victorian confidence that Man now has the upper hand and can afford to turn danger into romance: 'The land of dreams and romance, of fabulous wealth and fabulous poverty, of splendour and rags, of palaces and hovels, of famine and pestilence, of genii and giants and Aladdin lamps, of tigers and elephants, the cobra and the jungle, the country of a hundred nations and a hundred tongues, of a thousand religions and two million gods.'
Both Twain and Terry put their finger on an important truth: it was the animals dangerous to man that excited most interest and curiosity – the saltwater crocodile; the python, the cobra and its larger cousin found in Assam and the far eastern parts, the king cobra or hamadryad; the leopard, the wild hog and the bear. But two fearsome creatures above all dominated the eighteenth-century imagination: the tiger and the elephant; and those who care to speculate on the birth–death schema adumbrated in the introduction may care to note that the most famous poem about the tiger (symbolic of the creative imagination) was written by William Blake, born in the same year as Clive's great victory at Plassey. From the 1750s onwards tigers became the primary association with India in most British minds, as the conquest of Bengal brought India's most magnificent carnivore into direct contact with white soldiers and hunters. It is true that even before the British came to India tigers had been extensively displaced from their historical habitat by the conversion of lands for agriculture, but the East India Company's policies of land reclamation made further inroads into

the big cat's historical fastnesses and brought on many of the man-versus-tiger confrontations that so thrilled a reading population drunk on exotica. Burke, always acute to historical trends, explicitly had the tiger in mind when he discussed the association of fear with the sublime: 'Look at . . . [an] animal of prodigious strength, and what is your idea before reflection? Is it that this strength will be subservient to you? . . . No: the emotion you feel is, lest this enormous strength should be employed to the purposes of rapine and destruction . . . The Sublime . . . come upon us in the gloomy forest, and in the howling wilderness, in the form of . . . the tiger, the panther or rhinoceros.' George Stubbs, the most famous and original animal painter of his time who was just reaching his peak in 1759, liked to display combats of lion versus tiger, though he did not commit the egregious mistake made in James Ward's animal pictures painted later in the century where the lion symbolises Britain and the tiger India; in reality, as we know very clearly from the obscene animal fights staged by the Ancient Romans in the arena, the tiger would win such a fight every time.

Tigers in turn link by an inevitable association of ideas with elephants. The eighteenth-century rage for the new, the strange and the exotic, embracing savages both noble and ignoble from the Iroquois to the Polynesians of Tahiti, extended to the animal kingdom. The rhinoceros exhibited in Venice in 1751 and later the first giraffe sent to Europe by the Pasha of Egypt to the King of France were part of this trend. The elephant made an impact because the great pachyderm had been rarely seen in Europe since the Middle Ages (Louis XIV, the lucky recipient of one of the beasts, was a notable exception), since the early vogue for them in the Ancient World, as a shock weapon in war, in public spectacles in the arena or as status symbols, came to an end and they gradually became extinct in North Africa and the Middle East, the principal meeting points between eastern and western worlds. Once the Europeans gained a foothold in India the situation changed rapidly for elephants played a multi-faceted role in Hindu life. In the elaborate pantheon headed by the trinity of Brahma, Vishnu and Shiva, the elephant Airavata, mount of Indra, god of rain, and believed to have emerged from Brahma's eggshell, has an honoured role. And the two elephants Mahapadma and Saumanasa are the massive pillars of the Earth, who bear the world on their gigantic heads. Buddhism also co-opted the elephant: in his penultimate reincarnation, the future Buddha was Vessantara, son of a mighty king who derived his power from a miraculous elephant that granted his every wish; when Buddhism was forced to migrate from India to other parts of Asia, it took elephant myths, themes and iconography with it. At the purely pragmatic level, in India elephants were the visible symbol of kingly or princely power. Only great lords with huge wealth could afford to hunt dangerous big game from the safety of an elephant's howdah, for even a horseman was not safe against a charging tiger, leopard or buffalo. And by hunting tigers on elephants India's rulers proved their 'benevolence' – they were protecting villagers and their live-stock against a terrible threat – their courage and their majesty, thereby inculcating the all-important deference of 'inferiors' to superiors. For all these reasons – the pleasure in a dangerous 'sport', keeping the village toilers grateful and loyal and, most of all, demonstrating the 'ornamen-talism' of Empire – the incoming British rulers would eventually embrace the cult of tiger-hunting by elephant with almost more avidity than the native oligarchs they displaced.

The third aspect of the British in India is the most controversial. Exploitation, both in the technical economic sense of extracting a surplus, and in the cultural and moral sense, was an early reality, which some accepted as a fact of life but more thoughtful souls worried about. The question that still exercises our best minds – exactly what lies behind the huge differential in power and wealth between First and Third Worlds – was raised by Prince Rasselas in Johnson's 1759 classic but Johnson/Imlac typically provides an anodyne answer. Rasselas poses the question sharply: 'By what means are the Europeans thus powerful or why, since they can so easily visit Asia and Africa for trade or conquest, cannot the Asiatics and Africans invade their coast, plant colonies in their port, and give laws to their natural princes? The same wind that carries them back would bring us thither.' Imlac replies lamely that the Europeans have more knowledge, and knowledge is power, but that scarcely explains how a maritime nation of eight million could aspire to subdue a subcontinent of (in 1759) roughly 200 million. Imlac concedes the economic supremacy but not the moral: 'Europeans are less happy than we, but they are not happy. Human life is everywhere a state in which much is to be endured, and little is to be enjoyed.' But many more thoughtful observers thought that the conquest of India ought to have a clearer rationale, for otherwise it was vulnerable to the very charge of pointlessness that Voltaire brought against the French occu-pation of Canada. It was another of the leading writers of 1759, Edmund Burke, who would, some twenty years later, sum up the case against India when he spoke witheringly of the influx of the British:

> Animated with all the avarice of age, and all the impetuous ardour of youth, they roll in, one after another, wave after wave, while nothing presents itself to the view of the unhappy natives, except an inter-minable prospect of new flights of voracious birds of passage, with appetites insatiable for a food which is continually wasting under their

attacks. Every other conqueror, Arab, Tartar or Persian, has left behind him some monument, either of royal splendour or of useful benefi-cence. England has erected neither churches, nor hospitals, nor schools, nor palaces. If tomorrow we were expelled from Hindostan, nothing would remain to indicate that it had been possessed during the inglo-rious period of our dominion by any better tenants than the orang-outang or the tiger.

Few such voices were raised in 1759, when hegemony in India was thought a global prize more important than possession of North America.

And so it was that, halfway round the world and several continents away from North America or the Caribbean, another grim struggle for mastery was taking place. The Indian subcontinent was the next venue in the year of victories. In January 1759 the battle for Madras raged with a ferocity rare even in the far-from-gentle Seven Years War, as 8,000 French and Indian troops were attempting to batter their way into the fortress of Fort St George, occupied by 4,000 British and sepoy defenders. This citadel was the heart of the so-called 'white town' – the administrative centre of the British East India Company in southern India. Already the 'black town', home to more than 50,000 Indians, lay smouldering in ruins, more a bomb site or a charnel house than a centre for human habitation. Shells and mortar bombs screamed and whizzed overhead in an endless cacophony. The acrid stench of dead and dying human flesh mingled with the black smoke from a hundred fires. During the terrible two-month siege of Madras, which lasted from mid-December 1758 to mid-February 1759, at least one-third of the combatants became casualties. On the French side alone, the toll was 1,200 European troops killed, wounded or deserted. Out of 215 French officers, eighty-two were on the casualty roster. The sixty-strong Mauritius volunteers of the 'Île de France' company left forty-one dead before Madras. Other statistics are just as eloquent. The British defenders used up 1,768 barrels of gunpowder, 26,554 cannonballs, 7,502 mortar shells, 2,000 hand grenades and fired 200,000 cartridges from their muskets. Yet the French failed to take Madras, and many said that this was the fault of just one man, Thomas Arthur Lally, Comte de Lally-Tollendal.

Bonnie Prince Charlie may have been the highest-ranking Jacobite in France, but he was far from the only one caught up in the Seven Years War. The followers of the House of Stuart seemed indeed to be ubiq-uitous. In Europe Lord Clare, newly promoted as Marshal of France, had the highest profile, but in Prussia Frederick the Great leaned heavily on the advice of Earl Marischal Keith. The weakness of the Jacobite

The campaign for India, 1759

movement by this time was principally that both grandees cordially detested Charles Edward, and he them. But there were many other veterans of the '45 in significant positions, not least the Chevalier de Johnstone in Canada. The year 1758 saw the most notable diaspora within the Jacobite diaspora, for the Comte de Lally-Tollendal was nominated Syndic of the French East India Company, Commissary for the King and Commandant-General of all French establishments in India. Lally had distinguished himself at the Battle of Fontenoy in 1745, commanding a detachment of the Irish Brigade in the service of France (the 'Wild Geese') and had worked tirelessly for Charles Edward in the winter of 1745–46, when more vigorous French support for the Jacobite army in Scotland might well have led to a Stuart restoration in the three British kingdoms. His promotion was unexpected. As recently as early 1757 he had been a fairly minor intriguer, meeting secretly with the Bonnie Prince, the Duc de Richelieu and other pro-Stuart elements.

Lally made his mark with the Compagnie des Indes Orientales when he produced a well-argued memoir wholly endorsing the official line of the Compagnie in the controversy aroused by the administration of Joseph François, Marquis de Dupleix, who had been recalled to France from India in 1755. The directors of France's Compagnie were thereafter determined that Lally should have supreme command in India and lobbied tirelessly until they got their way. The supreme decision-maker at this stage was the Minister of War, Comte d'Argenson, who was finally unseated as minister by Madame de Pompadour in the murky period following the attempted assassination of Louis XV by Damiens in 1757. D'Argenson knew Lally of old and had worked closely with him during France's sincere but 'too little, too late' bid to assist the Jacobites in 1746. He recognised Lally's faults only too well. Lally was, said the War Minister, an intemperate, cross-grained man who did not suffer fools gladly – and by 'fools' he meant anyone who did not agree with him. Aged fifty-eight, Lally was imperious, short-tempered and despotic: he bullied subordinates and rowed with equals. The classic bull in a china shop, Lally was a hopeless politician, as he blurted out to their faces exactly what he thought of people and, since he possessed the gift of invective, such people rarely forgot or forgave the tirade. D'Argenson was right. Lally had made too many enemies and was far too inept to be given such a sensitive post as Indian supremo, which required a singular combination of political and military talents, plus the need for finesse and subtlety of mind.

Lally's expedition to India took an unconscionable time to establish itself in united form. First there was a dispute about the number of troops Louis XV could spare. At first projected as a massive enterprise, the force destined for India was gradually whittled down to a single regiment of Lorrainers and a regiment from Lally's Irish Brigade, each in two battalions of 510 men, together with a 150-strong detachment of the Royal Artillery. Added to the Compagnie's 1,000 troops, this would give the French in India an impressive fighting nucleus of more than 3,000 seasoned troops. These regiments were entrusted to a naval convoy commanded by the Comte d'Aché. The first division set sail as early as 30 December 1756 and spent eight months getting to India, making lengthy stopovers at Madagascar and Mauritius en route. D'Aché took even longer to transport Lally and the rest of the expedition. Leaving L'Orient in north-west France in early May, d'Aché's corps took a full year to get to India, after an interminable series of storms and diseases, which claimed the lives of nineteen officers and 307 enlisted men. Disease was also mainly the reason for the delay to the first division, but even without illness Lally's deputy the Chevalier de Soupire was already expressing grave doubts about the physique of the troops in the Lorraine regiment. When he arrived in India, on 8 September 1757, Soupire had further complaints. As he told the new Minister of War, the Marquis de Paulmy (by one of those quirks of the *ancien régime* he happened to be the Comte d'Argenson's nephew), the Commissary that Lally had been sent out to replace, Duval de Leyrit (a stop-gap appointment made after Dupleix's recall), had done nothing at all while in office. With French forces hugely outnumbering the British in terms of white troops on the Coromandel coast, Leyrit had failed to exploit his local military superiority, pleading lack of money.

But Leyrit was just a minor item on a long list of considerations that gave Lally pause as he too made his leisurely way to India. The Anglo-French struggle for mastery on the Indian subcontinent in many ways mirrored the similar conflict in North America and had a similarly protracted history. The story may be said to have begun on the last day of the sixteenth century when the London trading house known as the Honourable East India Company was given its charter by an ageing Queen Elizabeth I. The Mughal emperors had allowed the East India Company to set up its first trading post on the coast north of Bombay in 1613, and the Company added to its tally of stations in 1639, 1664 and 1696, with posts founded in, respectively, Madras, Bombay and Calcutta. By 1700 the Company had just one serious competitor for Indian trade: the French company based at Pondicherry on the south-east coast and its outpost at Chandernagore on the Hooghly river. But in the early eighteenth century the British East India Company was one of the great success stories of the financial revolution introduced in England after 1688. Satisfying what seemed like a limitless demand for tea, silks, fine china, chintz and calico, it declared annual dividends that never fell below 6 per cent, provided one-fifth of Britain's annual imports with yearly sales of £2 million and, during the War of Austrian Succession (1740–48) was even able to lend the British government £1 million. The star of the London stock exchange, it was a financial institution second only to the Bank of England itself.

It was the death of the last great Mughal emperor Aurangzeb, in 1707, that politicised the Company in India. The Mughal Empire, already financially bankrupt, was weakened still further by interminable wars of succession between Aurangzeb's sons. The vultures gathered for the feast over the ailing body. From 1739 on, Afghans and Persians poured across India's north-west frontier in a series of successful invasions. Farther south the empire disintegrated into a series of princely states: Bengal, Hyderabad, Oudh, Mysore and the increasingly powerful Maratha Confederacy in the Deccan. By the 1740s the East India Company was sufficiently alarmed by the chaos and threat to its position that it formed its own army and began recruiting sepoys. When war broke out in 1740 between Britain and France, the under-funded French Compagnie des Indes began cultivating the rulers of southern India in an attempt to increase its revenue and territories. A key event was the appointment in 1742 of Joseph François, Marquis de Dupleix, as Governor-General of the Compagnie, based in Pondicherry. Dupleix quickly realised two things: that a European power with a handful of European troops, and allied to local potentates, could be a major military player in India's martial maelstrom; and that the Compagnie could not survive as a trading company alone, but needed to become an imperial power, with sources of fixed revenues, taxes, tributes, tithes, monopolies and other privileges. Above all, the Compagnie had to make Indian operations pay for themselves, so that the surplus extracted from India covered all the expenses of local and European troops and still showed a profit.

For ten years, during his golden years, Dupleix scored dramatic successes. He made the Carnatic area of India virtually a French protectorate and extended his influence into central India and the Deccan. But his triumph was always built on shifting sands. India provided opportunities for great victories and personal fiefs, but was a snakepit of suddenly shifting personal alliances, of assassinations and *coups d'état*, where the careful work of a decade could be undone in a single day. Moreover, because Dupleix was a kind of uncrowned king, he had to conceal many of his ulterior political intentions from his paymaster, the Compagnie in Paris. And in France he had many enemies, jealous of his success and just waiting for his elaborately spun web in India to unravel. But his worst problem was the envy of the British. It was only the timely arrival of the Royal Navy in 1747 that prevented Madras from falling to the French, and by then the British were fully alerted to the threat to their position posed by Dupleix. From the autumn of 1750 the British East India Company had Dupleix firmly in its sights. Eager to avoid a general war, Louis XV placated the British by a series of conferences in London in 1753–54, where the two East India companies tried to resolve their differences. The end result was a treaty in December 1754 in which the French effectively repudiated the work of Dupleix.

One of the reasons for the demoralisation of the French was the rise of Britain's latest military genius, Robert Clive, who since 1746 had swept all before him, crowning his exploits with the incredible victory of Arcot near Madras in 1751, against odds of fifty to one. The English Governor of Madras and his French equivalent at Pondicherry had concluded a nominal peace in 1745 but it was a truce only, and the cessation of hostilities on the subcontinent was even more short-lived than in North America. The British fortified the capitals of their east coast 'presidencies' at Madras and Calcutta, and the French did likewise at Pondicherry and Chandernagore. Every move by one side was countered by the other. When the French under the Marquis de Bussy made forays into the interior in 1755, the British East India Company countered by sending an expedition to Hyderabad and Mysore on the plateau of the Deccan, beyond the high coastal mountain ranges. But by the end of 1755 the expedition to the Deccan hardly seemed necessary as the French trumped their own ace by recalling Dupleix to Paris to answer charges of corruption. The great French imperial genius was summoned home in disgrace.

When Louis XV and his Council decided, in the autumn of 1756, to send a major army and naval force to sustain the Compagnie des Indes, they could hardly have imagined that their English rivals would already be on the ropes, prostrated by a new enemy and from an unexpected quarter. The British used the lull in fighting the French to turn and deal with the Coromandel pirates who preyed on British and French shipping alike from their base at Geriah, 150 miles south of Bombay. The pirate chieftain Tulagree Angria attempted to blunt the force of the British offensive by trying to suborn their Maratha allies. At first the policy seemed hopeless, and the British stormed and took Geriah with surprising ease. Yet Angria's seed had fallen on fertile soil. The Nawab of Bengal, Alivardi Khan, a staunch British ally, died and was succeeded by his twenty-seven-year-old grandson Surajah Dowlah, who hated the foreigners. Treacherously he schemed against the British and then acted fast. His armies swarmed over Calcutta and took the East India Company citadel of Fort William after a three-day siege. The guardroom at Fort William, just eighteen feet square, became the scene of an atrocity known to every Victorian schoolboy – the 'Black Hole of Calcutta'. Crammed together with no water and scarcely able to breathe, forty-eight persons died on the night of 20–21 June 1756 and just twenty-three survived. The new Nawab thought he had cleared the British out of Bengal, but he reckoned without Clive. When news of Calcutta's fall reached Madras on 16 August, Clive made immediate preparations to embark troops for the north, even though it was the monsoon season and ships ventured out onto the Indian Ocean in these months only at extreme peril. His boldness paid off, and by January 1757 he was able to retake Calcutta. But his position was precarious. Hugely outnumbered by the Marathas, Clive was not even fully master in his own house, for that bane of the British in pre-1857 India – factionalism between the armed forces and the East India Company – once again made itself felt. Clive wanted to coordinate British strategy in Bengal but was thwarted by Sir Eyre Coote, designated as commander of Fort William by the supreme commander in the Indian theatre, Admiral Charles Watson.

Of Clive's military genius there can surely be no doubt. While Surajah Dowlah prepared a huge army to drive the British into the sea, the dauntless Clive advanced on the headquarters of the French in Bengal, Chandernagore; this was Clive's immediate reaction to the news that the Marquis de Bussy, the most experienced French commander in India, taking advantage of British troubles in the north, had opened a fresh offensive in the Carnatic region of southern India. The Seven Years War saw the British perfecting amphibious operations, and one of the earliest and best examples of the new expertise was the advance on Chandernagore. While Clive took three days to march north from Calcutta to Chandernagore, the Royal Navy ingeniously navigated the shoals, bars and man-made obstacles of the Hooghly river and was able to bring its guns to bear on the French presidency. Clive's brilliantly successful siege finished off the French in Bengal, but his worries were by no means at an end. He knew well enough, that, once the monsoon ended, the Royal Navy would have go south to Coromandel to defend the East India Company against Bussy's offensive, at which point Surajah Dowlah would undoubtedly strike again at Calcutta. Clive guessed correctly: the Nawab was even then in secret negotiations with Bussy for an alliance that would catch the British in a pincer. To overthrow the Nawab was crucial, but how could this be done? Time and numbers were against Clive, for the summer season would soon rule out effective campaigning and meanwhile how could 700 European troops and 2,000 sepoys contend against a Maratha army of 50,000–70,000?

Clive's brilliant and almost incredible victory at Plassey on 23 June 1757 was the answer. True, like Henry Tudor at Bosworth, he won because he had detached a vital part of the enemy army through treachery. Mir Jaffir, a key Indian ruler who hated and despised the Nawab, was a principal element in the Maratha army. Clive made him over, and at Plassey Mir Jaffir played the Lord Stanley of the piece, having finally decided that his future lay with the British rather than with the Nawab. In the turbulent aftermath of Plassey, Surajah Dowlah was overthrown and murdered while Mir Jaffir became the new Nawab of Bengal. It was therefore Lally's ill fortune that he arrived in India when all the high drama was over, the British were consolidated in Bengal, and the Royal Navy was free to leave Calcutta and concentrate against the French threat in the south. Lally was classically the wrong man in the wrong job at the wrong time, and his official instructions from the War Ministry might be thought to constitute a mission impossible, even if he had not been. Obsessed with financial crisis and the venality of its administrative personnel abroad, the French court gave Lally orders that were bound to bring him into conflict with the corrupt officials of the Compagnie des Indes. Where Dupleix had brought glory to France by his forward policy, Lally was told to forget about expansionism and concentrate on retrenchment and holding actions.

Lally, in effect, was ordered to curb the contumacity of Bussy and crack down hard on corrupt officialdom; unfortunately Louis XV's Council did not tell him where he was to acquire the political nous or even the day-to-day support to accomplish the task. Some of the wording in his official orders is no more than verbiage, pious hopes or bromides:

> Since the troubles in India have been the source of a great number of private fortunes, seemingly acquired overnight and those who have not yet hit the jackpot hope to do so by the same corrupt short-cuts . . . the Comte de Lally will take great pains to root out this spirit of greed and cupidity, and this will be one of the greatest services he could ever do for the Company. M. Lally is to forget about expansion in the interior and to disregard whatever the English are doing there; his entire concern is for the safety and security of the naval bases and the maritime forts.

The instruction to root out greed in India, when that was the sole motive for officers and officials serving there in the first place, may well be described as Versailles's equivalent of a papal bull against the comet. But Lally was also being asked to fight the British at the same time as changing human nature. Clive, in his later career, cleaned up the corruption in the British East India Company, but made so many enemies that he in turn was accused of embezzlement; he died with the shadow of defalcation over him and may even have committed suicide as a result of his malign reputation. Yet not even a genius like Clive could have cleansed the Augean stables and defeated the French simultaneously. Lally, no genius, was expected to perform the equivalent feat.

It was symptomatic of Lally's ill fortune that he went in harm's way even before landing in India. D'Aché, the naval commander, was already jealous of Lally, and was a stickler for protocol and paranoid about imagined slights; he was also a malcontent who groused eternally about the lack of support given him by the Ministry of Marine and was concerned always for the safety of his ships rather than the survival of France's Indian possessions. The day after sighting Pondicherry, he encountered the Royal Navy squadron under its energetic commander Vice-Admiral Sir George Pocock. Although the French had ten ships of the line and a frigate, against seven of the line on the enemy side, d'Aché was always nervous about engagements with the British. Nevertheless, on 29 April battle was joined at 3 p.m. and a furious fight continued until nearly 5 p.m., when d'Aché bore away with his entire squadron. The English had sustained severe damage in their masts and rigging, the French in the hulls of their vessels, reflecting the different gunnery tactics employed by the two sides. But one consequence of pouring roundshot into the hulls (the British approach) rather than chainshot and barshot into masts, yards and rigging (the French approach) was that French casualties were higher: 400 killed and wounded, as against 118 losses taken by the British. But the French tactics did have one clear advantage: their ships were able to bear away at speed, running before the wind while the British pursuers, with ripped and shivered sails and spars, limped along at about one-third the speed. Both sides were heavily criticised for the indecisive encounter. D'Aché had the perfect excuse, since he had sent Lally off in the seventy-four-gun *Comte de Provence* and the frigate to make landfall at Pondicherry, and now claimed that he could have won the duel with Pocock if only Lally had not taken his best warship. Pocock was heavily criticised for pursuing the French instead of making for Pondicherry and getting to windward of d'Aché, which would have prevented the French expedition from landing. But Pocock, it seems, was mesmerised by the recent tragic example of his cousin Admiral Byng, who had been executed for seeming not to fight hard enough at Minorca, and was determined that no one could fault him for reckless courage.

Meanwhile Lally landed at Pondicherry, but not before another singularly bad omen impressed the superstitious Irishman. As the *Comte de Provence* came alongside the harbour, an artillery salute boomed out for the new Governor but the artillery officers had forgotten to re-sight their guns and some of the shells hit the warship. The cross-grained Lally stormed ashore and immediately found fault with the military preparations, notably the lack of draft oxen and porters, and raged at Leyrit on the grounds that all preparations for the campaign should have been completed eight months ago. Lally gave orders to attack the East India Company trading station of Gondelour and its protecting fastness, Fort St David. This was a tough nut to crack without careful preparation, for Fort St David had the reputation of being the strongest fort on the Coromandel coast: although it lacked bomb-proof shelters, it had numerous outworks, which a clever defender could use tellingly during a long siege. Lally demanded 'action this day' and proceeded the day after his arrival to the French camp outside Gondelour. In vain did Leyrit lament, 'Is it my fault if M. de Lally rushes his operations and attacks works before he has provided himself with what he needs to attack them?' Lally wanted an immediate success to report to his superiors in Paris. Gondelour, a walled town but with decayed and worthless fortifications, looked like easy pickings. One mile south of Fort St David, it needed a large garrison to have any chance of being defended successfully and the commander of Fort St David could not spare the men. Lally therefore got his walkover victory: on 3 May he demanded the surrender of the town and got it the very same day.

Everyone realised that this easy victory was simply the prelude to an assault on the much tougher target of Fort St David. In a combat between Lally's army of 5,000, half of them French troops, and 400 European defenders of Fort St David, there could be only one outcome. There was a fortnight's lull during which Lally gradually brought up from Pondicherry the stores and artillery he needed. On 17 May 1758 he carried the outworks by storm. The British sepoys did not like the odds and deserted en masse before Lally's men got to grips with them; the British garrison soon learned to its chagrin that almost all the sepoys and local troops had fled into the countryside. On 26 May Lally, who had teased the fort hitherto by throwing merely a few random shells and mortars from Gondelour, opened the first of four breaching batteries and progressively began to pound the fort into submission. On 2 June the garrison surrendered, after the British Governor had reported to his superiors that most of the embrasures had been destroyed by enemy fire and that his effectives were down to 120 Europeans and 120 sepoys; additionally, he blamed the military commander, the Swiss officer Polier de Bottens, for not putting up as vigorous and protracted a defence as he might have done. Lally, though, introduced a new ruthlessness into the campaigns of the subcontinent and served warning that he intended to wage war in a new way. He ordered the fortress razed to the ground and all East India Company houses gutted. In fairness to him, it should be added that the new ruthlessness was in conformity with clear orders from the War Ministry. The way was now open for what seemed like the inevitable siege of Madras and its equally inevitable fall.

Yet at this crucial juncture Lally allowed himself to be sidetracked into a futile native war. Its objective was to compel the Prince of Tanjore to honour the bond for seventy lakhs (about twenty-four million livres) that he had given the French and their ally Chanda Sahib in 1749 as a war indemnity, to prevent the invasion of his territory; the Prince had actually never had the slightest intention of paying the sum. Why Lally chose this military diversion is disputed, but it is likely that he found himself acutely short of money. He had arrived in India with about two million livres of campaigning money, but this had been immediately swallowed up by Pondicherry's debts. The other reason for the failure to move immediately against Madras was that d'Aché would not cooperate and, in particular, refused to engage Pocock's fleet which lay unbeaten off the coast between Pondicherry and Madras. D'Aché was adamant that he could not attack Pocock until his fleet was better provisioned, and here he had the ghost of a case, for both sailors and soldiers in the French force openly grumbled about the poor quality of the food on offer. Yet it is likely that the motive uppermost in d'Aché's mind for refusing to cooperate was simply that he wished to cruise away south in search of some richly laden English Indiamen imminently expected in Indian waters.

Yet even if Lally was genuinely not yet ready to undertake the siege of Madras, he should at least have struck north, cleared the British out of the Arcot country, taken all posts and forts between Pondicherry and Madras, and confined the enemy in the latter town until he was ready to make his move. Whatever arguments might have been advanced for the Tanjore option, it was clear that its outcome would not affect France's overall Indian strategy; only the fall of Madras could do that. It has therefore been speculated that Lally fell under the malign influence of a Jesuit priest named Père Lavaur, who had been a confidant and agent of Dupleix. It was true that Lally was devout and susceptible to such an influence, but to suggest that priestcraft alone doomed France's Indian campaign would be absurd. The truth is that Lally had nearly as many enemies in Pondicherry as in Madras. Foremost among them was the old Governor-General Leyrit and his staff and cronies, with whom Lally had clashed violently since the day of his arrival. On 15 May Lally acted exactly as d'Argenson had predicted: he reproached Leyrit directly for his 'lethargy and indifference to the success of military operations' and accused him of having done nothing for eight months except dispute with Soupire about their respective prerogatives. Furious over the supply situation during the siege of Fort David, Lally also announced publicly that he would henceforth employ only honest men and would throw the peculators and speculators out of India. The side effect of this was to make the cold, bureaucratic and venal Leyrit a deadly enemy. It would not be long before Lally did the same thing with Bussy, a man (unlike Leyrit) of genuine ability.

Just before leaving for Tanjore, Lally tried to coordinate his military movements with Bussy, then campaigning in the Deccan. Lally's letter, though suffused with a friendly spirit and what he took to be wit and charm, implicitly insulted Bussy by stating that he was involved in a sideshow; and he scarcely sweetened the pill by going on to ask Bussy to send money. 'My mission from the king and the Company,' he wrote, 'is to throw the British out of India and it matters not to me in the slightest that an older brother might be disputing with a younger one in the Deccan or that such and such a rajah is at daggers drawn with such and such a nabob.' He ordered Bussy to make all haste to join him outside Madras with his troops, leaving the young Marquis de Conflans in charge in the Deccan with a policing force. While admonishing Bussy sanctimoniously that the days of expansionism and the forward policy were over, Lally illogically looked ahead to the day when, with Madras taken, they could press on together to the Ganges. But the letter was simply another in his litany of mistakes. To recall Bussy at this juncture, after twenty years' experience in India, and when he was at the height of his influence with the Indian princes and held the preponderance of power in the Deccan, was egregious stupidity. Bussy obeyed the order and made a magnanimous reply, but pointed out that the result of his obedience might well be the loss of the Deccan.

Lally then marched south in leisurely style, taking a month to arrive outside Tanjore. Everywhere he went, he astonished observers by his attitudes, which oscillated wildly between the cavalier and the authoritarian. Bored with detail, he seems almost to have thought that military expeditions should proceed by a kind of spontaneous locomotion; when structural inadequacies in logistics or Commissariat showed up, Lally looked around for a guilty individual on whom he could fasten responsibility. A martinet and petty disciplinarian, he could overreact or go over the top at a moment's notice. Most of all, he revealed his besetting fault as an India hand: the belief that sheer military force was all. He did not even remotely have Clive's gift for dealing with Indian rulers. There was no subtlety, no mixture of threat and blandishment, no antennae alive to the possibility of cajolery, corruption or co-optation. Lally's method was to threaten, then, if the Indians did not do his bidding, to use force against them. All the time he allowed the financial tail to wag the military dog. On 27 June Père Lavaur sidetracked him again by suggesting that there were four lakhs to be made by engineering a palace revolution in Udayarpalayam. When Lally occupied the Tanjorean seaport of Nagur, he sold the rights of plunder to a colonel of hussars for two lakhs.

Not surprisingly, then, the French campaign in Tanjore soon ended in debacle. It took them until 18 July to arrive at Tanjore city, as not enough bullocks had been requisitioned to transport the artillery and ammunition. Lally's men were already starving when they reached Devikottai. There they found a magazine of paddy but, because of incompetent administration, lacked the pestles to beat it into rice. Then the men started to go down with heatstroke because the Commissariat had failed to provide enough tents and the troops were forced to bed down under the broiling sun. Early in July the French army ran dangerously short of gunpowder, and only a frantic scrambling to Negapatam and Tranquebar to haggle with Dutch and Danish traders secured Lally the supplies he needed. At Tiravular, Lally lost his temper when a hunt for temple treasure proved unavailing; he seized six Brahmins and had them blown from cannons on the grounds that they were spies. Hoping to cow the Tanjoreans by these proofs of toughness, Lally succeeded only in convincing them that their best hope lay in helping the defaulting raja to defend their homeland. Even when Lally's army finally 'sat down' outside the walls of Tanjore, the troops found they were in no condition to press the attack as they were short of cannonballs and the infantry had just fifteen rounds per man.

As the French languished in the heat outside the walls, hostilities became largely a matter of bid and counter-bid. The recalcitrant ruler offered three lakhs; Lally demanded ten and an alliance against the British. When Lally finally made serious moves to attack the town by bringing up battering rams, the raja offered five lakhs, the provisioning of the army, 1,000 coolies and 300 horsemen. Lally dithered over whether to accept and finally did so, but the delay led to misunderstanding and finally withdrawal of the offer. Lally then raged that he would exile the raja to Mauritius when he caught him, which simply determined the Prince of Tanjore to resist to the bitter end. Lally's officers now convinced him that only frontal assault would cut the Gordian knot. He ordered batteries improvised, but these were vulnerable to Tanjorean sortie, since they were not protected by earthworks. But such was the shortage of ammunition that the French were forbidden to shoot back when fired on by the city batteries. At last the batteries were within range and the fall of the city seemed imminent. Suddenly news came through that Pocock had beaten d'Aché off Karikal and that Pondicherry itself was under threat. Lally called another council of war and explained the situation. The shortage of ammunition (still only twenty rounds per man) and gunpowder meant that all firepower would be exhausted in a successful assault on Tanjore, and Pondicherry would be left defenceless. Swallowing the tremendous loss of face involved in raising the siege, Lally withdrew to the coast, but not before he had to beat off with difficulty a major sortie from Tanjore. A dispirited, barefoot, half-naked, starving French army limped back to Pondicherry. By his stupidity and incompetence Lally had chalked up losses of 500 men killed, wounded or deserted.

Worse was to come. He reached Karikal on 18 August 1858 to learn that news of d'Aché's defeat had been wildly exaggerated. He had been worsted but by no means annihilated. The sequence of events was largely a function of the age-old regular military versus East India Company rivalry that plagued both sides. Almost as soon as Lally marched south to Tanjore, d'Aché announced that he intended to withdraw to Mauritius for the monsoon season. Since this would leave the British with naval mastery of the Coromandel coast at the precise moment Lally wanted to advance on Madras, the Jacobite commander sent his aide the Comte d'Estaing to Pondicherry with strict orders: not only was d'Aché not to withdraw to Mauritius, but he was to attack Pocock at once. In response d'Aché behaved oddly, obeying the first part but not the second part of the instructions. Finally, on 27 July, learning that Pocock was approaching, he set sail from Pondicherry but kept to windward of the English. The two fleets came in sight of each other on 1 August and spent two days manoeuvring for position. It was the afternoon of 3 August before they closed for action, and in a two-hour slugging match, beginning at about 1.20 p.m. the French fleet had the worse of it. The battle was indecisive in the sense that d'Aché's armada remained in existence, but in terms of losses it was a definite British victory: d'Aché sustained losses of 492 dead and wounded men against 197 in Pocock's ranks. But after this bruising experience d'Aché was jittery and no longer fancied the odds. Ignoring all instructions from Lally, he made ready to bear away to Mauritius, intending to re-equip his fleet with spars, sails and rope.

Lally arrived in Pondicherry before d'Aché got to sea and a bitter altercation ensued, with the Irishman raging, threatening and blustering, then calming down and trying cajolery. At first Lally tried to browbeat d'Aché, waving his commission from Louis XV and even ordering the ships' captains to obey him and disregard the Admiral. When this proved unavailing, Lally offered to give d'Aché a further 1,500 men who could act as marines and board Royal Navy vessels when the two sides came to close quarters. Finally Lally calmly stated an obvious truth: that unless the French navy stayed off the coast of India, not only could he not mount his offensive against Madras, but Pondicherry itself would be vulnerable to Pocock's incursions. But d'Aché was adamant: his own orders allowed him to exercise discretion when so many of his men were wounded or down with scurvy, and that was exactly what he intended to do. At a final, desperate interview on 2 September Lally asked d'Aché at least to delay his departure until mid-October. D'Aché flatly refused but, mindful of possible future courts martial, got all his captains to sign a document attesting that their departure for Mauritius was a unanimous decision. He sailed on 3 September and arrived at Mauritius on 13 October. He was able to perform a small service for Lally by sending on immediately a frigate from France carrying one million livres.

Once again Lally had proved that he lacked the abilities for supreme command in India. It is true that d'Aché was a prickly, difficult individual but Lally, for all his driving energy, had no idea how to win hearts and minds or to make common cause with awkward colleagues. Now his plan to assault Madras was more hazardous than it would have been had he pressed on with it in June. For one thing, the British defenders at Madras had been preparing assiduously for the coming conflict, laying in provisions and gunpowder, strengthening defences and even managing to secure a few hundred reinforcements from England. Military–civilian conflict was prevented by a standing order from the East India Company that, in the event of a threat to Madras, the civilian council was to be suspended and martial law assumed. Furthermore, all outlying posts and garrisons were evacuated and the troops pulled back to Madras. The only East India Company possession left between Pondicherry and Madras by autumn 1758 was a garrison at Chingleput, strategically placed to harry Lally's lines of communications. The intelligence with which the British made their plans demoralised the weak sisters in Pondicherry like Leyrit, who advocated attacking a soft target in the south, such as Trichinoroli. But at a council of war Lally easily secured backing for the attack on Madras. The key consideration was finance. The troops' pay was already in arrears, and the taking of Madras seemed the only way to sort out the financial mess in Pondicherry. As Lally put it in one of his magniloquent exhortations: 'Better to die fighting the enemy than starve to death.'

By the beginning of 1759, then, the stage was set for another major confrontation of the great powers in India. At Conjeveram, where Lally mustered his army, he assembled 3,266 European troops, 4,000 sepoys, twenty siege cannon and ten mortars. Against this force the British could oppose just 1,700 Europeans and 2,200 sepoys. As he advanced northwards in November 1758, Lally was amazed to encounter no resistance and to enter a series of deserted posts. Only the issue of Chingleput perplexed him and, as ever with Lally, he dithered about what to do. He could see that on paper this was a vital approach point that should be secured but he could spare neither the men nor the time to besiege the place, which was too strong to be taken by a single, escalade-like attack. He consoled himself with the thought that Madras should fall before this thorn in his rear could assume any significance, and on 12 December his advance guard began probing the outer defences of Madras. Because of the monsoon rains it took a long time for the French army to arrive and get into position, but Lally was cheered by the late arrival of 500 so-called elite cavalry from his Indian ally Raza Sahib.

The Madras of the 1750s was really two towns: the 'black town' where the Indians lived, unfortified and rigidly separated from the British quarter; and the 'white town' at St Thomas's Mount, where the Governor's palace, administrative offices and the residential quarter were located. There was also the citadel of Fort St George, into which the white defenders withdrew on the approach of the French. The British commander, Colonel Stringer Lawrence, had constructed the defences of Fort St George so that it was a tough nut for any attacker to crack. Facing the sea on one side, the citadel was protected on the landward side by a series of bastions, ravelins, reverse slopes, covered walkways and glacis. At the point nearest the 'black town', the outer defences were fortified by an inner wall, allowing a second line of defence. Although Pocock was now in the north and therefore the French, in theory, had control of the sea (though of course d'Aché and his fleet were absent), the defenders had two great advantages: their garrison at Chingleput posed an increasing hazard to French communications and could ambush their convoys; and they themselves enjoyed unanimity of purpose and high morale. The soldiers stuck to their task with grim enthusiasm, having been promised a gratuity of 50,000 rupees if they repulsed the French.

The French, on the other hand, though intermittently effective, were often no more than an indisciplined rabble. On 14 December 1758 Lally's men entered the 'black town'. Meeting no resistance, they sacked and looted in an orgy of rapine and pillage. The British, under their able field commanders Colonel William Draper and Major Cholmondeley Brereton, seized the opportunity to sortie in force: 600 men attacked the scattered

French, but soon became bogged down in confused street fighting. Bloody combat ensued: both sides lost nearly 300 dead and wounded and the British left behind two guns. Although the battle was indecisive, the consequences for French morale were grave, for a major row blew up involving Bussy.

It will be remembered that Lally had already made an enemy of Bussy by ordering him back from the Deccan. Smarting under the humiliation of the recall (which he never forgave), Bussy suddenly produced letters stating categorically that he was to be regarded as Lally's second-in-command. Since this meant that Bussy would then outrank all the regular officers Lally had brought with him (his favourites and cronies), Lally categorically refused to appoint him to the position of Senior Brigadier as clearly set down in the letters from Versailles. Even Lally's loyal officers thought this an arrogant step too far and advised him to confirm Bussy in the rank, but the Irishman, pigheaded as ever, would not listen. Serving as the lowliest Brigadier before Madras, Bussy received a hasty promotion when d'Estaing was captured in the sortie. An altercation then arose between Bussy and one of Lally's cronies, Colonel Crillon, as a result of which the raiders led by Colonel Draper were not cut off. Lally blamed Bussy for the failure and upbraided him publicly in a humiliating scene. Some authorities claim that Bussy was indeed at fault, but if so Lally should have demoted him or censured him in writing. Instead he did what he had already done to Leyrit and so many of the venal officials of the Compagnie des Indes: he humiliated him, making a mortal enemy, yet confirming Bussy in his position. Truly with Lally emotion always conquered reason.

After the dramatic sortie and hard-fought battle on 14 December, the siege of Madras for a short time entered a period of 'phoney war'. For three weeks the French guns remained silent, constrained by lack of ammunition; the British for their part attempted no more costly sallies. The first salvoes from French batteries fell into the town on 2 January 1759, but the defenders managed to knock out these guns temporarily. But on 6 January the first of the French big guns accurately found the range. Five days later a terrifying bombardment commenced; thirty-two artillery pieces shelled the defensive salient remorselessly while mortars obliterated the city with bombs. Yet it proved remarkably difficult to make any impression on the citadel. Consistently winkled out of defensive embrasures, the British as tirelessly re-formed themselves and retook the ground with formidable tenacity. The French managed to spring a mine, only to find that the resultant gap was completely commanded by one of the bastions, making it a killing ground. Man for man the British were unquestionably superior and the French had the disadvantage of bivouacking in the open. Soon morale in Lally's forces plummeted alarmingly: confidence was at rock-bottom, the siege seemed Sisyphean and drunkenness compounded the normal surly indiscipline. Not having been paid for several months, the troops complained vociferously, and, at the limit, deserted. The nadir was reached when 150 French deserters went over to the other side and fought valiantly as defenders.

Beset by myriad difficulties, Lally was not even able to give the siege his undivided attention. Now was revealed the fatuity of the decision to leave Chingleput as an island in the rear. Lally's thinking was that the troops he had left at Pondicherry would prevent any hostile forces from linking up with Chingleput. However, the 'king of the sepoys', Yusuf Khan, moved north from Trichinopoly with an Indian army, initially cutting the road from Pondicherry to Madras and then making a dangerous junction with the British garrison at Chingleput under Captain Achilles Preston. Yusuf and Preston then decided to take Lally's rear in the flank, relieving the pressure on Madras. Yusuf Khan advanced to the Mount and made a good showing against the French, repelling their first attack and capturing two guns. But the victory was dearly won, and Yusuf lost heart. Alleging that his men lacked provisions he retreated to Chingleput at speed, where a reluctant Preston was forced to follow him. Preston received orders to try again to relieve Madras and attempted to rouse Yusuf, but the sepoy army now seemed demoralised; Yusuf temporised and made excuse after lame excuse for not marching. Even though Major John Caillaud, a Clive protégé, managed to make yet another flank attack in February, he too was beaten back after a twelve-hour running fight among the garden walls of the 'white town'.

Lally still had reasonable hopes of eventual victory but, like Napoleon at Waterloo nearly fifty years later, the odds had already reduced to not much more than 60:40. The Blücher of the piece turned out to be Pocock in Bombay. He reasoned, correctly, that illness and lack of supplies would severely weaken the French during a long siege and, further, that the invest-ment of Madras could be prolonged if even a small flotilla of frigates carrying reinforcements got through, the monsoon notwithstanding. So it was that Lally with sinking heart saw a sail appear on the horizon on 30 January. The Royal Navy frigate ran the blockade and landed money and a small company of soldiers; more importantly, it brought the welcome news that the entire fleet was on its way with a fresh army. Animated by this news, the defenders were in good shape to repel the worst that Lally could throw at them. Lally for his part knew that it was now 'do or die'. He was achingly close to success, or so it seemed. The main bastion was destroyed, a breach had been opened up in the defence, the bombs had turned Madras into a wasteland and all houses and buildings lay gutted. Lally asked his officers for one last supreme effort, but they told him that, unless the defenders' big guns could be silenced, the attackers would be mown down in droves as they mounted a final assault. Nevertheless the French guns opened up a massed barrage on the English guns. The fusillade was without effect, and the failure spread a pall of gloom everywhere. Finally, on 16 February 1759, six Royal Navy vessels arrived with 600 troops. When Lally saw them disembark, he used the landing as the pretext for a face-saving withdrawal. The French raised the siege and retreated in two detachments, with Soupire's battalions going to Conjeveram and Lally's to Arcot.

Lally's failure at Madras, which would return to haunt him at the end of the Seven Years War, can be laid partly at his own door and partly at the lacklustre performance of the French artillery. Despite blasting apart virtually everything in sight, the artillerymen had been incompetent in the location of their big guns, their sighting and their accuracy. Their mining operations were hamfisted and they had no answer to the British sappers. Lally made matters worse by constant interference in the day-to-day operations of the artillery park and by ordering the guns to open fire prematurely, before they had the range of the enemy. Not a whit abashed by the debacle, Lally told his superiors that he felt no shame about having failed to take Madras. He wrote to Marshal Belle-Isle, the War Minister, to boast that he had won four battles during the siege and had destroyed Madras so thoroughly that it would not rise again from the ashes for a generation. For Lally, everyone and everything was wrong except himself. His men had been more interested in plundering the 'black town' than in besieging the fort; those who had not deserted he could not trust; and all in all he suggested that both officers and men under his command might do better to follow some trade other than war.

The French were now in a parlous state, with no money in the bank, the cupboard bare, their troops unpaid, all resources exhausted, and the choleric Commander-in-Chief peevishly contemplating throwing up his command. At some level Lally probably realised that by his failure to take Madras he had lost the struggle for India. His much greater British opponent, Robert Clive, certainly intuited this, as his first instinct was to counterattack in the Deccan. Even as Lally marched on Madras the ever-resourceful Clive sent an expedition under Colonel Francis Foorde to central India. Clive saw, even if Lally and his supporters then and since could not, that the French position in the Deccan was fragile, and that only the talents of Bussy had provided the glue to keep the rickety

Franco-Indian alliance in being. Bussy was a superb diplomat who knew the intrigue-sodden world of the Indian princes backwards and maintained French influence in central India as much by his personal authority as by force of arms. Once he was gone, the careful structure he had built up in the Decan collapsed like a house of cards. Clive seized the opportunity presented by the revolt of a power-hungry raja at Visagapatam and despatched Colonel Foorde with an army of 500 Europeans and 1,600 sepoys.

At Talapole on 3 December 1758 the Marquis de Conflans, left in charge after Lally's peremptory summons to Bussy, joined battle with Foorde's force. At first the French seemed to have the upper hand, but they made the catastrophic error of timing their major charge against the sepoys, mistaking them for the British troops because they were wearing red uniforms. Although the French crashed through the sepoy centre, they were then taken in the flank by the real British. Conflans, after losing 150 men plus baggage and artillery, retreated to Masulipatam, there to await the coming of the Indian allies under Salabet Jang. There Foorde caught up with him on 6 March 1759 and besieged him. Foorde's great exploit, a triumph of will power in the teeth of desertion, mutiny and the likelihood of being caught between two fires, has largely gone unsung in the annals of the British in India, overshadowed by the feats of Clive and the servants of the Raj who would come after him. Yet he prevailed. After a month of limp resistance Conflans surrendered, to universal obloquy; his position was not desperate and he was numerically almost equal to the enemy. The consequence was predictable: Salabet Jang, the principal power in the land and Bussy's old ally, declared for the British, disgusted that his former friend and ally was no longer on hand to help in his planned civil war against his brother Nizam Ali. The French lost for ever their position in the Deccan, to say nothing of the vast financial losses incurred in terms of trade and investment by both private individuals and the Compagnie des Indes. Private persons alone lost nine lakhs, and the Compagnie's losses must have been correspondingly greater.

April–June 1759 saw a lull in military activity. From Arcot Lally returned to Pondicherry, whence he sent a fast frigate to Mauritius, requesting the rapid return of d'Aché's squadron. He then decided on a lengthy period of rest and recreation at Chalembron, aping Tiberius on Capri. From his eyrie he announced that he would leave the affairs of India in good order and then return to France in October; to observers this seemed simply sulky peevishness. The British meanwhile were keen to seize the moment and go on the offensive, even though they could put only 1,000 into the field against Lally's 2,000. Clive, too, was concerned that he had to watch his back in Bengal, since the Dutch were already intriguing with the un-reliable Mir Jaffir. The other problem was that the hero of Madras, General Lawrence, was too old to campaign, so that the command devolved to Cholmondeley Brereton. Clive decided that Brereton was too junior to head a major offensive so he limited him to probes. As one of his colleagues recorded: 'Brereton's zeal and activity on service is very great, but he is warm, and has no idea of obstacles, which possibly arises from his never having been on subaltern's duty.' The judgement was sound, for Brereton always showed a disposition to exceed orders and acted as though he thought he could sweep the French away on his own. Now depressed and melan-cholic, Lally responded with a Fabian campaign and withdrew south, refusing to offer battle. Lacking numbers and resources to press on to Pondicherry, Lawrence contented himself by taking Conjeveram in April, but was then obliged by shortage of money to go into cantonment until August, being dispersed among various military stations instead of being held together in battle readiness.

Lolling at Chalembron, Lally brooded daily about Bussy, with whom relations had deteriorated steeply. When Lally announced that he no longer wanted to see or correspond with him, Bussy in turn asked for a congé to return to France. Lally spent most of his time in vindictive correspondence with his superiors in France, ripping into Bussy for a host of imagined faults. To the Compagnie he wrote that Bussy was to blame for the debacle in the Deccan and that his incompetence had cost the Compagnie four million livres in three years. To Marshal Belle-Isle, Lally paraded the supposed military shortcomings of his blockheaded colleague. Bussy, aware of what was going on, started his own corre-spondence with France. He pointed out that from the very beginning Lally had known nothing about Indian affairs, but had nonetheless tres-passed and rampaged through his (Bussy's) sphere of influence like a rogue elephant. Lally, he averred, was insanely jealous of his savoir-faire in matters Indian and of the prestige he enjoyed with the local princes and rajas, and could never hear a word of praise about any of his colleagues without throwing an angry scene. Bussy's letters to Belle-Isle were partic-ularly splenetic. And soon the two men ceased even to observe formal and ritual courtesies; their mutual resentment degenerated into public slanging. But Lally was forced to change tack for he suddenly received explicit orders from France. Comptroller-General Silhouette, obsessed by the grave financial crisis of the French state in 1759, decided that the first place for stringent economies was India. As a consequence, not only did Versailles recall most of Lally's officers and troops, but explicit instructions were sent out nominating Bussy as second-in-command on the subcontinent and making it clear that he was Lally's heir apparent in case of the latter's death.

The next stage of the 1759 campaign began when d'Aché's fleet at last got back from Mauritius. Incredibly, it was 15 August before d'Aché's squadron returned to Pondicherry. The problem was that d'Aché's abscondment to Mauritius had been very badly thought through, and the conclusion is inescapable that the French admiral went there mainly to escape another bruising encounter with the Royal Navy. Mauritius, with a population of 9,246, could barely feed itself, let alone cope with the extra mouths when French warships made their unwelcome visits. The situation had worsened since Clive's capture of Chandernagore in 1757 cut the regular supply of wheat and rice from Bengal which had sustained the French islands. For this reason d'Aché sent some of his fleet to the Dutch colony at the Cape of Good Hope: partly because they would be fed there and partly so that they could buy provisions for the inhabitants of the islands. But this in turn required money, so d'Aché found himself spending half of what had been remitted from France for the expenses of Pondicherry, where Lally in turn was desperately short of money. For all these reasons it took an unconscionable time for d'Aché to reassemble his ships before returning to India. But at least his warships were now better equipped and were carrying heavier armament than in 1758. The flagship *Comte de Provence*, for example, was now a seventy-four-gun vessel where before she had carried fifty-eight guns.

The tireless Pocock was waiting for the reappearance of his old foe and first sighted the sails of d'Aché's eleven ships of the line on 2 September, but the winds were too light on this occasion for battle to be feasible. Pocock lost sight of the French, so he headed for Pondicherry and there, on 8 September, came in sight of them once more. Finally on 10 September battle was joined. The French had a clear advantage, for the two hindmost ships in the English fleet were too far behind to take part in the mêlée, so that for all practical purposes it was eleven French warships against seven British. The battle was a more close-fought affair than the two previous encounters between d'Aché and Pocock. For two hours the two sides traded broadside for broadside and two English vessels, the *Tyger* and the *Newcastle*, suffered severe damage, with sail shot away so that the vessels would not answer to the helm. Yet the French lost their nerve first, and d'Aché furiously censured the captain of the *Fortune* for incompetence as the rearguard gave way. The truth was that d'Aché was a mediocre commander, outclassed by Pocock, though he set a good example to his lacklustre captains by falling wounded at the precise moment when the pilot ordered the flagship put about. Once again, despite some signal instances of French valour, the basic result was the same: an 'on points' victory for the British. They lost 569 killed and wounded as against 886 French casualties, but were too maimed in masts and rigging to pursue d'Aché into Pondicherry.

D'Aché's actions after the battle were typical of the man. He landed what remained of the money that had been sent out from France and immediately announced his intention of returning to Mauritius. This declaration was received with dismay by all in Pondicherry. Forgetting their myriad differences, Lally, Bussy, Leyrit and the venal officials whom Lally had alienated all joined forces and petitioned d'Aché not to leave the Carnatic at the mercy of the British. They said they would do anything to fit in with his plans and make his stay pleasant, provided only that he did not abandon them. Some of the appeals were aimed at his patriotism; others at his comfort, such as the suggestion that he winter in Ceylon rather than return to the French islands where he and his men risked dying of hunger. Leyrit and Lally both agreed they would sign an official document absolving d'Ache from any responsibility for harm or damage that might accrue to his fleet as a result of making such a patriotic gesture. Yet d'Aché was deaf to all overtures. The plain truth is that he was desperate not to have to test himself against Pocock again and, to mask his flight, spoke of sailing along the coast to stage an attack on Masulipatam. He set sail on 17 September, but was soon overtaken by a fast cutter bearing a new message. The citizens of Pondicherry had called an emergency council and unanimously decided to put their names to a declaration making d'Aché responsible for the possible loss of the French position in India. Lally, Bussy, Leyrit, all principal traders, citizens and members of the cloth put their signatures to the document. Mindful of the fate of Admiral Byng, d'Aché did not dare to disregard such a remonstrance blatantly so put about and anchored again at Pondicherry. On 28 September he conferred again with the triumvirate of Lally, Leyrit and Bussy and agreed, as a compromise, to disembark 500 of the troops he was supposed to be taking back to France. But he refused to remain on the Coromandel coast. On 1 October he set sail again, never to return. At Mauritius he met the same difficulties but covered himself by writing pointless letters to Lally, saying he would never abandon Pondicherry. The truth was that he already had, and the following year d'Aché used the excuse of a projected British attack on the French isles not to return to India.

D'Aché's abandonment of his compatriots seemed an even greater dereliction of duty in the light of an unexpected victory gained by Lally's fellow Irishman, Captain Geoghan, at Vandavachy on 26 September. An over-confident Brereton attacked with about 1,500 white troops and seemed at first to carry all before him; but Geoghan's counterattack with forces of about the same number swept the English out of their overnight gains and forced them back to Conjeveram. The fighting was short-lived but ferocious while it lasted, as evinced by the casualty figures: 600 British and 200 French. The victory had a marvellous effect on French morale and Lally at once let it be known that if, just a week earlier, he had had the reinforcement of the 500 men left behind by d'Aché, he could have annihilated Brereton. In his typically hyperbolic mode, dripping with sarcasm, Lally wrote: 'I expect they will say in Paris that M. d'Aché won this battle and I was the one who lost the naval battle.' The irony was particularly clever, since Lally himself had been nowhere near the Battle of Vandavachy. And he immediately displayed his strategic incompetence by detaching troops from the ranks of the victors and sending them on a pointless campaign in the south. This expedition captured the fort of Seringam near Trichinopoli, but meanwhile the weakened French troops in the more crucial sector were in no position to oppose the British who, granted this unexpected boon by Lally, regrouped and took Vandavachy, this time for good.

Meanwhile Lally forced himself to be reconciled to Bussy and sent him on a diplomatic mission to Bassalet Jang, brother of Salabet. Before allying himself with the French, Bassalet wanted a considerable sum of money (four lakhs) deposited with him as subsidy and a guarantee that he would be named Nawab of Arcot. But Lally, short of money, had already promised this prize to another potentate, Raza Sahib and had received the payment of 120,000 rupees for the title. Lally and Bussy now somehow had to square the circle and satisfy both Bassalet and Raza Sahib without also offending Nizam Ali, another claimant for French favours. After being delayed by heavy rains, Bussy met Bassalet in the Cuddapah country on 10 November 1759 and used all his charm and skill to win him over to the French cause but in vain. Bussy later blamed the fiasco on Lally's blundering folly with Raza Sahib; Lally, naturally, riposted that the fault had been Bussy's, because he was too slow and too Machiavellian in his intrigues. Lally was certainly behaving oddly in late 1759, to say the least. When a disappointed and disillusioned Bussy returned to Arcot on 10 December, he found a bizarre letter from Lally waiting for him. After the usual quota of Lallyisms, the letter came to the point: 'If I don't get word from you in two or three days, I intend to strike south and abandon to your care the other three-quarters of our empire here to do with as you will. I only wish I could hand the whole thing over to you.'

The finishing touch to French woes in India in 1759 was set by a wholesale mutiny in the army over arrears of pay. The outbreak began on 17

October when the Lorraine regiment refused to obey orders, quit their camp and marched off some distance, dragging the artillery with them. All the other regiments then joined in. Already ten months in arrears with their pay, the mutineers were adamant that they would not return to the colours until the entire amount of back pay was made good; they declared there would be no compromise and they would not call off their strike even if paid six months in arrears. Lally hastily summoned an emergency council and frantically tried to scrape together the money. He was forced to write to the Compagnie des Indes, protesting that he had never taken a sou of their money for his own purposes, as the mutineers' libels suggested. He also despatched an impassioned appeal to the mutineers not to bring disgrace on France, the King and their own wives and children. Together with this eloquent appeal he sent his aide M. de Crillon with 18,000 rupees in cash, enough to pay six months of the arrears. Despite their previous utterances, the mutineers accepted the ready money plus a promise to pay the rest by the end of the year as a fair settlement. But the ripples from the mutiny had far-flung effects. When Bussy met Bassalet Jang on 10 November, he found the Prince deeply troubled by exaggerated accounts of the mutiny. Aware that the French could not even pay their own people, Bassalet doubted that he would see a single rupee even if Bussy did agree to his demands, and this was the main stumbling block in the abortive negotiations which followed.

As the French waned, the British waxed. A battalion of fresh troops under Sir Eyre Coote had embarked for Bengal in April but, on reaching the Carnatic, were detached to deal the *coup de grâce* to Lally. In October Coote took the field at the head of the united British forces and on 19 November seized the forts of Wandiwash and Carangoly. The French were so demoralised that at Wandiwash they surrendered without agreeing any formal terms of capitulation. The local ruler, the Killedar, formerly a French ally, tried to curry favour with the British and had been in secret and treacherous negotiations with Coote even before the French threw in the towel. Much of the detail of the Killedar's clandestine overtures concerned his desire to evade the quasi-feudal tithes or tribute he owed to the pro-British Nawab – no fewer than five lakhs of rupees. In his reply, Coote insisted on payment of the full amount. But now the British in turn faced near-mutiny. The army claimed that they had refrained from plundering Wandiwash on the clear understanding that half of the five lakhs would be given to them as a bounty. At a council of war held on 2 December, Coote realised to his consternation that he would have full-scale revolt on his hands unless he bought his troops off; the army had cleverly pre-empted his likely moves by announcing publicly (and stating so in letters to

England) that Coote had a private and corrupt arrangement with the Killedar, whereby he would actually receive the five lakhs but claim only to have been given three. To contradict the rumours and bring his men to heel, Coote was obliged to issue a general order that the first 20,000 rupees received from the Killedar would be distributed as bounty to his soldiers.

Lally's position was now parlous. Fearing that if he abandoned his command he might be hauled before a tribunal or court martial in France, on 27 December 1759 he formally resumed his duties. Maybe he was also influenced by a minatory letter from Leyrit on 8 December, warning that the Governor had a verbatim record of all Lally's outrages and verbal tantrums and sketching all the ways this had harmed the French colony in India. Lally responded next day with another of his hyperbolic and emotional letters, appealing to Leyrit's better nature, exhorting him to let bygones be bygones and work together. The letter was almost a capsule psychological portrait of Lally, the man of extremes, the man with no middle range. This had always been his weakness in India. If, as was obvious, he was going to have to work with the venal officialdom of the Compagnie des Indes, what was the point of publicly denouncing their corruption? He boasted that he would cleanse the Augean stables but quite patently lacked the means and resources to do so. Lally always spoke before he thought and could never hold his tongue. But, on the credit side, he did not bear grudges, could not understand that others did, and thought that a simple apology could erase the record, no matter how extreme or wounding the things he had said. Contrary to the usual stereotype of the Irishman, Lally did not brood over ancient wrongs or masochistically savour the sting of an insult from twenty years ago. It was his misfortune that it was his enemies who most of all were guilty of the alleged *furor Hibernicus.*

At the end of 1759 the French position in India was critical but not yet desperate and the prestige of French arms was still, just, intact. True, they had lost the Deccan and Masulipatam, but it could be argued that the Compagnie des Indes had increased its power and consolidated its foothold by destroying Fort St David and occupying Arcot. If the fleet could return from Mauritius and substantial reinforcements of men and money arrived from France, there was still hope. But at a deep-seated level the omens were not good. France during the Seven Years War was bedevilled by money shortages and lack of credit, and Louis XV and his Comptroller-General Silhouette were already nearly as close to abandoning India as they were Canada. The chronic shortage of money made the French position on the Coromandel coast permanently precarious, and this much can be set down to 'necessity' and structural factors. But, at the level of contingency and 'conjuncture', the French were decisively outclassed by their British rivals. Clive had found a way to avoid the extremes of military versus Company factionalism, as Lally never did. Lally, moreover, was out of his depth in India. It really required a military genius like Clive to retrieve the French position on the Carnatic. Sadly, in the Seven Years War, France had few such people at their disposal.

SIX

WOLFE AT QUEBEC

The most significant work of literature published in the year 1759 was Voltaire's
Candide. *The sixty-five-year-old François-Marie Arouet had just become
domiciled at Ferney on the Swiss border after a notably peripatetic existence
and had found a new way to ridicule his lifelong enemy – established religion
(infamy or* l'infâme, *as he famously called it). The short thirty-chapter philosophical fable* Candide, *with its fast-moving narrative sustained almost entirely
through dialogue, carried to new heights Voltaire's typical method of ridicule
by teasing out the logical absurdities in any given tenet (what is often termed
the method of* reductio ad absurdum). *His targets this time were on the one
hand the Christian notion of a benevolent Providence and an all-powerful God
unlimited by evil and, on the other, Leibniz's idea that this world is the best of
all possible worlds. Traditional Catholic theology held that the notion of evil
comes from a 'partial' perception of the world; properly considered it is merely
negativity, the absence of good (*privatio boni *in St Thomas Aquinas's phrase).
But two tragic events in particular in Voltaire's lifetime made him consider this
view a form of secular blasphemy. One was the death in childbirth of his mistress
and great love, Madame du Châtelet, in 1749. The other was the great earthquake at Lisbon on 1 November 1755, when a massive tremor in the seabed to
the south-west of the city devastated the population, killing some in the crevasses
that opened up, more in the fires that followed and even more in the tidal wave
generated by the quake. Altogether at least 30,000 people perished.*

Candide *is the work of an angry man who knows that mere rage will not
influence a readership, but satire, wit and savage irony will. In a masterstroke
he provides his own version of a papal bull against the comet by having the
Portuguese proscribe future earthquakes by auto-da-fé. The eponymous hero
travels around Europe and South America as one picaresque adventure succeeds
another. Partly Voltaire is mocking devout allegories like Bunyan's* Pilgrim's
Progress *and partly he is developing the genre of the philosophical fable so
popular in the eighteenth century; such tales were widely read into the nineteenth century (Herman Melville's* Mardi *is a typical if obscure example) but*

in our own era have been subsumed in the genre of science fiction. Typically a hero undergoes a series of adventures in a number of exotic locations (in this case principally Portugal, Paraguay, Surinam, Venice and Turkey) before gaining new wisdom. The wisdom in this book is that all religion, all schemes of metaphysical speculation, and all search for a pattern in the universe is meaningless.

During Candide's travels in Paraguay, for example, Voltaire takes the opportunity to indulge in savage jibes at the expense of his old enemies the Jesuits. As it happens, this was notably unfair, for the Jesuit reductions in Paraguay, the nearest thing in human history to Plato's Republic, *were the only institution that protected Native American tribes from the ravages and exploitation of the European colonial powers. Voltaire's attacks on the smugness of priests and bishops who spoke blandly of 'God's will' after the Lisbon earthquake were more to the point and he linked them to his distaste for Leibniz, who is mercilessly parodied in the form of Dr Pangloss, the so-called mentor of Candide, who repeatedly parrots his mantra 'All is for the best in the best of all possible worlds'. Voltaire had other targets too, among them his old enemy and sometime associate Jean-Jacques Rousseau, famous for his irrationalism and his advocacy of the 'noble savage'. Rousseau's 'small is beautiful' view was that mankind had no business living in cities anyway and that the Lisbon earthquake was a kind of nemesis for human hubris in living crowded together and building seven-storey buildings. Rousseau conveniently ignored the tidal wave, which would have destroyed the Portuguese on the coast whether they were living in Lisbon or merely in the state of Nature.*

Candide *brought on the final rupture between Rousseau and Voltaire. The following year (1760) Rousseau wrote to Voltaire: 'I hate you, in fact, since that is what you want; but I hate you as one who would have loved you if that was how you wanted it. Of all the feelings my heart cherishes towards you, there now remains only admiration, which we can hardly refuse to your great genius and love of your writings. If there is nothing else but your talents I can respect, that is no fault of mine.' But in private, to a third party, his sentiments were rather more bitter:*

Voltaire pretends to believe in God but really believes only in the devil, as his so-called God is a malevolent being who, according to him, delights in causing misery. The absurdity of this doctrine coming from a man who possesses all the good things life has to offer is particularly egregious and offensive and it revolts me that a man who is happy himself should try to fill his fellow-men with despair, by imagining the very cruel and terrible calamities he himself has never suffered.

Rousseau despised Voltaire's worship of reason and stressed instead the primacy of instinct and emotion. He could see no merit in the idea that rationality is mankind's best hope, that without reason the world is random and without meaning, but that there is no supernatural pattern on which we can rely and that therefore we have to invent morality and order for ourselves, using reason as a lodestar. The intellectual content of Rousseau's conflict with Voltaire foreshadows the famous twentieth-century quarrels between, respectively, Camus and Sartre, or D. H. Lawrence and Bertrand Russell.

Yet to understand Voltaire and his 1759 masterpiece Candide properly, one must look at the turbulent course of Voltaire's eighty-four-year life, riven as it is with contradictions and paradoxes. Scion of a wealthy family, he was educated by Jesuits and from early youth displayed remarkable literary talent, completing a long poem on Henry IV and a successful tragedy Oedipe by his early twenties. But he was a natural rebel who chafed at any constraint by authority, whether paternal, social or political. He began by associating with a group of libertine freethinking intellectuals and, when his father tried to break this association by getting him a diplomatic post in Holland, he managed to get himself repatriated very soon after a scandalous love affair. Next he satirised the Regent, the Duc d'Orléans; the authorities responded by banishing him from Paris for a year. Voltaire returned to the capital and in 1717–18 composed a new attack, accusing the Regent of all manner of outlandish crimes. This time he was imprisoned for a year in the Bastille. Oedipe was meanwhile a huge success and by 1722, having speculated cleverly on the stockmarket with the profits, Voltaire was both rich and a favourite at court. But the imp of the perverse gnawed at him. He got into a quarrel with the influential Chevalier de Rohan-Chabot and began circulating caustic epigrams about him; the result was a further spell in the Bastille, from which he was released only on condition that he went into exile in England.

England was in many ways the making of him, for it was there that he fell under the spell of philosophy and science, particularly the empiricism of John Locke and the physics of Isaac Newton. Received at court by George I and welcomed by the Prime Minister Robert Walpole, Voltaire also associated with the philosophical and literary luminaries Jonathan Swift, George Berkeley, Alexander Pope, John Gay and William Congreve. He returned to France in 1729 determined to proselytise for Anglo-Saxon empiricist philosophy, and indeed Voltaire was the main eighteenth-century transmission belt by which English ideas entered the continent. With the pragmatic mixture of common sense and intellectuality that always delighted his admirers, Voltaire accumulated a second great fortune by purchasing shares in a government lottery and investing in the corn trade, having worked out that army contracts made this a virtually risk-free area for speculation. He was always a prolific writer, of *dramas, poetry, philosophy and scientific treatises, and so pleased Louis XV with his play the* Princesse de Navarre *(1745), performed on the occasion of the Dauphin's marriage, that he secured appointments as official royal historian and gentleman-in-ordinary to the King. A natural politician and accomplished flatterer when he chose to be so, Voltaire also charmed and cajoled the royal mistress Madame de Pompadour and the King's then court favourite the Duc de Richelieu, his womanising tendencies doubtless contributing to the rapport with the two personages in the kingdom at that time most noted for amatory dalliance.*

Yet probably the most bizarre incident in Voltaire's life was the three years he spent from 1750 to 1753 at the court of Frederick the Great of Prussia, officially as King's Chamberlain on a huge salary but really as Frederick's éminence grise. *Here he was undoubtedly aping the example of Plato, who attempted to put his philospher-king notion into practice by serving in a similar capacity with Dionysius the Younger, tyrant of Syracuse in the fourth century* B.C. *But, as with Plato, Voltaire's experiment ended badly. Always with a compulsion to be a gadfly, Voltaire grew bored in Berlin and started composing scurrilous verses about Pierre de Maupertuis, the French mathematician whom Frederick had appointed President of the Berlin Academy. In March 1753 Voltaire and Frederick parted acrimoniously and never met again, though they continued to correspond in a somewhat bitchy way thereafter. Curiously, Frederick seemed to concede Voltaire's implicit status as philosopher-king, as can be seen from his action after the Battle of Kunersdorf in August 1759 when he wrote almost as if in explanation for his defeat by the Russians:*

I wrap myself in stoicism as best I can. If you saw me you would hardly know me: I am old, broken, grey-headed, wrinkled. If this goes on there will be nothing left of me but the mania of making verses and an inviolable attachment to my duties and to the few virtuous men I know. But you will not get a peace signed by my hand except on conditions honourable to my nation. Your people, blown up with conceit and folly, may depend on this.

Voltaire was a mass of contradictions: avaricious yet generous, mean-spirited yet magnanimous, quarrelsome yet highly intelligent, vindictive yet humane. He despised kings and princes but had a soft spot for Bonnie Prince Charlie, whom he knew and admired and for whom he had written a stirring manifesto in 1745; a transmogrified Charles Edward even makes an appearance in Candide. *Voltaire was contemptuous of the common people whom he called a rabble (*canaille*), yet his basic impulses were towards democracy and against aristocracy. Although he described himself as having a 'lion's heart in the skin of a rabbit', this self-deprecation did not do justice to his obvious moral courage,* *as when he proved, to the wrath of the French establishment, that the Huguenot Jean Calas had been judicially murdered when innocent in 1762.*

As a literary figure Voltaire was highly talented, but he understood very little about philosophy proper, and his satire on Leibniz works only if one is ignorant of the true meaning of the great German's metaphysical work. And if Rousseau downgraded reason, Voltaire certainly underrated emotion, to the point where his poetry often reads like a mere metrical exercise. He was interested in science, but did not have the true scientist's objectivity, dedication and patience; Voltaire was impulsive, careless and apt to reject any evidence that did not fit his own a priori *theories. His denigration of and failure to understand Shakespeare is a serious strike against him, and he had no understanding of the psychology of religion and its role as consolation or myth; a pragmatist, he yet held the self-evidently absurd belief that, though human beings are fundamentally irrational, they can be led to truth through reason. In short, he combined massive erudition and ingenuity with a signal paucity of wisdom. Most controversial of all is his core criticism of Christianity: that those who ask us to believe absurdities will also ask us to condone atrocities.*

What distinguished Voltaire above all was his wit, which suffuses his work and is not surpassed by the figures with whom he is often compared in this respect: Jonathan Swift, Oscar Wilde, George Bernard Shaw. 'If God did not exist, it would be necessary to invent him' is justly famous but there are many other apophthegms just as good: 'The superfluous, a very necessary thing'; (of Louis XIV) 'he was not the greatest of men but he was the greatest of kings'; 'the best is the enemy of the good'; (on 'unnatural' sexual practices) 'once a philosopher, twice a pervert'; 'If God made us in his image, we have certainly returned the compliment'; 'God is on the side of the big battalions'; 'Never having been able to succeed in the world, he took his revenge by speaking ill of it.' He wrote histories of the reigns of both Louis XIV and Louis XV and was a shrewd student of Clio: 'History is just the portrayal of crimes and misfortunes'; 'One owes respect to the living, but to the dead one owes nothing but the truth'; 'All our ancient history . . . is no more than accepted fiction'; 'This agglomeration which was called and still calls itself the Holy Roman Empire was neither holy, nor Roman, nor an empire in any way.' From Candide *itself, his masterpiece and the* pièce de résistance *of 1759, we get the following: 'In this country [England] we find it pays to shoot an admiral from time to time to encourage the others' (his bitter satire on the execution of Admiral Byng in 1757); and 'Work banishes those three great evils, boredom, vice and poverty.' One of the most famous of all literary sign-offs comes at the end of* Candide *and clearly shows Voltaire as the detached but not cynical pragmatist: 'That's true enough,' said Candide, 'but we must go and cultivate our garden.'*

Voltaire was the leading light in the group known as the philosophes *(which translates better as 'sages' than 'philosophers'). The decade of the 1750s saw the* philosophes *at the height of their influence.* Montesquieu published De l'esprit des lois *in 1748,* Diderot the first volume of his famous Encyclopédie *in 1751,* Voltaire his Siècle de Louis XV *in the same year,* Condillac his Traité des sensations *in 1754, while* Rousseau chalked up two important works, the Discours sur les sciences et les arts *in 1750, and the revolutionary* Discours sur l'origine de l'inégalité *in 1754. But the* philosophes, *though united in their opposition to established religion, formed a coherent movement only in a very loose sense. Some were deists, others atheists; some were able to cohabit with the* ancien régime *in France, others had to go into exile to avoid persecution, censorship and book-burning.* Voltaire, keen on solidarity among those 'agin' things, often wrote to his fellow philosophes, especially Helvétius and d'Alembert, hailing them as brothers, speaking of the 'republic of letters' or referring to their common stand against religion in military terms: they were a battalion, a regiment, a division, an entire corps. But the philosophes were at least forty years ahead of French public opinion and resigned themselves to a steady drip-drip of propaganda to win round the public, organising themselves into clubs, gradually colonising the fashionable salons and eventually taking over the French Academy.*

Although the philosophes *disagreed violently among themselves and were often guilty of the besetting sin of radical groups – being more concerned with internal doctrinal wrangles than with confronting the common enemy – they overwhelmingly agreed on one thing: France's overseas colonies were a useless drain on resources, involving the motherland in a series of pointless conflicts with other nations, principally England. France, in this view, had been the dominant power in Europe in the seventeenth century and was so no longer, because she had dissipated her resources on overseas expansion. It was all very well for Spain to expand into the interior of South America or for Russia to press on eastwards, conquer Siberia and reach the Pacific, but these were both nations on the periphery of Europe; France's geographical position, on the other hand, made her destiny ineluctably European. French overseas colonies were absurd, the colonists the teeming refuse of French slums, and the entire colonial experiment merely a form of buffoonery or harlequinade in which all the participants were secretly despised by true French men and women. The detestation of overseas colonies by the* philosophes *has often been overlooked because of their abstract love of exotica and because their books teem with savage peoples: Persians, Peruvians, Turks, Mongols, Chinese, Hurons, Iroquois. But the interest of the* philosophes *in these people was superficial and specious: they merely wished to use them as handy weapons with which to hammer away at the absurdity of the culture, mores and folk ways of the* ancien régime.

It is true that in their anti-colonial campaign the philosophes *sometimes made an exception for the French West Indies, on the grounds that they produced useful tropical products that could not be grown at home and that the 'Antilles' were a theatre for private enterprise and mercantile entrepreneurship and so did not cost the French state anything.* Montesquieu's De l'esprit des lois *actually contains a eulogy of the French West Indies, and Voltaire often made favourable mention of the French Compagnie des Indes, perhaps mainly because he had shares in it. Yet his serious point was concerned with what would be called in later parlance 'comparative advantage'. All nations should play to their own strength: Britain's was the sea and navies, while France's was land and armies. Similarly, the population of French Canada was 59,000 while the British had millions of their colonists in North America. But in the West Indies France had a population of 414,000 against 245,000 in the British Caribbean islands, so French colonisation there made sense. Yet some* philosophes *were opposed to any colonies anywhere. In his* Lettres persanes, *Montesquieu made the classic anti-colonial statement:*

> *The normal effect of colonies is to weaken the mother country without populating or improving the said colonies. Men should stay where they are . . . When we are transported overseas we become sick in a number of different ways . . . In the few instances where colonies have succeeded, they have simply drained the strength of the founding nation, so that it ends up weaker, not stronger, than before . . . One can compare overseas empires to a great tree whose branches become too extended and simply suck the sap and vigour from the trunk while contributing nothing except shade.*

In his Fragments sur les Indes *Voltaire bitterly attacked the Spanish Empire in Latin America:*

> *The sole result of the European discovery of the Americas was devastation and the spilling of blood, just to bring back cacao, indigo, sugar, quinine, etc. The whole project was simply to put on the tables of bourgeois in London and Paris different kinds of provisions from those known before, to bedeck their women with jewels that in former centuries would have graced the necks of queens and to infect their noses with disgusting powders. In order to satisfy fantasies, by providing useless alcoholic liqueurs unknown to our forefathers, an enormous trade has arisen, disadvantageous to three-quarters of Europe. And it is to sustain this trade that the great powers wage wars, wherein a single cannon shot fired in our latitudes is the charge that sets off explosions from America to Asia.*

Here was one area where Voltaire and Rousseau could agree, for Rousseau saw colonisation as just another artefact of so-called civilisation, just like commerce, the arts, science and industry, which took mankind away from the ideal of the 'noble savage'. In the 1760s, inspired by Bougainville's voyages to the Pacific, Diderot composed a philosophical fable in which the Tahitian Orou inveighs against the vices and ambitions of Europeans and invites every last European to decamp from Polynesia. A minor philosophe, *Bernardin de Saint-Pierre, summed up in similar vein 'I will think I have performed a signal service to my country if I prevent a single honest man from emigrating.'*

But of all the targets for such anti-colonial thought the greatest, and a verit-able bête noire *for the* philosophes, *was Canada. The milder critics simply ignored New France altogether, and Diderot's* Encyclopédie *devotes just a dozen inconsequential lines to it. But Voltaire had something of an obsession with it and there are more than a hundred references to Canada in his letters, in the* Siècle de Louis XIV, Fragments sur les Indes, Les Moeurs et l'esprit des nations *and, naturally,* Candide. *Canada often seems to get into the act in the most unlikely contexts. When Voltaire wrote to Rousseau in 1755 to acknowledge receipt of the* Discours sur l'origine de l'inégalité, *his distaste for Canada almost edged out his dislike of Rousseau's work:*

> *I have received your new book directed against the human race and thank you for it. Never was such cleverness deployed for the purpose of making us all stupid. One longs, when reading your book, to walk on all fours. But as I have lost that habit for the last sixty years, sadly I feel unable to resume it. Nor can I embark in search of the savages of Canada, because the illnesses I suffer mean I need a European surgeon; because there is a war waging in those regions; and because by our example we have made the savages nearly as depraved as ourselves.*

Voltaire could never understand why anyone could be committed to a useless region, whose costs escalated every decade. France spent 300,000 livres on Canada in 1712, but by the 1730s the figure was 500,000 livres and by 1740 New France was costing more than one million livres; when war came in 1754 the figure went even higher. And all this expenditure went on 'frozen deserts, oceans of snow, sterile lands and savage terrains'. One hundred years of toil and a century of conflict with Britain had produced nothing worthwhile. France fell into the colonisation trap simply because

> *Two or three Norman merchants, on the vague hope of making a fortune from the fur trade, equipped some ships and established a colony in Canada,*

a country covered in ice and snow for eight months of the year, inhabited by savages, bears and beavers . . . involving us in continual warfare either with the natives or the English . . . the expenses of such wars cost far more than Canada could ever conceivably produce in a hundred years . . . Maybe one day, if France ever has a surplus population of one million, it might be to our advantage to populate Louisiana but it's much more likely that we'll have to abandon it.

When the Marquis de Chauvelin was Foreign Minister, Voltaire said that, if he dared, he would like to beseech him on bended knees to get rid of Canada. Two other Voltaire sayings may suffice to show his hatred of the very idea of New France. 'I wish Canada was at the bottom of an icy sea' and 'France can be happy and successful without Quebec.'

Voltaire chiefly blamed Louis XV for France's unhappy situation in Canada, for there was a head-on collision between the King and the 'republic of letters'. It was the monarch who aided and abetted overseas empires and grandiose colonial schemes and it was the job of the 'republic' to engage him in combat and win the battle for public opinion, without which Louis could not sustain his chimerical colonialism. It was clearly always going to be difficult for the King to engineer mass emigration to Canada, if the most famous scientists and finest minds in the kingdom unanimously declared that Canada was a land of no value and with no future. It would even be difficult for Louis to raise the money necessary to defend Canada if the philosophes won the hearts and minds of the moneyed classes on this issue. It is interesting that doubts about the value of Canada did not occur to an English-speaking intelligentsia until much later. In 1782 Thomas Paine wrote to the Abbé Raynal in terms which are almost an uncanny echo of Voltaire:

Respecting Canada, one or other of the two following will take place, viz. if Canada should become populous, it will revolt; and if it does not become so, it will not be worth the expense of holding . . . But Canada never will be populous; neither is there any occasion for contrivances on one side or the other, for nature alone will do the whole . . . I would not, were I a European power, have Canada under the conditions that Britain must retain it, could it be given to me. It is one of those kinds of dominions that is, and ever will be, a constant charge upon any foreign holder.

Yet if there were those on both sides who thought the struggle for Canada a waste of time, neither Montcalm nor Wolfe saw it that way. The man who commanded the British forces which sailed into the St Lawrence in June 1759 is one of those enigmatic figures who has always divided historians and always will. For generations of Victorian and Edwardian children, not to mention Sir Winston Churchill and his followers, James Wolfe was almost the avatar of the imperial paladin, a man of strength, courage and absolute integrity, the ideal type of imperial soldier, a figure of self-sacrifice and almost Christ-like sanctity. More sober-minded critics see a showman, a cross-grained individual with the gallery touch, a man promoted beyond his deserts by powerful connections and influential cliques, a darling of Fortune who was very lucky, a prima donna and, by modern standards, a war criminal. It is important neither to exaggerate the real qualities of Major-General Wolfe nor to overstate the very real dark side. War is always hell and is no business for the shrinking violet or the morally squeamish. Even so, Wolfe appears to moral disadvantage when compared with his great rival, Montcalm. And, despite the temptation to become bewitched by 'great men', we must remember that when Wolfe arrived at Louisbourg in the early summer of 1759 he inherited a highly efficient fighting machine for which he personally can take no credit. Pitt, in his desire to conquer North America for the English-speaking races, had made the conquest of Canada a supreme priority and had given Wolfe all the tools to complete the job.

Aged thirty-two, Wolfe was the eldest son of General Edward Wolfe, who died at seventy-four even while his son was on the wide Atlantic. Even though Parkman, with a flourish typical of that Bostonian Brahmin, refers to him as 'an officer of distinction', the truth is that Wolfe senior was an obscure and impecunious career officer. James Wolfe, who if nothing else was certainly a paragon of filial piety, loved his father and ostentatiously wore a crêpe band of mourning for him when he landed in Louisbourg and learned of his death. Yet an even more intense relationship existed with his mother, who endowed him with her own physical frailty but not her beauty. One of the most striking things about Wolfe was his physical ugliness. He was tall and thin with a gangling gait and awkward move-ments. He had a weak chin and a receding forehead, and his sharp upturned nose – too large a feature for the rest of his face – formed what one observer called 'the point of an obtuse triangle'. His mouth was small and his lips thin – the stereotypical features of the cruel despot – and his entire phys-iognomy was the butt of caricaturists, one of whom was his own Brigadier, George Townshend. Wolfe's ghostly pallor and long tapering fingers somehow set into bizarre relief his red hair, which he wore loose and long, disdaining the military wig that most officers still sported, even on the battlefield. His best feature was his eyes, clear, bright and piercing, denoting the resolution within. From his early days Wolfe had enjoyed poor health. He suffered from a number of complaints simultaneously, including chronic rheumatism, scurvy and diseases of the kidney and bladder (modern medical opinion is divided on what exactly was wrong with him) and had been the classical 'delicate child'. He compensated for this by being impetuous, headstrong and brave to the point of folly and from childhood dreamed of martial glory.

Wolfe began his army career at the age of sixteen, serving in Flanders during the War of Austrian Succession. He was present at the Battle of Dettingen in 1743 (the last occasion on which a British monarch took the field in person) and as regimental adjutant soon made his mark as an efficient, hard-working professional, who was popular with the ranks. Duly promoted, he was attached to the Duke of Cumberland's staff and served with the 'butcher' in the Scottish campaign of early 1746 against Bonnie Prince Charlie and the Jacobites, which ended with the disastrous defeat of the Highlanders at Culloden. As aide-de-camp to Cumberland's most slaughterous henchman, General 'Hangman' Hawley, Wolfe carried out murderous directives with relish and without compunction. Now a Major, he returned to Europe with Cumberland and was wounded at Lawfeldt in 1747.

Promoted to Lieutenant-Colonel in 1750, he commanded a regiment at Inverness for five years. This was an army of occupation in all but name, for Cumberland and his allies in the government lived for years in mortal fear that Prince Charles Edward Stuart would come again and there would be another bloody uprising in the Highlands. During the arduous tour of garrison duty in northern Scotland, Wolfe whiled away the time by learning Latin, improving his mathematics and devouring books on military tactics and strategy. But after five years he felt, as he wrote in a famous letter to his mother, that he was in danger of 'going native' – not in the sense that he harboured sympathies for the Scots or the Jacobites but that, exposed for so long to the 'barbarism' of the Highlands while exercising the powers of an absolute ruler, he seemed to be turning into a savage himself. He obtained leave of absence and spent the six-month furlough in Paris, mingling in high society, dancing with fine ladies and perfecting his skills in fencing and horsemanship.

In 1757 he was appointed Colonel of the newly raised 67th Foot and in this capacity took part in the abortive amphibious assault on Rochefort. This foundered both because of inter-service rivalry and through hesitation and indecision by the attackers, and led pessimists to conclude that the Royal Navy had declined disastrously since the days of Drake. Wolfe drew certain conclusions from this fiasco, which are often cited by his admirers as proof of his 'genius':

I have found out that an admiral should endeavour to run into an enemy's port immediately after he appears before it; that he should anchor the transport ships and frigates as close as can be to land; that he should reconnoitre and observe it as quick as possible, and lose no time in getting the troops on shore; that previous directions should be given in respect of landing the troops, and a proper disposition made for the boats of all sorts, appointing leaders and fit persons for conducting the various divisions. On the other hand, experience shows me that, in an affair depending upon vigour and dispatch, the generals should settle their plan of operations, so that no time may be lost in idle debate and consultations when the sword should be drawn.

Wolfe was an effective writer: vigorous, plain, lucid. His talent lay not so much in his military prescriptions, which are the merest common sense, but in his capacity for clear analysis of battle situations; it may be that, had he lived a long life, he might have rivalled the great practitioners in this sphere, from Julius Caesar to Ulysses S. Grant.

In 1758 Wolfe was transferred to North America, where he played a prominent part in the successful siege of Louisbourg. He then petitioned Amherst to be allowed to advance up the St Lawrence on Quebec. Amherst, to Wolfe's fury, procrastinated in his usual way. Impatiently Wolfe wrote to his father: 'We are gathering strawberries and other wild fruits of the country, with a seeming indifference about what is going on in other parts of the world. Our army, however, on the continent needs our help.' The impetuous Wolfe kept pressing Amherst, whom he increasingly despised while maintaining a front of extreme cordiality for decisive action. Amherst replied that he personally wanted to press on to Quebec but the Royal Navy had ruled out the attempt as impracticable so late in the season. Wolfe contumaciously answered that if the attempt on Quebec was not made, he and the army would be better off in Europe and, if that were not possible, he would prefer to resign his commission altogether. 'I beg pardon,' he wrote, 'for this freedom, but I cannot look coolly upon the bloody inroads of those hell-hounds the Canadians: and if nothing further is to be done, I must desire leave to quit the army.'

Amherst replied that Wolfe was too valuable an officer to let go and that he would not hear of his leaving the army. Wolfe responded with another splenetic outburst: 'An offensive, daring kind of war will awe the Indians and ruin the French. Blockhouses and a trembling defensive encourage the meanest scoundrels to attack us. If you will attempt to cut up New France by the roots, I will come with pleasure to assist.' Intuiting the violent nature of his subordinate, Amherst sought to placate Wolfe by sending him on missions which were really ill-disguised atrocities: the destruction of civilian settlements in the Gulf of St Lawrence. These villages had no military importance and the point of destroying them was to cow the population *in terrorem*. Although this sort of work was normally meat and drink to Wolfe, he construed being given such a mission as an insult and wrote to his father with heavy irony: 'Sir Charles Hardy and I are preparing to rob the fishermen of their nets and burn their huts. When that great exploit is at an end, I return to Louisbourg, and thence to England.'

Wolfe did indeed return to England. Amherst respected Wolfe's qualities as a fighter but did not think him suitable for high command and put in a brigadier over him at Louisbourg so that there would be one loose cannon less rolling around North America. Wolfe took this as an insult and sailed for home. He had a superlative view of his own abilities and at root despised all senior officers. One of his letters to his beloved mother gives the game away. 'If ever my opinion of myself,' he wrote, 'differs from my father's, 'tis certain to be in my own favour. I don't believe he ever thought better of me than I do of myself.'

In England Wolfe had many powerful patrons and influential admirers, especially Field Marshal Ligonier, Commander-in-Chief of the army, and he had courted them assiduously with his vivid and lucid letters, talking up his role in the taking of Louisbourg to the point where he appeared the 'onlie begetter' of the enterprise and Amherst a bumbling old woman. When he arrived in London, Wolfe found himself lionised as the hero of Louisbourg and, though his own inclinations were to serve in Europe, he let it be known, with breathtaking condescension, that he had 'no objections to serving in America and particularly in the river St Lawrence, if any operations are to be carried on there'. Ligonier recommended Wolfe to Pitt, who recognised a kindred spirit – they shared what one observer has called 'manic egotism'. Pitt altered his plans in late December and gave Wolfe an independent command, whose objective was the capture of Quebec. He even persuaded George II to promote Wolfe to the temporary rank of Major-General. Initially reluctant, the ailing monarch soon came round to Wolfe as wholly as Pitt had. When the Duke of Newcastle complained to the King that Wolfe and all his officers were too young and the expedition would have the appearance of a boys' crusade – Newcastle's real motive was hatred of meritocracy, for he believed fervently in the principles of patronage and seniority – George waved away the objections. When Newcastle then raised the issue of Wolfe's eccentricity and suggested that the young commander was mad, the King made the famous rejoinder: 'Mad, is he? Then I hope he will bite some others of my generals.'

When Pitt informed Amherst that Wolfe was to have an independent command, Amherst must have felt the appointment as a direct snub to himself. But he was a believer in the long game, where persistence and tenacity pay off rather than pyrotechnics and so, unlike Wolfe, he kept his emotions to himself. Yet it was in many ways a strange and even inappropriate appointment. Apart from his ill health – so acute that he himself thought he had not long to live – Wolfe was a psychological oddity, what psychoanalysts would doubtless call an example of 'masculine over-protest'. Two aspects of his personality are salient: his strange relations with women and his propensity towards savagery, atrocity and war crimes. His bachelor status undoubtedly links with his over-identification with his parents: Wolfe managed the neat trick of being both mother's boy and *fils à papa*. There is no evidence of any spontaneous feeling or desire for women and his interest in the sex seems to have been purely calculating: how far could they advance his career?

In the late 1740s Wolfe professed an admiration for a homely woman named Elizabeth Lawson, niece of General Mordaunt, a senior officer with influence at the Horse Guards. Although not overendowed with suitors, Miss Lawson grew tired of Wolfe's obvious lack of real feeling and his purely mechanical calculation (which he disguised as indecision) and decided not to marry him. The real reason for Wolfe's dithering was opposition to the match from his parents who thought Elizabeth Lawson not rich enough and instead proposed a wealthy heiress. It was typical of Wolfe that he then pretended to be mortified by Elizabeth's rejection, blamed his parents for 'interference', sulked and refused to see the heiress they had identified for him. Just before he left for Canada in 1759 he was betrothed to Catherine Lowther, sister of Sir James Lowther, an immensely wealthy MP, but a man so boorish and brutal that he was said to be the most hated man in England; the general opinion was that Lowther was a lunatic, but 'too rich to be confined'. Wolfe's very odd relations with women have led some biographers to speculate that he might have been a repressed or latent homosexual, and there is some circumstantial evidence to support this. What is certain is that he loved dogs more than human beings; his letters are full of huntin', shootin' and fishin' and paeans to the loyalty of his beloved canines.

The more serious strike against Wolfe was his inhumanity. This is distinct from his ruthlessness, which could be excused or attenuated as an aspect of his cynical (realistic?) view of life. Wolfe often stated that he did not believe in obstacles that were not proven to be so by trial and error; that chance and contingency played a large role in human and (especially) military affairs; that the end justified the means. He was also shrewd about the role of image, perception, psychology and credibility in human affairs.

He was obsessed in a somewhat compulsive way with the reputation of his country, but in one of his formulations of this principle we can discern much darker forces at work: 'In particular circumstances and times the loss of 1,000 men is rather an advantage to a nation than otherwise, seeing that gallant attempts raise its reputation and make it respectable; whereas the contrary appearances sink the credit of a country, ruin the troops, and create infinite uneasiness and discontent at home.' The inhumanity of this remark recalls Wolfe's unsavoury reputation during the suppression of the Jacobite rising, where he persecuted Jacobite women beyond reason and took the view that the only good Highlander was a dead one. He excused himself by the bogus and discredited notion that Prince Charles Edward had ordered the Jacobite troops to take no prisoners and wrote: 'The rebels, besides their natural incinations, had orders not to give quarter to our men. We had an opportunity of avenging ourselves for that and many other things, and indeed we did not neglect it. As few Highlanders were made prisoners as possible.'

When commanding at Inverness in the early 1750s, Wolfe evinced an extreme hatred of all Scots, male and female, and Highlanders in particular. Since Cluny MacPherson, leader of the MacPherson clan, had been 'out' with Prince Charlie in the '45 and was still skulking in Badenoch, Wolfe wanted to 'solve' this problem by massacring the entire MacPherson clan. He referred to Scots civilians as 'designing and treacherous' and spoke (significantly?) of the women as 'cold, coarse and cunning'. But it was not just Scots who excited Wolfe's visceral antipathy. Anyone who opposed his will, personally or impersonally, directly or indirectly, became the target of his murderous rage. He loathed the French and the Canadians as cordially as he did the Highlanders. He hated all North American Indians, even his allies, and in a letter to his uncle wholeheartedly approved of the English policy of massacring any Indians they encountered, without enquiring too closely into their allegiance: 'I take them to be the most contemptible *canaille* upon earth . . . these are a dastardly set of bloody rascals. We cut them to pieces whenever we found them in return for a thousand acts of cruelty and barbarity.'

Such a man was almost destined to make enemies, and one of the features of the 1759 campaign against Quebec was Wolfe's uncertain relations with his three brigadiers. The problem was compounded as all three, Robert Monkton, James Murray and George Townshend were the sons of peers, true aristocrats where Wolfe was 'merely' a scion of the upper classes. The prickly Wolfe was forever on the lookout for any signs of oligarchic condescension from the three but with Murray and Monkton he was on safe enough ground. Although Murray later proved by his humane actions that he must heartily have disapproved of Wolfe's harshness towards his opponents, Wolfe had specifically asked for him and for Monkton who, a veteran of the forcible expulsion of the Acadians, was a man much more after his own heart. The real problems arose with the third brigadier, who had been foisted on Wolfe by the War Office and was emphatically not his choice.

Townshend was a brave officer, notably cool under fire, but he was also aloof, quarrelsome, malicious, pompous and generally dislikeable. The acidulous Horace Walpole, himself no gleaming exemplar of generous humanity, said of him: 'George Townshend has thrust himself again into service; and as far as wrongheadedness will go, is very proper for a hero . . . [he is] of a proud, sullen and contemptuous nature . . . saw everything in an ill-natured light'. Townshend was also clever and witty. At the Battle of Lawfeldt, he was positioned right next to a German officer whose head was blown off by a shell. Townshend casually wiped the mess of blood and bones from his coat and remarked: 'I never knew that Scheiger had so many brains.' But most of all Townshend was a master of skilfully executed caricatures, and the most famous image of Wolfe is that composed by Townshend on the Atlantic voyage over. His caricatures invariably caused grave offence and one of them, of a corpulent Duke of Cumberland exactly as he was, with no flattering doctoring, so enraged Cumberland that Townshend's military career suffered. With such a man on his staff, Wolfe could rationally have expected nothing but trouble; indeed by the end of the campaign the two men loathed each other – a loathing in no way mitigated by Townshend's losing no opportunity to point out that he was superior in birth to his commander.

Wolfe, though, took no man's opinion seriously when it came to waging war; in his own mind he knew all there was to know, and what he knew was the consistent application of unremitting violence. It was not for nothing that he had spent his formative years with Butcher Cumberland and Hangman Hawley. Since the mythographic view of Wolfe still persists in some quarters, it is worth quoting a letter he wrote to Amherst on 6 March while he was still battling the high seas of the Atlantic:

> If, by accident in the river, by the enemy's resistance, by sickness or slaughter in the army, or, from any other cause, we find that Quebec is not likely to fall into our hands (persevering however to the last moment), I propose to set the town on fire with shells, to destroy the harvest, houses and cattle, both above and below, to send off as many Canadians as possible to Europe and to leave famine and desolation behind me; belle résolution & très chrétienne! but we must teach these scoundrels to make war in a more gentlemanlike manner.

At this stage Wolfe's plan was to land near Quebec between the St Charles river and Beauport and to advance across the St Charles. After the confluence of the St Lawrence and the St Charles rivers there was a three-mile stretch of flat land along the northern shore, and at the village of Beauport the hills began, turning steeper and steeper until the Montmorency river finally hurled itself from 300-foot clifftops in a mighty cataract. The falls here were spectacular, filled with what seemed more like milk and froth than water, a dazzling, whirling, churning mass of billows, breakers and foam-crests, sending up warm-grey mists from the boiling cauldron below. As with all great waterfalls, the main impact on the observer was of the tremendous, inexorable power of Nature.

Montcalm and his lieutenants had spotted that this was where the attack was likely to come and had acted accordingly, though it was late in the day that the French commander adopted the idea of the Chevalier de Lévis (his deputy) that the entire front from the St Charles to the Montmorency be fortified. Incredibly, the strong point named for the chevalier, the heights of Point Lévis, immediately across the St Lawrence from Quebec and only a mile from the city, was never fortified. But at least Montcalm had provided himself with a second line of defence on the west bank of the St Charles, in case the French were driven from the Beauport shore; he had also built three bridges across the St Charles, which could be blown up behind the retreating French once they withdrew from the eastern bank.

June 1759 saw French energy and enterprise at their height as they prepared for the ordeal to come, apprehensive but encouraged by the knowledge that two previous British attempts to take Quebec in 1690 and 1711, had ended in grievous fiasco. Montcalm's most impressive feat was the sheer number of men he mobilised for the defence of the city. He ordered Bourlamaque to withdraw in stages from Lake Champlain, mobilised the militia and accepted volunteers as old as eighty and as young as twelve. All the regulars in Canada except Bourlamaque's three battalions were with him: the Béarn, Guyenne, Languedoc, La Sarre and Royal-Roussillon regiments. He also had militiamen, sailors from the ships that had arrived with Bougainville in May, Indians (mainly Crees), refugee Acadians and even thirty-five scholars from the Jesuit seminary, in a unit that one wag called the *Royal*-Syntaxe. Out of a total population of 60,000, Montcalm had around 15,000 under arms, most of them in the field army. But the garrison troops, the Indians, sailors and the raw recruits played their part too.

Montcalm's chief weaknesses were twofold. The bribery and corruption of Vaudreuil's regime meant that the defences of Quebec were not nearly so formidable as they should have been: dishonest contractors, venal

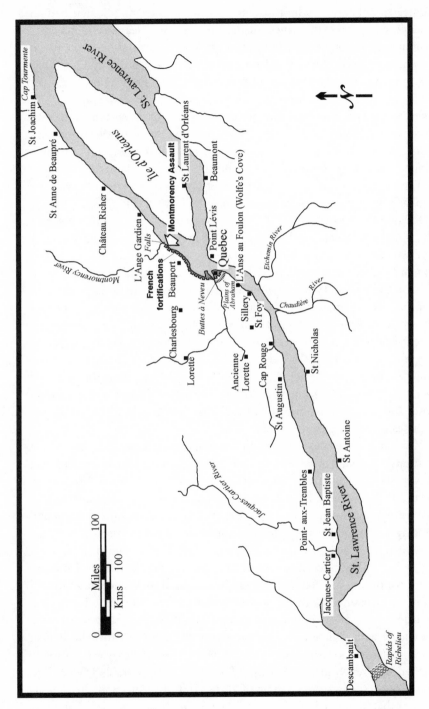

The St Lawrence campaign, June–September 1759

engineers, embezzling administrators and defalcating middlemen had all contributed to the malfeasance, misfeasance and non-feasance of schemes recommended by generals and military advisers. Bigot and his circle dined off wheat-fattened chicken and fine wines, while the ordinary Québécois were on a ration of two ounces of bread a day. New France now faced the enemy not just isolated from the mother country by British seapower but riven by internal divisions and jealousies, short of provisions and with defective fortifications. But Versailles must bear some of the blame, for during his winter mission of 1758–59 Bougainville had lobbied the French ministers tirelessly to implement Montcalm's plans to construct batteries to dispute the passage of any British fleet up the St Lawrence: particular emphasis was placed on having artillery at Point Lévis and on the Île d'Orléans. The so-called Isle of Orléans was a massive island that bisected the St Lawrence just north of the Montmorency Falls, carving the river into two narrow channels to west and east, and was a natural forward position for Quebec's defenders. But the Ministries of War and Marine declined to issue the necessary orders, doubtless in line with Belle-Isle's precept that the war in Canada in 1759 was to be a holding action only. Montcalm thus suffered from a dual disadvantage which, long-term, had a multiplier effect. He could not concentrate on Wolfe alone, for he knew that the army of Amherst was also in the field. On the other hand, Wolfe met no opposition whatever until he actually arrived before Quebec. This was a crucial factor in the summer campaign, for every week of delay brought autumn closer and hastened the day when the British would have to depart for the open sea or be caught in the ice.

Wolfe left Louisbourg for the St Lawrence on 4 June with his armada of twenty-two ships of the line and five frigates, but his vanguard had already started nibbling at the edges of the river. The British lived up to the tag of perfidious Albion, first by pressing a Canadian pilot into service by threatening to hang him otherwise, then by showing false colours and enticing a host of French Canadian pilots on board farther upriver; the benighted souls at first thought this was a French fleet and that salvation was at hand. Their services were invaluable, for they could tell from the merest ripple in the water where there were hidden rocks and could discern from the changing colour of the river whether sandbanks, mud or gravel lay below. Yet even with local pilots, the Royal Navy navigators astonished the enemy with their intrepidity. Vaudreuil later admitted that the British safely conveyed seventy-eight-gun warships through narrows normally avoided by French merchant ships. The more manoeuvrable frigates and transports actually made a show of their skippers' skills and the famous story is that Thomas Killick, master of the *Goodwill* transport, pointedly refused the services of a French pilot and then ostentatiously made light of the difficulties of St Lawrence navigation with a celebrated outburst: 'Damn me, if there are not a thousand places in the Thames fifty times more hazardous than this; I am ashamed that Englishmen should make such a rout about it.'

First contact between British and French can probably be dated to 20 May, when Admiral Durell anchored off Barnaby Island. Vaudreuil had ordered all French settlers on the lower St Lawrence to evacuate to Point Lévis and had sent Captain de Léry to oversee this operation, retaining all able-bodied males for military service. But the settlers refused to obey Vaudreuil's orders, claiming that they had oats to seed and anyway sceptical that a British invasion was imminent. A perplexed de Léry checked with Vaudreuil; he bowed to necessity, changed the orders and advised the settlers to take to the woods and hide. Wolfe enjoyed a serene passage upriver. There was no resistance except for the occasional militiaman's musket shot when a ship's boat ventured too close to the shore. The first skirmish occurred at the Île aux Coudres on 5 June. Admiral Durell landed troops on the island, which provoked the French to send a raiding party in retaliation. This accomplished nothing but took as prisoners three midshipmen who were on the island in defiance of orders. Durell pressed on to the Île d'Orléans, where the second armed encounter took place on 17 June. The French, having belatedly decided not to allow the enemy an uncontested landing at this major site, now captured a Royal Navy cutter and its eight-man crew. But when the whole British fleet hove in sight, they withdrew. Soon the massive Île d'Orléans come into view, its wooded sides kissed by a light fog. But in the clear light of day the British saw what looked like a land of milk and honey. The island was fertile and well cultivated with flax, barley, peas and wheat, and full of stone farmhouses and other signs of pacific civilisation: windmills, watermills, churches and chapels. Wolfe landed on the Île d'Orléans on the morning of 28 June, pushed on through the woods to the West Point and for the first time could see with his own eyes the scale of the problem he would confront at Quebec.

After viewing the elaborate French fortifications stretching from the St Charles river to the Montmorency Falls, Wolfe faced the ticklish problem of what to do next. His obvious move was to take the heights of Point Lévis opposite Quebec, but first he had to brush aside some gadfly attacks from the militia under de Léry and, more importantly, on the river itself. Then the elements lent a hand. On the afternoon of the 28th a violent storm hit the Royal Navy fleet, dashing the men-of-war together and destroying many of the flatboats from which troops had disembarked that morning. The weather seemed to be on the French side, but divine Providence, if so they interpreted it, would have made a more timely intervention a few hours earlier during the disembarkation when the loss of life would have been terrific. It was fortunate indeed that the storm subsided as suddenly as it had blown up, and that damage was not more widespread. French onlookers testified that the English mariners acquitted themselves well during this ordeal, and Wolfe's official reports made light of the 'squall', but one British naval officer testified to the momentary terror that the tempest had provoked: 'I never saw so much distress among shipping in my whole life,' he wrote. Those who had the leisure observed the impact on the Montmorency Falls, whose seething, boiling snow-white eddies seemed to become first grey and then black.

Having made no attempt to oppose the landing, the French decided that the time had come to use their seven fireships against the British vessels at anchor in the channel south of the big island. On the night of 28 June they launched their secret weapon. Sentries on the Point d'Orléans at first saw what looked like phantom ships coasting towards them. Suddenly the ghosts caught fire and there was a tremendous roar as the cocktail of fireworks, bombs, grenades, cannon, muskets and swivels exploded. But the result was fiasco. After the initial firework display and the choking clouds of acrid smoke and pitch, what should have been a blazing behemoth turned into a paper tiger. It seems that the ships had been fired too soon, giving the British ample warning, so, with consummate calmness, the Royal Navy ships either weighed anchor or cut their cables and sailed clear of danger while their boatmen rowed out and towed the fireships clear. Impotently fizzing and crackling on the shore, the would-be dragons blazed pointlessly until dawn. It is said that Vaudreuil watched the spectacle from the belfry of Beauport church, somehow hoping that a miracle would happen and that the towed fireships would be turned by the wind back onto their tormentors. The fireship failure was a blow to French morale. These vessels were meant to be the cutting edge of French defences, and the hard-pressed Ministry of Marine in Paris had spent one million francs on them. But, as one historian of Quebec in 1759 archly comments: 'The sight and sound of the blazing ships coming down the channel with their shotted guns exploding had frightened some of Wolfe's outposts on the island and caused a general alarm; this was all Louis XV got for his million.'

Suddenly, on 30 June, Montcalm spotted the danger to Point Lévis and asked Vaudreuil to send a strong party across from Quebec to seize the heights. For once Vaudreuil did not demur or wrangle, since this was the kind of operation he liked; the wooded landscape made Point Lévis ideal terrain for the bush-fighting of his Indians and Canadian irregulars. But one of the British prisoners somehow convinced his interrogators that

Wolfe's visible moves towards Point Lévis were a feint, to mask the real attack on Beauport and the St Charles. The Lévis operation was cancelled and the French dug in for the expected attack. All night they stood to arms, but there was no attack. At dawn the troops were dismissed, but had barely settled down to sleep in their hammocks when a false alarm led them to scramble back to the lines bleary-eyed. On 1 July Montcalm again ordered the heights of Point Lévis seized but again, incredibly, the operation was cancelled, this time because Vaudreuil personally interrogated the prisoner with the original disinformation and was gulled by him once more. While the French were still dithering, Brigadier Robert Monkton occupied the heights opposite the city. With Point Lévis now in British hands, the inevitable recriminations began among the French. Montcalm indited a furious letter of denunication and reproach to Vaudreuil, pointing out that he had disobeyed Louis XV's express orders that he was to defer to Montcalm in all operational matters. With typical patrician hauteur, Vaudreuil simply sent word that the letter 'was not accepted'. To be told that he had not written the letter and that his addressee had not received it simply enraged Montcalm further.

Wolfe meanwhile was ill and angry with his naval colleagues. Racked by pain in his bladder, he interviewed Admiral Saunders on 3 July and complained that French gunboats were wreaking havoc with his ships and that there seemed to be no effective answer to the enemy batteries. Patiently Saunders explained that the Royal Navy was not yet in full control of the Quebec basin and that there were particular problems in particular areas. For example, British warships could not close the range on the French positions around Beauport village because a wide bank of shallows meant it was too dangerous; if the vessels came in to bombardment range, they could well end up beached like turtles in the mud. But Wolfe countered that the navy captains seemed unwilling to come to close quarters with French batteries and gunboats in other sectors where such considerations did not apply and queried why the French gunboats seemed to be able to range freely without let or hindrance. He hovered close to accusing the Royal Navy of being cowards or 'gun-shy', but the phlegmatic Saunders did not allow himself to be provoked. Wolfe's temper was not improved when he finally gave up on another of his pet ideas, which was to approach Quebec from the west, at a place called St Michel (ironically not far from the Plains of Abraham) and establish an entrenchment there. His problem was that at this stage of the campaign he was not in a position to take his entire army west of the city. If he sent a detachment only, this offended against the principle of concentration of force. The likelihood was that he would be defeated piecemeal by a locally far superior enemy force. Even if he landed between Quebec and Cap Rouge, the first detachment onshore would be overwhelmed by superior forces before it could be reinforced.

Seemingly checkmated at all points, Wolfe returned to his initial idea of landing on the Beauport shore. Since this was too strongly defended, he fine-tuned this to a landing on the other side of the Montmorency Falls. On 8 July, leaving Major Hardy and a body of marines to hold the Point d'Orléans, Townshend and Murray embarked 3,000 men at night and landed before dawn at L'Ange Gardien, just the other side of the Montmorency Falls from the French. They dispersed the few Canadian outriders, climbed the heights and gained the plateau, from where they could look across the Montmorency gorge at the French army. Lévis and his Jacobite aide-de-camp Chevalier Johnstone watched all this and debated whether there was not a ford much lower down the Montmorency which would allow them to fall on the rear of the British interlopers. After an unseemly wrangle between Johnstone and Lévis, the Scotsman proved his point. An irritable Lévis sent his Indians to find this new ford; 400 men made the trip, worked round to the rear of the English newcomers and reported that the enemy could be destroyed at once if the French committed their main forces. Lévis hesitated and passed the buck to Vaudreuil, who was four miles away. His messenger brought back word that no risks were to be run, pending a full council of war. The disillusioned Indians opened fire anyway and were driven back with heavy losses, but not before they had consoled themselves by taking thirty-six scalps. This was a great opportunity lost, for in a battle in such terrain much would turn on woodcraft, and here the Canadians had a clear advantage.

The two armies now faced each other across the gorge of the Montmorency river. But Wolfe was really no nearer his ultimate objective. What should he do now? Attempt an attack across the Montmorency at one of the few points where it was fordable? Make a frontal amphibious assault on the Lower Town of Quebec from the Basin? Or somehow combine the two? On paper his position was dangerous, for he had one large force on the Montmorency river, another on Point Lévis and a third under Major Hardy on the Île d'Orléans; any one of the three – and especially Hardy's marines, could be overwhelmed before the others could reinforce them. For most of July Wolfe vacillated. Montcalm too was beset with uncertainty, indecisively weighing the options for offence and defence. On 9 July he outlined his ideas in a long letter to Lévis. There seemed to be four possible courses of action: to fight a limited offensive with the existing forces; to reinforce the Montmorency front with men from Quebec, cross the Montmorency fords by night and launch a surprise attack at dawn; to remain on the defensive ready to receive the British when they made their expected attack across the Montmorency; or to make the Montmorency lines impregnable by massive reinforcement, giving clear local superiority, but running the risk that Wolfe could re-embark and land in the rear between Beauport and St Charles, which would then by definition be scantily defended. At a council of war held later that day, and attended by Montcalm, Lévis, Vaudreuil and Bigot among others, there was considerable disagreement, with some (the sources do not make clear who) in favour of a bold attack, but the majority favouring the cautious policy of defence. Montcalm settled the issue by electing to stand on the defensive. He is alleged to have remarked of Wolfe: 'Let him amuse himself where he is. If we drive him off he may go to some place where he can do us harm.'

The second week of July saw phoney war at its height. The weather oscillated between extremes of heat and flash floods, so that men were either being drenched in their tents or plagued by mosquitoes. Envoys moved between the two camps under flags of truce, exchanging taunts and threats. When one messenger told Wolfe that he could destroy Quebec but could never take it, Wolfe flashed back that he would take the city if he had to spend the winter in the St Lawrence. There were naval skirmishes between French gunboats and British frigates, between rival bands of Indians and between Anglo-American Rangers and French *coureurs de bois*. The British awarded a bounty for enemy Indians killed, and the French Native American allies were further discomfited by the strides the redcoats had made in learning to fight them since the 'turkey shoot' at Monongahela four years earlier.

From the French point of view the most ominous development was the sudden increase in desertion. Several factors were involved here. The war of attrition was something French Canadians were not used to; they were hungry, bored and restless and could not understand why their commanders remained so supinely on the defensive. Some of them told their English captors that only the influence of their Catholic priests and fear that they would be massacred by Britain's Indian allies kept them loyal to Vaudreuil and Montcalm. Most of all their morale was low, and this was not helped by a dramatic development on 18 July when the Royal Navy finally ran the blockade from Quebec and burst through to the river above the town. Montcalm was immediately obliged to weaken his position at Beauport by despatching 600 troops to guard all accessible points in the cliffs between Quebec and Cap Rouge. Montcalm was now potentially under assault from three sides but, by the same token, Wolfe had spread himself dangerously thin and was vulnerable to counterattack in four distinct sectors. Yet overall the advantage henceforth lay with the British. Montcalm had assumed that no major warship could pass Quebec, but here were the British already at

Cap Rouge, able to interdict his food supplies and munitions of war.

While both sides marked time, Wolfe stepped up the bombardment of Quebec from Point Lévis, using six thirty-two-pounder guns and five thirteen-inch mortars. The target was the Upper Town and particularly the houses of the most wealthy and prosperous. So much destruction was caused that the merchants of Quebec actually petitioned Vaudreuil to be allowed to mount their own expedition to destroy the British batteries on the heights opposite. When Vaudreuil objected vociferously to the idea, the merchants went to Montcalm, who was only too happy to spite the Governor-General and give the scheme the nod. A group of 1,600 Canadian irregulars (many of them schoolboys and shopkeepers) under the command of Jean-Daniel Dumas, a veteran of Monongahela in 1755, volunteered for the task. Their aim was to take up a position on the heights overlooking the British battery and by sustained accurate musket fire to make the enemy position untenable. They began well by slipping across to the southern shore on the night of 11–12 July without being spotted but once ashore they ran into serious problems. Mere amateurs, lacking military training, discipline and cohesion and with no experience in the difficult art of bush-fighting, they soon literally became afraid of their own shadows and started shooting at their own men, thinking they were the enemy. Three times Dumas rallied his tatterdemalion army, but soon panic and confusion spread to the point where the force disintegrated. The ragged and unruly tiros began rushing back pell-mell to their canoes to re-embark. The irony was that the experienced Indian scouts who had been sent ahead found the British asleep and unsuspecting, so the operation could easily have been a success. But when the scouts returned to the main force, they found it no more. By first light the terrified amateurs were back on the northern shore. The British did not even learn of this ludicrous incident until five days later.

Wolfe issued a proclamation, calling on Canadians who were not in the regular army of France to remain neutral and promising that, if they did, their property and religion would be respected. If they did not, the Canadians should expect war to the knife, the destruction of houses, goods and harvests and no concessions made to civilians. In this vein he was happy to continue his campaign of aerial terror, raining down death from the skies for the whole month of July: 300 mortar bombs a day fell on Upper Quebec, which soon became a ghost town. The terrified citizens abandoned their homes and fled to the ramparts or into the fields outside the city. Their terror was particularly great since the city authorities, relying on supposedly authoritative reports from military engineers, had assured them that any bombardment from the Lévis heights could reach the Lower Town but not the Upper Town. Wolfe brought more and more armament into Point Lévis, adding four batteries brought ashore from the fleet on 20 July and two entirely new gun batteries, opened on 28 July and 28 August. All in all, by early September twenty-nine pieces of ordnance poured a death-hail into the city, causing particularly widespread damage with incendiaries and 'carcasses'. There were serious fires in Quebec on 16 July, then the whole of the Upper Town was gutted on 22–23 July. Something close to a firestorm occurred on the night of 8–9 August in the Lower Town when 152 houses were reduced to rubble. Quebec Cathedral and the Church of Notre Dame de Victoires, ironically given its name after the two triumphs of 1690 and 1711, were completely destroyed.

Since Quebec was a fortified city, the rules of war allowed its devastation and Wolfe explained his conduct as preparing the way for Saunders's fleet to pass safely by to the west and as the prelude to an amphibious assault on the Lower Town. But, as has been pointed out on many occasions, these objectives could have been secured simply by knocking out the ineffective city gun emplacements. Wolfe's real aim was to cow the Canadians by terror. There was nothing surreptitious or cryptic about this. He had warned Amherst that if he was frustrated at Quebec he would do the maximum damage to city and countryside and he was being as good as his word. Comparison of Wolfe with Sir Arthur 'Bomber' Harris and the aerial bombardment of German cities in 1941–45 may seem as far-fetched as the equal and opposite deification of Wolfe as Churchillian hero, but here, as elsewhere, he came very close to the thin line separating legitimate military action from war crimes.

On 28 July Vaudreuil revived the idea of fireships, albeit in a different form. He ordered a gigantic fire-raft constructed, 600 feet long, formed of more than seventy schooners, canoes, *chaloupes* and small boats chained together, all packed with grenades, old swivels, gun and pistol barrels loaded up to their muzzles, and other combustible material. This time the attack was better timed and ably directed by an intrepid Canadian irregular named Courval, supported by Bougainville, but the result was the same as before. Montcalm's opinion was that this time the French gunboats had not done their duty properly, letting Courval down by their timidity. Once more the Royal Navy jack tars performed brilliantly, rowing out to the blazing monster in their small boats, attaching cables and towing the menace away from the warships to the shore. One of the sailors was reported to have said to his comrade: 'Damme, Jack, did'st thee ever take Hell in tow before?' That night hearts of oak were fortified by an unparalleled grog order of half a pint of brandy per matelot; the Royal Navy knew how to reward its heroes.

Yet fire was becoming a constant in this grim war, not just the conflagration from the fireships or the inferno from gutted Quebec, but the casual toll taken by military insouciance and sometimes even arson. Captain John Knox, whose journal is an invaluable source for the entire siege of Quebec, relates one incident that must have been typical. British troops casually set fire to a farm, thinking it was uninhabited. Then, as the flames rapidly licked up to the roof, they were amazed and disconcerted to hear the terrified screaming of women and children (who had evidently been hiding) from within. Humanitarianism prompted a strenuous attempt at rescue but the men were beaten back by the ferocious flames and another hapless family joined the long list of casual victims of the war for North America.

Wolfe meanwhile cast about for some point above the city whence he could make his attack. He began by laying down an artillery barrage from his positions on the other side of the Montmorency gorge so intense that it was dangerous for French heads ever to peep over their entrenchments. This served two purposes: it diverted attention from operations above Quebec, and it acted as the necessary prelude should he later attempt amphibious landings anywhere along the Beauport–Montmorency line. But the plans for a major assault above the city soon came to nothing. It seems Wolfe was badly thrown off balance by Montcalm's counterattack with Dumas's 600 men, the Indian allies and Major François Le Mercier, commanding two eighteen-pounders and a mortar. Le Mercier's accurate gunnery forced the British ships anchored in the vicinity of the Anse de Mers to weigh anchor and stand away, which convinced Wolfe that his project for a landing above Quebec at St Michel was not feasible. Wolfe's critics have pounced on him for this non sequitur, for there were obviously other places above Quebec from which the city could be attacked (as indeed Wolfe discovered two months later). By abandoning his own principle that 'nothing is to be reckoned an obstacle to your undertaking which is not found really so upon trial', Wolfe created an impression of indecision and of being an ad hoc improviser rather than a general with a strategic vision. Some have dated his brigadiers' growing doubts about his competence to this contretemps at the end of July.

While he pondered his options, Wolfe kept the enemy guessing by sending a force under Sir Guy Carleton twenty miles upriver from Quebec to Pointe-aux-Trembles. The 600 men under Carleton were supposedly on the track of secret papers kept by the leading families of Quebec, again allegedly shedding light on ultimate French intentions, yet the enterprise seems to have been a fishing expedition in every sense. There was a skirmish with hostile Indians, who were soon flushed out, but Carleton's main achievement was to round up nearly a hundred women, children and very old men, who were sent back to Quebec under a flag of truce. Wolfe made a point of treating the grandest ladies among them to supper, where he tried to charm and flatter them. He joked that the French generals were mightily undistinguished since 'I have given good chances to attack me, and am surprised that they have not profited by them.' For propaganda purposes Wolfe encouraged his men to treat the lesser personages among the prisoners in a similarly benign way. Black cattle, sheep and hogs were slaughtered to provide a banquet, and the rankers made a point of sharing their rum and tobacco with the captives. All of this helped to increase the trickle of deserters from Quebec, which Wolfe hoped might develop into a flood.

Yet by the end of July he still lacked the decisive breakthrough he needed if the Quebec operation was to be completed before the winter of 1759; despite his public bravado, Wolfe had no intention of being ice-bound in the St Lawrence. Montcalm's Fabian tactics were beginning to wear him down and in the end he seems to have concluded that if Montcalm would not attack him or respond to any of the obvious baits, the only solution was for the British to attack him. It was very risky but it was better than the continuing stalemate. Wolfe had originally drawn up a plan for a two-pronged assault on the French Beauport–Montmorency positions, wherein Monkton's brigade would leave Point Lévis, ferry across the river and make a landing on the French right, between Beauport and the St Charles river; meanwhile on the French left another detachment of Monkton's Grenadiers were to attempt to seize one of the redoubts near the Montmorency river, and would be supported by troops coming down from the Montmorency gorge, crossing the ford in the French rear that the Indians had used when trying to attack them earlier. Now he abandoned the idea of assaulting the French right and concentrated on the Montmorency sector. In the opinion of many military analysts, he had exchanged a risky plan for a disastrous one. There is also the suspicion that when Wolfe consulted his brigadiers, they raised the awful possibility that Montcalm would acquiesce in the seizure of the redoubt and remain behind his entrenchments, thus making the flanking movement from the Montmorency gorge irrelevant. It is certainly true that Wolfe's strategy was predicated on Montcalm's willingness to fight in the open – the one thing he had hitherto consistently refused to do.

On 31 July, a clear hot day with a slight breeze – ideal for amphibious operations – Wolfe launched his attack. After an artillery duel between British warships and the most easterly French batteries, he boarded the *Russell* and again impressed everyone with his legendary coolness under fire: he was hit three times with shivering splinters from the ship's rigging and even had his cane knocked out of his hand by a missile. But when he got a close-up view of the redoubt, Wolfe did not like what he saw. It was much closer to the French entrenchments than he had thought when viewing it from a distance and now looked like a genuine death-trap; it was inconceivable that, even if they took it from under the noses of the French, the British could survive a counterattack or the relentless shelling from above. While Wolfe pondered whether to cancel the operation, lose face and affect morale, he noticed what he later described as 'confusion and disorder' among the French defenders. That decided him. He ordered Monkton at Point Lévis to bring his men across and Townshend, commanding at Montmorency, to make the diversionary flank attack; the batteries on the Montmorency gorge were to rain down fire on French positions until Townshend's men crossed the ford lower down the river. Wolfe was clearly playing double or quits for on the spur of the moment he had committed himself to a full frontal attack on the strongest French positions, employing 5,000 men against an enemy potentially twice as numerous. The marines and Grenadiers were in the boats ready to land by about 11 a.m. but many of the craft ran aground on hidden shoals. By the time the assault force had found a suitable place to disembark it was already about 5.30 p.m., with the tide out and the sky dark and lowering.

The thirteen companies of Grenadiers, first ashore, were supposed to form up on the beach in an orderly fashion until all the troops had left the boats. But there was a gung-ho spirit abroad among the Grenadiers that day – legend attributes it to doggerel verses composed by Sergeant Botwood of the 47th Grenadiers – and once they hit the beach, they broke loose and charged the redoubt. The French promptly abandoned it, but no sooner were the Grenadiers in possession than they suffered a hail of bullets from the enemy thronging the heights above them. The whizzing and pinging of the bullets did not deter the Grenadiers and they charged again, trying to climb the steep ascent. A second fusillade of musket-balls and buckshot from above dropped scores of men in their tracks. But there were enough survivors left, so grimly they fixed bayonets, encouraged by the thought that the French must by now be almost out of ammunition. At this precise moment a summer tempest burst over them. The rain fell in cascades, sheeting down so violently that the French defenders could no longer discern any targets coming up the hill. The Grenadiers meanwhile began slipping and sliding on the mud and wet grass until, finally, disconsolate, they retired to the redoubt. Wolfe then gave the signal for a general retreat. As the Grenadiers pulled out, the Indian allies of the French seized their opportunity to race down to the redoubt and scalp the fallen.

Meanwhile Townshend's brigade from Montmorency had crossed the ford lower down the river and was advancing for its putative flank attack. Suddenly word came that it was to retreat. This posed a fresh danger, for

Townshend's men had, so to speak, bought a one-way ticket, crossed the ford at low tide and were now in danger of being marooned on the wrong side of the river by the rapidly rising waters. Getting back across the ford in such conditions proved a ticklish business. Wolfe sent the 78th (Fraser's) Highlanders to cover the retreat across the ford, which they achieved with their customary Scottish heroism. Some of their comrades were with the landing force on the beach, and a notable wrangle ensued when Wolfe ordered the Highlanders back across the ford. They replied that they would not retire to the Montmorency gorge until satisfied that none of their clansmen had been left behind on the beach. Wolfe's low opinion of Scotsmen would not have been improved by this indiscipline. Finally, however, the Frasers were persuaded that their countrymen were safely re-embarked. Only then did they traverse the ford, but by this time the waters were so high that they made the crossing with difficulty, swimming rather than wading. All in all, the British had sustained their worst defeat since Ticonderoga in 1758 (significantly, also a frontal assault). Wolfe's casualty roster recorded 443 losses, including 210 dead. French casualties amounted to sixty dead and wounded, and all of these were sustained from the earlier cannonade from Montmorency.

Controversy raged about the defeat. The Grenadiers were adamant that they had been on the point of victory when the summer storm took a hand, but the French were just as convinced that the Grenadiers would have been massacred had they reached the entrenchment and interpreted the squall as another example of 'Protestant wind'. Much bitterness was caused by the scalping incidents when the Grenadiers withdrew from the redoubt, but this was to some extent palliated by a stirring narrative of French gallantry. Mortally wounded, a Captain Ochterlony was on the point of being scalped when a soldier from the Guyenne battalion intervened and held back the enraged Indian until French officers came up and removed the dying Ochterlony to a spot where he could expire peacefully. The captain's dying request was that his unknown saviour should be awarded a handful of guineas from his purse, but the Frenchman refused the offer. When Wolfe heard of the incident, he wrote to Vaudreuil with an offer of twenty pounds sterling for the hero; but Vaudreuil too turned down the offer, saying that the French soldier was simply following standard orders to prevent atrocities. Vaudreuil, indeed, was in rare high spirits, now confident that the only danger facing the French was on Lake Ontario. But Montcalm, imbued either with pessimism or realism, knew better and wrote to Bourlamaque: 'You see, monsieur, that our affair is undoubtedly only a prelude to something more important, which we are now waiting for.'

Truly there was something desperate about Wolfe's action on 31 July.

The initial plan, to coax Montcalm from his defensive position, was flawed and never likely to succeed; but the spur-of-the-moment decision, incredibly made at the very moment he saw all his earlier assumptions and calculations had been incorrect, poses severe problems to those who would portray Wolfe as a military genius. Surely Montcalm at Ticonderoga had shown clearly enough what would happen to a frontal assault on a well-defended position? And the risky head-on assault was not even made at the weakest end of the French position. Even if by some miracle Wolfe had established his army on the heights, the vast bulk of the French forces would simply have withdrawn across the St Charles river and formed up on the far bank, so that in a sense Wolfe would have been back where he started.

Wolfe was no master-strategist and he was also a prevaricator and ditherer. Yet Montcalm hardly emerges from 31 July with credit, since he told Lévis categorically a few days before that no such attack would or could take place. The struggle of Montcalm versus Wolfe has sometimes been elevated to the mythical pantheon, making it an analogue of Hector/Achilles or Arjun/Karna. Great issues were at stake in North America in 1759 but the two rival commanders, though talented, were very far from being military geniuses.

SEVEN

LAGOS BAY, PORTUGAL

Many are the myths that cluster round Bonnie Prince Charlie. Until recently it was thought that he was lowly sexed; that canard has now been laid to rest. More persistent is the perception that he was a blockhead, with a neurotic inability to adjust to reality; the unspoken premise here is that stoicism always represents intelligence, while voluntarism always represents stupidity. Yet Charles Edward Stuart, for all his faults – and they were many – was a highly intelligent man. Deeply versed in the thinking of the philosophes *(at one time or another he counted Voltaire, Montesquieu, Condillac and Helvétius among his personal friends) and a leading light in eighteenth-century freemasonry, he could be thoughtful and reflective, though his frustrated outbursts of rage often masked this. By 1759 he was deeply concerned that Jacobitism might be perceived as an outdated and discredited doctrine and he took advice, in particular from John Holker, on what to do about it.*

Holker was one of the great figures in industrial history. Born in 1719 at Stretford in Lancashire, he served his apprenticeship in Manchester and joined the Manchester Regiment in the Jacobite army when Charles Edward arrived there in November 1745. Imprisoned after Culloden, he escaped to France where, after a short period in Lord Ogilvy's regiment, he went into business in Rouen in 1749, bringing over from England the necessary men and machines to start a textile industry in France. Machault, then Comptroller-General of finances, promised to make him Manufacturer-Royal if he could beat the English at their own game. By 1755 Holker had succeeded to the point where he was made Inspector-General, in charge of foreign manufacturers. In the future lay even greater successes, when he brought back from England the first 'spinny jenny' and followed this with Arkwright's shuttle, enabling France to become a major force in the textile industry.

Holker never forgot his service with Charles Edward, to whom he was deeply and genuinely attached. In 1750 he risked his life by accompanying the Prince on his secret journey to London and in late 1758, hearing that the Prince had been abandoned by so many of his erstwhile followers, Holker took time out from his money-making to travel to Bouillon and confer with him. Charles Edward explained that there were signs the French were at last serious about helping him to regain the throne of his ancestors, but he worried that Scotland was no longer the base it had been in 1745. It was not just that the English government had smashed the clan system, confiscated Jacobite estates, forbade the wearing of traditional Highland dress, denuded the mountains and glens and cynically drained off Scotland's martial manpower by forming Highland regiments and sending them to North America to fight French and Indians. Jacobitism was now under threat from a number of ideological directions simultaneously. Many of the wretched of the Earth who had joined the Prince's standard from the slums of Edinburgh now saw greater attractions in the rising creed of Methodism. And the educated classes were increasingly drawn to the thinkers of what would later be termed the Scottish Enlightenment; almost to a man, Scotland's thinkers were hostile to the Stuarts and their ideology.

Holker tried to reassure the Prince. After all, there were few finer Scottish minds than that of Sir James Steuart, the economist, and he had suffered for his Jacobitism. This was true enough. In 1743 the thirty-one-year-old Steuart had married the sister of Lord Elcho, a fire-eating Lowland magnate who joined the Prince in 1745, while never liking him or achieving any rapport with him; in the many conflicts between the Prince and Lord George Murray during the '45, Elcho was always reliably to be found on Murray's side. Elcho was on a shortlist of Jacobite rebels who were to be expressly excluded from any future amnesty by the British government, and he blamed Charles Edward personally for his plight. Sir James Steuart was luckier and would eventually be pardoned in 1763. He had the good fortune to miss the Culloden debacle since he had been sent to Versailles in the autumn of 1745 as Charles Edward's personal envoy; he remained there to help plan the French invasion of England that never happened. In late 1758 Steuart and his wife were in Venice (where else for a Jacobite?), where they met and became friendly with Lady Mary Wortley Montagu. As Holker pointed out, Steuart had a most distinguished and subtle mind. Sometimes referred to as 'the last mercantilist', he was in some ways a kind of halfway house between the Scottish Enlightenment and earlier traditions.

As an economist Steuart evinced the same ambiguity, tacking as he did between a long-run quasi-Marxian labour theory of value and a short-term 'supply and demand' theory. He was the first to introduce the term 'equilibrium' into the economist's vocabulary and was an obvious forerunner of the classical and neoclassical schools. As an economist he advocated export subsidies and import tariffs and clung to the 'real bills' theory of money supply – a somewhat abstruse critique of what modern economists call the quantity theory of money. Whereas Hume would explain inflation in the Elizabethan era as the result of the influx of gold from the Americas, Steuart and Adam Smith believed that it was only when trade increased in Europe that the demand for gold became a factor, and it was this demand, rather than the raw influx of the gold itself, that triggered the inflation. But this was one of the few areas where Smith and Steuart did agree. It is perhaps significant that Smith's best-known book, The Wealth of Nations, *was intended as a thoroughgoing critique of Steuart; he thus had the rare distinction of being attacked by one of the prime theorists of capitalism and praised by the leading theorist of Communism, Karl Marx.*

Yet in 1759 Steuart was in exile and therefore not the force he would become in later years. As for the other members of the Scottish Enlightenment, it has to be conceded that the Bonnie Prince's fears were justified, since their attitudes towards the Jacobites ranged from, at best, ambivalence to, at worst, outright hostility. Although as a Scotsman, Hume had an instinctive sympathy for the House of Stuart and as a Tory he had no time for the Whig/Hanoverian ascendancy, he was no Jacobite. The accusation always amused him. In 1754, just after his history of the reigns of the first two Stuarts had been published, he wrote to his friend Balcarres that he was taken aback by the virulence of his many critics, according to whom 'I am as great an atheist as Bolingbroke, as great a Jacobite as Carte, I cannot write English, etc.' Perhaps this was partly his own fault, as he leaned rather too heavily in his History of Great Britain *on an earlier such history by the rabid Jacobite Thomas Carte (who died in 1754), sometimes to the extent of lifting entire phrases and passages.*

In the eighteenth century Hume's principal fame was as an historian not as a philosopher, and his multi-volume history of Great Britain was usually considered the finest such production in a crowded field. Curiously, Hume did not write it in chronological order: the first volumes, on the Stuarts, appeared in 1754, those on the Tudors in 1759, and the history of the British Isles from Julius Caesar to Henry VII was not published until 1761. It may be said that Hume served all the good wine first, since his work on the medieval world was marred by serious errors of scholarship, interpretation and sometimes even basic facts. Yet his history of the Tudors was in 1759 receiving generally good reviews. In his review that summer Tobias Smollett, a rival practitioner, said that Hume's work 'involved the reflections of a philosophical historian in the details of his facts, in a manner which throws lights upon every subject, without sensibly interrupting the course of the narration'. But there was little comfort in this work for the House of Stuart. In the famous controversy (that still rages today) about whether Mary, Queen of Scots was guilty of colluding in the murder of her husband Lord Darnley, Hume emphatically found Mary guilty.

The late 1750s and early 1760s saw a positive deluge of histories of Great Britain. Apart from Hume, there were major contributions from Smollett and

William Robertson, and from now forgotten figures like Robert Henry, Catherine Macaulay and Charles Coote; even Oliver Goldsmith tried his hand. After Hume's, easily the most interesting was by William Robertson, friend of Adam Smith and disciple of Henry, Lord Kames, another key figure in the Scottish Enlightenment. Kames had argued that history hitherto had evinced a fourfold pattern of human 'stages': first there were hunter-gatherers, then there were pastoral nomads, next came the agricultural society, and finally there was the modern or commercial society. In his History of the Reign of Emperor Charles V, *Robertson took this model and argued that the so-called 'Dark Ages' represented a reversion from the agricultural to the pastoral-nomadic stage, symbolised by the Goths, Vandals and Franks. The revival of agriculture was the seedbed of medieval feudalism, but meanwhile the fourth stage was already maturing in the agricultural womb in the form of the Mediterranean societies of Venice and Genoa, which in turn ushered in the fourth stage of general commercial civilisation in Western Europe. Just as Sir James Steuart's economics could be seen as proto-Marxian, so too could Robertson's emphasis on (though he never used such terms) the primacy of 'modes of production'. Kames and Robertson explained the diversity of contemporary society in terms of their four-fold model: so the Highland clans of Scotland and the Iroquois were alike still in the pastoral-nomadic stage, Russia was still in the agricultural stage but Britain and France, the two contenders for world supremacy, were clearly in the commercial stage. Kames's and Robertson's emphasis on 'stages in history' was seminal: it influenced Gibbon's work on the decline and fall of the Roman Empire, and its distant echoes can be seen in the work of the twentieth-century Arnold Toynbee's* Study of History.

Clearly an emphasis on 'modes of production' did nothing to serve the Jacobite cause, as British history was then construed not in terms of the divine right of kings but of purely contingent land grants. But if the Jacobites could take little comfort from Hume, Kames or Robertson, they could derive even less from Adam Smith, who showed no interest whatever, even implicit, in the fortunes of the House of Stuart. By common consent the most important production of the Scottish Enlightenment in the year 1759 was Smith's The Theory of Moral Sentiments, *which he himself rated above his much more famous* Inquiry into the Nature and Causes of the Wealth of Nations, *published seventeen years later. Smith was deeply influenced both by his old teacher of philosophy, Francis Hutcheson, and by Hume, but his two mentors had contradictory views on the nature of morality and Smith wanted to find a way to harmonise them. Hutcheson argued that morality was innate in human beings, but Hume stressed that morality was essentially a system of rewards and punishments that society had to impose on the individual from outside. It is important to be clear that for Smith moral philosophy meant providing an explanation for the actions and practices traditionally called 'moral' and was thus an empirical study of human history rather than, as in modern ethical theory, a normative enquiry, where one is concerned to justify a criterion for 'right' action. The collision between Hutcheson and Hume that concerned Smith was essentially the ancient clash between the Epicurean and Stoic principles. Stoics held that morality came naturally to human beings as they apprehended the basic order of the universe; Epicureans maintained that man was self-interested and morality simply a device to make sure that self-interest did not become self-defeating.*

Adam Smith appreciated the cogency of both perspectives. The natural morality of the Stoics would doubtless sustain people living in small communities or city-states of the kind Rousseau would champion in the Social Contract; *but for large, modern societies the Epicurean tradition of regulating individual self-interest came into its own. It seemed to him that the two different vantage points could be reconciled via what he called 'fellow feeling' and what we would call empathy. Since we are capable of identifying with other human beings, one of the vital functions of society is to hold a mirror up to ourselves. So, in one sense, it is only through living in societies that humans can become moral. 'Were it possible,' Smith wrote, 'that a human creature could grow up to manhood in a solitary place, without any communication with his own species, he could no more think of his own character . . . than of the beauty and deformity of his own face.' He thought that society enables us, as Burns later put it, 'to see ourselves as others see us' and that in moral terms we are all necessarily divided selves since we both pursue our own self-interest and yet are aware of its impact on others; we are both judges and judged and the ego needs the approval of our own judging self (which in normal language would be called conscience). This brings Smith to his master principle. All Scottish Enlightenment thinkers loved a master principle: with Hume it was 'opinion' and with Smith it was 'imagination'.*

Imagination is what enables us to carve out a specifically human sphere in the natural world. We yearn for order, and imagination is the faculty that enables us to satisfy that desire for order: so, in a sense all art, science, technology and religion are part of the web we weave to impose categories on the world. The richer our imagination, the more fellow feeling we can achieve, and hence the happier we become, as we also perceive happiness in others:

> *Our imagination, which in pain and sorrow seems to be confined and cooped up within our own persons, in time of ease and prosperity expands itself to everything around us. We are charmed then with the beauty of that accommodation which reigns in the palaces and economy of the great; and admire how everything is adapted to promote their ease, to prevent their wants, to gratify their wishes . . . We naturally confound [this ease and beauty] in our*

*imagination with the order, the regular and harmonious movement of the
system, the machinery by means of which it is produced.*

*True imagination, then, for Smith, does not work on envy or jealousy, but
sees how wealth-creation benefits all. What Smith calls the 'deception' of the
imagination is what motivates human beings at the deepest level:*

> *It is this which first prompted them to cultivate the ground, to build houses,
> to found cities and commonwealths, and to invent and improve all the sciences
> and arts, which ennoble and embellish human life; which have entirely changed
> the whole face of the globe, have turned the rude forests of nature into agree-
> able and fertile plains, and made the trackless and barren oceans a new fund
> of subsistence, and the great high road of communication to the different
> nations of the earth.*

*Since the truly rich man is the one with the most fecund imagination, finan-
cially wealthy men produce a surplus, beyond what they can produce themselves, and thus benefit all of mankind.*

The Theory of Moral Sentiments *shows Adam Smith trying to carry off
a delicate balancing act: between philosophical theory and the normal practices
of life; between jurisprudence and ethics; and between empiricism and philosophical rationalism. He tries to follow Hume in embracing the empirical world
and describing what actually exists, but is also drawn to theories of innate ideas
and a quasi-Kantian concern with categories as a way of making sense of the
world and imposing order. It was an ingenious book that made Smith famous
and earned plaudits from Burke, Hume and Kant but it can readily be appreciated how far removed it was from the nostalgic world-view of Jacobitism. As
Charles Edward correctly saw, the Scottish Enlightenment was at one level the
enemy of all he stood for, though doubtless purely at the level of kingship it
was, strictly speaking, irrelevant; how much did George II know or even care
about the ideas of Kames, Hume, Robertson or Smith? Those who emphasised
the features of the empirical world would have little use for theories of divine,
hereditary and indefeasible right; those who stressed the importance of credit
would have little time for Jacobites who inveighed against the National Debt
as an economic incubus; those wedded to the 'trickle down' theory of wealth
would pay little heed to the opposition who regarded conspicuous consumption
and money as evil, redolent of Oriental 'luxury', and who instead lauded the
virtues of landed wealth, spartan austerity and the virtuous qualities of the
Ancient city-states. John Holker could appreciate the inroads the new thinking
had made in the world, for some of it was implicit in the new industrial economy
of which he was a pioneer. But he knew that Charles Edward, like some later*

princes, wanted to be a 'people's prince,' someone who saw himself as a 'good man who did good things', so Holker encouraged him to concentrate his appeals on the dispossessed, not on the Enlightenment-influenced sophisticates.

Charles responded with gusto and produced a manifesto running to 107 clauses. From the tone of the declaration, it seemed that the Prince really thought his hour had struck and that he would soon be landing in England. He began by saying that his moderation in 1745–46 was itself a pledge for his future behaviour and claimed (disingenuously) to be speaking as Prince Regent with the full powers of Regency. He started with a general survey of the crimes and misdemeanours of the Hanoverian dynasty, claiming that the interest of Hanover was put before that of Britain, and that this involved Britain in unnecessary wars; denounced the standing army and expressed his hopes that a national militia would do away with this instrument of tyranny. Then he dealt in turn with his proposed policies and tried to reassure his audience on three different fronts: religious, financial and socio-economic.

He began with a long disquisition on Catholicism and admitted that he was now a Protestant, stressing however that his conversion was a matter of principle and conviction, not expediency. He pointed out that motives of self-interest should have made him change his religion in 1745 but at that time he was still sincerely convinced of the truth of the Catholic religion; similarly, motives of interest should have made him keep quiet about his switch to Anglicanism since. He continued:

The adversity I have suffered since that time has made me reflect, has furnished me opportunities of being informed, and God has been pleased so far to smile upon my honest endeavours as to enlighten my understanding and point out the hidden paths by which the finger of man has been introduced to form the artful system of Roman infallibility . . . In order to make my renunciation of the errors of the Church of Rome more authentic, and less liable afterwards to malicious interpretation, I went to London in the year 1750, and in that capital did then make a solemn abjuration of the Romish religion, and did embrace that of the Church of England as by law established in the thirty-nine articles, in which I hope to live and die.

Having established himself as a truly Protestant prince, Charles Edward moved on to the issue of finance. He denounced the excise tax as the major cause of smuggling – 'Can anything be more slavish than the penal laws made against frauds in the revenue?' – and then referred to his scheme to liquidate the National Debt by a sinking fund. The Debt was always a target of Jacobite propaganda, and here Charles Edward fulminated against a burden so great that the annual revenue raised in taxation could not service it, meaning that all future taxes would have to fall on manufacturing: 'If your own labour and industry cease to be exportable from high prices at home, your superior ability in trade will not long counterbalance the load of foreign importation and large annual remittances abroad in favour of your creditors.' The Prince then unveiled his master plan to upgrade industrial capitalism at the expense of financial capitalism (though naturally he did not use such words). After rehearsing the fiasco of the South Sea Bubble in 1720 and other signal instances of Hanoverian bribery and corruption, he declared that trade and trade alone would govern his foreign policy and (here the influence of Sir James Steuart is obvious) announced plans to increase the amount of specie in circulation:

> *As to that monstrous load of debt contracted upon government security, we fairly declare that we do not consider them as particularly prejudicial to the Crown, but in so far as they affect that of the people inseparably connected with it, and therefore we previously consent to their being paid off if that measure be approved of in parliament . . . If debts subsist, taxes are unavoidable, but we solemnly promise to consent to the abolition of the latter in proportion as the former shall cease to exist, and in all cases we shall establish such frugality in public expenses as to be able either to abolish the tax upon malt or the excise upon small beer, as being the most onerous upon the industrious poor of the nation.*

The mention of the poor brought the Prince neatly to the most original part of his manifesto:

> *Is not the poor in a starving condition? But what makes poor but a neglected education of youth, or heavy taxes? Are these poor cared for, notwithstanding the large fund raised upon the nation for that purpose? . . . We shall take under the protection of the state the children of poor parents, whereby the latter may be encouraged to propagate, and the former be properly cared for and become as by nature they are intended, the fountain of wealth in an industrious nature.*

There followed detailed prescriptions for enhancing industry and increasing exports, especially from the fisheries and the linen industry, which clearly showed the influence of Holker. In 1745 the Hanoverian government had sought to dissuade working men from joining the Jacobites by insinuating that the rising that year was purely about the technicalities of kingship; they argued that whoever sat on the throne, Hanoverian or Stuart, was a matter of complete indifference to the labourer in the field, the artisan in his forge or the tradesman in his shop, so why change the known for the unknown? Under Holker's influence Charles

Edward rose to the challenge and asserted that it would make all the difference. Certainly the pledge to put the poor under the protection of the state was a revolutionary undertaking and not something that was to be accomplished in Britain for another 200 years.

In the meantime Charles Edward and his agents kept hammering away at the French court, producing one ingenious proposition after another as to why France should now make an all-out effort on the Stuarts' behalf. Among the myriad arguments were the following: Louis XV and the Stuarts were bound by blood ties and a common interest in the divine right of kingship; a French invasion could never succeed without a second front in England and Scotland which only the Jacobites could provide; if France tried to go it alone, without the Bonnie Prince, the ordinary people of Britain would line up behind Pitt in a surge of patriotic fervour; all the crypto-Jacobites in the British army and the militia could not be energised if France acted unilaterally; if the Jacobites were privy to the French plans, they could bring horses, wagons and provisions to the landing point; since the Aldermen of London were (allegedly) Jacobite, if France went it alone, London would resist, but if the Prince was with her the capital would surrender without a fight; if Charles Edward was given a formal treaty of alliance like the one signed between France and the Jacobites at Fontainebleau in October 1745, the Prince would make sure that by the end of 1759 the English Parliament had ratified a treaty, not only defraying the entire expenses of invasion, but severing the alliance with Prussia and guaranteeing French possessions in the New World. But Choiseul no longer believed in the Prince or his powers. Whatever had to be done must be done by France alone; if that meant committing twice or three times the resources to the invasion of Britain that France had expended in 1745–46, then so be it.

Choiseul's original invasion plan envisaged a large flotilla of flat-bottomed craft sailing across the Channel from Boulogne and Ambleteuse with 50,000 troops on board. This plan was subjected to considerable modifications and finally changed out of all recognition, but throughout 1759 the French were in deadly earnest about descending on the British coast. The first 150 square-shaped flat-bottoms, 100 feet long, twenty-four feet broad and ten feet deep, each conveying either 300 infantry or 150 cavalry and with cannon at front and rear, were commissioned at Le Havre where 10,000 workmen received special contracts in the shipyards. A further 150 flat-bottoms were built in five other locations: Brest, St Malo, Nantes, Morlaix and Port Orient. Additionally, twelve armed escorts or *prames*, 130 feet long, thirty-six feet wide and nine feet deep, were constructed at

Dunkirk, Nantes and Bordeaux, each equipped with twenty thirty-six-pounders and two mortars and manned by 300 artillerymen. No expense was spared, and eventually another fifty-four flat-boats were commissioned. One estimate was that 100,000 livres a week was spent at Le Havre alone, but it is certain that by the end of 1759 thirty million livres had been spent on landing craft alone, enough to build thirty ships of the line. As one anxious member of the British ruling class, Lord Lyttelton, reported: 'They are certainly making such preparations as have never been made to invade this island since the Spanish Armada.'

Choiseul's plan was certainly a daring one, but his nervous colleagues on the Council of State (Belle-Isle excepted) thought the idea of crossing the Channel without the French fleet as escort was just too intrepid. The dispute on this point would eventually spell ruin for France, but it is to Choiseul's credit that he always insisted the men-of-war were, strictly speaking, irrelevant and that combined army and navy operations would simply repeat the fiasco of the Spanish Armada. If the French fleet at Brest was brought into the equation, the problems of mounting an invasion immediately multiplied, for in 1759 France was suffering a severe manpower shortage in its fighting ships. Manning problems had become acute for three main reasons: the capture of many ships and crews by the Royal Navy; the drain of competent personnel caused by privateering; and the high death rate in the French navy resulting from poor diet, lack of hygiene and disease. Additionally, resistance to pressing in France was robust, as it was widely known that the government did not pay seamen's wages on time, if at all; even when pressed, men deserted in droves, disgusted and disillusiuoned by brutalisation, victimisation and non-payment of wages. By the end of the War of Austrian Succession in 1748 sailors had to be paid five months' wages in advance before French warships could be crewed. When even the most draconian punishments like keelhauling failed to staunch the haemhorrage of desertion, the Ministry of Marine switched tack and tried kid-gloves treatment. At Brest by the spring of 1759 punishments were so mild that petty officers and matelots ran few risks through desertion. The consequences for French fleets were disastrous. By May the Brest squadron was short 3,507 petty officers and able seamen, the ships at L'Orient were 443 men shy while the Toulon fleet needed another 5,000 below-decks sailors to reach full strength.

The avid French preparations did not go unnoticed on the other side of the Channel, but at first Pitt remained remarkably complacent. The first emergency meeting of the British ruling elite to deal with the French threat took place at the house of Lord Anson, head of the Royal Navy, on 19 February. Present were Pitt, Newcastle, Earl Hardwicke, ex-Lord Chancellor and now Minister without Portfolio, Robert, Earl of Holdernesse, Secretary of State, northern division, John Carteret, Earl of Granville and President of the Council, and Field Marshal Ligonier, the army Commander-in-Chief. Anson, Admiral of the Fleet and First Lord of the Admiralty, opened proceedings by speaking confidently of the state of the Royal Navy. The fleet now had a record roster list of 71,000 men – a figure never previously attained – and there were 275 ships in commission in the fleet with another eighty-two 'in ordinary'. But Anson warned that these superficially encouraging figures masked a number of concerns. These ships were needed in a number of different theatres – the Mediterranean, the West Indies, the East Indies and North America as well as in home waters. This meant that fifty-nine of the 100 ships of the line were abroad or en route, leaving just forty-one at home, of which only twenty-one were fully manned and prepared. The French had forty-three ships of the line at home and thirty overseas. Anson was confident that all forty-one of his home ships could be on full alert in the Channel by May, but the problem of manning remained. Since all methods of recruitment had already been exhausted, and the shortages were largely due to sickness, scurvy and desertion, Anson proposed a number of emergency measures. Privateers should be impounded and crews taken from them, and meanwhile appeals should be issued by the Privy Council to mayors and magistrates to raise more men, rather as had been done during the 1745 rising. The ultimate aim should be for the Royal Navy to have 300 fully equipped ships for the first time in its history.

Ligonier was then asked to provide a similar *tour d'horizon* for the army. He explained that the total current manpower was 52,000, including the troops serving with Prince Ferdinand of Brunswick in Germany and the garrison at Gibraltar; a further 5,000 were stationed in Scotland and another 4,000 were performing military duties with the fleet. At a pinch he could raise 4,000 army pensioners for garrison duties, but his real problem was that, after attending to the defence of London and the naval ports, he would have only 10,000 men with which to oppose a French landing.

Pitt then intervened to make light of the difficulties. He refused to recall troops from any of the vital overseas theatres, but suggested stationing troops and transports on the Isle of Wight so that they could be rushed to any invasion point. He showed more sympathy for Anson than for Ligonier, declaring himself determined that the figure of 71,000 sailors cited should by July be a true statement of effectives and not just an 'on paper' muster. The number of sailors in home waters would therefore be increased from 18,000 to 25,000 and in addition no fewer than thirty-four new warships would be commissioned. Newcastle, ever the pessimist, took heart from Pitt's aplomb and suggested timidly that it was unlikely the French could mount an invasion before October. The general naval strategy was then agreed. The aim was at all events to prevent a union of the French fleets at Toulon and Brest and to this end Admiral Edward Boscawen, Commander-in-Chief of the Royal Navy in the Mediterranean, must ensure that the Toulon fleet never passed through the Straits of Gibraltar; if by some mischance it did, he was to engage it at once. It would be left to him to decide, in the light of local conditions, whether he would base himself outside Toulon or in the Straits themselves.

Pitt's team met at regular intervals throughout the spring and summer of 1759. Although Pitt, Newcastle, Anson, Ligonier, Hardwicke, Holdernesse and Granville hardly constituted a magnificent seven, they were an effective War Cabinet, much less racked by factionalism and intrigue than their counterparts on the French Council of State. They were far more single-minded, and part of the explanation was that they were dealing with a constitutional, not an absolute monarch. George II had many faults and was certainly less intelligent personally than Louis XV, but he did not rule by *lettres de cachet* and *lits de justice*; the English Parliament was at one with its king, whereas the French *parlement* remained locked in conflict even while France faced one of its worst ever crises. Pitt's War Cabinet also exhibited more of a 'can do' attitude than its French equivalent, which was too often concerned to find reasons why bold policies could not succeed.

Notable was the meeting at Holdernesse's house on 8 May, when John Russell, 4th Duke of Bedford and Lord Lieutenant of Ireland made up the heptarchy in the absence of Ligonier. Naturally enough, Irish affairs figured prominently on the agenda. It was known that the French were keen on landing in Ireland and stirring up the great latent discontent there, and it may even have been known – for the British secret service was highly efficient – that Louis XV had offered Charles Edward Stuart the crown of John Bull's other island, only to have it contemptuously rejected. Bedford pointed out that Ireland was in a pitiable state, with just 5,000 troops on the island and no possibility of reinforcing them. Pitt once more down-played the French threat, but agreed that measures should be taken to damp down the alarm. Knifing through to the heart of the problem, he argued that what was needed was decisive action to appoint a supreme naval commander in home waters, for it was by sea that any invasion force, whether destined for England, Scotland or Ireland, must come, and only at sea that it could be defeated.

The big question was: who would be appointed to this command? Rear-Admiral Sir Charles Saunders was Anson's favourite and preferred choice, but he was generally considered too junior to command the Channel squadron. Admiral Edward Boscawen was probably the form favourite in a talented field but he irritated Anson by turning down the senior naval post on the Quebec expedition with Wolfe, doubtless in the hope of being selected for the Channel. Anson gave Boscawen the consolation prize of Commander-in-Chief, Mediterranean and appointed Saunders to the Quebec position. Unless, therefore, Anson was to lead the fleet himself – which old age made him disinclined to do, though he had done so in a stopgap role in 1758 – the obvious man for the job was Admiral Sir Edward Hawke. The problem here was that both Pitt and Anson disliked Hawke, a tactless, indiscreet prima donna with no political skills or personal charm who had made many enemies and was sustained only by George II's partiality for him.

Hawke seems to have been a pure technician of seamanship, a man who scarcely existed when not at sea, and even his biographer finds nothing to say about his private life or outside interests. At fifty-four he was the hero of the Battle of Finisterre in 1747 but had enjoyed mixed fortunes so far in the Seven Years War. He succeeded the unfortunate Admiral Byng in the Mediterranean, but took part in a botched attack on Rochefort in 1757 and soon afterwards failed to intercept the Brest fleet. His darkest hour came in 1758. Anson sent out Captain Richard Howe (later a famous admiral) to command the transports in an amphibious attack on St Malo, with Hawke as overall fleet commander. Hawke somehow got it into his head that the combined operations assault was to be on Rochefort and that Howe had been sent out to replace him because he had failed at Rochefort the previous year. Impulsively he struck his flag and sent an intemperate letter to the Lords Commissioners of the Admiralty, washing his hands of the whole affair. For Hawke, this was a matter of honour, and the Admiralty had impugned his.

Hawke was summoned to a Board of Inquiry at the Admiralty. By now he had realised his mistake and attempted both to apologise for and to palliate his hasty actions. But the icy rebuke he received once again demonstrated Hawke's signal political naivety. The Lords of the Admiralty uttered as follows: 'That Sir Edward Hawke's striking his flag without order is a high breach of discipline; therefore notwithstanding the acknowledgement contained in the said minute [Hawke's apology], the Lords do not think proper to restore him to the command of the ships in the Channel, although in consideration of his past services, they have not proceeded to any further censure.' Anson took over the Channel fleet while Hawke retired on 'sick leave'. He was lucky. He could have been court-martialled or seen his career at an end by being ignored. Anson certainly found it hard to forgive him.

But Pitt, Anson and the others decided in May 1759 that Hawke's worth as a fighting admiral outweighed all personal considerations, and he was therefore appointed to command the fourteen warships at Spithead and the eleven at Plymouth. As his second-in-command he would have Sir Charles Hardy, another prima donna who was still fuming that Saunders, not he, had been given the Quebec naval command. Among the many talented captains assigned to Hawke were Robert Duff, John Storr, Augustus Hervey, Robert Digby, Sir Peter Denis, Augustus Keppel, Samuel Barrington, John Byron, George Edgecumbe, Witteronge Taylor and Richard Howe (his supposed nemesis from 1758), most of whom went on to be admirals themselves. The appointment of Hawke crystallised Pitt's anti-invasion preparations. At another meeting of the War Cabinet on 18 May, Pitt announced that an armed camp was being set up on the Isle of Wight, reinforcements were being rushed by troop transport to Ireland and Scotland, and the militia was being called out. Most significantly, Hawke was ordered to proceed immediately from Torbay and take up station outside Brest.

Ever since Choiseul first decided to invade the British Isles there had been constant skirmishing between the rival navies, usually in the form of one-on-one-combats in which the French invariably came off second-best: the *Vestal* against the *Bellone* in February; the *Iris* and the *Aeolus* against the *Mignone*, and the *Southampton* versus the *Danae* in March; the *Achilles* against the *Comte de St Florentin* in April; the *Venus* against the *Arethusa* in May. The effect on French morale was compounded when Hawke, having received the Admiralty's instructions for the blockade of Brest, began a close, continuous investment of the port. Whereas in 1756–58 the Royal Navy had kept a watch on Brest from bases in the west of England, they now instituted a system of unceasing surveillance and reconnaissance, maintaining station in relays. Hawke sent back his ships for refitting six at a time, rotating his capital vessels. In fact the roster did not work very efficiently, as the ships tended to stay too long at Plymouth, but the French did not realise this. Since they had never before had enemy warships sailing unchallenged at the entrance to Brest harbour, they experienced the close blockade as humiliation and worse, as there was an issue of credibility at stake: since their fleet of twenty-two men-of-war was virtually the same size as Hawke's (he had twenty-three), the French lost face in the eyes of Europe as it appeared that they dared not face the Royal Navy. And sheer geography and technology were working against the French invasion project. East of Brest there was no harbour suitable for a large fleet in the age of sail – no ports like Plymouth or Portsmouth – but only tidal harbours that could hold no more than a small number of craft.

And yet Hawke's position was by no means a bed of roses. He had to square the circle of watching the French constantly, while supplying and refurbishing his fleet. And he was bedevilled by inadequate and antiquated dockyards at Portsmouth and Plymouth as well as by manpower shortages. The shortfall in crews was serious but not critical: increased bounties for volunteers and a general press throughout the kingdom produced only 1,000 men, not the 7,000 Pitt had promised. But Hawke's real complaint – which brought him into dangerous conflict with the Admiralty – was Anson's arrangements for cleaning and refitting ships, which detained them unnecessarily in port. Hawke proposed that ships due for refitting should have their hulls boothose-topped only – in other words, they should be keeled over in shallow water, with a mixture of tallow and resin applied as a temporary protection. But Anson insisted on going through the full regulation procedures; the principal reason for the slow turnaround that so infuriated Hawke was Anson's cost-consciousness – he refused to hire more hands. And after the Board of Inquiry the year before, Hawke knew he had to tread carefully; after that fiasco Anson and the Admiralty would not cut him any more slack. The other problem concerned provisioning. Not only were the stores – and particularly the casks of beer – often sub-standard but the ships had to go all the way back to England to get them. During the summer Hawke persuaded the victuallers to come as far as Ushant to meet him so that his ships did not have so far to travel, but he knew that once the weather turned stormy, as businessmen unwilling to take losses they would not continue the arrangement.

Storms did indeed lend a hand in proceedings that summer and would do so throughout 1759. Early in June a severe gale forced the squadron blockading Brest off station and the ships were compelled to return to Torbay until the 17th. Hawke knew that the selfsame winds that drove him up the Channel on that occasion would keep the French in port, and that a change in the winds that enabled them to get out would also bring back the blockading force, but his abiding anxiety was that the French might be ready to clear from Brest the second the weather moderated, allowing them to sortie before the Royal Navy returned from the Channel. Moreover, a gale that forced him back to the Channel might also waft another French fleet (maybe even, horror of horrors, the Toulon squadron) into Brest. Storms also increased the sickness rate among his men and meant extra cleaning and refitting for the vessels that had to ride out the high seas. Nevertheless, in general in the war of nerves the British won hands down. Vigilance kept Royal Navy crews at a high pitch of readiness while the mere fact of being cooped up caused French morale to plummet. More than one French participant in the events of 1759 later testified that the unceasing blockade really bit deeply into French moral fibre. And British confidence grew as report after report told the same story: the French would not be ready to make a decisive move until autumn.

Hawke's blockade had two main aspects: attack and interdiction. As June turned into July, he increased his stranglehold on the French coast. While he himself remained off Brest, Commodore Boys and a cruiser squadron watched for any movement in the Flanders ports; another detachment of cruisers lay in the Downs in case the French tried to slip across from Boulogne and Ambleteuse; yet another force was on surveillance duties outside Le Havre, where the bulk of the flat-bottoms were being built; and a fifth force under Rear-Admiral Rodney, a critic and rival of Hawke, made ready in Spithead. First blood went to the audacious Rodney, who on 3–5 July in the sixty-gun *Achilles*, and with a mixed force of fifty-gun warships, frigates, sloops and bomb-ketches, raided Le Havre and destroyed large numbers of flat-bottoms and quantities of stores. Keen to see his own immediate command emulate Rodney, Hawke took particular pleasure from the exploit on 29 July when the *Rochester* chased an enemy convoy and four frigates into the River Vannes. But in the early summer most of his work involved interdiction. He prevented neutrals from entering Brest, starving the port of provisions and naval stores, and even risked a major incident, and playing into Choiseul's hands, when he intercepted four Swedish merchantmen and had them escorted to Plymouth. He also tried to stop supplies reaching the French by creating a special inshore squadron under Augustus Hervey, consisting of frigates able to navigate the rocky coast of Brittany and the dangerous lee shore, thus bottling up Brest even more tightly. Strictly speaking, all this was against international law, as blockades were meant to apply only to ships of belligerents or those carrying contraband of war, closely defined as money, arms or ammunition. But George II was no more punctilious an international lawyer than Elizabeth I had been.

With Boscawen's equally ceaseless vigil confining the French Mediterranean fleet inside the inner roadstead at Toulon, by mid-July Pitt's War Cabinet had grounds for cautious optimism. Pitt reverted to his earlier mood of jaunty contempt for French preparations, thus almost by pre-established harmony jolting the gloomy Newcastle into another bout of pessimism: 'I flatter myself that with the blockade of Guadeloupe we may have a very great success this year in North America. But to think of being able to extirpate the French from North America . . . is to be the idlest of all imaginations.' Nonetheless, Newcastle apart, the meeting of the War Cabinet at Holdernesse's house on 16 July saw Pitt and his colleagues in eupeptic, upbeat mood. To increase army numbers it was decided that proclamations be issued telling potential recruits they would not be sent out of the country, to Germany, North America, India or the Caribbean. Other military decisions taken in the flurry of mutual congratulation on 16 July included a resolution to raise a Highland regiment for service in Scotland (for the first time since 1745 the British elite felt it was safe to do this, and that the recruits would not immediately desert to the Jacobites); to raise another quite separate infantry regiment; another of light horse; and to attach militia companies to regular units with a view to eventual incorporation. Everywhere in the British Isles confidence was growing. Tobias Smollett, who was writing a history of England at this very time, included some (for the French) ominously loyal addresses from Irish Catholics to King George: 'They professed the warmest indignation at the threatened invasion of the kingdom, by an enemy who, grown desperate from repeated defeats, might possibly make that attempt as a last effort, vainly flattered with the imagined hope of assistance in Ireland.'

By mid-summer Choiseul's plans had matured well. Intensive naval preparations were taking place at Brest, Le Havre, Rochefort and Toulon and troops were being assembled at a number of points, principally Ostend, Dunkirk, St Omer, Lille and Vannes; 325 transports and flat-bottoms were nearing completion, including 100 at Le Havre specially designed to carry supplies, artillery and *matériel* and another 225 troopships; there had been a slight change of plan, in that now 125 of them were earmarked for cavalry and horses and 100 for infantry. The military agent Comte d'Hérouville went up to Le Havre to supervise embarkation and disembarkation drills and was delighted with the results: between six and seven minutes each way, coordinated for all 100 boats. Additionally, the twelve *prames* were giving every satisfaction. Altogether France had 48,000 men and 337 ships plus three months' supplies for Choiseul's great enterprise of England and Scotland.

Choiseul had by now decided that the departure port for Soubise's strike against England should be Le Havre rather than Dunkirk, for the simple reason that the troops could be cantoned at Rouen and taken down the Seine at the last moment, and it was much easier to get the fifty boats built in Dunkirk to Le Havre than the 100 at Le Havre to Dunkirk; moreover, because of tides the whole expedition could leave at the same time from Le Havre, but not from Dunkirk. But the famous privateer François Thurot would be given a small force with which to make a diversion in Ireland and to effect a smokescreen, for the Royal Navy reconnaissance ships would continue to report that preparations were going on at Dunkirk.

Ideas for expanding the invasion of Britain into a 'grand slam' exercise were already revolving in Choiseul's head, and he notified his friend the Duc d'Aiguillon, currently a popular hero after heavily defeating a raiding force of British marines that landed in Brittany in 1758, that he would be requiring his services soon as commander of an expedition to Scotland. By early June it was clear to Choiseul that he should launch two invasion forces: one against England under the Prince de Soubise and the other under d'Aiguillon against Scotland. The proposed Scottish expedition brought the Jacobites back into the picture. Given the potential multiplier effect of crypto-Jacobitism in England and, especially, Scotland, the pragmatic Choiseul felt he had to deal with supporters of the House of Stuart, despite his personal distaste for Prince Charles Edward. The Machiavellian Choiseul therefore decided to deal directly with Lord Blantyre, codenamed Leslie, and with Chevalier Alexander Mackenzie Douglas. He calculated, correctly, that these two men were genuinely keen to foment a rising in the Scottish Highlands, but did not approve of the Bonnie Prince's 'sulking in his tent' at Bouillon and might therefore collude in cutting the Prince out and marginalising him.

Choiseul kept his Jacobite agents in play with direct negotiation involving himself and d'Aiguillon while stalling and stringing Charles Edward along. Knowing how the Stuart prince's mind worked and how greatly he was ruled by pride, Choiseul proposed sending his secretary Jean-Louis Favier to Bouillon, calculating that an outraged Charles Edward would write back blusteringly, asking for someone of higher rank. The Bonnie Prince predictably fell into the trap. Further time was wasted while Choiseul 'looked for' someone suitable. Finally he sent his friend and kinsman Joachim Casimir de Béthune to Bouillon with instructions to prevaricate. A bemused Charles Edward told Béthune that he must know if Choiseul wanted him to take part in the French expedition so that he could warn his friends in England, who were getting conflicting messages. Béthune parroted the old formula 'Everything for the prince and nothing without him' and stressed that the French would not be ready to move until the autumn.

The extent of Choiseul's duplicity can be gauged from the instructions he was simultaneously giving to the French ambassador, the Marquis d'Affray, in Holland. Although Pitt at one time feared that the Dutch were so angry with Britain for flouting the neutrality laws governing ships on the high seas that they might join forces with the French, the situation was almost exactly the reverse. The Dutch were seriously alarmed by French preparations for invasion and sought assurances that it was not France's intention to restore the 'Pretender' or his son or to wage a religious campaign on behalf of Catholicism. D'Affray assured the States-General that France took no account of Charles Edward in its preparations. It was true that talks had been held with him, but only to gauge the extent of potential Jacobite strength in the Highlands. France's intention was to defeat Britain in Britain, to compel her to abandon her global pretensions and to make peace on terms favourable to France. She could hardly be waging a religious crusade, d'Affray pointed out, since Charles Edward was himself a Protestant. Choiseul clinched the matter by inditing a letter containing a scathingly contemptuous reference to the Stuart prince. Louis XV, he wrote, had no need of 'ghosts, spectres or scarecrows' in the rational pursuit of French policy aims. In the light of all this, there is something deeply pathetic about Charles Edward's plight (though he had only himself to blame for it). When Eugène Eleonore de Mézières, scion of a dynastic union between the English Jacobite Oglethorpe family and the great French aristocratic family, the Rohans, wrote to ask Charles Edward if he could accompany him on the expedition to England, the Prince wrote back on 12 June: 'I appreciate greatly the offer of your service and should be glad to have proper occasion to make use of it. I see frequent mention of a great expedition in the gazettes, but know no more of it. When I do, you shall be acquainted with it.'

Having sidelined the Bonnie Prince, Choiseul got down to serious business with Leslie and Douglas. Predictably, the two Jacobite agents did not see eye to eye. Douglas sent in a long memoir, recommending a landing at Bristol, with a turnpike road leading to London and the Welsh Jacobites in the catchment area. On the same day (13 June) Leslie dismissed the idea of a landing in Wales or the west of England as moonshine and advised Choiseul to concentrate on Scotland. Having shrewdly caught the drift of Choiseul's mind, he suggested that it would be a good idea to have a proclamation in Charles Edward's hand addressed to the Scottish clans, but stated baldly that there was no need for the Prince to stir from Bouillon. Basically, Leslie aimed at restoring the situation in Scotland to that obtaining in March 1746, just before Culloden, and to this end he mentioned Lord George Murray as someone who should be recruited. Murray, now an ailing old man of sixty-five living in exile in Holland, had been Charles Edward's Lieutenant-General in 1745–46 and the mastermind behind the Jacobite army. The problem, as Douglas well knew, was that the Bonnie Prince loathed him. Choiseul quickly picked up on the veiled anti-Charles hostility in Leslie's remarks. He replied that Louis XV valued all these suggestions and had always had a special feeling for Scotland. He himself thought the Lord George Murray suggestion a good one but, given Charles Edward's known feelings about him, it was probably best to wait until French troops had actually landed in Scotland before approaching the veteran Lieutenant-General.

The energetic Leslie followed up Choiseul's approving nod and, on

15 June, had a long meeting with the Prince de Soubise, commander-designate of the expedition to England. Leslie advised him that Scotland was a crucial aspect of the invasion of Britain, that a foothold be gained on the west coast of Scotland and that either Charles Edward or his father James should issue a royal warrant for the raising of clan regiments. The ultimate aim should be the establishment of a Scots government friendly to France (in effect a resurgence of the 'Auld Alliance'), complete with a parliament and Privy Council that would restore the ancient laws and customs of Scotia. Leslie promised to engineer another Jacobite rising in Scotland but asked that his offer be kept a secret from the English Jacobites (and presumably also from Charles Edward himself).

Encouraged by Soubise, Leslie next sent Choiseul a list of twenty-three peers and sixty-five knights, baronets and gentlemen who could be relied on if the French landed in Scotland; he promised to put 20,000 clansmen in the field, provided only that a minimum of 7,000 of France's best troops made landfall on the west coast, bringing arms, equipment and some experienced officers and engineers. Leslie's next memorandum was commendably thorough, containing as it did maps and landing points (he highlighted Greenock and Montrose) and the recommendation that the invasion flotilla follow a westabout track round Ireland because of the currents in the Channel. As a veteran of Louis XV's 'King's Secret', Leslie particularly relished backroom diplomacy and backstabbing, and his disloyalty to Charles Edward was pronounced. But other Jacobites, wishing to curry favour with Choiseul, and seeing the Bonnie Prince as a man undone, were even more treacherous. Dominique O'Heguerty recommended that the Stuart prince be given a take-it-or-leave-it offer: either become King of Ireland or be cast adrift. It was even suggested that James Stuart, the Old Pretender, be summoned from Rome to meet Louis XV and then offered the crown of Ireland, thus cutting out Charles Edward altogether. And since James was by now very angry with his son for his intransigence – to the point where he refused to sign articles of abdication or a certificate of Regency for Charles – the idea was not so far-fetched as it might look at first sight.

With his lucid mind and ruthless single-mindedness, Choiseul was able to cut through the tangle of factionalism, spite, petty rivalry and sheer cloud-cuckoo-land that was the Jacobite movement by 1759 to excerpt exactly what he needed to win over his wavering colleagues on the Council of State. The moment of truth came at the Council meeting on 14 July (attended by Belle-Isle, Berryer, Silhouette, d'Estrées and Soubise) when a confident Choiseul began by amusing the King and the other ministers with an account of his Machiavellian handling of Charles Edward. Because

Jacobite support would be invaluable to us, he said, he had been forced to negotiate directly with the Stuart prince but to a large extent he had managed to detach Blantyre (Leslie) and work with him. Blantyre was told that the French expedition was independent of Charles Edward but that His Most Christian Majesty was not averse to any benefits that could accrue to the House of Stuart from the invasion. It was quite likely that all the negotiations with the Highland clans would come to nothing, but it was thought necessary to try them. As for Charles Edward himself, once Soubise or d'Aiguillon landed at their respective destinations, the true value of his support would become clear and at that point France would know what to do about the Prince. Louis XV emphasised that a decision had been taken not to make any formal agreement with Charles Edward and that his commanders were under strict orders to make no commitment of any kind to him. His intention was that once the invasion was launched, the Stuart prince would be informed and invited to take part in person.

Belle-Isle, who always oscillated between having a soft spot for the Prince and being exasperated by him, asked for a summary of the negotiations so far between Choiseul and Charles Edward. Choiseul replied that the Prince had made a number of efforts to get in on the secret, but that he had fobbed Charles Edward off and given nothing away. It was then that Choiseul revealed his true hostility and contempt for the Prince. He explained that Charles Edward had been held at arm's length for three main reasons: the Prince was not a stable person and had not a calm and collected head ('*pas assez bien faite*'); he was surrounded by spies and venal riff-raff; and there was a danger that Holland and Sweden would panic and join the British if France supported him openly, even though he had changed his religion. Having dealt with the Stuarts, Choiseul outlined the manpower situation and the state of readiness of the navy. Despite Leslie's recent memorandum, warning against landings on the south coast of England, Choiseul reassured the Council that the Soubise expedition would set out as originally intended from Le Havre and make landfall at Portsmouth. Admiral la Clue would be ordered to sortie from Toulon with the Mediterranean fleet, so that British attention was distracted to that arena. After destroying the dockyards, arsenal and naval installation in Portsmouth, Soubise would make it the base of his operations in England and the nerve centre of communications with France. Thurot's force would meanwhile decoy the Royal Navy so that it kept much of its strength on the Downs but, when the time was right, Thurot would break out and make for Ireland, where he would create another diversion. Choiseul's thinking was that, with Hawke watching Brest and the rest of his fleet on the Downs, Soubise and his men would sail through the gap in the middle.

The recent alarming raid on le Havre by Rodney had made the British complacent and convinced them there was no longer a threat at Le Havre.

Choiseul next turned to his *pièce de résistance*. Twenty-five battalions of infantry and a regiment of dragoons under the Duc d'Aiguillon would leave Brest in September, bound for Scotland and accompanied by Admiral Marshal Conflans and the Brest fleet as far as the open Atlantic; at this point six of Conflans's warships would detach and accompany d'Aiguillon to landfall in the Clyde and with the other sixteen Conflans would head for Martinique. Once at sea he would open sealed orders telling him to proceed to the West Indies to search out and destroy Admiral Moore prior to retaking Guadeloupe and then maybe even proceeding to capture Jamaica. D'Aiguillon's army meanwhile, after landing at Glasgow, should proceed to the capture of Edinburgh, which would form the base for the conquest of Scotland. Now came the icing on Choiseul's cake. Conflans's six warships would then sail round Scotland into the North Sea, head for Ostend and there pick up yet another army, 20,000 strong, which was even then being prepared by the veteran general Chevert. This new strike force, intended as the *coup de grâce*, would land at Maldon in Essex, whence the French army would march swiftly over flat terrain to take London by surprise. Choiseul argued that by the sheer law of probability, provided measures were concerted properly, at least two out of the four projects (Portsmouth, Glasgow, Maldon, Martinique) had to work. Even supposing the Chevert and Soubise forces were interdicted by the Royal Navy, d'Aiguillon would establish himself in Scotland, pick up armed support from the Highland clans and be ready to invade England from the north in the spring of 1760 with an army of 40,000.

But Choiseul ignored three crucial considerations. The plans for the invasion of England were too sketchily drawn and no detailed coordination or war-gaming had been attempted between the Soubise and Chevert armies. Choiseul's timetable, envisaging Soubise landing about a month ahead of Chevert, ran the obvious risking of seeing both French armies defeated independently. The d'Aiguillon/Conflans scenario was in many ways even worse, for Conflans had to break the Royal Navy blockade at Brest and pick up d'Aiguillon's army from the Morbihan and the Quiberon peninsula 100 miles away. This plan – assembling an army at one port and a fleet at another – was precisely the egregious error that had defeated the Spanish Armada in 1588. Finally, there was a distinct whiff of 'too clever by half' about Choiseul's complex strategy, and in this respect it eerily pre-echoes Napoleon's attempt to outwit Nelson in 1804–05. If things went wrong in any one of the four enterprises (five, if we count the Thurot diversion), this could have a knock-on or multiplier implication for the others. Once again we can discern the besetting sin of France during the Seven Years War: dissipation of resources and inability to concentrate on a single clear objective. It had been the same story in 1746 when France, in a position to deliver a knockout blow to Britain, initiated three enterprises simultaneously: assistance for Charles Edward in Scotland, the expedition to Cape Breton and the campaign in Flanders. For all Choiseul's talents, he had not learnt the lesson of concentration of force. Pitt by contrast refused to halt any of his overseas campaigns even when his colleagues became almost hysterically anxious about the French invasion threat.

Having outlined his ingenious plan, Choiseul asked for comments from his fellow ministers. To his annoyance, Soubise made a number of supremely unhelpful and at times fatuous points. First he expressed anxiety about attempting a Channel crossing without a covering fleet, when it was obvious that to concede to him on this was to abandon both the West Indies venture and d'Aiguillon's invasion of Scotland. Soubise opposed embarking at Le Havre, since this was an obvious signal to England that Portsmouth was the target; if on the other hand the invasion left from Dunkirk, this could mean that the target was Dover, the Thames, Maldon or even the east coast of Scotland. Absurdly he asked if it would be possible for the 337 boats to be launched from Dunkirk, when Choiseul had made clear at previous meetings that this was no longer practicable.

The bookish Silhouette was much more positive: he pointed out that ancient descents on England in the reigns of Louis XI and Henry VI had proved that such landings were possible but he thought Choiseul was being over-optimistic in circling the month of September on the calendar. Given the tightness of the Royal Navy's blockade of Brest and the necessity for Conflans's fleet to sortie and then sail 100 miles south-east to pick up the invading force, it would surely be winter before the enterprise could be launched, for only then would storms drive the Royal Navy ships from the sea. As a consequence, Soubise in turn would not be able to cross the Channel until much later and would have to wait for the south or south-westerly winds of winter. If all these objections could be overcome, he would simply tweak the Soubise project by having him land at the Isle of Wight instead of Portsmouth. Silhouette backed the sending of the fleet to the West Indies and urged Choiseul to continue trying to win Sweden over, so that a joint landing could be made on the east coast of Scotland. But in general, and despite the financial hardship the invasion would cause, he warmly approved of Choiseul's ideas; indeed, in the present circumstances, with Canada, India and the West Indies at risk, what else could the King do?

Marshal d'Estrées proved as negative as Soubise, to the point where Choiseul must almost have suspected that the army had a vested interest in seeing the descent on Britain fail. He began with a pointless lament that the French navy was so weak – philosophically and historically correct certainly, but worse than useless as an attitude in a would-be decision-maker. Then he played Mark Antony praising Brutus by claiming to accept Choiseul's plan in outline yet subjecting every aspect of it to criticism. First he whinged lamely that the Royal Navy was bound to intercept any vessels trying to cross the Channel either from Le Havre or Dunkirk – and so he out-Soubised Soubise in pure negativity. Then he insisted that Conflans should fight a sea battle with Hawke before even trying to pick up d'Aiguillon's men. Everything would hinge on that battle: if Conflans lost it, then everything else was lost. Given the state of army–navy rivalry in France, Choiseul could have been forgiven for believing that d'Estrées was expressing an unconscious wish. Finally, he dissected the arrangements for the Soubise crossing. Since there were always about a dozen British warships cruising around the Isle of Wight and cruisers prowling outside Le Havre whatever the conditions, Soubise would need an exceptionally favourable turn in the weather. And even if he did get to sea, could anyone really imagine a huge flotilla of 337 vessels being able to cross the Channel without being seen? If they were observed, there would be no chance of evasive action and they would simply be destroyed. D'Estrées backed his fellow army marshal Soubise in asserting that the *prames* alone were not sufficient defence and that Soubise needed Conflans's fleet to protect him. Even if all these obstacles could by some miracle be overcome, the capture of Portsmouth in icy winter weather was itself a tall order. Suppose the attack was successful. Where would the victorious troops be cantoned? And would not the Royal Navy simply recall every last warship to the Channel and cut Soubise off from France?

D'Estrées, in short, wanted to subordinate the Soubise expedition to the d'Aiguillon one, concentrate on Scotland and make the descent on England contingent on a successful landing in the Clyde. Bit by bit he was trying to force Choiseul to the one policy position he did not want to adopt: ordering Conflans to engage Hawke before anything else could be attempted. Stung by this barrage of criticism, Choiseul counterattacked and gnawed away at the edges of d'Estrées's arguments. The idea of Soubise being marooned in Portsmouth was an absurdity, he pointed out, since with 50,000 men already landed, he could march on London and compel its surrender; with the capital city captured, whatever the Royal Navy did at sea was irrelevant. But Berryer then weighed in on the side of the marshals. While paying tribute to Choiseul's 'noble' plan and accepting that something had to be done urgently, since the very worst thing was supine inaction, Berryer thought that time was too short, French resources too feeble and the enemy too strong for Choiseul's strategy to have a happy outcome. Could Soubise really cross the Channel without Conflans's fleet? He doubted that the *prames* would be ready in time and even that the flat-bottoms would be complete before the end of October, which meant that the entire operation would have to take place in mid-winter. Somewhat self-contradictorily, Berryer then accepted that Soubise must depart from the Seine with the *prames*, that the Scottish project and the West Indian scheme should proceed.

Louis XV hated it when no clear consensus emerged at Council, but tried to take the sense of the meeting. He ruled that Conflans would have to protect d'Aiguillon's army and escort it to Scotland, and that it should then return to escort Soubise across the Channel. The Thurot diversion would still stand but the West Indies and Chevert ideas would have to be shelved, at least temporarily. Although the King and the ministers congratulated Choiseul warmly on the boldness of his thinking, in his own mind the Council meeting of 14 July counted as a defeat for his ideas and an endorsement of the two military weak sisters, Soubise and d'Estrées.

Truly Choiseul was beset by sceptics and cynics on all sides. Although the Paris mob was hugely enthusiastic about the prospect of landing on the soil of the ancient enemy, the intellectual classes and the *philosophes* thought the whole idea chimerical. Writing to a friend about the many rumours circulating in Paris (including the canard that Charles Edward himself had landed in Scotland with a Russo-Swedish force), Voltaire remarked scathingly that the whole thing sounded like something out of the *Arabian Nights*. In puckish mood he continued: 'As for our descent, 280 English ships is 280 Newtonian problems for our Cartesians to solve.'

Yet despite warnings from his confidante, La Pompadour, that the invasion plans might founder on the rock of finance rather than under the guns of British warships, Louis XV was determined to press ahead, well aware that the descent on Britain was the only card he had left to play. He ordered Silhouette to find the necessary money and Silhouette responded with an issue of seventy-two million livres, financed by tax farming. Spain under its new king finally decided to make a loan, and the Court Banker and Farmer-General Jean-Josephe de Laborde received four million livres in Portuguese money, specifically earmarked by Madrid to finance Thurot's landing in Ireland. Doubtless behind-the-scenes manoeuvring by Pompadour on behalf of her protégé Soubise explains the sequel to the 14 July conference. At the next meeting of the Council of State, on 22 July, Louis XV decided to suspend the Soubise expedition and reinstate the cross-Channel coup by

Chevert, who would now depart for Maldon from Ostend, thus making use of the Austrian Netherlands card. To ensure that d'Aiguillon's invasion force got to Scotland, Admiral La Clue was ordered to sortie from Toulon, evade the British under Boscawen and join Conflans at Brest. There they would have temporary local superiority over Hawke, which would give them time to embark d'Aiguillon's troops.

In the Mediterranean, Boscawen had taken over from Rear-Admiral Thomas Broderick in May and had followed his predecessor's policy of making audacious raids on the coast of France to disconcert the French and keep them guessing. With twenty-five ships (thirteen men-of-war and twelve frigates) under his command, he had official orders to maintain a close blockade of Marseilles and Toulon and secret ones making the safety of Gibraltar a priority, but nothing was said about an invasion. Boscawen's unceasing activity made the French think that another descent in force on their coastline was envisaged by the enemy, so they deployed ten battalions of infantry between Toulon and Marseilles. Boscawen increased the fear and uncertainty by sending two frigates on a daring raid right under the shore battery at Toulon. In his seamanship and derring-do, Boscawen was another Hawke, but in personality no two more unlike commanders could be imagined. Where Hawke was socially and politically inept and gauche, Boscawen knew how to manipulate the Georgian elite system for maximum advantage. Still only forty-nine, he could count among his honours and achievements the following: Admiral of the Blue, Lord of the Admiralty, member of the Privy Council and General of Marines at a salary of £3,000 a year (roughly £200,000 in present-day terms). He enjoyed a happy home life, devoted to his intellectual wife Frances, who returned the compliment and bore him five children. The only attribute Boscawen did not possess was Napoleon's essential: luck. He would die of a mysterious fever in January 1761, which his physicians ascribed to having spent too many years at sea.

At the end of June, Boscawen relaxed the blockade and headed west to the coast of Spain for water. On board his flagship, serving as a gunnery assistant, was one of the most remarkable figures of the eighteenth century, a black youth named Olaudah Equiano, later to be a notable writer and an inspiration for Afro-Americans. Equiano was the son of a chief in Benin, who had been captured by slavers when he was eleven. Having survived the notorious 'Middle Passage', he arrived in America where, in 1757, aged twelve, he was bought by a Royal Navy lieutenant named Michael Pascal. In 1759 Pascal was assigned to Boscawen's command, and this was the reason for Equiano's presence on the flagship. Equiano's intellect and powers of recall were formidable and he memorably recollected the terrible gale that assailed Boscawen's fleet at this juncture: 'The sea ran so high that, though all the guns were well housed, there was great reason to fear their getting loose, the ship rolled so much; and if they had it must have proved our destruction.'

Since Boscawen remained in Salou Bay near Tarragona until the end of July, this would have been the ideal time for La Clue to clear from Toulon and head out through the Straits of Gibraltar to join Conflans at Brest. It was typical of the muddle, indecision and sheer bad fortune of the French that Louis XV's order to this effect did not reach La Clue until the end of the month, by which time Boscawen had arrived at Gilbraltar for revictualling. For a whole month Boscawen took a huge risk and relied on 'open blockade': he left two frigates behind for surveillance duties, one off Malaga and the other cruising the Straits between Estrepona and Ceuta. His thinking was that La Clue might be tempted to sortie, and he (Boscawen) could then finish him off. On 3 August Boscawen received new orders, this time making the danger of invasion a priority and enjoining him at all costs to prevent the juncture of the Brest and Toulon fleets; he was expressly commanded to follow La Clue wherever he would venture, if he managed to get clear of the Straits into the Atlantic. As always the French took an unconscionable time to get to sea. It was 5 August before La Clue was finally convinced the British were not lurking in ambush outside Toulon and so set sail. He had twelve ships of the line and three frigates in his fleet, including his flagship, the eighty-gun *L'Océan*, the pride of the French navy. Although Louis XV had foolishly allowed his navy to decline during his reign, it was widely acknowledged that, in terms of shipbuilding, eighteenth-century French warships were the finest in the world, and *L'Océan*, a new warship launched at Toulon in 1756, was a prime specimen.

La Clue's intentions were to approach the Straits of Gibraltar along the Barbary coast and then crowd on sail at night so as to pass through the narrow entrance undetected. At first luck was with him and he made good progress with the aid of a stiff easterly breeze. He was almost through the Straits undetected, east of Ceuta at nightfall, when a patrolling Royal Navy frigate spotted his ships and raised the alarm. La Clue had done well, since Boscawen's fleet was still refitting, with his flagship *Namur* with sails still unbent and most of the crews on shore leave; Boscawen himself and his senior officers had so little sense of danger that they were away dining with the Governor of San Roque. But someone on the Admiral's flagship, following previous orders, gave the signal to unmoor. The dinner party broke up instantly, and there was a stampede to get back to the ships. Boscawen's speed of recovery was remarkable: by 10 p.m. eight vessels had got under way, and an hour later Boscawen was in full pursuit off Cabritra

Point. This was a stunning feat of seamanship and it is hardly surprising that historians of the Royal Navy have always gone into rhapsodies about the achievement. In three hours an entire fleet, moored in a difficult harbour at night, with sails unbent and the Admiral absent, had set sail. La Clue had seen the British frigate signalling his presence and realised that his best-case scenario hopes were in vain. He was now involved in a race. He was confident that *L'Océan* could outstrip her pursuers. But what about the lesser ships in his fleet?

At midnight La Clue made a fateful decision. His standing orders had called for a rendezvous at Cadiz – a wise precaution in view of the differential speeds of his ships and the uncertain weather in the Atlantic, which might scatter them. So far he had been making way with all lights extinguished but now, with the wind set fair and confident that all his craft were tightly bunched around him, he signalled with his poop-lantern that the entire armada should instead make for Cape St Vincent. Why this signal was not seen by all is not clear, but no fewer than five men-of-war and three frigates (the *Fantasque*, *Lion*, *Trito*, *Fier*, *L'Oriflamme*, *La Chimère*, *Minerve* and *Gracieuse*) failed to obey the new signal and made for Cadiz, following the original instructions. Some have speculated that La Clue's captains did not like the new order and deliberately ignored it, but the best testimony suggests that the hindmost vessels were too far away at midnight to read the signal and, by the time they caught up between 2 and 3 a.m., La Clue had extinguished the lantern for fear he was simply lighting the way for Boscawen. Once again Louis XV's neglect of the French marine must take some part of the blame, for the French had no night-compass signals. The eight breakaway French ships spent the next day trying to find *L'Océan*, then gave up and put into Cadiz, convinced they would find the flagship there. Arriving on 19 August, they were at once bottled up by Admiral Brodrick and there they remained impotently until New Year's Day 1760. When the French ships split up, Boscawen made the right decision: ignore the small fry and follow the flagship.

At 6 a.m. on the morning of the 18th, La Clue saw some ships toiling in his rear and, thinking they were his rearguard, stopped to let them catch up. Finally, when Brodrick's division (Boscawen's rearguard) also appeared on the horizon, a mere head count revealed that this must be the enemy. To his horror La Clue realised that his own rear was nowhere to be seen and he had foolishly waited for the enemy to close on him. Now, with just seven French ships to the leeward of him, some thirty miles short of Cape St Vincent, and their rearguard mysteriously vanished, Boscawen engaged in a metaphorical licking of the lips. In his own words: 'The wind was strong at east; the weather fine, the water smooth; and we soon perceived that we gained exceedingly fast upon the enemy; which were plainly discovered to be seven large ships of the line, and one of them carrying a French admiral's flag.' He signalled his fleet as he later recalled: 'the ships to engage as they come up, without regard to the line of battle. The enemy's ships were formed in a line a-head and crowding away from us under a press of sail . . . we had a fresh gale and came up with them very fast.'

For five hours, from about 8 a.m. to 1 p.m., both fleets made fast progress to the north-west, with the British gradually gaining. Shortly afterwards both fleets showed their colours and Boscawen signalled to attack. Even so it was 2.30 p.m. before HMS *Culloden* came to close quarters with the seventy-four-gun *Centaure*, captain M. de Sabran Grammont.

Although he had brought the enemy to battle, Boscawen was not at first pleased with the progress of the engagement. His official report was terse: 'About half past two, some of the headmost ships began to engage; I could not get up to the *Océan* till near four.' But his private correspondence shows that he was displeased when five of his warships crowded in on the *Centaure*. In Boscawen's mind, Brodrick and the rearguard could easily take care of the French rear, and in the meantime his best ships should be pursuing the flagship. Nor could he perform his favourite manoeuvre of attacking in inverted order, whereby each successive ship used its comrade already engaged as a shield and thus got alongside the next enemy vessel, until every single one of the enemy craft from rear to van was engaged in rotation. Olaudah Equiano recalled that Boscawen passed three French ships to get close to *L'Océan* and was fired on by all three but 'notwithstanding which our admiral would not suffer a gun to be fired at any of them, to my astonishment, but made us lie on our bellies on the deck till we came quite close to the *Océan*, who was ahead of them all; when we had orders to pour the whole three tiers into her at once.'

But meanwhile Boscawen had a fight on his hands with the *Centaure*, which battled tigerishly for five hours. Two hundred French mariners were killed or wounded in the furious combat, while Captain de Sabran Grammont himself was wounded in nine places. And when Boscawen got the *Namur* close enough to *L'Océan* around 4 p.m. so that a running fight developed, *Namur* had the worse of the encounter and had to sheer off after half an hour, but not before she had inflicted severe casualties of eighty-six dead and more than 100 wounded on the French. Olaudah Equiano was carrying powder to the guns during the fight and described the encounter as grim and deadly:

I ran a very great risk for more than half an hour of blowing up the ship. For, when we had taken the cartridges out of the boxes, the bottom of many of them proving rotten, the powder ran all about the deck, near the match tub; we scarcely had water enough at the last to throw on it. We were also, from our employment, very much exposed to the enemy's shots; for we had to go through the whole length of the ship to bring the powder.

La Clue, with one arm broken and the other seriously wounded, temporarily handed over command to the Comte de Carne Marcein. Disabled, having lost mizzen mast and both topsail yards, Boscawen's flag-ship fell astern and as it did so he encountered the *Centaure*, which was now (7.15 p.m.) striking after its battering by five Royal Navy ships. While *L'Océan* crowded on sail, Boscawen had to transfer his flag to the *Newark*. He ordered a general chase that would last all night, with the fifty-gun *Guernsey* in the British van. The heroic captain de Sabran Grammont was meanwhile taken prisoner to Gibraltar.

For the French it was now a case of *sauve qui peut*. By the morning of 19 August, La Clue had at *L'Océan*'s side only the three seventy-four-gun ships *Redoutable*, *Téméraire* and *Modeste*; the other two were making way on independent tracks, one bound for Rochefort, the other for the Canaries. Boscawen reported: 'I pursued all night and in the morning of the 19th saw only four sail standing in for the land of Lagos.' Unable to escape his pursuers but determined not to surrender, La Clue ran his magnificent flagship onto the rocks, with flag flying and every sail set; 'every mast went by the board and fell over the bows,' the watching Boscawen reported. The *Redoutable* followed suit, but the *Téméraire* and the *Modeste* anchored under the guns of some Portuguese batteries in Lagos Bay. In flagrant disregard of Portuguese neutrality, Boscawen sent his ships in to take the French vessels as prizes. *L'Océan* and *Redoubtable* were put to the torch where they lay. It seems there was still plenty of gunpowder on board *L'Océan*, for Olaudah Equiano describes the sequel: 'About midnight I saw the *Océan* blow up, with a most dreadful explosion. I never beheld a more awful scene. In less than a minute the midnight for a certain space seemed turned into day by the blaze, which was attended with a noise louder and more terrible than thunder, that seemed to reveal every element around us.'

Carne Marcein and his officers were taken prisoner; La Clue escaped captivity, having previously taken himself off to Lisbon on a cutter. Lagos was a stunning victory for Britain. The French lost five ships and 500 killed and wounded as against casualties of 252 for Boscawen, but it was in its strategic implications that the battle was so decisive. Conflans was now on his own against the combined might of the Royal Navy and the chances of a successful French invasion considerably diminished. Unable to find the other two French vessels, Boscawen reported his success to Pitt and Hawke and announced on 20 August that he was returning home, leaving Brodrick and seven ships on patrol.

The demoralised French were reduced to unseemly three-way polemics between La Clue, the Ministry of Marine and the captains of the ships that had run into Cadiz. A marathon of epistolary self-exculpation and blame-shifting ensued, with La Clue pointing the finger at the captains now bottled up in Cadiz and they in turn protesting that the Admiral had not made his intentions plain, had changed his mind and then not sent clear signals. La Clue blithely wrote to Choiseul that he was not guilty but simply unlucky; all that seamanship could do he had done but the caprice of Fortune had undone him. French public opinion expressed itself disgusted with the whole affair, from which no one except Captain de Sabran Grammont had emerged with credit; indeed, he was universally conceded to have performed as valiantly as warriors of old and was expressly singled out for plaudits by his British captors in Gibraltar. As always, the French government proved absurdly indulgent towards its failed admirals. La Clue was made Lieutenant-General in 1764 and Castillon, one of the captains who skulked in Lagos, was promoted in 1765. The Marquis de Saint-Aignan, the lacklustre commander of the *Redoutable*, went on to reach the highest rank in the navy.

The gloom in Paris contrasted with the euphoria in London, where news of the great victory arrived on 6 September. Even the congenitally downbeat Duke of Newcastle allowed himself to breathe new optimism: 'Now Boscawen will come back,' he wrote, 'with seven ships and three French ones, and two regiments from Gibraltar. I own I was afraid of invasion till now.' Adam Smith, revelling in the success of his book on moral sentiments, told his friend Gilbert Elliott (in a letter dated 10 October) that he was very pleased about Lagos but nobody took the threatened invasion seriously anyway. Arriving almost simultaneously with the news of the victory at Minden in Germany, Boscawen's tidings convinced Pitt that Providence was with the British this year. But he and Newcastle forgot the ancient wisdom about cornered rats. Now almost out of options, Choiseul and his ministers would fight desperately to ensure that d'Aiguillon and his invasion force got to Scotland.

EIGHT

MINDEN

The surprise literary hit of 1759 was The Life and Opinions of Tristram Shandy *(the first two parts appeared this year and a third part a few years later), written by an obscure forty-seven-year-old clergyman named Laurence Sterne; within a year this classic 'shaggy dog story' would catapult Sterne to fame and fortune.*

Although the 1750s were a decade when writers experimented with the new craze for self-conscious narration, Tristram Shandy *– with its fragmented narrative, lack of chronological sequence, interior monologue, association of ideas, stream of consciousness, ludic excursions into problems of authorial voice and reader participation, plus mock-academic excursuses, digressions and mini-essays which interrupt the tenuous plot – was the culmination and, some would say, the* reductio ad absurdum *of the process. Those who thrill to the mere idea of the avant-garde and think that to jumble up beginnings, middles and ends is the last word in profundity will always warm to this book. Its influence has been enormous: on Joyce, Beckett and a hundred Gallic imitators from Robbe-Grillet to Nathalie Sarraute. Beckett's famous line from* Murphy *– 'he cursed the day of his birth then, in a daring flashback, the moment of his conception' – is a straight steal from the opening chapter of* Tristram Shandy *when the author laments that his mother was thinking about a clock instead of concentrating on sexual congress at the moment of his conception. But Sterne revelled in so-called plagiarism, trying to make the point that there really is nothing new under the sun. One of the best-known passages in* Tristram Shandy *reads as follows: 'Shall we for ever make new books, as apothecaries make new mixtures, by pouring only out of one vessel into another? Are we for ever to be twisting and untwisting the same rope?' Sterne's in-joke is that this passage is itself taken almost word-for-word from Robert Burton's* Anatomy of Melancholy, *and that Burton in turn took it from another source; attempts to avoid plagiarism usually involve one in an infinite regress.*

Tristram Shandy was a strange book to have emerged in any era, but perhaps especially so in the midst of a global war. Dr Johnson later (in 1776) passed the judgement with which many subsequent readers have concurred: 'Nothing odd will do long. Tristram Shandy *did not last.' Johnson turned out to be as wrong about that as about Berkeley's metaphysics when he 'refuted' it by kicking a stone. But it is hard not to see Sterne's* magnum opus *as a creative cul-de-sac. It is perhaps the ultimate fantasy of the man for whom writing is more important than living and the talisman of all those who elevate art above life. Sterne's supporters have always spoken of his 'ambiguity', by which they mean that any clear proposition about him can always be contested, but it is better to view it as the dead-end that occurs when Hume's method of scepticism is applied not to philosophy but to literature. Nihilism and relativism will always have admirers and defenders but Sterne is surely guilty of launching what would ultimately become the twentieth century's hoariest cliché – the novel about writing a novel. And it is interesting that the 'off-duty' Sterne was nothing like so relativistic as his own implicit doctrine required him to be, for when it came to politics relativism came to a juddering halt. The character of Dr Slop (based on the historical Dr John Burton) shows Sterne pouring out all his venom on Jacobites and Jacobitism. Suddenly the relativistic world-view goes out of the window and we learn that Jacobitism is unmitigated evil and the Whig/Hanoverian/Protestant ascendancy the ultimate good; quite how this is squared with the general world-view of* Tristram Shandy *is not explained.*

For the student of the Seven Years War what is interesting about Tristram Shandy *is the amount of space Sterne devotes to military matters. Apart from Parson Yorick, who operates in the novel as a kind of extension of Sterne himself, the author lavishes most sympathy on the character of Captain Toby Shandy (Uncle Toby), a military veteran who sustained a groin injury while campaigning in Europe and is fanatically dedicated to military history and the art of siegecraft. The majority of the most-quoted lines in the novel are put into Uncle Toby's mouth. 'Our armies swore terribly in Flanders,' cried my uncle Toby, 'but nothing to this.' 'I wish,' quoth my uncle Toby, 'you had seen what prodigious armies we had in Flanders.' Toby is supposed to have fought in the wars against Louis XV from 1689 to 1697 and 1702 to 1713, and there are frequent mentions of the battles of Steinkirk and Namur and the campaigns of Marlborough during the War of Spanish Succession that ended with the Treaty of Utrecht in 1713. To display Toby's erudition in military science, Sterne drags in all the most famous names concerned with the theory of war in the hundred years from c. 1650 to 1750 – names now lost in the mists of time but well known to educated audiences in 1759: Marolis, de Ville, Lorini, Van Cochorn, Skeeter, Depagan, Blondel and, above all, Marshal Vauban, most famous of all military engineers to date, whose work on siegecraft and fortifications appeared in the early 1740s. Moreover, Sterne likes to sprinkle his text with obscure and technical words relating to offensive and defensive operations during sieges: redan, talus, parallel, glacis, banquette, orgues, horn-work, bastion, demi-bastion, saps, epaulments, tenaille, double tenaille, half-moon, ravelin, counter-scarp, counterguard, blinds, gabions, cuvettes, ballista, terebra, scorpio, sally-port, paderero, demi-culverin.*

Sieges and fortifications played their part in the Seven Years War but these were mainly the concern of the principal belligerents. As Sterne's Uncle Toby makes clear, the presence of the British army on the continent was always perceived on both sides as an unusual and even singular event, both because the Royal Navy was perceived to be *the* military arm of the island kingdom and because there was a natural tendency to send troops to the colonies rather than European theatres. But there were times when the preferred system of paying subsidies to a land-based ally was not enough and the ally required actual redcoats in the field. Such a stage had been reached in the Seven Years War by 1759, but the British army was in many ways outdated in its ideas, so its generals had to learn the new techniques pioneered by Frederick the Great of Prussia, including cadenced marching.

Frederick wanted to be the master of warfare rather than merely its servant, constrained in a deterministic way by logistical, topographical, climatic and even social factors. Since Prussia did not have an unlimited population base and 154,000 was about the maximum possible size of its army, Frederick had to husband resources carefully and avoid heavy casualties. Vauban's ideas on siegecraft helped, as they emphasised capitulation after reasonable resistance rather than protracted sieges and no-holds-barred stormings. To this Frederick added disrupting lines of communication and rapid movement plus the avoidance of battle if possible, though he was more ready to risk everything on a single engagement in the field than most of his contemporaries. Pitched battles tended to produce pyrrhic victories, as Marlborough's triumphs, involving 20–25 per cent losses, showed; to an extent this was a function of primitive medicine since one in three battle casualties died from septicaemia and other (on paper) non-lethal wounds. And it was Frederick's heavy losses at Leuthen and Rossbach in 1757 that had ended his early run of success and turned the tide against him by 1759.

Frederick influenced many by his rigid system of discipline – it was said the aim was to make soldiers fear their own officers more than the enemy – his emphasis on logistics, commissariat and proper supply lines, his dislike of sieges and his emphasis (and here one can surely detect the influence of the *philosophes*) on reason as the guiding principle in military science. Yet one can make a case that technology rather than human agency was still the real determinant. Probably the most important revolution in eighteenth-century warfare was the increase in importance of infantry and artillery and the relative decline of cavalry. Flintlock muskets and the socket bayonet gradually replaced the pike and matchlock during the War of Spanish Succession, while a further improvement to infantry was made when Frederick revived the marching disciplines of the Ancient world and replaced manoeuvring in open-order columns with swift and coordinated movements orchestrated with fife and drum. The Prussian approach, which the British army copied during the Seven Years War, was to emphasise increased fire-power and in military academies and the officers' mess debate ranged over the advantages of deploying in line rather than column. The line – three ranks ranged elbow-to-elbow – was thought to maximise available musketry and to be superior to the French column, which was perceived as favouring the bayonet over firepower. French thinking was that the bayonet was a superior weapon to the musket to which it was attached; twenty-one inches long, a bayonet made gaping wounds that could not be sutured, and those who survived the stabbing usually died from infection. Ironically, this repre-sented a complete reversal of roles from the War of Spanish Succession, when it had been the French who relied on firepower and Marlborough and Eugene of Savoy on cold steel.

The British army then, once committed to fighting in Europe, habitu-ally entered the field in columns that shifted into lines two ranks deep, shoulder-to-shoulder; a third line of men filled up the gaps when the infantry ahead fell under enemy fire. Once within twenty to thirty yards of the enemy, the troops would fire one or two volleys before charging with the bayonet. The idea was to deliver the shock-power of a devastating volley at close range, followed by a bayonet charge. Since each defender aimed his gun at the man in front of him, the British took advantage of the exposed area below the left arm, which was raised and extended to support the gun barrel. Each redcoat was trained to shift at the last moment and, in a coordinated surprise movement, plunge his bayonet into the heart or stomach to the left of the enemy. The legend was that this was how 'Butcher' Cumberland's army had won at Culloden, though such drill played in fact only a minuscule part in the victory on Drummossie Moor that day. But more important than this drill was what happened before the troops got to close range. The British army aimed to provide a continuous rippling barrage as platoons fired at different times from along the line. These platoons cut across the normal structure of regiment–battalion–company since a battalion of ten companies would break down into eighteen platoons or 'fire-units' responsible for the three firings that would ensure the enemy was under a constant fusillade. In practice neither the serried ranks depicted in military paintings nor the choreography of the parade ground obtained, as discipline was constantly at war with the human instinct for self-preservation. The battlefield reality was independent fire, and this departure from orthodoxy was all the more marked when the redcoats could free themselves from the pre-requisites of German commanders-in-chief, like Ferdinand of Brunswick, trained in the Frederick tradition. In 1759 North American warfare was thus less structured and conventional than the fighting in Germany.

The average rate of fire from a musket was two to three rounds a minute, the process speeded up by the metal ramrods that replaced the old wooden ones, and by priming and loading from the same cartridge paper. Priming and loading involved a four-step process, but crack troops could load and fire every fifteen seconds. The basic method was to point the gun at the enemy, hoping that in a crowded field the massed volley would find targets through sheer probability. Accuracy and reliability were scarcely possible with eighteenth-century muskets, as the chain reaction of flint, spark and powder often failed to ignite the charge in the barrel and the barrel itself was not perfectly straight. At a distance greater than fifty yards the musket was a poor weapon but at shorter range it was deadly. It was a low-velocity weapon, so the energy of the spherical musket balls decreased rapidly with distance. A carefully delivered volley therefore produced a lethal 'weight' lacking in long-distance fire. If you opened fire too soon, it was likely that you would only wound the enemy. Conversely, at close range the heavy lead musket balls did frightful damage, and eighteenth-century battlefields were dreadful scenes of carnage, with men running around without eyes, noses or other extremities, which had been taken clean off by a musket ball.

Rifles were also available for eighteenth-century fighting men, and their maximum range was 300–400 yards, as against 80–100 for a musket, largely because the spiral groove inside the rifle barrel caused a bullet to rotate and fly a straighter course. But because it took longer to load and lacked a bayonet, the rifle could not be issued as standard equipment for infantry and was better suited for use as a sniper's weapon or for long-range work in the North American forests. The rifle took longer to load because the powder had to be measured from a horn instead of being pre-measured in a paper cartridge, and the ball, wrapped in a cloth patch, had to be forced down the narrow barrel, which quickly became clogged with the powder's residue and had to be cleaned after every five or six shots. Moreover, a musket was more useful in the open battlefield since its heavier lead ball could stop a man in his tracks and usually stayed inside the body, doing terrible damage to flesh and organs until all momentum was spent; the smaller rifle bullet, on the other hand, tended to pass through the body.

France made the fatal mistake in the Seven Years War of devoting most of her energies to continental warfare, largely fought on behalf of Maria Theresa of Austria, instead of concentrating on the crucial areas where the battle for world supremacy with Britain would be decided: in North America, the West Indies and India. The most intelligent British policy on the continent would have been to confine land-based military activity to the periphery, as was done in the Napoleonic Wars until 1814. This option was not open to Britain in the Seven Years War because of its Achilles heel, the Electorate of Hanover. By placing the Elector of Hanover on the British throne in 1714, the new post-1688 elite gave hostages to continental fortune for a hundred years thereafter. The plain fact was that, in terms of British interests, George II as both King of England and Elector of Hanover was a liability. One can even say that the entire genesis of the controversial 1757 Militia Act was George's obsession with Hanover. Hessian and Hanoverian troops had been rushed to England in 1756, in the face of a major invasion threat from France but, once the scare subsided, they were sent back to Germany to protect Hanover, leaving the gap to be plugged by a newly formed militia. British ambivalence about the militia found expression in a dog-in-the manger attitude towards the Hanoverian troops: although their arrival in 1756 had been resented, so too was their departure. From 1757 British troops joined their Hanoverian allies in a so-called 'Army of Observation' in western Germany, and at the beginning of April that year George II's favourite son, the Duke of Cumberland, was appointed Commander-in-Chief of the force, despite his dismal record against the French military aces, Marshals Saxe and Lowendahl, in the War of Austrian Succession. Defeated by the French at Hastenback on 26 July 1757, Cumberland signed the humiliating Convention of Kloster-Zeven in September, acquiescing in French occupation of Hanover. Both French and British commanders were disgraced by this event. George II repudiated the treaty, snubbed his favourite son and ordered him into retirement and disgrace. The French commander, the Duc de Richelieu, was accused of having given Cumberland lenient terms and was himself shortly afterwards recalled and exiled to his estates.

In an attempt to lend credibility to his continental endeavours, George II cast about for a suitable replacement for the discredited Cumberland. He lit on Prince Ferdinand of Brunswick, Frederick of Prussia's brother-in-law, a middle-aged man of undistinguished appearance, just five feet six inches in height and with a pock-marked complexion, a highly regarded professional soldier with a commission in the Prussian army, a man of will-power and endurance who also had the ability to improvise. Appointed commander in November 1757, Ferdinand accepted on the strict condition that he would have direct access to George II, and would have plenipotentiary military, disciplinary, administrative and financial powers. The title of the Anglo-German force was changed to 'His Britannic Majesty's Army under the order of His Serene Highness, Prince Ferdinand of Brunswick and of Luneburg'.

Ferdinand at once showed himself a first-class administrator and immeasurably improved supplies, munitions, rations, pay and even field hospitals. Imitating Shakespeare's Henry V and anticipating Napoleon, he made a point of joining his troops around the fireside in freezing weather, full of hearty encouragement and morale-boosting praise and exhortation, always visible in a distinctive greatcoat covered in medals. He had a wonderful propaganda weapon to hand, for the French soldiers in Westphalia and Hanover in 1757 had gone on the rampage. Although the extent of the atrocities was exaggerated by the British and Prussians, there is no doubt that the *poilus* had enjoyed an orgy of theft, looting, plunder and rape and that the lazy, sybaritic commander Richelieu, as indisposed to instil discipline as to practise it himself, had ignored or connived at it. Richelieu, hero of a thousand bedroom conquests, was not the man to lick this indisciplined rabble into shape, and his incompetence played into the hands of Ferdinand, who was able to exploit the anger and desire for revenge entertained by the Hanoverian and Hessian troops. But Ferdinand was not just a master of administration and propaganda. In a six-week winter campaign in March–April 1758 he showed his mettle, driving the French back across the Rhine with huge losses, while suffering only about 200 casualties himself. He captured Bremen and Emden without fighting a battle and displayed a phenomenal talent for winter campaigning. French stategic calculations were thrown into chaos. Versailles had hoped to deploy two huge armies against Frederick of Prussia from the west while the Russians and Austrians crashed in on his eastern flank. Now, it seemed, one of these French armies would have to remain in western Germany to deal with Ferdinand's Anglo-Hanoverian force. Now more than ever France rued the day Richelieu had allowed his defeated foe to depart for their hearths and homes, instead of taking Cumberland and his men prisoner.

Rarely had military fortunes changed so rapidly. In September 1757 the French thought they had won definitively in western Germany and only a few mopping-up details remained. By May 1758 the tables were turned, Ferdinand had an army 40,000 strong and France was floundering. Richelieu's replacement on the western front proved an even greater disaster than his philandering predecessor. Now in his fiftieth year, Louis de Bourbon-Condé, Comte de Clermont, a prince of the blood, was an oddity in that he had been destined for holy orders but then given a papal dispensation to become a soldier, after which he had fought at Dettingen, Fontenoy and Raucoux during the War of Austrian Succession. The peculiarity of his position was that he retained his clerical benefices as Abbot of St Germain-des-Prés and was known mockingly by his troops as the 'Général des Bénédictines'. Evidently Clermont had a line in gallows humour, for it is said that he wrote to Louis XV as follows on taking up his command: 'I found Your Majesty's Army divided into three parts. The part which is above ground is composed of pillagers and marauders; the second part is underground; and the third is in hospital. Should I retire with the first or wait until I join one of the others?'

Clermont was hardly exaggerating. French losses in the winter campaign amounted to more than 16,000 in dead, wounded, prisoners and deserters with another 10,000 sick. But as one of the great aristocrats of the *ancien régime*, Clermont had pull. With the able collaboration of Belle-Isle at the War Ministry, he made good the numbers. By May he could muster 32,000 infantry and 12,000 cavalry, and Belle-Isle promised him he would have an army nearly double that size by the end of June. Clermont was an efficient if unimaginative soldier and he was taken unawares by the energetic Ferdinand, who crossed the Rhine near the Dutch border on 1–3 June after constructing a pontoon bridge. Madame de Pompadour, now secure in Louis XV's favour and always keen to take the rest of the Bourbon family down a notch or two, wrote to him witheringly: 'What a humiliation, monsieur, to allow the enemy to build a bridge across the Rhine and land 6,000 men a day on the other side.' But Clermont's humiliation was not yet complete. Despite the reassurances from his friend Belle-Isle that Ferdinand was now dangerously exposed, Clermont could make no impression on him. He did at least hold his own in the indecisive battle at Rheinberg on 12 June 1758 but nine days later Ferdinand won a hard-fought victory at Krefeld. Faced with the threat that Ferdinand might invade the Netherlands, Belle-Isle had to detach to Clermont's aid a second French army, which was supposed to be helping Maria Theresa and the Austrians in Bohemia.

Seven thousand British troops joined Ferdinand after Krefeld, but the Anglophone and German-speaking troops did not meld seamlessly. Differences in culture and military tradition were compounded by the language barrier, except in the case of the officer class who usually spoke French to one another. The British troops were indisciplined, prone to illness and lacked the hygiene of their German counterparts while their officers were touchy and arrogant, inclined to treat the Hanoverians as natural inferiors. There were numerous niggling items of discord between the two sides: the Germans, for example, resented the extra forage required by the horse-loving British. The choice of British commander was perhaps especially infelicitous. The 3rd Duke of Marlborough, though modest and generous, was ignorant, careless and insouciant, and was a particularly poor diplomatic choice in that in the previous war he had complained vociferously about the behaviour of German troops. But Marlborough died before Krefeld, in October 1757, and the British command fell to his deputy – an even more disastrous appointment, as it turned out.

At forty-two, Lord George Sackville, second son of the Earl of Dorset, was sharp-tongued, arrogant, ambitious, unsure of himself, depressive and hypersensitive to criticism. A heavily set, melancholy-looking individual, with clear blue eyes, protruding lower lip and an ugly snout of a nose, Sackville was a scion of the Anglo-Irish aristocracy, who had been educated at Trinity College, Dublin, and had fought at Fontenoy with Cumberland (also later in the Jacobite rising and under Wolfe in Scotland). MP for Dover since 1741, he was an important political figure whom Pitt and Bute had wanted as their Secretary of State for War in 1757. But the great barrier to Sackville's political and military advancement was the hatred of George II. Sackville had attached himself to the rival court clustered round the King's hated eldest son Frederick and his son George (later George III). Sackville's drive and energy were not matched by tact or an ability to make himself popular. His joining the Anglo-German army was a case in point. Leicester House favoured military raids on the French coast and was strongly opposed to German entanglements, but by accepting the position with Marlborough Sackville showed poor political nous. His appointment was simply Pitt's way of co-opting Leicester House into a German adventure but the Prince of Wales did not see it that way. Sackville simply weakened his status with Bute and Leicester House without commending himself to George II. He made fresh enemies without making any new friends.

Although in retrospect the partnership of Prince Ferdinand and Lord Sackville was an accident waiting to happen, in 1758 Sackville confined himself to complaining about Ferdinand's Fabian policy and the continual retreats. After Krefeld, though, even his mouth was shut. Krefeld was a setback to France almost as serious as Rossbach. In England, where Ferdinand was lionised as a hero, Pitt realised the potential value of the western front. Properly reinforced, Ferdinand's Anglo-Hanoverian army could pin down huge French forces, not only preventing them from fighting Prussia on the eastern front but also making it impossible for Versailles to reinforce its beleaguered garrisons in India and North America. Expertly

14. 'A man undone.'
1759 was the last chance of Bonnie Prince Charlie

15. Pitt the Elder,
the architect of victory

16. Sugar. The prize for victory in the West Indies.

17. The Montmorency Falls, scene of Wolfe's initial failure

18. Canadian landscape: snow and ice were the common enemy

19. Niagara Falls,
the acme of the Sublime

20. Voltaire: he thought Canada
not worth the bones of a single soldier

21. Elephant fight: potent symbol of the clash of empires

22. Tiger hunting: the eighteenth-century was obsessed with the exotic orient

23. General Robert Clive: the French had no-one to match him

24. General James Wolfe, hero of Quebec

25. Frederick the Great,
Britain's only ally on the continent

26. The war in
Germany,
France v. Britain:
the first round

27. The Battle of Minden,
a day of glory for British arms

28. Wolfe's night
landing near the
Plains of Abraham

29. Wolfe's victory
at Quebec

30. Death of Montcalm

31. Death of Wolfe

32. Robert Rogers of the Rangers

33. Rogers' Rangers in action

34. Admiral Hawke, victor of Quiberon

35. Victory on the high seas: the Battle of Quiberon

managed by the Duke of Newcastle, Parliament voted to send to Germany another five battalions of infantry and fourteen squadrons of cavalry. After a further embarrassment with the fall of Düsseldorf (July 1758), Clermont meanwhile was replaced by the fifty-four-year-old Louis-Georges Erasme, Marquis de Contades, who had a long and distinguished military career, beginning in Italy and Corsica in 1734–35, extending through the war of 1740–48 and most recently taking in the battles of Hastenbeck and Krefeld.

Contades showed more respect for Ferdinand than Clermont had, and played cat-and-mouse with him, probing and making contact with his vanguard, but never allowing Ferdinand's main army to get close to him. There was stalemate as both sides faced each other across the Erft river from 14 to 24 July, but the French grew stronger every day as Belle-Isle made good his promises about increased numbers. Ferdinand, still waiting for the British reinforcements before making a decisive move, resolved to withdraw and put the Rhine between himself and the French, but Contades moved north swiftly to hem him in between the confluence of the Roer and Meuse rivers. Ferdinand was now in deadly peril, in imminent danger of having his communications cut, and Contades came within an ace of a stunning victory, but he narrowly failed to take the all-important bridge at Mehr that would have sealed Ferdinand's doom.

Belle-Isle now decided that the only way to finish off Ferdinand before he became even more powerful with extra contingents from Britain was to use a second army against him. This force was commanded by the vanquished Marshal of Rossbach, Charles de Rohan, Prince de Soubise. Another of the great French aristocrats, Soubise was a member of the influential Rohan family, had been Louis XV's aide-de-camp in the War of Austrian Succession and had served as Governor of Flanders and Hennegau. Something of a French Cumberland, Soubise was notorious for the catastrophe at Rossbach but his many supporters at court would talk up a minor victory at Lutterberg in Hesse rather as Cumberland's cronies had portrayed his walk-over victory at Culloden as a glittering triumph of the military art. The truth was that, aged forty-three, Soubise was a nonentity, timid and indecisive as a commander, possessing no military talent and owing everything to his being a favourite of Madame de Pompadour, who assiduously pushed for his promotion far beyond his intrinsic abilities. Realising Ferdinand's military calibre, Belle-Isle urged caution and close coordination between the armies of Contades and Soubise. Resentful and envious of each other, Contades and Soubise each waited for the other to act and refused to collaborate on a detailed strategy.

September found both of them writing peevishly to Belle-Isle to know what the other proposed to do. Belle-Isle fulminated at his two generals for being the passive dupes of Ferdinand, warned that French military honour was being compromised, and advised them that France was becoming the laughing stock of Europe. Finally Soubise stirred himself and began marching towards Hanover. But he seems to have taken fright at his own decisiveness, feared he was over-exposed and, blaming Contades for having been slow to support him, withdrew to Kassel. There, stiffened by the Duc de Fitzjames, the timid Soubise finally felt strong enough to give battle. Marginally victorious at Lutterberg on 12 October – though some critics thought the battle drawn – he failed to support Contades when he in turn finally made a move and threatened Münster, an important allied base. This was another timid probe, carried out too late and with too small forces to be a serious threat.

By the end of 1758 all of Belle-Isle's efforts had produced a null result in west Germany. Despite all the reinforcements he had thrown into the western front, the French armies were again suffering numerical shrinkage and under-equipment. That winter Belle-Isle wrote to the future Duc de Choiseul (then Comte de Stainville, French ambassador in Austria): 'Two-thirds of our infantry are without clothes and consist either of men who have had no rest for fifteen months, or of recruits who are not strong enough to withstand the cold and rain of this late season.' Meanwhile his past, present, future, actual and putative generals spent most of their energy intriguing against each other and trying to discredit or belittle each other in the eyes of Louis XV: Soubise, Richelieu, d'Estrées, Broglie, St-Germain, Contades and Clermont were only some of the principals involved in the Machiavellian and disgraceful game, for the Dauphin himself had petitioned his father hard to be allowed to succeed Clermont as Commander-in-Chief. The truth was that Louis XV had no one of the calibre of Marshal Saxe in the last war, or even of Lowendahl, and some jeremiahs lamented that in France military science had gone into a tailspin. Ferdinand, by contrast, had been a brilliant success. At the beginning of 1758 the French had occupied most of Hanover but by the end they occupied not an inch of it. Understandably George II was the great champion of Ferdinand. In September he awarded him £2,000 a year for life and in December Frederick of Prussia appointed him a Field Marshal. But Ferdinand seemed to some critics to be running out of ideas, and it was noteworthy that he went into winter quarters in mid-November 1758 and did not try to repeat his exploits of the previous year.

On 4 February 1759 Soubise, appointed commander of the army projected for the invasion of England, handed over to the forty-year-old Duc de Broglie. Victor François, Duc de Broglie, would prove to be the most capable French army commander in the Seven Years War, and the year 1759 would have gone better for France if he had been confirmed as supreme commander in Germany. He inherited a much healthier situation than at the beginning of 1758 for, under Belle-Isle's energetic leadership, the two French armies in Germany had been extensively re-equipped and retrained. Broglie's Army of the Main contained fifty squadrons of cavalry and fifty battalions of infantry – a total of 31,000 men. Contades's Army of the Lower Rhine was much larger, with ninety-one squadrons and 100 battalions (66,000 men). With this army of nearly 100,000 men, Belle-Isle intended to drive the pestilent Ferdinand across the Weser river. With Broglie's army in support, Contades was to cross the lower Rhine in June, capture Münster and Lippstadt and sweep the enemy before him. The obvious snag was that Ferdinand might take the offensive first. To pre-empt this and give themselves a sound base of operations, the French seized the free city of Frankfurt on New Year's Eve. They used an underhand trick to secure admission, then overpowered the garrison while the citizens were sleeping. Frankfurt became the base for French operations during the rest of the war; it was easily defended and could be supplied by the river.

Five miles north-east of Frankfurt the French fortified the strong natural position of Bergen covering the approaches from Kassel and sought to make it all but impregnable. This single fact determined allied strategy for 1759. Ferdinand strengthened his bases at Münster and Lippstadt, with subsidiaries at Nienburg, Hameln Stade and Hamburg, and patiently built up his total numbers to nearly 72,000 by April 1759, including two new companies sent from England. Originally he had been planning to attack the French in Hesse but that scheme was aborted when Frederick of Prussia told him he had no troops to spare. Lacking the manpower to tackle Hesse, Ferdinand now played cat and mouse with the French in a winter campaign lasting through January–February 1759, but found himself outpointed by Broglie. Initially threatened on his right flank, Broglie neatly turned the tables on Ferdinand by trying to punch through his right. Perhaps realising that he faced an opponent of real military calibre, Ferdinand finally sheered off after a face-saving, protracted and confusing (confused?) war of manoeuvre. At length he made up his mind to attack the main French strength at Frankfurt. He left Münster on 22 March, determined to test to the limit the strength of the French position at Bergen.

French military planners had not been exaggerating when they boasted that Bergen was the dream defensive position, difficult to outflank and high enough to provide an overview of any approaching enemy forces while providing plenty of cover. Two miles north-east of Frankfurt was where Broglie intended to begin drawing up his forces. The battleground he selected was adjacent to flat and marshy country on the right which ran to the steep escarpment topped by Bergen. On the left the terrain was not so steep. Wooded and striated by streams, with open country between the woods and Bergen, it was cut across by two sunken roads, impeding any attack from the east. Bergen itself was enclosed by a fortified wall, eighteen feet high and three feet thick, outside which were farms, orchards and enclosures, surrounded by banks and hedges. In front was the hill of Am Hohen Stein, offering some protection to an attacker on its eastern slope; but the western slope, extending to the scarp on the right and the woods on the left, was devoid of cover. North-west of Bergen, 1,000 yards away and set on a knoll, was a tower, the Bergen Warte, dominating Bergen and the 1,000 yards of open land between it and the village. South of Bergen the escarpment ran westwards until it hit the River Main. Here Broglie awaited Ferdinand's coming with some 30,000 men, eight battalions in Bergen itself and another thirteen held in reserve. On his left, behind the woods, were the Saxons; in the centre, behind the Bergen Warte, were the cavalry; the artillery was in the centre, between the sunken roads. Ferdinand, relying on false estimates of enemy strength from his scouts and an irrational belief that the French were not present in strength, was confident that Broglie could not hold his position and proposed to attack 30,000 seasoned defenders with a numerically inferior force, computed at 24,000–27,000 troops.

Ferdinand began by sending General von Gilsa into the orchards, where he quickly cleaned out the French. Broglie, commanding a panorama of the battlefield from his obsevation post on the Bergen Warte, ordered his reserves to counterattack. Emerging in a cloud from behind the walls of Bergen, they quickly repulsed the enemy. The seesaw battle in the orchards continued when Ferdinand ordered his Brunswickers into the fray and they in turn began to push the French back. One hundred yards from the walls the French dug in and a furious struggle commenced. Sensing that this was the moment to commit the last of his reserves, Broglie gave the signal to his veterans who decisively repelled the Brunswickers. Ferdinand next ordered his artillery to come to the aid of the Brunswickers but his gunners were caught by a murderous fire from the French artillerymen at the western end of the sunken road. Ferdinand's principal lieutenant, Johann Kasimir, Prince of Isenburg, rallied his men for another charge but was counter-attacked on the flanks; he fell, mortally wounded, and his men broke and fled. Ferdinand now expected an all-out assault but Broglie had no intention of going over onto the attack, as this would mean leaving his strong position and meeting the enemy in the open. This gave Ferdinand a welcome breathing space, so once again he rallied his men before withdrawing them to the Am Hohen Stein, vainly hoping that Broglie would pursue him there. When Ferdinand's big guns were in position, he prepared for a final attack but cancelled the assault when he saw movements on the French side indicating an imminent charge. Broglie, though, was simply strengthening his left flank by positioning more artillery there and moving up his last six reserve battalions from the Bergen Warte. A period of phoney war developed, with the artillery exchanging shots and each side waiting for the other to make the first move, and so it continued until dusk. Ferdinand withdrew under cover of night but had sentries posted at dawn, waiting for what seemed like an inevitable attack. But it never came. Broglie, having been left on the field and with 1,800 casualties against Ferdinand's 2,500, claimed the victory.

Ferdinand withdrew to the north, still in dread that Broglie would strike his slow-moving column; he was especially vulnerable now, with a tired, hungry and demoralised allied army. But the Anglo-Hanoverians were left to recoup in peace, as Broglie made no attempt to exploit his victory and indeed huddled fearfully near Frankfurt, apprehensive that Ferdinand would attack again. Both sides were left to ponder the implications of French success in the first campaign of 1759. Broglie's performance was efficient rather than brilliant, since he fought from a well-nigh impregnable position, outnumbered the enemy in men and guns and had fresh troops who were not afraid of Ferdinand since they had not been involved in the 1758 defeats under Clermont and Contades. His failure to pursue Ferdinand was deplorable and showed once again that the tradition of Condé, Turenne, Saxe and Lowendahl was dead. Broglie had many enemies at court, who immediately tried to spread the rumour that his victory was really a defeat. The friends of the Prince de Soubise were particularly forward in this regard and even spread the canard that Broglie had abandoned his field hospital during the battle. Soubise's champion was Madame de Pompadour and she in turn had the ear of the King. Broglie would not get his Marshal's baton for a while yet. But if Broglie had been excessively timid, Ferdinand had been rash, complacent and over-confident, and perhaps the victories of 1758 had made him gravely underrate the French. That seems the most likely explanation for his extraordinary decision to make a frontal attack in a piecemeal fashion and without proper artillery support, though the false estimates produced by his scouts hardly helped. Ferdinand did not relish the task of reporting to Frederick, but for once the Prussian king did not nag him mercilessly, contenting himself this time with the suggestion that Ferdinand should at once increase his complement of heavy guns. Secretly Ferdinand blamed Frederick for his defeat, since the Prussian preoccupation with the eastern front meant that he had not been able to open his offensive at the beginning of March, as he wanted.

April–July 1759 was a very bad patch for Ferdinand, and now for the first time his Achilles heel became manifest. He cultivated a persona of professionalism and unflappability, but his mask of serene courtesy concealed anxiety and insecurity; some have speculated that he had a chip on his shoulder about Frederick, that Brunswick always felt itself to be in the shadow of Prussia and suffered the same feelings of inferiority that Poland has always had about Russia. Studies of the accident-prone invariably show depression lurking in the shadows, and it is surely significant that on 30 June, while riding with his aide-de-camp the Duke of Richmond, Ferdinand fell off his horse into a deep water-filled ditch and was almost drowned before being rescued.

Ferdinand's principal anxiety was that when the French marched north in June on the summer campaign, they would have an army twice as strong as his. His difficult relationship with Frederick simply made his problems worse, for when he asked the King's advice, Frederick soon lost patience with his 'defeatism': the King's replies were initially cordial, shortly became peevish and thereafter downright insulting. The beginning of the summer campaign underlined Ferdinand's worst fears. Advancing slowly but surely, the French took Münster and then Minden. The Marquis d'Armentière's first attempt to capture Münster was beaten back with heavy losses, but he brought up reinforcements, forcing the defenders back into the citadel where, after a perfunctory defence, the garrison of 3,600 surrendered. Armentière then proceeded to Lippstadt to lend his weight to the siege being conducted there by the Duc de Chevreuses. Minden was another French triumph. Learning that the town was weakly garrisoned, Broglie sent his brother (the Comte de Broglie) with 1,500 infantry and 1,200 cavalry to seize it; the coup was successful but Minden was then looted in a way not seen since the Thirty Years War and it was with difficulty that the French commanders restored order.

The day before Minden fell (11 July) Ferdinand received another carping letter from Frederick, chiding him for his Fabian tactics. Exhorting him to remember Rossbach, Frederick admonished his brother-in-law that it was better to join battle with the enemy and lose than demoralise the troops by constant retreat; in a particularly nasty jibe, Frederick suggested that Ferdinand was a second Cumberland. At the same time George II was growing anxious about the lack of good news from Germany and was also starting to nag him for results. The effect on a man already suffering self-doubt can be imagined. His particular current anxiety was that the French would move on Hanover and cut him off from his communications with Frederick; perhaps the Prussian king had spoken more truly than he knew and it was now to be his (Ferdinand's) fate to suffer Cumberland's 1757 humiliation. This was the moment when his secretary, Christian Heinrich Philipp Edler von Westphalen, stiffened his resolve with a famous letter, urging Ferdinand to follow his own lights and not just agree with the last person he spoke to. From a secretary, this sounds at first like impertinence, but Westphalen had already shown that, when the occasion demanded, he was prepared to waive protocol and to go beyond the bounds of his formally subordinate station. Devoted to Ferdinand, having been with him at the battles of Lobositz, Prague and Rossbach, Westphalen was the Prince's chief planning officer and strategist, a devotee of boldness and imagination as against the sound space-time logistics of the military manuals. Ferdinand trusted him, listened to him and always took his advice seriously. On this occasion his response to Westphalen's written homily was as decisive as his secretary could have wished. Ferdinand decided he would make no attempt to retake Münster but would march to the Weser river and establish himself on both sides of the river, daring Contades to dislodge him.

Contades though, exhibited the usual inertia of French commanders in Germany in the 1750s. Excessively circumspect, by covering all possible options he left himself with insufficient troops to mount an offensive. Even the capture of Minden was something of an embarrassment to him, as his distribution of numbers left him in no real position to take advantage of it. Nonetheless he decided that the town gave him another impregnable base from which to operate, so he dug in there. Ferdinand then tried all the ruses he knew to get Contades to leave his Minden position and fight before French reinforcements arrived, but Contades refused to take the bait. There were constant skirmishes along the Weser and both sides' big guns blazed away pointlessly at each other. After failing to coax Contades out of his prepared positions, Ferdinand tried to threaten his communications at Minden by a march on Lübbecke. This operation he entrusted to his favourite commander, the twenty-four-year-old Erbprinz of Brunswick, Karl Wilhelm Ferdinand, who had won Ferdinand's undying respect and affection by serving under him even after his father (the Duke of Brunswick) had forbidden it. Ferdinand's thinking was that Contades would have to deal with this threat either by turning south or giving battle. When the Erbprinz with his force of nearly 10,000 men brushed the French aside at Lübbecke on 28 July, Contades decided this was a challenge he could not ignore and sent the Duc de Brissac to intercept him. Brissac was told to buy time until reinforcements, expected under the command of the veteran Lieutenant-General, the Comte de St-Germain, arrived, guaranteeing overwhelming numerical superiority. The vanguards of the two armies collided near Bünde on 31 July, but this did not halt the Erbprinz's probe and soon he had advanced as far as Kirchlengern and Quernheim. Now in serious alarm at the threat to his communications, Contades realised that inaction was no longer an option. But would he plump for retreat or battle? Ferdinand made contingency plans for either eventuality, detaching a liaison force under General Gilsa to make sure he was in constant touch with the Erbprinz, but meanwhile disposing his army so that it could operate at a moment's notice in the Minden plain.

Contades had been in Minden for sixteen days, in a position of great strength, with his right resting on the Weser and Minden and his left covered by the Bastau marshes. Situated at the confluence of the rivers Bastau and Weser, Minden looked out to the north-west over a plain where on the horizon could be seen the villages and hamlets of Hahlen, Stemmer, Kutenhausen and Maulbeerkamp; the principal features on the skyline were a windmill and a cemetery. As one headed north and east from Hahlen, the landscape became more choppy, broken up by smallholdings, plantations and orchards abutting the hamlets. Contades's idea was to recall Armentières from the protracted siege of Lippstadt, leaving Chevreuse to invest it and with the Armentières and St-Germain forces to overwhelm Ferdinand. Contades was irritated that the Brunswick prince had given him the slip since Bergen and wanted to finish him off in one go. His preference was to wait for Ferdinand to attack him, but he was under the same sort of nagging pressure from Belle-Isle and Versailles as Ferdinand was experiencing from Frederick and Berlin. He wanted to win the glory of being the French commander who made the definitive conquest of Hanover, and it was also in his mind that Versailles needed a decisive breakthrough in west Germany so that it could switch some of the 100,000 troops there to the invasion of the British Isles.

Contades therefore decided to launch a surprise attack on Ferdinand. But first he had to extricate his troops from the bottleneck – perfect for defence but not offence – between the Bastau marshes and Minden and this, he decided, was best done at night. Because of the difficult terrain, the infantry would have to be on the flanks of the cavalry instead of the other way round as in normal circumstances. Meticulous planning was necessary for the surprise attack, since while this night manoeuvre in unorthodox formation on a narrow front was going on, Broglie's troops would have to be brought over from the other side of the river. At 6 p.m. on 31 July, therefore, Contades summoned his generals and issued his orders. Broglie was to march at dusk, cross the Weser by a stone bridge, proceed through Minden and link up with the artillery and eight battalions of Grenadiers. Situated on Contades's right, at dawn he would launch a sudden attack of unparalleled ferocity,

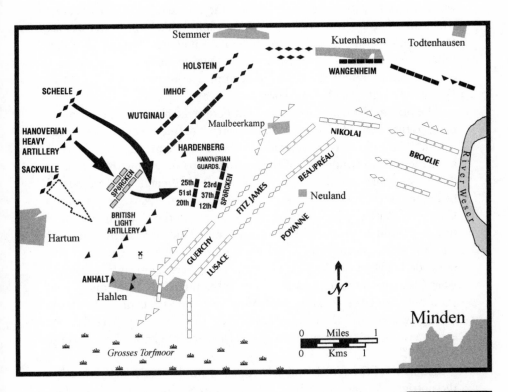

Stemmer

HOLSTEIN

Kutenhausen Todtenhausen

WANGENHEIM

SCHEELE

IMHOF

WUTGINAU

Maulbeerkamp

NIKOLAI

HANOVERIAN
HEAVY
ARTILLERY

HARDENBERG

BROGLIE

SACKVILLE

HANOVERIAN
GUARDS.

SPÖRCKEN

25th 23rd
51st 37th
20th 12th

SPÖRCKEN

FITZ JAMES

BEAUPRÉAU

Neuland

BRITISH
LIGHT
ARTILLERY

POVANNE

River Weser

Hartum

GUERCHY

LUSACE

ANHALT

N

Hahlen

Minden

Grosses Torfmoor

0   Miles   1

0   Kms   1

Allies   French
▲ Artillery △
◆ Cavalry ◇
■ Infantry ▢

The Battle of Minden, 1 August 1759

exposing Ferdinand's left flank. The main army meanwhile would cross the Bastau by bridge and draw up, ready for daybreak, with the infantry on the flanks and the cavalry in the centre; artillery would cover the cavalry by enfilading fire from both flanks. Between Broglie's corps and the right of the main army, a third column, eight battalions strong under General Nikolai (yet another veteran who would have to wait until his sixties to receive a Marshal's baton) would support Broglie's left and make sure the enemy could not drive a wedge between Broglie and Contades. Nikolai, whose forty-seventh birthday it was on the morrow, hoped to celebrate with a notable victory. Contades's left meanwhile would be protected against flank attack by the Duc d'Havre and four battalions. Making sure that proper contact was maintained with the Duc de Brissac in the reserve, d'Havre would initiate the action by feinting across the causeway towards Ferdinand's right just before dawn.

The plan might have worked had not Ferdinand almost simultaneously decided that *he* would launch a surprise attack on the French after a night march. The army was to be ready to march at 1 a.m., the right was to seize the Hahlen windmill and the left to occupy the hamlet of Stemmer. The best scholarship discounts the idea that Ferdinand was forewarned of French intentions by a peasant who brought him a package containing Contades's battle orders; what is not explained in the traditional story is how a peasant with anti-French sentiments could have been entrusted with top-secret documents – and ones, moreover that were in clear and not coded. The most likely explanation is that Ferdinand simply intuited what Contades intended and beat him to the punch. By this time he too probably wanted a decisive confrontation. The strain on him of the chivvying and carping George II and Frederick was not assuaged by an extremely difficult relationship with the British commander, Lord George Sackville.

Estimates of Sackville's character range from the moderately critical to the outright denunciatory. According to Lord Shelburne, who knew him well, Sackville was the avatar of all the vices: he was incompetent, cowardly, an intriguer, a vindictive enemy, a lover of low company and an unbalanced individual who swung violently from spurious optimism to false pessimism. The reference to 'low company' was code for the consistent canard that Sackville, even though he was married and would sire five children, was a homosexual. Even his friends conceded that he was a difficult man, reserved, haughty and socially isolated even among his peers and equals. Relations between Ferdinand and Sackville by 31 July 1759 were icy, and it is clear that at one of the many conferences Ferdinand liked to convene, Lord George had given deep offence by something he had said. The most plausible explanation is that Sackville expressed his frustration with the constant retreating before the French and threatened to pull the British troops out of the campaign. The threat could not be presumed to be idle, for in the War of Spanish Succession the great Duke of Marlborough had done just that to his ally Prince Eugene of Savoy.

The upshot of the two converging night marches was that by dawn on 1 August Contades's army was drawn up along a line stretching from Hahlen to Maulbeerkamp and Ferdinand's from Hartum to Stemmer. The British troops during their night march had noticed that the fields and hedgerows were teeming with wild red and yellow roses, so they picked the flowers and put them in their hats. Broglie's corps completed the march as planned, made contact with the enemy left at about 5 a.m. and opened fire. Lieutenant-General Georg August von Wangenheim, the Hanoverian commander who enjoyed the best relations with the British – he had been a battalion commander in England in 1756–57 during the invasion scare – was taken by surprise as a heavy pre-dawn thunderstorm drowned the noise of the approaching attackers. But the French plans began to unravel almost immediately. Instead of pressing home his advantage, Broglie waited for Nikolai to come up in support, giving Wangenheim time to get his big guns ready. There followed a pounding artillery duel, in which Broglie's leading troops, the Grenadiers, took heavy casualties. By 6 a.m., with Wangenheim's artillery gaining the advantage, Broglie sent Nikolai to try to loop round the enemy and occupy Kutenhausen. But, cautious like all French commanders, he first reconnoitred and seems to have persuaded himself that a German cavalry charge was imminent.

Contades, realising that his plans were already behind schedule, sent a mounted messenger to find out why Broglie had not advanced. Broglie then wasted further time by galloping over to Contades's headquarters to explain his fears. In the meantime Contades, as dithering as his second-in-command, became alarmed by a supposed threat to his left, so told Broglie to return and contain the enemy right, until the situation on the left wing was sorted out; he even discussed with Broglie contingency plans for withdrawal. So, only two hours into the battle, things had already gone seriously awry; instead of launching a dawn attack, Broglie was now in limbo and even thinking of retreat. He could scarcely feel pleased with the morning's work. He should not have waited for Nikolai, but attacked Wangenheim without delay; since Wangenheim was caught unawares, Ferdinand's left would then have been turned. Broglie showed himself indecisive: he mistook a movement by Wangenheim's men when taking up their position as an attack and therefore decided to wait for Nikolai. And so Broglie's advance, on which the whole battle plan of Contades was supposed to turn, petered out. The unintended consequence was that he spent the rest of the battle containing Wangenheim – a stalemate that was compatible with Ferdinand's tactics, but not with Contades's.

Meanwhile Contades's infantry had been delayed crossing the Bastau. They saw the sky lit up by flashes of gunfire and assumed that Broglie's attack was proceeding as planned. The consequence was that the Comte de Lusace, on the French left, commanding fifteen battalions of Saxons, came to a halt near Hahlen at dawn, in close contact with another sixteen French battalions who were already in the village. This was the precise moment when Ferdinand, unaware that the enemy was present in strength, ordered forward Karl, Prinz von Anhalt-Bernburg and his men to occupy the village. Luck was with the Germans that morning. As they stormed forward into a potential death-trap, houses on the western side of the village caught fire, probably from incendiary shells. The wind caught up the fire and fanned it into the faces of the French defenders, who were driven back by the fierce heat and blinding smoke. The first British troops seriously engaged in battle in Germany now came into play as Foy's Light Infantry Battalion collided with the French at the windmill just north of Hahlen. Seeing his attack now well under way on the right, Ferdinand ordered Wangenheim on the left to advance, and also gave the signal to Spörcken's corps on the right centre to close the gap left as Anhalt advanced.

General Freiherr von Spörcken was, at sixty-one, the oldest officer on the field that day, an unspectacular plodder as a soldier but very popular with his men. Although nominally a German column, Number Three column (Spörcken's) was actually comprised largely of British troops, including the Royal Welch Fusiliers, the King's Own Yorkshire Light Infantry (51st Foot) and the other troops commanded by General Waldegrave and Colonel Kingsley, six regiments all told. Spörcken's column came on at the double, at first hidden by woods, then deploying as it emerged from the sylvan darkness. To his alarm Ferdinand noticed Spörcken's men getting ahead of the rest of the army and sent word for them to slow down. They made a brief halt in a copse but then recommenced their advance at the same rapid pace. Swerving to the left, and thus not hitting their intended target, they caught the left flank of the French cavalry. So on Ferdinand's right, the situation was that the leading British and Hanoverian infantry were not only ahead of the rest of their comrades but had cut across them and were beginning to crowd them out. Nobody knows exactly why Spörcken's men decided to fight virtually at running pace. Some say the orders were garbled in transmission because of language problems, but since Spörcken was in command this hardly makes sense. Others say the British wanted to show the other regiments their mettle, as they had been criticised for being raw troops. Doubtless a combination of élan and naivety caused the near-fiasco. Having dislocated the order of battle and being caught alone out in the open, they should have been severely punished and defeated in detail. But luck was with Ferdinand in all sectors this morning.

The battle for Hahlen now settled into a grim slugging match between the big guns of the French and those of Spörcken. This was a critical moment in the battle for, as Spörcken's men stumbled towards them, the French infantry should have been able to seize the big guns before the artillery duel began. Unaccountably they failed to do so – later it was said they had been blinded by smoke and dust from the battle. That Ferdinand's artillery was able to engage the French big guns was a hugely significant development, as the French were thereby prevented from sweeping away the opposition facing their own cavalry. Had these German guns not come into play at this juncture, the right flank of the British infantry would have been at the mercy of the French guns, causing heavy casualties and possibly affecting the entire result of the battle. In a letter to his mother written on the afternoon of the battle, Lieutenant Hugh Montgomery of the 12th Regiment of Foot explained the atmosphere that morning:

> We advanced more than a quarter of a mile through a most furious fire from a most infernal battery of 18-pounders, which was at first upon our front, but as we proceeded, bore upon our flank, and at last upon our rear. It might be imagined, that this cannonade would render the regiments incapable of bearing the shock of unhurt troops drawn up long before on ground of their own choosing, but firmness and resolution will surmount almost any difficulty.

Relentlessly the British battalions pressed forward onto the French cavalry, 7,000 strong, who could do nothing to stop them as they were equipped with sabres and pistols, and not muskets. Seeing that they were in danger of becoming sitting targets, the cavalry commander gave the order to charge. Commanding the cavalry was the Duc de Fitzjames, yet another forty-seven-year-old at Minden that day. Grandson of James II of England and son of the Duke of Berwick, the Jacobite warrior who was killed at Philipsburg in 1734 (the young Fitzjames was at his side when he died), the Duc de Fitzjames was a veteran of a dozen battlefields, first in the War of Austrian Succession and more recently at Hastenbeck, Krefeld and Lutterberg. Now he ordered the Marquis de Castries to lead the first cavalry wave of eleven squadrons in a daring attempt to demoralise and rout the enemy. Spörcken's infantry had just one round apiece, after which it would be a combat of bayonets against sabres. Every round had to tell.

A series of crashing volleys from the superbly disciplined British regiments tore the heart out of the French cavalry; those who survived the deadly fire and got through to the enemy were finished off with the bayonet. As the French retreated, their tormentors reloaded and stood ready for the next charge. Fitzjames then ordered his second line – twenty-two squadrons – to charge. Now, if ever, the British proved their calibre for their casualties were mounting and yet there was no sign that they were losing their heads or becoming downhearted. Lieutenant Montgomery summed up the situation nonchalantly: 'These visitants [i.e. the first French cavalry wave] being thus dismissed, without giving us a moment's time to recover the unavoidable disaster, down came upon us like lightning the glory of France in the person of the Gens d'Armes.' Once again murderous volleys tore holes in the careering horsemen; once again a few French horsemen got through only to be skewered at point-blank range; once again the German infantry reloaded and stood ready. This time they did not wait for a third charge but surged forward. In so doing they exposed their right flank, and the Comte de Guerchy on Fitzjames's left saw his opportunity.

Forced to turn their second line half-right to meet this new challenge, the hard-pressed Spörcken's infantry now had just three battalions to pit against a new enemy nearly three times as strong. It would have gone hard with them, had not Ferdinand spotted the new development and ordered to their support five battalions of Scheele's men (situated on Spörcken's right) and a brigade of heavy artillery. Ferdinand had only just plugged this hole when the French launched another cavalry attack, this time under General de Poyanne and 2,000 horsemen. This was not a frontal attack like Fitzjames's but an enveloping movement on Spörcken's left flank and rear. This was the crux of the battle, for Poyanne's attack was the most dangerous French movement so far. Lieutenant Montgomery continued his recital: 'The next who made their appearance were some regiments of the Grenadiers of France, as fine and terrible looking fellows as ever I saw. They stood us a tug, notwithstanding we beat them off to a distance, where they galded [goaded] us much, they having rifled barrels, and our muskets would not reach them. To remedy this we advanced, they took the hint and ran away.' But how much longer could the British regiments really withstand this dual envelopment, by infantry to the right and cavalry to the left and rear?

This was the supreme moment of glory for the Royal Welch Fusiliers, who have had Minden among their most prized battle honours from that day on. Ably supported by the Hanoverian Guards, they fought like lions, taking the brunt of a frenzied attack from front, flank and rear. The hind-most ranks turned and faced about, knowing there was no reserve behind them. For a brief moment they wavered and looked likely to break. Vicious fighting ensued with the French tearing large holes in the defence and the British holding firm and closing the gaps. Again and again Guerchy's infantry tried to make the breakthrough but were driven off by close, precise fire, with the Anglo–Hanoverian artillery joining in during the final stages of the titanic struggle. Finally Ferdinand was able to get reinforcements to the vital arena. Wutginau's column (from the centre and thus immediately to the left of Scheele's) came up, and its right wing, composed of Hanoverians and Hessians, caught the French in the flank. More slaughterous close-quarter and often hand-to-hand fighting resulted. Poyanne's cavalry were the first to snap. Soon the flower of French horsemen, the Gendarmerie and Carabineers, were streaming away in defeat, having lost half their numbers. By this time General Imhoff's column on the Anglo–German left centre had come into line. They were late onto the field partly because they had marched all night and partly because Spörcken's column crowded them out by advancing so quickly and impetuously. Their arrival completed the disarray of the French who had been trying to rally. The remaining French cavalry were especially devastated. As Fitzjames desperately tried to get them to regroup and mass, the big guns further decimated them. Finally Fitzjames ordered his remaining horsemen to charge, but their attempt was flung back with ease by an allied army already confident of victory.

It was now about 9 a.m. and Anhalt sensed a great opportunity not just to defeat but to annihilate the French army. Ferdinand sent orders to Lord George Sackville to enter the fray and tip the balance decisively with his fresh troops. Sackville had found the waiting period exasperating and began to fume at the delay and inaction. But now began one of the most disgraceful incidents in the Seven Years War. Two separate aides arrived from Frederick but with what Sackville claimed were contradictory orders, making no sense and in no way conforming with the battle plans discussed the day before; further confusion arose from the fact that the two messages were deliv-ered independently and no one could agree which of the aides had arrived first. In the end Sackville rode to Ferdinand to find out exactly what his orders were. Ferdinand, already nursing a giant grievance against the British commander for the threat to leave him in the lurch, listened to Sackville's explanation of confusion with icy politeness and then replied: 'My lord, the situation has changed, my dispositions of yesterday can no longer have any effect; and in any case it is enough that I want it so and I beg you to do it immediately.' Sackville bowed and withdrew but then took an uncon-scionable time about drawing up his cavalry on the heath and getting them into position. What was the reason for this slowness? Was Sackville confused by the earlier contretemps and still slightly dazed at Ferdinand's words? Was he simply incompetent at cavalry tactics? Or was he, as his critics suggest and as seems most likely from his psychological profile, deliberately dragging his feet and 'working to rule' in rage at Ferdinand's publicly delivered rebuke?

The battle continued without Sackville's intervention. The French centre was by now decisively broken, but Contades riposted by throwing his sole hitherto uncommitted troops into the struggle. Eight battalions of Beauprieu's in the right centre, to the left of Broglie and Nikolai, were just preparing to launch a shock attack when they were overwhelmed by a combined onset of nineteen Prussian and Hanoverian cavalry squadrons, backed up by four bayonet-wielding Hessian infantry battalions. Contades's last forces were thrown back onto the pitiful remnants of the French cavalry. The only part of the French line still holding firm was the axis formed by Beaupréau's second line and the ten squadrons of cavalry from Broglie's left flank. But at this precise moment Wangenheim, hitherto on the defensive, unleashed his cavalry, all sixteen squadrons, who smashed through Nikolai's two brigades and collided with Broglie's cavalry. The thrusting, slashing combat of horseman against horseman was almost Contades's last throw. On the left the Comte de Lusace and his Saxons meanwhile made a last effort against Spörcken's infantry and performed valiantly. The Saxons actually forced the British heroes of the earlier struggle to give way, only to be beaten off when they came under artillery fire north of Hahlen. Seeing the day lost, Contades reluctantly ordered a general retreat. He was in danger of rout and annihilation, and all that was needed was the charge of the twenty-four cavalry squadrons that Sackville continued to manoeuvre around Hartum. They never appeared on the field. While Sackville was away receiving his reprimand from Ferdinand, his deputy Lord Granby actually ordered the cavalry forward on his own responsibility and they were just setting off at a trot when the peevish Sackville, smarting from the 'insult' offered by Ferdinand, returned from the interview and countermanded the order.

Ferdinand's other chances for destroying Contades also came to nothing. Wangenheim's infantry were slow to leave their entrenchments and in the end did so only after direct orders from Ferdinand, so whatever pursuit there was of the French right came from the heavily encumbered artillerymen. Broglie successfully covered the retreat of the French right, and by 11 a.m. the French were back across the Bastau, with Broglie occupying a position protected by Minden fortress. Even so he was hard pressed and soon found himself retreating right back through Minden itself. Brissac, covering the retreat of the French left, was theoretically in danger from the Erbprinz's mobile columns, for Ferdinand had intended that he should envelop Brissac and close the road behind him, thus trapping the French left between Minden and the Porta Westfalica. But the Erbprinz, instead of pressing on to the bank of the Weser, allowed his worries about the forces under Armentières and Chevreuse to prey on his mind; in short, he feared that while he sought to trap Brissac, he might be ambushed himself and the two French commanders not at Minden might suddenly appear on his flank with superior numbers. At any rate the French made good their escape and by noon all firing had ceased; Contades got his army across the Weser and did not stop retreating until he reached Kassel.

The allies pitched their camp between Hahlen and Friedewalde and started sifting through the battlefield wreckage. Ferdinand had every reason to be proud. He had successfully enticed Contades to come out and fight, the French had been driven from Westphalia and Hanover was no longer threatened. The victory at Minden was crucial. Since Frederick of Prussia was defeated by the Russians at Kunersdorf on 12 August, if Ferdinand had lost at Minden and been forced to retreat east to Prussia, Frederick would have been in a desperate situation. Indeed, he came close to losing his nerve altogether after his defeat. A brilliant beginning to the battle, when he broke the Russian left wing and captured 180 cannon, petered out after furious fighting, when he was first thrown back and later routed. He had two horses killed under him and for two days could barely speak with rage and disappointment. To his favourite Frenchman, d'Argens, he wrote: 'Death is sweet in comparison to such a life as mine. Have pity on me and it; believe that I still keep to myself a great many evil things, not wishing to burden or disgust anybody with them, and that I would not advise you to escape these unlucky countries if I had any ray of hope. Adieu, mon cher.'

Frederick was in the doldrums, but Ferdinand's reputation, in danger of dipping after his first twelve months on a roll, was now once again sky-high. He had proved himself a good general who could think quickly and turn subordinates' mistakes to his advantage. He had handled his artillery superbly, especially on the right as, but for the big guns, Spörcken's corps would have been badly mauled and perhaps 'eaten up'. Bergen had taught Ferdinand the importance of artillery and he had learned the lesson well. A delighted George II awarded him £20,000 and the Order of the Garter when he received news of Minden.

But for Contades the battle was a disaster and his reputation was in tatters. Belle-Isle wrote to his friend the Marquis de Castries, who at thirty-two had now added Minden to a long list of battle honours (Dettingen, Fontenoy, Roucoux, Lawfeldt, Rossbach, Lutterberg; he probably saw more front-line service than any other senior French commander in the eighteenth century): 'I can't understand why sixty squadrons at the height of their powers could not break nine or ten battalions of infantry, especially as the same British infantry also put to flight four of our infantry brigades who on their own were numerically superior to them.'

So alarmed and despondent was Belle-Isle that he sent the veteran sixty-four-year-old Marshal d'Estrées, now also a member of Louis XV's elite Council of State, to Germany, officially as Contades's 'adviser' but really to oversee operations and report directly to the War Minister, since Belle-Isle had lost confidence. As all the senior French commanders were madly jealous of each other, it was not surprising that d'Estrées immediately found much to criticise. He wrote to Versailles as follows:

> I can't recover from my surprise when I reflect that, in less than two months, a strong French army of 100,000 men has been reduced to about half that number. Here are the finest regiments in the French Army and one can hardly recognise them. To help poor Contades, against whom the duc de Broglie, the comte de Saint-Germain and Saint-Pern make such loud and derisive cries, I have made the least wounding report possible to the Court; but despite that, the mere reading of a factual recital of this battle is enough to ensure his immediate recall, unless he receives the protection of the woman of whom we have spoken so many times [i.e. Madame de Pompadour].

D'Estrées did not like what he saw in Germany and cannily resisted pressure from Versailles (and the despondent Contades himself) to take over command. But if Contades clearly had to be replaced to restore morale and credibility, who could replace him? Broglie was the obvious choice but he was not popular at court and was junior in rank to many would-be marshals who considered themselves just as good he was. But in the end Austrian pressure was decisive, and Broglie was confirmed as French Commander-in-Chief in Germany in November.

In many accounts of the Seven Years War in Germany, Minden receives scant mention compared with Rossbach and Krefeld, and especially the terrible maulings Frederick took from the Russians on the eastern front. But it is worth emphasising that it was a colossal military achievement. With 41,000 troops ranged against Contades's 51,000, Ferdinand's army inflicted 11,000–12,000 casualties; among the French infantry alone, six generals and 438 officers were killed. Ferdinand's total losses amounted to

2,762, of whom 1,392 were from the heroic six British regiments, which lost an incredible 30 per cent of their fighting strength. These six regiments had seen off altogether thirty-six squadrons of cavalry and forty battalions of infantry; truly, as was said at the time, 'at Minden the impossible was achieved'.

Although Minden relieved the pressure on Frederick, it was not the decisive battle it might have been had the war in west Germany been a self-contained affair. Ferdinand quickly cleared Hesse of the French and wanted to take Frankfurt and then push the French back to the Rhine. But he wasted time on triumphalism, with Te Deums being sung and fireworks (*feux de joie*) being let off. And after Kunersdorf Frederick's pleas for help became so insistent that Ferdinand had to abandon his more ambitious plans. Frederick pressed him to move on Leipzig instead of Frankfurt, but Ferdinand was unwilliing to move to the eastern front until he had cleared the French out of Münster; otherwise they would retain it as a base for future threats on Hanover. Since Münster did not surrender until 22 November, it was only then that Ferdinand felt able to transfer troops to Frederick. Once again the western front restored Frederick's fortunes. His defeats at Maxen (20 November) and Meissen (3–4 December), which made 1759 as black a year for Prussia as it was for France and Louis XV, restored the balance of continental fortunes to the Austrian coalition, even after Ferdinand (and his replacement Wangenheim, during the Prince of Brunswick's frequent absences to confer with Frederick) had checkmated the initial moves of the new French commander, Broglie.

Ferdinand had one further piece of business to attend to in 1759: settling accounts with the 'coward of Minden', Lord George Sackville. He was in a difficult position, for British troops had just won a glorious victory and complaint about their commander might appear churlish; nevertheless Ferdinand was determined that Sackville should not use the 'glorious First' as a way of wriggling out of the consequences of his infamous conduct. He began by praising the valour of the British regiments at Minden and singled out for praise Sackville's deputy, the Marquis of Granby, pointedly saying nothing about Sackville. This summary of Minden was promulgated throughout the army. Ferdinand then issued further public orders, speaking of Granby as if he had commanded the British and again failing to mention Sackville. The intemperate Lord George then appealed to Ferdinand, repeating his story about confused and ambiguous orders, but the ground was cut from under this version of events when Granby refused to back him up in the implausible fiction. Icily Ferdinand responded that all his standing orders stood and were immutable, that he was weary of disputation in his army and refused to enter into any further discussion of Sackville's conduct. But in a letter to George II on 13 August Ferdinand unleashed a genuine thunderbolt:

> Sire,
>
> I find myself obliged, sire, to represent to Your Majesty, that if He wishes me to continue in the very honourable appointment of Commander-in-Chief of His Allied Army in Germany, he should be graciously pleased to make a notable change in this army by recalling Lord George Sackville commanding the British troops. His behaviour on the day of the 1st was not such as to help either the Cause in general or me in particular, and that at the very point at which affairs might have been within an ace of being lost; on the other hand, the success of this day was not so perfectly brilliant and complete as it would have been, had I been able to use all the means available. As the matter is so very grave, I dare to insist on the recall of the said Lord George Sackville; I dare also very humbly hope that Your Majesty will give it serious atten- tion by making this essential change at once. Otherwise, I find myself obliged to state frankly that I will not be responsible for what might follow; and that, without this prompt change, I will be of no more use to this army. Force of circumstance and zeal for the service of Your Majesty and the Cause in general compel me to make this approach. My conscience demands it; my natural character would never incline me to take such a step.

Sackville's fate was essentially in the hands of Pitt and George II, since the Duke of Newcastle only ever revealed his hand when he was sure he was on the winning side and was temperamentally incapable of standing up to the King on such a matter even if he wanted to. But he did not wish to: for Newcastle the only principles were those of survival as political kingmaker and the corrupt means needed to achieve that end; the idea of a principled stand was something the Duke's decayed intellect would have regarded as inherently risible. Sackville could hope for nothing at the hands of George II, who hated him, and his slender chances were anyway less- ened when Leicester House decided to use the entire unsavoury affair as a means of baiting the monarch. The Prince of Wales stirred the pot by announcing that it was 'pretty pert for a little German prince to make public any fault he finds with the British commander, without first waiting for instructions from the king on so delicate a matter'. That left just Pitt. For him personal considerations had no meaning – he could not under- stand friendship and had no real friends – and everything was judged by the strict canons of political expediency. In a masterpiece of double-talk

Pitt announced that Sackville had been 'given leave' to return to England, as if that was something Lord George himself had requested; he thus obfuscated the reality that George II took brutal delight in dismissing Sackville instantly. His sacking from the army cost him £7,000 a year but what hurt Sackville more was the gradual realisation that, while not being put on trial, he was the object of universal derision. He began a sustained campaign of lobbying the Cabinet for 'justice'. Finally Pitt lost patience and ordered a general court-martial on the capital charge of disobeying a commander in the face of the enemy. The court-martial found Sackville guilty as charged, struck him off the list of Privy Councillors and ordered his sentence of disgrace read out at every army parade – something usually done only in the case of an execution. The consensus opinion on Sackville was that he was probably more stupid and incompetent than cowardly in the normal sense. But even his supporters conceded that his behaviour after the battlefield reprimand from Ferdinand – deliberately dragging his feet while he manoeuvred the cavalry – constituted 'contumacious slowness' – eighteenth-century code for what we would call dumb insolence.

NINE

THE PLAINS OF ABRAHAM

It will already be clear that 1759 was a good year for literature. Apart from the classics that have endured, there was a host of now forgotten works that made an impact in their day. To take the example of Britain alone the Scots cleric Alexander Gerard made what was then considered an important contribution to aesthetics and the debate about the sublime in his An Essay on Taste, *while the English clergyman Richard Hurd in his* Moral and Political Dialogues, *using the conceit of quizzing literary figures from the past on various subjects, was taken seriously at the time, even though for posterity he was totally eclipsed by Hume and his* Essays Moral and Political. *Sarah Fielding produced a kind of proto-Gothic novel,* The History of the Countess of Dellwyn, *in some ways anticipating the motifs that Horace Walpole would make famous five years later in* The Castle of Otranto. *The Irish actor and dramatist Charles ('Mad Charlie') Macklin was hard at work on two plays,* The Married Libertine *and* Love à la Mode.

Yet another figure almost totally forgotten today was the poet Edward Young, who in 1759 penned his Conjectures on Original Composition – *his last significant writing. As with so many other productions of this year, one can almost discern the first shoots of the Romantic movement breaking through. Young was the first to articulate fully the now familiar notion of artist as genius – his work was a case of 'what oft was thought but ne'er so well expressed' – and to stress that the author is creative artist, not a mere craftsman with technique. Young popularised the idea of the genius as a kind of transmission belt for divine inspirations – what a later age would call the workings of the unconscious:*

Nor are we only ignorant of the dimensions of the human mind in general but even of our own. That a man be scarce less ignorant of his own powers than an oyster of its pearl or a rock of its diamond; that he may possess dormant, unsuspected qualities, till wakened by loud calls, or stung by striking emergencies, is evident from the sudden eruption of some men, out of perfect obscurity, into public admiration, on the strong principle of some animating occasion; not more to the world's great surprise than their own.

Perhaps the one thing lacking in English literature this year was any first-class poetry, with Pope and Thomson dead, Young declining and the Romantics still some way over the horizon. In 1759 Oliver Goldsmith, whose Deserted Village *was still a decade away, was then a hack with aspirations, writing ruefully to his brother in February: 'Could a man live by it, it were not unpleasant employment to be a poet.' With a background as erratic Trinity College, Dublin, scholar, failed emigrant, failed parson, failed physician, sometime pharmacist's assistant, amateur flautist, Grub Street hack and now apprenticed and penurious scribbler, Goldsmith hardly seemed destined for fame and fortune. The one quality he did have was energy. In 1759 he not only contributed prolifically to Smollett's* British Magazine *and even founded his own publication* The Bee *but wrote an angry treatise entitled* Enquiry into the Present State of Polite Learning in Europe, *in which he documented the decline of the arts in Europe as a result of a lack of enlightened patronage and the bad influence of dry criticism and academic scholarship. Although critics dismissed it as too short an essay to do justice to its broad ambit, it was undoubtedly fresh, invigorating and convincing when it dealt with the London Grub Street scene.*

Goldsmith had seen for himself the bitter disappointment of hungry would-be novelists, the poverty of poets, the slow or non-existent rewards of genius, the mercantile greed and low standards of London publishers and booksellers. He upset David Garrick with his attack on genteel, sentimental comedy – 'a kind of mulish production with all the defects of its opposite parents and marked with sterility' – and evinced a delight in epigrams and saws that drew him, inevitably, to the circle of Samuel Johnson. To be 'dull and dronish', he observed, was 'an encroachment on the prerogative of the folio' and he inveighed particularly at the straitjacket or cul-de-sac into which society forced poetry. 'Does the poet paint the absurdities of the vulgar, he is low, *does he exaggerate the features of folly to render it more ridiculous, he is very* low. *In short, they have proscribed the comic or satirical muse from every walk but high life, which, though abounding in fools as well as the humblest station, is by no means so fruitful in absurdity.'*

The greatest living English poet was Thomas Gray, but his masterpiece had appeared eight years earlier. There are probably more famous tags from his Elegy Written in a Country Churchyard *– 'paths of glory', 'far from the madding crowd', 'wade through slaughter to a throne', 'full many a flower is born to blush unseen', 'some village Hampden', etc, etc – than from any other poet but Shakespeare. Gray was singularly unlucky in love: his schoolfriend Richard West died young, he was snubbed by fellow homosexual Horace Walpole* *and spent the last years of his life in a fruitless passion for the young Swiss traveller Charles Victor Bonstetten. Celibate and depressive, Gray was particularly interested in the progress of the Seven Years War and quizzed his friend George Townshend (Wolfe's deputy) about the campaign in Canada. In January 1760 he reported the result of his conversation to Thomas Wharton: 'You ask after Quebec. General Townshend says it is much like Richmond-Hill, and the River as fine (but bigger) and the vale as* riant, *as rich and as well cultivated.' There is much more evidence of Gray's interest in military affairs. On 8 August 1759 he commented as follows on the Battle of Minden:*

> The season for triumph is at last come; I mean for our Allies, for it will be long enough before we shall have reason to exult in any great action of our own and therefore as usual we are proud for our neighbours. Contades' great army is entirely defeated: this I am told is undoubted, but no particulars are known yet; and almost as few of the other victory over the Russians, which is lost in the splendour of this great action.

Yet there are even more intimate links binding Gray to the world of military action, for possibly the best-known story about General Wolfe at Quebec involves the Elegy Written in a Country Churchyard. *John Robison, later Professor of Natural History at Edinburgh University, was in 1759 a young midshipman on the* Royal William. *He told Robert Southey (who passed it on to Sir Walter Scott) that on the night of 12 September during the British army's night passage on the St Lawrence, Wolfe pulled a copy of Gray's works from his pocket and began declaiming the* Elegy. *When the reading was received in silence by his officers, Wolfe upbraided them: 'I can only say, gentlemen, that if the choice were mine, I would rather be the author of these verses than win the battle which we are to fight tomorrow morning.' In another version of the story, one of Robison's students, James Lurie, remembered the Professor saying that someone else recited the* Elegy *from memory and that Wolfe then said: 'I would rather have been the author of that piece than beat the French tomorrow' – a giveaway remark that led the company to infer that there would be a battle next day, since Wolfe had so far confided in no one. The story became widely known after William Hazlitt repeated it in the* Literary Examiner *in 1823. The severest, most straitlaced scholars have always affected to disbelieve the story, on three main grounds: there is no mention of this anecdote in eighteenth-century literature; it does not fit what we know of the character and personality of Wolfe; and lines like those about the flower blushing unseen and wasting 'its sweetness on the desert air' scarcely square with the mentality of a self-publicist. But it is known that Wolfe's fiancée Katharine Lawler had given him a copy of Gray's poems just before he left England. The consensus is that the story is probably true in its main outline. The prime irony was that Gray never knew that one of Britain's great military heroes had made this most famous tribute to his most famous poem.*

Cast down and depressed by the debacle at Montmorency, Wolfe contemplated the likelihood that he would soon have to depart for Louisbourg, Halifax or even London, leaving a holding force on the Île-aux-Coudres against his return with another army in the spring of 1760. But his anger with the French found expression in a third proclamation in early August (the first had been on 27 June) which made it clear that, since they had spurned his earlier offer of amnesty, the full fury of war would now be visited on them. The Canadians, he alleged, 'had made such ungrateful returns in practising the most unchristian barbarities against his troops on all occasions, he could no longer refrain in justice to himself and his army from chastising them as they deserved'. What particularly infuriated Wolfe was the behaviour of Montcalm's Indians, particularly the Ottawas and Micmacs, and their habit of scalping and mutilating prisoners or the sentries they often overpowered in the darkness in the remote British outposts. There were suspicions, too, that the French Canadians did their own scalping and mutilating and passed it off as the work of their benighted Indian allies, whom 'unfortunately' they could not control. But when Wolfe officially remonstrated to Vaudreuil, the Governor gave him short shrift. Since both sides had always used Indians as allies in their struggle for mastery in North America, it was arrant humbug for the British to raise the issue now just because Wolfe had scarcely a native man in his ranks. Indian atrocities, though regrettable, were part of the 'fortunes of war' that both sides had to suffer stoically in this increasingly bitter conflict.

It may be that Wolfe had the Indians particularly on his mind at this juncture through an association of ideas with another enemy. By the beginning of August his relations with Townshend had deteriorated alarmingly, but meanwhile Townshend had added to his portraiture portfolio by proving the first authentic sketch of an Ottawa warrior in full fighting fig. In the small hours of 8 August 1759 this brave swam the ford below Montmorency Falls, making landfall where he hoped to pick off an unwary British sentry. But luck was against him; the Ottawa found himself staring down the muzzle of a redcoat's musket; within minutes the warrior was hauled before Brigadier Townshend. The Indian pretended not to understand anything said to him, even though there were many in the encampment who spoke the Ottawa tongue. Regarding with aristocratic hauteur 'a very savage looking brute and naked all to an arse clout', Townshend was sufficiently intrigued to make a quick sketch of his prisoner. This initial sketch became the first of a series of watercolours that Townshend completed during the campaign – invaluable as the only known images of North American Indians produced by an eyewitness during the Seven Years War. The would-be scalper was manacled and stowed on board a British warship, with the intention that he should be taken back to England as a present for George II, but the nimble Ottawa slipped his chains a few nights later and slid into the dark waters of the St Lawrence. Search parties were launched but no trace of the escapee was found, and the natural inference is that such an intrepid swimmer made his way safely back to the French lines.

According to Wolfe's interpretation of the rules of war, the French use of Indians and the masking of their own atrocities as the uncontrollable actions of the painted savages gave him the justification he needed to harry the inhabitants of the St Lawrence with fire and sword. Although he had given the Canadians until 10 August to change their ways, he decided to get his reprisals in first and on 4 August sent a company of Rangers to put the settlement of St Paul's Bay to the torch on the ground that the people there had fired on British boats. The man he chose to lead the group – one of Rogers' Rangers named Joseph Gorham – was an Indian-hating fire-eater who went about his work with a relish that Wolfe would have recognised from his time in Scotland with Cumberland and 'Hangman Hawley'. Wolfe's standing order of 27 July prohibited the Rangers from scalping (one of the Indian customs they had taken over with avidity, unless the enemy comprised Indians or Canadians dressed as Indians). But the Rangers simply scalped whomever they pleased, then claimed that the enemy had been 'masquerading' as Ottawas. Two days later Wolfe told Monkton that if any further shots were fired at his boats, he intended to burn every single house in the village of St Joachim, although 'churches must be spared – I shall give notice to Vaudreuil obliquely, that such is my intention'. The scorched-earth policy is a measure of Wolfe's desperation, for he clearly hoped that a reign of terror would force the French out of their entrenchments to defend their own kith and kin. Civilians in the St Lawrence were caught in a horrible dilemma: Vaudreuil had already warned them that if they collaborated with the enemy, he would unleash his Indians against them, and now here was Wolfe warning that if they did not collaborate, he would burn hearth and home down around their heads.

After gutting Baie St Paule, Gorham and his marauders moved on to Malbaie (Murray Bay) where he burned down forty houses and barns, then crossed the river to Ste Anne de la Pocatière, where he torched fifty more. Throughout August the sky over the St Lawrence was blackened as if by a mighty forest fire, as smoke from burning farmhouses blotted out the sun. On both sides of the river the inferno raged, as Gorham's Rangers fired every sign of human civilisation. By the middle of the month they had completed the destruction of all houses, farms and barns between the Etchemin river and la Chaudière. On the 23rd it was the turn of the villages on the north shore between Montmorency and St Joachim to taste the pyromania of Wolfe's arsonists. The Ile d'Orléans was swept into the conflagration. At the beginning of September Major George Scott, commanding a mixed force of regulars, Rangers and seamen, proceeded downriver and began destroying all buildings, flocks and harvests on the south shore, following Wolfe's threat to 'burn all the country from Camarasca to the Point of Levy'. In a fifty-two-mile march, Scott and his destroyers burned 998 buildings (Scott kept a precise count), took fifteen prisoners and killed five Canadians for the loss of two killed and a handful wounded. The final tally of destruction in Wolfe's campaign of terror was more than 1,400 farmhouses which, a New England newspaper gloatingly reported, it would take half a century to rebuild. Nor was this all. British sources kept quiet about the accompanying atrocities but the modern historian Fred Anderson sums up with terse under-statement: 'No one ever reckoned the numbers of rapes, scalpings, thefts and casual murders perpetrated during this month of bloody terror.'

The terror tactics were probably counter-productive as they solved the Canadians' dilemma for them. They now had little choice but to oppose the British, since Wolfe allowed them no way out. Ferocious guerrilla warfare was the inevitable upshot, with particularly bitter fighting on the north shore below Montmorency. The principal guerrilla leader was a priest named Portneuf, whom the sources confusingly refer to as both the Abbé de Beaupré and the Curé de St Joachim. Evidently a confidant of Vaudreuil, Father Portneuf tried to mitigate the worst savagery in the guerrilla warfare and deal with the British officers opposing him in a civilised way. His chivalry and gallantry were brusquely rebuffed by officers who were under orders from Wolfe to wage war to the knife. Frustrated at the priest's able defence, Wolfe sent reinforcements to the north shore and on 23 August 300 fresh troops and field artillery arrived on the scene. A ferocious artillery barrage on Portneuf's position at Ste Anne drove the defenders into the open, where they were butchered mercilessly. Thirty men and Portneuf himself were killed and scalped; the British used the lame excuse that the defenders had disguised themselves as Indians. No quarter was given or prisoners taken. Ensign Malcolm Fraser of the Highlanders had already promised two of the men their lives but he was overruled by the bloodthirsty local commander Captain Alexander Montgomery, who ordered all captives slaughtered in cold blood. Montgomery celebrated his hecatomb of Portneuf's guerrillas by gutting all the houses in Ste Anne and gratu-itously reducing the Château Richer to ashes.

Wolfe had once again proved himself an able disciple of Cumberland. In Tacitus's words he had created a desert and called it peace. Even Townshend, no bleeding heart, was revolted and wrote to his wife: 'I never served so disagreeable a campaign as this. Our unequal force has reduced our operations to a scene of skirmishing, cruelty and devastation. It is war of the worst shape. A scene I ought not to be in, for the future believe me, my dear Charlotte, I will seek the reverse of it.'

Wolfe's apologists, beginning with the intellectually dishonest Parkman, claim that his scorched-earth policy and his massacres were simply tit-for-tat retaliation for far worse war crimes meted out by Vaudreuil, Montcalm and their allies. This is scarcely convincing. The atrocities committed on the French side, as at Fort William Henry in 1757 and elsewhere, were the results of French inability to control their Indian allies, on whom they were forced to depend because of the massive superiority in numbers enjoyed by the British. There was no general *guerre à outrance* order of the kind that Wolfe issued in August and it is quite clear that his orders were regarded as egregious or received with stupefaction. Quite apart from the disgust evinced by those such as Malcolm Fraser and Townshend, there is Monkton's querying of Wolfe's draconian instructions and the British government's censoring of Wolfe's despatch to Pitt on the subject. The most that can be said in Wolfe's defence is that warfare in North America in the eighteenth century was always a nasty and barbarous business. But is it not a logical implication of that, as Wolfe's defenders seem to think, to accept that atrocity and barbarity should therefore be raised exponen-tially to new heights. If the Indians were benighted savages, what was it that justified supposedly civilised European officers behaving with equal savagery? Moreover, as was famously said of Napoleon's murder of the Duc d'Enghien, it was more than a crime, it was an error. Wolfe's atroci-ties did nothing to advance his ultimate aims, since the Québécois could no more be drawn out by the sufferings of their compatriots than by the 'strategic bombing' of their fair city.

While this cruel devastation of the Quebec hinterland went on, Wolfe probed the area of the St Lawrence above the city for some foothold or landing place, trying also to make contact with Amherst and cut Montcalm's communications. Brigadier Murray commanded this venture, and a game of cat and mouse developed with the French, the British making temporary landfall at various points, the French ponderously following them along the shore. Atrocity bade fair to follow Murray upriver for, after a repulse on the northern shore by Bougainville on 8 August, which cost the invaders 140 men killed and wounded, Murray switched to St Antoine on the southern shore, where he threatened to raze every dwelling to the ground if the inhabitants opened fire on him. On 18 August he re-embarked, gave Bougainville the slip, landed at Deschambault farther upriver on the northern shore and destroyed Montcalm's spare baggage and equipment.

This raid was sufficiently worrying to Montcalm to draw him temporarily from Quebec. Fearing that his communications would be cut, he rushed to Bougainville's assistance, only to learn that the British had already withdrawn. Montcalm confessed himself relieved, for if Murray had established a bridgehead in force at Deschambault, he lacked the forces to dislodge him. But he worried about the shape of possible similar things to come, unlike the bone-headed Vaudreuil, who could see no point in Montcalm's sortie and thought he was merely panicking. The August probe upriver stuttered out in stalemate: Montcalm returned to Beauport and Murray to Point Levis, summoned back post-haste by an increasingly jumpy Wolfe. But Murray came back with something of infinite value: news that Fort Niagara had fallen and the would-be French counterattack beaten off. When Montcalm received this intelligence, he was justifiably alarmed and sent off the Chevalier de Lévis and 800 troops to reinforce the crumbling western theatre. These were men he could ill afford to spare for, as it was, defending a front that extended from the Montmorency Falls to the northern shore of the St Lawrence upriver from Quebec, he was stretched almost to snapping point even before he detached Levis.

Wolfe, unaware of Montcalm's grave concerns, was himself undergoing a crisis in August, and perhaps we can understand the atrocities of that month as the fanatical actions of a man who had essentially lost sight of his aim. His problems were twofold: he was ill and he was at odds with his brigadiers. For most of August he was scarcely well enough to leave his sick-bed. Barely recovered from a grave attack of fever, he suffered from a steadily worsening tubercular cough and was weak from the constant blood-letting to which his physicians subjected him. High on opium and other painkillers, he could often not even urinate without terrible pain. Situated thus, he was scarcely able to deal with the accumulated hostility of all three of his brigadiers.

Wolfe had got off on the wrong foot with Townshend – admittedly not a difficult thing to do – and the cryptic diary evidence for 7 July indicates that there had been a stand-up row between the foppish aristocrat and his commander, with Townshend threatening to foment a 'parliamentary inquiry' into the behaviour of his commanding officer. There was further tension during the rest of July, and it seems clear that Wolfe gradually alienated Murray also during this period. The commander lost face considerably as a result of the Montmorency fiasco on 31 July, after which we find Deputy Quartermaster General Guy Carleton, previously a Wolfe favourite, joining the dissenters. Then, in the middle of August, Wolfe additionally fell foul of Monkton. The details are obscure, but on 15 August we find Wolfe apologising with 'hearty excuses' for any unintentional offence offered when the commander withdrew men from Monkton's posts and thus weakened them. On 16 August Wolfe wrote again almost pleadingly to Monkton, saying: 'I heartily beg you forgiveness.' Captain Thomas Bell, whose diary is an important source for the Quebec campaign, relates that Wolfe destroyed his diary for the period after August but that this deleted section 'contained a careful account of the officers' ignoble conduct towards him in case of a Parliamentary enquiry'.

It was 27 August before Wolfe felt well enough to convene a council of war with the three brigadiers he had so seriously alienated. Wolfe almost certainly had no great opinion of their strategic abilities but consulted them, partly because such a council was a cultural norm in eighteenth-century military life and partly so that he could not later (maybe in a parliamentary inquiry?) be accused of having acted in a high-handed and authoritarian way. The council took place on 28 August. Wolfe began by outlining three possible courses of action, all of them involving an attack on the Beauport lines. The first idea was to catch the French forces between two fires, with both a frontal attack and an attack in the rear by a large force which would have crossed the Montmorency by the upper ford. The second was essentially a rerun of 31 July, with an attempt being made once more to recapture the upper redoubt, with Townshend's men establishing a beachhead and Monkton's crossing from Point Levis for the *coup de grâce*. The third was essentially a combination of the first and second scenarios. All the proposed actions were in effect simply variations on the old strategy that had failed so dismally on 31 August.

Wolfe's apologists, anxious to rescue him from the obvious charge of bankruptcy of ideas, allege that he was simply 'flying a kite', that he had already decided on an alternative strategy but was determined to get his brigadiers to commit themselves in writing to a final rejection of all attacks on the Beauport front. The alternate and much more likely explanation is that Wolfe simply had no idea what to do next. Whatever the reason for his spectacularly unimaginative memorandum, it is certain that his brigadiers rejected it decisively. They suggested instead that Wolfe abandon all idea of forcing the Beauport–Montomorency front and concentrate instead on finding somewhere upriver to land the next blow. This would threaten Montcalm's food supplies from the west and finally force him to emerge from his entrenched eyrie in Quebec. Landing at some location above Quebec would have the further advantage that the British army could concentrate, instead of, as hitherto, being vulnerable to French local superiority. Crucially, if defeated at Quebec, Montcalm would no longer have the option of being able to retreat west and continue the struggle there; the battle for Quebec would, under the new dispositions, settle the entire struggle for mastery in North America.

By the beginning of September the British had assembled a formidable naval force in the river above Quebec. On 28 August the frigate *Lowestoft*, the sloop *Hunter* and smaller vessels managed to slip past the French shore batteries and join the handful of ships already upriver. On the night of 31 August–1 September five more vessels, including the frigate *Seahorse*, forced passage above Quebec. Wolfe thus had covering fire for any force he tried to land to the south-west of the city (i.e. upriver). His brigadiers now took in hand a skilful evacuation of the Montmorency camp, transporting the troops first of all to the Île d'Orléans. Leaving a holding force on that island to protect the base camp, hospital and stores, and another strong garrison on Point Lévis, where all the heaviest artillery was stationed, the British commanders conveyed the entire besieging army to the mouth of the Etchemin river on the south bank (south-west of Point Levis), ready for the eventual move upriver. The evacuation was another great success for amphibious operations. Monkton feinted towards the right of the French defences by the mouth of the St Charles river, while Wolfe dragged his feet about the final withdrawal of men from Montmorency, keeping five battalions there until 3 September in the hope of tempting the French commander to a rash sortie. Montcalm could not be tempted, but many observers on both sides thought he had lost a great opportunity to sow chaos during the intricate process of embarkation.

Both commanders had their problems. Wolfe was not sanguine about the outcome of the new strategy and confessed to Pitt that he had acquiesced in it with great misgivings. In his last letter to his mother, written on 31 August, Wolfe was equally pessimistic:

> My antagonist has wisely shut himself up in inaccessible entrenchments, so that I can't get at him without spilling a torrent of blood and that perhaps to little purpose. The Marquis de Montcalm is at the head of a great number of bad soldiers, and I am at the head of a small number of good ones, that wish for nothing so much as to fight him – but the wary old fellow avoids an action doubtful of the behaviour of his army.

In his last letter to Pitt, dated 2 September, Wolfe complained about the difficulty of campaigning in Canada where the terrain was against him and the St Lawrence river itself attenuated his superiority in numbers and *matériel*. He also stressed the growing casualty roster: since the end of June he had lost 850 men dead and wounded, including two colonels, two majors, nineteen captains and thirty-four subalterns, and now there were signs that disease too was lending a hand, further reducing his effective manpower. Wolfe admitted that he had only grudgingly accepted his brigadiers' plan to cut Montcalm's line of communications between the Jacques Cartier and Cap Rouge rivers and the subtext of all his final messages indicated a man preparing for ultimate failure, half-accepting his responsibility for this and half-wishing to slough it off onto others – though, to be fair, when he tried to blame the navy for some of the setbacks and Admiral Saunders vociferously objected, Wolfe agreed to remove the offending words. Referring to the debacle of 31 July, Wolfe even displayed magnanimity, for his letter to Saunders reads as follows: 'I am sensible of my own errors in the course of the campaign; see clearly wherein I have been deficient, and think a little more or less blame, to a man that must necessarily be ruined, of little or no consequence.'

Vaudreuil considered that the British abandonment of the Montmorency camp and the removal of their forces upriver, combined with the lateness of the season, meant that Wolfe had in effect accepted defeat, and on 1 September he wrote to Bourlamaque thus: 'Everything proves that the grand design of the English has failed.' Montcalm was nothing like so sanguine, for many reasons. In the first place, Quebec continued to be shelled until 4 September. The English batteries set the Lower Town on fire again, burning down 167 buildings in a single night. At the General Hospital, thankfully not in the direct line of fire from the big guns at Point Levis, every inch of space was packed with sick, wounded and refugee women and children from the town, to say nothing of a gaggle of Ursuline nuns. Secondly, both the inhabitants of Quebec and the troops in the Beauport lines were on starvation rations, and only the lucky chance of an early harvest in Montreal had enabled them to survive so far. The French were already eating bread from new wheat and the desertion rate increased daily and alarmingly, with many troops not caring who won or what happened next as long as they could fill their bellies. Montcalm was depressed that his favourite officers, Bourlamaque and Levis, were not with him and, like Wolfe, he was no longer in the best of health. Where Vaudreuil was always a heady optimist, Montcalm remained pessimistic and suspicious of British intentions. Where the euphoric Vaudreuil took seriously the expedient exaggerations of British renegades (for the tide of desertion was not all one-way) to the effect that the Royal Navy would give Wolfe only one more week in the St Lawrence, Montcalm was convinced he would have to hold out at least another month. His letters to Bourlamaque provide an accurate barometer of his falling spirits:

> The night is dark; it rains; our troops are in their tents, with clothes on, ready for an alarm; I in my boots; my horse saddled. In fact, this is my usual way. I wish you were here; for I cannot be everywhere, though I multiply myself, and have not taken off my clothes since the twenty-third of June . . . I am overwhelmed with work, and should often lose temper, like you, if I did not remember that I am paid by Europe for not losing it.

The second week of September saw a determined effort by the British to cut Montcalm's communications with Bourlamaque and the west. By 7 September the entire British flotilla had cleared from south of Point Lévis and the Etchemin river, having begun on the 4th by launching the flat-boats and the baggage and floating them unscathed past the French guns at Quebec. The 5th and 6th saw Murray, Monkton and Townshend embarking their regiments aboard dangerously crowded ships. On the 7th the squadron was off Cap Rouge, where Bougainville and his intercepting force watched it warily. On the 8th the British feinted towards Cap Rouge while heading for their real destination at Pointe-aux-Trembles, a further score of miles up the St Lawrence, where they hoped to establish a beachhead; five battalions stood ready for the landings. But the landfall never materialised, as heavy, torrential rains caused the postponement of the operation. A despondent Wolfe, observing no break in the skies, began cruising down the river, hoping for inspiration. Yet the rain continued its pelting and, on 9 September, the Pointe-aux-Trembles landings were definitely abandoned. Exhausted men, standing to in overcrowded transports, were starting to drop with sickness, so the commanders landed 1,500 men from the most crowded vessels at St Nicholas on the south shore, telling them to wait there until they could be re-embarked. Some have criticised Wolfe for not pressing on with the landings, rain notwithstanding since, it is argued, Bougainville's defenders would have been bogged down in the quagmires of mud and unable to offer effective resistance. But meanwhile, on this same day, something happened that made Wolfe regard the entire Pointe-aux-Trembles theatre as an irrelevance.

Almost out of the blue, Wolfe decided to disembark a force near Quebec, just below St Michel, where he had previously considered landing. The spot chosen was known as l'Anse au Foulon, ever afterwards named Wolfe's Cove. Where did this idea come from? The usual answer is that Captain Robert Stobo, a colonial officer who knew Quebec intimately after being imprisoned there, suggested it. A prisoner of war from 1755 to the spring of 1759, Stobo had served with Washington, was handed over as a hostage at Fort Duquesne and thence removed to Quebec. In Quebec he was not even under house arrest, but was allowed to mingle with high society and form business partnerships. After Braddock's disaster at Monongahela in 1755, the French inspected his baggage and discovered a detailed plan of Fort Duquesne, drawn by Stobo contrary to the terms of his prisoner status. The enraged French tried Stobo as a spy, found him guilty and sentenced him to death; he escaped the gallows only because the sentence was sent to Versailles for confirmation, where the minister ordered it suspended. After two unsuccessful attempts to escape confinement, Stobo finally led an eight-prisoner breakout on 1 May 1759. He sailed down the St Lawrence to Louisbourg, narrowly missed Wolfe there and then retraced his steps in the wake of the British expedition until he found the commander. There, according to his own account, he fed the idea of l'Anse au Foulon to Wolfe, stressing that it was the one weak spot in French defences, the one location habitually left lightly guarded.

There are considerable difficulties with this story. If Stobo told Wolfe about l'Anse au Foulon he must have done so in July, for there would have been no point in guarding such a vital secret, or indeed of following Wolfe back up the river. If Stobo did tell Wolfe in July, the General either discounted or disregarded his advice. All his correspondence until 12 September breathes uncertainty, doubt and despondency. Those who claim that Wolfe had a secret master plan up his sleeve all the time are committed to the absurd notion that he would have involved his army in the disaster of Montmorency, and the entire detailed planning for seizing Pointe-aux-Trembles for no reason and at the very moment when time was running out with the approach of winter. Hagiographers of Wolfe have argued that black is white by seizing on any and all cryptic or delphic utterances in Wolfe's letters and claiming that they hinted at a secret plan. All of this is utterly implausible, if only because we have Wolfe's own refutation of such far-fetched theories. In the very last report sent to London on 9 September, Wolfe mentioned his grudging acceptance of his brigadiers' proposal to seek a solution upriver above St Lawrence. He went on:

> I agreed to the proposal, and we are now here, with about 3,600 men, waiting an opportunity to attack them when and wherever they can best be got at. The weather has been extremely unfavourable for a day or two, so that we have been inactive. I am so far recovered as to do business, but my constitution is entirely ruined, without the consolation of having done any considerable service to the State, *or without any prospect of it* [the italics are mine].

In other words, on 9 September Wolfe had no inkling of a probe at l'Anse au Foulon. Nor can Stobo have whispered in the General's ear at that point, even apart from the inherent implausibility of such an eleventh-hour pitch, since he had left the besieging army on 7 September, sent by Wolfe with letters to Amherst. It is of course possible that Wolfe during his reconnoitring suddenly saw l'Anse au Foulon and remembered Stobo's earlier words. But even if he had observed through his spyglass that the location seemed skimpily defended, Wolfe was too old a warrior not to know that Montcalm might simply be baiting a trap; after all, this was a stratagem he himself had employed again and again around Montmorency, albeit without ever being able to tempt Montcalm. The suspicion arises that the hard intelligence about l'Anse au Foulon was provided by a French deserter at the very point when Wolfe was in almost terminal despair.

So strong is the presumption of an 'inside job' that entire conspiracy theories have arisen. The most full-blown such theory posits that Bigot and Cadet, knowing their peculations were finally about to be unmasked, contrived to bring about the fall of Quebec to mask their own villainy. In short, they sent an agent to Wolfe to tell him l'Anse au Foulon would be unguarded. Cadet certainly had the clout to withdraw guards from the Foulon but the question is: did he really add treason to his other crimes? The idea of Bougainville being decoyed by the charms of Madame de Vienne, the wife of his cousin, so that he failed to concentrate on his military tasks seems to belong to the realm of romantic fiction rather than history. The only cogent point the conspiracy theorists have is that Cadet warned all French posts along the river that friendly provision boats would be on the water on the night of 12 September, and that the provision boats were then cancelled without the sentries being warned. There is certainly something of a mystery here, but simple incompetence seems a more plausible explanation than elaborate conspiracy. The most likely explanation is that Wolfe was tipped off about l'Anse au Foulon by a French deserter in one of those freak moments of contingency on which history so often turns. Whatever the explanation, once the idea was planted in his mind, Wolfe acted with energy and despatch. He now possessed two cardinal advantages: knowledge of an unguarded area in the French soft underbelly; and the ability to concentrate all his forces. Whereas when operating far upriver at Pointe-aux-Trembles he had to keep more than 1,000 men to guard his base camp at the Île d'Orléans and his battery on Point Lévis, now that he was attacking so close to Quebec he could afford to throw those forces too into the coming venture, raising his strength to 4,600 troops. Detailed instructions were sent out to assemble the Point Lévis and Île d'Orléans soldiers ready for a major offensive at 4 a.m. on 13 September and for the rendezvous of flat-bottomed landing craft and the escorting men-of-war. But Wolfe did not tell his brigadiers what the objective of the new operation was. A few hours before the assault was due to begin, they were still in the dark. In some alarm, Monkton, Townshend and Murray composed a respectful letter asking what the General's aims and intentions were. Wolfe wrote a grudging reply, dated 8.30 p.m. on the evening of 12 September, confirming that l'Anse au Foulon was the objective and insinuating that they should have been able to work this out for themselves after the reconnaissances he had conducted with them on the 11th. It was an extraordinary performance from a commander expecting the last ounce in commitment and morale from his brigadiers. What is the explanation? Wolfe's defenders stress 'security' and claim, even more bizarrely, that withholding his plans from his subordinates was 'proof of his genius'. But the truth seems to be that it was a petty, mean-minded exercise in power, evincing contempt and disdain for the officers who had so often implicitly queried his competence.

Montcalm and the French, meanwhile, had totally failed to divine Wolfe's intentions. An over-confident Montcalm wrote to Bourlamaque when the British pulled out of Montmorency: 'As for things here, I think Wolfe will act like a player of *tope et tingue* [a now obsolete French gambling game] who, after having played to the left of the *tope*, plays to the right and [then] to the middle. We shall do our best to see him off.' He expected a central assault on the Beauport lines or on Quebec. He was not entirely unmindful of the threat above Quebec, but seems to have assumed this would be limited to trying to cut French supply lines to tempt him out. Covering his options, Montcalm switched the Guyenne regiment from east of Quebec, near the St Charles river, to the west, actually quite close to l'Anse au Foulon, and incorporated it in Bougainville's roving defence force. But then, astonishingly, he ordered it back to its former station twenty-four hours later. From this imbroglio arose the later legend that it was Vaudreuil who had ordered the regiment to return to the St Charles behind Montcalm's back, and the counter-legend that when Montcalm ordered it back, Vaudreuil had protested vociferously. These later exercises in blame-shifting are only natural when one considers that for twenty-four hours the Guyenne regiment had been stationed in the exact location that would have ruined Wolfe's new plan. Some scholars try to make sense of the confused and contradictory accounts by stating that there was no countermanding of orders on the 6th and that the Guyenne regiment, in its role as mobile reserve either above or below Quebec, was not situated athwart the path from l'Anse au Foulon to the city of Quebec but only somewhere in the general area.

Whatever one's reservations about Wolfe's overall performance in 1759, it has to be acknowledged that the embarkation on the night of 12–13 September was a military masterpiece. Whether Wolfe was secretly one of the first disciples of scientific warfare, or whether the Royal Navy did the leg-work for him, he managed to select the one night in September 1759 that perfectly answered his purposes – floating down the river unobserved on an ebb tide. It cannot have been pure luck, unless we immediately jettison all our notions of probability and with them any pretence to a rational view of cosmology. As Rear-Admiral Charles Holmes, the expert in running ships past Quebec, lucidly expressed it, there were three main problems about departing from an anchorage at St Nicholas and coming safely to landfall at l'Anse au Foulon: the distance to the landing place; the strength of the tide; and the darkness of the night. The distance from embarkation to disembarkation has been exactly calculated as 7.6 nautical (8.7 statute) miles, and the length of time taken to cover this distance depended both on the exact time the tide turned in the St Lawrence and on the speed of the tidal currents. It seems quite clear that Wolfe deliberately chose the night of 12–13 September to give him the ebb tide he needed, since he wanted to spend no more than two hours on the water, necessitating an average speed of 3.8 knots. As it happened, his boats achieved a maximum speed of 5.7 knots. The ebb current began to run shortly after midnight and was beginning to flow strongly past St Nicholas at 2 a.m. Needing to be ashore well before sunrise (at 5.34 local time), Wolfe's forces cast off at 2 a.m. and were clambering ashore at l'Anse au Foulon at about 3.45 a.m.

Two lanterns hoisted on the maintop of HMS *Sutherland* were the signal for the start of the operation. To divert attention from this sector, Admiral Saunders ordered his sailors to row noisily back and forth between Beauport and the St Charles river, having previously placed buoys in the channel off Beauport as if to mark the route for landing craft to follow. Although it has often been asserted that Wolfe made his move on a moonless night, this is a misunderstanding. His army did not navigate in pitch blackness but benefited from the light of the moon. What happened was that a large quarter-moon rose at 9.48 p.m. (local time) on 12 September and remained in the sky for the rest of the night, illuminating Wolfe's flotilla. The crucial factor was not the darkness, but the direction of the moonlight. French sentries looking upriver towards Wolfe's anchorage could see little of the stretch where Wolfe was crossing, though the Île d'Orléans and Point Lévis were clearly visible. Only a last quarter-moon in the eastern sky provided the British with near-perfect conditions of tide and moon for the approach to l'Anse au Foulon. Wolfe's cleverness should not be underrated. There was only one other date in the September calendar that would have given him the right ebbing tide (the night of 28–29 September), but on that date the moon would have set at midnight and the journey would have had to proceed in almost total darkness. If he had made his bid twenty-four hours later, or twenty-four hours earlier, conditions would likewise have been against him. Embarking on 11–12 or 13–14 September, he could not have got all his men ashore by daybreak. It may well be that such technical considerations, based on minute scientific and mathematical calculations, explain why he did not fall in with his commanders' advice to land much farther up the St Lawrence.

The irony is that by his very secretiveness Wolfe damaged his reputation, for the events of 12–13 September give new meaning to the hackneyed phrase 'the science of war'. Wolfe never lived to explain exactly how he had made his calculations but, although he was not in general an inspired commander, he rose to the necessary heights on this crucial night. As the flotilla moved from south to north shore, Wolfe was in the vanguard, dressed in a new uniform, his mind apparently pulsating with thoughts of death; a few hours earlier he had handed over for safe keeping to Lieutenant John Jervis of the Royal Navy a will, personal papers and a miniature of his fiancée. Even though the light was against them, the French sentinels could clearly make out the passing of a large flotilla. They bawled out a challenge, to which French-speaking officers replied that they were convoying supplies down from Batiscan and Cap Rouge. Since the sentries had been warned of this precise eventuality, they did not press the matter further. French incompetence at this point seems over-determined. No one has ever been quite clear who cancelled the provision convoy or why, but at the very least Bougainville, in command of the western sector, knew of the cancellation and should have alerted all sentries in that theatre. To compound their folly, the French were not using a password. The best evidence suggests that when challenged the British did no more than utter the words '*la France*' and '*Vive le roi*', at which point the sentries, satisfied, yelled out: 'Let them pass, they are our people with the supplies.'

Well before dawn the first wave hit the gravelly beaches at the cove. Here the cliffs rose 175 feet above the St Lawrence, and on the east bank of a small stream that ran down into the cove a path ran transversely upwards across the face of the cliff. Far from being the winding and fractuous path of legend, it was a good, usable track up which heavy guns could be hauled. A detachment of Light Infantry under Colonel William Howe began scrambling up the track. From the top of the cliff a French sentry challenged them. A resourceful French-speaking Highlander – the sources dispute whether his name was Fraser or MacDonald – replied with outraged protests at such ingratitude and explained that they were a new

French detachment sent by Bougainville as reinforcements; he pushed his luck even farther by ordering the man to return to his camp and call off all other over-zealous sentries. The ascent recommenced. This was no easy task, for the shale surface caused the troops to slip and slide and they could often make progress only by hauling themselves up on the branches of trees and bushes. Their first objective was the 100 men under M. de Vergor, ostensibly guarding the Foulon. Once at the top of the cliff they brushed aside with ease the small camp of bleary-eyed Frenchmen and sentries sleeping on the job, the task made easier because the absurd Vergor had allowed some of his men to go home to work on their farms. Before being taken prisoner Vergor just had time to send a runner to Montcalm, warning that the British were already established on the Heights of Abraham.

Once Wolfe's troops scrambled to the top of the cliffs, the military advantage shifted decisively in his favour. There had been a handful of casualties during the landing when the French battery at Samos, west of the Foulon, opened up on the second wave, but overall the operation had been a staggering success. Negotiating tides and a gravelly beach without being detected would have tested the greatest exponents of amphibious warfare, for landing troops on a hostile shore in the dark with pinpoint accuracy calls for naval skills of the very highest order. Both the army and the navy acquitted themselves well: the navy with their precise, professional boatwork; the army with the smoothness whereby three successive waves of invaders were conveyed to the clifftops with minimal resistance. Wolfe's best-case scenario had allowed for a massive French counterattack once his men reached the summit – assuming that could be obtained; his worst-case envisaged a contested landing followed by retreat. Some students of Wolfe have seen him in full death-wish mode this night, expecting to fall during a repulse by superior French numbers dug in along the foot of the cliffs – the repulse to be followed by a retreat ordered by Monkton, who would then assume command. But events had turned out even better than Wolfe could have imagined in his wildest fantasies. When his men formed up with their backs to the river below, with Sillery to their left and Quebec to their right, there was still no sign of the counterattack. Scarcely believing his luck, Wolfe edged forward cautiously towards the open land on the Plains of Abraham, searching for the best ground on which to give battle. By 8 a.m. the entire force of some 4,600 was drawn up in readiness.

The Wolfe mythographers, however, have to contend with one awkward fact. When Wolfe reached the clifftop with the first wave (the three brigadiers were still below, struggling onto the beach), he lost his nerve and ordered Major Isaac Barre at the cove to halt the operation. Barre took one look at the host of incoming boats and concluded that Wolfe did not know the true state of affairs below; he therefore 'interpreted' Wolfe's orders as meaning a temporary halt only, so as not to cause a traffic jam on the upward-slanting path. But if Wolfe had momentarily buckled, the French were by now in full panic mode. The feint towards Beauport by Admiral Saunders had totally nonplussed Montcalm, and the fiasco over the cancelled food convoy further added to the confusion. Montcalm had been up all night at Beauport, fully expecting a British landing there. So intent were the French officers on this sector that they 'missed' the first signal from Quebec, warning that something was going on to the west of the city. Not even the arrival of a breathless courier from Vergor's camp shook their aplomb, for when he blurted out the story of the real British landing, one of Montcalm's aides concluded that he had taken leave of his senses.

But soon came more heralds and couriers, confirming the original 'incredible' story. At last the commander himself was informed and was at first disbelieving. When shooting was heard in the area of l'Anse au Foulon, Montcalm's worst fear was that his supply flotilla had been captured. He rounded on his aides and asked why he had not been alerted sooner. The answer, they replied, was simple. The arrival of Vergor's messenger, with word that the British were already on the heights, was at first disbelieved, since they themselves were so sure that no landing could be made in that sector that they concluded the lacklustre Vergor had simply panicked, possibly disorientated by the 'captured' food convoy. When yet another message came in to say that the enemy had landed in force at l'Anse au Foulon, the 'will to believe' in the invulnerability of the cliffs west of Quebec was such that further psychological 'denial' was manifested. The commandant of Lower Quebec opined that, since there had been a volley of musketry that had now ceased, the British must have landed briefly and then disembarked. Only in the clear light of morning did the full horror of the situation dawn on Montcalm as he rode across the St Charles river to the Plains of Abraham. Stunned and incredulous, he learned to his stupefaction that the famed Guyenne regiment had been nowhere near the danger area and that Vaudreuil had waited until Wolfe's forces were clearly visible, drawn up in battle order, before sending to Bougainville to bring his power with all speed.

What Montcalm saw on the Plains of Abraham further depressed him. Seven British battalions now stretched across the Grande Allée (the main road into Quebec), less than a mile from Quebec's western wall. Behind them could be seen a further five battalions of reserves and a large body of colonial skirmishers. From l'Anse au Foulon sailors from the twenty ships at anchor in the cove were manhauling artillery up the track. Wolfe had made good dispositions across the 1,000-yard breadth of the plains, waiting for Montcalm's next move. An eyewitness reported that Montcalm sat on his horse a long time as if hypnotised by the sight of the redcoats: 'it seemed as though he felt his fate upon him'. What most of all disconcerted Montcalm was that the double rank of redcoats seemed untroubled by the angry, bee-like whizzing and pinging of bullets as Canadian militiamen and Indian sharpshooters calmly picked their targets from nests behind the city walls. This level of discipline outstripped anything he could expect from his own troops.

Quickly Montcalm made mental calculations and reviewed his options. His best course was to wait for Bougainville's mobile force, but, given that the messenger had not been sent to the camp at Cap Rouge until 6.45 a.m., it would surely take him another three hours to arrive on the battlefield. Could he wait that long? Military prudence said yes but considerations of morale said no. Quebec was starving; the British were now blocking any possible avenue of resupply; and the city walls in this sector, around the Bastion of St Louis, were particularly weak and could not compare with the trench network around Beauport and Montmorency – it had been assumed that the sheer cliff walls provided a much more secure protection than any man-made structures around the city. Additionally Montcalm mistakenly thought the British were entrenching around the Buttes à Neveu (the high ground in front of Quebec), preparatory to opening a siege. Immediate action therefore seemed imperative. Yet could he win with just 4,500 effectives, about the same number as the enemy, but man-for-man far inferior in quality?

Wolfe's battle-line used the Louisbourg Grenadiers and the Fraser Highlanders as its spine. To cover the long front across the plateau to the St Charles, they were drawn up two deep only. Monkton, the senior Brigadier, commanded the right wing, Murray the left, while Townshend deployed two battalions of Royal Americans at right angles to the main line to deal with the threat to the left from Canadian militiamen and Indians. Later another battalion of Royal Americans was detached to guard the landing places at the Foulon, in case Bougainville put in an appearance. With Howe's Light Infantry forming the rearguard and Royal Navy mariners manfully hauling six-pounders up the path to the heights, Wolfe had every reason to feel pleased with his dispositions. In the confusion the French had had less time to think of refined tactics but Montcalm had drawn up his white-uniformed regulars in the centre, with Quebec militiamen and Indians on the flanks, both wings protected by waves of Canadian and Native American sharpshooters. Both sides were about 4,500 strong but unequal in discipline, élan, morale and even calorie intake; it was not quite a case of British professionals against French amateurs but at level numbers Montcalm must have known that his chances were very slender.

Once the last units had joined his line at about 8 a.m., Wolfe ordered his men to lie down so that they would not present easy targets for the snipers. On both sides – in the woods to the British left and in the corn-fields between the British right and the cliff edge – the Canadian and Indian sharpshooters had been eerily accurate and effective since first light. Wolfe feared the winnowing effect on his men if they remained upright, for in his mind he had to wait for Montcalm to make the first move so that he could deliver a close-quarter musketry broadside and end the battle within minutes. Howe's Light Infantry made some early sorties to try to drive the snipers from their positions, but they in turn were driven back at around eight o'clock when the French artillery opened up. When Montcalm's five fieldpieces began lobbing cannonballs towards the British lines and the redcoats could see the lethal projectiles often skipping over the grass towards them like bouncing bombs, it was the merest common sense to fall prone and present the smallest possible target. Wolfe osten-tatiously walked up and down the lines, as if tempting the snipers and artillerymen to take him out. But he would remain a worried man until Montcalm ordered a charge. Time was against him, for if Bougainville arrived soon, Wolfe might be caught in an almost perfect three-way trap, between snipers, Montcalm and Bougainville, with no escape route except the perilous descent to l'Anse au Foulon.

Since time was on his side, Montcalm should at all cost have waited for Bougainville. But his impatience with that officer was like that of Napoleon with Marshal Grouchy at Waterloo fifty-six years later. After asking exas-peratedly where Bougainville was, at 9.30 a.m. Montcalm gloomily told his chief of artillery: 'We cannot avoid action; the enemy is entrenching, he already has two pieces of cannon. If we give him time to establish himself, we shall never be able to attack him with the sort of troops we have.' He then added with a grimace: 'Is it possible that Bougainville doesn't hear all that noise?' Had Montcalm known that Wolfe was not entrenching, he would have taken heart. But fatalistically he gave the order to his men to advance. Nothing better exposes Montcalm's limitations as a commander, for the order to an army largely composed of irregulars to charge a disci-plined red line could have only one outcome. Since the British line extended virtually from the St Charles's escarpment on Montcalm's right to the St Lawrence cliffs on his left, there was no room to maneouvre and no prospect of encircling or outflanking the enemy. It would be a desperate, bloody affair of musketry and bayonets, where Wolfe's redcoats were bound to win. Montcalm should have corralled his impatience and waited for Bougainville to arrive, however agonising the wait. So it is a fair judgement to say that the outcome of the battle hinged on Bougainville. What was he doing while all these dramatic developments were unfolding?

The sober answer is that Bougainville's movements on the night of 12–13 September are hidden from documented history; the scope for the historical novelist and the conspiracy theorist is clear, especially as educated speculation can really shed no light on the matter. According to one version, Bougainville went upriver from Cap Rouge to Pointe-aux-Trembles. Most likely he simply remained inactive and supine at Cap Rouge. Bougainville was a great man, as his later career would prove, but the night of the 12th–13th was not his finest hour. He must have seen the British flotilla going downriver but too glibly assumed that it was the French supply convoy. Yet since it is inconceivable that he did not know the sailing of this convoy had been cancelled, his failure to act seems incredible. The traditional explanation is that he could not reinforce Montcalm as soon as news of the landing at l'Anse au Foulon came in, because his men were worn out by the constant marching and counter-marching involved in the surveillance of the British fleet. But the last movement of the British fleet in Bougainville's sector had been the abandoned upriver landings on 9 September. While not necessarily as fresh as paint, his men should have been ready for a forced march on the morning of the 13th. Bougainville's apologists stress that it was Vaudreuil who was liaising with Bougainville and that he did not send a clear order to march towards Quebec when he wrote to Bougainville at 6.45 a.m that morning, nearly three hours after the British landing. This in turn allows one faction of the conspiracy theorists to switch attention away from Bigot and Bougainville and locate the trouble once again in Vaudreuil's insane jealousy of Montcalm. Could it be that Vaudreuil did not issue the order to Bougainville because he did not want Montcalm to win a victory that day? But nothing can really absolve Bougainville just as nothing could later absolve Grouchy. Whatever the clarity or turbidity of orders, it must always be the duty of a subsidiary commander to march towards the sound of the guns unless the supreme commander has already given explicit orders not to.

At 10 a.m. Montcalm finally gave the order to attack. But even before full battle was joined, there had been some ferocious, bloody fighting on the St Charles side of the lines (the British left) as French colonial regulars and militiamen clashed with the Royal Americans. A running fight, sometimes involving hand-to-hand combat, developed around a pair of farmhouses, which changed hands at least once and were finally gutted when caught in the middle of a grim artillery duel. Even while this sanguinary encounter was being played out, Montcalm gave the signal to advance. The French whooped with delight and came on at the double, much too fast given that they had to cover 500 yards to the British lines. It soon became apparent that Montcalm's policy of melding militia and regulars in a regular battalion was a disaster, as Major Malartic of the Béarn battalion explained: 'We had not gone twenty paces when the left was too far in rear and the centre too far in front.' At 'half musket shot' (between 125 and 150 yards) the French halted, went down on one knee and fired a stuttering volley. The regulars fired in platoon volleys, but the militiamen discharged wild shots. Even worse, each executed the manoeuvre in a totally different way. The regulars remained standing upright in ranks to reload, while the militiamen, accustomed to forest fighting where one sought cover before reloading, threw themselves prone on the ground and began fumbling with their muskets; as Malartic remarked acidly, reloading from the prone position was not easy. He summed up the indiscipline of Montcalm's force: 'The Canadians who formed the second rank and the soldiers of the third fired without orders, and according to their custom threw themselves on the ground to reload. This false movement broke all the battalions.'

Many of the attackers never advanced beyond this point but seemed to have veered off to the right when they picked themselves off the ground. Those of the French who did advance progressed to within forty yards of the British lines, where the redcoats awaited them impassively. They then discharged a devastating relay of fire, with each battalion commander judging the killing ground for himself and firing when ready. Despite the hyperbolic chauvinism of Sir John Fortescue, who claimed that the French ran into 'the most perfect volley ever fired on a battlefield' – an obvious exaggeration since nobody could coordinate a single volley along such a widespread line – it is clear that the French reeled under the impact. When the smoke cleared, the British advanced a few yards and fired again. This time there does seem to have been a more coordinated volley, for the result was described as 'like a cannonshot'. At a range of maybe twenty to thirty yards eighteenth-century musketry doled out fearful damage. After a few terrible minutes the French wilted under this cannonade, broke and began fleeing back towards Quebec. With a cry of 'Claymore!', the Frasers swept after them with the broadsword, but this time the famous Highland charge did less damage than on other notable occasions. So rapid was the rout of the French that the pursuers never caught up with the main army.

It was probably the first French volley, 150 yards out, that dealt Wolfe his death-stroke. Standing on a rise near the Louisbourg Grenadiers, he first sustained a shattered wrist (which he bandaged with a handkerchief), and then a fatal wound in the right of his chest; there may have been an additional hit from a spent bullet in the groin or lower belly. Haemorrhaging uncontrollably, he remained conscious long enough to learn that he had been victorious. Many Wolfe students are convinced that he went into battle certain that he had but a short time to live and determined to pre-empt disease by a glorious death in combat. Certainly the evidence is over-whelming that he deliberately exposed himself to gunshot, and his most vehement critics even assert that in his overpowering death-wish he actu-ally neglected the interests of his troops and exposed them to great peril on the Heights of Abraham, from which only Montcalm's folly in seeking an early battle rescued them.

In death Wolfe won the eternal glory he lusted after. One of the most famous of all historical paintings, by Benjamin West, shows his senior offi-cers clustered around him, listening to words of wisdom from the fallen hero, while an Indian ally looks on pensively. Need we say that there was no Indian ally present and that his officers did not cluster round him? The most accurate account of Wolfe's last moments records that he rejected the ministrations of a surgeon on the grounds that he was too far gone. Then, hearing the words 'They run!', Wolfe enquired who it was that ran. An officer replied: 'The enemy, sir; Egad, they give way everywhere.' Wolfe replied: 'Go one of you, my lads, to Colonel Burton; tell him to march Webb's regiment with all speed down to Charles's River, to cut off the retreat of the fugitives from the bridge.' He then turned on his side and said: 'Now, God be praised, I will die in peace.' Within seconds he was dead.

By a bizarre synchronicity Montcalm was mortally wounded only minutes later, during the confused rush of the defeated French back to Quebec. There is dispute about whether he was wounded by grapeshot from a British six-pounder or was deliberately and cynically taken out by British snipers. His wounds were in the lower part of the stomach and thigh and although he did not bleed to death on the field like Wolfe, he was a dying man and he knew it. Three soldiers supported him in the saddle as he rode painfully back to the city; he lingered on until 4 a.m. on the 14th. Like Wolfe, he became the subject of myth-making. Jean-Antoine Watteau's painting *The Death of Montcalm* is a visual riposte to Benjamin West. Once again we see the hero dying on the battlefield (in fact Montcalm was buried in the Ursuline convent), and once again Mohawk warriors, never at the centre of the action historically, occupy a prominent position in the iconography. Montcalm's death had more immediate effects. Since his two brigadiers, Fontbonne and Senesergues, had also received mortal wounds, there was a power vacuum in the French army. All was chaos, with no one knowing casualty figures or those of the enemy, Bougainville's whereabouts unknown and Vaudreuil still in the Beauport camp, dithering and procrastinating.

When the Frasers unsheathed their claymores and charged off in pursuit of the stricken French, they were soon followed by the English regiments with fixed bayonets, all advancing across a field where the scattered showers of the morning had given way to sunshine. It was in this sunlit aftermath of the battle proper that the heaviest casualties occurred. In the woods just east of the spot where Montcalm had formed his line, hundreds of Canadians, now in their element among the gloomy trees, turned to face their pursuers. A particularly sanguinary fight ensued between the 78th Fraser's Highlanders and the Canadians, both wilderness fighters of high calibre. Murray later reported that the enemy 'killed and wounded a great many of our men, and killed two officers, which obliged us to retire and form again'. It was only with the aid of the 58th Highlanders and the Royal Americans that the Frasers were finally able to flush their doughty opponents out of their wooded foxholes and drive them down the hill and over the St Charles, though in the latter stages the Highlanders came under fire from the Canadian hulks in the mouth of the St Charles. This valiant rearguard action enabled the defeated French army to make good its escape over the bridges to the Beauport camp. Meanwhile the Louisbourg Grenadiers on the British right had also taken some punishment from the snipers who still remained in the corn field. It was at this stage that Townshend assumed command and at once called off the pursuit.

Townshend has been criticised for excessive caution in not pursuing the French at all costs. But he sensed that in the post-battle blood-lust his troops were losing their discipline and degenerating into a rabble. It was important to restore order before Bougainville put in an appearance. It took time for his officers to reinstate discipline and the British army had only just re-emerged as a fighting force rather than a rabble when Bougainville's force duly arrived. Outnumbered two to one in this theatre, Townshend faced around and placed two battalions and two big guns across the path Bougainville would have to tread in order to relieve Quebec. Taken aback by the enemy's boldness and stupefied to learn that Montcalm had already been defeated, Bougainville did not stop to consider that he had a local superiority, but sheered off to the Sillery Woods to contemplate his next move. Townshend's actions were correct, for the power vacuum following Wolfe's death left the British troops concentrating on gung-ho mopping-up operations instead of moving swiftly to cut off the French retreat. But there was a lack of leadership for a vital hour and in that time a great opportunity was missed. Nobody followed up on Wolfe's dying prescription that the St Charles bridges be seized, and the result was that the French army, though defeated, was not destroyed. The long-term consequences were that Britain had to campaign in North America in 1760, and for that Townshend, most unfairly, was held to blame.

The battle on the Plains of Abraham was a notable victory, but it was expensively purchased. British casualties amounted to 658, including fifty-eight killed. Fraser's Highlanders bore the brunt of the losses, with 168 dead and wounded, and the attrition rate was high among the officer classes, with Monkton, Carleton and Barre all wounded. Vaudreuil posted losses of about 600 men and forty-four officers. Normally the losers in an armed encounter suffer casualties way above those of the defeated, but in this case the near-equality of suffering is explained by the damage done by Canadian snipers before the battle and by the colonial militia in the bloody post-battle combat with the Highlanders in the woods. Yet the French were utterly demoralised and it was 6 p.m. that evening before Vaudreuil could collect his wits sufficiently to convene a council of war. It was put to him that he had but three choices: he could make a fresh attack on the enemy; surrender the whole of New France; or retire to continue the fight on the Jacques Cartier river. Because of the demoralised state of the army and the lack of provisions, only withdrawal made sense. Abandoning all heavy artillery and much of their ammunition, the French soldiers stole away along the east bank of the St Charles river and made a forced march to Pointe-aux-Trembles on the 14th whence they continued to the Jacques Cartier.

The useless Vaudreuil, having fled with the army, further ruined French prospects by three separate actions. He failed to move any of the food and supplies from the Beauport camp into Quebec to help the besieged garrison and civilians he left behind. He wrote out draft articles of capitulation for the use of the hapless individual he left as commandant of Quebec, Jean-Baptiste de Ramezay. And he told Ramezay that on no account was he to hold out in Quebec beyond the exhaustion of his food supplies; this effectively meant an order to surrender in three days. Vaudreuil compounded his fatuity by drafting long letters to Versailles, pinning the blame for the recent defeat on Montcalm, maligning the dead hero and mendaciously suggesting that Montcalm had only ever achieved military success when he followed his (Vaudreuil's) prescriptions.

Ramezay was thus left with a mission impossible – having to defend Quebec with little more than 2,000 demoralised men, while being plagued with the defeatism of 4,000 civilians, sick and wounded, all of them on the brink of starvation. His only option was to play for time and hope that Lévis, the new commander, could relieve him. Outside the walls the British guns were silent, but their grim determination was evident, as they could be seen setting up batteries and redoubts within 1,000 yards of the weak and feeble western wall. Soon Ramezay was beset by a clamour, even from the militiamen whom he hoped would defend the city, that he should surrender immediately.

On 17 September Lévis arrived at the Jacques Cartier river and took command of the stricken French army. He at once decided that the retreat had been an egregious error and browbeat Vaudreuil into marching the army back to Quebec. Lévis's idea was that they do everything possible to prevent the fall of Quebec but that, if the city proved indefensible, they should raze it to the ground before abandoning it so that the incoming British would inherit a mere blazing shell of a town. Unfortunately for him, it took a further twenty-four hours to get the army properly supplied and on the road. In this crucial time-lapse Ramezay's nerve had given way, beset as he was both by defeatism within and the evidence of British determination without; it was obvious from the disposition of the Royal Navy warships that they intended to blow apart the Lower Town while Townshend's batteries pulverised Upper Quebec. In a further comedy of errors, Vaudreuil sent urgent despatches to Ramezay telling him to hold out at all costs, but the mounted courier managed to lose them on the road to Quebec. When contact was finally made by a cavalry detachment on the night of 17–18 September, a rueful Ramezay told them they were too late. He had offered Vaudreuil's terms of capitulation to Townshend and they had been accepted.

The surrender terms were formally signed in Townshend's tent on the morning of the 18th. The garrison was to be allowed the honours of war and was to be embarked for France as soon as possible. The property rights of the Québécois and their Catholic religion would be respected and full safeguards offered to all luminaries and dignitaries of Quebec society. To an extent the accord was an embarrassment to both sides. Ramezay felt a fool when he realised Lévis was marching to his aid, but said he had known nothing of this and meanwhile had yielded to the pleas and imprecations of people who were starving. Besides the fault, if any, lay with Vaudreuil, who had left behind such explicit instructions and such a carefully drafted surrender document. Townshend, too, foresaw that he would be criticised for leniency, and pointed out that both the approach of winter and the persistence of Lévis made his position precarious. Any kind of protracted siege would expose him both to attack in the rear and, more pertinently, to the ravages of winter. A winter investment of Quebec would be madness and for the fleet to tarry any longer would mean that it would either be iced up in the St Lawrence or struggling back across the Atlantic in the teeth of full winter gales. He need not have worried: his 'leniency' was condoned in the euphoria of victory; it was

Ramezay who took the full weight of opprobrium in Paris, not the Machiavellian Vaudreuil, who should have been held responsible.

The first British troops entered Quebec on the evening of the 18th. Townshend was as good as his word: there were no reprisals, no looting, no atrocities. He knew that it was vital to secure the cooperation of a civilian population that could not be held down indefinitely by force, especially since Lévis would probably return in the spring with heavy artillery and siege impedimenta. From the French point of view, the British occupation of Quebec even had some advantages for, on the Jacques Cartier river, their army was free from worries over food supplies and meanwhile, in Quebec, the relief of a famished population was a British problem which would further drain their resources. Townshend now saw himself in a race against the winter and set sail at once for England. Since Monkton had to journey to New York for urgent medical treatment, Murray was left in Quebec for the winter as Governor and military commander. Most of the troops stayed with him, but the navy withdrew on the 26th, heading for winter anchorage at Halifax and intending to return in the ice-free spring of 1760. The bitterly disappointed Lévis withdrew to the Jacques Cartier river and built a fort ready for the following year's campaign. Vaudreuil decamped to Montreal, where he spent his time composing further mendacious apologias and blame-shifting memoranda. He consoled himself with the thought that he had at least fulfilled Belle-Isle's minimum requirements and had retained a foothold in the New World until 1760. It remained to be seen whether the French Minister of War could perform a miracle and pull some unexpected rabbit out of his conjuror's hat.

The taking of Quebec was probably the most spectacular success in the year of victories and certainly had the most momentous consequences. From this exploit has arisen the legend of Wolfe as, even more than Clive of India, the true begetter of the first British Empire. Seldom has historical inevitability been more blatantly confused with the contingent, the adventitious and the aleatory. For the truth is that Wolfe was above all almost supernaturally lucky. The landing at l'Anse au Foulon was, objectively considered, a foolish gamble rather than an act of military genius. It presupposed the unlikely concatenation of a string of separate French errors. The most scholarly study of Quebec in 1759, by C. P. Stacey, lays the blame mainly at Bougainville's door:

> Bougainville botched the task of guarding the area above Quebec. He failed to ensure that the posts nearest to the city were fully watchful; he failed to provide adequate communication from those posts to the Beauport camp and his own headquarters; he failed to see to it that the

posts were warned of the cancellation of the movement of the provision boats on the fatal night of 12–13 September; finally he failed to observe what was happening and to march to counter Wolfe's action, with the consequence that Wolfe landed without difficulty and Bougainville himself was too late to cooperate with his chief on the Plains of Abraham at the critical moment the following morning. His inefficiency had much to do with the French disaster.

Later generations might point out that Wolfe, for all his brilliance as a tactician, was a poor strategist; that his brigadiers' plan to land the army at Cap Rouge and cut the St Lawrence in two was a much sounder basis for action than the gambler's landing at l'Anse au Foulon. But in the late autumn of 1759 all most people perceived was the well-nigh incredible fact of his heroic victory. The English-speaking colonies went wild, with pealing bells, bonfires and illuminated windows lighting up all the great cities of the eastern seaboard, from Boston through New York to Philadelphia. Yet even these celabrations were dwarfed by the effusions of joy that hit London in late October when news of Wolfe's triumph finally arrived. Elite opinion, fuelled by Wolfe's pessimistic despatches, had given up on Canada and accepted that there would be no progress until 1760. The always gloomy Duke of Newcastle wrote to his henchman Earl Hardwicke on 15 October in particularly despondent fashion. Picking up on the phrase about 'without any prospect' in Wolfe's last letter to London, the acidulous Horace Walpole commented: 'In the most artful terms that could be framed he left the nation uncertain whether he meant to prepare an excuse for desisting or to claim the melancholy merit of having sacrificed himself without a prospect of success.' But when Pitt read Townshend's account of the Canadian triumph he and the city of London with him went overboard in an outpouring of frenzied joy that reads from contemporary accounts as if it were collective hysteria. Bumpers were raised, cannon fired, huzzas shouted, bells pealed, beacons lit and bonfires lit on every patch of green or common. The fact that Wolfe had died in the very moment of victory appealed as much to the English ruling elite and middle classes as it would to their similarly sentimental Victorian counterparts.

Horace Walpole, quickly changing his tune, argued that the taking of Quebec was stranger than fiction and a mythic event that outstripped anything that had come down from the ancient legends of Greece and Rome. Not even Pitt's eloquent oratory, he thought, so much in evidence in his triumphalist speech to the House of Commons on 21 October, could do justice to the occasion:

The incidents of dramatic fiction could not be conducted with more address to lead an audience from despondency to sudden exaltation than accident prepared to excite the passions of a whole people. They despaired, they triumphed, and they wept, for Wolfe had fallen in the hour of victory . . . [Pitt's attempts to find] parallels . . . from Greek and Roman history did but flatten the pathetic of the topic . . . The horror of the night, the precipice scaled by Wolfe, the empire he with a handful of men added to England, and the glorious catastrophe of contentedly terminating life where his fame began – ancient history may be ransacked, and ostentatious philosophy thrown into the account, before an episode can be found to rank with Wolfe's.

Yet the universal British ecstasy overlooked one inconvenient fact. The French had been worsted in North America but in Europe they still posed a clear and present danger to the island empire.

TEN

ROGERS' RANGERS

It is hard to convey adequately the awed fascination with which educated Europe viewed the Indian tribes of North America. Hard at work on his history of the British Isles, the Scottish author Tobias Smollett took time off to compile a short history of Canada, which appeared in the British Magazine *in instalments, beginning in January 1760. Naturally the most sensational 'copy' was that relating to the Iroquois, Micmacs, Ottawas, Chippewas and Crees. When he came to write* Humphry Clinker *ten years later, Smollett made very effective use of his new-found knowledge in his devastating satire of the Duke of Newcastle, always his* bête noire. *Having mistaken Mr Melford for someone he called 'Sir Francis' at a reception, Newcastle plunges on as follows:*

> *My dear Sir Francis . . . Pray when does your excellency set sail? – For God's sake have a care of your health, and eat stewed prunes in the passage – Next to your own precious health, pray, my dear excellency, take care of the Five Nations – Our good friends the Five Nations – The Toryrories, the Maccolmacks, the Out-o-the ways, the Crickets and the Kickshaws – Let 'em have plenty of blankets, and stinkubus, and wampum, and your excellency won't fail to scour the kettle, and boil the chain, and bury the tree, and plant the hatchet – Ha, ha, ha!*

But what was a joke for Smollett was deadly serious to most denizens of the London salons. Even Samuel Johnson, ever on the lookout for a way to transmute raw material into a quip or apophthegm, was given pause by the horrific tales coming out of North America. 'The Indian war cry,' he wrote, 'is represented as too dreadful to be endured, as a sound that will force the bravest veteran to drop his weapon, and desert his rank; that will deafen his ear and chill his breast; that will neither suffer him to hear orders or to feel shame, or retain any sensibility but dread of death.' Yet it was not so much the blood-curdling war-cry in itself that terrorised so much as what it portended, and Europeans fighting in North America genuinely did feel that to be taken alive by whooping, painted savages was a fate worse than death. It was the quartet of torture, human sacrifice, cannibalism and scalping (all of which had ritualistic significance in Indian culture) that particularly exercised their imaginations. Being roasted to death was probably the greatest fear. One of the British survivors of Monongahela in 1755 was tied to a tree and burned alive between two fires while the Indians danced around; when the man's agonised lamentations grew too insistent, one of the warriors ran in between the two fires and cut off his genitals, leaving him to bleed to death, so that the ululations would cease. Rufus Putnam, a private in the Massachusetts provincials, recorded on 4 July 1757 that a soldier taken by the Indians was 'found barbecued at a most doleful rate, for they found him with his nails all pulled out, his lips cut down to his chin, and up to his nose, and his jaw lay bare; his scalp was taken off, his breast cut open, his heart pulled out and his bullet pouch put in the room of it; his left hand clenched around his gall, a tomahawk left in his bowels and a dart stuck through him; the little finger on his left hand cut off and the little toe of his left foot cut off.'

In the same year the Jesuit Father Roubaud met a band of Ottawas leading several English prisoners through the forest with halters round their necks. Shortly afterwards Roubaud caught up with this war-party and pitched his tent near theirs. He saw a large band sitting around the fire and eating roast meat on sticks, as if it were kebabed lamb. When he asked what the meat was, the Ottawas told him it was roast Englishman, and they pointed to a kettle in which other parts of the butchered body were boiling. Nearby sat eight terrified prisoners, forced to watch the grisly feast and in that extremity of terror described by Odysseus in Homer's poem, when the monster Scylla had snatched some of his comrades off the ship and set them down by her cave, ready to be devoured at her leisure. The horrified Roubaud tried to remonstrate but the Ottawas waved his objections away. One young warrior said to him gruffly: 'You have French taste; I have Indian. This is good meat for me.' He then invited Roubaud to share their meal and seemed offended when the priest declined.

The Indians were particularly severe with those who fought them in their own style or could come close to matching their woodcraft, and for this reason the forest-roving irregulars were specially at risk. Private Thomas Brown, in Captain Thomas Spikeman's company of the green-uniformed Rogers' Rangers, was wounded in a snowfield battle with the Abenaki in January 1757, crawled from the battlefield and fell in with two other wounded men, one called Baker, the other Captain Spikeman himself. In pain and misery, they foolishly thought it safe to light a fire and were almost instantly set on by the Abenaki. Brown managed to crawl away from the fire and hide in the bush, from which he watched the unfolding tragedy. The Abenaki began by stripping Spikeman and lifting his scalp while he was still alive; then they departed, taking Baker with them. Brown describes the sequel:

> *Seeing this dreadful tragedy, I concluded, if possible, to crawl into the woods and there die of my wounds: but not being far from Capt. Spikeman, he saw me and begged me for God's sake to give him a tomahawk that he might put an end to his life! I refused him, and exhorted him as well as I could to pray for mercy, as he could not live many minutes in that deplorable condition, being on the frozen ground, covered with snow. He desired me to let his wife know if I lived to get home of the dreadful death he died.*

Shortly afterwards Brown was captured by the Abenaki who returned to the scene of the scalping to put Spikeman's head on a pole. Brown survived his captivity, but Baker did not:

> *The squaws cut pieces of pine, like Scures [skewers], and thrust them into his flesh, and set them on fire, and then fell to pow-wowing and dancing around him; and ordered me to do the same. Law of Life obliged me to comply . . . With a bitter and heavy heart I feigned myself merry. They cut the poor man's cords, and made him run backwards and forwards. I heard the poor man's cries to Heaven for mercy, and at length, through extreme anguish and pain, he pitched himself into the flames and expired.*

Yet of all Indian practices it was scalping that attracted the most horrified European attention – a pattern that would continue into the nineteenth century. Despite some absurd attempts by bien-pensant *revisionists to claim that scalping originated in Europe – possibly among the Visigoths, Franks or Scythians – it is abundantly clear that it was practised in North America long before Europeans arrived. Scalps played a serious role in Native American culture, for they could fulfil any (or all) of three different needs: to 'replace' dead tribal members – it is worth recalling that Indians always worried about heavy casualties in war and thus depopulation – to appease the spirits of the departed, and to assuage the grief of the relict. French veterans of the Seven Years War in North America left many graphic descriptions of this gruesome form of mutilation. Here is Pouchot: 'As soon as a man has fallen, they run to him, put their knee between his shoulders, take a lock of their hair in one hand, and with their knife in the other give a blow separating the skin from the head and tearing off a piece. This is a thing quickly done; then showing the scalp they utter a cry they call the death cry.' And here is a valuable eyewitness account from the Frenchman known only by his initials J. C. B.:*

The savage quickly seizes his knife, and makes an incision around the hair from the upper part of the forehead to the back of the neck. Then he puts his foot on the shoulder of the victim, whom he has turned over face down, and pulls the hair off with both hands, from the back to the front . . . When a savage has taken a scalp, and is not afraid he is being pursued, he stops and scrapes the skin to remove the blood and the fibres on it. He makes a hoop of green wood, stretches the skin over it like a tambourine, and puts it in the sun to dry a little. The skin is painted red and the hair on the outside combed. When prepared, the scalp is fastened to the end of a long stick, and carried on his shoulder in triumph to the village or place where he wants to put it. But as he nears each place on his way, he gives as many cries as he has scalps to announce his arrival and show his bravery. Sometimes as many as fifteen scalps are fastened on the same stick. When there are too many for one stick, they decorate several sticks with scalps.

Nothing can diminish the savagery and cruelty of the Native Americans, but their actions must be viewed both within the context of their own warrior cultures and animistic religions and within the larger picture of the general brutality of life in the eighteenth century. The citizens and intellectuals who expressed fascinated horror at cannibalism, torture, human sacrifice and scalping were quite content to attend public executions where (until the coming of the 'drop' method) the condemned man or woman took half an hour to die an agonised death. They did not cavil when 'traitors' were subjected to the barbaric ritual of being hanged, drawn and quartered, as the Jacobite rebels were after the '45. They raised no particular objection when the heads of rebels were placed on pikes and displayed outside cities as an awful warning. They tolerated hanging in chains, keelhauling sailors (usually a fatal punishment) and army floggings so brutal and severe that many men expired under the lash. Eighteenth-century European soldiers were terrorised into military discipline by the lash; Native American braves made war for prestige, glory or the perceived general good of the clan or tribe. Moreover, the mass sack, pillage and wholesale rape that followed most successful sieges in European warfare exceeded anything the Iroquois or Abenaki were able to achieve. Holocausts of horror like the sack of Magdeburg in the Thirty Years War make the Fort Henry atrocities seem like small beer. And in this very year of 1759, at Quebec, Wolfe was quite content to fire-bomb the city with incendiaries, heedless of the suffering caused to innocent civilians, and to lay waste the countryside with scorched-earth tactics. The war in North America was a bloody, brutal and horrifying business, but it would be naive to see it as a struggle of civilisation against barbarism.

Besides, the specific issue of scalping invites a rejoinder of its own. In the first place Europeans, and especially irregular groups like Rogers' Rangers, responded by scalping and maiming on their own account, their descent into savagery abetted by the routine bounties of £5 per scalp offered – a massive bonus for a Ranger on basic pay. The spiral of atrocity and counter-atrocity became more vertiginous, especially after 1757. When Louisbourg fell, the victorious Highlanders chopped off the heads of any Indians they encountered. One eyewitness reported: 'We have killed a great many Indians, and the Rangers and Highlanders give no quarter to anyone, and are scalping everywhere so you cannot know a French from an Indian scalp.' So rampant did the European scalping epidemic become that in June 1759 Amherst was forced to issue express orders: 'No scouting party or other in the Army under his command shall whatsoever opportunity they may have scalp any women or children belonging to the enemies. They are to bring them away if they can, if not they are to leave them unhurt.'

But what use was such a military directive when everyone knew that the civilian authorities were offering premium rates for scalps? In May 1755 Governor William Shirley of Massachusetts offered £40 for Indian male scalps and £20 for female. That might have seemed in line with a degenerate warriors' code, but Governor Robert Hunter Morris of Pennsylvania made clear his genocidal intentions by targeting the child-bearing sex: in 1756 he offered bounties of £30 for a male, but £50 for a female. In any case, the despicable practice of offering bounties for scalps backfired badly, as Indians proved adept at scams. First there was obvious fraud, when the Native Americans manufactured 'scalps' from horsehide. Next came the practice of killing so-called friends and allies just to make money: in a well-documented case in 1757 a band of Cherokees killed a friendly Chickasaw just to get the bounty. And finally, as virtually every single chronicler of the war noted, Indians were adept at dividing single scalps, and the Cherokees were reputedly so expert at this that they could make four scalps out of every man they killed.

It was now September 1759. Quebec had fallen, but at Crown Point Amherst was in the dark about this crucial development. It was too late for regular campaigning, but he still had hopes for great things from his irregulars and summoned his favourite officer for a briefing. Amherst's favourite was one of the most controversial characters on the American frontier, a man who had already succeeded in ruffling feathers in the British army establishment and in incurring the deep enmity of two of the major players in North America, Sir William Johnson, the 'Mohawk Baronet', and Brigadier-General Thomas Gage, Amherst's second-in-command and formerly commander of the light infantry.

The twenty-eight-year-old Major Richard Rogers was by now something of a legend in the back country. Six feet tall, immensely strong, with a huge, long straight nose, fleshy face and bull neck, he had turned himself into the foremost authority in bush-fighting on the Anglo-American side. Professional jealousy explains the hostility of Gage and Johnson, his rivals in the business of irregular warfare, but many others had reservations about Rogers, whose background and reputation alike were unsavoury and whose ambitions were overweening – when only in his mid-twenties he was petitioning for a colonelcy and boasting about a future knighthood. Consumed with an obsession about one day locating the North-West Passage and thereby making his fortune, Rogers was known to be both careless and dishonest with money, fond of gambling and drinking, forever in debt and always on the lookout for get-rich-quick schemes. His care-free attitude concealed a very dark side, which manifested itself in merci-less flogging of men under his command who disobeyed orders and in recurrent nightmares about dying in prison – he always said this was a fate worse than death and that he would rather be scalped by the Indians. Nursing a hatred of Indians, the French and anyone set in authority over him, Rogers was a familiar figure at Crown Point, often to be seen smoking his clay pipe or quaffing hot buttered rum. The only man he respected was Amherst, and this may only have been because the Commander-in-Chief once told Rogers that he had no respect for irregulars in general but immense admiration for him personally.

Born in Massachusetts in 1731 of yeoman farming stock, Rogers moved with his family to New Hampshire in the late 1730s, but war between Britain and France in 1744 adversely affected his fortunes. In August 1745 Abenaki marauders from St Francis in Quebec province (southern Canada) raided the Rogers farm and compelled the family to flee with other settlers to the security of the garrison town of Rumford. Others were not so fortu-nate: the Abenaki ambushed a party of eight militiamen, killed five and carried off another two for ritual torture. Rogers heard the stories of what had happened to the dead men: they had been scalped, eviscerated and all extremities (including genitals) lopped off. From this event dated his hatred of Indians, and it is significant that when the local militia commander called for volunteers, the broad-shouldered fourteen-year-old was among those who raised his hand.

Further bitterness was excited in 1748 when his militia company arrived too late to save his family farm in Mountalona from destruction. Ever afterwards Rogers spoke with bitterness about the charred and gutted remnants of the once-flourishing homestead that he picked over: the smoke billowed thickly into the atmosphere, cattle lay butchered all around in the spring sunshine and the Rogers' prize fruit trees had all been destroyed, except for a solitary survivor. When the war ended (at the close of 1748), young Robert Rogers was already a grizzled veteran of a hundred tracking expeditions and was deeply versed in woodcraft. Uneducated, unsocialised and thus unfit for civilian life, he drifted into crime and shady entrepreneurship. He had a long apprenticeship with a gang of counterfeiters, then diversified into smuggling. Concealing his hatred, he went north and traded furs and other contraband goods with the French and Abenaki in return for gold. On these trips he picked up a good knowledge of French and learned much valuable lore and wisdom about the Abenaki, which he carefully stored away for future use. By the time hostilities between Britain and France broke out again (in 1755) he had an unrivalled knowledge of the woods, streams and mountain passes of the vast wilderness country between New Hampshire and southern Canada.

The war gave Rogers the chance to combine his campaigning background with his taste for entrepreneurship. He contacted the Massachusetts authorities and offered to recruit men to an irregular company provided he was given the command. He began recruiting for Massachusetts but, when New Hampshire also decided to raise troops, he took his volunteers there and secured from the Governor the terms he required. In April 1755 Rogers was appointed Captain of Number One Company of the putative New Hampshire Regiment and saw service along the Hudson river and in Albany. Governor William Shirley of Massachusetts was now Commander-in-Chief, North America, and wanted to counterattack the French under Baron Dieskau, who had attacked Sir William Johnson at Lake George and faced the problem that his Mohawk allies had refused to campaign. Rogers was recommended to him as an expert in irregular operations and performed scouting probes into French territory with great skill, making use of the woodcraft dinned into him in the 1740s. His reputation as an aggressive guerrilla, prepared to take the fight to the enemy, soared.

His reward came in March 1756 when Shirley summoned him to Boston and put him in command of an entirely independent second company of Rangers, to be raised and employed forthwith. Pay was to be three shillings a day, with sergeants receiving four, ensigns five, lieutenants seven and Rogers (as Captain) ten – liberal pay by the standards of regular army emoluments. Rogers appointed his brother Richard as his First Lieutenant and his friend John Stark as Second Lieutenant. The snag was that the Rangers' existence was not guaranteed: they would always only be as good as their last exploit. Yet Rogers soon showed that he was no mean politician: he managed to parlay this humble beginning for the forest guerrillas to the point where eventually there would be ten companies of Rangers, including two of Stockbridge (pro-British) Indians, with their own war chiefs as officers. By July 1756 he had secured his brother Richard (who died soon after from smallpox) as commander of the third company and by 1757, having raised a further seven companies, Rogers himself was promoted to Major, in overall command of all ten.

Rogers tried to beat the Indians at their own game and to turn irregular warfare into a kind of science. His instruction manuals and verbal briefings gave advice on where to find trees of apples, pears, plums, cherries and wild strawberries; and hints on fishing, whether on catching mackerel and cod at the seashore or salmon and eighteen-pound bass in the swift rivers. His green-uniformed men were taught to use ice-skates and snow-shoes, carry supplies on sleighs and use dogs to track Indians; to canoe by night and lay up by day; and to appear on roll-call each evening with full kit and packed knapsack. He taught the Rangers how to survive freezing rains and blinding snows without lighting fires; how to avoid frostbite and snow-blindness; how to survive on iron rations; how to hide one's own track and follow an enemy trail; how to conceal boats and portage them across rapids; how to hide in trees and imitate animal and bird calls; how to make silent signals in the depth of the forest. His nineteen-article 'bullet points' express in pithy and homespun language the code of the Ranger:

1. Don't forget nothing.
2. Have your musket clean as a whistle, hatchet scoured, sixty rounds powder and ball and be ready to march at a minute's warning.
3. Tell the truth about what you see and what you do. There is an army depending on you for correct information.
4. You can lie all you please when you tell other folks about the Rangers, but don't never lie to a Ranger or officer.
5. Don't never take a chance you don't have to.
6. When we're on the march, we march single file, far enough apart so that one shot can't go through two men.
7. If we strike swamps or soft ground, we spread out abreast so it's hard to track us.
8. When we march, we keep moving till dark, so as to give the enemy the least possible chance at us.
9. When we camp, half the party stays awake while the other half sleeps.
10. If we take prisoners, we keep 'em separate till we have had time to examine them, so they can't cook up a story between 'em.
11. Don't ever march home the same way. Take a different route so you won't be ambushed.
12. No matter whether we travel in big parties or little ones, each party has to keep a scout twenty yards ahead, twenty yards on each flank

and twenty yards in the rear so the main body can't be surprised and wiped out.

13. Every night you'll be told where to meet if surrounded by a superior force.

14. Don't sit down to eat without posting sentries.

15. Don't sleep beyond dawn. Dawn's when the French and Indians attack.

16. Don't cross a river by a regular ford.

17. If someone's trailing you, make a circle, come back onto your own tracks and ambush the folks that aim to ambush you.

18. Don't stand up when the enemy's coming against you. Kneel down, lie down, hide behind a tree.

19. Let the enemy come up till he's almost close enough to touch. Then let him have it and jump out and finish him up with your hatchet.

Rogers' Rangers really made their mark in 1756. Rogers and his men showed their contempt for the French by skating down Lake George past Ticonderoga, then hiding in the forest, emerging to burn barns, kill cattle and lay ambushes. Rogers capped these exploits in October with a daring raid on Ticonderoga itself, when he and a couple of Rangers walked straight up to a French sentry, bamboozled him with some heavily accented French brogue and then took him prisoner. But perhaps Rogers's most substantial feat happened that summer. He and his men rowed ten miles down Lake George in whaleboats, portaged them six miles over a mountainous gorge and relaunched them on Lake Champlain. Then they concealed the boats and hid in the woods by day while hundreds of French boats criss-crossed the lake looking for them. When dusk fell they rowed overnight, came on a schooner and two sloops, overcame them, sank the ships, laden with wine, brandy and flour, took eight prisoners, hid the boats on the western shore and came home on foot with their prisoners. A month later Rogers returned to the concealed whaleboats, embarked, reconnoitred the lake, again hid the boats (this time eight miles north of Crown Point), took some more prisoners and carried them to Fort William Henry. Abercromby was delighted, for the Rangers had proved that the British need not slumber impotently in winter quarters during the great 'white-out' from November to March, but could carry the fight to the enemy.

Rogers's audacity led to the first major firefight for the Rangers – the so-called first 'Battle of the Snowshoes'. In January 1757 seventy-four Rangers left their base at Fort Edward and travelled through the snows to Fort William Henry, where they spent two days making snowshoes. On the

17th they set out and marched down the frozen Lake George. On the 19th they reached the western shore, marched north-west and bivouacked in the mountains. Changing course next morning for a north-easterly track, they looped round Ticonderoga undetected and paused overnight some five miles distant. They made camp in the usual way, scraping away the snow from their snowshoes, piling it up into a bank to resemble a drift and then making beds of spruce boughs before being lulled to sleep by the campfire in the hollow. Next morning they trekked in drizzling rain through the dripping forest and came to the banks of Lake Champlain. Here they captured some sledges, seven men and six boats plying on the frozen lake between Ticonderoga and Crown Point, but then noticed to their discomfiture that some more-distant sledgers had seen them and were returning to the enemy forts to alert the French. On questioning the prisoners, they learned that both French and Indians were present in large numbers at Ticonderoga, from which Rogers knew at once that a severe reckoning was at hand. He returned to his overnight bivouac, lit fires, dried out all the dripping guns and then began marching south through the forest. All his favourite comrades were with him: John Stark, Thomas Spikeman (or Speakman) and another man known only as Captain Kennedy.

In the afternoon the French sprang an expert ambush, forcing the Rangers to retreat in some disarray, though Stark and the rearguard covered the withdrawal valiantly with a brisk fire. Then the united party dug in at a natural hollow, stubbornly held their ground and beat off the French attack. Outnumbered at least two to one, Rogers feared being outflanked, and indeed the French twice tried this manoeuvre, only to be beaten back by a reserve that Rogers had held back for this very purpose. The French tried to break down their will to resist, calling out that it was useless to persevere since the Rangers were completely surrounded, and even yelling out to Rogers by name. The Rangers held on until darkness, taking heavy losses: Spikeman and Kennedy were killed and Rogers himself wounded twice, first with little more than a graze but later taking a shot in the wrist. Finally the Rangers were able to withdraw under cover of night, having lost fourteen killed and six wounded. They marched all night, reached Lake George the next morning, camped by The Narrows the next night and got back to Fort William Henry the following day. Vaudreuil, who falsely claimed that forty Rangers had been killed and only three survived, said that his fighting force was 179 strong, which probably means it was rather larger (perhaps 200) but not as large as Rogers claimed (250). But since Vaudreuil admitted thirty-seven killed and wounded on his side, French losses were probably higher.

The spring and summer of 1757 were a quiet period for Rogers. He took time to recover from his wounds and then went down with smallpox. The Rangers took no part in the climactic events of Montcalm's siege of Fort William Henry, since Loudoun sent them north on the abortive Louisbourg campaign. Yet Rogers had to be at his political best this year since he was challenged both from within and without. General Gage, his bitter enemy, secured permission from Loudoun to form his own companies of 'Rangers' or irregulars, who would operate under the same pay and conditions of service as the regular regiments. This was widely perceived as (and indeed was) an attempt to marginalise Rogers prior to mothballing his independent Rangers. Yet Rogers could do little, for he was barely recovered from the smallpox that carried off his brother when he went down with an attack of scurvy. Command of the Rangers temporarily devolved on John Stark, who seemed not to have Rogers's charisma. At any rate, on a scouting expedition to Ticonderoga in November 1757, the Rangers disobeyed one of Rogers's most express orders and began shooting at game on the march; they then compounded this by going against the standing order that only half the Rangers should sleep at any one time. Captain James Abercrombie, a regular officer accompanying Stark, was shocked to find that not a single sentry had been posted at midnight and everyone was asleep.

Hard on the fiasco of this scouting probe, a further scandal arose when two Rangers were caught stealing rum from the army stores at Fort Edward in December and sentenced to a whipping – the normal punishment for regulars. Their comrades refused to accept this judgement, chopped down the whipping post, released the two culprits from the guardhouse and prepared to shoot it out with the regulars. The camp commandant Colonel Haviland arrested the ringleaders and instituted court-martial proceedings for mutiny. Rogers had to rise from his sick-bed and confront Haviland. When the commandant refused to give him satisfaction and referred the matter to General Abercromby, Rogers bearded the General in his lair at Albany and won him over by a mixture of firmness and charm. Abercromby then passed the buck to Loudoun in New York. In January 1758 Rogers had an interview with Loudoun there and persuaded him that the entire affair was a storm in a teacup, some Rangers horseplay which the by-the-book martinet had blown out of proportion. Not only did Loudoun accept this version of events but he gave formal endorsement to the continuance of Rogers's Rangers as a regiment, with ten companies each of 100 men, two of them formed from the Mohegan and Stockbridge Indians of Connecticut. Rogers's political victory in January 1758 was as considerable as his military triumph in the snow twelve months earlier.

Back at Fort Edward the enraged commandant Haviland made life as difficult as possible for Rogers and the Rangers. There was a public slanging match between the two on 19 February, confirmed by some good eyewitness reports. The Machiavellian Haviland thought up what was virtually a suicide mission for the Rangers: he proposed that a Major Putnam of Connecticut make a probe towards Ticonderoga, followed closely by an attack on Crown Point by 400 Rangers. Rogers saw through this at once: any deserter or prisoner from Putnam's mission would certainly tip off the French about the second wave directed against Crown Point. As predicted, Putnam returned minus a deserter. Haviland insisted that the second expedition proceed and then made his malevolence clear by reducing the strike force to 180, sugaring the pill only by stating that the target should be Ticonderoga rather than Crown Point. Rogers was now certain that his party was marked down for destruction, but feared the capital that Gage and other enemies might make if he refused to go on the mission. Full of gloomy foreboding, Rogers led his 180 men out of Fort Edward on 10 March 1758, passed Lake George on the ice by night and donned snowshoes for a trek round the foot of the mountains that would bring them down behind the French. The Rangers split into two divisions, one led by Rogers, the other by Captain Charles Bulkeley. Trouble arrived faster than he had expected it, for the French Indians picked up their snowshoe tracks at Trout Brook, a gorge opening on the west to the valley of Ticonderoga. At about 3 p.m. on 12 March, Rogers spied a party of about 100 Indians seemingly unaware of their presence. He decided to attack and passed the word to Captain Bulkeley, commanding the second company. The second 'Battle of the Snowshoes' was about to begin.

A devastating volley dropped many warriors in their tracks. The jubilant Rangers broke cover and pursued the fleeing Indians, only to run into a hailstorm of fire that scythed down about fifty of them, including Bulkeley. The French trap had been perfectly baited, for what Rogers thought was the main body was simply a decoy, and here now was the main body, tearing the heart out of the foolishly incautious Rangers. Aware of his desperate situation, Rogers formed his men in a defensive position on the slope of a hill, and there they fought courageously and stoically until sunset, twice repelling an all-out attack. Sometimes shooting at the enemy from a twenty-yard range and sometimes grappling hand-to-hand with hatchets and tomahawks, the Rangers somehow held out until at last a large body of Indians turned their right flank. The surviving Rangers broke and fled as night came on, leaving eight officers and more than 100 of their comrades dead or wounded on the snow. Rogers and about twenty followers escaped up the mountainside but a running fight continued all night. Finally the Rangers reached Lake George, taking further losses, but it was not until after a further two days of suffering and misery that they limped into Fort Edward, having eaten nothing but juniper berries and tree bark for the last forty-eight hours. It was the grimmest fight Rogers was ever in. Against his losses of about 125 the French had sustained casualties at least as great, and so heavy were Indian losses that in revenge they murdered most of their prisoners. Lieutenant William Phillips, one of three regular officers who accompanied Rogers on this march of death, was tied to a tree and then hacked to pieces. None of the wounded survived. Parkman sardonically notes: 'The Indians brought in 144 scalps, having no doubt divided some of them, after their ingenious custom.' As always in the wilderness war, numbers were bitterly disputed on both sides. The Chevalier de Lévis says that the French force was only 250 strong but it must have been considerably larger, though still some way short of Rogers's estimate of 700 (his head counts were always hyperbolic). Rogers himself was at first reported killed because, it seemed, he threw off his overcoat in the heat of conflict and it was later found on the field with his commission in the pocket. The story that he survived by sliding on his snowshoes down the precipice of 'Rogers Rock' appears to be apocryphal.

No doubt to Haviland's disappointment, Rogers not only survived the battle but, somewhat curiously in the circumstances, gained kudos from his heavy defeat. He took part in the abortive attack on Ticonderoga in the summer of 1758, but had to wait until August for his next noteworthy exploit. Abercromby had sent him down Lake George once again on the now familiar route across the mountain ridge to Lake Champlain, but Rogers and his Rangers were just eighty men in a larger combined force of 800 and this probe was beset by a plethora of contradictory orders, of instructions issued and then countermanded. Doubtless disillusioned and grown cynical, Rogers started to become careless. He forgot his usual caution when in the wilderness and, on 8 August, he and Lieutenant Irwin of the infantry entered into a sharpshooting contest, whose reports could be heard for miles around. The shots reached the ears of a mixed party of French and Indians under the command of the notable guerrilla leader Marin, a sort of French Richard Rogers. Marin planned a perfect ambush, into which the British walked like tiros, and a terrible fight ensued. 'The enemy rose like a cloud and fired a volley upon us . . . the tomahawks and bullets flying around my ears like hailstones,' was how one Ranger recalled it. At first the French had the advantage but gradually superior numbers told and the French stole away, breaking into small parties to evade pursuit. Nonetheless, Rogers's self-indulgence as a sharpshooter had cost the Rangers dear: forty-nine of them lay dead and were buried on the field.

1759 was the year when Rogers's reputation would acquire an international cachet, largely, be it said, through his own talents as a self-publicist. But the year did not start auspiciously for him. In February his old enemy General Gage succeeded General John Stanwix as commander of the northern district in the American theatre and at once began a systematic attempt to destroy the Rangers as a separate corps and to replace Rogers as their commander. It would have gone very hard for Rogers had not the new Commander-in-Chief, General Amherst, been a huge admirer of his methods. Pitt was impatient with commanders in North America who could not deliver and, having replaced Loudoun with Abercromby in early 1758, allowed that General only six months before replacing him in turn with Amherst, who was the hero of the hour after his taking of Louisbourg. Gage imagined that Amherst would know nothing of Rogers and would be swayed by his black propaganda about the Rangers, but Amherst was shrewd, saw through Gage's self-serving tactics and largely ignored his representations.

By March Gage was trying to insist that the Rangers come under the direct control of the regular army and that any Ranger refusing to serve under a regular officer should be court-martialled for mutiny; moreover, any Ranger officer resigning in protest would be deemed to have deserted. Gage did himself no favours with Amherst by seeming to take an eclectic view of the Commander-in-Chief's orders, obeying those he liked and ignoring those he did not, and gradually lost credibility. Moreover, generals whom Amherst esteemed more highly than Gage spoke favourably of Rogers. The ultimate accolade came when Wolfe, known to have a low opinion of American troops, asked for Rogers and his Rangers to take part in the siege of Quebec. Amherst, whose view of Wolfe must have been at best ambivalent, surely took pleasure in refusing this request. But when he interviewed Rogers in Albany in May, he was very taken with him. 'I shall always cheerfully receive your opinion in relation to the service you are engaged in,' Amherst told Rogers, and went on to assure him that his rank was safe, as was the independence of the Rangers, and this would be publicly announced in army orders. To make the point clear beyond misapprehension, Amherst kept Rogers and his company with him at Fort Edward, ready for his summer campaign against Ticonderoga.

Nothing Rogers did that summer disappointed Amherst, whose journal is full of admiring remarks, as in this entry for 5 August: 'I . . . sent Mr Rogers on the other side of the lake to see for the best place for cutting timber to erect the Fort [on the site of Crown Point], gave him leave to shoot deer; he killed three and seven bear.' And now at last Amherst authorised Rogers to take a step which the Rangers' leader had been advocating since 1756: an offensive against the Abenakis in their village of St Francis across the Canadian border from New Hampshire. His letter of instructions to Rogers dated 13 September 1759 leaves no doubt that this was to be a revenge mission on a large scale:

> You are this night to set out with the detachment ordered yesterday, viz of 200 men, which you will take under your command, and proceed to Misisquey Bay, from whence you will march and attack the enemy's settlements on the south side of the river St Lawrence, in such a manner as you shall judge most effectual to disgrace the enemy, and for the success and honour of His Majesty's arms. Remember the barbarities that have been committed by the enemy's Indian scoundrels on every occasion, where they had an opportunity of shewing their infamous cruelties on the king's subjects, which they have done without mercy. Take your revenge, but don't forget that though those villains have dastardly and promiscuously murdered women and children of all ages, it is my orders that no women or children are to be killed or hurt. When you have executed your intended service, you will return with your detachment to camp or to join me wherever I may be.

What possessed Amherst to order a raid that has engendered controversy ever since? We may discern a threefold motivation. In the first place, Amherst loathed Indians and was enraged by the Abenakis' latest move. Amherst had sent two officers, Captain Kennedy and Lieutenant Hamilton, northwards with orders to hit the St Lawrence and proceed to Quebec to find out how Wolfe was faring; four Stockbridge Indians accompanied them, bearing a flag of truce and requesting safe passage. Early in September Amherst received a letter from Montcalm (delivered under a flag of truce) telling him that the Abenakis had taken the two officers prisoner. In Amherst's view this was double-barrelled treachery, for he only learned about the Abenakis' action from the very system they themselves had violated. In any case, by 1759 Amherst was disgusted with Indians of all tribes and wanted a settlement of accounts with them. An incident in Nova Scotia that January had particularly angered him. A party of eleven redcoats and Rangers failed to return from a woodcutting expedition, and next day a patrol found the bodies of five of them. According to John Knox, they had been shot, then scalped while still alive: 'Their limbs were horribly distorted, truly expressive of the agonies in which they died; in this manner they froze, not unlike figures, or statues, which are variously distributed on pedestals in the gardens of the curious.' As for the general detestation, Amherst confided to Gage: 'I know what a vile brew they are and have as

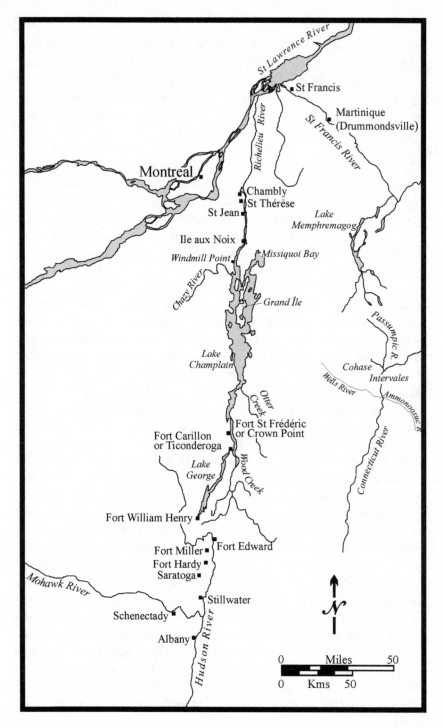

Rogers' Rangers' raid on St Francis, October 1759

bad an opinion of those lazy rum-drinking scoundrels as anyone can have
. . . [but because the French feared them] . . . I shall for that reason engage
as many of them as I can.' Further outrage was caused by the Abenaki on
2 July 1759 when sixteen men of the Jersey Blues on a woodcutting expedition were ambushed by a large party of Abenakis within sight of their
camp on Lake George. An eyewitness reported:

> They killed and scalped six, wounded two, took four prisoner, and only
> four of the whole party escaped. They showed themselves plainly to the
> whole army after they got the scalps, gave a hollow [sic] and then made
> off to their bateaux, which were not more than two miles from the head
> of the lake. A large party was ordered out after them but in vain. They
> butchered our people in a most shocking manner by cutting pieces of
> flesh out of their necks, thighs and legs.

Second, there was at stake an issue of credibility. Ever since 1755 it had
been widely believed in the British army that the Indian tribes were invincible in wilderness warfare, and this was a belief that Amherst badly wanted
to lay to rest. The memory of Braddock's defeat at Monongahela haunted
the collective imagination, and officers often chewed over the details of
that black day in the army's history. It was 9 July 1755 when Braddock's
forces entered the forest ten miles from Fort Duquesne and found themselves in a natural killing ground. Whereas most forests in North America
were choked with vegetation and undergrowth, the 637 Indian members
of the French strike force – mainly Ottawas, Mississaugas, Wyandots and
Potawatomis from the west, the so-called *pays d'en haut* – had used this
stretch of woods as a hunting ground and had cleared the undergrowth to
flush out small and big game and to allow their hunters to move and
manoeuvre easily. Firing from the cover of the trees, yet able to move
swiftly and freely so as not to present a counter-target, within minutes the
Indians threw Braddock's men into confusion and penned them into an
area 250 yards long and only about 100 feet wide. Unable to see their foe,
the British troops soon realised that they were in a kind of human abat-
toir. Confusion became disarray, and disarray soon turned to panic as the
forests became a sensory hell. All around them was smoke, gunfire and the
screams of wounded men and stricken horses. From the dark forest depths
came the blood-curdling war-cries of the Indians – 'ravenous Hell-hounds,
yelping and screaming like so many devils' – all the more terrifying to men
who had been fed on tales of Native American torture, mutilation and
scalping.
So strongly inculcated was the British discipline of platoon formation

and successive volleys that the redcoats fired broadsides at trees where no enemy lurked and, behaving like automata yet fundamentally confused about what they were doing, ended by firing volleys into each other. Braddock's men stood their ground for three hours, but their American auxiliaries either fled at once or took cover behind trees, where they were often mistaken for Indians and killed by 'friendly fire'. The redcoats' training and Braddock's mistaken notion of courage were suicidally counter-productive that day for, instead of adapting his tactics and improvising to deal with a strange enemy with novel methods of fighting, Braddock continued his parade-ground 'stand fast' approach, assuming that sooner or later the Indians must give way before the regulars. But by the time the redcoats reached the Monongahela river, their ranks were so thinned by their adversaries' murderous fire that they could finally take it no longer, broke and ran. Seeing men screaming in terror and running round in circles, the Indians broke cover and charged in among them, wielding tomahawk and scalping knife. Braddock's force disintegrated: in the battle and the rout that followed he lost two-thirds of an army that began the day 2,200 strong. For the eighteenth-century British army it was a disaster as great as the Battle of Isandlhwana would be in the nineteenth century, fighting against a similar 'savage' enemy: the Zulus.

Yet even more than the desire to erase for ever the stain of Monongahela, what actuated Amherst was revenge for the army's second-greatest disaster in this Indian war, the massacre of British troops after Colonel Monro surrendered to Montcalm following the siege of Fort William Henry in 1757. 'Remember William Henry' was as much a watchword in the British army in North America in the late 1750s as 'Remember the Alamo' would be in Texas eighty years later. Monro surrendered on the basis that his troops could march out unarmed but with full honours to Fort Edward. Montcalm was sincere in offering such terms, but when he explained to his Indian allies, who fought only for booty, prisoners and scalps, not honour, that the British were to be allowed to depart unharmed and that the arms, *matériel* and food stocks left behind in the fort were not to be plundered – and all this as the consequence of surrender terms about which they were not consulted – they reacted with incredulity. Listening in sullen silence to Montcalm's (to them) incomprehensible words, they decided they would take what was rightly theirs, whatever the white 'Father' said.

As the British soldiers and their families trooped dejectedly out of Fort William Henry at dawn on 10 August 1757, hundreds of warriors of all races (but with Abenakis in the majority) clustered round them, demanding that they surrender arms, clothes and equipment. The regulars in the van of the column were protected by a French escort but the provincial troops and irregulars were not and fell easy prey to the painted warriors. First the Indians began carrying off women and children, then they turned their fury on the wounded, hacking and scalping before stripping their victims of anything of value. Next the Abenaki turned on the men and women in the extreme rear of the column and began tomahawking them without mercy. Although the killing lasted just a few minutes, the slaughter spread panic among the rest of the rearguard, who broke formation and ran panic-stricken into the woods. The Abenaki easily rounded up these terrified refugees and made them prisoner but now Montcalm compounded the disaster. With the best of intentions he ordered that the Indians release their prisoners; rather than stomach this 'dishonour' the warriors preferred to kill them. By the time Montcalm managed to restore order, more than 100 Americans lay dead (the most careful computation says a minimum of sixty-nine and a maximum of 185) and between 300 and 500 had been taken prisoner. If one wants to number-crunch, one can say that a fatality of between 2.8 and 7.5 per cent hardly constitutes a 'massacre' and it is true that if all 1,600 of Montcalm's Indian allies had fallen on the column simultaneously for the same length of time, there would have been few survivors at all. But 100 deaths in such circumstances still represents a war crime, and in any case human feelings are governed by perceptions, not facts.

For this 'massacre' the Abenaki were held mainly responsible, though not all the slaughtering Indians were Abenaki. So why was Amherst's hostility so pronounced towards this one tribe? Two factors were salient: the Catholicism of the Abenaki and their geographical location. Whereas most of France's Indian allies were located in and around the Great Lakes area, the Abenaki occupied the north-eastern corner of North America, thus in tribal terms catching the British between two fires, since the territories of their Iroquois allies were penned between two different sets of hostile tribes. As for religion, not only had the Abenaki been converted to Catholicism in around 1640, but the converters had been the hated Jesuits, and even now the well-known Jesuit Joseph Antoine Roubaud, friend of Montcalm, had his headquarters at the Abenaki village of St Francis, though his life was itinerant and peripatetic. The Jesuit success was at first sight surprising, since Indians generally struck back vengefully when visited by the white man's diseases, and the Abenaki had been twice devastated, first by plague in 1617 and then by smallpox in 1633–34. It seems that the Jesuit doctrine of redemption through suffering for sin struck an unexpected chord. The Abenaki interest in theology surprised and often amused their French 'fathers'. In 1757 Vaudreuil tried to engineer an alliance between the Abenaki and the Delawares, and the Abenaki insisted on taking their

Jesuit priest with them to the conference at the Delaware lodge. The Delawares said they were interested in what their 'grandchildren' the Abenaki had to say, whereupon the Jesuit priest launched into a rousing sermon. Not to be outdone, a Delaware convert to the Moravian faith got to his feet and harangued the visitors, making a spirited theological rejoinder to the Jesuit that might have pleased a medieval schoolman, comparing the Trinity to the hierarchies found in an Indian tribe.

The Abenaki (they called themselves Wabanaki), the so-called 'people of the dawn' because their lands lay at the easternmost extremity of North America, were an Algonquian-speaking 'super-tribe' whose sub-septs included the Sokokis of the middle and upper Connecticut river, the Conasucks farther upriver, the Missisquois on the north shore of Lake Champlain, the Pennanacooks of New Hampshire's Merrimack Valley, the Pigwallets of the White Mountains, the Androcoggins of western Maine and, farther east, the Penobscots, Norridgewocks, Wawenocks and Kennebecs. The Abenaki homeland covered a vast area, from the St Lawrence Valley to northern Massachusetts. Anthropologists sometimes distinguish between the Eastern Abenakis of Maine and the Western Abenakis of Vermont, but no clear differentiation along these lines is possible, and some experts prefer to distinguish between them on religious rather than geographical grounds: on this model the Western Abenaki are those who view the Champlain Valley, the scene of their creation stories, as the centre of their spiritual universe; the Eastern Abenaki are those who look to the numinous power of Mount Katahdin in Maine; the St Francis Indians against whom Rogers was campaigning were therefore the Western Abenaki.

The Abenaki were hunters who ran a diversified economy combining hunter-gathering with agriculture (especially the growing of corn) and fishing, and they liked to locate their villages in valleys to take advantage of the spring fish runs. They were skilled artisans, whose expertise in making moccasins, snowshoes and canoes was highly prized. Village life was seasonal: communities came to life when bands of related families got together for the spring fishing and planting, and broke up when families dispersed for the autumn and winter hunting. They had always been pro-French, for when contact with the white man was first made, it became clear that the French were interested only in beaver pelts and baptism, whereas the English wanted their lands and demanded cultural integration. The Abenaki raids that so terrorised New England were, from the British viewpoint, the barbaric assaults of bloodthirsty savages; but to the Abenaki they were simply an assertion of their sovereignty, for the white men who had settled on their ancient lands and displaced them farther north were thieves, trespassers and usurpers. The drawback about the

Abenakis as military allies, as Montcalm discovered, was that they liked to raid, avoid set-piece battles, dodge pursuing militias and evacuate villages when in danger so as to avoid heavy losses; despite occasional European propaganda about mindless hordes of savages, North American Indians always liked to avoid heavy casualties.

Father Roubaud, the intermittently resident priest at St Francis, gives interesting details on the everyday life of the Abenaki and describes a war council:

Imagine a great assembly of savages adorned with every ornament most suited to disfigure them in European eyes, painted with vermilion, white, green, yellow and black made of soot and the scrapings of pots. A single savage face combines all these different colours, methodically laid on with the help of a little tallow, which serves for pomatum. The head is shaved except at the top, where there is a small tuft, to which are fastened feathers, a few beads of wampum, or some such trinket. Every part of the head has its ornament. Pendants hang from the nose and also from the ears, which are split in infancy and drawn down by weights till they flap at last against the shoulders. The rest of the equipment answers to this fantastic decoration: a shirt bedaubed with vermilion, wampum collars, silver bracelets, a large knife hanging on the breast, moose-skin moccasins, and a belt of various colours always absurdly combined. The sachems and war-chiefs are distinguished from the rest: the latter by a gorget, and the former by a medal, with the King's portrait on one side, and on the other Mars and Bellona joining hands, with the device, *Virtus et Honor* . . . They proceed to nominate the chiefs who were to take command. As soon as one was named he rose and took the head of some animal that had been butchered for the feast. He raised it aloft so that all the company could see it and cried: 'Behold the head of the enemy!' Applause and cries of joy from all parts of the assembly. The chief, with the head in his hands, passed down between the lines, singing his war-song, bragging of his exploits, taunting and defying the enemy, and glorifying himself beyond all measure. To hear his self-laudation in these moments of martial transport one would think him a conquering hero ready to sweep everything before him. As he passed in front of the other savages, they would respond by dull broken cries jerked up from the depths of their stomachs, and accompanied by movements of their bodies so odd that one must be well used to them to keep countenance. In the course of this song the chief would utter from time to time some grotesque witticism; then he would stop, as if pleased with himself, or rather to listen to the thousand confused cries of applause that greeted his ears. He kept up his martial promenade as long as he liked the sport; and when he had enough, ended by flinging down the head of the animal to show that his warlike appetite craved meat of another sort.

Amherst and Rogers were now determined that the Abenaki would sustain such severe casualties that they would never again raid in areas settled by English-speaking pioneers. On the early evening of 13 September 1759 Rogers reviewed his men. Their green uniforms, chosen for camouflage in the woods, at once distinguished them from the redcoated regulars. Over a buckskin shirt they wore two layers: a kind of sleeved waistcoat and an outer body-warming short sleeveless jacket; both these garments were lined with green serge. Over their trousers they sometimes wore an imitation kilt or philibeg and always thigh-length brown leggings with moccasins on their feet. On parade they wore tricorne hats, but once in the bush they switched to flat Scots bonnets. They carried regulation-issue muskets, and a leather sling on the left side, hanging from a belt that ran over the right shoulder, held a bayonet and tomahawk, while at the waist was a sheathed scalping knife; they also had a cartridge box and (under the right arm) a powder horn suspended from a belt looped over the left shoulder. Blankets were carried in rolls except when worn for extra warmth on the march, and their knapsacks contained the iron rations on which they would eke out a living in the wilderness. The officers carried a small compass fixed in the bottom of their powder horns. It was Loudoun who had first agreed to uniforms for the Rangers, though Rogers's enemies constantly groused that the cost of supplying this special apparel and the general costs of the Rangers – some £35,000 a year – could have been better diverted to providing another two regiments of regulars for the same price. Relations between Rogers and the military administrators and accountants were always uneasy and there was a permanent dialogue of the deaf. The army's bookkeepers resented the Rangers' indiscipline and suspected Rogers himself of being financially dishonest; while he reacted with incredulous stupefaction to their demands for receipts and proper accounting procedures after fighting battles in snows and swamps.

Rogers was in no doubt about the scale of the task Amherst had set him. The Abenaki village of St Francis, or Odanak, lay 150 miles to the north of Crown Point, for the most part through an uncharted wilderness; it was enemy territory where the Abenaki knew the terrain and would hold all the cards. Crossing Lake Champlain, the first part of the journey, would be comparatively easy, but only comparatively, since the northern lake was still controlled by the French navy, known to boast at the very least a brigantine, a schooner, a topsail ship and at least a dozen gunboats, any of which would make short work of the Rangers' whaleboats if they encountered them on the open lake. Once to the north of Lake Champlain, a gruelling trek through a green hell awaited the Rangers; they would have to loop round Fort Île-aux-Noix seventy miles south of their target and then avoid a series of smaller posts. Rogers had the element of surprise on his side, but if once the French were alerted to his presence, there would be no hiding place. Thousands of troops could be mobilised, especially given the proximity of Montreal to St Francis. Once the raid was successfully accomplished, the hue and cry would be raised and the Rangers would be in a grim struggle for survival, pursued by Abenaki war-bands and hunted by French regulars from the forts of Chambly, St Jean and Île-aux-Noix. Even in the best-case scenario, Rogers had to expect a shooting match at some stage of the journey. The raid on St Francis was a feat beyond anything the Rangers had yet attempted, since even in the two 'Snowshoes' battles they were only two days' trek from safety and in country they knew and had often reconnoitred. On top of this, Rogers knew that he faced discipline problems, for Amherst had lumbered him with provincials and regulars in addition to his Rangers, and among them were known troublemakers.

Once it was fully dark, Rogers gave the order and 200 men shoved off into the inky blackness from the shallow beach at Crown Point. Among them were Stockbridge Indians and, according to tradition, thirteen Mohawks whom Rogers was taking along under protest, on Amherst's orders. The Mohawks were the people of his old enemy Sir William Johnson, and Rogers thought that Amherst had been gulled, allowing Johnson to muscle in on action that was the Rangers' and the Rangers' alone. Also along was a renegade Abenaki named Pissenne, who was supposed to be their guide beyond Lake Champlain. Once launched, the whaleboats stayed within sight of each other, the oarsmen pausing between strokes to record a beat in the silence, straining their ears for any sounds of French craft on the water. No exact details of the itinerary were recorded, but eyewitness accounts, Rogers's journals, French sources and even archaeological evidence allow us to reconstruct the journey with a fair degree of confidence.

At dawn they made for the shore, probably Button Bay, intending to lay up all day and proceed overnight. Rogers sent his scouts overland to find the French boats, and they came back to report that they were cruising off the projecting mouth of the Otter river, a few miles north, where the lake narrowed. The Otter river cut its way through the hills east of Lake Champlain before it flowed into the lake along a narrow spit of land jutting one mile into the lake, forming two bays where it debouched. Above the tongue of land was North Otter Bay, with its deep waters; below was South Otter Bay, known for its dangerous shoals. Rogers and the Rangers spent their second night dragging their boats through the shallows of South Otter Bay before portaging them over the spit of land and concealing them with brushwood in North Otter Bay. Since scouts brought back word that there were three French sloops between the river mouth and Diamond Island, there was nothing for it but another day of concealment and patient waiting.

It was at this stage that Rogers suffered his first manpower shrinkage. First Captain Willyamos, a regular officer, nearly managed to blow himself and a few others up in a gunpowder explosion; then two more men were wounded by an accidental firearms discharge; next the provincial militia-men under Captain Butterfield started to report sick. Finally Rogers had his showdown (which he may have planned) with the Mohawks. When they refused to carry out scouting duties, he had the pretext he needed to send them back to Crown Point. By the third day, having sent Mohawks, sick and wounded back to Amherst, Rogers had lost forty men (one-fifth of his force) before they had even seen the enemy. It was hardly an auspicious beginning. But at least Fortune favoured him with the weather, for his force was able to slip past the French when cold rains began, which would produce five successive nights of storms and squalls on the lake. Champlain spread out more widely before them and they held a course by Split Rock and the Winooski river before seeing the wooded contours of Île la Motte and Grand Île. On 20 September they camped in pelting rain on the flat land on the shore opposite Grand Île, and the next day watched from their hiding place as four French scouting canoes looked into cove after cove on the western shore, at one point passing within half a mile of where the Rangers lay hidden, perfectly camouflaged behind their screen of brushwood. The Rangers then turned into the narrow corridor (East Bay) lying between the eastern shore and Grand Île, trusting that the shallow bar between island and mainland would deter pursuers, and on 22 September camped on the peninsula separating the swamp-fringed shoreline of Missisquoi Bay at the extreme northern end of the lake from Champlain proper. Rogers marched over a short stretch of solid ground in the north-eastern corner of the bay (near present-day Philipsburg), beached the boats in dense brushwood and cached a store of provisions there. He left behind two Stockbridge Indians as sentinels, with instructions 'to lie at a distance in sight of the boats and there to stay until I [Rogers] came back, except the enemy found them; in which case they were with all possible speed to follow on my track'.

On 23 September the Rangers plunged into unknown country, heading north-east into the wilderness, carrying two weeks' provisions. They began plodding through dense forests, thick undergrowth and marshy ground, plagued by mosquitoes. It took them two days to reach the northern end of Missisquoi Bay and at the end of that trek the two Indians left behind came running into camp to report that the whaleboats had been discovered. An Indian canoe had found their landing place and then followed the trail to the concealed whaleboats (this on the evening of the 24th). A party of 400 Frenchmen had landed in Missisquoi Bay and half of them were now on their track; since the Stockbridge Indians had made the journey in twenty-four hours on the double, it followed that the French pursuers were only a day behind them. As Rogers put it:

> This unlucky circumstance . . . put us in some consternation . . . Being so far advanced in their country, where no reinforcement could possibly relieve me, and where they could be supported by any numbers they pleased, afforded us little hopes of escaping their hands. Our boats being taken, cut off all hope of a retreat by them; besides the loss of our provisions left with them, of which we knew we should have great need at any rate, in case we survived, was a melancholy consideration.

Gloomily Rogers called a council of war. He explained that as St Francis lay near the top of an inverted 'V' at the base of whose left leg Crown Point was situated, their best hope was to follow the St Francis river to its fork, then keep to its southerly branch down the right leg of the 'V' to Lake Memphremagog and the Connecticut river and there to the base of the right leg at Fort Number Four, which was in British hands. But since they could not hope to get all the way to Number Four on their existing provisions, they should agree a rendezvous point at the lower end of the so-called Cohase Intervales (the big curves in the upper Connecticut river) where the Ammonoosuc and Wells rivers ran into the Connecticut virtually opposite each other. At this triple junction, at the mouth of the Ammonoosuc, was another fort, sixty miles north of Number Four and possibly now abandoned. What was needed was for Amherst to send provisions for 150 men to that point. Rogers therefore sent back the lamed and limping Lieutenant McMullen and six ailing Rangers to take this vital message to Amherst, making for Crown Point as directly as he could. Rogers was now down to just 153 men.

McMullen set off on 26 September, evaded the French who stood between him and his objective, and reached Crown Point nine days later. The letter he brought from Rogers made the Rangers' plight clear and Rogers added a telling remark about Number Four: 'that being the way I should return if at all'. Realising the need for speed, Amherst engaged

Lieutenant Samuel Stevens of the Rangers to head the relief party, since Rogers claimed that Stevens knew the Number Four region well. Amherst wrote to Stevens:

> Herewith you will receive a letter from me to Mr Bellows at No. 4 . . . Who is thereby directed to furnish you provisions sufficient to victual Major Rogers and his party . . . and with said provisions, and a competent number of men, which Mr Bellows is likewise ordered to furnish you with, to be aiding . . . in conveying them to Wells River. You will proceed thither, and there remain with said party as long as you shall think there is any probability of Major Rogers returning that way.

Stevens departed for Number Four (now Charleston, New Hampshire) on 4 October.

After leaving the northern end of Missisquoi Lake, the Rangers entered a spruce bog, with water at least a foot deep and sometimes deeper, where the current had carved brook-like channels. For nine days they splashed through mud and icy water, often stumbling and sometimes falling full-length into the noisome tarn. There was no firm ground anywhere, and the entire area was plashy marsh, with water everywhere between the trees, concealing irregularities in the ground. Young and choked trees of every height provided invisible tripwires; huge trunks lay rotting in the water with small spruces sprouting thickly along them; there were dead branches sharp as razors concealed in the water and if a man trod on them, he would be raked from ankle to thigh on jagged points. It seemed as if living malevolent branches clutched and tore at their clothes, gored them through the holes, plucked the caps from their heads and tried to scratch their eyes out. The Rangers suffered from sore feet, trench foot and chilblains, while their clothes were soaked and they could not light fires to dry them out or warm themselves. With water halfway to their knees, exhausted Rangers at dusk chopped down young spruces, placed three together, lopped the limbs from the upper sides and made a kind of platform held above the water by the limbs below. Using knapsacks as pillows they munched their spartan rations of sausage, cornmeal and rum and spent a miserable, wet and cold night, shivering and only half-fed. In the morning the more hopeful ones would climb trees to try to descry dry land, but there was none to be seen. Stoically they prepared for the day's trek, which would see them covering no more than nine miles, eating their meals where they stood in the bog. Soon their beards were sprouting and their clothes reduced to scarecrows' apparel. Their moccasins became so pulpy that they had to take them off and hang them round their necks. Not surprisingly, the weaker brethren cracked under the constant misery. They lost a straggler on 29 September and another the next day, and two more vanished on 2 October. What made matters worse was that the Rangers did not know for certain that the losses had not been caused by the pursuing French catching up with the back markers, though Rogers assured them that the disappearances were accidental: the men had fallen into deep holes or quicksand and drowned.

They were in the spruce bog for nine days, tacking between a north-westerly and north-easterly course, seeing no game, or even so much as a squirrel. Probably the route ran near modern Frelighsburg and then looped around Lake Selby and Brome Lake before cutting across the swamplands between Roxton Falls and Actonville. On 4 October a smooth bed of pine needles provided the first *terra firma* since Missisquoi Bay. Gradually the water became shallower and by noon they were sinking in only as far as their ankles. By sundown there was solid ground everywhere, except for scattered puddles in hollows. Finally to be able to sleep on dry earth seemed an impossible luxury. But their ordeal was far from over.

Next morning they hit the St Francis river, thirty to forty yards wide at this point, surging between high gravel banks that looked like cliffs, and were covered with maple, beech and oak, their leaves dark scarlet, blazing red and sere yellow. The stream was swollen and turbulent, its brown current swirling in waterpools, but this was the river they had to cross to be on the same side as Odanak, or the St Francis village. Rogers tested the depth with a spruce pole, then invited the biggest, strongest Ranger to link arms with him while he anchored himself with the pole; a third then went into the water to link arms with the second to form a human chain and they began edging tentatively out into the river; the idea was to construct a firm human anchor, giving a point of leverage to the next link in the chain. Gradually they edged towards the middle of the river, where the water was five feet deep and splashing over the men's heads. Finally a man reached the far bank and hooked his arms round a tree. There was a veritable causeway of Rangers standing firm against the boiling, yellowish foam, and the smaller men then made their way along the causeway, inching from link to link like a mountaineer on a sheer rock-face. Those crossing had to carry extra muskets to compensate for the men in the human chain, who could barely maintain their balance against the rushing water as it was, and would have been capsized by the extra weight of firearms. Those crossing therefore had to endure the clanking of unwieldy muskets against the chin and their chafing against the flesh, the flintlocks digging into the stomach. All the time they had to keep a precarious foothold on the slippery stone of the river bed and endure the discomfort of an icy, chest-high current and the roar of an engorged torrent. One man slipped, got his arm tangled in the straps of his knapsack and drowned, because to save him would mean snapping the chain and perhaps losing even more. Two men lost muskets and the Indians had to dive into the icy waters and recover them lest they be borne downstream to St Francis and give the game away. Six more men were wrenched from the chain by the seething waters and spewed back up on the far bank. Rogers ordered them left there; they would have to take their chances.

One by one the human chain-links emerged shivering from the river before retreating to high land to dry out. Tradition places the spot near modern Joachim de Courval. Rogers called the roll: 142 Rangers were left, five of them without muskets. Rogers now led them south along the clear Indian trail by the high river bank, on a march that was no more than a stroll on flat land after their recent travails. It was 5 October and the Rangers were cutting south to the village of Odanak fifteen miles away. When three miles from his target, Rogers climbed a tree and saw swirls of smoke ascending in the twilit sky. He then exhorted his men and pointed out that at last they were to have their satisfaction: they had marched for twenty-two days, with no fires, no cooked food, no shelter, no dry blankets and no clean clothes, but the hour of reckoning was at hand. Rogers took Lieutenant Turner and Ensign Avery, and possibly Pissenne, to reconnoitre the village.

Odanak or St Francis consisted of sixty framed and windowed houses covered with boards and stone, twelve built in the French style with lofts and cellars and grouped round a square. The rest were log cabins and plank-built dwellings, with unglazed 'windows', some just black holes, others covered with paper on which were painted fish, birds and animals. There was a Jesuit church and, nearby, the Council House, solidly constructed for defence with embrasures and notched musket holes. In the clearings by the houses were cultivated patches of corn, melon and pumpkin. Rogers and his men made their reconnaissance at about 8 p.m. that evening, after which he made his final dispositions. He felt reasonably confident, for a wedding feast was going on, following nuptials at which a French priest had officiated. Abenaki were reeling round the streets drunk and the deafening noise would surely mask any mistakes by less-than-circumspect Rangers.

Rogers issued his final orders. They would surround the village, cutting off all escape paths, with Captain Ogden ordered to seal off the obvious downstream get-away route. They were to show no mercy and to kill all Indians (no mention here of Amherst's strict injunction not to kill women and children), taking care they did not shoot at their own Stockbridge allies; but they were enjoined not to kill any of the white captives held in the village. The time set for the assault was just before dawn. The men moved close to the village, dumped their knapsacks and blankets, fixed bayonets over their musket-sights and waited.

This is the point where sober history begins to unravel and a mass of mutually contradictory oral testimony crowds in on our attention. There is agreement on almost no aspect of Rogers's famous raid on St Francis. Some say the Abenaki were forewarned: by an Indian girl who was not believed because she was female; by Pissenne; by disgruntled Indians in Rogers's party; or even by the French, who had sent couriers ahead after the whaleboats were discovered. Some claim the Jesuit priest was still in Odanak when Rogers attacked; others that he had already left. The most absurd story is that Joseph Antoine Roubaud himself was in the village, was captured during the attack and led out of the church with a rope around his neck. There is not even general agreement on the nature of the evening's riotous festivities, with some claiming that it was a victory cele- bration and others a corn dance; it seems certain, however, that it was a wedding feast. The idea that the Abenaki were forewarned makes no sense in the light of what happened. What is certain is that most, but by no means all, of the warriors were absent on a hunting expedition. Here Amherst and Rogers were badly at fault for, if they really wanted to destroy the Abenaki for ever, they should have staged their raid in the spring when they could have been certain of finding the entire fighting strength of Odanak in one spot. Out of a total population in the village of 500, as esti- mated by the Jesuit Roubaud, there were perhaps 200 present when Rogers launched his attack.

At around 5.17 a.m., half an hour before dawn, Rogers ordered his men to close in and begin firing. The first that many Abenaki knew about their fate was when the Rangers' musket butts came crashing through their doors. A few were slain as they slept, but most escaped the murderous first wave of shooting and bayoneting. Bleary-eyed, they groped for their weapons, many by their own later admission blaming their comrades for not having muskets to hand. One Abenaki escaped from his hut, then remembered he had left a child behind, climbed back through the window and retrieved the infant just before the Rangers broke down the door. A surprising number, drunk, stupefied or sleep- befuddled though they might have been, managed to find refuge in a bolthole about which the Rangers knew nothing: a ravine just east of the St Francis river as it flowed north–south; here was a pine-covered hollow, about forty feet wide at the river and then tapering down narrowly for a length of about 300 yards. Those who ran for the canoes fared the worst, being shot down by the forty Rangers under Ogden posted at the river for this purpose; many got clear of the river bank in their boats only to be shot in the river while they tried to balance their canoes in the strong current. Some braves made a token resistance from doorways or windows but were soon despatched, allegedly chanting death-songs as they fell. Now it was time for the Rangers to torch the village. They hurled fire-brands and flambeaux into the huts, gutting everything except the three buildings Rogers had identified as containing corn. The Jesuit church was a magnet for plunder: the Rangers swept up the sacramental silver chalice and a silver image of the Virgin weighing about ten pounds. According to one report, the Jesuit priest Father Aubery was butchered while kneeling at the foot of the cross in the church, but this seems to be a later embellishment; the best evidence is that the priest who offici-ated at the wedding had already departed.

By about 6.10 a.m. the firing ceased. St Francis was now a smoking ruin, the air thick with smoke and the stench of burning flesh. Nothing is more controversial than the alleged death-toll. Rogers claimed he had killed 200 Indians, but we may safely discount such a high figure, as this would mean he had annihilated every last human being in the village. Clearly he was deeply mortified that he had not found and slaughtered the main body of Abenaki warriors and rationalised his rage and disap-pointment by claiming such a large body count. But the dominant Abenaki oral tradition, which claims only thirty killed, twenty of them women and children, cannot be accurate either, as it conflicts with a mountain of circumstantial evidence. Unfortunately the story of Rogers's raid on St Francis has become distorted and politicised by the ideologies and received opinions of the late twentieth century. Whereas in the nine-teenth century oral history was treated with contempt, there is nowadays a tendency to elevate it above archive-based sources. The facts, as we can see in the famous case of the conflicting narratives of Sir Samuel Baker and the people of Uganda in 1872, are that both European and indig-enous sources usually contain some aspect of the truth but neither should be treated as an oracle.

So, in this case, did Rogers kill 200 or thirty? Almost certainly the answer is neither. The figure quoted in Abenaki oral tradition cannot be right, for Rogers had the village surrounded, and his own casualty figures – one Stockbridge Indian killed, seven Rangers, including Ogden, badly wounded – suggests considerable resistance from a surprised foe. Besides, there is a mass of circumstantial evidence suggesting a higher Abenaki casualty rate, and the eyewitness accounts surely cannot have colluded to perpe-trate a falsehood. If just ten males died, who were all the people at the wedding and all those caught sleeping? There are many possible explanations of the huge discrepancy between the Abenaki and Rogers versions. Maybe only bodies found lying in the village were counted, and not those of the dead swept away in the river or burned beyond recognition in the flames; maybe casualties among the really old were not counted – only those of accredited warriors and nubile women and children. But the most likely explanation is that an original figure of thirty dead plus twenty women and children was converted into 'thirty dead *including* women and children'. If all the factors mentioned operated together, we could well approach a fatality number in three figures; the most likely number is somewhere in the region of fifty deaths.

At any rate the carnage and destruction were considerable, and the Rangers justified it by pointing to more than 600 scalps of whites dangling on lodge poles. Altogether Rogers took twenty-one prisoners, let fifteen of them go and rescued six captives of English origin: three of them were Rangers captured in earlier encounters; the other three were George Barnes of Durham, New Hampshire, a prisoner since 1756, a German woman from Dutch Flats and – most troublesome of all – Jane Chandler, who had been abducted at the age of five and now, full grown, was more Abenaki than white. She had been adopted by a chief and her Abenaki spouse had just been killed in the holocaust. Her biting tongue and hellion tactics infuriated Captain Jacobs, chief of the Stockbridge Mohegans and his twenty-three tribesmen with Rogers, to the point where they came within an ace of cutting her throat; unlike many of the Rangers, Jane Chandler survived and was taken back to Crown Point. But the most intriguing story of a white 'gone native' concerns Jonathan Dore, taken captive aged twelve at Rochester, New Hampshire, by a raiding Abenaki party. Brought up among the Abenaki, given a wife and made a full warrior, Dore actually took part on the Abenaki side in the blood-letting at Fort William Henry in 1757. The story goes that, tomahawk in hand, he seized a colonial by the hair and was about to finish him off when he recognised a friend of his boyhood and released him. What is certain is that Dore was fully adopted by the Abenaki, married an Indian wife and had a family, but was absent from St Francis when Rogers raided it. When he returned and found his family slaughtered, it seemed to sever all ties with the Abenaki in a moment. He returned to Rochester, married and settled in Maine, where he died in 1799.

The fate of the Indian prisoners taken by Rogers was less happy. Careful questioning revealed that most of them were willing to cooperate, which is partly why Rogers released fifteen of them unharmed. They revealed to him that there was a large party of at least 300 French troops and Abenaki not far downriver, expecting the Rangers' blow to fall on an Abenaki settlement on the Yamaska river ('river Wigwam Martinic'); and, from the discovery of the whaleboats, it was known for certain that the Rangers were at large. Interrogation of the captives on the circumstances of the finding of the boats matched in every detail the version Rogers had from his own Stockbridge Mohegans, so he knew he was not being lied to. His situation was very serious, with one hostile party at least advancing up the St Francis and the original bloodhounds still on his trail, perhaps even then descending the selfsame river. Rogers's scouts told him that Pissenne had run off into the bush during the killing, doubtless full of guilt and remorse, and would not be available to guide them on the return journey. Rogers thought he could get all the information he needed from three teenage Abenaki girls whom he was bringing back with him. This trio behaved circumspectly and survived the return journey, only to succumb to smallpox in Albany within months of the raid. It was a chief's wife, one of the extended Abenaki Gill family, who drew the full ire of Rogers' Rangers. Marie-Jeanne Gill appeared docile and later in the journey offered to lead a party of the raiders by a shortcut to Lake Champlain, but her real intention was to decoy them to the French fort at Île-aux-Noix. Doubtless unaware that the Rangers had compasses, she began leading them in the wrong direction, but the Stockbridge Indians at once noticed her treachery and slit her throat before the senior officer present, Lieutenant Jenkins, could intervene. The other two captives were also hostages, being two sons of Chief Gill, Xavier and Antoine. Both survived, and Antoine returned to St Francis having acquired some English schooling.

With the day now dawning clearly, Rogers was anxious to quit Odanak without a moment's delay, before the searching French parties found them. Ordering his men to fill their knapsacks with corn and to jettison all loot, he called a quick conference of his officers to confirm that the route to Lake Memphremagog was still the favoured one. All agreed that retracing their steps or trying to descend the St Francis river was suicide; even if they managed to catch one party of pursuers off guard, they would take casualties and be easy prey to another group, most likely the one that had been tailing them since Missisquoi. To ascend the St Francis to Quebec was also out of the question for the same reason, but Rogers told the released captives that was what he intended to do, and 'proved' it by striking north, intending of course to turn south at the fork in the river.

The Rangers marched fast that day, covering seventeen miles on a firm-surfaced Indian trail. Only when they were two miles past the 'ford' where they had waded across the St Francis on the way downriver did Rogers consent to pitch camp, and even then he allowed only five or six hours' sleep before pressing on again in the moonlight. By dawn, when they stopped for food, the trail, smooth to this point, started to become less so, with frequent wet patches. With the path petering out into watercourses, the Rangers started having to climb over or crawl under trees blocking the path. By now all the bologna sausage and rum was gone and food comprised mainly just mouthfuls of corn. Making fourteen to fifteen miles a day, they started to bear south-east, with the river moving in serpentine loops and the trail vanishing into bogs. On the fourth day out from St Francis they started to experience really tough going, with the hills getting steeper, the brooks more torrential and the boulders in them larger and more slippery. Six days out and they began to see real mountains in their path. By now even the corn was in short supply and those who had filled their knap-sacks with loot instead of food began trying to trade it, but without finding many takers. All the time northerly winds lashed them with freezing rain. After eight dreadful days they were relieved to sight Memphremagog, a beautiful narrow lake set among sawtooth hills.

It was now 13 October and across the lake the Rangers could see daunting mountain peaks ahead. They had hoped that, once at Memphremagog, Rogers would let them hunt and fish, but he insisted it was too dangerous and that they must press on. At this the Rangers came close to open mutiny. Another council of war was held and it was decided to split into small groups, both to have a better chance of finding and catching game and to baffle their pursuers. The rendezvous was still the same: where the Ammonoosuc ran into the Connecticut river opposite the Wells. How many detachments they split into is disputed: some said twelve, others, possibly more plausibly, ten. Some nominally independent groups thought better of their autonomy and stuck close to Rogers's tracks. Others, more boldly, decided to strike overland directly for Lake Champlain and Crown Point. One such was the group nominally commanded by Lieutenant Jenkins and mainly composed of the Stockbridge Indians. With them was Marie-Jeanne Gill and, when she tried to steer them in the wrong direction, the Mohegans cut her throat, as previously related. Maddened by hunger, the Indians then dismembered part of her body, roasted the flesh and ate it; the Europeans with them refused to touch the grisly meal and some died of starvation as a result, including Lieutenant Jenkins himself, who expired on the banks of the Missisquoi.

The Abenaki were also hot on the Rangers' trail. One war-party caught up with a band of about twenty, under Lieutenants Dunbar and Turner, and killed or captured nearly all of them. Ensign Avery, leading another party, also had a narrow escape, as related by Rogers: 'Two days after we parted Ensign Avery of Fitche's fell in on my track, and followed in my rear; and a party of the enemy came upon them, and took seven of his party prisoners, two of whom that night made their escape and came in to me next morning. Avery with the remainder of his party joined mine.' Two of the remaining five prisoners were later exchanged. One of these was Frederick Curtiss, who subsequently recounted that starvation had made his party unwary – they had subsisted on nothing but mushrooms and beech leaves – with the result that the Abenaki got to within a couple of feet of them before being observed. He told of rough treatment and beatings, and of the killing of a Ranger named Ballard, and named the two Rangers who escaped as Hewet and Lee. Two of the other prisoners were tortured to death in St Francis by Abenaki women. As a French source puts it, Canadians tried to save the captives but they 'became victims of the fury of the Indian women'.

Perhaps predictably, the party that fared best was the one commanded by Rogers, but there is much that is unclear about Rogers's route to the Connecticut river and many traditions, possibly apocryphal, have accumulated about the running fights he was supposed to have had with the Abenaki. In one version Rogers pressed on to Big Forks (modern Sherbrooke) where, realising that the Abenaki were in close pursuit, he devised a cunning stratagem. He sent a small detachment ahead to Little Forks (present-day Lennoxville) with instructions to build a huge fire and make the Abenaki think the main party was camped there. He then prepared an ambush on high ground at Big Forks, took the pursuers by surprise as they hurried forward to their would-be prey, and inflicted such heavy casualties on them that they gave up the chase. This sounds like a tall story concocted *a priori* from Rogers's manual with its recommendation for doubling back on pursuers, and Rogers himself does not mention such an engagement. But then there is the puzzling feature that the chief source for the story is an Abenaki chief, who would hardly have invented the account of his own defeat. All we know for certain is that after Lake Memphremagog, Rogers's group plunged into a labyrinth of hills and mountains, where a tourbillon of swirling winds seemed to blow in circles and confused rainstorms appeared to lash them from all directions at once. Survivors' accounts speak of streams turning at right angles, in steep chicanes or hairpin bends; at best the watercourses in this area were serpentine. Others speak of wooded ravines 200 feet deep, with turbulent streams at the bottom. Above all there was gnawing hunger, with nothing to eat but beech nuts, the occasional minnow scooped out of a pool, or a skimpy squirrel or cadaverous crow if they managed to get off a lucky shot. Rogers spoke laconically of 'many days tedious march over steep rocky mountains or through dirty swamps, with the terrible attendants of fatigue and hunger'. Even when the heavy rains stopped on 16 October, the clearer daytime weather brought severe nightly frosts.

At last, nearly dead of hunger, on 20 October they caught their first glimpse of the Connecticut Valley and soon they were in the Cohase Intervales, a fertile valley in two stages, first an upper shelf of flat land and then a second valley bottom. This was the first time they had come out of the woods since leaving St Francis. Emerging at the confluence of the Nuchegan and the Connecticut, they could see further great mountain ranges on the other side of the river; somewhere to the south the Ammonoosuc would flow in and they should be safe. Still with nothing to eat save groundnuts and roots, suffering from stomach cramps and bent over like old men, with wild, dark-ringed eyes staring from deep-sunk sockets and with deep grooves or furrows between the eyes giving them the look of bald eagles, the Rangers plodded down the Connecticut across rain-engorged tributaries, still finding no game. At last they picked up a blazed trail – the first since the long stretch from St Francis on the morning of the 6th – and finally they saw the imagined journey's end, the Ammonoosuc. By now starting to lose their balance from hunger cramps, the exhilarated men nonetheless quickened their pace, making twelve miles on 21 October and fifteen on the 22nd.

On 23 October they reached the rendezvous point but here was no cornucopia – only another starvation camp. They were the victims of fiasco, for Lieutenant Stevens with the relief column had been here, waited two days and then gone. From the smoke of recent fires that still smouldered Rogers reckoned that Stevens could not be more than two hours' march away, but in the present condition of the Rangers that might as well be two weeks. Stevens had done as instructed, taken men and provisions from Number Four up the Connecticut, but lost his nerve when Rogers was not at the rendezvous. Claiming it was too dangerous to explore farther up the Cohase Intervales, and clearly terrified that he would be the victim of a surprise attack, Stevens obeyed the letter but not the spirit of his instructions. He and his men went daily overland to the Wells river and fired shots as a signal. According to one barely believable account, on 22 October they fired their guns and heard answering shots. Rogers testified that his men heard a salvo and fired shots in reply, but that, unaccountably, was the end of the matter. Stevens's defence was that shortly after his men had fired their shots, two hunters appeared in a canoe and confessed that they had been firing, whereupon Stevens returned to camp.

When Rogers and the Rangers arrived at the rendezvous point to discover not only that there was no food, but that Stevens had actually been there and gone away again with the provisions, not surprisingly they gave themselves over to despair. As Rogers reported: 'Our distress upon this occasion was truly inexpressible; our spirits, greatly depressed by the hunger and fatigues we had already suffered, now almost entirely sunk within us, seeing no resource left, nor any reasonable ground to hope that we should escape a most miserable death by famine.' At the time Rogers hid his feelings, ordered his men to build fires and tried to encourage them by pointing out that they could now sleep their fill. Improvising desperately, he set them to work digging up roots and groundnuts, and prepared meals of *katniss*, a kind of tuber – 'the wretched subsistence as the barren wilderness could afford' – and boiled and cured *tawho*, the tiger-lily plant. Meanwhile Rogers began building a raft in which he hoped to float down to Number Four to get food. Heavy rains delayed its construction, which required a combination of alder, willow and red spruce; spruce roots knotted together functioned as ropes, and alder and willow shoots, laced from log to log and bound with the spruce roots, held the logs firmly in place; swamp maples were used as paddles. Rogers and the three men who were to accompany him lashed a spruce sapling across the middle of the raft, leaving a row of branches standing up like the teeth of a comb, and to these they tied their muskets, powder horns, knapsacks and blankets. Leaving Lieutenant Grant in charge and promising to return within ten days – without, however, saying what Grant should do if he did not – Rogers launched onto the river on 27 October. With him went the mysteriously recovered Ogden, one other Ranger and one of Chief Gill's sons.

They floated down the foaming waters, barely able to control the raft in the rapid current. The next day they came to the formidable cataracts of White River Falls, where the raft was swept into the rapids and destroyed; Rogers and his comrades were lucky to be able to scramble on shore with their muskets before the craft became uncontrollable. They watched despondently as the raft was tossed contemptuously among the white-flecked waves, shivered and then disintegrated into its constituent logs. Rogers takes up the story:

Our little remains of strength however enabled us to land, and to march by them [the falls]. At the bottom of these falls, while Captain Ogden and the Ranger hunted for red squirrels for a refreshment, who had the good fortune likewise to kill a partridge, I attempted the forming a new raft . . . Not being able to cut down trees, I burnt them down, and then burnt them off at proper lengths. This was our third day's work after leaving our companions. The next day we got our materials together, and completed our raft, and floated with the stream till we came to Wattockquitchey Falls, which are about fifty yards in length.

Here they paddled the raft into the shore before the current could catch it. Rogers then went to the bottom of the falls, stripped and swam out into the icy, seething waters to catch the raft, while Ogden tried to lessen the speed of descent by paying it out on a rope made of hazel withies. Rogers's account is notably understated: 'Captain Ogden held the raft, till I went to the bottom, prepared to swim in and board it down, and if possible paddle it ashore, this being our only resource for life, as we were not able to make a third raft in case we had lost this . . . I had the good fortune to succeed.'

Snow was beginning to wisp the first few flakes onto the trees when they re-embarked. On 31 October they came on a party of woodcutters, who gave them food and shelter and helped them to the fort. Within half an hour of arriving at Number Four, more dead than alive, the exhausted Rogers had sent provisions upriver to Grant and the Rangers, where they arrived four days later, ten days after Rogers had left them and to the very day he had promised. He also sent canoes with provisions to help any stragglers on other rivers such as the Merrimack, and it was as well that he did, for Lieutenant George Campbell's group had meanwhile gone through even worse nightmares than Rogers's detachment. Thomas Mante, who interviewed the survivors, gave this account in his later history of the war in North America:

These were, at one time, without any kind of sustenance, when some of them, in consequence of their complicated misery, severely aggravated by their not knowing whither the route they pursued would lead, and, of course, the little prospect of relief that was left to them, lost their senses; whilst others, who could no longer bear the keen pangs of an empty stomach, attempted to eat their own excrements. What leather they had on their cartouch boxes, they had already reduced to a cinder, and greedily devoured. At length, on the 28th of October, as they were crossing a small river, which was in some measure dammed up by logs, they discovered some human bodies not only scalped but horribly mangled, which they supposed to be those of some of their own party. But this was not the season for distinctions. On them, accordingly, they fell like cannibals, and devoured part of them raw; their impatience being too great to wait the kindling of a fire to dress it by. When they had thus abated the excruciating pangs they before endured, they carefully collected the fragments and carried them off. This was their sole support, except roots and a squirrel, till the 4th of November, when Providence conducted them to a boat on the Connecticut River, which Major Rogers had sent with provisions to their relief.

At Number Four, Rogers allowed himself two day's rest before starting back upriver. He wrote an account of his exploits to Amherst, working from memory since he had lost his daily notes, and also sent letters to all the towns and villages of New Hampshire asking for aid and succour for any of his men who might be found straggling there. On 2 November he returned to the Ammonoosuc, taking more provisions and search parties to beat the woods for his missing detachments. One detachment came in of its own accord, having gone down the Passumpsic Valley to the Connecticut river (some Rogers scholars even think Rogers travelled that way, but their evidence is not cogent). A few more men staggered in, and Rogers remained at Number Four until late November hoping there would be more until at last even he gave up and made the snowy journey to Crown Point where Amherst received him as a hero. Rogers's first missive from Number Four, written on 1 November 1759 and received in Crown Point six days later, had set off an explosion of euphoria, especially given his exaggerated estimate of the casualties he had inflicted on the Abenakis and the downplaying of his own losses. On 8 November Amherst wrote about Rogers's report: 'I . . . assure you of the satisfaction I had on reading it as every step you inform me you have taken has been very well judged and deserves my full approbation.' He ordered Lieutenant Stevens's arrest and his court martial was set for April 1760. At the hearing Stevens protested that Amherst had given him no definite time-scale and that he had exercised his (admittedly) faulty judgement in good faith. Amherst and the military command were in no mood to listen to excuses, especially now that the St Francis raid was being touted as the expedition that saved New England from future Indian raids. Stevens was found guilty and dismissed from the service.

Controversy has always dogged the Odanak raid. Undoubtedly many of the Rangers looted and pillaged like desperadoes, ransacked the church at St Francis and brought back silver-plated copper chandeliers, a solid sterling statue of the Virgin Mary, two golden candlesticks, an incense vessel, a gold case and many other valuables. For years there were stories of Rangers returning to the wilderness to find the stashes of gold and silver they had cached on the way home. There seems to have been some fire behind this smoke, for Amherst recorded in his journal for 24 December 1759 that some Rangers returned loaded with wampum and other trade goods, and that the estimated value of the loot Rogers's men brought back with them was $933. Scurrilous rumours ran round Crown Point that Rogers was a major beneficiary, that he had made a deal with the looters to let them have food in return for a cut of the loot and had then taken food from the starving to give to his accomplices in greed. Others said that Rogers made a fortune out of the raid by claiming to have advanced money to now deceased Rangers, which he insisted on having the army repay to him. But the principal charge against Rogers was that he waged a campaign of deliberate extermination against the Abenaki. Terms like 'genocide' have been flung about wildly, though these hardly square with the simultaneous assertion that Rogers killed only a handful at St Francis. In the moral scale there is little to choose between Rogers's murderous raid and the Abenaki 'massacre' at Fort William Henry in 1757 (and presumably especially so if we follow the revisionists and 'downsize' the casualty rosters in each case), though of course Anglo-Americans purporting to represent 'civilisation' hardly had the excuse that their overall culture warranted their actions.

The war in the wilderness of North America was a nasty, brutal, vicious war, fought without quarter on both sides. In strictly military terms, Rogers's raid on St Francis in October 1759 was pointless and gratuitous, especially when we consider that Rogers lost three officers and forty-six men of other ranks while probably inflicting scarcely any more casualties himself. It did not even stop the raiding, for the Abenaki hit back in June 1760 when they probed as far south as Charlestown, New Hampshire, and abducted the entire family of Joseph Willand. Perhaps the most sober judgement on Rogers' Rangers was that they were never anywhere near as good or effective as their legend requires them to be, though Rogers worked tirelessly to make them an elite guerrilla force, and that the French irregulars and their Indian allies were far superior as wilderness fighters. When the expedient exaggerations of Rogers's vainglorious self-publicity are diminished by careful historical analysis, he becomes no longer the colossus of frontier mythology, but a man of blinkered horizons, neither totally honest nor scrupulous; a less educated version of the Amherst Indian-hating type, yet endowed with boundless energy and a superhuman will. Of his physical courage there can be no doubt, but his greatest historical importance is that he acted as a role model for backwoods heroes and guerrilla leaders to come. On the one hand, we can see him as the spiritual forefather of Daniel Boone, Davy Crockett and Kit Carson; on the other hand, he aligns with John Brown, Lawrence of Arabia and Orde Wingate. One does not want to go as far as the Abenakis, who called Rogers *Wabo Madahondo* – the 'White Devil' – but he was clearly of the Cortés species, a man whose activities we deplore while admiring his courage. In any case, human beings do not live by historical fact alone, but also by ideology, collective images and mythology. This is why the events of October 1759 in North America, and the legend of Rogers and his Rangers, have made an indelible impression.

ELEVEN

QUIBERON BAY

'I was in great pain lest the enemy should have escaped you . . . Allow me to add that no man in England can be more pleased with your good fortune, nor more rejoice to see you reap those advantages from it which you so truly merit.' Admiral Hawke's letter to his fellow admiral on 14 September 1759, congratulating him on the victory at Lagos, must have been written with clenched teeth, for Hawke thought himself a better man than Boscawen and secretly resented the way his 'brother' officer had been given first refusal on the naval command of the expedition that accompanied Wolfe to the St Lawrence, and then been handed the Mediterranean command. In early September Hawke worried away about how he could sustain the close blockade of France's Atlantic ports. At the moment he and the Admiralty were involved in a wrangle with the naval victuallers. Hawke and Boscawen might be driven by dreams of glory, but the victuallers were entrepreneurs who cared about the bottom line. The new system of supplying warships at sea was hazardous and there was a high wastage and damage rate, which ate into the entrepreneurs' profit margins. Although Hawke was angry with the victuallers for their lack of patriotism, he realised that, with people outside navy discipline, conflict meant a war he could not win. He therefore issued two orders that in effect were a capitulation to the businessmen's demands. He ordained that any merchant sustaining damage while loading should issue a certificate for the damages to the ship's master, which would form the documentary evidence against which compensation would be paid. And he gave strict orders to his captains that they were never to impress seamen in the employment of the victuallers, who had a certificate of 'protected' status.

In September, then, Hawke was concerned mainly with the technicalities of continuing his innovation of close blockade. The French, by contrast, had to weigh the consequences of Lagos while still grappling with the implications of inter-service rivalry – that fatal malaise that had led them to assemble an army of invasion in one port and the accompanying fleet of warships in another. They had spent most of the year preparing an invasion force and supporting flotilla, hampered by money shortages, corrupt administrators and agents, and prima-donna admirals and generals, but so painfully protracted was the process that the enemy had had time to blockade the Atlantic ports and even master the art of revictualling at sea. Commodore Boys was patrolling outside Dunkirk, Rodney along the Normandy coast, Duff was watching Morbihan, while Hawke and Hardy hovered off Brest. Lagos was the writing on the wall and on any rational basis the French should now have jettisoned their invasion project. But there was a serious issue of credibility at stake. It was too late now to back down, and to disband d'Aiguillon's army would be to make a public admission of naval impotence. Besides, the invasion of Britain was supposed to be the master-stroke that would redress the calamitous losses in India, the West Indies and Canada. If this project was abandoned, what was the fall-back plan or worst-case scenario? The dreadful truth was that there was none. Not surprisingly then, after Lagos, Choiseul, Belle-Isle and Berryer bent all their energies to thinking up a new stratagem.

The odds against a happy outcome for France were massive, but a naval victory was not totally inconceivable and even one such triumph, followed by the landing of troops in Britain, could lead to an honourable peace. Louis XV and his ministers therefore decided to place all their bets on Admiral Conflans. This gamble was not totally unwarranted. Conflans had had his successes in the War of Austrian Succession and his record in the years 1740–48 was a good one; he had captured two ships of the line, one of them the prestigious *Severn* finally retaken by Hawke in October 1747. The Minister of Marine had marked him down as a possible star, promoting him from the rank of Lieutenant-General (thus leaving his eight peers behind him) to one of only two Vice-Admirals in 1756 and thence in 1758 to full Admiral, the only one at the top of the French naval tree. In the same year, in recognition of more than fifty valiant years at sea, Conflans received a baton as a Marshal of France, the first naval commander to be so honoured since Admiral Tourville in 1692. Such a promotion was supposed to be a reward for great exploits already achieved. It was an obvious objection to the theory, that Conflans had as yet accomplished nothing, but the marshalship was supposed to act as a morale-boosting fillip to the navy and as a strong hint to Conflans that great things were expected of him. On 26 August Conflans received his formal instructions from Louis XV, which basically enjoined him to get his fleet out of Brest and onto the open sea as soon as possible. Another set of instructions, of which Conflans must have been aware, was issued on the same day to Bigot de Morogues, who was to command a six-ship convoy assembling at

Morbihan, which was to act as the escort for d'Aiguillon's invasion force.

Meanwhile Choiseul continued his unhappy collaboration with Prince Charles Edward Stuart and his representatives. He summoned Murray of Elibank on 2 August for a full-scale dressing-down of the Jacobites and their 'Bonnie Prince', mentioning a number of indiscretions committed both by individual supporters of the Stuart prince and by the man himself. Some of the complaints were pointless rants about matters over which Murray had no control anyway, such as the allegedly stupid and brutal behaviour of members of the Irish Brigade in French ports. Choiseul explained that twenty-four million francs had already been spent on the invasion project but that, because of unforeseen difficulties with barges and transports, the expedition was behind schedule. But he advised Murray that d'Aiguillon would soon be leaving for his headquarters in Brittany and suggested that the Stuart prince come to Paris to confer with the commander before he left. Needless to say, Charles Edward ignored the advice and remained sulking in his tent; his only significant action was to write to Belle-Isle to complain that he had heard nothing of French plans and that his 'friends in England' were growing impatient. Both France and the Jacobites were exaggerating the strength of their position. Versailles had secretly already decided to take no account of the Prince in its invasion plans, though he did have more drawing power in Scotland than they realised. For his part, the Prince kept up a mantra about 'his friends in England', for whose existence no documentary evidence can be found – nor did the Prince provide it to ministers at the time.

When news of Lagos came in, Mackenzie Douglas, always a shrewder reader of the runes than Murray, immediately saw its likely implication: the French might press ahead with the landing in Scotland but they would certainly abandon the descent on the English coast. But, as ever, Charles Edward continued to insist he was not interested in any scheme that did not involve the French landing in England. When this message was conveyed to him, Choiseul immediately assumed that there was a complete lack of interest in the Scottish expedition and therefore asked Murray, presuming that the Prince did not wish to journey to Scotland, to get his master to issue a manifesto, calling on the loyal clans to rise. Murray replied that he was not authorised to make any such declaration; he would have to consult the Prince. Choiseul, wearying of Charles Edward's dog-in-the-manger attitude (he would not go to Scotland as in 1745 but did not want the French to go there without him either), decided to play him at his own double game. On 7 September he wrote to the Prince to tell him that all previous arrangements were unchanged (he even reiterated the tired old formula 'everything will be for and with the prince and nothing without him'). But three days later d'Aiguillon received from Louis XV a true statement of Versailles's attitude to the Jacobites: he was reminded forcibly that he was not to enter into any engagements whatever with the House of Stuart. A subsidiary anonymous memorandum contained the explanation: 'This prince has not a steady enough head for him to direct an enterprise so momentous or for anyone to direct it when advised by him . . . He is surrounded by very dubious persons of both sex who, it appears likely, betray him at every point.'

On 13 September, the day Wolfe was winning glory on the Plains of Abraham, Belle-Isle wrote to d'Aiguillon with further, more detailed instructions. After making landfall at Glasgow, d'Aiguillon was to march to Edinburgh and make that city his principal base of operations. Once safely ensconced in Scotland, a second army under Soubise would follow (it is perhaps significant that Belle-Isle did not spell out whether Soubise's army was still destined for England or had been switched to Scotland as the second wave). There are even hints in the letter that Belle-Isle was not entirely happy with the vanquished General of Rossbach being given such an important role, but both he and d'Aiguillon knew that Soubise was a puppet whose strings were pulled by La Pompadour. Two days later a personal letter from Louis XV, countersigned by Berryer, was delivered to Bigot de Morogues, captaining the *Magnifique*. He was ordered to take d'Aiguillon's force to the west of Scotland, having first circumnavigated Ireland, to make landfall at Irvine on the Clyde. After conferring with local pilots and fishermen, Bigot de Morogues was to decide the exact spot for disembarking troops, always of course in consultation with d'Aiguillon. If for any reason a landing was not practicable, he was to sail round the north coast of Scotland to make another landfall on the east coast, where the army would be disembarked. In case of a major setback, he was to burn his ships and proceed to dry land to serve under d'Aiguillon. Both memoranda were long on daring strategic vision but short on practical detail. The cynical conclusion would be that they were both textbook examples of vagueness, where nothing had really been thought through and everything left to chance. Micawberism as military planning would be a good title for the two documents.

The vain and self-regarding Conflans exploded when he heard of these memoranda. If Bigot de Morogues was given such an independent command, this would mean that his battle fleet would lose six men-of-war and, in his opinion, the French squadron even at full strength was no match for the Royal Navy. Moreover, without those six ships, the balance of power shifted subtly in favour of the army, so that in any joint enterprise d'Aiguillon, and not the Marshal-Admiral, would be the senior partner.

Conflans bombarded Choiseul, Belle-Isle and Berryer with letters of protest, revealing himself a true prima donna and principal player in the inter-service rivalry stakes. Choiseul and Belle-Isle were in a dilemma. They had, so to speak, put all their eggs in the Conflans basket, and so to repudiate him or fail to give him what he wanted quite obviously would jeopardise the entire enterprise. Conflans was confirmed as the supreme leader of the expedition, with Bigot de Morogues firmly under his command; there would be a united fleet and no separate naval support for d'Aiguillon. But since Conflans now had to engage the blockading British *and* escort d'Aiguillon's army, the ministers had to think up some ingenious way of squaring the circle. They came up with the lame suggestion that Conflans must attack the blockading squadrons but that, after that, it would be left to his discretion whether he kept to sea or returned to Brest, ready to make a fresh sortie when the Morbihan flotilla was ready. It was thought so important to keep Conflans sweet that on 14 October Louis wrote to his Marshal-Admiral, modifying his earlier (26 August) orders at the Admiral's request. So much for Bourbon absolutism. Tactful and almost deferential, the King reassured Conflans and reminded him that the paramount objective was the safety of the Morbihan flotilla. Louis included a Parthian shot by saying that, if Conflans were to accompany d'Aiguillon instead of Bigot de Morogues, he must then either go the whole way with him to Scotland or detach six warships (plus some frigates and corvettes) to convey the flotilla to safe anchorage in Scotland.

Meanwhile at Dunkirk a subsidiary expedition under the famous corsair François Thurot was being assembled. A protégé of Belle-Isle, Thurot had won a great reputation as an intrepid privateer. In 1757, in his flagship the *Maréchal de Belle-Isle*, named for his protector, and commanding a small group of frigates he had harried British commerce on the North Sea, the Irish Sea and the Baltic, perfecting the technique of never staying long enough in any one area to be tracked down by the Royal Navy. Sweeping in huge arcs from Lough Swilly in Ireland to Bergen in Norway and the Faeroe Islands, Thurot took many prizes and severely disrupted trade between Liverpool and North America. His success in 1758, when France was on the retreat in most theatres in the world, determined Belle-Isle to use him in the great 1759 invasion project. Lionised at Versailles, where he was received by Louis XV and became a great hit with the ladies, Thurot was in 1759 at the very peak of his achievement and reputation. Belle-Isle's idea was to employ him on a feint to Ireland that would keep the enemy guessing and that could bring him and his financial backers great riches. The conquistadores had gone to the New World to serve God and grow rich; Thurot, a latterday conquistador, aimed to serve France and grow rich.

Thurot raised the capital for his venture in an early example of public–private initiative, securing 500,000 livres from Berryer as the state's contribution and attracting large amounts of capital from private investors and banks in Paris, St Malo, Boulogne and Dunkirk. Apart from the forty-four-gun flagship, his flotilla contained the thirty-eight-gun *Begon*, the twenty-four-gun *Terpsichore* and the eighteen-gun *Amaranthe*, as well as a small cutter, the *Faucon*. Meanwhile 1,500 troops were earmarked for the Irish venture, under the command of Brigadier Flobert. Unfortunately, right from the start Thurot and Flobert did not get on. Flobert despised the great corsair for his humble origins and resented having to be under his command. When Belle-Isle realised that there was bad blood between them, he should immediately have replaced Flobert; instead, for reasons unknown, he simply decided that the two men should exchange copies of their written instructions. It was pellucidly clear from Louis XV's orders that Thurot was to be the unquestioned leader. But Flobert was not Thurot's only problem. The long wait at Dunkirk ate into his financial reserves and soon his creditors began clamouring for their money. It was only when the Prince de Soubise wrote a letter pledging payment of any debts incurred by Thurot that a Dunkirk merchant withdrew his threat to impound the *Maréchal de Belle-Isle* as surety for unpaid bills.

By the summer of 1759 Louis XV had another of his changes of mind. He decided to reinstate Soubise as commander of an expedition to England, and gave Chevert a consolation prize by making him Intendant of Dunkirk; there, if it was thought necessary to reinstate the Maldon *coup de main*, Chevert would be on hand. Now aged sixty-four, General François Chevert was, like Thurot, a man of no 'birth', the bravest of the brave and the toughest of the tough. Old enough to be Thurot's father (Thurot was just thirty-three in 1759), he was a good choice to liaise with the privateer and make straight his ways. Chevert was given the difficult task of ensuring that none of Thurot's creditors prevented him from leaving Dunkirk, while not appearing to flout the spirit of the law. When pressed hard by a Thurot creditor named Tugghe, Chevert passed the buck to Belle-Isle, who 'leaned on' the merchant as only an *ancien régime* grandee could, telling Tugghe he should waive his claims for the time being, 'it being very detrimental that Thurot's departure should be held up for any reason other than the winds'. Unfortunately, by the time Thurot was finally ready to sail, on 6 September, the British blockading squadron was in place outside Dunkirk, with Commodore Boys having three men-of-war, thirteen frigates and seven cutters on station outside the port. As a consequence Thurot's fleet sat idle in Dunkirk Roads, waiting for favourable winds, while all the time the embarked soldiers languished and fell sick in their cramped bunks aboard ship. By the end of September Chevert told Thurot that if the fleet did not get away soon, the troops would have to be brought ashore. As it was, when Thurot did get the chance to sail at a moment's notice, he had to leave 360 of his troops behind.

The contrast between the bickering, indecision, negativity and self-destructive impulses of the French and the aplomb of the British in the autumn of 1759 can hardly be over-stated. Between 21 August and 22 October the bellringers at York Minster were paid four times for celebrating victories, beginning with Minden and ending with Quebec. If anything, the British were over-confident. Pitt, animated by Minden, wanted to send 10,000 new troops to Europe and ostentatiously refused to be distracted from his objectives in Europe and North America by the French invasion threat. The Duke of Newcastle, who always fumed and fretted whenever an invasion threat from France loomed, thought Pitt rash to the point of folly and his words to his crony Earl Hardwicke on 25 October, reporting Pitt's triumph with the news of Quebec, do not sound entirely happy: 'No one will have a majority at present against Mr Pitt. No man will, in the present conjuncture, set his face against Mr Pitt in the House of Commons.' Pitt's argument, made again and again to a sceptical Newcastle, was that the habit of being mesmerised by French invasion threats was precisely what had led to the absurdly defensive strategy in 1756 and hence the loss of Minorca. The situation was utterly unlike that in 1745–46, both as regards the Jacobites and North America. In the War of Austrian Succession Britain had to abandon the conquest of Canada after taking Louisbourg, because the French hit back by invading the Low Countries. This time they did not have to worry about French designs on the Low Countries, precisely because of the reversal of alliances.

Hawke was still on ceaseless patrol outside Brest. Having perfected the technique of revictualling at sea, he was now mainly concerned with maintaining the health of his 14,000 sailors and, in particular, preventing scurvy. His correspondence with the Admiralty is full of references to beer, bread and fresh meat. Although the importance of vitamin C was not yet appreciated, the sailors' improved diet just enabled them to scrape by without contracting the dread disease. Although vegetables sometimes featured in the ships' menus, the all-important greens and citrus fruit did not; ironically apples, low in scorbutic acid, were plentifully supplied. Some have speculated that Hawke's personal hygiene-mania helped to ward off typhus, but whether the 'cleanliness is next to godliness' ethos of the Admiral percolated to the lower decks must be considered doubtful. But it is clear that Hawke had to battle throughout his blockade with dishonest provisioners and peculating officials: there are frequent complaints about the shortage of cheese and, especially, about poor-quality beer – often so bad that ships' captains simply ordered it thrown overboard. Bread was another problem: sometimes loaves were found to be crawling with weevils and maggots and thus threatening to contaminate all the good bread. Although the Admiralty responded to Hawke's complaints about the beer by ordering wine to replace it, they could do little to prevent swindling contractors supplying stinking and brackish water, and since it was customary on board to mix Guernsey wine with water, Hawke often found himself back at square one in terms of providing his men with a decent beverage.

By September the Royal Navy's efforts had shifted away from bottling up Conflans's warships to finding and destroying the transports. On 26 August, Hawke announced this new bearing in policy (explicitly mandated by the Admiralty) when he ordered Reynolds to cruise between Port Louis and Nantes and attempt to destroy the French flat-bottoms and other troop carriers; he was not to get diverted into chasing enemy cruisers. Reynolds began by blockading Nantes with a ship of the line and twelve cruisers. Evidently Reynolds did not act with the élan Hawke required, for in mid-September we find the Admiral proposing that Reynolds come under Duff's command. But before this change could be implemented, Reynolds reported that he was in pursuit of the Nantes transports, which had emerged from the Loire and given him the slip and, accompanied by three frigates, were sailing north to join the troopships at Vannes. Hotly pursued, the French found refuge at Auray, where Reynolds could not pursue them. Both Auray and Vannes were secure havens for Morbihan, an extensive inlet on the north-east side of Quiberon Bay, which was indented by shoals and islets, and led to Vannes and Auray by a series of narrow, twisting channels. To penetrate this labyrinth required the services of expert pilots, and none was available to the British.

Duff meanwhile arrived at the entrance to Morbihan on 22 September and conferred with Reynolds. Together they and other captains landed on the island of Meaban at the entrance to the Morbihan gulf and climbed to an eminence from where there was a clear view of the Auray river. Having viewed the maze for himself, Duff made the obvious conclusion that the Royal Navy could not harm the transports where they were; on the other hand, he could not see how the French could ever sortie from their fastnesses onto the open ocean. Duff therefore left most of his squadron in Quiberon Bay to watch the French flotilla and took up station in the *Rochester* with some frigates off the Île de Croix, where he could bottle up St Louis.

There was good news from other theatres. Although Rodney's attack on flat-bottoms in September had to be called off because of high seas, which threatened to smash his ships onto the coast, the endeavour confirmed his opinion that flat-bottoms could operate only on a millpond sea, and as autumn wore on there would be fewer and fewer of those. Then, at the end of September, Commodore Hervey directed a daring boat attack close to the entry of Brest harbour, engaged four ships in Camaret Bay and captured a schooner. The blockade was hurting the French badly, as they later admitted. Even at the simplest level, their matelots were cooped up in inaction and inertia while constant vigilance meanwhile kept Royal Navy crews at a high pitch of readiness.

One of the crosses Hawke had to bear was that the Admiralty constantly nagged him and tried to micro-manage his blockade, forcing him to pile up a mountain of paperwork in which he justified his every action. The Lords of the Admiralty put a negative 'spin' on Hawke's demands by giving out that he required a superiority in capital ships before he would take decisive action against the French. Anson and Hawke were particularly at odds over the putative threat from Bompart's West Indies squadron. Hawke's only concern was that this might try to reinforce Conflans at Brest, possibly catching the Royal Navy between two fires, but he felt confident enough to intercept Bompart if he made for Rochefort without breaking stride on the blockade of France's northwest coast. Anson, though, was adamant that Hawke had to have local superiority at Brest, and instructed him (with some asperity) that if Bompart did not interfere with the blockade and headed straight for Rochefort, Hawke should ignore him. Reluctantly accepting these orders, but hoping to make a virtue of necessity, Hawke decided to forget about Rochefort altogether and transferred Geary's squadron there to the Brest theatre, to reinforce his local superiority. In Hawke's opinion, the entire Admiralty brouhaha about Bompart was a storm in a teacup since, to move from the metaphorical to the actual realm, the hurricane season in the Caribbean (August–September) meant it was extremely unlikely that Bompart would soon sail for France anyway.

October saw the pace of French preparations quickening, especially when the Duc d'Aiguillon arrived at his command headquarters at the Jesuit seminary in Vannes. Conflans had a golden opportunity to clear from Brest in mid-October when ferocious storms battered the Royal Navy. Reynolds, on surveillance at Île de Croix, was forced to rejoin Duff at Quiberon Bay when heavy gales blowing continuously from 11 to 14 October obliged his ships to strike topgallant masts. The united force contemplated an attack on the transports in the River Auray as a way to turn the storms to immediate advantage, but a council of war on the *Rochester* on 15 October concluded that an attack on the Morbihan transports was far too dangerous, especially as the *Achilles* struck a rock and was nearly wrecked; treacherous or venal pilots were blamed for the mishap. Off Ushant, Hervey was buffeted by heavy gales from the south-west, which swept in on a long heavy swell. Forced back to the Lizard peninsula, he was however able to return to Ushant when the weather moderated and to report that there was still nothing stirring at Brest. Hawke, aware that his men were weary after six months' cruising in unpleasant waters, raised the blockade of Brest and returned to Plymouth, where he took the opportunity to lay in a three-month supply of fresh water. Normally the onset of winter meant an end to naval campaigning, and Hawke might have been confident that Conflans would not put to sea in such weather. But these were not normal times and nothing could be taken for granted. Ominously, when Boys was driven off station at Dunkirk by a violent gale on 15 October, Thurot took the opportunity to escape with five frigates and 1,100 men. It was perhaps fortunate for Britain that he was detained by bad weather in Gothenburg and then again at Bergen.

Since for five days (15–20 October) there were no significant forces investing the French Atlantic ports, why did Conflans not put to sea, pick up the transports and proceed to Scotland, especially as he had just received a direct order from Louis XV to counterattack the blockade at Brest and Morbihan? Conflans, though, was no seafaring buccaneer in the Nelson or John Paul Jones mould, but a by-the-book plodding precisian. He was still bombarding the Ministry of Marine with requisitions, refusing to put to sea until he was completely crewed and victualled. He pointed out that provisioning was a particular problem, since storeships destined for Brest had been driven by the Royal Navy into Quimper and the victuals then had to be unloaded and trundled for 100 miles over very bad roads to Brest. On 7 November Conflans wrote a letter to Berryer that positively drips with sarcasm: 'I see neither money nor ship's timber nor workers nor provisions. I am sure you made arrangements to deal with all these contingencies.' To an extent one can sympathise with him. The horse transports had been rotting away in the roads for the past three years and the battleships were not ready for action, except for the occasional star like the eighty-cannon *Soleil Royal* – state-of-the art warship and pride of the French navy. But Conflans was not just short of supplies and stores. Manpower was an even bigger headache, with Captain Guébriant of the *Orient* complaining that he had only thirty good seamen in his entire ship. It was all very well to press raw recruits, but they were incompetent at carrying out the complex battle manoeuvres necessary in any meaningful engagement with Hawke. Whatever the excellence of Conflans's reasons for delay, the King and the ministers at Versailles were tearing their hair out. Infuriated with Conflans, Choiseul tried to encourage d'Aiguillon by mendaciously assuring him in October that Sweden was secretly with France and was only waiting for the French landing in Scotland to show its hand and declare war on Britain.

The weather 'window' passed, and on 20 October Hawke resumed his station off Brest. His confidence was rising daily, especially when he learned that Conflans's ships were still nowhere near ready to come out, as all their topmasts and topgallants were still down. He also heard from Duff that, although there were now five regiments at Auray and eight at Vannes, all sixty vessels there had their sails unbent. Hawke had recently received reinforcements from Boscawen's fleet, and was particularly pleased to be joined by Captain Sir John Bentley, a veteran of both battles of Finisterre in 1747, a fleet captain in the Royal Navy, and recently knighted for his sterling performance at Lagos. The only irritant was that the Admiralty had now changed its mind on the Bompart squadron. It turned out that after all they did want Hawke to intercept it, so he suggested sending Geary back to Rochefort to do the job. Confident that his advice would be accepted Hawke sent Geary on his way, only to be forced to recall him when the Admiralty lords, possibly heeding Bocsawen, who thought Geary was an idiot ('a stupid fellow'), ordered Hawke to do so and suggested that he was not keeping the principal objectives (the blockades of Brest and Morbihan) clearly enough in the forefront of his mind. Hawke might have been justified in asking the noble lords whether the information about Bompart was meant to be taken at some metaphysical level only.

From the beginning of November it was the wind and waves rather than the tactical acumen of the rival naval commanders that determined the progress of the campaign. The volatility of the weather can be tracked in wind direction and velocity: westerly at the end of October, the wind then blew from the south-south-east on 1–2 November, from the south-south-west on the 3rd, from the south-west on the 4th and from the north-north-west on the 5th, when it began blowing a full gale. By this time Conflans was being deluged with urgent messages from Versailles, and Choiseul especially, demanding that at least the d'Aiguillon part of the invasion should be attempted, with Conflans picking up the transports at Morbihan before clearing for Scotland via the west coast of Ireland. Having evaded Hawke, Conflans was to blast passage through Duff's blockading squadron off Morbihan; if a general engagement became necessary, Louis XV would accept the risk. The Admiralty's spies intercepted Choiseul's latest letter and the order went out from Anson that all ships should converge at Brest for a general engagement. These orders reached Hawke on 5 November, just as the sea began making up alarmingly. On the very same day Conflans wrote to Minister of Marine Berryer that he was determined not to abort the invasion project but would try to avoid a general engagement at sea. Naturally, if caught he would fight hard and acquit himself well, but the evasion of Hawke by stealth remained the prime objective. Conflans's critics allege that this determination to avoid battle finally became an obsession, with disastrous results.

The bitter westerly gale of the 5th became a ferocious storm by the night of 6–7 November. Hawke's fleet was battered mercilessly by heavy squalls of wind and rain as it tried unsuccessfully to work to the westward. As the wind backed gradually from northerly to westerly, the damage to the ships increased inexorably, with split sails and damaged masts. Topgallant yards were got down and topsails close-reefed, but the heavy western swell bore the armada increasingly off station. On the morning of the 7th Hawke reluctantly gave up the unequal struggle and bore away for Torbay. Duff and the cruisers were left to watch Brest and to send a frigate to Torbay if Conflans sortied. Later the very same day the winds of storm that had sent Hawke back to England brought Bompart's squadron from the West Indies into Brest. Here was serendipity. Not only did Bompart learn from an unimpeachable source that Hawke's fleet was no longer blockading, but Conflans's crewing problems were solved at a stroke: although Bompart's vessels were no longer battle-worthy, he simply transferred the seasoned crews and the supplies and *matériel* to his own battle fleet. But the French wrongly concluded that Hawke had returned to England for the winter. Had the Duke of Newcastle had his way, this would indeed have been the outcome. Afraid that the fleet would sustain severe damage if it had to struggle further with the winter storms, Newcastle strongly counselled the path of discretion. But, after some warm exchanges of opinion, Pitt, adamant that Hawke must put to sea again, had his way.

In Torbay, Hawke chafed in inactivity and frustration. Although a period of rest and recuperation was necessary for the storm-tossed ships, many of which had suffered badly split sails, Hawke worried that this lull might play straight into Conflans's hands. But the hard gales of 10–11 November meant that getting out to sea was not possible. On the 12th the wind moderated, and Hawke momentarily hoped he could return to station. He cleared with nineteen men-of-war and two frigates, but he was barely into the Channel before the wind speed and wave height increased steeply. Faced with a south-west gale and a heavy swell, and with the warships again suffering split sails while not even out of sight of land, Hawke hung on grimly until the morning of the 13th when the savage state of the foam-flecked seas forced him to return to Torbay. At least there was some consolation, for Admiral Saunders and the Quebec fleet arrived back in England after a perilous Atlantic crossing. After his heroic work on the St Lawrence, Saunders would have been justified in taking leave, but he immediately volunteered himself and his ships for Hawke's service. The British Quebec fleet for the French West Indian one, Saunders for Bompart: truly all paths now seemed to be leading to Quiberon Bay. There was a general sense of anticipation in the air as Anson rushed additional workmen to Portsmouth and Plymouth to get every available warship ready for sea-going.

It was not until 14 November that the storms abated sufficiently to allow the first of Hawke's fleet to put to sea; many did not get away until the 19th. He was supremely confident in his own abilities and those of his sailors, whose morale, diet and health he had worked on so assiduously. Perhaps his only worry was that he had not been able to achieve a systematic charting of the French coast, so that he did not have an accurate picture of the reefs, shoals, fathom soundings, tides, anchorage grounds and batteries in all the Atlantic locations. Even as he toiled down the Channel towards Ushant on the 16th, Hawke met four victualling boats, whose captains informed him that Conflans had emerged from Brest on the 14th and the day before had been just sixty miles from Belle-Île, the large island off the coast of the Quiberon peninsula. Since it was obvious that the Admiral-Marshal was heading for Morbihan, Hawke sent fast cutters to all his captains to alert them that the prey was afoot. He wrote to the Admiralty: 'I have carried a press of sail all night with a hard gale at S.S.W. and make no doubt of coming up with them at sea or in Quiberon Bay.' The timorous Duke of Newcastle, who earlier glumly concluded that nothing could now prevent a French invasion – though he thought it was aimed at Ireland – wrote ecstatically to the Duke of Bedford: 'It is thought almost impossible that M. Conflans should escape from Sir Edward Hawke . . . As to fighting him, which is given out by the French, my lord Anson treats that as the idlest of notions.'

Once he cleared from Brest, Conflans stood away to Morbihan on a north-west breeze; he was just over 100 miles from his destination and had a 200-mile lead over Hawke. In his fleet were twenty-one ships of the line in three divisions, under Budes de Guébriant, St André du Verger and the Chevalier de Bauffremont; but, fatally, there were just five cruisers to watch for enemy movements. By midday on 16 November Conflans was halfway from his target, about sixty-nine miles west of Belle-Île. But that afternoon the wind blew in fiercely from the east and built up into a gale, with heavy, breaking seas. Forced to run before the wind, and unable to stop until they were 120 miles west of Belle-Île, the French in effect lost three days to the storm, being exactly in the same position three days later. It

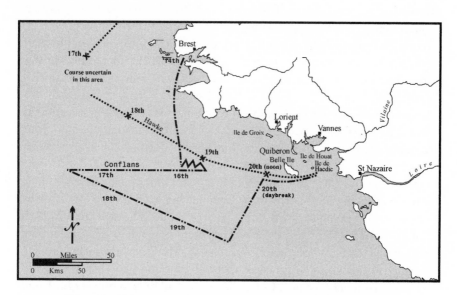

The Quiberon campaign, 14–20 November 1759

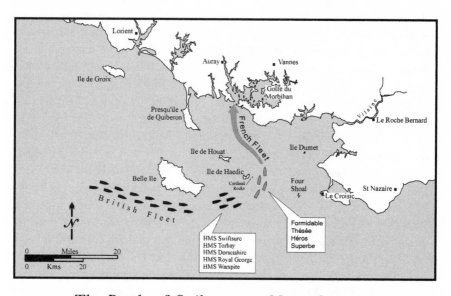

The Battle of Quiberon, 20 November 1759

was only on the 18th that Conflans could start reaching back, and even then not on a true course. The wind had settled in the north-north-east, which meant that to make easting he had to stand away far to the south. When the breeze died away on the afternoon of the 19th, he found himself becalmed about seventy miles south-west of Belle-Île. Incredibly, he was no nearer his destination than when he had been spotted by the British victualling ships on the 15th. Conflans has been bitterly criticised for his tardy performance but, although his crews may not have been as skilful as Hawke's, the adverse weather explains most of the delay. Some poor seamanship there may have been, but Hawke did not clock up a much better mileage with a superior fleet.

It was not until nearly midnight that the wind sprang up again, now blowing from the west-north-west. From having been becalmed, Conflans was soon once again exposed to the fury of a gale. The seas were so high that he dared not approach close to land, even though he had issued orders late on the 19th to prepare for landing at Morbihan the next day. He signalled to his ships to proceed under short canvas, to ensure they did not reach land before dawn. Compelled to reef all sails to prevent his being driven onto the shore, Conflans lolled perilously on the waves, hove to about twenty-one miles west of Belle-Île and there, at daybreak, Duff's five-ship patrol spotted them. The French had no difficulty in chasing off the patrol, but now the secret of their position was out. Fortune meanwhile had smiled on Hawke. At first the winds drove his fleet westward, but on 18–19 November, though variable, they were more favourable, so Hawke followed a south-easterly track. By now he was running parallel with Conflans on a north-north-east wind and got to within seventy miles of Belle-Île before the following wind ceased. By noon on the 19th he found himself beset by heavy squalls from the south-east, west by north of the island, flying double-reefed topsails. The gale that hit Conflans at midnight reached Hawke five hours earlier, so that at 7 p.m. he signalled the fleet to send up topgallant masts, shake out reefs and make for Morbihan under a press of sail. The night, which began with light south-westerly breezes and fine weather, ended with gale-force westerly winds, together with cloudy skies and heavy squalls. He held on until 3 a.m while Conflans was hove to, but was then forced to lie to until 7 a.m. with topsails backed. At dawn on the 20th Hawke was forty miles west by north of Belle-Île.

If there was a hero on the morning of 20 November it was surely Commodore Duff. There was nearly a disastrous breakdown in communication between him and Hawke, as the Admiral had sent a Lieutenant Stewart on the sloop *Fortune* to liaise with Duff, but Stewart reprehensibly got sidetracked into an attack on a French frigate. Only apprised at

3 p.m. on the 19th that Conflans was at sea, by superb seamanship Duff got his ships out to the open ocean. He discovered Conflans at dawn on the 20th and then led the French a dance back towards Hawke's fleet. When Conflans saw Duff's squadron, he ordered a general chase, with all ships cleared for action. Duff divided his squadron and stood inshore, sending half of his ships south and the other half north, hoping the French would disperse. Conflans took the bait and divided his force in three: the vanguard and centre were to pursue the two detachments of British frigates separately while the rearguard marked time and identified some strange sails just starting to appear on the seaward horizon. The French fleet was becoming badly scattered in the pursuit of Duff's vessels when they suddenly changed tack and veered off. To his horror, Conflans was now aware of Hawke's presence and frantically signalled to his own ships to abandon the pursuit of Duff and close up on the flagship. Hawke already had his ships in line of battle, all abreast 'at the distance of two cables asunder', and, seeing that the enemy was not in battle formation, immediately signalled a general chase. By noon the vanguard of the chasing Royal Navy vessels were just nine miles west of Belle-Île on a northerly bearing.

By now Conflans had signalled to his fleet to make for the entrance to Quiberon Bay in single file. For this decision he has been much criticised, especially by his own countrymen, and it is true that by this time he had allowed himself to be psychologically intimidated by Hawke, to the point where he feared the very thought of a sea battle, even though he was little inferior in numbers. His motives, as he later explained them, were three-fold. He feared that he was no match for Hawke in the open sea on a lee shore in bad weather. Secondly, he thought that if he got all his ships inside Quiberon Bay before the British could enter, he could haul to the wind, form battle line on the weather side of the bay and thus redress his numerical superiority. Hawke would then be put in the tricky position of having to decide whether to come in close and risk the myriad shoals and reefs. Thirdly, Conflans could then embark the army of invasion and wait for the weather to drive Hawke away, as it had done twice already in this autumn campaign. But most of all, he considered that Hawke would not pursue him in such wild seas; to fight during a storm was against all the precepts of naval warfare. As he put it to the Minister of Marine:

> The wind was very violent at west-north-west, the sea very high with every indication of very heavy weather. These circumstances, added to the object which all your letters pointed out, and the superiority of the enemy . . . determined me to make for Morbihan . . . I had no grounds

for thinking that, if I got in first with twenty-one of the line, the enemy would dare to follow me. In order to show the course, I had chosen the order of sailing in single line. In this order I led the van; and in order to form 'the natural order of battle' I had nothing to do but take my station in the centre, which I intended to do . . . as soon as the entire line was inside the bay.

Certainly it was against all the canons of naval warfare to fight a battle in such weather. Under a thunderous cobalt-grey sky the *Royal George* crowded on sail in pursuit of the French, spray scudding from her bows as she drove before the wind. Hawke was pushing as hard as he dared, and his officers anxiously scanned the cracking and heaving canvas above them. All hands stood ready at sheets and braces, and the decks were cleared for action. At about 10 a.m. the *Royal George* shook out the second reef in her topsails and set studding sails. Seeing land ahead – which he took to be Belle-Île – Hawke hoist his colours and ordered the topgallant sails set, a very risky manoeuvre in such high seas. Hawke's other ships did not find his hard driving easy to accommodate: the *Magnanime* sustained damage in the topgallants and had to slow for repairs. The atmosphere in the other vessels is best described as controlled panic. Several ships stove in their launches and longboats and jettisoned them, while the *Burford* threw its livestock overboard. At noon the wind was blowing so hard that the *Royal George* was forced to take in two reefs in her foresails. As Hawke explained conditions to the Admiralty: 'All day we had very fresh gales at north-west and W.N.W. with heavy squalls. M. Conflans kept going off under such sail as all his squadron could carry and at the same time keep together; while we crowded after him with every sail our ships could carry.'

Conflans might have been justified in thinking that the enemy would not attempt to follow him into Quiberon Bay – even if high seas were not running, there were simply too many Royal Navy ships. And there were other rational grounds for his action. All he had to do was wait until the next westerly gale blew Hawke off station, which would enable the invasion flotilla to come out. French critics always think Conflans should have fought and risked his fleet to put Hawke out of action. Against this was the consideration that, even if the two fleets knocked each other out, there were still dozens of Royal Navy frigates left to destroy d'Aiguillon's transports. The fallacy in Conflans's thinking was, however, twofold. For even if he was not being pursued by his most deadly foe, how did he hope to get all *his* ships through the narrow harbour entrance while such a ferocious storm was blowing? And, however strategically sound Conflans's ideas, in war so much depends on the unexpected. Doubtless nobody could have foreseen that Hawke would hurl himself onto a lee shore with a press of sail, when the shoreline was known to be studded with reefs and shoals. But a commander must always try to read his opponent and gauge his desperation. Here was Hawke, who had been itching to finish off the enemy since the beginning of the year, and obsessed with the notion that he was plagued by supernatural ill luck. Conflans should have known Hawke was desperate, and a desperate man, like a gambler, will risk the entire pot on a single throw.

If courage is the art of taking minutely calculated risks, Hawke was a great practitioner of the art. Ever since Finisterre in 1747 he had been working on a range of battle orders that would cover every contingency. Part of the fleet drill was that in a general chase the warships nearest the enemy should form line of battle and engage without regard to their position in the overall battle line; as new ships came up, they would also engage without worrying about their regular stations. Since Howe was now in the van with seven men-o war, these conditions were fulfilled. Undeterred by the weather, Hawke hoist his flags and set topgallant sails, despite the rising sea, and the other ships were compelled to follow his example. This was an extremely dangerous manoeuvre and, like everything Hawke did that day, strictly against the book. There was nearly an early disaster, for Keppel carried so much sail that water poured into his lee ports and he had to come up into the wind very quickly to avoid capsizing. All this time the wind speed was increasing from the west-north-west, with heavy gusts, driving rain and sudden squalls. Not even Hawke dared to flout the odds in such conditions, so he very soon took in his topgallant sails, while ordering them reset the moment the wind abated.

The result of Hawke's headstrong, risky pursuit was to wreck Conflans's plan for getting all his ships to safety before the British could engage. Making way with perilous rapidity on a rising sea, Howe in the *Magnanime* began to gain on the enemy. Conflans realised he might not have time to get all his ships inside the bay and then form line under the shelter of the western shore. Now it looked as though the French would not have time to haul to the wind and come about. To his incredulity, the rising gale, high seas and dangerous lee shore coruscating with rocks and shoals did nothing to make the British slacken their speed, and the *Magnanime* and *Royal George* were even prepared to set their topgallants. The Bay of Biscay was in full ferocity, with pyramidal waves, a heavy swell and foam-flecked confused seas, where the dark green of the ocean, the grey of the 'white caps' and the lowering black clouds on the horizon produced an atmosphere of Stygian gloom even at midday. The menacing seas found their complement in the rocky shore – one of the most dangerous of all Atlantic coastlines. The French were making for the entrance to the bay between Dumet Island and the Cardinal rocks to port – the last of the long range of rocks and islets that continue the Quiberon peninsula; beyond that was a lee shore sticklebacked with reefs. By noon Hawke was off the south coast of Belle-Île and could see huge breakers smashing against the cliffs. In the distance he could make out the foam-drenched Hoedik rocks and the surf-beaten Cardinals. A heavy breaking sea was crashing over the Guérin and other rocky banks flanking the approach to the southern entrance to Quiberon Bay, which lay between the Cardinals and the Four shoal to starboard, a perilous rocky bank about seven miles east-south-east.

For two hours the Royal Navy steadily closed the gap between their vanguard and the four ships in the French rear – *Formidable, Thésée, Héros* and *Superbe*. At around 2 p.m. the leading vessel in the British van, the *Coventry*, came under fire from the French. But as the French stood in for land, Howe, commanding the British van, signalled to his crews to keep their nerve and refrain from firing back until they were close enough to touch the muzzles of the enemy guns. But the gunners on HMS *Warspite* disregarded the orders and, without any word of command from their captain (Sir John Bentley), opened up on the hindmost enemy ship, which was out of range. It was about 2.30 p.m. when Conflans in his flagship the *Soleil Royal* reached the Cardinal rocks. As he entered and hauled round them, Conflans heard the sound of gunfire and realised that his slow rear had been caught. The four French ships toiling along eight to ten miles behind their Admiral were now being attacked by nine Royal Navy warships. Conflans, who had already committed the grave error of not using his flagship as a focus around which his other vessels could cluster, now committed another by not turning round and going to their rescue; there was still time to save the rearguard before Hawke's main force came up. His excuse was that when he saw the rearguard giving a good account of itself, he thought it could escape without his help. Moreover, he could not turn round until he had shown the way into Quiberon Bay to the ships immediately behind him.

By this time, isolated and abandoned, the four French ships in the rear were fighting tigerishly against the nine men-of-war in the Royal Navy van. By about 2.45 p.m. *Magnanime, Swiftsure, Torbay, Dorsetshire, Resolution, Warspite, Montague, Revenge* and *Defiance* were within gunshot of the French, with Hawke and the rest of the British fleet about six miles behind. Just before 3 p.m. the *Revenge* engaged the eighty-gun *Formidable*, flagship of Rear-Admiral St André du Verger, but the Frenchman stood away to rake the *Magnifique*, which soon had its topmast and foreyard carried away. The captains of the *Dorsetshire* and *Defiance* decided that their colleagues were strong enough to deal with the French rear and overtook them, taking fire as they went, hoping to catch up with Conflans. Soon after the action began, the elements took a hand and a heavy squall struck both fleets, with the Royal Navy ships taking a particular battering. The *Temple* was forced to double-reef her topsails; the *Dorsetshire*, with lee ports under water, had to luff in order to clear the water between decks; and the *Torbay* almost broached to and took so much water in the lee ports that the captain had to bring her up in the wind with all speed. At about 3.17 p.m. Hawke's fleet was hit by such a heavy squall that the *Chichester*'s fore-topsail was carried away. The *Magnanime*, *Warspite* and *Montague* ran foul of each other, and in the collision all three lost jib-booms and sprit-sail yards. The *Montague* later reported the loss of jib-boom, spritsail, spritsail-topsail yard, driver boom and spare anchor as well as severe damage to the main chains and quarter.

The collision of the three Royal Navy ships momentarily halted the pursuit, but once the *Magnanime* got clear she overhauled the *Formidable* and engaged her in ferocious combat. Soon joined by the *Warspite*, the Royal Navy ship began to make steady inroads on the *Formidable*'s defences; in half an hour, despite much heroism, the French ship was fought to a standstill. But the *Formidable*'s stupendous performance should never be forgotten: completely surrounded, she battled on like a wounded panther, taking fire from successive ships. The admiring British assailants reported that she looked like a gigantic colander and still continued to fight, though virtually a floating wreck. At about this time the *Magnanime* detached to pursue the seventy-four-gun *Héros*, which had been in the thick of the fighting and had lost fore and mizzen topmasts. As the French vessel tried to make off for the south, the *Magnanime* overhauled her and raked her. The *Chatham* too came up, and shortly afterwards the *Héros* struck its colours. The devastation wrought by the *Magnanime* was such that every officer down to the rank of midshipman had been killed. There were 400 dead and wounded on board, the helm was shot away and the decks were strewn with wreckage. The surrendered *Héros* came to anchor but the gale was so fierce that no boats could be lowered to board her.

Just before the *Héros* struck, an even greater disaster hit the French. Shortly after 4 p.m. the seventy-four-gun *Thésée* bore down to engage the *Torbay*. Manoeuvring in a giant swell, both ships took the imminent risk of being swamped in order to use their main batteries. The French ship blasted four of the enemy sails and had the better of the gunnery, but Captain Kersaint de Coetnempren of the *Thésée* lacked Keppel's brilliance as a seaman. Keppel flung the *Torbay* round into the wind as soon as water began to burst into his gun-ports. But the *Thésée* suddenly shipped an enormous sea through the cannon holes, capsized and went to the bottom in seconds. Kersaint, one of the rising stars of the French navy, perished alongside 650 of his men; only twenty-two survived. Horrified by the sea's cruel treatment of a fellow mariner, Keppel launched boats into the seething sea-cauldron. His courage was matched by the grit of his tars: one boat's crew picked up nine French survivors and floundered in the savage sea until after dark, when it finally found its way back to the *Torbay*. Part of the problem here was that Keppel after his narrow escape took his ship alongside the stricken *Formidable* to finish her off, administering the *coup de grâce* with a double broadside. On board the French ship were scenes of horror. After seeing his ship's fore-topmast shot away, the wounded Duverger continued to direct operations from a chair on the quarterdeck until he received a fatal shot; his brother then took over and was shot in the same way; finally a second captain assumed command until he too was killed; then at last the *Formidable* struck, to the *Resolution*. It was no more than a floating carcass, its decks littered with corpses and torn to pieces by bullets and cannon-shot.

The saga of woes of the ships in the French rearguard was not yet ended. By this time the running battle had taken the combatants to the edge of the Cardinals where Conflans in the *Soleil Royal* had emerged at the entrance, still hoping to form his ships up in battle line or at least to double the Four head near Croisic and thus draw the English fleet away onto the open sea. The attempt to form line just inside the bay soon had to be abandoned as a total disaster; Conflans did not even manage to take up station in the centre. Before he could draw up his ships in a tight, defensive formation, they all had to be inside the bay, and they were not. Then the *Magnanime* swept into the bay, with French assailants swarming around her like killer whales around a rorqual. Before long other Royal Navy ships had come to her rescue, but by then Conflans's would-be defensive line was thrown into confusion by a fresh development. The wind shifted to the north-west, making it impossible for the French to go about. They were now in a funnel with rocks on one side and the Royal Navy on the other.

With fifty ships of the line crammed into an area five miles long and six and a half broad, hemmed in by islands and shoals, Conflans's fleet had no room to manoeuvre. There was a press of French ships in the bay, with the Royal Navy slavering nearby and the whole drama being played out under a grey, darkening sky, lit up by fires and mottled by clouds of smoke. Thousands of spectators, who had run out from Croisic and nearby villages, watched as the British and French ships rolled heavily on the great ocean swell that had followed them into the bay. Total confusion reigned and in places seemed likely to turn into pandemonium. A French officer wrote: 'The confusion was dreadful when the van, in which I was, tried to go about. Part could not do it. We were in a funnel, as it were, all on top of each other, with rocks on one side of us and ships on another.' Seeing that it was impossible to form a defensive line, Conflans opted for the escape scenario. Having now definitely decided to make for the open sea, accompanied by two other ships, he was making rapidly for the exit when Hawke in the *Royal George* rounded the Cardinals. Conflans was unlucky. On the way out he had shot up the *Swiftsure*, destroying her fore-topsail yard and causing her to broach to; in the open ocean this would have been the end of her. Taking additional damage in her tiller rope, the *Swiftsure* limped out of action, and lay to under a mizzen – the only sail she had left to set. But the ten-minute delay in sweeping her out of his path meant that Conflans did not get clear before Hawke spotted his ensign.

Hawke ordered the *Royal George*'s master to lay her alongside the *Soleil Royal*. The master protested vociferously that, in failing light and with a rising sea, such a manoeuvre was madness. It was then that, according to legend, Hawke made his famous reply: 'You have done your duty in apprising me of the danger; let us next see how well you can comply with my orders. I say, lay me alongside the French Admiral!' Hawke's flagship caught up with Conflans and his flotilla at about 4.25 p.m., only to receive a heavy broadside from all three French ships. The two flagships exchanged broadsides, but then swept past each other as more ships became sucked into the confused mêlée, partly by osmosis, partly because they were uncontrollable in the weather. Astern of Hawke's vessel other ships (the *Union*, *Mars* and *Hero*) were coming up to help him. Seeing Hawke manoeuvring to rake Conflans, the seventy-gun *Intrepide*, the only survivor of the five French ships in the rearguard, interposed itself between the two flagships and took the full force of the murderous gunnery from the *Royal George*. At 4.41 p.m. she sank almost instantly, dragging down with her 630 Breton sailors. There were no survivors and the tragedy was made more poignant as these were poor, conscripted peasants who had never been to sea before Conflans cleared from Brest. The fact that Captain Monthalais was himself a Breton did nothing to assuage the depression that fell on north-western France, as Brittany mourned its lost sons for months.

Meanwhile, while manoeuvring to avoid being raked by the *Royal George*, the *Soleil Royal* fell to leeward and then, in trying to tack, fouled two of the ships following her. Consequently she was unable to weather the Four and had to run back and anchor off Croisic. It was now past 5 p.m., the dark of a winter's night had descended, it was blowing harder than ever and high seas were running even inside the bay; outside in the ocean enormous waves were building up. Hawke considered his options. Ahead of him lay the wave-besieged shore of Dumet Island, while close at hand and uncharted were the killer rocks and shoals of Croisic; even more peril lay to the south in the form of a seething chaos of breakers and combers washing around the dangerous Four shoal. All around him were unknown reefs and shoals just waiting for an unwary vessel, while outside in the Atlantic it sounded from the din of crashing surf as if the world was coming to an end.

Hawke had been lucky so far and he knew it; but he also knew when to cut his losses and not push his luck. At 5.30 p.m. he hauled down the signal for engagement, though not all his captains heeded the signal, continuing the fight until around 6 p.m. in their eagerness to prevent the enemy's escape. Some of the Royal Navy ships thus came within an ace of running aground in the dusk. Finally, just after six o'clock, all firing ceased. It was said that the very last shots fired were by *L'Orient*. Then Hawke gave the signal to anchor – two guns fired from the flagship, without lights, so that only the vessels directly adjacent to the *Royal George* knew where it was anchored. Most of Hawke's fleet anchored between Dumet Island and the Cardinals, but a few spent the night at rest in another part of the bay, while some intrepid souls (*Swiftsure*, *Revenge*, *Dorsetshire* and *Defiance*) actually stood out to sea.

Both sides spent the night in some anxiety and uncertainty, but the French were most beset by gloom. All that terrible day they had endured the moaning of the savage gale, the ceaseless rattle of blocks and creaking of yards. While the storm crashed around them, the infernal din was counterpointed by the slatting of canvas and the clatter of sheets, the booming of guns, the crash of falling spars, the shivering and splintering of woodwork, the groans of wounded men and the shrieks of poor souls drowning in the foam-flecked brine. Even the pitch, roll and yaw of the ships and the thrumming of backstays had been an agony to their taut-stretched nerves. And now they had to face the uncertainty of a hellish, black night. The French were the first to crack. Seven of their ships, led by Villan de Brosse in the *Glorieux*, tacking to avoid the rocks and shoals they at least knew about and which lay all around them, made their way deeper and deeper towards the estuary of the River Vilaine. Another French ship, the *Juste*, got out of the bay and headed north to the Loire estuary. Since both captains (the brothers Saint-Allouarn) had been killed, the First Lieutenant took command and managed to navigate the vessel out onto the open sea. They survived the storm and struggled all night to repair the smashed rigging and plug leaks but in vain. Next morning they had a fair wind for entering the Loire and made for St Nazaire. Miscalculating the falling tide and thus coming too close to land, the *Juste* struck a rock, pitching its complement into the sea. Although the crew took to the boats as the ship broke up, only a handful of the 630 men on board survived – and again the dead were all Bretons.

Unknowingly, Conflans had anchored right in the middle of the Royal Navy vessels and when morning came would be easy prey. There was no hope of rescue for eight ships were already out of the reckoning, seven in the Vilaine river and another a wreck on the Brittany coast. The masters of these ships had at least acted for the best according to their own lights. But in the case of Conflans's deputy, the Chevalier de Bauffremont, the suspicion of cowardice, incompetence or dereliction of duty must be entertained. Bauffremont's pilot warned him that to stay in the bay in the middle of reefs and shoals was supremely hazardous and advised him to make for the open sea. Bauffremont (on the *Tonnant*) conferred with his nearest colleague, Captain Guébriant of the *L'Orient*, whose pilot gave him the same advice. Concluding that Conflans 'must have' been similarly warned and must therefore be exiting the bay, Bauffremont, without sending out boats to try to locate the flagship, simply headed out to sea and sailed down to Rochefort. He claimed to be astonished to discover both that five vessels from the fleet were already there and that Conflans was not one of them. Taxed with running away, Bauffremont pointed out that a return to Brest was out of the question because of contrary winds, and that six ships (including his own) from three different divisions in the fleet had all independently come to the same conclusion he had reached; they had not all arrived at Rochefort together. Moreover, he was simply obeying standing orders, which stated that in the aftermath of a lost battle a captain should always steer for the nearest unobstructed port.

The morning of the 21st dawned, still stormy. The bulk of the Royal Navy fleet was anchored about three miles from Dumet Island at the mouth of the Vilaine river. To his astonishment, Hawke saw the *Soleil Royal* anchored nearby and only eight other French vessels in sight, beyond and inshore of the British line. Finally understanding his desperate position, Conflans slipped anchor and tried to reach Croisic Roads where there were protecting batteries. Hawke sent the *Essex* in pursuit but both she and her quarry ran aground on Four shoal, hard by the *Héros*, similarly disabled. This was now a veritable graveyard of ships, for at 10 p.m. the night before the *Resolution* had also struck a reef here and run aground. Hawke meanwhile weighed anchor and gave the signal to attack the other French ships in the Vilaine. But it was blowing so hard from the north-west that he finally considered the attempt suicidal and struck topgallant masts. With the aid of the storm and a favourable wind, the French vessels managed to cross the bar into the Vilaine river – a feat they could probably not have achieved in any other weather conditions; as it was, they had to jettison all guns and gear to get to safety. The conjuncture of the tides and the freak high-water level in Quiberon Bay combined to provide a unique, unrepeatable opportunity.

All that day the gale raged ferociously and unceasingly. Not until evening did Hawke dare even to lower boats to rescue the crew of the stricken *Essex*. It was only on the 22nd that Hawke sent in three ships to finish off the *Soleil Royal* and the *Héros*. Seeing the British about to descend on him, Conflans set fire to his flagship and escaped; he did not even tarry to save the magnificent artillery on board. The British arrived and boarded the blazing flagship but had no time to do more than carry off the golden-rayed figurehead. Duff's men then completed the French discomfiture by burning the *Héros*. Hawke worked up as far as the Vilaine estuary and even found an anchorage, but concluded there was no way he could reach the other French ships. Duff and his captains reconnoitred the lower reaches of the Vilaine in small boats and at first there was some hope that they could send in fireships, but this later proved chimerical. The French ships were now, at any rate, out of the war, though some did return to service a year later. Hawke now proceeded to tighten his hold on the Brittany coast. He sent Keppel with a flying squadron to investigate French ships said to have taken refuge in the Basque Roads, but these vessels proceeded up the River Charentin, out of reach of the Royal Navy, so Keppel returned to Quiberon Bay. And he seized Belle-Île, a wonderful base for raids on France's west coast.

In the euphoria of victory Hawke did not observe the precise rules of warfare as understood by eighteenth-century international law, and this embroiled him in an acrimonious and abrasive correspondence with d'Aiguillon. Although he sent the French wounded ashore, he reserved the right to extract the big guns from the *Soleil Royal* and set about their removal. D'Aiguillon and his second-in-command, the Marquis de Broc, protested that the *Soleil Royal* and the *Héros* had never struck, so that Hawke could not claim them and all their contents as lawful prizes of war. When Hawke disregarded the protests, d'Aiguillon ordered local militia-men to open fire on any British working parties attempting to remove artillery from the *Soleil Royal*. Matters quickly escalated: Hawke opened fire on Croisic and threatened a systematic bombardment if his men were attacked again. He then seized the Île d'Yeu, halfway down the coast to Rochefort, destroyed its defences, rounded up all the cattle there and slaughtered them to feed his hungry sailors. At the end of the year Hawke returned in triumph to England, handing over the continuing blockade of Quiberon to Boscawen.

Quiberon Bay was one of the great naval victories in world history. It may lack the totality of Nelson's later triumphs at the Nile and Trafalgar, if only because many of the French ships never got into the fight; and it was not a decisive event in the sense that Salamis, Actium and Tsushima were. It did not even have the obvious drama of Lepanto. But a sea battle fought in a violent storm will surely remain a unique event in all the chronicles of the ages. Hawke never really got the praise he deserved and there is even something defensive in the way he described the battle to the Admiralty:

> In attacking a flying enemy, it was impossible in the space of a short winter's day that all our ships should be able to get into action or all those of the enemy brought to it . . . When I consider the season of the year, the hard gales on the day of the action, and the coast they were on, I can boldly affirm that all that could possibly be done has been done. As to the loss we have sustained, let it be placed to the account of the necessity I was under of running all risks to break this strong force of the enemy. Had we but two hours more daylight, the whole had been totally destroyed or taken; for we were almost up with their van when night overtook us.

At Quiberon, Hawke lost two ships and 300–400 men. The French lost five, including their flagships *Soleil Royal* and *Formidable*, and more than 2,500 men, most of them drowned. Additionally, four of the seven vessels that had taken refuge in the Vilaine ended up with their backs broken. Essentially Hawke's victory was the result of superior seamanship and his readiness to risk all to defeat the enemy. His was a stunning achievement in such weather. Ungenerous critics say that Hawke was above all lucky in meeting the victuallers when he did near Ushant, while Conflans lost three days to gales. But against this counterfactual can be set another, which says that if Hawke had not arrived at Quiberon Bay until 22 November, he would have entered the bay and won an even more spectacular victory while Conflans was trying to embark d'Aiguillon's invading force. Certainly Hawke always attracted contrary opinions. At the very moment of his victory, the British mob, frustrated with the lack of a decisive breakthrough, was burning him in effigy. When news of the victory reached London it was of course a different story. Horace Walpole wrote to his confidant Mann: 'You would not know your country again. You left it a private little island, living upon its means. You would find it the capital of the world. St James's Street crowded with Nabobs and American chiefs, and Mr Pitt attended on his Sabine farm by Eastern monarchs, waiting till the gout has gone out of his foot for an audience.' For all that, Hawke himself was ill requited. He was awarded a £2,000-a-year pension, but nothing else. Since Pitt did not like him and Anson was jealous of him, he waited in vain for further recognition for his triumph at Quiberon. After Finisterre in 1747 he had been raised to the peerage, but the ruling elite, still full of Wolfe-mania, ignored a far greater hero.

But for Conflans and the French, Quiberon was an utter catastrophe. The general opinion in France was that Conflans deserved to live in eternal infamy for the events of 20 November 1759. Opinion in the streets of Paris was inflamed, but not more so than in Brittany, where the people turned violently against the whole idea of foreign invasions; in Vannes the locals tore down theatre posters and would not allow the actors of the Comédie Française to perform for d'Aiguillon and his officers. Conflans lamely told Berryer that he had done his best and acted with 'firmness and wisdom'. The problem, in his view, was the quixotic attempt to mount an invasion in winter. To d'Aiguillon the day after the battle he was blunter: 'What can we do with such marked naval inferiority? At least this debacle should put an end to these ill-coordinated land and sea combined operations.' He left the navy soon afterwards and died, forgotten, in 1777. Conflans was a mediocre by-the-book admiral who did not seriously confront his own errors. Obsessed with avoiding a battle at all costs, he was indecisive for the whole of 20 November. First he headed towards the enemy, then he fled in such haste as to leave his rear unprotected. Once at Quiberon he dithered again: first he wanted to get inside the bay, and then he wanted to get out. As the true hero of the day on the French side, Saint-André du Verger remarked: 'The circumstances of this day's work are a disgrace to our Navy, and show only too well that it has but a handful of officers with initiative, courage and skill; that nothing else will do but to reorganise the service from top to bottom, and to provide it with commanders who are capable of commanding.'

Yet the real villain of 20 November was Bauffremont, who disobeyed standing orders and also the particular command from Conflans that he should never lose sight of the flagship. He was later accused of having deliberately ignored signals from Conflans out of jealousy and personal dislike; the fact that he was aided and abetted by Bigot de Morogues, still smarting after Conflans went above his head to Choiseul, adds circumstantial colour to the charge. That Bauffremont acted like a coward or a dullard seems scarcely disputable; the only serious argument is about whether he was guilty of treason or just terminally stupid. Bauffremont's protestation that he acted on his pilot's advice is irrelevant, if that meant ignoring explicit orders. But he soon added bluster to his other blemishes and indignantly wrote to Berryer to know why he was being cross-questioned. When Berryer on 1 December ordered him and all the ships at Rochefort to clear at once for Brest, Bauffremont sulkily replied that it was impossible, yet he would try to perform the miracle requested. On 21 December he sent a long screed of apologia to Berryer. Surely his action in sailing for Rochefort, thus saving eight ships, was better than staying with Conflans, where these vessels would either have been gutted or bottled up, useless, on the Vilaine? He then got on his high horse and declared that he should by now have had Berryer's express commendation for what he had done. Bauffremont remained completely unapologetic and, in a bellicose letter to Choiseul in 1762, demanded to know why he was being held responsible for the disaster at Quiberon when French commanders genuinely responsible for debacles like Crefeld and Minden were never censured. The Ministry of Marine formed its own opinion on Bauffremont and made him wait until 1764 for the Lieutenant-Generalship he solicited two years earlier.

The contrast between the mild treatment of Conflans and Bauffremont by France and the savagery meted out by England to Admiral Byng in 1757 is clear. One shudders to think of the likely treatment of Bauffremont by the Admiralty. His self-defence (all the later blustering aside) was essentially twofold: he always obeyed orders but did not see Conflans's signals; and he exercised the sort of discretion that he imagined his leader was even then exercising. But Bauffremont really could not have it both ways. If he was not in command, then he had to obey Conflans's orders; the transparent fiction that he did not see the Marshal's signals fooled nobody, and he was anyway under a strict professional obligation not to lose sight of the *Soleil Royal*. He also overlooked his clear duty as chief of squadron – which was to inform all ships in his division of his decision to run for Rochefort. He could not therefore logically state that other captains took the *sauve qui peut* decision to run for Rochefort independently, but he did so because it was one of the main planks of his defence. Bauffremont therefore stands convicted on a number of moral counts. He neglected his duty both to his superior and his subordinates and sinned against discipline and against the honour of the French Marine. Like other captains guilty of dereliction of duty he forgot the cardinal rule: all initiatives must not be independent but within the context of the Commander-in-Chief's general orders. By trying to exculpate himself with a number of different arguments, Bauffremont simply impaled himself with self-contradiction.

Bauffremont probably escaped court martial only because Berryer had more important things on his mind. On 25 November he informed d'Aiguillon that the expedition to Scotland was officially suspended. The troops at Morbihan, almost atrophied from months of inaction, were given furlough. However, because of the continued presence of the British on the Atlantic coast, d'Aiguillon's army was not disbanded and transferred to service in Germany, but broken up, cantoned, dispersed along the coast and used to repel invaders in Brittany and Gascony. The Basque roads and Belle-Île were now being used as anchorages by the Royal Navy who were so confident of quasi-permanent occupation that they used several islets as extended vegetable gardens. The mighty French fleet had been humiliated and, like the German Grand Fleet after Jutland, never put to sea again during the Seven Years War. Although naval captains and Jacobites continued to lobby Versailles to attempt an invasion of Britain with unescorted transports, the ministers had gone sour on 'descents'. The debacle at Quiberon played into the hands of those members of the Council of State who wished to concentrate on continental warfare, and even Berryer's prime interest in the ships that had got away to Rochefort was to disarm them so that he could save money.

For Pitt, Quiberon was the victory that set the seal on the year of victories. 1759 had been like a dream for him. He had made the Royal Navy the pivot of his global strategy and had been successful beyond anything he could have imagined. Seapower had enabled him to win the struggle for the West Indies, to defeat France in the battle for mastery in North America and to devastate all Choiseul's counter-offensives. With Anson and Hawke, a talented team, he had successfully introduced the innovation of a fleet-in-being, for no armada like Hawke's had ever been at sea for so long, or would be again for forty years. Britain was now incontestably a great power – perhaps the greatest of all time at this moment – and controlled the world's sea lanes: to North America, to the Caribbean and to the Orient. Pitt's triumph gave new heart to Frederick of Prussia, currently at the nadir of his fortunes. By diplomatic finesse had kept Spain out of the war, though Pitt knew that Spain was still fearful that Britain was now all-powerful in all theatres, and that ill-considered schemes, such as Newcastle's ambition to control the Baltic by seapower, were likely to alienate her and make new enemies. Even so, Anson was able to announce that in 1760 the Royal Navy would have an unprecedented strength of 301 ships and 85,000 sailors. But most of all, Quiberon destroyed for ever any lingering hopes of a Jacobite restoration. Bonnie Prince Charlie might sulk in his lair at Bouillon, like Achilles in his tent, but no deputation of despairing French Achaeans would ever visit him to beg him to re-enter the fray.

The one minor blemish on the Royal Navy's glorious record in 1759 was its inability to track down Thurot. It will be remembered that British cruisers withdrew from Ostend in mid-October, allowing Thurot to escape. The thinking was that even if he broke out, he must be making for Newcastle or the east coast of Scotland, so he could easily be picked up later by vessels cruising between Yarmouth and the Dutch island of Texel. But on 17 October Thurot and his ships, with 1,100 troops on board, gave the English frigates the slip and vanished into the mists of the North Sea. He then entered the Kattegat strait and anchored at Gothenburg on 26 October, declaring: 'I am here for political reasons and out of caution.' The circumspection was warranted. Commodore Boys learned from the Dutch that Thurot had headed north-east from the Texel and therefore made straight for Edinburgh with eight frigates; another squadron was stationed off Yarmouth just in case Thurot tried to double back and make a landing on England's east coast. But by now the secret of Thurot's real destination was out, leaked both by British agents in Dunkirk and in Gothenburg. The Duke of Bedford, Lord Lieutenant of Ireland was notified accordingly. Meanwhile Thurot wrote confidently to Belle-Isle: 'Do not be surprised if you hear nothing from me for a very long time; I am planning to lose the enemy. The advancing season may delude the English into thinking that the project is abandoned. All these preparations are necessary because of the preparations which the English have undertaken.'

On 14 November the French fleet sailed from Gothenburg, only to be caught next day in a ferocious storm, which scattered the ships. In accordance with the secret instructions Thurot had given to each of his captains at Dunkirk, he headed for Bergen, designated as the first rendezvous point in the event of separation; failing that, there would be a second rendezvous in the Faeroe Islands. In Bergen Thurot waited for three weeks with four ships, hoping in vain that the *Begon* and the *Faucon* would rejoin him. But the masters of these two vessels had sustained such heavy damage in the storm that they disregarded Thurot's instructions and sailed haltingly back to Dunkirk. The loss of the *Begon* was an especially heavy blow, since she carried 350 men – a quarter of the landing force. Yet Thurot decided to press on, pausing only to write to Belle-Isle 'to expect no further news of me, but of my success or total destruction.' He cleared from Bergen on 5 December but did not fetch the Faeroes until 28 December, battling high seas and severe gales all the way. Supplies were running low and the men were suffering from the unbearably cramped conditions below deck. Mutiny was in the air when a council of officers voted almost unanimously on New Year's Day 1760 to turn back. But Thurot insisted that the honour of France demanded a landfall in Ireland and in this he was backed by Cavenac, Flobert's second-in-command.

Thurot took on what provisions he could and waited for favourable winds. Finally, on 26 January, the four frigates set sail for Ireland and, four days later, sighted the northern coast. Again short of food, Thurot decided to attack the city of Derry (Londonderry) but once again the winds and waves were against them, so that it was 7 February before they reached the entrance to Lough Foyle. At a council of war Thurot laid out his plans: he would land Flobert and the troops outside the city, while he sailed into the port to destroy enemy shipping. But Flobert refused to go along with the plan, claiming that the landing point was too far from Londonderry and they would be attacking the town blind, in total ignorance about the size of its garrison or the strength of the defences. Grudgingly he agreed to a modified plan, whereby 200 men under Cavenac would support Thurot's attack on the harbour. For three days Thurot waited for favourable winds that would waft him into Lough Foyle, but in vain. When a breeze did finally appear it was in the form of an adverse wind, followed by a gale, which drove the ships far to the north; once again the fleet was scattered and the *Amaranthe* took advantage of the excuse provided by storm and separation to set a course for France round the west coast of Ireland. Seriously short of provisions and now down to three vessels manned by near-mutinous sailors, Thurot reluctantly agreed to abandon his attack on Londonderry. He ordered a return to Bergen, prior to a homeward track down the North Sea, but only after the army commander on the *Terpsichore* told him that his ship intended to return to France, whatever commands Thurot gave.

On 13 February the winds reversed their direction, so Thurot announced that the ships would make their way home through the Irish Sea; in reality he was still hoping to find a pretext for another attempt on Londonderry. Colonel Rusilly, the contumacious commander on the *Terpsichore*, saw what Thurot's game was and led an outright mutiny, forcing the ship's captain to steer away to Scotland. An angry Thurot brought the *Maréchal de Belle-Isle* alongside and threatened to rake her unless Rusilly surrendered. The *Terpsichore* struck and it was agreed that Thurot's orders would now be obeyed, provided he landed to take on provisions. Thurot agreed and secretly set a course for Londonderry. But Flobert was no fool and discovered they were not on a track for France. There was another crisis, this time with Flobert threatening to arrest Thurot and take over command himself. When Thurot defied him to do his worst, Flobert tried to get his Grenadiers to arrest Thurot, but they hesitated and, while they were still undecided, Thurot read out Louis XV's instructions, making it clear that his arrest would be an express act of mutiny attracting the death penalty. The revolt subsided, but the sailors and soldiers remained sullen and uncooperative, so Thurot reluctantly gave the orders to set course for Scotland.

He reminded Flobert, however, that there was no question of being able to land troops and seize provisions – the option open to them in Ireland – since Louis XV's express orders forbade any attack on Scotland, as a possible ally; all they were allowed to do in Scotland was pay for supplies by cash or credit. Flobert gloomily accepted that they would have to return to France via the Irish Sea.

Once again Thurot duped his followers. On 20 February he informed Flobert that he intended to enter Carrickfergus Bay that evening, prior to an attack on Carrickfergus and Belfast. His motive was not so much the glory of France, which he urged his officers to uphold – there had been a gloomy dinner on the evening of 15 February while anchored off the Scottish island of Islay, when a local MacDonald laird gave them news of Quiberon – as loot; the money paid to ransom a city like Belfast would surely be considerable. As a corsair, Thurot was also a businessman and he realised that if he returned to France empty-handed he would be a ruined man. Once again Flobert opposed the plan, but finally agreed to a landing on the understanding that Carrickfergus alone should be attacked; Flobert argued, plausibly enough, that they lacked the manpower to overwhelm both Belfast and Carrickfergus at the same time.

On 21 February French forces at last set foot on Irish soil. The remaining 600 men were given the last of the brandy before rowing ashore in longboats. The local British commander, Colonel Jennings, had only 200 men to defend Carrickfergus, but decided to make a stand. The British defenders were soon flushed out of the village of Kilroot and the French pursued them into Carrickfergus, where they quickly gained control of the town except for the castle, into which the British troops retreated. When the French guardsmen tried to break down the gates of the citadel with axes, they took such heavy casualties that they soon withdrew, Flobert being among the wounded. Since Cavenac was absent, Commandant du Soulier now assumed command. He threatened to raze the town if the garrison in the castle did not surrender. Jennings did not like the odds and was soon induced to sign articles of capitulation.

But things were not working out well for Thurot. He had lost nineteen men killed and thirty wounded during Flobert's absurd charge of the gates and still there was no likelihood of substantial financial returns, unless he pressed on to Belfast. Once again Flobert objected, arguing that his own soldiers were too weak to march to Belfast; that the garrison there was at least 600 strong; that the local militia was being called out; and that Carrickfergus could not even supply them with enough food as it was. Thurot therefore sent a message to Belfast, demanding food. The Mayor of Belfast agreed, but stalled, hoping for reinforcements to arrive. General

Strode, commanding the Belfast garrison, did not think his men were strong enough to hold out and sent urgent pleas for reinforcement to Bedford in Dublin. Bedford received the news with consternation. He had stationed all his troops in the south of Ireland, expecting that d'Aiguillon might land there, and since Quiberon had assumed that the heat was off. He wrote to Pitt that he should expect the fall of Belfast and said he would not reinforce it, since he suspected a French feint prior to a main blow that would fall on Dublin or Cork. Meanwhile at Carrickfergus Thurot's anger with Flobert's intransigence boiled over into an irate slanging match, with both men threatening court-martial proceedings when they got back to France. Flobert displaced his rage onto the Mayor of Belfast. When supplies had still not arrived on 23 February, he sent the Mayor a threatening letter promising the stone-by-stone destruction of Belfast if the provisions did not arrive by 10 a.m. next day. The Mayor sent a single wagon full of salted beef; this was the only food the French obtained during their entire stay in Ireland.

Despairing of making any further progress, seeing his bluff called, unaware of Bedford's pusillanimous attitude and fearful that it must be only a matter of time before Royal Navy vessels found them, Thurot reluctantly began re-embarking his men on 25 February, but he did not manage to complete his sailing preparations until the evening of the 26th. In the end it was midnight on the night of 27–28 February before he cleared from Carrickfergus Bay, as he was detained by strong contrary winds. They were only four hours out to sea when Thurot's worst fears were realised: three thirty-six-gun Royal Navy frigates came upon them. Seeing that flight was impossible, Thurot signalled the *Blonde* and *Terpsichore* to rally, but they bolted, leaving the *Maréchal de Belle-Isle* to fight alone. Abandoned so ruthlessly, Thurot knew his only chance lay in boarding one of the frigates and capturing her; the troops on board his ship, evidently superior to anything the frigates possessed, made this seem anything but quixotic. But before he could implement this plan, the British gunners disabled the *Maréchal de Belle-Isle*, shooting away both the mizzen mast and the bowsprit. Thurot's ship started taking on water and was likely to sink but he refused to strike, despite the fervent pleas of his officers. He was urging his gunners to fire a final broadside when he was shot in the chest and killed instantly. The British commander, Captain John Elliott, ordered Thurot to be buried at sea and took the floating hulk of the *Maréchal de Belle-Isle* as a prize. He reported five British dead and thirty-one wounded as against 250 French casualties; 1,100 French prisoners were taken to Whitehaven, Belfast and Kinsale.

Thurot's raid, uncannily prefiguring the landing in Ireland in 1798 of

Humbert and the French with similarly small forces, achieved nothing significant either militarily or financially. Some historians have claimed that Thurot might have been able to achieve great things, had he had a military commander of talent instead of the useless Flobert, an officer so lacklustre that even Cavenac, his deputy, openly despised him. But the real effect of the Irish venture was on French morale. Like the Hoche landing in 1796 and the Humbert adventure two years later, it proved that the Royal Navy was not infallible and that it was eminently possible for French forces to land in the British Isles. France went wild with joy over the capture of Carrickfergus – a joy only slightly dented by news of Thurot's defeat and death. His exploits conjured up memories of the great days of the French corsairs, when men like Jean Bart, Dugay-Trouin and the Comte de Forbin were much-feared figures in the Channel. France had once again shown that it was not only England that could produce Francis Drakes. Thurot was installed as a great hero in the French pantheon, a position confirmed even in the Revolutionary era of the 1790s. Madame de Pompadour may have exaggerated when she said that France would have won at Quiberon if Thurot rather than Conflans had commanded, but it is true that he represented a kind of indomitable fighting spirit that would next be seen in the person of John Paul Jones. For all that, Carrickfergus in 1760 was no more than a sideshow to a sideshow. By the main battle at Quiberon the British had made themselves masters of the world.

CONCLUSION

1759 effectively made Britain the global superpower of the eighteenth century; it was the first time a genuine British Empire could be discerned, and it laid the foundations for the dominance of the English language in the modern world. Although British victory was not officially acknowledged until the Treaty of Paris in 1763, the rest of the war consisted in 'mopping up' operations.

Although 1760 saw a hard-fought campaign in Canada, with the French at one point coming close to retaking Quebec, the issue was never really in doubt, and the fall of Montreal led to the surrender of New France. In India Sir Eyre Coote won the decisive battle of Wandiwash in 1760, and Lally and the French surrendered Pondicherry early in 1761, ending France's stay on the subcontinent. In the West Indies, Martinique, which had evaded capture in 1759, gave up the ghost very rapidly when faced with a second British invasion in 1762. Everywhere the French were in retreat, and the process did not end even when Choiseul finally manoeuvred Spain into the war on his side. Although Spanish participation in the conflict ended Pitt's hegemony – for he resigned in pique when his colleagues would not agree to a pre-emptive strike on Spain before she entered the war – almost the sole effect of Charles III's commitment to his Bourbon cousin Louis XV was that he sustained terrible losses in his overseas empire: both Havana and Manila went down to British naval superiority in 1762.

One clear sign of British global mastery was the plethora of rebellions against their suzerainty in the 1760s and the hard-nosed imperial backlash and crackdown. The fall of Pondicherry in 1761 and the Battle of Plassey in 1757 delivered all of eastern India to the triumphant East India Company, which in 1765 effectively replaced the Mughal Empire as the supreme power on the subcontinent by obtaining the *diwan*, allowing it to collect directly the revenues of Bengal. When sepoys had struck the year before, 'John Company's' servant Hector Munro blew them to pieces with four six-pounders. While the Indian peasantry paid half their crops in rent, the weavers, silk-winders and other skilled craftsmen were forced into debt bondage or introduced to the new, draconian disciplines of the factory and the Industrial Revolution. While the year 1769 saw the import into Britain of 700,000 pounds of silk, double the previous year's import, India itself suffered a famine in which one-third of its population perished. Perhaps the very last year when there was any real hope for a non-British India was 1763, when Mir Kasim was defeated. But India was not the only cockpit for the struggle between the new master of the world and the subjugated peoples who were destined to provide the labour on which British capital would feed. Tacky's Rebellion in Jamaica in 1760, the Whiteboy movement in Ireland (beginning in 1761), Pontiac's Indian Rising in Michigan (1763–66), land wars in the Hudson Valley in 1765–66 and the outbreak of 'regulators' in North Carolina (1765–69) were all direct or indirect responses to the definitive appearance of Britain as the first global superpower.

Why were the British so successful in the Seven Years War? Some economic historians attempt to explain it all by the ease of access to credit. It is true that Britain found it easier than France to raise loans but the French managed to raise them nonetheless under a more cumbersome financial system, so this new version of economic determinism does not carry us very far. One is tempted to emphasise sheer contingency more, and to pose the questions asked by counterfactual history. The Battle of Quebec, for example, is a battle that Montcalm should not have fought, or at least not when and how he fought it; had he waited for reinforcements, he would probably have won. There is really no other explanation for the lacklustre military performance of French commanders than sheer historical bad luck in terms of the conjuncture of the war. Britain had Clive, Wolfe, Hawke and Boscawen; France had Lally, Vaudreuil, Soubise, Contades, d'Estrées and Conflans. It is more than interesting to compare French military performance in the War of Austrian Succession, fought in the previous decade, with their poor showing in the Seven Years War. Marshal Saxe was a military genius and the Comte de Lowendahl was a highly talented general, but no such figures appeared in 1756–63.

To contrast Britain and France in the Seven Years War is to compare two oligarchic elites, one united and self-confident, the other riven by conflict, factionalism and self-doubt. The continuing struggle between King and *parlement*, the devout and the *philosophes*, the ultramontane Catholics and the anti-Jesuits, when combined with the endemic factionalism of Louis XV's Ministers of State, fatally weakened French decisionmaking, resolution and morale. Some historians have even alleged that

France during the years of the Seven Years War teetered on the edge of civil war or a premature outburst of the revolution that swept away the Bourbons after 1789. Although the hagiographic accounts of William Pitt have been overdone, and the consensus now is to see him as leader of a hard-working team rather than an individual maverick of genius, he headed a remarkably single-minded and even ruthless War Cabinet. Pitt cut the powers of his commanders-in-chief in a way that Louis XV never contemplated; weak, indecisive and vacillating, Louis could always be talked round by La Pompadour in favour of one of her protégés, however useless; the case of Soubise is the most obvious one. Pitt's ruthlessness comes through above all in his attitude to the struggle in North America. When it became clear that numbers alone could not achieve victory – as was evident when Montcalm at Fort Ticonderoga in 1758 defeated 15,000 attackers with just 3,800 defenders – Pitt threw money at the problem. He spent £5.5 million on the army, nearly £1 million on the navy and more than £1 million on paying colonial assemblies for their troops, reversing the policy of his predecessors and virtually bribing the North American colonists to cooperate with him; it has been estimated that in 1755–60 France spent just one-tenth of that total sum.

France could have matched that sum – a fact that the 'economic determinism' account of British success overlooks – but chose to dissipate its resources on a two-front war. Although modern historians affect to disdain the older ideas about Madame de Pompadour's baneful influence on the Seven Years War, nobody has convincingly explained the rationale of the famous 'reversal of alliances' or why a pointless war in Germany waged against Prussia was perceived to be in the national interest. A ditty current in France during the war expressed some of the bitterness felt on this issue:

> Let us shed all our blood for the queen of Hungary;
> Let us give her all our money for Silesia;
> At least she knew how to truckle to Pompadour.

Louis XV's stubbornness in defence of the indefensible was notable. When Choiseul's predecessor as Foreign Secretary, Cardinal de Bernis, tried to raise with the King in 1758 the question of whether it was wise or expedient to persist with the continental war when France was in imminent danger of losing her colonial possessions abroad, Louis cut him off brusquely: 'You are like all the rest, an enemy of the Queen of Hungary.' What is astounding is that Louis should have acknowledged that all thinking people were against the European war but that he was determined to persist with it.

Britain decisively won the war, but at huge cost to herself, and some of these costs enabled France to strike back in revenge in the 1770s, but without ever regaining her global position. Pitt effectively mortgaged future generations to achieve his year of victory in 1759. The Jacobites may not have understood credit and finance but they were not entirely wrong when they harped on about the crushing burden of the National Debt. In the eighteenth century British ministers financed their frequent wars with long-term loans which led to spectacular increases in the annual budget. Incremental expenditure occasioned by the War of Spanish Succession amounted to 74 per cent, by the War of Austrian Succession 79 per cent, and by the Seven Years War close to 100 per cent. In other words, the British government had to double its budget to pay for the war and this could only be done by new loans and new issues of bonds. The National Debt rose from £74.6 million in 1756 to £132.6 million in 1763 – a staggering and in the view of some, a ruinous, increase. The wartime tax burden had to be sustained after the war to cover the interest charges and this led the government in search of new taxes, often with catastrophic results. Ministers began gently with a cider tax – provoking an uproar in the west of England – but soon they had unleashed a plethora of new taxes, most of them designed to make the North American colonies pay for their own security: the Sugar Act, the Stamp Act, the Quartering Act, and so on. These taxes were peculiarly ill-judged as they meant in effect the reassertion of metropolitan control over North America, coming immediately after Pitt's generous, and even pampering, treatment of the colonies. And following the removal of the French threat in North America by the Seven Years War, it is very clear in retrospect that the end of the road in the New World would be the revolt of the colonies. Yet even without the crisis precipitated in North America by new taxation, British ministers had a delicate financial balancing act to pull off. By 1760 customs and excise duties amounted to 68 per cent of all government revenue. Since British workers could only consume the heavily taxed imports of sugar, tobacco and tea if they were in regular employment, British exports were vital, so the government was forced to pursue mercantilist policies contrary to the main economic currents of the age.

The summing-up is simple: no 1759, no victory in the Seven Years War; no victory in North America, no expansionist British Empire, no break-away colonies and therefore, conceivably; no United States of America. The consequences of 1759 were momentous; it really was a hinge on which all of world history turned. And so, although there would be worrying developments for the rest of the century, which would enable Napoleon to stage a partial French comeback after 1798, so that the British Empire was not on a totally secure footing until 1815, it is easy to appreciate the national mood at the end of the year of victories. The eighteenth century had a tradition of Christmas pantomimes or farces, and in December 1759 the great hit was David Garrick's *The Harlequin's Invasion*, a mixture of broad farce and jingoistic patriotism. At one point in the entertainment the singer Richard Champness advanced to the footlights to sing a new song, with words by Garrick and music by William Boyce. 'Hearts of Oak', still performed today by Royal Navy bands, has had many versions and had many even in the eighteenth century, being infinitely adaptable to almost any circumstance, whether the revolt of the North American colonists or the threat of invasion from Napoleon. It is chauvinistic and triumphalist but, in its original version, it explicitly makes the connection between seapower, repelled invasion and the dawning of true empire. It is worth quoting just to show how the year of victory seemed to British men and women, almost intoxicated on pealing bells and festive bonfires:

> Come, cheer up, my lads,
> It's to glory we steer,
> To add something more
> To this glorious year
>
> To honour we call you
> As free men not slaves
> For who are so free
> As the sons of the waves
>
> Our worthy forefathers,
> Let's give them a cheer,
> To climates unknown
> Did courageously steer
>
> Through oceans to deserts
> For freedom they came
> And by dying bequeathed us
> Their freedom and fame.

PRIMARY SOURCES: UNPUBLISHED

1. ENGLAND

Royal Archives, Windsor Castle, Stuart Papers, vols 350–400
Additional MSS, British Library, 32,850–32,900
Admiralty Records, PRO, 1/84, 89, 92, 93; 2/83, 84, 526, 1331

2. FRANCE

Ministère des Affaires Etrangères, Quai d'Orsay. Archives Etrangères,
Correspondance Politique:
Angleterre 428, 441, 442
Amérique 10, 11, 21, 24
Espagne 523–526
Hollande 501–502
Russie 59–61
Suède 237

Ministère des Affaires Etrangères, Quai d'Orsay, Archives Etrangères,
Mémoires et Documents:
Angleterre 40, 41, 54, 58, 156

Vincennes, Archives de la Guerre, Séries A1: 3512–3526

Archives Nationales, Ministère de la Marine, Séries B/4: 68, 74, 78, 80,
82, 83, 86, 87, 88, 90, 94, 299, 300, 313

3. VATICAN CITY

Archivio Segreto Vaticano, Francia, vols 506, 507, 513, 522

Anonymous, *A Soldier's Journal* (1770)

Anonymous, *The Journal of the Expedition up the River St Lawrence* (Boston, 1759)

Bissett, Andrew, ed., *Memoirs and Papers of Sir Andrew Mitchell* (1850)

Burnaby, Andrew, *Travels through the middle settlements in North America in the years 1759 and 1760* (1775)

Casgrain, H.R., ed., *Collection des Manuscrits du Maréchal de Lévis*, 12 vols (Montreal, 1895)

Connell, Brian, ed., *The Siege of Quebec and the Campaigns in North America 1757–60 by John Knox* (1976)

Dannigan, Brian Leigh, ed., *Memoirs on the late war in North America between France and England by Pierre Pouchot* (Youngstown, NY, 1994)

Dawes, E.C., ed., *Journal of General Rufus Putnam kept in northern New York during the four campaigns of the old French and Indian War 1757–1760* (Albany, 1886)

Doughty, A.G., ed., *Historical Journal of the Campaigns in North America for the years 1757, 1758, 1759 and 1760 by Captain John Knox*, 3 vols (Toronto, 1916)

Doughty, A.G., & Parmelee, G.W., eds., *The Siege of Quebec and the Battle of the Plains of Abraham*, 6 vols (Quebec, 1901)

Fraser, Malcolm, 'Journal', *Journal of Army Historical Research* 18 (1939) pp. 135–68

Frederick the Great, *Politische Correspondenz: Friedrich's des Grossen*, 46 vols (Berlin, 1882)

Grant, Anne, *Memoirs of an American Lady*, 2 vols (1809)

Hamilton, Edward P., ed., *Adventure in the Wilderness: The American Journals of Antoine de Bougainville* (Norman, Ok., 1964)

Hamilton, Milton W., ed., *The Papers of Sir William Johnson* (Albany, NY, 1962)

Hervey, William, *Journal in North America and Europe* (Bury St Edmunds, 1906)

Humphreys, David, *An Essay on the Life of the Honourable Major-General Israel Putnam* (1788)

James, A.P., *The Writings of General John Forbes Relating to his Service in North America* (Wisconsin, 1938)

Johnstone, Chevalier de, *A Dialogue in Hades* (Quebec, 1887)

Kimball, Gertrude S., ed., *Correspondence of William Pitt . . . with Colonial Governors and Military and Naval Commanders in America*, 2 vols (NY, 1906)

Lewis, W.S., ed., *The Yale Edition of Horace Walpole's Correspondence*, 48 vols (Oxford, 1984)

Lincoln, Charles H., *The Correspondence of William Shirley* (NY, 1912)

Mackay, Ruddock F., *The Hawke Papers, A Selection: 1743–1771* (Navy Records Society 129, Aldershot, 1990)

Malartic, M., *Journal des Campagnes au Canada de 1755 à 1760* (Paris, 1890)

Mante, Thomas, *The History of the Late War in North America* (1772)

Marshall, P.J., ed., *The Writings and Speeches of Edmund Burke* (Oxford, 1991)

Martin, Eveline, ed., *Journal of a Slaveowner by Nicholas Owen* (1930)

Moseley, Benjamin, *A Treatise on Tropical Diseases; on Military Operations; and on the climate of the West Indies* (1803)

Murray, James, *Governor Murray's Journal* (Toronto, 1939)

O'Callaghan, E.B., *Documents relating to the Colonial History of New York*, 10 vols (1858)

Pargellis, Stanley, ed., *Military Affairs in North America 1748–1765: Selected Documents from the Cumberland Papers in Windsor Castle* (Hamden, Conn., 1969)

Ramsay, David, *Military Memoirs of Great Britain* (Edinburgh, 1779)

Roby, Luther, ed., *Reminiscences of the French War* (NH, 1988)

St Paul, Horace, *A Journal of the First Two Campaigns* (Cambridge, 1814)

Stevens, Sylvester K., ed., *J.C.B. Travels in New France* (Harrisburg, Pa., 1941)

Tomlinson, Abraham, ed., *The Military Journals of Two Private Soldiers* (Poughkeepsie, 1855)

Vaisey, David, ed., *Thomas Turner, The Diary of a Georgian Shopkeeper* (Oxford, 1984)

Voltaire, François Marie Arouet, *Œuvres Complètes*, ed. Moland (Paris, 1885)

Voltaire, François Marie Arouet, *Correspondance*, ed. Besterman (Geneva, 1967)

Webster, J.C., ed., *Journal of Jeffrey Amherst* (Chicago, 1931)
Webster, J.C., ed., *Journal of William Amherst in America* (1927)
Wilentz, Elias S., ed., *The Journals of Robert Rogers* (NY, 1961)
Wood, William, ed., *The Logs of the Conquest of Canada* (Toronto, 1909)

BIBLIOGRAPHY

Abler, T.S., 'Scalping, torture, cannibalism and rape: An ethnocultural analysis of conflicting cultural values in war', *Anthropologica* 34 (1992) pp. 7–9

Acerra, Martine, Merino, José, & Meyer, Jean, eds, *Les Marines de guerre européennes, xviie –xviiie siècles* (Paris, 1985)

Acerra, Martine, Poussou, Jean-Pierre, Verge-Franceschi, Michel, & Zysberg, André, eds, *Etat, marine et société: Homage à Jean Meyer* (Paris, 1995)

Alam, Muzaffar, *Crisis of Empire in Mughal North India: Awadh and the Punjab 1707–48* (Oxford, 1992)

Alden, J.R., *General Gage in America* (Baton Rouge, 1947)

Ali, S.A., 'The Moghul emperors of India as naturalists and sportsmen', *Journal of the Bombay Natural History Society* 31 (1927) pp. 833–861

Anderson, Fred, *A People's Army: Massachusetts Soldiers and Society in the Seven Years War* (Chapel Hill, NC, 1984)

Anderson, Fred, *Crucible of War: The Seven Years War and the Fate of Empire in British North America 1754–1766* (2000)

Anderson, M.S., *War and Society in the Europe of the Old Regime 1618–1789* (Leicester, 1988)

Antoine, Michel, *Louis XV* (1989)

Aquila, Richard, *The Iroquois Restoration* (Detroit, 1983)

Auger, Leonard A., 'St Francis through the Years', *Vermont History* 27 (1959) pp. 287–304

Auth, F., *The Ten Years War: Indian-White Relations 1755–1765* (NY, 1989)

Axtell, J., *The European and the Indian: Essays in the Ethnohistory of Colonial North America* (NY, 1982)

Axtell, J., 'The White Indians of Colonial America', *William and Mary Quarterly* 32 (1975) pp. 55–88

Axtell, J., & Sturtevant, W.C., 'The unkindest cut, or who invented scalping?' *William and Mary Quarterly* 37 (1980) pp. 451–72

Ayling, Stanley, *The Elder Pitt, Earl of Chatham* (NY, 1976)

Bahadur, K.P., *A History of Indian Civilization* (1983)

Baker, Keith Michael, *Inventing the French Revolution* (Cambridge, 1990)

Baker, Keith Michael, *The Political Culture of the Old Regime* (NY, 1987)

Baker, K.M., Lucas, C., & Furet, F., eds, *The French Revolution and the creation of modern political culture*, 3 vols (1989)

Barcham, William L., *The Religious Paintings of Giambattista Tiepolo: Piety and Tradition in Eighteenth-Century Venice* (Oxford, 1989)

Barnett, Richard B., *North India between Empires: Awadh, the Mughals and the British 1720–1801* (Berkeley, 1980)

Basham, A.L., ed., *A Cultural History of India* (1984)

Bate, Walter Jackson, *Samuel Johnson* (NY, 1977)

Baugh, Daniel A., 'Great Britain's "Blue Water" Policy 1689–1815', *International History Review* 10 (1988) pp. 35–58

Beaglehole, J.C., *The Life of Captain James Cook* (Stanford, Ca., 1974)

Beers, H.P., 'British Commanders in Chief in North America 1754–1783', *Military Affairs* 13 (1949) pp. 79–94

Beeson, David, *Maupertuis* (Oxford, 1992)

Bellico, Russell P., *Sails and Steam in the Mountains: A Maritime History of Lake George and Lake Champlain* (NY, 2001)

Bence-Jones, Mark, *Clive of India* (1974)

Bewell, Alan, *Romanticism and Colonial Disease* (Baltimore, 1999)

Black, Jeremy, *Britain as a Military Power 1688–1815* (1999)

Black, Jeremy, *European Warfare 1660–1815* (1994)

Black, Jeremy, *From Louis XIV to Napoleon* (1999)

Black, Jeremy, *Pitt the Elder: The Great Commoner* (1999)

Black, Jeremy, *Warfare in the Eighteenth Century* (1999)

Black, Jeremy, ed., *Knights Errant and True Englishmen: British Foreign Policy 1600–1800* (Edinburgh, 1989)

Black, Jeremy, ed., *The Origins of War in Early Modern Europe* (Edinburgh, 1987)

Black, Jeremy, ed., *War in the Early Modern World 1480–1815* (1999)

Black, Jeremy & Woodfine, P.L., eds, *The British Navy and the Use of Naval Power in the Eighteenth Century* (Leicester, 1988)

Blackburn, Robin, *The Making of New World Slavery from the Baroque to the Modern 1492–1800* (1997)

Blackmore, H.L., *British Military Firearms 1660–1815* (1961)

Bonney, Richard, ed., *Economic Systems and State Finance* (Oxford, 1995)

Bonney, Richard, ed., *The Rise of the Fiscal State in Europe c.1200–1815* (Oxford, 1999)

Bonomi, Patricia U., *A Factious People: Politics and Society in Colonial New York* (NY, 1971)

Bourguet, A., *Choiseul et l'Angleterre* (Paris, 1908)

Boutry, P., *Choiseul à Rome 1754–1757* (Paris, 1895)

Bowen, H.V., *Revenue and Reform: the Indian Problem in British Politics 1757–1773* (Cambridge, 1991)

Bowen, Huw, *War and British Society 1688–1815* (1998)

Brecher, Frank W., *Losing a Continent: France's North American Policy 1753–1763* (1998)

Brewer, John, *The Sinews of Power: War, Money and the English State 1688–1783* (1989)

Brice, Andrew, *The Channel Islands in 1759* (1986)

Broadie, Alexander, ed., *The Scottish Enlightenment* (Edinburgh, 1999)

Brown, Peter Douglas, *William Pitt, Earl of Chatham: The Great Commoner* (1978)

Brown, Stewart, ed., *William Robertson and the Expansion of Empire* (1997)

Browning, Reed, *The Duke of Newcastle* (New Haven, 1975)

Brumfitt, J.H., 'Voltaire and Bonnie Prince Charlie: Historian and Hero', *Forum for Modern Languages Studies* 21 (1985) pp. 322–37

Brumwell, Stephen, '"Rank and File": A Profile of One of Wolfe's Regiments', *Journal of the Society for Army Historical Research* 79 (2001) pp. 3–24

Brumwell, Stephen, *Redcoats: The British Soldier and War in the Americas 1755–1763* (Cambridge, 2002)

Brumwell, Stephen, '"Service Truly Critical": The British Army and Warfare with North American Indians 1755–1764', *War in History* 5 (1998) pp. 146–75

Butel, Paul & Lavalle, Bernards, eds, *L'Espace Caraïbe: Théâtre et enjeu des luttes impériales, xviie –xixe siècles* (Bordeaux, 1996)

Butler, Rohan, *Choiseul* (Oxford, 1980)

Calder, Isabel M., *Colonial Captivities, Marches and Journeys* (NY, 1935)

Calloway, Colin G., *New Worlds for All: Indians, Europeans and the Remaking of Early America* (Baltimore, 1997)

Campadour, Emile, *Madame de Pompadour et la cour de Louis XV* (Paris, 1867)

Campbell, Peter R., *Power and Politics in Old Regime France 1720–1745* (1996)

Carretta, Vincent, 'Olaudah Equinao or Gustavus Vassa? New Light on an Eighteenth Century Question of Identity', *Slavery and Abolition* 20 (1999) pp. 96–105

Carter, A., *The Dutch Republic during the Seven Years War* (1871)

Cash, Arthur H., *Laurence Sterne: The Early and Middle Years* (1992)

Cash, Arthur H., *Laurence Sterne: The Later Years* (1992)

Chapais, Thomas, *Le Marquis de Montcalm 1721-1759* (Quebec, 1911)

Charland, Thomas F., *Les Abenakis d'Odanak* (Montreal, 1964)

Charland, Thomas F., 'The Lake Champlain Army and the Fall of Montreal', *Vermont History* 28 (1960) pp. 287–301

Chartraud, R., *The French Soldier in Colonial America* (Ottawa, 1984)

Chartraud, R., *The Heights of Abraham 1759: The Armies of Wolfe and Montcalm* (Oxford, 1999)

Chaudhuri, K.N., *The Trading World of Asia and the English East India Company 1660–1760* (Cambridge, 1978)

Chaudhuri, Sushil, *From Prosperity to Decline: Eighteenth-Century Bengal* (New Delhi, 1995)

Chaussinard-Nogaret, G., *La noblesse au XVIIIe siècle: De la féodalité aux lumières* (Paris, 1976)

Childs, John, *Armies and Warfare in Europe 1648–1789* (Manchester, 1982)

Clark, Charles E., *The Eastern Frontier: The Settlement of Northern New England 1610–1763* (NY, 1970)

Codignola, Luca, *Guerra e Guerriglia nell'Americana Coloniale: Robert Rogers e la Guerra dei Sette Anni 1754–1760* (Venice, 1977)

Cole, H., *The First Gentleman of the Bedchamber* (1965)

Colley, Linda, *Captives* (2002)

Coolidge, Guy Omerson, *The French Occupation of the Champlain Valley from 1609 to 1759* (NY, 1979)

Coquelle, P., *La Hollande pendant la guerre de Sept Ans* (Paris, 1899)

Corbett, Julian S., *England in the Seven Years War: A Study in Combined Strategy*, 2 vols (1918)

Corkran, David, *The Cherokee Frontier: Conflict and Survival 1740–1762* (Norman, Ok., 1996)

Corvisier, A., *L'Armée française de la fin du XVIIe siècle au Ministre de Choiseul*, 2 vols (Paris, 1964)

Corvisier, A., *Armées et sociétés en Europe de 1494 à 1789* (Paris, 1976)

Costanzo, Angelo, *Surprising Narrative: Olaudah Equiano and the Beginnings of Black Autobiography* (NY, 1987)

Cross, Michael & Kealey, Gregory S., *Economy and Society during the French Regime to 1759* (Toronto, 1983)

Cruickshanks, Eveline, ed., *Ideology and Conspiracy* (1979)

Cuneo, John R., *Robert Rogers of the Rangers* (NY, 1959)

Curtin, Philp D., *The Atlantic Slave Trade* (Madison, Wis., 1969)

Daunton, M., & Halpern, R., eds, *Empire and Others: British encounters with indigenous peoples 1600–1850* (1999)

Day, Gordon M., 'Rogers' Raid in Indian Tradition', *Historical New Hampshire* 17 (1962) pp. 3–17

Day, Gordon M., *The Identity of the St Francis Indians*, National Museum Canadian Ethnology Service Paper 71 (Ottawa, 1981)

Dayan, Joan, *Haiti, History and the Gods* (California, 1996)

De Categno, P., *James MacPherson* (Boston, Mass., 1989)

Desprat, Jean-Paul, *Le Cardinal de Bernis 1715–1794* (Paris, 2000)

Dickson, P.G.M., *The Financial Revolution in England: A study in the development of public credit 1688–1756* (1967)

Dole, George F., *A Scientist Explores Spirit: A Biography of Emanuel Swedenborg with Key Concepts of his Theology* (1997)

Donaldson, Gordon, *Battle for a Continent: Quebec 1759* (Garden City, NY, 1973)

Doughty, A.G., *The Siege of Quebec* (1901)

Dowd, Gregory Evans, *A Spirited Resistance: The North American Indian Struggle for Unity 1745–1815* (Baltimore, 1992)

Downs, Randolph C., *Council Fires on the Upper Ohio: A Narrative of Indian Affairs in the Upper Ohio Valley until 1795* (Pittsburgh, 1940)

Doyle, W., *The French Parlement and the crisis of the Old Regime* (Chapel Hill, NC, 1986)

Doyle, W., *Old Regime France 1648–1788* (2001)

Doyle, W., 'Was there an aristocratic revolution in pre-revolutionary France?' *PP* 57 (1972) pp. 97–122

Duffy, Christopher, *Fire and Stone: The Science of Fortress Warfare 1660–1860* (1996)

Duffy, Christopher, *The Military Experience in the Age of Reason* (1987)

Duffy, Christopher, *The Military Life of Frederick the Great* (1986)

Duffy, M., *Soldiers, Sugar and Seapower: The British expeditions to the West Indies and the war against Revolutionary France* (Oxford, 1987)

Duffy, Michael, ed., *Parameters of British Naval Power 1650–1850* (Exeter, 1992)

Dunmore, John, *Pacific Explorer: The life of Jean-François de la Pérouse 1741–1788* (Sydney, 1985)

Dunnigan, B.L., *Siege 1759: The Campaign against Niagara* (Youngstown, NY, 1986)

Dussauge, A., *Le Ministère de Belle-Isle* (Paris, 1914)

Eccles, W.J., *The Canadian Frontier 1534–1760* (Albuquerque, NM, 1983)

Eccles, W.J., 'The social, economic and political significance of the military establishment in New France', *Canadian Historical Review* 52 (1971) pp. 1–22

Eccles, W.J., *France in America* (NY, 1972)

Eccles, W.J., 'The History of New France according to Francis Parkman', *William and Mary Quarterly* 18 (1961) pp. 163–75

Eccles, W.J., ed., *Essays on New France* (Toronto, 1987)

Edwardes, M., *Plassey: The Founding of an Empire* (1970)

Edwards, Paul, ed., *The Life of Olaudah Equiano* (Essex, 1989)

Fage, J.D., 'African Societies and the Atlantic Slave Trade', *PP* 125 (1989) pp. 97–115

Flexner, J.T., *Mohawk Baronet: Sir William Johnson of New York* (NY, 1959)

Fenn, Elizabeth A., 'Biological Warfare in Eighteenth Century North America: Beyond Jeffrey Amherst', *Journal of American History* 86 (2000) pp. 1552–1580

Ferling, John E., *The First of Men: A Life of George Washington* (Knoxville, Tenn., 1988)

Ferling, John E., *A Wilderness of Miseries: War and Warriors in Early America* (Westport, Conn., 1980)

Fluchere, Henri, *Laurence Sterne, de l'homme à l'œuvre: Biographie critique et essai d'interprétation de Tristram Shandy* (Paris, 1961)

Ford, F.L., *The Regrouping of the French Aristocracy after Louis XIV* (Harvard, 1953)

Forrest, George, *The Life of Lord Clive*, 2 vols (1918)

Forster, H., *Edward Young: Poet of the Night Thoughts* (1986)

Fortescue, J., 'Guadeloupe', *Blackwood's Magazine* 234 (1933) pp. 552–66

Frazier, Patrick, *The Mahicans of Stockbridge* (Lincoln, Neb., 1992)

Fregault, Guy, *Canada: The War of Conquest* (Toronto, 1969)

Fregault, Guy, *François Bigot administrateur français*, 2 vols (Montreal, 1948)

Furber, Holden, *Rival Empires of Trade in the Orient 1600–1800* (Minneapolis, 1976)

Fussell, Paul, *Samuel Johnson and the Life of Writing* (1972)

Gallet, Danielle, *Madame de Pompadour ou le pouvoir féminin* (Paris, 1985)

Galloway, Colin G., *New Worlds for all: Indians, Europeans and the Remaking of Early America* (Baltimore, 1997)

Galloway, Colin G., *The Western Abenaki of Vermont 1600–1800* (Norman, Ok., 1990)

Gallup, Andrew, & Shaffer, Donald F., *La Marine: The French Colonial Soldier in Canada 1745–1761* (Maryland, 1992)

Garrett, Richard, *General Wolfe* (1975)

Gay, Peter, *Voltaire's Politics: The Poet as Realist* (NY, 1975)

Geggus, David, 'Haitian Voodoo in the Eighteenth Century', *Jahrbuch für Geschichte Lateinamerikas* 28 (1991) pp. 21–51

Gipson, Lawrence Henry, *The British Empire before the American Revolution*, 8 vols (1954)

Godfrey, William G., *John Bradstreet's Quest: Pursuit of Profit and Preferment in Colonial North America* (Waterloo, Ontario, 1983)

Gooch, G.P., *Louis XV* (1976)

Grandish, Stephen F., *The Manning of the British Navy during the Seven Years War* (1980)

Graves, Donald E., *Fighting for Canada: Seven Battles 1758–1945* (Toronto, 2000)

Graymont, Barbara, *The Iroquois in the American Revolution* (Syracuse, NY, 1972)

Greene, Donald J., *Samuel Johnson* (Boston, 1989)

Gupta, Ashin Das, & Pearson, M.N., eds, *India and the Indian Ocean 1500–1800* (Calcutta, 1987)

Hamilton, Charles, ed., *Braddock's Defeat* (Norman, Oklahoma, 1959)

Hamilton, Edward P., *The French Army in Canada* (Ottawa, 1967)

Hamilton, Edward P., *The French and Indian War* (1962)

Hamilton, Milton W., *Sir William Johnson: Colonial American 1715–1763* (NY, 1976)

Hanley, S., *The lit de justice of the kings of France: Constitutional ideology in legend, ritual and discourse* (Princeton, 1983)

Harding, R., *Amphibious Warfare in the Eighteenth Century: The British Expedition to the West Indies 1740–1742* (Woodbridge, Suffolk, 1991)

Hargreave-Maudsley, W.N., *Eighteenth Century Spain 1700–1788* (1979)

Haudrere, Philippe, *La compagnie française des Indes au 18e siècle (1719–1795)*, 4 vols (Paris, 1989)

Haviland, William A., *The Original Vermonters: Native Inhabitants Past and Present* (Hanover, NH, 1981)

Hayes, J., 'Scottish Officers in the British Army 1714–63', *Scottish Historical Review* 37 (1958) pp. 23–33

Herman, Arthur, *The Scottish Enlightenment* (2001)

Hinderaker, Eric, *Elusive Empires, Constructing Colonialism in the Ohio Valley 1673–1800* (NY, 1997)

Hitsman, J.M., & Bond, C.L.J., 'The Assault Landing at Louisbourg, 1758', *Canadian Historical Review* 35 (1954) pp. 314–30

Howes, Alan B., ed., *Sterne: The Critical Heritage* (1974)

Hubert-Robert, Regine, *Le lys et le lion en Amérique, une guerre franco-anglaise 1534–1760* (Paris, 1980)

Hutchison, T.W., *Before Adam Smith: The Emergence of Political Economy 1662–1776* (Oxford, 1988)

Jacobs, Wilbur R., *Diplomacy and Indian Gifts: Anglo-French Rivalry along the Ohio and North West Frontiers 1748–1763* (Stanford, Ca., 1950)

Jacobs, Wilbur R., *Francis Parkman, Historian as Hero: The Formative Years* (Austin, Texas, 1991)

Jennings, Francis, *The Ambiguous Iroquois Empire: The Covenant Chain*

Confederation of Indian Tribes with English Colonies from its Beginnings to the Lancaster Treaty of 1744 (NY, 1984)

Jennings, Francis, *Empire of Fortune: Crowns, Colonies and Tribes in the Seven Years War in America* (NY, 1988)

Jennings, Francis, *The Invasion of America: Indians, Colonialism and the Cant of Conquest* (Chapel Hill, NC, 1975)

Jennings, Francis, 'Francis Parkman: A Brahmin among Untouchables', *William and Mary Quarterly* 42 (1985) pp. 305–28

Jennings, Francis et al., eds, *The History and Culture of Iroquois Diplomacy: An Interdisciplinary Guide to the Treaties of the Six Nations and their League* (Syracuse, NY, 1985)

Johnson, D., *Sketches of Indian Field Sports* (1827)

Johnson, W.W., *Richard Jack, assistant engineer in the expedition to Guadeloupe 1758–9, facts and hypothesis* (Oxford, 1994)

Kaplan, Steven L., *Bread, Politics and Political Economy in the Reign of Louis XV*, 2 vols (The Hague, 1976)

Keegan, John, *Fields of Battle: The Wars for North America* (1996)

Keeley, Lawrence H., *War before Civilization: The Myth of the Peaceful Savage* (NY, 1996)

Kennet, L., *The French Armies in the Seven Years War* (Durham, NC, 1967)

Kimbrough, Mary, *Louis Antoine de Bougainville* (1990)

Kirwan, Robert H., *Angels in Action: What Swedenborg Saw and Heard* (1994)

Knollenber, P., 'General Amherst and Germ Warfare', *Mississippi Valley Historical Review* 41 (1954) pp. 489–94

Koehn, Nancy F., *The Power of Commerce: Economy and Governance in the First British Empire* (Ithaca, NY, 1994)

Kopperman, P.E., *Braddock at the Monongahela* (Pittsburgh, 1977)

Kreiser, Robert, *Miracles, Convulsions and Ecclesiastical Politics* (Princeton, 1978)

Lapierre, Lauier L., *1759: The Battle for Canada* (Toronto, 1990)

Laugier, Lucien, *Le duc d'Aiguillon* (Paris, 1984)

Lawford, James P., *Britain's Army in India from its Origins to the Conquest of Bengal* (1978)

Leckie, Robert, *'A Few Acres of Snow': The Saga of the French and Indian Wars* (NY, 1999)

Lee, David, 'The Contest for Isle-aux-Noix 1759–60: A Case Study in the Fall of New France', *Vermont History* 37 (1969) pp. 96–107

Leech, Douglas Edward, *Arms for Empire: A Military History of the British Colonies in North America 1609–1763* (NY, 1973)

Leech, Douglas Edward, *Roots of Conflict: British Armed Forces and Colonial Americans 1677–1763* (Chapel Hill, NC, 1986)

Lehmann, William, *Henry Home, Lord Kames and the Scottish Enlightenment* (The Hague, 1971)

Levey, Michael, *Painting in Eighteenth Century Venice* (1994)

Lewis, Meiwether Liston, *Montcalm the Marvelous Marquis* (NY, 1961)

Lloyd, Christopher, *The Capture of Quebec* (1959)

Lock, F.P., *Edmund Burke: Vol. 1 1730–1784* (Oxford, 1998)

Long, John Cuthbert, *Lord Jeffrey Amherst: A Soldier of the King* (NY, 1933)

Long, John Cuthbert, 'Amherst in 1759', *New York History* 15 (1934) pp. 50–58

Lunn, Jean Elizabeth, 'Agriculture and War in Canada 1740–1760', *Canadian Historical Review* 16 (1935) pp. 123–36

Lynch, John, *Bourbon Spain 1700–1808* (1993)

McCardell, Lee, *Ill-Starred General: Braddock of the Coldstream Guards* (Pittsburgh, 1958)

McClellan, James E., *Colonialism and Science: Saint-Domingue in the Old Regime* (Baltimore, 1992)

McConnell, Michael N., *A Country Between: The Upper Ohio Valley and its Peoples 1724–1774* (Lincoln, Neb., 1992)

McIntyre, Ian, *Garrick* (1999)

McLynn, Frank, *Bonnie Prince Charlie* (Oxford, 1991)

McNairn, Alan, *Behold the Hero: General Wolfe and the Arts in the Eighteenth Century* (Liverpool, 1997)

Mack, Robert L., *Thomas Gray: A Life* (2000)

Mackay, R.F., *Admiral Hawke* (Oxford, 1965)

MacDonogh, Giles, *Frederick the Great: A Life in Deed and Letters* (1999)

Mackesy, Piers, *The Coward of Minden: The Affair of Lord George Sackville* (1979)

Macleod, Peter, *The Canadian Iroquois and the Seven Years War* (Toronto, 1996)

Mahon, J.K., 'Anglo-American Methods of Indian Warfare 1696-1794', *Mississippi Valley Historical Review* 45 (1958) pp. 254–75

Maine, Catherine, 'L'église et la nation. Du dépôt de la vérité au dépôt des lois: la trajectoire janséniste au XVIIIe siècle', *Annales ESC* 5 (1991) pp. 1177–1205

Malone, P., *The Skulking Way of War: Technology and Tactics among the New England Indians* (Baltimore, 1993)

Manning, Patrick, *Slavery and African Life: Occidental, Oriental and African Slave Trades* (Cambridge, 1990)

Marcus, G., *Quiberon* (1960)

Marion M., *La Bretagne et le duc d'Aiguillon, 1753-1770* (Paris, 1898)

Marion M., *Machault d'Arnouville* (Paris, 1891)

Markovitz, Claude, ed., *A History of Modern India 1480–1950* (2002)

Marshall, P.J., *British Bridgehead: Eastern India 1740–1828* (1987)

Marshall, P.J., *East Indian Fortunes: The British in Bengal in the Eighteenth Century* (Oxford, 1976)

Marshall, P.J., & Williams, Glyndwr, *The Great Map of Mankind: British Perceptions of the World in the Age of Enlightenment* (1982)

Marshall, P.J., & Williams, Glyndwr, eds, *The British Atlantic Empire before the American Revolution* (1980)

Mason, Haydn, *Voltaire: A Biography* (1981)

Masson, F., *Le Cardinal de Bernis depuis son ministère 1759–1794* (Paris, 1903)

May, R., & Embleton,G., *Wolfe's Army* (Reading, 1997)

Merrick, J.W., *The desacralization of the French monarchy in the eighteenth century* (Baton Rouge, LA, 1990)

Metraux, Alfred, *Le Vaudou Haïtien* (Paris, 1958)

Middleton, Richard, *The Bells of Victory: The Pitt-Newcastle Ministry and the Conduct of the Seven Years War 1757–1762* (Cambridge, 1985)

Mintz, Sidney W., *Sweetness and Power: The Place of Sugar in Modern History* (NY, 1985)

Moon, Penderel, *The British Conquest and Dominion of India* (1989)

Morgan, Kenneth, *Bristol and the Atlantic Trade in the Eighteenth Century* (Cambridge, 1993)

Morrison, Kenneth M., *The Embattled North-East: The Elusive Ideal of Alliance in Abenaki-European Relations* (Berkeley, 1984)

Mossner, Ernest, *The Life of David Hume* (Oxford, 1954)

Mukherjee, S.N., *Sir William Jones: A Study in Eighteenth Century British Attitudes to India* (1987)

Muller, Jerry Z., *Adam Smith in his time – and ours* (NY, 1993)

Namias, J., *White Captives: Gender and Ethnicity on the American Frontier* (Chapel Hill, NC, 1993)

Neal, Larry, 'Integration of International Capital Markets: Quantitative Evidence from the Eighteenth to the Twentieth Centuries', *Journal of Economic History* 45 (1985) pp. 219–26

Nester, William R., *The First World War: Britain, France and the Fate of North America 1756–1775* (Westport, Conn., 2000)

Nicolai, M.L., 'A Different Kind of Carnage: The French Military and Canadian Irregular Soldiers during the Seven Years War', *Canadian Historical Review* 70 (1989) pp. 53–75

Nobles, Gregory H., *American Frontiers: Cultural Encounters and Continental Conquest* (1997)

Nolhac, P. de, *Madame de Pompadour et la politique d'après des documents nouveaux* (Paris, 1948)

Norton, David Fate, ed., *The Cambridge Companion to Hume* (Cambridge, 1993)

Nosworthy, B., *The Anatomy of Victory: Battle Tactics 1689–1763* (NY, 1992)

O'Brien, Conor Cruse, *The Great Melody: A Thematic Biography and Commented Anthology of Edmund Burke* (1992)

O'Brien, P.K., & Mathias P., 'Taxation in Britain and France 1715-1810: A comparison of the social and economic incidence of taxes collected for the central government', *Journal of European Economic History* 5 (1976) pp. 601–50

O'Brien, P.K., & Hunt, P., 'The rise of a fiscal state in England 1485–1815', *Historical Research* 66 (1993) pp. 129–76

Ogude, S.E., 'Facts into Fiction: Equinao's Narrative Reconsidered', *Research in African Literature* 13 (1982) pp. 31–43

Olson, Donald W., et al, 'Perfect Tide, Ideal Moon: An Unappreciated Aspect of Wolfe's Generalship at Quebec 1759', *William and Mary Quarterly* 59 (2002) pp. 957–74

Pagden, Anthony, *Lords of All the World: Ideologies of Empire in Spain, Britain and France c.1500 to c.1800* (New Haven, 1995)

Pares, Richard, *War and Trade in the West Indies 1739–63* (Oxford, 1936)

Pares, Richard, *Yankees and Creoles: The Trade between North America and the West Indies before the American Revolution* (NY, 1956)

Pargellis, S., *Lord Loudoun in North America* (Yale, 1933)

Parissien, Steven, *The Adams Style* (1992)

Parry, J.H., *A Short History of the West Indies* (1965)

Pencak, William, *War, Politics and Power in Colonial Massachusetts* (Boston, 1981)

Peters, Marie, *The Elder Pitt* (1998)

Peters, Marie, 'The Myth of William Pitt, Earl of Chatham, Great Imperialist. Part One: Pitt and Imperial Expansion 1738-1763', *Journal of Imperial and Commonwealth History* 21 (1993) pp. 31–74

Peters, Marie, *Pitt and Popularity: The patriot minister and London opinion during the Seven Years War* (1980)

Philips, Kevin, *The Cousins' War: Religion, Politics and the Triumph of Anglo-America* (NY, 1999)

Picciola, André, *Le Comte de Maurepas: Versailles et L'Europe à la fin de l'Ancien Régime* (Paris, 1999)

Pitman, Frank W., *The Development of the British West Indies 1700–1763* (New Haven, 1917)

Pocock, J.G.A., *Barbarism and Religion: The Enlightenment and Edward Gibbon* (Cambridge, 2000)

Potkay, Adam, 'Olaudah Equiano and the Art of Spiritual Autobiography', *Eighteenth Century Studies* 27 (1994) pp. 677–92

Potkay, Adam, *The Passion for Happiness: Samuel Johnson and David Hume* (Ithaca, NY, 2000)

Prapaditya, Pal, *Elephants and Ivories in South Asia* (1981)

Pritchard, J., *Louis XV's Navy 1748–1762* (Kingston, Ontario, 1987)

Rao, P. Setu Madhava, *Eighteenth-Century Deccan* (Bombay, 1963)

Reid, John Philip, *A Better Kind of Hatchet: Law, Trade and Diplomacy in the Cherokee Nation during the Early Years of European Contact* (Pennsylvania, 1976)

Reid, Stuart, *Wolfe: The Career of General James Wolfe from Culloden to Quebec* (2000)

Reilly, Robin, *The Rest to Fortune: The Life of Major-General James Wolfe* (1960)

Rice, W., *Tiger Shooting in India* (1857)

Richardson, Alan, 'Romantic Voodoo: Obeah and British Culture 1797–1807', *Studies in Romanticism* 32 (1993) pp. 3–28

Richter, Daniel K., *The Ordeal of the Longhouse: The Peoples of the Iroquois League in the Era of European Colonization* (Chapel Hill, NC, 1992)

Richter, Daniel K., 'War and Culture: The Iroquois Experience', *William and Mary Quarterly* 40 (1983) pp. 528–59

Richter, Daniel K., & Merrell, James, eds, *Beyond the Covenant Chain: The Iroquois and their Neighbours in Indian North America 1600–1800* (Syracuse, NY, 1987)

Riley, James C., *The Seven Years War and the Old Regime in France* (Princeton, 1986)

Roberts, W.A., *The French in the West Indies* (1942)

Rodger, N.A.M., *The Insatiable Earl: A Life of John Montagu, 4th Earl of Sandwich 1718–1792* (1993)

Rodger, N.A.M., *The Wooden World: An Anatomy of the Georgian Navy* (1986)

Rogers, A., *Empire and Liberty: American Resistance to British Authority 1755–1763* (LA, 1974)

Rogers, H.C.B., *The British Army of the Eighteenth Century* (1977)

Ross, Ian, *Lord Kames and the Scotland of His Day* (Oxford, 1972)

Rousseau, F., *Règne de Charles III* (Paris, 1907)

Russell, Peter E., 'Redcoats in the Wilderness: British Officers and Irregular Warfare in Europe and America 1740–1760', *William and Mary Quarterly* 35 (1978) pp. 629–52

Rykwert, Anne, *Robert and James Adam: The Men and the Style* (1985)

Samuels, Sigmund, *The Seven Years War in Canada 1756–1763* (Toronto, 1934)

Sarkar, Jadunath, *The Fall of the Mughal Empire*, 4 vols (New Delhi, 1992)

Sarrailh, J., *L'Espagne éclairée de la seconde moitie du XVIIIe siècle* (Paris, 1952)

Savory, Reginald, *His Britannic Majesty's Army in Germany during the Seven Years' War* (Oxford, 1966)

Schutz, John A., *William Shirley, King's Governor of Massachusetts* (Chapel Hill, NC, 1961)

Schwartz, Seymour I., *The French and Indian War 1754–1763: The Imperial Struggle for North America* (NY, 1994)

Schweizer, Karl W., *England, Prussia and the Seven Years War* (Lampeter, 1989)

Schweizer, Karl W., *Frederick the Great, William Pitt, Lord Bute and the Anglo-Prussian Alliance 1756–1763* (1991)

Selesky, Harold E., *War and Society in Colonial Connecticut* (New Haven, 1964)

Sen, Siba P., *The French in India 1763–1816* (New Delhi, 1971)

Sharp, Andrew, 'Scots, Savages and Barbarians: Humphrey Clinker and the Scots' Philosophy', *Eighteenth Century Life* 18 (1994) pp. 65–79

Sheridan, Richard B., *Sugar and Slavery: An Economic History of the British West Indies 1623–1775* (Barbados, 1974)

Showalter, D.E., *The Wars of Frederick the Great* (Harlow, 1996)

Smelser, M.T., *The Campaign for the Sugar Islands 1759: A Study of Amphibious Warfare* (NY, 1955)

Smith, John Graham, *The Origins and Early Development of the Heavy Chemical Industry in France* (Oxford, 1979)

Soltau, R., *Choiseul* (Paris, 1909)

Sosin, Jack M., *The Revolutionary Frontier 1763–1783* (NY, 1967)

Spear, Percy, *Master of Bengal: Clive and His India* (1975)

Stacey, C.P., 'Quebec 1759: Some New Documents', *Canadian Historical Review* 47 (1966) pp. 344–55

Stacey, C.P., *Quebec 1759: The Siege and the Battle* (Toronto, 1959)

Stafford, Fiona, *The Sublime Savage: James MacPherson and the Poems of Ossian* (Edinburgh, 1988)

Stanley, G.F.C., *New France: The Last Phase 1744–1760* (Toronto, 1968)

Starkey, Armstrong, *European and Native American Warfare 1675–1815* (Norman, Oklahoma, 1998)

Steele, Ian K., *Betrayals: Fort William Henry and the 'Massacre'* (NY, 1990)

Steele, Ian K., *Warpaths: Invasions of North America* (NY, 1994)

Stein, Robert L., *The French Slave Trade in the Eighteenth Century* (Madison, 1979)

Stein, Robert L., *The French Sugar Business in the Eighteenth Century* (Baton Rouge, La, 1988)

Stephens, L., *Robert Clive and Imperialism* (1981)

Stone, William L., *The Life and Times of Sir William Johnson* (Albany, 1865)

Stotz, Charles Morse, *Outposts of the War for Empire: The French and English in Western Pennsylvania: Their Armies, Their Forts, Their People 1749–1764* (Pittsburgh, 1985)

Stove, B., 'Robe versus sword: The parlements of Paris and the French aristocracy 1774–1789', *French Historical Studies* 9 (1975) pp. 278–303

Sutherland, L.S., *The East India Company in Eighteenth Century Politics* (Oxford, 1952)

Suzuki, D.T., *Swedenborg: Buddha of the North* (1996)

Swann, Julian, *Politics and the Parlement of Paris under Louis XV 1754–1774* (Cambridge, 1995)

Stewart, M.A., ed., *Studies in the Philosophy of the Scottish Enlightenment* (Oxford, 1990)

Syrett, D., 'The British Landing at Havana: An Example of an Eighteenth-Century Combined Operation', *Mariner's Mirror* 55 (1969) pp. 325–31

Syrett, D., 'The Methodology of British Amphibious Operations during the Seven Years War and American Wars', *Mariner's Mirror* 58 (1972) pp. 269–80

Tallant, Robert, *Voodoo in New Orleans* (NY, 1974)

Tapie, V.L., *L'Europe de Marie Thérèse* (Paris, 1973)

Taylor, Stephen, Coono, Richard & Jones, Clyne, eds, *Hanoverian Britain and Empire: Essays in Memory of Philip Lawson* (Woodbridge, 1998)

Terrall, Mary, *The Man Who Flattened the Earth: Maupertuis and the Sciences in the Enlightenment* (Chicago, 2002)

Thayer, T., 'Army Contractors for the Niagara Campaign 1755–1756', *William and Mary Quarterly* 14 (1957) pp. 31–46

Thomas, P.D.G., *John Wilkes: A Friend to Liberty* (Oxford, 1996)

Tracy, Nicholas, *Manila Ransomed: The British Assault on Manila in the Seven Years War* (Exeter, 1995)

Trantman, T.R., *Lewis Henry Morgan and the Invention of Kinship* (NY, 1987)

Turnell, Curtis D., & Newcomb, William W., *A Lipan Apache Mission* (Austin, 1969)

Uglow, Jenny, *Hogarth: A Life and a World* (1997)

Uglow, Jenny, The *Lunar Men: The Friends Who Made the Future* (2002)

Ultee, M., ed., *Adapting to Conditions: War and Society in the Eighteenth Century* (Tuscaloosa, Ala., 1986)

Upton, L.F.S., *Micmacs and Colonists: Indian-White Relations in the Maritimes 1713–1867* (Vancouver, 1979)

Van de Water, Frederic F., *Lake Champlain and Lake George* (NY, 1969)

Van Kley, Dale, *The Jansenists and the Expulsion of the Jesuits from France 1757–1765* (New Haven, 1975)

Van Kley, Dale, *The Damiens Affair and the Unravelling of the Ancien Régime 1750–1770* (1984)

Vaucher, P., *La Grande-Bretagne, l'Irlande et les colonies britanniques au XVIIIe siècle* (Paris, 1978)

Verdier, H., *Le duc de Choiseul* (Paris, 1969)

Waddington, Richard, *La Guerre de Sept Ans* (Paris, 1904)

Waddington, Richard, *Louis XV et le renversement des alliances* (Paris, 1896)

Wade, Ira O., *Voltaire and Candide* (Princeton, 1959)

Wallace, Anthony F.C., *The Death and Rebirth of the Seneca* (NY, 1969)

Wallace, Anthony F.C., *Teedyuscung, King of the Delawares 1700–1763* (Syracuse, NY, 1990)

Wallace, Paul A.W., *Conrad Weiser 1796–1770: Friend of Colonist and Mohawk* (Philadelphia, 1945)

Walvin, James, *An African's Life: The Life and Times of Olaudah Equiano 1745–1797* (Washington, 1998)

Warner, Oliver, *With Wolfe to Quebec: The Path to Glory* (Toronto, 1972)

Waugh, W.T., *James Wolfe: Man and Soldier* (Montreal, 1928)

Weddle, Robert S., *San Juan Bautista: Gateway to Spanish Texas* (Austin, 1968)

Weddle, Robert S., *The San Saba Mission* (Austin, 1964)

Weigley, Russell F., *The Age of Battles: The Quest for Decisive Warfare from Breitenfeld to Waterloo* (Bloomington, Ind., 1991)

Wells, John & Wills, Douglas, 'Revolution, Restoration and Debt Repudiation: The Jacobite Threat to England's Institutions and Growth', *Journal of Economic History* 60 (2000) pp. 418–41

Wheeler, D., 'A Climatic Reconstruction of the Battle of Quiberon Bay, 20 November 1759', *Weather* 50 (1995) pp. 230–39

White, Richard, *The Middle Ground, Indians, Empires and Republics in the Great Lakes Region 1650–1815* (NY, 1991)

Whitworth, Rex, *Field-Marshal Lord Ligonier* (Oxford, 1958)

Williamson, T., *Oriental Field Sports* (1807)

Wilson, Kathleen, *A Sense of the People: Politics, Culture and Imperialism in England 1715–1785* (Cambridge, 1995)

Winch, Donald, *Adam Smith's Politics* (Cambridge, 1978)

Winthrop, Sargent, *History of an Expedition against Fort DuQuesne in 1755* (Philadelphia, 1855)

Winyates, F.A., *The Services of Lieutenant-Colonel Francis Downman* (Woolwich, 1898)

1759

Wolpert, Stanley A., *A New History of British India* (Oxford, 1997)
Woodbridge, John D., *Revolt in Prerevolutionary France: The Prince de Conti's Conspiracy against Louis XV 1755–1757* (1995)
Yaple, R.L., 'Braddock's Defeat: The Theories and a Reconsideration', *Journal of the Society for Army Historical Research* 46 (1968) pp. 194–201

INDEX

Abenakis, the 35, 36, 41, 42, 43, 131, 315-16, 319, 320, 328, 330, 331-6, 341-5, 347, 352
Abercrombie, Captain James 324
Abercromby, General James 44, 47, 138, 154, 322, 324, 326
Ache, Comte d' 168, 173, 175, 178-9, 180, 184, 186-8
Achilles, HMS 236, 238, 363
Adam, Robert 4
Aeolus, HMS 236
Affray, Marquis d' 240-1
Ahmed Shah 10
Aiguillon, Emmanuel-Armand, Duc d' 239-40, 243, 244, 245, 246, 248, 253, 356, 357-8, 362, 364, 378, 379, 380, 381-2
Aix-la-Chapelle, Treaty of (1748) 6
Alembert, Jean Le Rond d' 25, 197
Algonquin Indians 30, 132
Alivardi Khan 170
Alompra Aloung P'Houra 11
Amaranthe 359, 384
Amherst, General Jeffrey 19, 44, 45
  hatred of Indians 129, 132, 328, 330, 331, 332
  Quebec campaign 138, 140, 146, 153-7, 203-5, 207, 210, 217, 290, 318
  and Rogers 319, 327-8, 335, 336, 337, 338-9, 351, 351
Angria, Tulagree 170
Anhalt-Bernburg, Karl, Prinz von 274, 277
Anse au Foulon, Canada 295-8, 299, 302-3, 305, 311, 312
Anson, Admiral Lord George 25, 98, 104, 139, 232, 233, 234-5, 237, 362, 366, 380, 382
Antigua 93, 101, 102, 110, 112, 116
Antilles, the 93, 95
Arethusa 236
Argenson, Marc Pierre de Voyer de Paulmy, Comte d' 52, 64, 68, 69, 70, 75, 167, 168, 176
Armentière, Marquis d' 268, 270, 279
armies
  British 256, 257-8, 261-2, 330-1
  Prussian 256-7

Arne, Thomas 4
Arnouville, battle of (1759) 114
Atlantic Ocean 23-5, 38
Attakullakulla (Little Carpenter), Chief 18, 19, 141
Aubeterre, Comte d' 65, 88
Aubry, Charles Philippe 149, 151
Aurangzeb, Mughal Emperor 10, 169
Austria/Austrians 7, 59, 71, 74, 80, 85-6, 260, 261
Avery, Ensign 341, 346-7

Bahamas, the 101
Barbados 101, 102, 105, 116
Barnard, John 4
Barnes, George 344
Barre, Major Isaac 301-2, 309
Barrington, General John 104-5, 112, 113-14, 115-16, 119
Barrington, Captain Samuel 236
Bassalet Jang 188, 189
Basse Terre *see* Guadeloupe
'Battles of the Snowshoes': (1757) 322-3, (1758) 325-6
Bauffremont, Chevalier Louis de 366, 377, 380-1
Beauharnois, François, Marquis de 117
Beaumont, Christophe de, Archbishop of Paris 67
Beauport, Canada 208, 212, 213, 215, 291, 302
Beaupréau, General 278
Beckett, Samuel: *Murphy* 254
Beckford, William 99-100
Bedford, John Russell, 4th Duke of 234, 366, 383, 386
Begon 359, 383
Bell, Captain Thomas 292
Bellamy, George Ann 34
Belle-Isle, Charles-Louis Fouquet, Comte 52, 70, 71, 117, 183, 185
  and Canadian war 135, 136, 210, 311
  and Choiseul 61, 70, 81
  German campaign 261, 263-4, 265, 270,

279-80
and invasion of Britain 232, 355, 357, 358, 383
and Prince Charles Edward Stuart 79, 80, 81, 82, 83, 84, 242, 243
Bellone 236
Benedict XIV, Pope 61, 67-8
Bentley, Captain Sir John 364
Bergen, battle of (1759) 265-7
Berkeley, George 91, 194, 255
Bernis, Cardinal François-Joachim de 52, 54-5, 59-60, 68, 69, 70, 73, 74, 75, 87, 105-6, 390
Bernstorff, Baron Johan von 86-7
Berryer, Nicolas 50-1, 52, 69, 70-1, 75, 380-1, 382
and Canadian war 133, 135, 137-8
and invasion of Britain 242, 246-7, 355, 357, 358, 359, 363, 365, 381
and West Indies 93, 118
Bertin, Henri 69
Berwick, HMS 111
Béthune, Joachim Casimir de 240
Bigot, François 39-40, 46, 52, 133, 136, 137, 142, 210, 215, 297, 305
Bigot de Morogues, Sébastien-François 355-6, 357, 358, 380
Blake, William 90, 123
'The Tyger' 162
Blantyre, William Stuart, Lord ('Leslie') 80, 240, 241-2, 243
Blonde 386
Bombay 168
Bompart, Admiral Maximin de 113, 114, 115, 116, 118, 365
Boscawen, Admiral Edward 6, 234, 235, 238, 248-53, 354, 364, 378
Boswell, James 159
Botwood, Sergeant 220
Bougainville, Louis Antoine de 9, 25-6, 28-9, 51-2, 143, 199
and Canadian war 25, 38, 47-9, 50, 51, 52-3, 132-3, 135, 136-7, 138, 143, 210, 217, 290-1, 295, 297, 300, 302, 303, 304, 305, 308, 311-12
Boulogne, Jean-Nicolas de 69
Boulton, Matthew 3
Bourlamaque, General François-Charles de 38, 154, 155, 156, 208, 294, 295
Montcalm's correspondence with 134, 145, 221, 294, 298
Boyce, William 392
Boys, Commodore William 238, 355, 359, 363, 383
Braddock, General Edward 6, 34-5, 125, 148, 296, 330, 331
Bradstreet, Colonel John 47, 153
Brereton, Major Cholmondeley 180, 185, 188
Brest, France 231, 232, 236-8, 239, 244, 245,

248, 355, 360, 362, 363, 364
Bridgewater, Francis, Duke of 3
Brissac, Louis de Cossé, Duc de 269, 272, 279
Broc, Marquis Louis-Antoine de 378
Brodrick, Admiral Thomas 248, 250, 251, 253
Broglie, Victor François, Duc de 59, 71, 264-7, 268, 270, 272, 273-4, 278, 280
Brown, Private Thomas 315-16
Budes de Guébriant, Captain 363, 377
Bulkeley, Captain Charles 325
Burford, HMS 370
Burke, Edmund 164-5, 228
Philosophical Inquiry into the Origin of our Ideas of the Sublime and the Beautiful 122-4, 126
Burma 11
Bussy, Charles-Joseph Patissier, Marquis de 171, 172, 176, 181, 184, 185, 186, 187, 188, 189
Butterfield, Captain 337
Byng, Admiral John 108-9, 173, 196, 381
Byron, Captain John 236

Cabot, John 23
Cadet, Joseph 40, 297
Cadiz, Spain 250, 253
Caillaud, Major John 182
Calas, Jean 196
Calcutta 168, 170, 171
Campbell, Lieutenant George 350
Canaletto (Antonio Canale) 55
Cap Rouge, Canada 215-16
Carleton, Sir Guy 218, 292, 309
Carne Marcein, Comte de 252
Carolinas, the 15, 18-19, 49, 52
Carte, Thomas: *History of Great Britain* 225
Cartegena, siege of (1741) 106
Casanova, Giacomo Girolamo 54-5
Castillon, Captain 253
Castries, Marquis Charles de 275, 279-80
Catawbas, the 30
Catherine II ('the Great'), of Russia 13
Caughnawagas, the 36, 42
Cavenac, Captain 383, 384, 387
Cayugas, the 26, 27
Centaure 251, 252
Centurion, HMS 139
Champlain, Lake 49, 134, 136, 146, 154, 155, 156, 322, 335-6, 337
Champlain, Samuel 144
Champness, Richard 392
Chandernagore, India 168, 170, 171
Chandler, Jane 344
Charles III, of Spain 12, 14, 88, 388
Chatham, Earl of *see* Pitt, William
Chatham, HMS 373
Cherokees, the 15, 18-19, 30, 140-1, 318
Chesterfield, Philip Stanhope, 4th Earl of 22, 96

Chevert, General François 52, 244, 248, 359-60
Chevreuse, Duc de 268, 270, 279
Chichester, HMS 373
Chimère, La 250
Chingleput garrison, India 179, 180, 182
Chippewas, the 32-3, 153, 314
Choiseul, Antoine de, Archbishop of Cambrai 63, 84
Choiseul, Etienne-François de Stainville, Ducde 12, 52, 59, 60-4, 65, 66, 70-1, 264, 355, 382, 388
and Prince Charles Edward Stuart 75, 81-4, 240-3, 356
and Louis XV 61, 62, 67, 68, 69, 74-5, 82, 247
plans for invasion of Britain 72, 81, 85-7, 88, 231-2, 238, 239-47, 253, 356, 358, 364
Choiseul-Romanet, Madame de 61
Citoyenne, Lucie 74
Clancarty, Robert McCarthy, 5th Earl of 79
Clare, Lord 165
Clement XI, Pope 66-7
Clement XIII, Pope 4, 13, 54
Clermont, Louis de Bourbon-Condé, Comte de 260-1, 263, 264, 267
Clive, Robert 161, 162, 170, 171-2, 173, 177, 182, 183-4, 185, 186, 191
Colbert, Jean-Baptiste 14
Compagnie des Indes Orientales 167, 168, 169, 170, 172, 181, 184, 185, 189, 190, 198
Comte de Provence 173, 174
Comte de St Florentin 236
Condillac, Etienne de 197, 223
Conflans, Admiral Hubert de Brienne, Marquis de 176, 184, 244, 246, 247, 252, 355, 357-8, 361, 363-5, 366, 368-73, 374-5, 377-8, 379, 380-1
Conjeveram, India 185, 188
Contades, Louis-Georges-Erasme, Marquis de 263-4, 265, 267, 270, 272-3, 278-80
Conti, Louis-François, Prince de 52, 71, 74, 80
Contrecoeur, Captain Claude-Pierre de 33, 35
Cook, Captain James 9, 11, 25, 139
Cooper, Fenimore: *The Last of the Mohicans* 42, 132
Coote, Sir Eyre 171, 189-90, 388
Cope, Sir John 76
Corte-Real, Gaspar and Miguel 24
Coupier, Ann 74
Coventry, HMS 372
Crillon, Colonel de 181, 189
Crown Point, Canada 36, 153, 155, 156, 157, 318, 325, 327
Cuba 101
Culloden, battle of (1746) 77, 257, 202, 257, 263
Culloden, HMS 251

Cumberland, William Augustus, Duke of 34, 35, 36, 43-4, 86, 95, 99, 202, 207, 257, 259, 262, 263
Cumming, Thomas 99
Curaçao 101
Curtiss, Frederick 347

Dahomey 92
Damiens, Robert 68, 75, 167
Danae, HMS 236
Danton, Georges Jacques 5, 95
Dawkins, Jeremy 81, 160
Defiance, HMS 372, 376
Delawares, the 19, 30, 31, 32, 33, 35, 41, 42, 46, 141, 142, 143, 147, 157, 332-3
Denis, Captain Sir Peter 236
Denmark 85, 86-7
Denny, Governor William 142
Deschambault, Canada 291
Dettingen, battle of (1743) 202, 261, 280
Diderot, Denis 58, 199
  Encyclopédie 197, 199
Dieskau, Ludwig August, Baron 35, 36, 48, 320
Digby, Captain Robert 236
Dinwiddie, Robert 33, 34
  disease 36, 43, 45, 105, 106, 109, 110, 111, 112, 113, 115, 116, 132, 324
Dominica, island of 101, 109, 113, 115, 118
Dominican Republic 101
Dore, Jonathan 344
Doreil (emissary) 48
Dorsetshire, HMS 372, 373, 376
Douglas, Sir Alexander Peter Mackenzie 59, 80, 84, 240, 241, 356
Douglas, Sholto 88
Draper, Colonel William 180, 181
Duff, Captain Robert 236, 355, 361, 362, 364, 365, 368-9, 378
Dumas, Jean-Daniel 216
Dunbar, Lieutenant 346
Dupleix, Joseph François, Marquis de 167, 168, 169-70, 172, 175
Durant, George 117
Durell, Admiral Philip 139, 146, 211
du Verger, Captain St André 366, 372, 374, 380

earthquakes 20-1
East India Company, British 11, 84, 102, 162-3, 165, 168-9, 170, 171, 173, 174, 175, 178, 179, 388
East India Company, French *see* Compagnie des Indes Orientales
Easton conferences 46, 141-2
Eddystone Lighthouse 3-4
Edgecumbe, Captain George 236
Elcho, David Wemyss, Lord 58, 224
Elibank Plot 78, 79

Elliott, Captain John 386
Equiano, Olaudah 248-9, 251-2
Eries, the 27
Essex, HMS 377, 378
Estaing, Henri, Comte d' 178, 181
Estrées, Marshal d' 70, 75, 242, 246. 247, 264, 280

Fantasque 250
Faucon 359, 383
Favier, Jean-Louis 240
Ferdinand VI, of Spain 14, 65, 87
Ferdinand of Brunswick, Prince 258, 259-60, 261, 262-4, 265-70, 272-9, 280-2, 283
Fielding, Sarah: *The History of the Countess of Dellwynn* 4, 284
Fier 250
Fitzjames, Duc de 264, 275-6, 277
Fleury, Cardinal Claude 15, 60, 67, 69, 70
Flobert, Brigadier 359, 383, 384-5, 386, 387
Fontenoy, battle of (1745) 7, 167, 261, 262, 280
Foorde, Colonel Francis 183, 184
Forbes, General John 18, 44, 47, 125, 141
Formidable 372, 373, 374, 379
Fort Carillon *see* Ticonderoga
Fort Duquesne (*later* Fort Pitt; Pittsburgh) 33, 35, 44, 47, 125, 142-3, 152, 157, 296
Fort Edward, Canada 42-3, 324-5
Fort Frontenac, Lake Ontario 47
Fort Louis, Senegal river 99, 111, 112, 113
Fort Niagara, Canada 34, 47, 134, 138, 146, 147, 148, 149-50, 153, 291
Fort Oswego, battle of (1756) 41, 42
Fort Prince George 18, 19
Fort Royale, Martinique 106, 107, 108, 109, 115
Fort St David, India 174-5, 176, 190
Fort St Frederic, Crown Point 34, 36, 41, 44, 48
Fort St Michael, Goree 99
Fort William Henry, Canada 36, 42-3, 45-6, 132, 322, 331
Fortescue, Sir John 306
Fortune (French) 186
Fortune (British) 368
Foy, General 274
Frankfurt, Germany 265
Franklin, Benjamin 4-5, 28
Fraser, Ensign Malcolm 289, 290
Frederick II ('the Great'), of Prussia 4, 85, 88, 165
  campaigns 2, 7, 50, 98, 98, 104, 279, 280, 382
  and Ferdinand of Brunswick 264, 265, 267-8, 272, 277, 281
  and Jesuits 13, 64
  military techniques 256-7
  and Voltaire 62, 195

Frederick, Prince 96, 98, 99, 262
freemasonry 4, 79, 80, 84

Gage, General Thomas 153, 318, 319, 324, 327, 328
Gambia, the 99
Gardiner, Captain Richard 106, 116
Garrick, David: *The Harlequin's Invasion* 392
Geary, Admiral Sir Francis 362, 364
Geoghan, Captain 187-8
George II, of England 78, 204, 228, 234, 235, 238, 288
  and Duke of Cumberland 35, 86, 259
  and Ferdinand of Brunswick 259, 260, 264, 268, 272, 279, 282
  and Pitt 62, 95, 96, 98, 99, 100, 104, 204
  and Sackville 262, 282, 283
George III, of England 262, 282
George, Lake 36, 42, 153, 154, 322
Gerard, Alexander: 'An Essay on Taste' 4, 284
Ghazi-ud-Din 10
Gibbon, Edward: *Decline and Fall of the Roman Empire* 160-1, 226
Gibraltar 248, 249, 253
Gill, Marie-Jeanne 345, 346
Gilsa, General Philipp von 266, 270
Glorieux 376
Goldoni, Carlo 56-7, 58
  Gl'Innamorati 56
  I Rusteghi 57
  L'Uomo Prudente 57-8
Goldsmith, Oliver 61, 226, 285
  Enquiry into the Present State of Polite Learning in Europe 285
Gondelour, India 174
Goodwill 210
Goree, island of 99, 100
Gorham, Joseph 288-9
Gracieuse 250
Granby, John Manners, Marquis of 278, 281
Grande Terre *see* Guadeloupe
Grant, John 59
Grant, Lieutenant (Black Watch) 112
Grant, Lieutenant (Rogers' Rangers) 349, 350
Granville, John Carteret, Earl of 233, 234
Gray, Thomas 285-6
  Elegy Written in a Country Churchyard 285, 286-7
Great Lakes, the 125-6, 156
Grenada 118, 119
Guadeloupe (Basse Terre; Grande Terre) 81, 92, 101, 102, 105, 109-21, 244
Guarani Indians 12, 13
Guardi, Francesco 55
Guerchy, Claude Régnier, Comte de 276, 277
Guernsey, HMS 252
Guinness, Arthur 3

Haidar Ali 11

Haiti 92, 101
Haldimand, Colonel Frederick 147
Halifax, Nova Scotia 21, 146
Halley's Comet 21
Hamilton, James 19
Hanover, Germany 98, 99, 259, 264, 281
Hanway, Jonas 3
Hardwicke, Philip Yorke, 1st Earl 104, 232-3, 234, 312, 360
Hardy, Sir Charles 204, 236, 355
Harman, Captain William 111
Harrison, John 9
Hastenbeck, battle of (1757) 259, 263, 275
Haviland, Colonel William 324-5, 326
Havre, Duc d' 272
Havrincourt, Marquis d' 85
Hawke, Admiral Sir Edward 235-8, 243, 246, 248, 253, 354, 355, 360-1, 363, 364-6
  at Quiberon Bay 366, 368-73, 375-6, 377-80, 382
Hawley, General Henry 'Hangman' 202, 207
Hazlitt, William 286
'Hearts of Oak' 392
Hébécourt, Captain 154, 155
Helvétius, Claude-Adrien 4, 58, 197, 223
Hénault, Charles 69, 70
Héro, HMS 375
Héros 372, 373, 377, 378
Hérouville, Comte d' 239
Hervey, Commodore Augustus 236, 238, 362, 363
Hiawatha 27
Hispaniola 101
Hodenosaunee League 26; see Iroquois Confederacy Holdernesse, Robert, Earl of 233, 234, 238
Holker, John 223-4, 228-9, 230
Holmes, Rear-Admiral Charles 299
Home, John 5
Hooghly River 168, 171
Hopken, Anders Johann von 86
Hopson, General Peregrine Thomas 104, 106, 107-9, 110-11, 112, 113, 116
Howe, George, Viscount 44, 45
Howe, Captain Richard (later Admiral) 235, 236, 371, 372
Howe, Colonel William 300-1, 303, 304
Hughes, Captain Edward 139
Hume, David 5, 91, 122, 224, 226-7, 228, 255
  Dialogues Concerning Natural Religion 92
  Essays Moral and Political 284
  History of Great Britain 225
Hunter, HMS 293
Hurd, Richard: Moral and Political Dialogues 4, 284
Hurons, the 27, 35, 42
Hutcheson, Francis 226, 227

Île aux Coudres, Canada 211, 287

Île-aux-Noix, Canada 154, 156
Île d'Orléans, Canada 210, 211, 214, 289, 293, 297
Imhoff, General Gustaaf 277
Intrepide 375
Ireland, French invasion of 383-7
Iris, HMS 236
Iroquois Confederacy 26-33, 34-5, 36, 46, 129, 141, 142, 146-7, 150-1, 152-3, 156-7, 314
Isenburg, Johann Kasimir, Prince of 266
Isle of Wight 245, 246

Jacobites 58-9, 75, 78, 80, 81, 82, 83, 84, 85, 86, 87, 88, 122, 124, 165, 167, 202, 223, 224, 225, 226, 229, 239, 240-1, 242, 356, 357, 382, 391
  '45 Rising 34, 36, 76-7, 78-9, 81, 206, 224, 230, 317
Jacobs, Captain 344
Jamaica 93, 99, 101, 102, 109, 389
James II, of England 58, 75
Jansenists 12, 63, 66-8, 71, 75
Jefferson, Thomas 2, 28
Jenkins, Lieutenant 345, 346
Jennings, Colonel 385
Jervis, Captain John (later Lord St Vincent) 139, 300
Jesuits 12-13, 27, 35, 52-3, 63-4, 68, 71, 73, 75, 175, 193, 194, 208, 315, 332-3, 341, 343
Johnson, Dr Samuel 5, 124, 131, 158, 255, 285, 314
  Rasselas 158-60, 164
Johnson, Sir William 146, 147, 149, 150, 151, 152-3, 157, 318, 319, 320, 326
Johnstone, Chevalier James 59, 167, 214
Joncaire brothers 148
Joseph I, of Portugal 13
Jung, Carl 90, 91
Juste 376-7

Kaende, Chief 150
Kames, Henry, Lord 226, 228
Kant, Immanuel 90, 91, 122, 228
Karl Wilhelm Ferdinand, Erbprinz of Brunswick 269-70, 279
Keith, Earl Marischal George 58, 59, 81, 88, 122, 165
Kelly, George 79
Kennedy, Captain 323
Keppel, Captain Augustus 236, 371, 373-4, 378
Kersaint, Armand de Coetnempren, Comte de 373-4
Killick, Thomas 210-11
Knox, Captain John 128, 129, 218, 328
Krefeld, battle of (1758) 261, 262, 263, 275, 381
Kunersdorf, battle of (1759) 195, 279, 281

Laborde, General Jean-Joseph de 63, 247
La Clue, Admiral 243, 248, 249-50, 252, 253
La Corne, Saint-Luc de 148
Lagos Bay, battle of (1759) 250-3, 354, 355, 356, 364
Lally-Tollendal, Thomas Arthur Lally, Comte de 59, 79, 165, 167-8, 172-86, 187, 188-9, 190, 191, 388
Lancaster, Treaty of (1744) 30, 31
La Pérouse, Comte Jean-François de 9, 25
Lavaur, Père 175, 177
Lawfeldt, battle of (1747) 7, 202, 207, 280
Lawrence, General John Stringer 180, 185
Lawson, Elizabeth 205
Leeward Islands 102, 109, 119
Le Gosier, Guadeloupe 113
Le Havre, France 239
Leibniz, Gottfried 122, 159, 192, 193, 196
Le Mercier, Major François 218
'Leslie' see Blantyre, Lord
Leuthen, battle of (1757) 256
Lévis, François-Gaston, Duc de 37-8, 50, 153, 208, 214, 215, 222, 291, 294, 309, 310, 311, 326
Leyrit, Duval de 168, 174, 175-6, 179, 181, 187, 190
Ligneris, Captain 148, 149, 150, 151, 152
Ligonier, Field Marshal Sir John 44, 96, 98, 204, 233, 234
Lion 250
Lippstadt, siege of (1759) 265, 268, 270
Lisbon earthquake (1755) 20, 192
Little Carpenter see Attakullakulla
Longhi, Pietro 55
Loring, Captain 155
Loudoun, John Campbell, 4th Earl of 36, 41-2, 43, 44, 140, 324, 335
Louis XIV, of France 14, 67, 69, 70, 163, 196
Louis XV, of France
  assassination attempt 68, 75, 167
  and Duc de Choiseul 61, 62, 67, 68, 69, 74-5, 82, 242, 247
  foreign policies 7, 59, 71, 87-8, 89, 93, 234, 247-8, 355, 358, 363, 390
  in Canada 26, 34, 35, 37, 39, 40, 49, 51, 134, 135, 142, 212, 213
  in India 168, 170, 172, 190
  and French navy 249, 250
  and Jansenism 66-8
  and Madame de la Pompadour 7, 26, 52, 68, 69, 72-5, 247, 265, 267, 390
  and ministers 59-60, 62, 64, 65, 66, 68-70, 71-2, 264, 280, 389, 390
  mistresses 61, 72-3, 74; see also Madame de la Pompadour (above)
  and Prince Charles Edward Stuart 76, 77-8, 80, 82, 83, 231, 234, 241, 242, 243, 357
  and Thurot 358, 359, 384, 385

  and Voltaire 195, 196, 200
Louis, Dauphin of France 77, 84, 195, 264
Louisbourg 93, 116, 117, 138, 139
  battles and sieges: (1745) 32, 144; (1757) 41-2, 43; (1758) 44, 45, 203, 204, 318
Louisiana 1, 2, 36, 39, 50, 52, 92
Lowendahl, General Comte de 60, 259, 389
Lowestoft, HMS 293
Lowther, Sir James 205
Lowther, Catherine 205, 286
Lübbecke, battle of 269
Lunar Men 3
Lusace, Comte de 274, 278
Lutterberg, battle of (1759) 263, 264, 275, 280
Lyttelton, Governor William Henry 18-19

Machault d'Arnouville, Jean-Baptiste de 64, 68, 93, 223
MacIntosh, William 161
Macklin, Charles
  Love à la Mode 4, 284
  The Married Libertine 284
McMullen, Lieutenant 338
MacPherson, Cluny 206
Macpherson, James 5
  Fragments of Ancient Poetry 5
Madras 81, 168, 170
  siege of (1759) 165, 175, 179, 181-2
Magnanime, HMS 370, 371, 372, 373, 374
Magnières, Comte de see O'Heguerty, Dominique
Magnifique 357, 372
Mahicans, the 132, 141
Malartic, Major 306
Malplaquet, battle of (1709) 95
Mante, Thomas: The History of the Late War in North America 350-1
Marathas, the 10-11, 169, 170, 171, 172
Maréchal de Belle-Isle 358, 359, 384, 386
Maria Theresa, Queen of Austria 7, 63, 74, 259, 261
Marie, Queen of France 73, 75, 77
Marie Galante, island of 116, 117
Marin (guerrilla leader) 149, 326
Marlborough, Charles Spencer, 3rd Duke of 262
Marlborough, John Churchill, 1st Duke of 95, 255, 256, 273
Mars, HMS 375
Marseilles 248
Martin, Abraham 144
Martineau, Harriet 126
Martinique 92, 93, 100-9, 113, 114-15, 117, 119, 120
Marx, Karl 28, 225
Maryland 31, 101, 131
Massachusetts 140
Massey, Colonel Eyre 151-2
Massiac, Marquis de 69

Maupertuis, Pierre de 5, 21, 58, 195
Maurepas, Jean-Frédéric de 64, 69, 93
Mauritius 178, 179, 184, 186, 187
Menominees, the 42
Mézières, Eugène de 241
Miamis, the 32, 42, 147
Micmacs, the 35, 287, 314
Mignone 236
Militia Act (1757) 98, 259
Minden 268, 269
  battle of (1759) 270, 272-81, 286, 360, 381
Minerve 250
Mingoes 31, 33, 35, 42, 143
Minorca 7, 79, 82, 87, 103, 108, 120, 172, 360
Mir Jaffir 172, 185
Modeste 252
Moffat, William 3
Mohawks, the 26, 27, 31, 33, 36, 141, 147, 157, 307, 326, 337
Mohegans, the 132, 324, 344, 345, 346
molasses trade 101, 109, 117
Monkton, Brigadier Robert 138, 206, 207, 213, 219, 220, 288, 290, 292, 293, 295, 298, 301, 303, 309, 311
Monongahela, battle of (1755) 35, 45, 124, 131, 152, 216, 296, 315, 330-1
Monongahelas, the 27
Monro, Colonel George 42-3, 331
Montagu, Lady Mary Wortley 54, 160, 224
Montague, HMS 372, 373
Montcalm, Angélique de (née du Boulay) 37, 47
Montcalm Gezan, Louis Joseph, Marquis de 37-8, 39, 40-1, 44, 48-52, 135-6
  and battle of Ticonderoga (Fort Carillon) (1758) 45, 46, 47, 49, 50, 133, 154, 222, 390
  and Bougainville 25, 38-9, 48-9, 52-3, 135, 136-7, 138
  conflict with Vaudreuil 39, 40, 41, 44, 46-8, 50-1, 133-5, 139, 291, 298, 305, 309
  death 307
  and defence of Quebec (1759) 139, 140, 142, 143-6, 153, 156, 200, 208, 210, 212-19, 221-2, 291, 292-3, 294-5, 298, 302-6, 308, 389
  and fall of Fort William Henry (1757) 42-3, 331
  and Indian allies 41, 42, 43, 132, 139, 140, 142, 218, 287, 290, 328, 331, 332, 334
  and Wolfe 201, 215, 222
Montesquieu, Charles de Secondat, Baron 58, 223
  De l'esprit des lois 197, 198
  Lettres persanes 198
Montgomery, Captain Alexander 289-90
Montgomery, Lieutenant Hugh 275, 276
Monthalais, Captain 375
Montmorency Falls 208, 211, 212, 287

Montmorency River 208, 214-15, 218, 219, 220
Montreal 44, 136, 139, 146, 153
Moore, Admiral Sir John 93, 105, 106, 108-9, 110, 111, 112, 113, 114-15, 116, 119, 244
Moras, Marquis François Marie Peyrence de 52, 69, 93
Morbihan, France 361, 363, 364, 368
Moreau de Seychelles, Jean 69
Morris, Governor Robert Hunter 318
Mughal Empire 10, 160, 161, 168, 169, 388
Muhammad Shah 10
Mundy, Peter 161
Munroe, Hector 388
Münster 268, 281
Murray, Alexander 79, 82
Murray, Lord George 58, 224, 241, 356
Murray, Brigadier James 138, 206-7, 214, 290-1, 295, 298, 303, 308, 311
Murray, Captain William 111

Nadau du Treil, Charles-François 113, 117
Namur 249, 251
Napoleon Bonaparte 1-2, 5, 8, 54, 259, 290, 304, 391
National Debt 8, 66, 228, 229-30, 391
Neptune, HMS 139
Nevis, island of 93, 101
New York 31, 93, 146
Newark, HMS 252
Newcastle, HMS 186
Newcastle, Thomas Pelham-Holles, 1st Duke of 34, 95, 96-8, 103-4, 117, 204, 232, 233-4, 238, 253, 263, 282, 312, 314, 360, 365, 366
Newfoundland/Newfoundland Banks 14, 23, 25, 100
Niagara see Fort Niagara
Niagara Falls 126-7
Nikolai, General 272, 273, 278
Nizam Ali 184, 188
Nova Scotia 21, 34, 35, 138, 146

Océan, L' 249, 250, 251-2
Ogden, Captain 341, 343, 349-50
O'Heguerty, Dominique (Comte de Magnières) 79, 242
O'Heguerty, Pierre André 79
Ohio country 6, 15, 30-1, 32-3, 34, 42, 46, 47, 134, 138, 139, 141, 142, 149, 152, 157
Ojibwas, the 35, 42
O'Murphy, Louise 74
Oneidas, the 26, 27, 141
Onondaga, the 26, 27, 30, 31, 32, 141, 147
Ontario, Lake 47, 48, 49, 134, 136, 138, 146, 148, 153
Orient, L' 363, 376, 377
Oriflamme, L' 250
Orry, Philibert 69

Ortiz Parilla, Diego 20
Oswego (Chouagen) 146-7, 153; see also Fort
  Oswego
Ottawas, the 29, 32-3, 35, 42, 140, 287-8, 314,
  315, 330
Otter river, Canada 336-7

Paine, James 4
Paine, Tom 4, 200
Palmer, Benjamin 4
Paris, Treaty of (1763) 7, 388
Paris-Monmartel brothers, the 63
Parkman, Francis 35, 37, 47, 96, 97, 130, 154,
  201, 290, 326
Pascal, Lieutenant Michael 248
Paulmy, Marquis de 52, 168
Pembroke, HMS 139
Pennsylvania 19, 32, 41, 131, 141, 142, 147,
  149
Phillips, Lieutenant William 326
philosophes 4, 5, 14, 21, 25, 58, 63, 68, 71, 75,
  90, 197-8, 199, 200, 223, 247, 256
Pisquetomen 46, 141, 142, 143
Pissenne 336, 341, 342
Pitt, William, the Elder (Earl of Chatham)
  95-6, 98-9, 388, 391
  and French invasion plans 231, 232, 233-4,
    235, 236, 237, 238, 240, 245, 253, 360
  and George II 62, 95, 96, 98, 99, 100, 104,
    204
  and Duke of Newcastle 95, 96, 97-8, 103,
    360
  and North American and Canadian war 43-4,
    113, 116, 131, 138, 139, 140, 146, 201,
    204-5, 290, 312-13, 390
  and Sackville 262, 282-3
  and victory in Quiberon Bay 365, 379-80,
    382
  West Indian policy 92-3, 99-100, 101, 102-4,
    110, 112, 113, 116, 117, 120
Pittsburgh 149, 157; see Fort Duquesne
Plains of Abraham 144, 145
  battle (1759) 301-9
Plassey, battle of (1757) 172, 388
Pocock, Vice-Admiral Sir George 173, 175,
  178, 179, 180, 182, 186, 187
Point Levis, Canada 145, 208, 211, 212-13,
  216, 217, 220, 291, 293, 297
Pombal, Sebastião José de Carvalho e Mello,
  Marquis of 12-13, 63-4
Pompadour, Madame Jeanne de (née Poisson)
  72, 73-4, 77, 167, 195, 387
  favourites and protégés 52, 61, 63, 69, 71,
    72, 84, 106, 247, 263, 280, 357
  influence on Louis XV 7, 26, 52, 55, 59, 68,
    69, 72-3, 74-5, 267, 390
Pondicherry, India 168, 169, 170, 172, 174,
  175, 178-9, 186, 187, 388
Pontiac, Chief 140-1, 389

Pope, Alexander 194, 285
Portneuf, Father 289, 290
Portugal/Portuguese 11, 12-13, 24, 64
Post, Christian 141
Potawatomis, the 35, 42, 330
Pouchot, Captain Pierre 148-9, 150, 151, 152
Poyanne, General de 276, 277
Praslin, Comte de Choiseul, Duc de 63, 64,
  75
Preston, Captain Achilles 182
Prideaux, Brigadier-General John 146-8, 149
privateers 100-1, 102, 105, 109, 116, 118, 120,
  137; see also Thurot, François
Prussia 7, 71, 256; see also Frederick II
Puerto Rico 101
Putnam, Major 325
Putnam, Private Rufus 315
Puysieux (French minister) 69

Quebec 44, 48, 49, 134-5, 139, 143-5, 146
  British campaigns for (1759) 203, 207-8,
    210-22, 290-313, 317, 327, 389
Quiberon Bay, battle of (1759) 366-82

Ramezay, Jean-Baptiste de 309, 310, 311
Rangers 138; see also 'Rogers' Rangers'
Raza Sahib 180, 188
Redoutable 252, 253
Resolution, HMS 372, 374, 377
Revenge, HMS 372, 376
Reynolds, Captain 361, 362
Richelieu, Armand, Duc de 60, 62, 79, 88,
  167, 195, 259, 260, 264
Rippon, HMS 108
Robertson, William 5, 228
  History of Great Britain 226
  History of the Reign of Emperor Charles V 226
Robison, John 286
Rochester, HMS 238, 361, 362
Rodney, Admiral George 238, 244, 355, 361-2
Rogers, Major Richard 320-1, 324
Rogers, Major Robert 130, 318-28, 333, 335-9,
  340, 341-2, 343, 344-5, 346-53
'Rogers' Rangers' 42, 45, 130, 288, 315,
  317-18, 320-3, 324-6, 335-53
Rossbach, battle of (1757) 51, 68, 256, 263, 269,
  280, 357
Roubaud, Father Joseph Antoine 315, 332,
  334-5, 342
Roucoux, battle of (1746) 7, 261, 280
Rouille (French minister) 69
Rousseau, Jean-Jacques 58, 193-4, 196, 197,
  199
  Discours sur l'origine de l'inégalité 197, 199
  Social Contract 227
Royal George HMS 370, 371, 375, 376
Royal Navy 102-3, 106, 109-10, 135, 136, 139,
  170, 171, 182-3, 202-3, 210-11, 217, 234-6,
  237-8, 250, 256, 360-1

Rusilly, Colonel 384
Russell, HMS 219
Russia/Russians 7, 9, 20, 50, 71, 80, 85, 86, 260, 279, 280

Sabran Grammont, Captain M. de 251, 252, 253
Sackville, Lord George 262, 272-3, 277-8, 281-3
Saint-Aignan, Marquis de 253
Ste Anne, Guadeloupe 113, 114
Ste Anne de la Pocatière, Canada 288-90
St Charles River 144, 145, 208
Saint Contest (French minister) 69
St Francis, raid on (1759) 328, 332, 333, 334, 335, 336, 341-4, 351-2
St Francis river 340-1, 342
St François, Guadeloupe 113
Saint-Germain, Claude-Louis, Comte de 264, 269, 270, 280
St Kitts 101
St Lawrence River 44, 45, 49, 136, 144, 145, 156, 208, 210-11
St Lucia 101, 116
St Paul's Bay, Canada 288
Saint-Pierre, Bernardin de 199
St Vincent 101, 116
Salabet Jang 184, 188
San Teodor, battle of (1759) 20
Santo Domingo 101, 102
Saunders, Admiral Sir Charles 139, 213, 217, 234, 235, 236, 294, 299, 302, 365-6
Saxe, Maurice, Comte de 60, 259, 389
scalping 288, 315-18
Scheffer, Ulric 85
Schiller, Friedrich von 5
Scott, Major George 289
Seahorse, HMS 293
Senecas, the 26, 27, 28, 29-30, 31, 141, 147, 149, 150, 157
Senegal 99, 100
Serrant, Comte François Walsh de 88
Seven Years' War (1756-63) 2, 6, 7, 9, 25, 29, 39, 64, 74, 87, 245, 255, 256, 388, 389-91
Severn, HMS 355
Shawnees, the 19, 27, 30, 31, 33, 35, 143, 147
Shingas, Chief 32
Shirley, Governor William 35, 36, 41, 318, 320
Silhouette, Etienne de 64-5, 69, 70, 185, 190, 242, 245
Six Nations *see* Iroquois Confederacy
slave trade 92, 93, 99, 100, 102, 116, 119, 248
Smeaton, John 3
Smith, Adam 5, 122, 226, 253
  Inquiry into the Nature and Causes of the Wealth of Nations 225, 226
  The Theory of Moral Sentiments 226-8, 253
Smollett, Tobias 158, 225, 239, 285, 314
  Humphry Clinker 97, 314

smuggling 100-1
Soleil Royal 363, 372, 374, 375, 377, 378, 379, 381
Soubise, Charles de Rohan, Prince de 70, 75, 82, 84, 239, 240, 242, 243, 244, 245-7, 263-4, 267, 357, 359, 390
Soupire, Chevalier de 168, 176, 183
Southampton, HMS 236
Spain 6, 11-14, 20, 65, 83, 87-8, 101
Spikeman, Captain Thomas 315-16
Spikeman (or Speakman), Thomas 323
Spörcken, General Freiherr von 274-5, 276, 277, 279
Stacey, C.P.: *Quebec 1759* . . . 311-12
Stainville, Marquis de 60
Stanwix, General John 327
Stark, John 320, 323, 324
Sterne, Laurence: *Tristram Shandy* 123, 124, 159, 254-6
Steuart, Sir James 224, 225, 226, 230
Stevens, Lieutenant Samuel 339, 348, 351
Stobo, Captain Robert 295-6, 297
Stockbridge Indians 320, 324, 328, 336, 337, 338, 341, 343, 344, 345, 346
Storr, Captain John 236
Strode, General 385-6
Stuart, Charles Edward ('Bonnie Prince Charlie') 58-9, 75-85, 86, 88, 165, 167, 195, 202, 206, 223-4, 228-31, 234, 240-3, 247, 356, 382
Stuart, James ('The Old Pretender') 75-6, 80, 83, 88, 242
Stubbs, George 163
sugar trade 92, 93, 100, 109, 114, 117, 118, 120
Superbe 372
Surajah Dowlah 170-1, 172
Sutherland, HMS 299
Sweden 85, 86, 90, 91, 243
Swedenborg, Emanuel 90-1
Swift, Jonathan 158, 194, 196
Swiftsure, HMS 372, 375, 376

Tanaghrisson, Chief 29-30, 31, 32, 33
Tanjore, India 176, 177-8
Tanjore, Prince of 175, 177
Taovayan Confederation 20
Taylor, Captain Witteronge 236
Teedyuscung, Chief 19, 41, 46, 141, 142
Téméraire 252
Temple, HMS 373
Terpsichore 359, 384, 386
Terry, Edward: *Purchas his Pilgrimes* 161-2
Thésée 372, 373-4
Thurot, François 239, 243, 244, 247, 358-60, 363, 382-7
Ticonderoga (Fort Carillon) 36, 41, 42, 43, 44, 48, 127
  battles (1758) 46, 47, 49, 50, 133, 138, 221,

222; (1759) 153, 154-5, 156
Tiepolo, Giovanni Battista 55-6
Tiercelin, Jeanne-Louise 74
Tipu Sultan 11
Tonnant 377
Torbay, HMS 372, 373
Tournelle, Marquis de 79
Townshend, Brigadier George 138, 201, 206, 207, 214, 220-1, 286, 287-8, 290, 291, 292, 295, 298, 303, 308, 309, 310-11, 312
Trinidad 101
Tripoli: earthquakes (1759) 20
Trito 250
Turner, Lieutenant 341, 346
Tuscaroras, the 27, 31
Twain, Mark 162
Tyger, HMS 186

Union, HMS 375
Utrecht, Treaty of (1713) 12, 14, 100

Vandavachy, battle of (1759) 187-8
Vauban, Sébastien Le Prestre, Marquis de 255, 256
Vaudreuil, Pierre de Rigaud, Marquis de 35-6, 52, 136
conflict with Montcalm 36-7, 39, 40, 41, 44, 46-8, 50-1, 133-5, 139, 291, 298, 305, 309
and Indians 41, 287, 288, 332
and Quebec campaign 138, 139, 142, 149, 154, 208, 210, 211, 212-13, 215, 216, 217, 221, 288, 294, 302, 308, 309, 310, 311
and Rogers' Rangers 323
and Wolfe 287, 288, 290
Venice 54-9, 163
Venus, HMS 236
Vergor, Captain Duchambon de 301, 302
Versailles, Treaty of (1756) 7
Vestal, HMS 236
Villan de Brosse, Captain 376
Villars, Claude, Duc de 95
Villiers, Coulon de 33
Virgin Islands 101
Virginia 18, 19, 30, 31, 32, 49, 101, 131, 149
Vivaldi, Antonio 55
Voltaire (François-Marie Arouet) 14, 56, 58, 62, 63, 73, 109, 127, 164, 192, 193-7, 198, 223, 247
Candide 123, 159, 160, 192-4, 195, 196, 199
Fragments sur les Indes 198
Oedipe 194
Princesse de Navarre 195

voodoo 92
Vorontzov, Chancellor 86

Walkinshaw, Clementina 78, 81
Wall, Ricardo 13-14, 87-8
Walpole, Horace 34, 96, 97, 104, 105, 207, 284, 285, 312-13, 379
Walpole, Sir Robert 96, 98, 104, 194
Walsh, Antoine 79-80
Wandiwash, India 189, 388
Wangenheim, General Georg August von 273-4, 278, 281
War of Austrian Succession (1740-48) 6, 7, 32, 76, 169, 202, 232, 259, 261, 263, 275, 355, 360, 389, 391
War of Spanish Succession (1702-13) 7, 12, 255, 273, 391
Warspite, HMS 372, 373
Washington, George 4, 33
Waters, George Jean 79
Watson, Admiral Charles 171
Watt, James 3
Watteau, Jean-Antoine 55
The Death of Montcalm 307
weaponry 109-10, 133, 257-9
Webb, General Daniel 41-3
Wedgwood, Josiah 3
Wesley, John 22-3
West, Benjamin: *The Death of General Wolfe* 307
Westphalen, Christian Heinrich Philipp Edler von 269
Wilkes, John 60-1, 158
Willand, Joseph 352
Willyamos, Captain 337
Wolfe, General Edward 201
Wolfe, General James 200-7, 286-7
at battle of the Plains of Abraham 301-9
death 306-7, 308-9, 312
hatred of Indians 132, 203, 206, 287, 288
at Louisbourg (1758) 44, 45, 203
Quebec campaign (1759) 132, 208, 210-22, 287, 289-94, 295-309, 311, 312, 317, 327, 328
St Lawrence campaign 131, 138, 139, 146, 153, 156, 203-4
Wyandots, the 32, 35, 330

Young, Edward: *Conjectures on Original Composition* 284-5
Yusuf Khan 182